Lecture Notes in Computer Science　　9543

Commenced Publication in 1973
Founding and Former Series Editors:
Gerhard Goos, Juris Hartmanis, and Jan van Leeuwen

More information about this series at http://www.springer.com/series/7410

Sihan Qing · Eiji Okamoto
Kwangjo Kim · Dongmei Liu (Eds.)

Information and Communications Security

17th International Conference, ICICS 2015
Beijing, China, December 9–11, 2015
Revised Selected Papers

 Springer

Editors
Sihan Qing
Institute of Information Engineering
Chinese Academy of Science
Beijing
China

Eiji Okamoto
Graduate School of Systems
  and Information Engineering
University of Tsukuba
Tsukuba
Japan

Kwangjo Kim
School of Computing
KAIST
Daejeon
Korea (Republic of)

Dongmei Liu
Westone Corporation
Beijing
China

ISSN 0302-9743   ISSN 1611-3349   (electronic)
Lecture Notes in Computer Science
ISBN 978-3-319-29813-9   ISBN 978-3-319-29814-6   (eBook)
DOI 10.1007/978-3-319-29814-6

Library of Congress Control Number: 2016931281

LNCS Sublibrary: SL4 – Security and Cryptology

This Springer imprint is published by SpringerNature
The registered company is Springer International Publishing AG Switzerland

Preface

The 17th International Conference on Information and Communications Security (ICICS 2015) was held in Beijing, China, during December 9–11, 2015. The ICICS conference series is an established forum that brings together people from universities, research institutes, industry, and government institutions who work in a range of fields within information and communications security. The ICICS conferences give attendees the opportunity to exchange new ideas and investigate developments in the state of the art. In previous years, ICICS has taken place in Australia (1999), China (2013, 2011, 2009, 2007, 2005, 2003, 2001, and 1997), Hong Kong (2012, 2014), Singapore (2002), Spain (2010, 2004), UK (2008), and USA (2006). On each occasion, as on this one, the proceedings have been published in the Springer LNCS series.

In total, 148 manuscripts from 21 countries and districts were submitted to ICICS 2015, among which 24 regular and 19 short papers from 13 countries and districts were accepted. The accepted papers cover a wide range of disciplines within information security and applied cryptography. Each submission to ICICS 2015 was anonymously reviewed by at least three reviewers. We are very grateful to members of the Program Committee, which was composed of 82 members from 19 countries and districts; we would like to thank them, as well as all the external reviewers, for their valuable contributions to the tough and time-consuming reviewing process.

ICICS 2015 was organized and hosted by the Institute of Software, Chinese Academy of Sciences (CAS), the Institute of Software and Microelectronics, Peking University, and the State Key Laboratory of Information Security of the Institute of Information Engineering, Chinese Academy of Sciences (CAS). The conference was sponsored by the National Natural Science Foundation of China under Grant No. 61170282.

We would like to thank the authors who submitted their papers to ICICS 2015, and the attendees from all around the world. Finally, we would also like to thank Chao Zheng for managing the conference website and EasyChair system, Publicity Chair Yongbin Zhou for making the wide distribution of the call for papers, Publication Chair Dongmei Liu for her time and expertise in compiling the proceedings, and other local Organizing Committee members for providing logistic support.

December 2015

Sihan Qing
Eiji Okamoto
Kwangjo Kim

Organization

Program Committee

Man Ho Allen Au	The Hong Kong Polytechnic University, Hong Kong, SAR China
Joonsang Baek	Khalifa University of Science, Technology and Research, UAE
Feng Bao	Huawei, Singapore
Zhenfu Cao	East China Normal University, China
Chin Chen Chang	Feng Chia University, Taiwan
Kefei Chen	Hangzhou Normal University, China
Liqun Chen	Hewlett-Packard Laboratories, UK
Songqing Chen	George Mason University, USA
Zhong Chen	Peking University, China
Kam Pui Chow	The University of Hong Kong, Hong Kong, SAR China
Sherman S.M. Chow	Chinese University of Hong Kong, Hong Kong, SAR China
Frédéric Cuppens	Telecom Bretagne, France
Xiaomei Dong	Northeastern University, China
Junbin Fang	Jinan University, China
Josep-Lluís Ferrer-Gomila	University of the Balearic Islands, Spain
Steven Furnell	University of Plymouth, UK
Debin Gao	Singapore Management University, Singapore
Dieter Gollmann	Hamburg University of Technology, Germany
Dawu Gu	Shanghai Jiao Tong University, China
Yong Guan	Iowa State University, USA
Matt Henricksen	Institute for Infocomm Research, Singapore
Shoichi Hirose	University of Fukui, Japan
Qiong Huang	South China Agricultural University, China
Chi Kwong Hui	The University of Hong Kong, Hong Kong, SAR China
Lech Janczewski	The University of Auckland, New Zealand
Chunfu Jia	Nankai University, China
Sokratis Katsikas	University of Piraeus, Greece
Howon Kim	Pusan National University, Korea
Byoungcheon Lee	Joongbu University, Korea
Yingjiu Li	Singapore Management University, Singapore
Zichen Li	Beijing Institute of Graphic Communications, China
Bogang Lin	Fuzhou University, China

Dongdai Lin	IIE, Chinese Academy of Sciences, China
Hua-Yi Lin	China University of Technology, Taiwan
Javier Lopez	University of Malaga, Spain
Chuangui Ma	Information Engineering University of PLA, China
Ding Ma	People's Public Security University of China, China
Masahiro Mambo	Kanazawa University, Japan
Atsuko Miyaji	Japan Advanced Institute of Science and Technology, Japan
Yuko Murayama	Iwate Prefectural University, Japan
David Naccache	École normale supérieure, France
Takashi Nishide	University of Tsukuba, Japan
Takao Okubo	Institute of Information Security, Japan
Siani Pearson	Hewlett-Packard Laboratories, UK
Raphael Phan	Multimedia University Malaysia
Josef Pieprzyk	Queensland University of Technology, Australia
Kai Rannenberg	Goethe University of Frankfurt, Germany
Kyung-Hyune Rhee	Pukyong University, Korea
Bimal Roy	Indian Statistical Institute, India
Rajeev Anand Sahu	C.R. Rao AIMSCS, University of Hyderabad Campus, India
Pierangela Samarati	Università degli Studi di Milano, Italy
Yu Sasaki	NTT, Japan
Qingni Shen	Peking University, China
Miguel Soriano	Technical University of Catalonia, Spain
Hung-Min Sun	National Tsing Hua University, Taiwan
Neeraj Suri	TU Darmstadt, Germany
Willy Susilo	University of Wollongong, Australia
Wen-Guey Tzeng	National Chiao Tung University, Taiwan
Claire Vishik	Intel, UK
Guilin Wang	Huawei, Singapore
Huaxiong Wang	Nanyang Technological University, Singapore
Lihua Wang	NICT, Japan
Lina Wang	Wuhan University, China
Weiping Wen	Peking University, China
Andreas Wespi	IBM Zurich Research Laboratory, Switzerland
Wenling Wu	Institute of Software, Chinese Academy of Sciences, China
Yongdong Wu	Institute for Infocomm Research, Singapore
Guoai Xu	Beijing University of Posts and Telecommunications, China
Shouhuai Xu	University of Texas at San Antonio, USA
Rui Xue	IIE, Chinese Academy of Sciences, China
Alec Yasinsac	University of South Alabama, USA
Ching-Hung Yeh	Far East University, Taiwan
Sung-Ming Yen	National Central University, Taiwan
Siu Ming Yiu	The University of Hong Kong, Hong Kong, SAR China

Fangguo Zhang   Sun Yat-sen University, China
Rui Zhang   IIE, Chinese Academy of Sciences, China
Ye Zhang   Google Inc., USA
Yongbin Zhou   IIE, Chinese Academy of Sciences, China

Additional Reviewers

Chang, Bing	Li, Yan	Wang, Liangliang
Chen, Hua	Limniotis, Konstantinos	Wang, Licheng
Chen, Jiageng	Lin, Hsi-Chung	Wang, Qian
Chen, Jie	Liu, Hui	Wang, Weijia
Chen, Yikang	Liu, Junrong	Wang, Xiuhua
Cheng, Yao	Liu, Ximing	Wang, Yanfeng
Cui, Xingmin	Long, Yu	Wei, Lifei
Espes, David	Ma, Sha	Wu, Qiuxin
Formoso, Saul	McDonald, Todd	Wu, Shuang
Hachana, Safaa	Neogy, Sarmistha	Yaich, Reda
He, Debiao	Nieto, Ana	Yampolskiy, Mark
He, Kai	Osada, Genki	Yang, Po-Hung
Hegen, Marvin	Pape, Sebastian	Yang, Shuzhe
Hu, Ziyuan	Rangasamy, Jothi	Yang, Wenbi
Huang, Jianye	Rios, Ruben	Yang, Wenbo
Huang, Tiancheng	Saraswat, Vishal	Yeung, Cheuk Yu
Huang, Xinyi	Su, Chunhua	Yiu, Siu Ming
Junod, Pascal	Sui, Han	Yu, Xingjie
Kanayama, Naoki	Tanaka, Satoru	Zerkane, Salaheddine
Kang, Xin	Tarrière, Clément	Zhang, Huiling
Kiribuchi, Naoto	Tesfay, Welderufael	Zhang, Rocky
Kuo, Tsung-Min	Tian, Haibo	Zhang, Tao
Kywe, Su Mon	Veseli, Fatbardh	Zhao, Yongjun
Lai, Russell W.F.	Wang, Ding	Zhou, Xuhua
Li, Qi	Wang, Jingxuan	

Abstracts

Challenges in Post Quantum Cryptography Standardization

(Lily) Lidong Chen

NIST, USA

Abstract. Over the past three decades, public-key cryptographic schemes such as RSA and Diffie-Hellman have been standardized and deployed in wherever protection is needed. The quantum computers have capabilities that can lay to ruin all of the public-key cryptographic systems currently in use. In recent years, post quantum cryptography has been an extremely active research area. Many quantum computing resistant schemes are proposed and analyzed. To plug these new schemes into the applications, standards need to be developed. This presentation will overview the major families of quantum resistant cryptosystems and the initial standard activities. The presentation leads discussions on the challenges in post quantum cryptography standardization and explores the possible paths to deploy the next generation cryptographic standards.

Usable Security - A Personal Perspective

Jeff Yan

Lancaster University, UK

Abstract. My first usable security paper was written with Cambridge colleagues in 1999–2000, and it became publically available in 2000 [1]. It took about five years to get the paper published in a peer-reviewed venue, but virtually no revision was made. The paper has been highly cited, and it is still cited each year. Nowadays, usable security papers are readily published at top venues such as Oakland, CCS and Usenix Security. The change is simple: usable security is no longer an ignored area, but has become mainstream. In this keynote, I will briefly talk about my involvement in this exciting development.

I will begin with how we started to work on usable security long before it is so called.

Security and usability are often competing requirements, and it's considered inherently hard to create solutions that are both secure and usable. However, with a number of exemplary results taken from my own work (on passwords, graphical passwords and Captchas), I'll show that it is feasible to develop novel, well-engineered and scientifically evaluated solutions which achieve security and usability simultaneously, rather than at each other's expense.

As a more recent latest development, usable security has been evolving into security psychology, a discipline that is much broader and deeper. Along this line, my recent joint project with Cambridge has yielded interesting results in the understanding of deception, which is not only the basic problem underlying security and cybercrime, but is central to human behaviour.

Contents

Minimizing Databases Attack Surface Against SQL Injection Attacks   1
  Dimitris Geneiatakis

Ensuring Kernel Integrity Using KIPBMFH   10
  Zhifeng Chen, Qingbao Li, Songhui Guo, and Ye Wang

Bitsliced Implementations of the PRINCE, LED and RECTANGLE Block
Ciphers on AVR 8-Bit Microcontrollers   18
  Zhenzhen Bao, Peng Luo, and Dongdai Lin

On Promise Problem of the Generalized Shortest Vector Problem   37
  Wenwen Wang and Kewei Lv

Secret Key Extraction with Quantization Randomness Using Hadamard
Matrix on QuaDRiGa Channel   50
  Xuanxuan Wang, Lihuan Jiang, Lars Thiele, and Yongming Wang

Practical Lattice-Based Fault Attack and Countermeasure on SM2
Signature Algorithm   62
  Weiqiong Cao, Jingyi Feng, Shaofeng Zhu, Hua Chen, Wenling Wu,
  Xucang Han, and Xiaoguang Zheng

The Security of Polynomial Information of Diffie-Hellman Key   71
  Yao Wang and Kewei Lv

How to Vote Privately Using Bitcoin   82
  Zhichao Zhao and T.-H. Hubert Chan

Multidimensional Zero-Correlation Linear Cryptanalysis on 23-Round
LBlock-s   97
  Hong Xu, Ping Jia, Geshi Huang, and Xuejia Lai

Traceable CP-ABE on Prime Order Groups: Fully Secure and Fully
Collusion-Resistant Blackbox Traceable   109
  Zhen Liu and Duncan S. Wong

Generic Construction of Audit Logging Schemes with Forward Privacy
and Authenticity   125
  Shoichi Hirose

A Novel Post-processing Method to Improve the Ability of Reconstruction
for Video Leaking Signal   141
  Xuejie Ding, Meng Zhang, Jun Shi, and Weiqing Huang

TMSUI: A Trust Management Scheme of USB Storage Devices for
Industrial Control Systems   152
   Bo Yang, Yu Qin, Yingjun Zhang, Weijin Wang, and Dengguo Feng

Characterization of the Third Descent Points for the k-error Linear
Complexity of 2^n-periodic Binary Sequences   169
   Jianqin Zhou, Wanquan Liu, and Xifeng Wang

QRL: A High Performance Quadruple-Rail Logic for Resisting DPA
on FPGA Implementations   184
   Chenyang Tu, Jian Zhou, Neng Gao, Zeyi Liu, Yuan Ma,
   and Zongbin Liu

Strategy of Relations Collection in Factoring RSA Modulus   199
   Haibo Yu and Guoqiang Bai

Ultra High-Performance ASIC Implementation of SM2 with SPA
Resistance   212
   Dan Zhang and Guoqiang Bai

Multi-input Functional Encryption and Its Application
in Outsourcing Computation   220
   Peili Li, Haixia Xu, and Yuanyuan Ji

A Multivariate Encryption Scheme with Rainbow   236
   Takanori Yasuda and Kouichi Sakurai

Efficient and Secure Many-to-One Signature Delegation   252
   Rajeev Anand Sahu and Vishal Saraswat

Fully Secure IBE with Tighter Reduction in Prime Order Bilinear Groups . . .   260
   Jie Zhang, Aijun Ge, Siyu Xiao, and Chuangui Ma

A Secure Route Optimization Mechanism for Expressive Internet
Architecture (XIA) Mobility   269
   Hongwei Meng, Zhong Chen, Ziqian Meng, and Chuck Song

An Entropy Based Encrypted Traffic Classifier   282
   Mohammad Saiful Islam Mamun, Ali A. Ghorbani,
   and Natalia Stakhanova

Modelling and Analysis of Network Security - a Probabilistic
Value-passing CCS Approach   295
   Qian Zhang, Ying Jiang, and Liping Ding

An Improved NPCUSUM Method with Adaptive Sliding Window
to Detect DDoS Attacks   303
   Degang Sun, Kun Yang, Weiqing Huang, Yan Wang, and Bo Hu

Dynamic Hybrid Honeypot System Based Transparent Traffic
Redirection Mechanism 311
  Wenjun Fan, Zhihui Du, David Fernández, and Xinning Hui

Leveraging Static Probe Instrumentation for VM-based Anomaly Detection
System 320
  *Ady Wahyudi Paundu, Takeshi Okuda, Youki Kadobayashi,
  and Suguru Yamaguchi*

MB-DDIVR: A Map-Based Dynamic Data Integrity Verification
and Recovery Scheme in Cloud Storage 335
  Zizhou Sun, Yahui Yang, Qingni Shen, Zhonghai Wu, and Xiaochen Li

Chameleon: A Lightweight Method for Thwarting Relay Attacks
in Near Field Communication 346
  *Yafei Ji, Luning Xia, Jingqiang Lin, Jian Zhou, Guozhu Zhang,
  and Shijie Jia*

A Solution of Code Authentication on Android 356
  Xue Zhang and Rui Zhang

Verifiable Proxy Re-encryption from Indistinguishability Obfuscation 363
  Muhua Liu, Ying Wu, Jinyong Chang, Rui Xue, and Wei Guo

Higher-Order Masking Schemes for SIMON 379
  Jiehui Tang, Yongbin Zhou, Hailong Zhang, and Shuang Qiu

An ORAM Scheme with Improved Worst-Case Computational Overhead 393
  Nairen Cao, Xiaoqi Yu, Yufang Yang, Linru Zhang, and SiuMing Yiu

A Self-Matching Sliding Block Algorithm Applied to Deduplication
in Distributed Storage System 406
  Chuiyi Xie, Ying Huo, Sihan Qing, Shoushan Luo, and Lingli Hu

Suffix Type String Matching Algorithms Based on Multi-windows
and Integer Comparison 414
  Hongbo Fan, Shupeng Shi, Jing Zhang, and Li Dong

Security-Enhanced Reprogramming with XORs Coding in Wireless
Sensor Networks 421
  Depeng Chen, Daojing He, and Sammy Chan

Preserving Context Privacy in Distributed Hash Table Wireless
Sensor Networks 436
  Paolo Palmieri

Prior Classification of Stego Containers as a New Approach for Enhancing
Steganalyzers Accuracy 445
  Viktor Monarev and Andrey Pestunov

Eavesdropper: A Framework for Detecting the Location of the Processed
Result in Hadoop 458
    Chuntao Dong, Qingni Shen, Wenting Li, Yahui Yang, Zhonghai Wu,
    and Xiang Wan

Secret Picture: An Efficient Tool for Mitigating Deletion Delay on OSN 467
    Shangqi Lai, Joseph K. Liu, Kim-Kwang Raymond Choo,
    and Kaitai Liang

A De-anonymization Attack on Geo-Located Data Considering
Spatio-temporal Influences 478
    Rong Wang, Min Zhang, Dengguo Feng, Yanyan Fu, and Zhenyu Chen

Author Index 485

Minimizing Databases Attack Surface Against SQL Injection Attacks

Dimitris Geneiatakis[✉]

Electrical and Computer Engineering Department,
Aristotle University of Thessaloniki, 54124 Thessaloniki, Greece
dgeneiat@auth.gr

Abstract. Lately, end-users and database administrators face continuously personal data exposures. Among different type of vulnerabilities an adversary might exploit, to gain access to this data, SQL injections are considered one of the most serious vulnerabilities, which remain at the top twenty most known vulnerabilities more than a decade. Though various defenses have been proposed against SQL injections for database protection, most of them require "modifications" on the underlying infrastructure, such as proxy interposition, middleware drivers, *etc.*, while they cannot be employed transparently. In this paper, we propose a practical framework that enables the transparent enforcement of randomization to any given database for enhancing protection against SQL injection attacks, while being agnostic to the underlying database and completely transparent to end-user. We demonstrate a methodology for identifying automatically SQL statements on a given database application, and we introduce a runtime environment for enforcing the randomization and de-randomization mechanism in a completely transparent way, without requiring access to its source code. We evaluate in terms of overhead our approach using the well-known MySQL database under different configurations. Results indicate the employment feasibility of the proposed framework.

1 Introduction

End-users' personal data in Internet era, gain more and more value and attention as are considered the basic functional block for digital services provision. Service providers rely upon them to offer personalized services to their customers, while adversaries try to get access to this data for fun and profit as well. These data, structured or unstructured, are stored in most of the cases in databases that provide the appropriate Application Programming Interface (APIs) to the employed applications and services for handling them. Specifically, these interactions are accomplished through Structured Query Language (SQL) [6] offering in such a way a transparently access to the data requested by different applications and sources. Though beneficial might SQL be for data management, adversaries exploits their structure to gain access to otherwise private data. To do so, they inject (legitimate) SQL commands to the input data of a given application for

© Springer International Publishing Switzerland 2016
S. Qing et al. (Eds.): ICICS 2015, LNCS 9543, pp. 1–9, 2016.
DOI: 10.1007/978-3-319-29814-6_1

modifying the initial SQL command, and gain access or modify private information. This type of flaw is known as SQL Injection Attack (SQLIA) [9], in which adversaries exploit the fact that database makes no differentiation between end-users' actual data and SQL commands. Note that, SQLIA remains at the top twenty most known vulnerabilities more than a decade, though, various countermeasures such as [3,11] *etc.*, have been proposed in literature. This trend endures because most of existing protection approaches either focus on specific applications or they cannot be applied transparently to existing databases.

Defensive programming could be considered an alternative solution for enhancing database security, however, in this case is supposed that the developed application is "error" free *e.g.,* by introducing sanitazation techniques on end-users' inputs, which is not the case under all the circumstances. Furthermore, developers do not take into consideration the details for securing securing the developed application [4,19]. On the other hand, SQL injections vulnerabilities could be easily identified and exploited using open source tools *e.g.,* Grabber[1]. Thus, we believe that other solutions orthogonal to existing ones are required to enhance databases security.

In this paper, we propose a practical framework that enables the transparent enforcement of randomization to any given database for enhancing protection against SQLIA. Our main goal is the employment of a solution that requires as little as possible intervention, while building on the advantages of well-known practical security mechanisms. This way, we elaborate on enhancing database security against SQLIA on otherwise "unprotected" databases, minimizing their attack surface. To the best of our knowledge this is the first work in its kind. In this direction, we introduce a methodology building on the benefits of static and dynamic analysis towards SQL statements randomization [3] for any given database related application, and enforcing a runtime environment for SQL de-randomization without requiring to modify neither database source code nor middleware interfaces. We evaluate our framework in terms of introduced overhead using the well-known MySQL database under different configurations. Outcomes indicate the feasibility employment of the proposed framework.

The rest of the paper is structured as follows. In Sect. 2 we describe in detail our proposed framework for applying randomization technique transparently on any given databases application. In Sect. 3 we evaluate our framework in terms of its effectiveness with regard to introduced overhead. In Sect. 4 we discuss the related work and introduce a comparison with our approach. Finally, in Sect. 5 we conclude this paper giving some pointers for future work as well.

2   Proposed Framework

The core protection mechanism of our framework builds around the randomization protection mechanism [1,10]. This is because, randomization is considered among the most effective solutions for protecting services against injection attacks. So, it should be noted that the access to the Server Side Script (SSS) is

---

[1] https://github.com/neuroo/grabber.

mandatory if there is a need to employ such a technique, as is the input point to access database and through it the attack vectors are created. This is exactly the case of binary randomization [16], meaning that if there is not access to the binary itself, it cannot be employed the randomization countermeasure.

Briefly, the proposed framework is composed of three main components (a) SQL statements identification (b) SQL randomization, and (c) the run-time enforcement. So, assuming the availability of the SSS, we parse it through a meta-compiler for identifying all the SQL statements included in it. Afterwards, the identified queries are randomized through a function f and the SSS is updated correspondingly. As the SSS generates and forwards randomized ("SQL") statements, according to users' inputs, to the database, the latter will not be in the position of "understanding" these ("SQL") statements. Consequently, the database should incorporate the de-randomization function for transforming the incoming randomized statement to a "normal" SQL statement, otherwise the SQL statement could not be executed successfully. The runtime enforcement realizes this functionality in a transparent way, indicating that no access to database source code is required as well as is agnostic to the underlying database.

2.1   SQL Statements Identification

To automatically identify SQL statements in any give application, we assume that the SSS is available for analysis, as mentioned previously. To do so, we built a meta compiler based on the well-known tools *lex* and *yacc* [14]. In this point one might argue that SQL statements could be identified by simply searching inside the SSS for the corresponding SQL keyword. Indeed, this could be the case for "explicit" SQL statements definitions, corresponding to statements build in a "single" line. However, in that case there is no way to identify or variables that include part of an SQL and influence the final SQL statement *e.g.,* part of SQL statement might be included in a conditional statement. This is because "searching" tools have no any capability of identifying data flows between variables. For instance, consider the code example illustrated in the Listing 1.1 in which a variable x is concatenated to the *sql* if "userinput" equals to 1. This means that the content of variable x should be protected, since it is a part of the SQL statement, otherwise the database remains vulnerable to SQLIA.

```
1 indirect SQL code] sql = select * from table where id = ;
2 if (userinput == 1 ){
3   x = 5 ;
4   sql = sql.$x$;
5 }
```

Thus, our proposed SQL identification solution defines a sample SSS programming language, *e.g.,* PHP like[2]. We rely on such a type of grammar to

---

[2] We focus on this type of languages as most of the malicious inputs are generated through web based applications.

build a parser able to identify all the available SQL parts consisting an SQL statement that included in a given SSS *i.e.,* variables, function parameters, *etc.,* that should be protected. This means that variables are "tainted", to identify whether or not include an SQL statement, and monitor if there are variables influence the initial statement. If this is the case the variable is also tainted.

The start rule is the program consisted of series of statements. We have defined various types of statement, *e.g.,* VARIABLE POINTER STRING '(' expr_list ')', CMD expr_list, however, in this version of the grammar we consider a limited number of statements included in the PHP server side script. We are planning to extend this grammar for including all the available statements in a future work.

First the SSS is split in tokens through lex that are passed to yacc to compute program's statements and expressions included in the server side script to evaluate each of the whether or not includes an SQL code. All variables, function parameters, *etc.* are evaluated whether or not include an SQL statement. If this is the case the variable is marked and "monitored" if influence other variables as well that consequently marked. The analysis tool reports on the parts of the code that include SQL statements that should be randomized. This evaluation is accomplished by simple keywords identification on the values of the variables.

2.2 SQL Statements Randomization

Instruction set randomization technique was initially proposed in [1,10] to protect software against code for protecting binaries against code injection attacks. In this approach the code is transformed through a transformation function *i.e.,* F to a new executed code. This transformation is known only to the system in which it will be executed, so it can be translated to the original code. This approach assumes that the adversary is not aware of this transformation, and as a result any type of code injected towards to the application generates unknown commands causing the application rejection. Indeed, in case that the attacker knows the transformation it can inject and execute malicious code without being identified.

In this direction, Boyd and Keromytis [3] apply the concept of randomization for protecting databases against SQL injection attacks. Specifically, in their initial design they transform the SQL keywords to new types of keywords by appending a "random" integer to them. As this transformation is only known to the database adversaries injected code is transformed to unknown statements and consequently rejects its execution. To enforce a runtime environment for implementing the proposed framework (randomization) in a transparent way, meaning that no access to the underlying database source code is required, we rely on the advantages of adaptive defenses [7]. This is because, adaptive defenses enable software "virtual" partitioning based on its innate properties.

To do so, we build a database execution monitor using Intel's Pin [13] dynamic binary instrumentation framework. We rely on Pin because it can run executables as is, while enables developers to instrument any executable, and develop tools supervisioning various aspects of its execution at different granularity level. In our case, we implemented a Pin tool that injects small pieces of monitoring code before every function entry as well as their parameters. To identify the appropriate hook point we execute a series of a software supporting (1) a database SQL connection and (2) a SQL statement execution. Using our monitor we record all the function calls for the both cases. Afterwards, we analyze the collected "traces" to determine execution differentiation points that constitute potential SQL hooks. The analysis of discovering the differentiation point is based on the formula (1). This is a heuristic based on the observation that the software supports the database SQL connection feature generates a subset of function calls of the software supports the execution of SQL statement. The outcome of this analysis provides a set of *possible* hooks for employing the de-randomization function for our case.

Since this analysis might produce more than one hooks as results shows a further process is required to determine the appropriate point. This further process includes the analysis of the parameters and return values of the possible SQL hook points. Note this information is recorded also by our monitor tool. We choose as the appropriate hook point the first function builds a complete SQL statement either as a return value, or as a parameter of a function call. If the complete SQL statement does not exist in such locations, because the database uses a global variable to store the statement, then the current approach fails to determine such a point, however, in our results we do not identify such a case. We develop and test this procedure on x86 Linux over two well known databases *i.e.,* MySQL and PostgreSQL. We consider these database as they belong to the most employed one. To do so, we implement the corresponding clients incorporating the SQL connect and statement execution using the C programming language APIs for both databases. The analysis outcomes identifies the following functions as possible hooks (a) _Z16dispatch_command19enum and (b) pg_parse_query(char *) correspondingly.

We validate the outcomes of this analysis by employing the complete scheme of the protection framework, so the incoming statements can be executed note that in case that we send randomized statements are not possible to be executed by the database. We control also the CFG for showing that the identified calls are executed before the statement execution. The other way around to validate outcomes analysis is through code inspection. Note that these are possible points so other functions could be suitable for the employment–meaning that every function before statement execution is a suitable candidate hook point. We believe that the identification procedure cannot be employed manually by inspecting the source code as we do not have any hint of the SQL statements execution as well as the code base of databases are thousands of lines.

As the appropriate point of SQL hook point is identified, the de-randomization should take place on the database side. The enforcement could take different implementations *i.e.,* modify the database source code directly, function interposition, or database instrumentation. However, to do it transparently we develop another tool based on Pin instrumenting the identified SQL point before its execution and modify the corresponding parameters. We report in detail on database performance under different configurations in Sect. 3.

3   Evaluation

We develop the proposed approach on MySQL ver. 5.5.44 database, as it is one of the most employed open source databases, using the MySQL *select*-benchmark. As randomization function we relied on XOR transformation using a key length of eight bytes. The database server runs on a single host featuring an i5 Intel processor with 4 GB of RAM running Ubuntu OS (14.04.3 LTS). All the experiments were repeated 40 times, while the client and the server executed on different machines. We use various configurations to demonstrate the performance implications under different employments. We run the benchmark on MySQL database natively both without and with randomization protection enabled, as well as over null and randomization enabled Pin tools, and using Pin probe mode for function interposition.

Figure 1 demonstrates the time required to complete the MySQL select-benchmark under these configurations. Note that the native and Pin null tool configurations are used as a point of reference to indicate the introduced overhead of the protection enabled scenarios. The native execution of MySQL-select benchmark without enabling database protection requires on average 96 s to accomplish its tasks, while the native enforcement of the runtime environment requires 112 s corresponding to an overhead of 16 %. When the runtime environment is implemented as a Pin tool the overhead increases significantly almost 330 %, which affects highly the performance of the database. However, using the Pin probe mode for function interposition scales down the overhead up to 2.2x times, whereas in comparison with native runtime enforcement the overhead is as little as 20 %.

4   Related Work

The very first approaches for protecting services against SQLIA were focusing on end-users' input sanitazation. They were implemented as a built-in functionality in web based frameworks such as PHP, ASP.Net, *etc.*, as well as in intrusion detection systems *i.e.,* SNORT[3] in which the incoming traffic is inspected through pre-defined signatures. Though effective these approaches might be adversaries could by pass them, while rely on developers and administrators capabilities to develop the appropriate controls which is not always the case. Thus, various other approaches combining static and dynamic analysis have been proposed in literature in order to enhance database security.

Halfond *et al.* in [8] introduce a model based approach to detect malicious SQL statements generating by users' inputs. Briefly, this model is consisted of two parts (a) the static one which builds the legitimate statements model that

---

[3] www.snort.org.

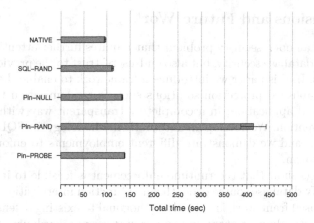

Fig. 1. Total execution time for MySQL select-benchmark under different implementations of our proposed framework. Native and Pin null tool are used as a reference to demonstrate protection enforcement introduced overhead.

could be generated by an application, and (b) the dynamic which inspects the generated statements at runtime and compares them with the statically built model. In the same direction, Bisht *et al.* in [2] propose an approach based on symbolic execution, instead of static analysis, for constructing applications' legitimate SQL statements.

Su *et al.* in [17] introduce a solution named SqlCheck in which the syntactic structure of original SQL statements are compared with those generated by end users inputs in order to detect SQLIA. Complementary Wei *et al.* [18] focus on stored procedure protection against SQLIA. In their approach they rely on static analysis to model SQL statements as a Finite State Automata (FSA), while they check at runtime whether the generated statements follow the static analysis model.

SQLProb [12] employs a dynamic user input extraction analysis taking into consideration the context of query syntactic structure to detect SQLIA, however, in contrast to other solutions incorporates a black box approach. Mitropoulos *et al.* in [15] propose a novel methodology for preventing SQLIA by introducing a middleware interface between the application and the underlying database. In alternative approach, Felt *et al.* [5], towards the employment of the least privilege principle, introduce the notion of *data separation* in database related applications where each application develops a policy describing its access rights in the database. This way, different applications' data are isolated among each other. This policy is enforced through a proxy server.

Boyd and Keromytis [3] consider the very first employment of randomization for database protection against SQLIA enabling their prevention. As mentioned previously, they suggest applications' SQL statement randomization by appending a random integer to them, while its enforcement requires a proxy server in order to forward de-randomized SQL statements to database.

5　Conclusions and Future Work

SLQIA is still an open security problem that requires further attention not only for enhancing database security, but also end-users' trust to the provided Internet based services. In this paper we introduce a framework to enable the applicability of well established protection solutions such as randomization to any given database related application, in a completely transparent way with as little as possible intervention. We develop an automatic methodology for SQL statements randomization, and we demonstrate different employments to enforce the protection mechanism.

Our findings show that the runtime enforcement is feasible to implemented, without modify database source code, through function interposition. We believe that the proposed framework is not only orthogonal to existing defenses, but also enables database administrators and server side scripts developers to minimize database attack surface against SQLIA. Currently, we are looking to extend the SQL statements identification approach by including also other server side programming languages as well as enabling it on binary applications. In addition we intend to accomplish a more thorough evaluation using various well-known reversible transformation *i.e.*, AES.

References

1. Barrantes, E.G., Ackley, D.H., Palmer, T.S., Stefanovic, D., Zovi, D.D.: Randomized instruction set emulation to disrupt binary code injection attacks. In: Proceedings of the 10th ACM Conference on Computer and Communications Security, CCS 2003. ACM (2003)
2. Bisht, P., Madhusudan, P., Venkatakrishnan, V.N.: CANDID : dynamic candidate evaluations for automatic prevention of SQL injection attacks. ACM Trans. Inf. Syst. Secur. **13**(2), 14:1–14:39 (2010)
3. Boyd, S.W., Keromytis, A.D.: SQLrand: Preventing SQL Injection Attacks. In: Jakobsson, M., Yung, M., Zhou, J. (eds.) ACNS 2004. LNCS, vol. 3089, pp. 292–302. Springer, Heidelberg (2004)
4. Chess, B., West, J.: Secure Programming With Static Analysis: Software Security Series, NZ1. Addison-Wesley, Boston (2007)
5. Felt, A.P., Finifter, M., Weinberger, J., Wagner, D.: Diesel : applying privilege separation to database access. In: Proceedings of the 6th ACM Symposium on Information, Computer and Communications Security, ASIACCS 2011. ACM (2011)
6. A.N.S. for Information Systems. Database language - sql, November 1992
7. Geneiatakis, D., Portokalidis, G., Kemerlis, V.P., Keromytis, A.D.: Adaptive defenses for commodity software through virtual application partitioning. In: Proceedings of the ACM Conference on Computer and Communications Security, CCS 2012. ACM (2012)
8. Halfond, W.G.J., Orso, A.: AMNESIA : analysis and monitoring for neutralizing SQL-injection attacks. In: Proceedings of the 20th IEEE/ACM International Conference on Automated Software Engineering, ASE 2005. ACM (2005)
9. Johari, R., Sharma, P.: A survey on web application vulnerabilities (SQLIA, XSS) exploitation and security engine for SQL injection. In: Proceedings of the International Conference on Communication Systems and Network Technologies, CSNT 2012. IEEE Computer Society (2012)

10. Kc, G.S., Keromytis, A.D., Prevelakis, V.: Countering code-injection attacks with instruction-set randomization. In: Proceedings of the 10th ACM Conference on Computer and Communications Security, CCS 2003. ACM (2003)
11. Lee, I., Jeong, S., Yeo, S., Moon, J.: A novel method for SQL injection attack detection based on removing SQL query attribute values. Math. Comput. Modell. 55(1–2), 58–68 (2012)
12. Liu, A., Yuan, Y., Wijesekera, D., Stavrou, A.: SQLProb : a proxy-based architecture towards preventing SQL injection attacks. In: Proceedings of the ACM Symposium on Applied Computing, SAC 2009. ACM (2009)
13. Luk, C.-K., Cohn, R., Muth, R., Patil, H., Klauser, A., Lowney, G., Wallace, S., Reddi, V.J., Hazelwood, K.: Pin : building customized program analysis tools with dynamic instrumentation. In: Proceedings of the ACM SIGPLAN Conference on Programming Language Design and Implementation, PLDI 2005. ACM (2005)
14. Mason, T., Brown, D.: Lex & Yacc. O'Reilly & Associates Inc., Sebastopol (1990)
15. Mitropoulos, D., Spinellis, D.: SDriver : location-specific signatures prevent SQL injection attacks. Comput. Secur. 28(3–4), 121–129 (2009)
16. Portokalidis, G., Keromytis, A.D.: Fast and practical instruction-set randomization for commodity systems. In: Proceedings of the 26th Annual Computer Security Applications Conference, ACSAC 2010. ACM (2010)
17. Su, Z., Wassermann, G.: The essence of command injection attacks in web applications. SIGPLAN Not. 41(1), 372–382 (2006)
18. Wei, K., Muthuprasanna, M., Kothari, S.: Preventing SQL injection attacks in stored procedures. In: Australian Software Engineering Conference, April 2006
19. Zhu, J., Xie, J., Lipford, H.R., Chu, B.: Supporting secure programming in web applications through interactive static analysis. J. Adv. Res. 5(4), 449–462 (2014). Cyber Security

Ensuring Kernel Integrity Using KIPBMFH

Zhifeng Chen[✉], Qingbao Li, Songhui Guo, and Ye Wang

State Key Laboratory of Mathematical Engineering and
Advanced Computing, Zhengzhou, China
xiaohouzi060123@gmail.com

Abstract. Kernel-level malwares are a serious threat to the integrity and security of the operating system. Current kernel integrity measurement methods have one-sidedness in selecting the measurement objects, and the characters of periodic measurement make TOC-TOU attacks unavoidable. The kernel integrity measurement methods based on hardware usually suffer high cost due to the additional hardware, while the kernel integrity measurement methods based on host are always likely to be passed. To address these problems, a kernel integrity protection approach based on memory forensics technique implemented in Hypervisor (KIPBMFH) is proposed in this paper. We first use memory forensics technology to extract the static and dynamic measurement objects, and then adopt time randomization algorithm to weaken TOC-TOU attacks. The experimental results show that KIPBMFH can measure the integrity of the operating system effectively, and has reasonable performance overhead.

Keywords: Kernel integrity · TOC-TOU · Memory forensics · Time randomization · Hypervisor

1 Introduction

The security of operating systems (OS) is one of the most important issues of computer security. As the kernel is the basic component of OS, its security impacts heavily on the security of OS.

Integrity measurement technique provides a comprehensive description of the system security through the measurement, verification and evaluation of the coincidence of the expectant and actual situation.

Current kernel integrity measurement methods can be divided into three categories according to their deployment levels, which are host-based, hardware-based and hypervisor-based, respectively.

The host-based methods [1–3] are most widely used. They mainly measure the static kernel objects such as system call table, which do not consider the dynamic object, cannot find the data-only attacks, and the use of periodic analysis techniques make them exist TOC-TOU (Time-of-Check to Time-of-Use) problem [4]. Besides, the objects of their methods are also limited.

The hardware-based methods [5, 6] solidify the detection tools at hardware level, which are isolated with the objects to be detected. They maybe tamper-resistant and

© Springer International Publishing Switzerland 2016
S. Qing et al. (Eds.): ICICS 2015, LNCS 9543, pp. 10–17, 2016.
DOI: 10.1007/978-3-319-29814-6_2

non-bypass, but due to the need for additional hardware support and high cost, they have not been widely used. In addition, they also have the TOC-TOU problem.

Given the isolation, insight and safety advantages of virtual machine technology, it has been used to measure and protect the integrity of kernel in recent years. The hypervisor-based methods [8–10] deploy the measurement tools in the hypervisor layer, which improve the safety of measurement tools to some extent. They bring additional load and performance loss, and only focus on measurement objects related to the process, do not consider other objects, such as modules, network connections, etc., resulting in inaccurate measurement results. The reasons are two-folded. One is the introduction of the intervention of virtual monitoring; the other is the lack of adequate upper semantic information.

Therefore, to solve these problems, a Kernel Integrity Protection Method Based on Memory Forensics in Hypervisor (KIPBMFH) is proposed, which is deployed in the Hypervisor layer. This method extracts the measurement objects in kernel memory space based on forensics technology. It uses lightweight hypervisor Bitvisor, which thus reduces the system cost and performance loss. This method also uses randomization time-triggered measurements, which makes extraction, analysis and measurement not follow the periodic rule any longer. So it can avoid the attacker to control the measurement rule, and weaken TOC-TOU attacks.

2 Problem Overview

The fundamental problem of the integrity measurement is obtaining measurement objects accurately, timely and comprehensively. However, existing kernel integrity measurement methods have one-sidedness in obtaining the objects. So to solve this key issue is important for improving the effectiveness of the integrity measurement.

Memory forensics technology is one of the currently popular digital forensics analysis techniques, which focuses on obtaining information from the computer memory, such as processes, files network connection status and other activities. It provides large amounts of information of system running status about network intrusion.

As integrity measurement objects exist in memory, the basic idea of memory forensics technology can be used to obtain the measurement objects. However, the memory forensics technology does not involve related discussions on the measurement objects. In addition, the memory forensics technology only simply provides a mechanism; it does not discuss how to set the measurement points and how to measure.

Therefore, applying the memory forensics technology on the kernel integrity measurement needs to address the following issues. Firstly, the memory forensics provides a method of extracting the measurement objects, but which measurement objects in memory to be obtained and how to get the measurement objects in the Hypervisor are the most important issue. Secondly, attackers can bypass the periodical integrity measurement to achieve attacks. So how to distribute the measurement points reasonably to reduce the possibility of escaping measurement without the use of real-time monitoring is another difficulty issue to be addressed.

3 Kernel Integrity Protection

3.1 Memory Forensics Based on EPT

Random Memory Extraction. Memory forensics methods to obtain physical memory contents can be divided into hardware-based and software-based methods [11]. These methods copy the entire contents of the physical memory to the storage devices. With the increase of physical memory, the time overhead grows fast. In fact, for a running operating system, the kernel space of physical memory is limited, and kernel memory analysis is also targeted to extract specific measurement objects, so dumping the entire contents of the memory to the external storage device is unnecessary.

Since the measurement objects are distributed in memory discretely, to overcome the deficiencies of the existing memory extraction method to realize on-demand extraction is to design a random extraction method. However, the address received by Hypervisor is the guest physical address, and access memory through host physical address. While the guest VM accesses the memory through guest virtual address. So to achieve memory access in Hypervisor has to design an algorithm which translates the guest virtual address into a host physical address. Therefore, we first need to do address translation, which translates the guest virtual address into the guest physical address, and then translates the guest physical address into the host physical address. Finally, we achieve access to the host physical memory in Hypervisor, thereby extracting arbitrary physical memory contents. In this paper, we take the Intel processor as the experimental environment. So we give the address conversion method based on the EPT as example.

Selectable PMCE (Physical Memory Contents Extraction) is designed and implemented according to the above ideal. Selectable extraction means that users can choose any address or address scope to get memory contents. This algorithm completes the memory randomly access and memory contents extraction, which solves the mapping problem of physical address and logical address. The algorithm is shown in Table 1, step 2–3 of the algorithm are corresponding to the address mapping process.

Kernel Memory Analysis. The memory contents extracted by PMCE are formatted with binary, so the next step is to identify the measurement objects from the contents. While the best solution is that determine the objects which influent the integrity of running kernel.

(1) determining the measurement objects. We determine the measurement objects according to the basic composition and running mechanism of kernel, and attacked objects. As we know, the objects like kernel code section, Interrupt Description Table(IDT), system call table(SCT), etc., have persistent values during the kernel running. Once they are destroyed, the expectation behavior of system will change, which means the integrity of kernel is destroyed. As they are persistent, we call them the static measurement objects. In addition, there are dynamically changed objects, such as processes, modules, network connection, and so on, we call them the dynamic measurement objects. Although they change dynamically, they have certain characteristics.

Table 1. Physical memory contents extraction algorithm

Algorithm 1. PMCE
Input: u32 beginaddress, u32 endaddress
Output: char[] MC//physical memory contents
(1) len=endaddress-beginaddress;
(2) gphy=gvtogp(beginaddress);//translate VM virtual address into VM physical address
(3) hphy=gptohp(gphy);//translate VM physical address into host physical address based on EPT
(4) while(len>0)
(5)   MC[i]=read_hpys_b(hphy);//access physical memory contents after memory map
(6)   len--;hpy++;i++;
(7) return MC;
Function: u32 gvtogp(u32 va)
(1) u32 cr3=get_guest_cr3();//guest VM CR3
(2) u32 gpgde =gptohp(cr3) +8*va>>39; //pgd
(3) u32 hpgde=gptohp(gpgde);
(4) u32 gpude=readaddress(hpgde) &0xfffff000+8*(va>>30&0x1ff);//pud
(5) u32 hpude=gptohp(gpude);
(6) u32 gpmde=readaddress(hpude) &0xfffff000+8*(va>>21&0x1ff);//pmd
(7) u32 hpmde=gptohp(gpmde);
(8) u32 gpte=readaddress(hpmde) &0xfffff000+8*(va>>12&0x1ff);//pt
(9) u32 hpte=gptohp(gpte);
(10) u32 gpa=readaddress(hpte) &0xfffff000+8*(va&0x1ff);//pa
(11) return gpa;

For example, the processes in Linux satisfy the relation: run_list⊆all-tasks or all-tasks==ps-tasks, where run_list represents the schedule processes, all_tasks represents the whole processes of system, ps-tasks represents the processes got by system tools.

Based on the above analysis, the measurement objects can be divided into static measurement objects and dynamic objects. They distribute in different memory positions, so next we will discuss how to reconstruct them from the memory.

(2) analyzing the measurement objects. The kernel symbol table of operating system is the entry point for memory analysis. The kernel symbol table stores the memory address of key data objects. Linux kernel symbol table names System.map, which stores thousands of symbol addresses, but we only concern with the contents related to integrity measurement. In addition, the definition of critical kernel data structures and offset of each field are also the important factors for memory analysis.

Now we take the analysis of the Linux system process analysis as an example to show the basic idea of memory analysis. Process information is stored in the task_struct structure, all of the processes are linked by double-linked list, shown in Fig. 1. Process #0 is the parent of all other processes, which stays in memory forever. So the analysis begins with Process #0. First, translate the logical address of Process #0 in System.map into host physical address, and then extract the contents of this process in memory by Hypervisor, and reconstruct PID, running status, process name and so on assisted by data structures definition of the operating system. Next, take Process #0 as the starting point, and then analyze the other processes through the double-link field of the process structure.

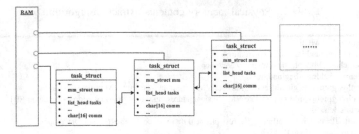

Fig. 1. Process structure and its organization on memory

In summary, when analyzing physical memory, we extract memory addresses of the measurement objects based on the kernel symbol table, and then reconstruct the measurement objects according the relation of addresses and critical kernel data structures.

3.2   Time Randomization Based Measurement Time Distribution Method

Due to the presence of TOC-TOU vulnerability of periodical measurement, attackers can bypass the integrity measurement by using this vulnerability. We set the value of the interval for T. The attackers can break the rule if they find out this vulnerability. Therefore, in order to avoid an attacker to grasp the rule of integrity measurement, we propose time randomization measurement method, which distributes the measure operations randomly into the time domain. However, some randomized algorithms may lead to measurement time points too dense or too sparse. The former will bring the system load increasing, while the latter will lead to measurement accuracy decline, so the distribution of measurement points cannot be arbitrary randomization.

According to the impact on system load caused by measurement time sequences of different time ranges and the measurement accuracy, we define the random seed in the [T/3, 6*T/5] range. This practice ensures that the distributions of measurement points meet the requirements, but also ensures that the measurement time is random. The specific process is as follows.

(1) Generate the seed s_seed at a given time range [T/3, 6*T/5];
(2) Select a largest prime number between 1 and n and an additional number of multiplier adder. And then calculate the value of s_time by formula (((multiplier*s_seed+adder)≫16)% (6*T/5)). If s_time is less than T/3, then the value of s_time should plus T/3 to obtain a time point RS. otherwise s_time is the final time point.
(3) Repeat step (2) until the number of time points is equal to n, and then finish the generation of time sequence.
(4) Synchronize the system time with the time sequences. Take the current system time as the first measure point, and then make each time point of the time sequence accumulate the system time in turn.

4 Experimental Results and Analysis

In this section, we provide the effectiveness and performance evaluation of KIPBMFH. Experimental environment is as follows.

Guest operating system is Ubuntu 12.04-x86, kernel version is 3.2.43, CPU is Intel (R) Core(TM) i5-750 @ 2.67 GHz, memory size is 4 GB. Using Bitvisor as Hypervisor, whose version is 1.4. Select rootkit, such as kbeast, enyelkm and suckit etc. as a test suit.

4.1 Effectiveness Evaluation

we verify the effectiveness of KIPBMFH through a variety of different rootkits, which use different methods to perform attacks. Table 2 shows the integrity measurement results comparison of KIPBMFH and other measurement tools in a variety of rootkit attacks, where "√" indicates a successful measurement, "×" indicates failure to measure the integrity of the system, "—" indicates that the system does not test this rootkit.

Table 2 shows that KIPBMFH successfully finds out variety of rootkit attacks,

Table 2. KIPBMFH and other tools' measurement for kinds of rootkit attacks

Rootkit	Attack level	KIPBMFH	Copilot	Osck	Gibraltar
ddrk	User, Kernel	√	—	—	—
wnps v0.26	Kernel	√	√	√	√
enyelkm v1.2	Kernel	√	√	√	√
adore-ng 0.56	Kernel	√	√	√	√
allroot	Kernel	√	√	√	√
mood-nt	Kernel	√	—	—	—
Knark-2.4.3	Kernel	√	√	—	√
suckit v2.0	Kernel	√	√	—	—
lrk v5	Kernel	√	×	×	×

while Copilot [5], Osck [8] and Gobraltar [6] only find out part of rootkit attacks. In conclusion, the measurement accuracy of KIPBMFH is higher than the existing measurement tools.

In addition, KIPBMFH not only can discover attacks, but also can get more fine-grain attack information, such as the number of system call, system call name, hidden processes information, the hidden network connection information, and so on. So KIPBMFH has a stronger analytical capability than other measurement tools.

4.2 Performance Evaluation

In this section, we take integrity measurement time as performance index to evaluate the efficiency of KIPBMFH. Measurement time refers to the time from the memory forensic analysis to obtain the integrity measurement results.

In addition, measurement time has a guiding role to determine the period time T. Integrity measurement time includes the time of physical memory analysis and integrity measurement. Table 3 shows the time and the total time required for each part. The measurement time is approximately 161.05544 ms.

Table 3. Time cost of part of measure process

	Physical memory analysis	Integrity measurement	All
Time (ms)	159.45004	1.6054	161.05544

In addition, as KIPBMFH needs to read memory to measure the guest, we use Stream to test the memory bandwidth of guest OS. The evaluation shows that the system load of KIPBMFH is only 0.18 % in the case of 15 s. Compared to 2 % – 6 % of Osck and 3.6 % – 48.3 % of SBCFI [7], the system load of KIPBMFH is negligible. Compared to 0.49 % of Gibraltar and 0.84 % of Copilot, KIPBMFH not only has small load, but also provide certain security. Therefore, KIPBMFH has certain advantages in time overhead and system load comparing with these measurement tools.

5 Conclusion

In this paper, KIPBMFH is proposed aiming at address the overhead, TOC-TOU problem and one-sidedness of measurement objects of the existing measurement methods. Compared with the periodical measurement tools, the measure ability and accuracy of KIPBMFH is higher.

References

1. Wang, Y.M., Beck, D., et al.: Detecting stealth software with strider ghostbuster. In: Proceedings of the International Conference on Dependable Systems and Networks (2005)
2. Joy, J., John, A.: A host based kernel level rootkit detection mechanism using clustering technique. In: Nagamalai, D., Renault, E., Dhanuskodi, M. (eds.) CCSEIT 2011. CCIS, vol. 204, pp. 564–570. Springer, Heidelberg (2011)
3. Liu, Z.W., Feng, D.G.: TPM-based dynamic integrity measurement architecture. J. Electron. Inf. Technol. **32**(4), 875–879 (2010)
4. Bratus, S., D'Cunha, N., Sparks, E., Smith, S.W.: TOCTOU, traps, and trusted computing. In: Lipp, P., Sadeghi, A.-R., Koch, K.-M. (eds.) Trust 2008. LNCS, vol. 4968, pp. 14–32. Springer, Heidelberg (2008)
5. Petroni, Jr. N.L., Fraser, et al.: Copilot - a coprocessor-based kernel runtime integrity monitor. In: Proceedings of the 13th Conference on USENIX Security Symposium (2004)
6. Baliga, A., Ganapathy, V., Iftode, L.: Automatic inference and enforcement of kernel data structure invariants. IEEE Trans. Dependable Secure Comput. **8**(5), 670–684 (2011)

7. Petroni Jr. N.L., Hicks, M.: Automated detection of persistent kernel control-flow attacks. In: Proceedings of the 14th ACM Conference on Computer and Communications Security (2007)
8. Hofmann, O.S., Dunn, A.M., et al.: Ensuring operating system kernel integrity with OSck. In: Proceedings of the 6th International Conference on Architectural Support For Programming Languages and Operating Systems (2011)
9. Li, B., Wo, T.Y., et al.: Hidden OS objects correlated detection technology based on VMM. J. Softw. **24**(2), 405–420 (2013). (in Chinese)
10. Lin, J., Liu, C.Y., Fang, B.X.: IVirt runtime environment integrity measurement mechanism based on virtual machine introspection. Chin. J. Comput. **38**(1), 191–203 (2015). (in Chinese)
11. Carvey, H.: Windows Forensic Analysis and DVD Toolkit, pp. 59–63. Elsevier: Syngress, Burlington (2009)

Bitsliced Implementations of the PRINCE, LED and RECTANGLE Block Ciphers on AVR 8-Bit Microcontrollers

Zhenzhen Bao[1,2]([✉]), Peng Luo[1,2], and Dongdai Lin[1]

[1] State Key Laboratory of Information Security, Institute of Information
Engineering, Chinese Academy of Sciences, Beijing, China
{baozhenzhen,luopeng,ddlin}@iie.ac.cn
[2] University of Chinese Academy of Sciences, Beijing, China

Abstract. Due to the demand for low-cost cryptosystems from industry, there spring up a lot of lightweight block ciphers which are excellent for some different implementation features. An innovative design is the block cipher PRINCE. To meet the requirement for low-latency and instantaneously encryption, NXP Semiconductors and its academic partners cooperate and design the low-latency block cipher PRINCE. Another good example is the block cipher LED which is very compact in hardware, and whose designers also aim to maintain a reasonable software performance. In this paper, we demonstrate how to achieve high software performance of these two ciphers on the AVR 8-bit microcontrollers using bitslice technique. Our bitsliced implementations speed up the execution of these two ciphers several times with less memory usage than previous work. In addition to these two nibble-oriented ciphers, we also evaluate the software performance of a newly proposed lightweight block cipher RECTANGLE, whose design takes bitslicing into consider. Our results show that RECTANGLE has very high ranks among the existing block ciphers on 8-bit microcontrollers in the real-world usage scenarios.

Keywords: PRINCE · LED · RECTANGLE · Bitslice · Block cipher ·
Lightweight · Cryptography · Microcontroller · Wireless sensor · AVR ·
ATtiny · Implementation

1   Introduction

In several emerging areas and in the Internet of Things (IoT) era, where hundreds billion of highly constrained devices are interconnected, working together and typically communicating wirelessly, security and privacy can be very important. Cryptographic techniques will be required for those devices and will be implemented on more devices at present and in the future. For different application scenarios, there are different efficiency measures to evaluate whether a cryptographic technique can be applied to the scenarios. For hardware implementation, dominant metric are gate count (power, cost), energy, latency etc. The

© Springer International Publishing Switzerland 2016
S. Qing et al. (Eds.): ICICS 2015, LNCS 9543, pp. 18–36, 2016.
DOI: 10.1007/978-3-319-29814-6_3

corresponding application examples are RFID and low-cost sensors, healthcare devices and battery-powered devices, memory encryption, in-vehicle devices and industrial control systems. For software implementation, memory (ROM/RAM) and execution time are important measures. Again, application examples are in-vehicle devices, sensors and consumer electronics.

Compare with general purpose cryptographic algorithms, lightweight cryptographic primitives which relax implementation requirements have more advantages in those scenarios. In this paper, we mainly talk about block ciphers which are the most versatile of the symmetric ciphers. Lightweight block ciphers can overcome limitations of gate count in small chips, for examples a state of the art AES-128 [1] hardware implementation uses 2400 GE (Gate Equivalent) [7], while PRESENT-128 [5], LED-128 [3,4] and SIMON-128 [6] can respectively offer a 1391 GE [8], a 1265 GE [4] and a 1234 GE [6] implementation. As the gate count is small, energy consumption is small. In applications where instantaneous response is highly desired, lightweight primitives such as PRINCE [2] and SIMON can achieve same or less latency of AES with respectively 1/40 and 1/52 gate counts at 130 nm low-leakage Faraday libraries. In other applications, such as sensor nodes or RFID tags, the equipped inexpensive microprocessor and microcontroller typically have a limited power budget and severely constrained memory (RAM and flash). For example, the ATtiny45 [11] has just 4 KBytes of flash, 256 bytes of RAM. There are lightweight ciphers, such as PRIDE [9] that can use no RAM and achieve similar throughput of AES with 1/2 flash bytes.

Over the last decade, cryptographic community has made significant efforts in the development of lightweight block ciphers. Following as a result, there are now more than a dozen of lightweight block ciphers for industry to choose from, including PRESENT [5] and CLEFIA [12], which have become ISO/IEC lightweight block cipher standards, and many other lightweight block ciphers, such as HIGHT [13], KATAN/KATANTAN [14], KLEIN [15], LBlock [16], LED [3], TWINE [17], PRINCE [2], SIMON and SPECK [6], PRIDE [9], RECTANGLE [18] etc. They are all excellent with respect to certain features. We refer to a web page [19] for a complement lightweight block cipher list. Consequences are the work and projects to improve and evaluated the performance of those lightweight block ciphers. With respect to software implementation on microcontrollers, there are several survey papers and open projects provide benchmarking results and reports on the performance of lightweight block ciphers [20–33].

On [25], a web page of ECRYPT II project, compact implementation and performance evaluation of 12 low-cost block ciphers on AVR ATtiny45 8-bit microcontroller are presented. The set of analyzed ciphers includes the low-cost ciphers designed until the corresponding paper [24] publication and thus it does not contain recent designs. The authors introduce a comparison metric that takes into account both the code size (ROM and RAM), the cycle count and the energy consumption. Implementation of the 12 ciphers comes from 12 different designers and codes are written in assembly. Both encryption, decryption and key management routines have to be implemented, and there is no usage scenarios (message length and mode of operation) involved. The authors of [29] implemented 21 low-cost (5 classical and 16 lightweight) block ciphers on the WSN430 sensor which is based on 16-bit TI MSP430 microcontroller. This is the biggest collection of low-cost ciphers implementations available on 16-bit microcontroller. However, as [32] points out, some of the implemented ciphers do not verify the test vectors. Both of the two above projects are not active for a long time.

Recently, a new benchmarking framework [32] was presented at the NIST Lightweight Cryptography Workshop 2015 [36]. Learn from the strengths and weakness of those previous benchmarking frameworks, the authors manage to design a more flexible and powerful framework for evaluation of lightweight ciphers on different embedded devices commonly used in the IoT context. By the publication, they have studied software performance of 13 lightweight block ciphers on three different devices, 8-bit AVR, 16-bit MSP and 32-bit ARM. Their evaluation consideration involves two most typical usage scenarios that resemble security-related operations commonly performed by real-world IoT devices. They also maintain a web page [34] with the most recent results. Triathlon challenge [33] are announced to improve those results and collect more implementations and more performance evaluations of more newer designs. They introduce a "Figure of Merit" (FOM) according to which an overall ranking of ciphers can be assembled.

Based on their current results in [32], the NSA designs Simon and Speck, AES and LS-designs are among the smallest and fastest ciphers on all platforms. Unfortunately, PRINCE which is superior as for low-latency and LED which is very compact as for hardware implementation get the lowest rank. Some newly proposed designs are also not included in their list, such as RECTANGLE [18] which is published in 2014 and presented at the NIST Lightweight Cryptography Workshop 2015 [36].

In this paper, we aim to contribute to the performance benchmarks of PRINCE, LED and RECTANGLE on 8-bit microcontrollers. Generally speaking, we expect to improve the performance of those ciphers on 8-, 16- and 32-bit microcontrollers. While, it seems reasonable to begin with 8-bit microcontroller, since the performance of those ciphers on 16- and 32-bit microcontrollers will be much better than that they can achieve on the 8-bit, and 8- and 16-bit microcontrollers constituted an overwhelming part of the total microcontroller market [35]. Moreover, optimizations on the 8-bit microcontrollers can have strong reference meanings for that on the 16- and the 32-bit.

1.1 Related Work

For nibble-oriented and byte-oriented ciphers, people usually use look up tables (LUTs), which may need large memory to achieve high throughput. Both of PRINCE and LED can be seen as nibble-oriented. Specifically, the original components of the ciphers can be described as operations on nibbles (intra-nibbles and inter-nibbles). For PRINCE, there are two related efforts which aim to improve the software performance on 8-bit AVR microcontrollers. In the first work [37], two implementations of PRINCE are presented. The first is T-table implementation which combines different operations within a round into a single table lookup operation. The second is block-parallel implementation which stores two nibbles in one register and processes them in parallel wherever possible. The S-boxes are stored as two 256-byte tables. In these two implementations, LUTs are too large to store in RAM. Thus they are coded in the programmable flash memory to which each access takes 1 more clock than that takes to the RAM.

The second work [38] presents a nibble-sliced implementation which stemming from bitslicing. Nibble-slicing is custom-made for nibble-oriented permutation layers. Similar to the block-parallel implementation in the first work, two nibbles are stored in one register. However, there is a difference between the two work: the block-parallel implementation processes nibbles within one block in parallel, while the nibble-sliced implementation processes two blocks in parallel, specifically, two nibbles in the same position of two blocks are stored in one register. Thus, it needs 16 registers to store states of two blocks. As in the first work, the second work also uses byte-oriented LUTs, which are 256-byte tables stored in flash memory for the S-boxes computation. Due to the nibble-slicing manner, the S-boxes computation and the SR operations can be merged together, which helps to reduce execution time. In the second work, cycle count and memory consumption are derived using AVR Studio simulations. Code in both of the two work was implemented in assembly. Performance evaluation in the first work involved cycles and code for nibble reordering, while it is unclear whether cycles and code for the nibble slicing are taken into account in the second work. Usage scenarios are not considered in both of the two work.

Work to improve the performance of LED on 8-bit AVR microcontrollers is quite rare. We can only refer to [34] for open source software implementation of LED on 8-bit microcontrollers. Unfortunately, the performance achieved by those C implementations in [32,34] are quite unsatisfactory.

1.2   Our Contributions

This work aims to improve the software performance of PRINCE and LED on 8-bit microcontrollers in two usage scenarios. By using bitslice technique instead of LUTs, we can minimize the requirement for memory and at the same time keep high throughput. In our implementations, by inventively rearrange the state bits, each message block can be processed in fine granularity parallel. By minimizing the number of instructions needed by each operation (S-boxes, MixColumns, ShiftRows etc.) of these ciphers, high throughput and low memory usage are achieved at the same time. Thus, these implementations can be used in serial message processing scenarios (corresponds to Scenario 1 in Section 2) in which the work [38] is hard to be used. It is quite natural to processing two blocks in parallel using our bitslice methods. Thus, in scenarios where message blocks can be processed simultaneously (corresponds to Scenario 2 in Section 2), our implementations also reduce the memory usage and execution time.

With respect to PRINCE, in Scenario 1, we achieve **2.88×** boost in throughput with **1/1.23** RAM and **1/2.18** flash memory comparing with [32], achieve **1.28×** boost in throughput comparing with [37]. In Scenario 2, we achieve **4.67×** boost in throughput with the same RAM and **1/2.09** flash comparing with [32], achieve similar throughput with $1/9.17$ RAM and similar flash comparing with [38]. For LED, comparing with [32], our implementation achieves $6.12\times$ boost in throughput with $1/2.09$ RAM and $1/2.17$ flash in Scenario 1, and $11.27\times$ boost in throughput with the same RAM and $1/2.72$ flash in Scenario 2. As shown in this work, PRINCE which gets a low rank in [32] is actually very efficient on 8-bit AVR devices.

We also aim to contribute performance benchmarks in the real-world usage scenarios of a newly proposed cipher RECTANGLE. Our results show that RECTANGLE gets very high ranks in those scenarios and can parallel SIMON in performance, see Table 3.

Table 1. Results for Scenario 1 (encryption of 128 bytes of data using CBC mode)

Cipher	Implementation	Code [Bytes]	RAM [Bytes]	Time [Cycles]
I: Encryption + Decryption (including key schedule)				
PRINCE	Triathlon [32]	5358	[c](374 − 70) 304	243396
	This work[a]	**2454**	**248**	**84656**
LED	Triathlon [32]	5156	[c](574 − 88) 486	2221555
	This work[a]	**2374**	**232**	**362889**
RECTANGLE	**This work**	**682**	**310**	**60298**
II: Encryption (without key schedule)				
PRINCE	Triathlon [32]	4210	[c](174 − 46) 128	121137
	Block-Parallel [37]	[b]1574	[b]24	[b]52048
	This work[a]	**1746**	**0**	**40736**
LED	Triathlon [32]	2600	[c](242 − 66) 176	1074961
	This work[a]	**1412**	**0**	**180384**
RECTANGLE	**This work**	**250**	**0**	**29148**
III: Decryption (without key schedule)				
PRINCE	Triathlon [32]	4352	[c](198 − 70) 128	122082
	This work[a]	**1746**	**0**	**40976**
LED	Triathlon [32]	3068	[c](280 − 88) 192	1146226
	This work[a]	**1414**	**0**	**182128**
RECTANGLE	**This work**	**252**	**0**	**29788**

[a]State rearrangement operations on plaintext, ciphertext and round-keys are all included.

[b][37] evaluates the encryption of one block (3253 cycles), and the cost of dealing with the encryption mode is not included. We use $3253 \times 16 = 52048$ to estimate the cycles count.

[c]In this table and in Tables 2 and 3, we subtract the stack consumption from the RAM usage of implementation in [32,34] to make a comparison considering the problem explained in Sect. 6.

Table 2. Results for Scenario 2 (encryption of 128 bits of data using CTR mode)

Cipher	Implementation	Code [Bytes]	RAM [Bytes]	Time [Cycles]
PRINCE	Triathlon [32]	4420	(68 − 44) 24	17271
	Nibble-Slice [38]	[a]2382	[a]220	[a]3606
	This work (FixOrder)	**2118**	**24**	**3696**
	This work (ReOrder)	**2642**	**24**	**4236**
LED	Triathlon [32]	2602	(91 − 67) 24	143317
	This work (FixOrder)	**956**	**24**	**12714**
	This work (ReOrder)	**1480**	**24**	**13254**
RECTANGLE	**This work (LessTime)**	**582**	**24**	**3405**
	This work (LowFlash)	**428**	**24**	**3995**

[a]In [38] (processing two blocks in parallel in nibble-slicing), it is unclear whether cost of reordering the nibbles and dealing with the encryption mode are considered.

Table 3. Updated results for ciphers performance in Scenario 1 and Scenario 2

Scenario 1 (encryption of 128 bytes of data using CBC mode)					Scenario 2 (encryption of 128 bits of data using CTR mode)				
Cipher	Code [Bytes]	RAM [Bytes]	Time [Cycles]	p_i	Cipher	Code [Bytes]	RAM [Bytes]	Time [Cycles]	p_i
Speck[b]	560	280	44264	3.21	Speck[b]	294	24	2563	3.00
Simon[b]	566	320	64884	3.86	Simon[b]	364	24	4181	3.87
REC[b]	682	310	60298	3.92	REC[b]	428	24	3995	4.01
PRIN[b]	2454	248	84656	7.36	AES[a]	1246	(81 − 49) 32	3408	6.90
AES[a]	3010	(408 − 70) 338	58246	8.15	LED[b]	956	24	12714	9.21
PRES[a]	2160	(448 − 46) 402	245232	11.13	PRIN[b]	2118	24	3696	9.65
LED[b]	2374	232	362889	13.44	PRES[a]	1294	(56 − 32) 24	16849	11.97

$p_i = \sum_{m \in M} (w_m \times \frac{v_{i,m}}{\min_i(v_{i,m})})$, where $M = \{$the code, the RAM, the cycles$\}$, $w_m = 1$ [32].

[a]Results for assembly implementations in [34]. [b]Results for assembly implementations by this work.

Tables 1 and 2 summarize our results on the performance of PRINCE, LED and RECTANGLE in Scenario 1 and Scenario 2, in which we also include the results of previous work to make comparisons.

The rest of the paper is organized as follows. Section 2 clarifies our target device, considering scenarios and performance measurement metrics. Sections 3, 4 and 5 respectively demonstrate how to achieve high software performance of PRINCE, LED and RECTANGLE on the AVR 8-bit microcontrollers using bit-slice technique. For each cipher, after a brief description, we exhibit how to rearrange the state bits, and how to implement its main operations in bitslicing with minimal number of instructions in two usage scenarios. Section 6 summarizes the results of this work.

2 Our AVR Implementations, Considering Scenarios and Performance Measurement

The specific target device in this work is the AVR ATmega128 8-bit microcontroller, which has 128 KBytes of flash, 4 KBytes of RAM and 32 8-bit general purpose registers. The ATmega128 uses an 8-bit RISC microprocessor. The arithmetic and logical instructions are usually destructive source operand, i.e. destination register is one of the source registers. And most of the numeric processing instructions take one clock cycle. Instructions which load data from and store data to RAM take 2 clock cycles and that access to flash memory take 3 clock cycles. Opcode of most instructions uses 2 bytes, some special types uses 4 bytes. For a detailed introduction of 8-bit AVR instructions, please refer to [10,32]. To achieve optimal performance, we code the ciphers in assembly and the assembly code was written in and compiled using Atmel Studio 6.2. Cycle counts, code sizes and RAM usage are also determined using this tool.

For each cipher, we have implementations targeting to two scenarios which are introduced in [32].

Scenario 1 - Communication Protocol [32]. This scenario covers the need for secure communication in sensor networks and between IoT devices. Sensitive data is encrypted and decrypted using a lightweight block cipher in CBC mode of operation. Data length exchanged in a single transmission is fixed to 128 bytes. The master key is stored in the device's RAM, from which, round keys are computed using the key schedule and then stored in RAM for later use. The key schedule does not modify the master key. The data that have to be sent as well as the initialization vector are also stored in RAM. Encryption is performed in place to reduce the RAM consumption.

Scenario 2 - Challenge-Handshake Authentication Protocol [32]. This scenario covers the need of authentication in the IoT. In the authentication protocol, the block cipher is used in CTR mode to encrypt 128 bits of data. The device has the cipher round keys stored in Flash memory and there is no master key stored in the device and consequently no key schedule is required. The data that has to be encrypted is stored in RAM, as well as the counter value. To reduce the RAM usage, the encryption process is done in place.

We consider the same three metrics of ciphers performance as considered in [32], including code size, RAM and execution time. Code sizes include the value of the Code and Data sections. Code section contains the bytes used by the binary code, Data section contains global initialized variables (such as the flash used by round constants etc.). The measurements do not consider the main function's code size, where all the cipher operations are put together. RAM usage includes scenario specific RAM data, such as data to encrypt, master keys, round keys and initialization vectors. The execution time is expressed in number of processor cycles spent executing those procedures, such as encryption, key schedule or decryption. In addition, our measurement includes the cost taken by rearrangement operations on the plaintexts, ciphertexts and round keys.

3   PRINCE AVR Implementations

In this section, we present the first (to our knowledge) bitsliced implementation of the PRINCE cipher on 8-bit AVR microcontroller.

3.1   The PRINCE Cipher

PRINCE operates on 64-bit blocks and uses a 128-bit key k which composed of two 64-bits elements, k_0 and k_1. It is based on the so-called FX-construction. The 128-bit key is extended to 192 bits by the mapping: $(k_0||k_1) \rightarrow (k_0||k_0'||k_1) = (k_0||(k_0 \ggg 1) \oplus (k_0 \gg 63)||k_1)$. k_0 and k_0' are used as whitening keys, while k_1 is the 64-bit key used without updates by the 12-round block cipher refer to as PRINCE_{core}. PRINCE has an α-reflection property. Decryption can reuse the exact same procedure of encryption by simply XOR a constant α to the third element k_1 of the extended key and exchange the used order between k_0 and k_0'. While, both procedures use the inverse round function as well as the round function.

The round function of PRINCE is AES-like, operates on a 4×4 state matrix of nibbles, which can be seen as composed of the following operations: KeyXor (correspond to k_i-add in the cipher specification) and RCXor (corresponds to RC_i-add), S-box (corresponds to S-Layer), MixColumns (corresponds to The Matrices M'-layer) and ShiftRows (corresponds to SR, and $SR \circ M' = M$ which is called the Linear Layer), among which only MixColumns is an involution. Thus, the implementations of the PRINCE have to instantiate the following operations: the KeyXor and RCXor, the S-box and inverse S-box, the MixColumns, the ShiftRows and Inverse ShiftRows. For more details about PRINCE please refer to [2].

We implement all of those operations in bitslicing, while all previous work is nibble-oriented and based on LUTs. Before the demonstration of those bitsliced implementations of each operation, we show how we slice the state.

3.2   PRINCE AVR Implementations

State Bits Rearrangement. The original arrangement of the state can be seen in Fig. 1. In this arrangement, successive four bits from right to left is called a *nibble*, successive four nibbles from right to left is a *row*. Successive four bits from top to bottom is a *slice*, successive four nibbles from top to bottom is a *column* [40]. Bits are indexed in the form of xyz, where x is the column index (0 to 3 right-to-left), y is the row index (0 to 3 top-to-bottom) and z is the slice index (0 to 3 right-to-left) within a column. Then the right up corner can be seen as the origin of the state.

To bitsliced implement the operations, we gather the bits with index $*yz$, i.e. bits with same row index and same slice index are gathered together. We call the resulted bit set a *lane*[1], in which all bits will be settled in the same register in our implementations. And we rearrange the state in a way as depicted in Fig. 2a.

---

[1] This name is borrowed from names of KECCAK-f state parts [42] .

row																
303	302	301	300	203	202	201	200	103	102	101	100	003	002	001	000
313	312	311	310	213	212	211	210	113	112	111	110	013	012	011	010
323	322	321	320	223	222	221	220	123	122	121	120	023	022	021	020
333	332	331	330	233	232	231	230	133	132	131	130	033	032	031	030

nibble   column   bit   slice

Fig. 1. The original arrangement of the state of bits for PRINCE

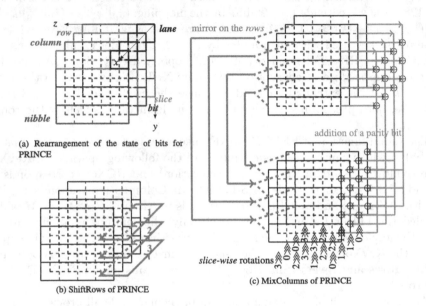

(a) Rearrangement of the state of bits for PRINCE

(b) ShiftRows of PRINCE

(c) MixColumns of PRINCE

Fig. 2. Rearrangement of the state of bits, ShiftRows and MixColumns of PRINCE

We then use the following conventions. Let $\mathbf{S}$ denotes the complete state, then $\mathbf{S}[*, y, z]$ denotes a particular lane. In implementations for Scenario 1, two lanes of one state $\mathbf{S}[*, y, z]$ and $\mathbf{S}[*, y+2, z]$ ($y \in \{0, 1\}$, $z \in \{0, \ldots, 3\}$) are stored in one register, in the lower half and the high half respectively. In Scenario 2, two lanes of two states $\mathbf{S}[*, y, z]$ and $\mathbf{S}'[*, y, z]$ ($y \in \{0, \ldots, 3\}$, $z \in \{0, \ldots, 3\}$) are stored in one register to process two blocks in parallel.

The rearrangement of the state takes 2 clocks per bit using rotate through carry instructions (ROL and ROR). Thus, rearranging the input state and back rearranging the output state take 4 clocks per bits.

Bitsliced Implementation of the KeyXor and RCXor. Since we have rearranged the encryption state, we should also rearrange the key and the round constant state in the same way. The KeyXor and RCXor operations can be merged together. In Scenario 1, during the key schedule procedure, the master key is extended and the resulted 3 sub-keys are rearranged and XORed to the pre-rearranged round constants to generate round-key-constant materials. The resulted round-key-constant materials are then stored in RAM. In Scenario 2, the resulted round-key-constant materials is extended (to encrypt two blocks in parallel) and coded in flash memory.

Bitsliced Implementation of the S-Box and the Inverse S-Box. By rearranging the state bits, we can implement the S-box and inverse S-box using logical operations instead of LUTs. In our rearrangement, 4 lanes within one row respectively correspond to the 4 input-outputs of S-boxes, thus 8 S-boxes can be computed in parallel using a logical instruction sequence operating on 8-bit registers, since 2 lanes share one register.

We firstly managed to find the bitsliced implementation of the 4×4 S-box (resp. inverse S-box) of PRINCE using an automatic search tool [41]. Operations in the resulted bitsliced implementations use the '*operator destination, source$_1$, source$_2$*' instruction format. While in AVR ATtiny, instructions destination register is one of the source register, i.e. it uses '*operator destination, source*' instruction format. Thus, we translate the primary instruction sequences into two-operator instruction sequences manually. In our translation, we try to minimum the required clock cycles and realize in place process, i.e. the outputs are in the same registers as the inputs.

The primary bitsliced implementation of the S-box (resp. inverse S-box) of PRINCE need 17 (resp. 16) terms. Translating into AVR instructions, it turns to be an instruction sequence with length of $17+4 = 21$ (resp. $16+6 = 22$) with 4 (resp. 6) additional copy register (MOV) instructions. Taking advantage of the copy register pair (MOVW) instruction, and processing 16 S-boxes together instead of 8 S-boxes, the S-layer (inverse S-layer) of PRINCE needs $17 \times 2+4 = 38$ (resp. $16 \times 2 + 6 = 38$) instructions, instead of $21 \times 2 = 42$ (resp. $22 \times 2 = 44$).

Bitsliced Implementation of the MixColumns. According to observations on the linear layer of PRINCE in [39,40], MixColumns of PRINCE can be seen as being composed of three compositions: mirror on the *rows*, addition of a parity bit, *slice-wise* rotations by 0,1,2 or 3 positions. Thus, it can be expressed as the parallel application of 16 independent transformations operating on one *slice* of the internal state. Figure 2c explains those transformations in a 3-dimensional way.

In our way of state bits rearrangement, 4 bits in same position within 4 different *slices* are stored in same register. Thus, parity bits of 8 *slices* can be computed in parallel. Mirror on the *rows* and *slice-wise* rotations can be combined to be a bits exchanging among different *lanes*.

In our implementation for Scenario 1, since the lower half and the high half of one register hold lanes in two rows (lane $S[*, y, z]$ and lane $S[*, y+2, z]$), addition of parity bit takes 7 instructions for 4 slices. Thus, addition of parity bit for the whole state takes 28 instructions per state. Since column $S[0, *, *]$ and column $S[3, *, *]$ in state S of PRINCE go through same MixColumns operations M_0, slice $S[0, *, z]$ and slice $S[3, *, z]$ within column $S[0, *, *]$ and column $S[3, *, *]$ go through same mirror and rotation operations for $z \in \{0, \ldots, 3\}$. Thus, bit 0 and bit 3 in a register, and bit 4 and bit 7 in a register go through same operations. Likewise, since column $S[1, *, *]$ and column $S[2, *, *]$ in state S go through same MixColumns operations M_1, bit 1 and bit 2 in a register, and bit 5 and bit 6 in a register go through same operations. Finally, we achieve a 4-way parallel implementation for the combination between mirror on the *rows* and *slice-wise* rotations. That takes $2 \times 9 + 2 \times 8 = 34$ instructions per state.

In our implementation for Scenario 2, since the lower half and the high half of one register hold some lanes in two states (lane $S[*, y, z]$ and lane $S'[*, y, z]$), addition of the parity bit takes 8 instructions for 8 slices. Thus, addition of parity bit for the whole state takes 32 instructions for two states (thus 16 instructions per state). Similar to the implementation for Scenario 1, the 0, 3rd, 4th and 7th bit in a register go through same operations, and the 1st, 2nd, 5th and 6th bit in a register go through another set of operations. We also achieve 4-way and 8-way parallel implementations for the combination between mirror on the *rows* and *slice-wise* rotations. That takes $4 \times 16 = 64$ instructions for 2 states (thus 32 instructions per state).

On the whole, in respect of Scenario 1, the MixColumns takes $28 + 34 = 62$ instructions per state. And in respect of Scenario 2, the MixColumns takes $16 + 32 = 48$ instructions per state.

Bitsliced Implementation of the ShiftRows and the Inverse ShiftRows. In our way of state bits rearrangement, ShiftRows and Inverse ShiftRows correspond to rotate bits in *lanes*, which are depicted in Fig. 2b. Thus that needs to rotate high the half and the lower half of 8-bit registers separately in our implementation. We implement this by logical AND (AND), logical shift left and right (LSL and LSR), bit load from the T flag in SREG to a bit in register (BLD) and bit store from bit in register to T flag in SREG (BST) instructions.

With respect to Scenario 1, it takes $4 \times 19 = 76$ instructions to implement ShiftRows (or Inverse ShiftRows) per state. With respect to Scenario 2, it takes $4 \times 19 + 2 = 78$ instructions to implement ShiftRows (or Inverse ShiftRows) per 2 states (thus 39 instructions per state).

4   LED AVR Implementations

In this section, we present the first (to our knowledge) bitsliced implementation of the LED cipher on 8-bit AVR microcontroller.

4.1   The LED Cipher

LED is a 64-bit block cipher, uses a key size from 64 to 128 bits, bases on an substitution-permutation network (SPN). The two primary instances, 64-bit key LED (named LED-64) and 128-bit key LED (named LED-128), respectively has 32 rounds and 48 rounds. In this paper, we will focus on LED-128. The key schedule of LED is very simple. In the case of LED-128, the master key k is composed of two 64-bit subparts, $k = k_1||k_2$, alternatively XORed to the internal state every 4 rounds. The 4-round operation between two key addition is called a *step*. The whole encryption process of LED is described using key addition and *step* operation.

Similar to the round function of PRINCE, the round function of LED is also AES-like, which operates on a 4×4 state matrix of nibbles. It also uses the following operations AddConstants (round constant addition), SubNibbles (corresponds to SubCells in [4]), ShiftRows, and MixColumnsSerial. None of those operations is involution. Thus, we should also implement their inverse operations. For more details about LED, please refer to [4].

4.2 LED AVR Implementations

State Bits Rearrangement. We follow the same naming convention for PRINCE state mentioned above in Fig. 2a to define the names of parts of LED state. Our rearrangement of LED state is quite similar to that of PRINCE state. A difference is that, in Scenario 1, each lane of LED state is stored in a whole 8-bit register, i.e. only the high half of the 8-bit register holds meaningful bits. Thus, 16 lanes $S[*, y, z]$ are respectively stored in 16 8-bit registers, leaving the lower half part of register empty. In Scenario 2, the lower half part of those 16 registers hold 16 lanes in another block state.

Bitsliced Implementation of the MixColumnsSerial. In MixColumnsSerial, each column of the internal LED state is transformed by multiplying it once with MDS matrix M, where $M = A^4$. It can also be viewed as four serial applications of a hardware-friendly matrix A, which can be implemented using XOR and bit-permutation. Bit-permutation is free in hardware, but usually not free in software implementations. However, by observing the iterative processing procedure of $M = A^4$, which is depicted in Fig. 3, we find that after 4 times of matrix multiplication, the four bits in each nibble switched from the order (3,2,1,0) to the order (1,0,3,2). Since each register in our implementation stores bits at same position within different nibbles, this switching operation corresponds to an exchanging operation between registers. Since bits needed to be exchanged are located in same nibble, this switching operation can be combined with the S-box operation, thus there is no need to exchange registers in real. Thus, we can implement the MixColumnsSerial using sequential XOR instructions, and implement a bit-permutation variant of the original S-box. In addition, because of the four columns of the LED state go through same MixColumnsSerial operation, and due to our rearrangement of the state of bits, MixColumnsSerial operations on four columns are done in parallel. In Scenario 1, we achieve a 4-way parallel implementation which needs 64 instructions per state, and in Scenario 2, we achieve an 8-way parallel implementation using 64 instructions for two states.

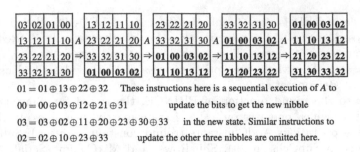

$01 = 01 \oplus 13 \oplus 22 \oplus 32$ These instructions here is a sequential execution of A to

$00 = 00 \oplus 03 \oplus 12 \oplus 21 \oplus 31$ update the bits to get the new nibble

$03 = 03 \oplus 02 \oplus 11 \oplus 20 \oplus 23 \oplus 30 \oplus 33$ in the new state. Similar instructions to

$02 = 02 \oplus 10 \oplus 23 \oplus 33$ update the other three nibbles are omitted here.

Fig. 3. MixColumnsSerial of LED operate on one column

Bitsliced Implementation of the S-Box and the Inverse S-Box. LED uses the PRESENT Sbox. There are previous work in which bitsliced implementation of PRESENT Sbox is studied. In [38], the authors aim to improve the throughput of PRESENT using bitslice technique. Their 19-instruction AVR implementation of the PRESENT S-box based on the 14 terms representation found by Courtois in [43]. Using the automatic search tool [41], we try to find optimal bitsliced implementations of both PRESENT S-box and the inverse S-box. The best solutions also need 14 terms for PRESENT S-box and it needs 15 terms for the inverse S-box.

Similar to our work on PRINCE S-box, we also try to find the best translation from those general solutions to instruction sequences in AVR instruction set. Through our manual optimization, there are 4 additional instructions (mov) penalty to implement the S-box on AVR based on the 14 terms (resp. 15 terms) sequences. When take advantage of the MOVW instruction, and deal with two sets of 8-bit registers together, 32 instructions (resp. 34 instructions) are needed to finish 16 S-boxes (in Scenario 1, since the lower part of a register is left empty, it takes 64 instructions to execute 16 S-boxes).

As mentioned above, our implementation of MixColumnsSerial for LED does not execute the last switching operation, instead, we combine this switching operation with the S-box operation. To encrypt, the input of S-boxes are switched between bit 0 and bit 2, and between bit 1 and bit 3. To decrypt, the output of inverse S-boxes are switched similarly. Thus, in our implementation, we actually implement a bit-permutation version of the S-box and the inverse S-box, and the final instruction number is 33 for the 16 input-switched S-boxes and 34 for the 16 output-switched inverse S-boxes.

Bitsliced Implementation of the ShiftRows and the Inverse ShiftRows. ShiftRows and the Inverse ShiftRows of LED are same with that of PRINCE. The difference between the implementations of the two ciphers is caused by the difference in the arrangement of the state bits in Scenario 1. $4 \times 12 = 48$ instructions are needed in Scenario 1 to rotate 16 lanes in one state and $4 \times 19 = 76$ instructions are needed in Scenario 2 to rotate 32 lanes in two states (thus 38 instructions to rotate 16 lanes in average).

5   RECTANGLE AVR Implementations

Presented at [36], RECTANGLE [18] is the most recent cipher discussed here, which is not involved in the analyzed cipher list in [32]. Thus, in this paper, we aim to provide a software performance benchmark for this cipher to [34].

5.1   The RECTANGLE Cipher

RECTANGLE operates on 64-bit cipher state. The key length can be 80 or 128 bits. In this paper, we mainly focus on the 128-bit key version (named RECTANGLE-128). The encryption is also based on an SP network. The substitution layer consists of 16 4×4 S-boxes in parallel, which is called SubColumn. The permutation layer is composed of 3 rotations, which is called ShiftRows. For more details about RECTANGLE, please refer to [18].

5.2   RECTANGLE AVR Implementations

State Bits Arrangement. Since the main idea of the design of RECTANGLE is to allow fast implementations using bitslicing techniques, the state arrangement in the bitsliced implementation is quite straightforward. Each 16-bit row of the cipher state is held by 2 registers, thus 8 registers are needed to hold the cipher state.

Bitsliced Implementation of the S-Box and the Inverse S-Box (Sub-Columns). Similar to our work on PRINCE and LED S-box, we first find the optimal general bitsliced implementations of the S-box and the inverse S-box, both of which requires 12 terms. Then we try to get the best translation from those general solutions to instruction sequences in AVR instruction set. Our manual optimization needs 2 (resp. 3) additional instructions (mov) penalty to implement the S-box (resp. inverse S-box) on AVR. When take advantage of the MOVW instruction, and deal with two sets of 8-bit registers together, $26 = 12 \times 2 + 2$ (resp. $27 = 12 \times 2 + 3$) instructions are needed to finish 16 S-boxes.

Bitsliced Implementation of the ShiftRows. The 1-bit rotation of the 16-bit row can be carried out using AVR's logical shift left (LSL), rotate left through carry (ROL) and add with carry (ADC) instructions, together with an all 0 register. We mainly focus on implementing the 12-bit and 13-bit rotation of the 16-bit row with a minimized number of instructions. Thanks for our optimization on the 4-bit rotation (both left and right) of 16-bit row using swap nibbles (SWAP), copy register pair (MOVW), logical AND with immediate (ANDI) and exclusive OR (EOR) instructions and 2 temporary registers, it only needs 7 instructions to perform 12-bit rotation (both left and right) of the 16-bit row. Thus the total ShiftRows and the inverse ShiftRows only need 20 instructions per state.

Bitsliced Implementation of the Key Schedule and Adding Round Key. The 128-bit key state are arranged as a 4×32 matrix. The key schedule for RECTANGLE-128 consists of applying the 4×4 S-boxes to the 8 rightmost columns of the four 32-bit rows of the key state, 1-round generalized Feistel transformation on the 4 rows and 5-bit round constant XORing on a single row. The 64-bit round key rk consists of the 16 rightmost columns of the four 32-bit rows.

In our implementation, applying the 4×4 S-boxes to the 8 columns takes 14 logical instructions (28 bytes and 14 cycles), the 1-round generalized Feistel transformation takes 18 instructions (36 bytes and 18 cycles), the 5-bit round constant XORing takes 2 instructions (4 bytes and 4 cycles). There are two key bytes shared between every two successive round keys. According to this observation, we can use $8 + 25 \times 6$ bytes instead of 26×8 bytes to store 26 round keys. Meanwhile, by reordering the key bytes and using two additional registers, we can use 6 load instructions instead of 8 when adding the 8-byte round keys during encryption and decryption.

Our results are consistent with that shown in [18], while evaluation in this paper considers the two typical real-world usage scenarios. In addition, we develop a high throughput implementation (LessTime) and a low flash implementation (LowFlash) in Scenario 2. In the high throughput implementation, two blocks are processed simultaneously. Thus, it allows to load the subkeys one time every two blocks and reduce the cycles by sacrificing 146 bytes of flash than that in the low flash implementation which processes blocks one by one using a loop.

6   Results Summary and Comparisons

The vast majority of instructions used in our bitsliced implementations are types of instruction which takes one clock cycle and 2 bytes. And there is no memory access except for load inputs, load round keys, load round constants and store outputs. We write the whole program in assembly code. And executions of operations in our implementations are all in place in registers. Thus, there is no extra RAM used to store local variables during the whole executions of encryption, decryption and key schedule. While, that inevitably gives rise to difficulty when making a comparison with the inline assembly implementation in [32] or [34], in which stack RAM is needed and PUSH and POP instructions are used to store and restore all modified registers. Thus, in Tables 1, 2 and 3, we subtract the stack consumption from the RAM usage of implementation in [32] or [34] to make a comparison. Besides, it would be hard to process blocks in parallel if comply with the C interface provided in [31].

All of our implementations have verified the test vectors provided in the cipher specifications, and the source codes are available on a web site [45].

For Scenario 1, our implementations include the key schedule and encryption, inverse key schedule (when needed) and decryption procedures. State rearrangement operations on the plaintext, ciphertext and round-keys are all included in our measurement. For Scenario 2, we only need to implement the encryption procedure, no decryption and no key schedule procedure are needed. Since encryption of 128-bit data using CTR mode, data is XORed with the output of the encryption procedure with counters as the input. There are two conventions on the usage of the two counters in our implementation for PRINCE and LED, because we rearrange the input of the encryptions. In the first convention, these two counters must be rearranged before going through the encryption procedure and must be back rearranged after the encryption procedure before XORed to the 128 bits message. We denoted this convention ReOrder. In the other convention, we encrypt the two counters directly and XOR the output with the 128-bit message without rearrangement of the state bits. We denoted this convention FixOrder. In our opinion, FixOrder convention does not relate to the security issues and is more efficient, thus it can be used as the final performance benchmark.

Our results on the performance of PRINCE, LED and RECTANGLE are summarized in Tables 1 and 2, in which we also include the results of previous work to make comparisons. In addition, we have also implemented Simon and Speck in assembly according to the method provided in [44]. If use our results to update the results in [34], we get Table 3. Since AES and PRESENT are coded in assembly, we only include this two ciphers to make comparisons. As shown in Table 3, RECTANGLE get a higher rank than AES and slightly lower rank than SIMON both in Scenario 1 and Scenario 2. PRINCE and LED respectively get a higher rank than AES in Scenario 1 and higher rank than PRESENT in Scenario 2. We believe that comparison in [34] is inevitable unfair since only AES, PRESENT, SIMON and SPECK are coded in assembly. Several other ciphers may also get a performance improvement if coded in assembly. And as pointed above, there is also unfairness when making a comparison between an implementation using pure assembly code and an implementation using inline assembly code. Besides, it is difficult to compare the performance between ciphers which supports parallelization and which does not. We remain the optimization work on other ciphers and a more fair comparison to the future.

Acknowledgement. Many thanks go to the anonymous reviewers. The research presented in this paper is supported by the National Natural Science Foundation of China (No.61379138), the "Strategic Priority Research Program" of the Chinese Academy of Sciences (No.XDA06010701).

References

1. Daemen, J., Rijmen, V.: The Design of Rijndael - AES - The Advanced Encryption Standard. Springer, Heidelberg (2002)
2. Borghoff, J., Canteaut, A., Güneysu, T., Kavun, E.B., Knezevic, M., Knudsen, L.R., Leander, G., Nikov, V., Paar, C., Rechberger, C., Rombouts, P., Thomsen, S.S., Yalçın, T.: PRINCE – a low-latency block cipher for pervasive computing applications. In: Sako, K., Wang, X. (eds.) ASIACRYPT 2012. LNCS, vol. 7658, pp. 208–225. Springer, Heidelberg (2012)

3. Guo, J., Peyrin, T., Poschmann, A., Robshaw, M.: The LED block cipher. In: Preneel, B., Takagi, T. (eds.) CHES 2011. LNCS, vol. 6917, pp. 326–341. Springer, Heidelberg (2011)
4. Guo, J., Peyrin, T., Poschmann, A., Robshaw, M.: The LED block cipher. http://eprint.iacr.org/2012/600
5. Bogdanov, A., Knudsen, L.R., Leander, G., Paar, C., Poschmann, A., Robshaw, M.J.B., Seurin, Y., Vikkelsoe, C.: PRESENT: an ultra-lightweight block cipher. In: Paillier, P., Verbauwhede, I. (eds.) CHES 2007. LNCS, vol. 4727, pp. 450–466. Springer, Heidelberg (2007)
6. Beaulieu, R., Shors, D., Smith, J., Treatman-Clark, S., Weeks, B., Wingers, L.: SIMON and SPECK: block ciphers for the internet of things. http://eprint.iacr.org/2015/585
7. Moradi, A., Poschmann, A., Ling, S., Paar, C., Wang, H.: Pushing the limits: a very compact and a threshold implementation of AES. In: Paterson, K.G. (ed.) EUROCRYPT 2011. LNCS, vol. 6632, pp. 69–88. Springer, Heidelberg (2011)
8. Poschmann, A.: Lightweight cryptography cryptographic engineering for a pervasive world. PhD Dissertation, Faculty of Electrical Engineering and Information Technology, Ruhr-University Bochum, Germany (2009)
9. Albrecht, M.R., Driessen, B., Kavun, E.B., Leander, G., Paar, C., Yalçın, T.: Block Ciphers – Focus on the linear layer (feat. PRIDE). In: Garay, J.A., Gennaro, R. (eds.) CRYPTO 2014, Part I. LNCS, vol. 8616, pp. 57–76. Springer, Heidelberg (2014)
10. Atmel Corporation. 8-bit AVR Instruction Set. http://www.atmel.com/images/doc0856.pdf
11. Atmel Corporation. AVR 8-bit Microcontrollers. http://www.atmel.com/products/microcontrollers/avr/default.aspx
12. Shirai, T., Shibutani, K., Akishita, T., Moriai, S., Iwata, T.: The 128-bit blockcipher CLEFIA (Extended Abstract). In: Biryukov, A. (ed.) FSE 2007. LNCS, vol. 4593, pp. 181–195. Springer, Heidelberg (2007)
13. Hong, D., Sung, J., Hong, S.H., Lim, J.-I., Lee, S.-J., Koo, B.-S., Lee, C.-H., Chang, D., Lee, J., Jeong, K., Kim, H., Kim, J.-S., Chee, S.: HIGHT: a new block cipher suitable for low-resource device. In: Goubin, L., Matsui, M. (eds.) CHES 2006. LNCS, vol. 4249, pp. 46–59. Springer, Heidelberg (2006)
14. De Cannière, C., Dunkelman, O., Knežević, M.: KATAN and KTANTAN — a family of small and efficient hardware-oriented block ciphers. In: Clavier, C., Gaj, K. (eds.) CHES 2009. LNCS, vol. 5747, pp. 272–288. Springer, Heidelberg (2009)
15. Gong, Z., Nikova, S., Law, Y.W.: KLEIN: a new family of lightweight block ciphers. In: Juels, A., Paar, C. (eds.) RFIDSec 2011. LNCS, vol. 7055, pp. 1–18. Springer, Heidelberg (2012)
16. Wu, W., Zhang, L.: LBlock: a lightweight block cipher. In: Lopez, J., Tsudik, G. (eds.) ACNS 2011. LNCS, vol. 6715, pp. 327–344. Springer, Heidelberg (2011)
17. Suzaki, T., Minematsu, K., Morioka, S., Kobayashi, E.: TWINE: a lightweight block cipher for multiple platforms. In: Knudsen, L.R., Wu, H. (eds.) SAC 2012. LNCS, vol. 7707, pp. 339–354. Springer, Heidelberg (2013)
18. Zhang, W., Bao, Z., Lin, D., Rijmen, V., Yang, B., Verbauwhede, I.: RECTANGLE: a bit-slice ultra-lightweight block cipher suitable for multiple platforms. Sci. China Inf. Sci. **58**(12), 1–15 (2015)
19. CryptoLUX: Lightweight Block Ciphers. http://www.cryptolux.org/index.php/Lightweight_Block_Ciphers
20. Law, Y.W., Doumen, J., Hartel, P.H.: Survey and benchmark of block ciphers for wireless sensor networks. ACM Trans. Sensor Networks (TOSN) **2**(1), 65–93 (2006)

21. Eisenbarth, T., Kumar, S., Paar, C., Poschmann, A., Uhsadel, L.: A survey of lightweight-cryptography implementations. IEEE Design & Test of Computers **24**(6), 522–533 (2007)
22. Kerckhof, S., Durvaux, F., Hocquet, C., Bol, D., Standaert, F.-X.: Towards green cryptography: a comparison of lightweight ciphers from the energy viewpoint. In: Prouff, E., Schaumont, P. (eds.) CHES 2012. LNCS, vol. 7428, pp. 390–407. Springer, Heidelberg (2012)
23. Knežević, M., Nikov, V., Rombouts, P.: Low-latency encryption – is "Lightweight = Light + Wait"? In: Prouff, E., Schaumont, P. (eds.) CHES 2012. LNCS, vol. 7428, pp. 426–446. Springer, Heidelberg (2012)
24. Eisenbarth, T., Gong, Z., Güneysu, T., Heyse, S., Indesteege, S., Kerckhof, S., Koeune, F., Nad, T., Plos, T., Regazzoni, F., Standaert, F.-X., van Oldeneel tot Oldenzeel, L.: Compact implementation and performance evaluation of block ciphers in ATtiny devices. In: Vaudenay, S., Mitrokotsa, A. (eds.) AFRICACRYPT 2012. LNCS, vol. 7374, pp. 172–187. Springer, Heidelberg (2012)
25. Eisenbarth, T., Gong, Z., Güneysu, T., Heyse, S., Indesteege, S., Kerckhof, S., Koeune, F., Nad, T., Plos, T., Regazzoni, F. et al.: Implementations of Low Cost Block Ciphers in Atmel AVR Devices, February 2015. http://perso.uclouvain.be/fstandae/lightweight_ciphers/
26. Matsui, M., Murakami, Y.: Minimalism of software implementation extensive performance analysis of symmetric primitives on the RL78 microcontroller. In: Moriai, S. (ed.) FSE 2013. LNCS, vol. 8424, pp. 393–409. Springer, Heidelberg (2014)
27. Cazorla, M., Marquet, K., Minier, M.: Survey and benchmark of lightweight block ciphers for wireless sensor networks. http://eprint.iacr.org/2013/295
28. Cazorla, M., Marquet, K., Minier, M.: Survey and Benchmark of Lightweight Block Ciphers for Wireless Sensor Networks. In: Samarati, P. (ed.), SECRYPT 2013 - Proceedings of the 10th International Conference on Security and Cryptography, Reykjavík, Iceland, 29–31 July 2013, pp. 543–548. SciTePress (2013)
29. Cazorla, M., Marquet, K., and Minier, M.: Implementations of lightweight block ciphers on a WSN430 sensor, February 2015. http://bloc.project.citi-lab.fr/library.html
30. Dinu, D., Biryukov, A., Großschädl, J., Khovratovich, D., Corre, Y.L., Perrin, L.: FELICS - fair evaluation of lightweight cryptographic systems, July 2015. http://csrc.nist.gov/groups/ST/lwc-workshop2015/papers/session7-dinu-paper.pdf
31. CryptoLUX.: FELICS (Fair Evaluation of Lightweight Cryptographic Systems), 15 August 2015. http://www.cryptolux.org/index.php/FELICS
32. Dinu, D., Corre, Y.L., Khovratovich, D., Perrin, L., Großschädl, J., Biryukov, A.: Triathlon of lightweight block ciphers for the internet of things (2015). http://eprint.iacr.org/2015/209
33. CryptoLUX.: FELICS Triathlon, 12 August 2015. http://www.cryptolux.org/index.php/FELICS_Triathlon
34. Dinu, D., Corre, Y.L., Khovratovich, D., Perrin, L., Großschädl, J., Biryukov, A.: FELICS block ciphers brief results and FELICS block ciphers detailed results, 1 October 2015 http://www.cryptolux.org/index.php/FELICS_Block_Ciphers_Brief_Results, http://www.cryptolux.org/index.php/FELICS_Block_Ciphers_Detailed_Results
35. Processor Watch, 8 January 2013. http://www.linleygroup.com
36. National Institute of Standards and Technology (NIST). Lightweight Cryptography Workshop 2015. http://www.nist.gov/itl/csd/ct/lwc_workshop2015.cfm

37. Shahverdi, A., Chen, C., and Eisenbarth, T.: AVRprince - an efficient implementation of PRINCE for 8-bit microprocessors. Technical Report, Worcester Polytechnic Institute (2014). http://www.ashahverdi.com/files/papers/avrPRINCEv01.pdf
38. Papapagiannopoulos, K.: High throughput in slices: the case of PRESENT, PRINCE and KATAN64 ciphers. In: Sadeghi, A.-R., Saxena, N. (eds.) RFIDSec 2014. LNCS, vol. 8651, pp. 137–155. Springer, Heidelberg (2014)
39. Canteaut, A., Fuhr, T., Gilbert, H., Naya-Plasencia, M., Reinhard, J.: Multiple differential cryptanalysis of round-reduced PRINCE. Presentation at Fast Software Encryption FSE 2014, London, 25 March 2014. http://fse2014.isg.rhul.ac.uk/slides/slides-09_4.pdf
40. Canteaut, A., Fuhr, T., Gilbert, H., Naya-Plasencia, M., Reinhard, J.: Multiple Differential Cryptanalysis of Round-Reduced PRINCE (Full version). eprint.iacr.org/2014/089
41. Gladman, B.: Serpent S Boxes as Boolean Functions. http://www.gladman.me.uk/
42. Bertoni, G., Daemen, J., Peeters, M., Van Assche, G.: The Keccak Reference, January 2011. http://keccak.noekeon.org/
43. Courtois, N.T., Hulme, D., Mourouzis, T.: Solving circuit optimisation problems in cryptography and cryptanalysis. In: Electronic Proceedings of 2nd IMA Conference Mathematics in Defence, Swindon (2011)
44. Beaulieu, R., Shors, D., Smith, J., Treatman-Clark, S., Weeks, B., Wingers, L.: The Simon and Speck Block Ciphers on AVR 8-bit Microcontrollers (2014). http://eprint.iacr.org/2014/947
45. Bao, Z., Zhang, W., Luo, P., Lin, D.: Bitsliced Implementations of Block Ciphers on AVR 8-bit Microcontrollers, October 2015. http://github.com/FreeDisciplina/BlockCiphersOnAVR

On Promise Problem of the Generalized Shortest Vector Problem

Wenwen Wang[1,2,3] and Kewei Lv[1,2(✉)]

[1] State Key Laboratory of Information Security,
Institute of Information Engineering, Chinese Academy of Sciences,
Beijing 100093, China
{wangwenwen,lvkewei}@iie.ac.cn
[2] Data Assurance Communication Security Research Center,
Chinese Academy of Sciences, Beijing 100093, China
[3] University of Chinese Academy Sciences, Beijing 100049, China

Abstract. In 2009, Blömer and Naewe proposed the Generalized Shortest Vector Problem (GSVP). We initiate the study of the promise problem (GAPSAM) for GSVP. It is a promise problem associated with estimating the subspace avoiding minimum. We show $GAPSAM_{c \cdot n}$ lies in $coNP$, where c is a constant. Furthermore, we study relationships between GAPSAM of a lattice and the nth successive minimum, the shortest basis, and the shortest vector in the dual of the saturated sublattice, and obtain new transference theorems for GAPSAM. Then, using the new transference theorems, we give various deterministic polynomial time reductions among the promise problems for some lattice problems. We also show $GAPSAM_\gamma$ can be reduced to the promise problem associated to the Closest Vector Problem ($GAPCVP_\gamma$) under a deterministic polynomial time rank-preserving reduction.

Keywords: The generalized shortest vector problem · The saturated sublattice · Transference theorems · Polynomial time reduction

1 Introduction

A lattice is the set of all integer combinations of n linearly independent vectors in $\mathbb{R}^m$, where n is the rank of the lattice, m is the dimension of the lattice, and the n linearly independent vectors are called a lattice basis. Let $B = [b_1, b_2, \ldots, b_n]$ be a basis of the lattice L. The ith successive minimum $\lambda_i(L)$ of the lattice L is the least number r such that the sphere centered at the origin with radius r contains i linearly independent lattice vectors. The length of a basis B is $g(B)$, that is, $g(B) = \max_i \|b_i\|$, and $g(L)$ is the minimum value of $g(B)$ over all bases B of L. Some important lattice problems are defined below, where $\gamma \geq 1$ is a function of rank:

SVP (Shortest Vector Problem): Given a lattice L, find approximate nonzero lattice vector v such that $\|v\| \leq \gamma \cdot \lambda_1(L)$.

© Springer International Publishing Switzerland 2016
S. Qing et al. (Eds.): ICICS 2015, LNCS 9543, pp. 37–49, 2016.
DOI: 10.1007/978-3-319-29814-6_4

CVP (Closest Vector Problem): Given a lattice L and a target vector t, find a lattice point v such that $dist(v, t) \leq \gamma \cdot dist(L, t)$.

SIVP (Shortest Independent Vector Problem): Given a lattice L of rank n, find n linearly independent lattice vector $s_1, s_2, \ldots, s_n$ such that $\|s_i\| \leq \gamma \cdot \lambda_n(L), i = 1, 2, \ldots, n$.

SBP (Shortest Basis Problem): Given a lattice L, L is generated by basis B, find an equivalent basis B' such that $g(\mathcal{L}(B')) \leq \gamma \cdot g(L)$.

These lattice problems have been widely studied, and it is known that all of these problems are NP-hard [1,7,13,14]. Aharonov and Regev [3] showed that approximating SVP and CVP lie in $NP \cap coNP$ within a factor of $\sqrt{n}$. Goldreich and Goldwasser [11] showed that approximating SVP and CVP lie in $NP \cap coAM$ within a factor of $\sqrt{n/O(\log n)}$. Boppana et al. [8] found that approximating SVP and CVP within a factor of $\sqrt{n/O(\log n)}$ is not NP-hard unless the polynomial hierarchy collapses. Ajtai, Kumar and Sivakumar [2] proposed a sieve method for computing SVP under a randomized $2^{O(n)}$ time algorithm. Blömer and Seifert [7] proved that approximating SIVP and SBP within any constant factor are NP-hard and within a factor of $O(n/\sqrt{\log n})$ are $NP \cap coAM$. Guruswami et al. [12] proved that SIVP lies in $coAM$ within an improved approximation factor of $O(\sqrt{n/\log n})$ and is in $coNP$ within an approximation factor of $O(\sqrt{n})$. Blömer and Naewe [5] proposed the Generalized Shortest Vector Problem (GSVP) and gave polynomial-time reductions from SVP, CVP, SIVP, and SMP (Successive Minima Problem) to GSVP. They also proved that there exists a randomized algorithm in single-exponential time which approximates the GSVP within a factor of $1 + \epsilon$, where $0 < \epsilon \leq 2$, with success probability $1 - 2^{-\Omega(n)}$ for all ℓ_p norms. This result implies that in single-exponential time there exists an approximation algorithm for all above-mentioned lattice problems for all ℓ_p norms for $1 \leq p \leq \infty$. Micciancio [16] gave efficient reductions among approximation problems and showed that several lattice problems that are equivalent under polynomial-time rank-preserving reductions.

Transference theorems reflect relationships between the successive minima of a lattice and its dual lattice. As a consequence of transference theorems, it was shown in [15] that, under Karp reduction, $SVP_{O(n)}$ can not be NP-hard unless $NP = coNP$. Banaszczyk [4] proved that the following inequality: for a lattice L of rank n with dual lattice L^*, $1 \leq \lambda_1(L) \cdot \lambda_n(L^*) \leq n$. Cai [9,10] generalized the transference theorems of Banaszcyk to obtain the following bounds relating the successive minima of a lattice with the minimum length of generating vectors of its dual: for a lattice L of rank n with dual lattice L^*, $1 \leq \lambda_{n-i+1}(L) \cdot g_i(L^*) \leq C \cdot n$ for all $1 \leq i \leq n$ and some universal constant C. The lattice quantity $g_i(L)$ is defined as follows. First, $g(L)$ is the minimum value r such that the ball $\mathcal{B}(0, r)$ centered at 0 with radius r contains a set of linearly independent lattice vectors that generate the lattice L. Define a saturated sublattice L' such that a sublattice $L' \subset L$ satisfies $L' = L \cap span(L')$ [10]. Then, $g_i(L)$ is the minimum value r such that the sublattice generated by $L \cap \mathcal{B}(0, r)$ contains an i dimensional saturated sublattice L' for $1 \leq i \leq dim(L)$.

From [10], $\lambda_i(L) \cdot g_{n-i+1}(L^*) \leq C \cdot n$ and $g_n(L) = g(L)$ for all $1 \leq i \leq n$, the proof used the discrete Fourier transform and discrete potential functions.

Our Contributions. The first contribution is to present the promise problem GAPSAM associated with GSVP and construct new transference theorems for GAPSAM using the algorithm from [16] and properties of subspace. We obtain the following inequalities:

$$1 \leq \lambda_M(L) \cdot \lambda_n(L_1^*) \leq c \cdot n, \tag{1}$$

$$1 \leq \lambda_M(L) \cdot g(L_1^*) \leq d \cdot n, \tag{2}$$

where n is the rank L_1 and L_1^* is the dual of L_1, c and d are constants. The subspace avoiding minimum $\lambda_M(L)$ of a lattice L with respect to some subspace $M \subset span(L)$ is the smallest real number r such that there exists a vector in $L \backslash M$ of length at most r.

By Regev's result [17], we also prove that for a lattice L of rank l and a subspace $M \subset span(L)$,

$$1 \leq \lambda_M(L) \cdot \lambda_1(L_1^*) \leq n, \tag{3}$$

where L_1^* is the dual of a saturated rank n sublattice L_1 of L.

The inequality (2) is similar to Cai's, but our proof is simper. In [9,10], Cai presented the inequality $1 \leq \lambda_1(L) \cdot g(L^*) \leq C \cdot n$, which reflects the relationship between the shortest lattice vector of L and the shortest basis of the dual lattice L^*. Our result, $1 \leq \lambda_M(L) \cdot g(L_1^*) \leq d \cdot n$, associates the minimum length of lattice vectors in $L \backslash M$ to the shortest basis of dual saturated sublattice L_1 generated by intersecting L with a subspace $V \subset span(L)$, where $V \oplus M = span(L)$.

By these results, we prove that $GAPSAM_{cn}$ is in $coNP$, where c is a constant. We also give polynomial reductions between GAPSVP, GAPSIVP, and GAPSBP and GAPSAM. We also obtain the following inequalities: $1 \leq \lambda_1(L) \cdot \lambda_n(L_1^*) \leq c \cdot n$; $1 \leq \lambda_1(L) \cdot g(L_1^*) \leq d \cdot n$; $1 \leq \lambda_1(L) \cdot \lambda_1(L_1^*) \leq n$, where L_1^* is the dual of a saturated rank n sublattice L_1 of L. These inequalities show the relationships between the lattice and the dual of the saturated sublattice.

The second contribution is that for any $\gamma \geq 1$, we give a deterministic polynomial time rank-preserving reduction from $GAPSAM_\gamma$ to $GAPCVP_\gamma$.

Micciancio [16] considered SVP$'$ as a variant of SVP which is a new less standard problem on lattices. The problem SVP$'$ is to minimize the norm $\|Bx\|$ where $x = (x_1, \ldots, x_i, \ldots, x_n)$ and $x_i \neq 0$ for some i. Here, we propose the promise version GAPSVP$'$ for SVP$'$ and show that there exist rank and approximation preserving reductions from $GAPSAM_\gamma$ to $GAPSVP'_\gamma$ and $GAPSVP'_\gamma$ to $GAPCVP_\gamma$. Hence, $GAPSAM_\gamma$ can be reduced to $GAPCVP_\gamma$ under deterministic polynomial time rank-preserving reduction.

Organization. The paper is organized as follows. In Sect. 2, we introduce basic notations for lattices and some promise versions of lattice problems. In Sect. 3, we first study of the promise problem GAPSAM for GSVP. Then, we present variants of transference theorems for GAPSAM. From these relationships, we give polynomial time reductions from GAPSAM to other lattice problems. In Sect. 4, we show that GAPSAM_γ can be reduced to GAPCVP_γ.

2   Preliminaries

Let $\mathbb{R}^m$ be an m-dimensional Euclidean space. For every vector $\boldsymbol{x} = (x_1, x_2, \ldots, x_m) \in \mathbb{R}^m$, the ℓ_2-norm of $\boldsymbol{x}$ is defined as $\|\boldsymbol{x}\|_2 = \sqrt{\sum_{i=1}^m x_i^2}$. The scalar product of two vectors $\boldsymbol{x}$ and $\boldsymbol{y}$ is $\langle \boldsymbol{x}, \boldsymbol{y} \rangle = \sum_i x_i y_i$. $\text{dist}(\boldsymbol{x}, \boldsymbol{L})$ is the minimum Euclidean distance from $\boldsymbol{x} \in \mathbb{R}^m$ to any vector in $\boldsymbol{L}$. All definitions and results in this paper are based on the ℓ_2 norm.

A lattice $\boldsymbol{L}$ is the set of all linear combinations generated by n linearly independent vectors $\boldsymbol{b}_1, \ldots, \boldsymbol{b}_n$ in $\mathbb{R}^m (m \geq n)$, that is,

$$L = \{\sum_{i=1}^n x_i \boldsymbol{b}_i | x_i \in \mathbb{Z}, 1 \leq i \leq n\}.$$

The integer n is the rank of the lattice and m is the dimension of the lattice. The sequence of linearly independent vectors $\boldsymbol{b}_1, \ldots, \boldsymbol{b}_n \in \mathbb{R}^m$ is called a basis of the lattice. We can represent $\boldsymbol{b}_1, \ldots, \boldsymbol{b}_n$ as a matrix $\boldsymbol{B}$ with m rows and n columns, that is, $\boldsymbol{B} = [\boldsymbol{b}_1, \ldots, \boldsymbol{b}_n] \in \mathbb{R}^{m \times n}$. The lattice $\boldsymbol{L}$ generated by a basis $\boldsymbol{B}$ is denoted by $\boldsymbol{L} = \mathcal{L}(\boldsymbol{B}) = \{\boldsymbol{Bx} : \boldsymbol{x} \in \mathbb{Z}^n\}$. A lattice has many different bases. Two matrices $\boldsymbol{B}$ and $\boldsymbol{B}'$ are two bases of the same lattice $\mathcal{L}$ if and only if $\boldsymbol{B} = \boldsymbol{B}'U$ for some unimodular matrix U. If $\mathcal{L}(\boldsymbol{S})$ is a sublattice of $\mathcal{L}(\boldsymbol{B})$, then any lattice point from the lattice $\mathcal{L}(\boldsymbol{S})$ also belongs to $\mathcal{L}(\boldsymbol{B})$. We denote this by $\mathcal{L}(\boldsymbol{S}) \subseteq \mathcal{L}(\boldsymbol{B})$.

For a lattice $\boldsymbol{L}$, the dual lattice $\boldsymbol{L}^*$ is a set of all vectors $\boldsymbol{y} \in span(\boldsymbol{L})$ that satisfy $\langle \boldsymbol{x}, \boldsymbol{y} \rangle \in \mathbb{Z}$ for all $\boldsymbol{x} \in \boldsymbol{L}$, that is,

$$L^* = \{\boldsymbol{y} \in span(\boldsymbol{L}) : \forall \boldsymbol{x} \in \boldsymbol{L}, \langle \boldsymbol{x}, \boldsymbol{y} \rangle \in \mathbb{Z}\}.$$

The dual lattice $\boldsymbol{L}^*$ is a lattice.

Successive minima are fundamental constants of a lattice. The first successive minimum of a lattice $\boldsymbol{L}$, denoted by $\lambda_1(\boldsymbol{L})$, is the length of the shortest non-zero lattice vector. Formally, $\lambda_1(\boldsymbol{L}) = min\{\|\boldsymbol{x}\| : \boldsymbol{x} \in \boldsymbol{L} \backslash \{0\}\} = min_{\boldsymbol{x} \neq \boldsymbol{y} \in \boldsymbol{L}} \|\boldsymbol{x} - \boldsymbol{y}\|$. The ith minimum $\lambda_i(\boldsymbol{L})$ of a lattice $\boldsymbol{L}$ is the smallest value r such that $\mathcal{B}(0, r)$ contains i linearly independent lattice vectors, that is, $\lambda_i(\boldsymbol{L}) = min\{r : dim(\boldsymbol{L} \cap \mathcal{B}(0, r)) \geq i\}$ where $\mathcal{B}(0, r)$ is an open ball of radius r centered in $\boldsymbol{0}$.

Let $g(\boldsymbol{B})$ be the maximum length of vectors $\boldsymbol{b}_i$ in the basis $\boldsymbol{B}$, that is, $g(\boldsymbol{B}) = \max_i \|\boldsymbol{b}_i\|$. We define $g(\boldsymbol{L})$ as the minimum value of $g(\boldsymbol{B})$ over all bases $\boldsymbol{B}$ of $\boldsymbol{L}$, that is, $g(\boldsymbol{L}) = \min_{\boldsymbol{B}} g(\boldsymbol{B})$.

The following are several important lattice problems. Here we only concentrate on promise problems for approximate lattice problems.

Definition 1 (GAPSVP$_\gamma$). (L, r) *is an instance of GAPSVP$_\gamma$, where $L \subseteq \mathbb{Z}^m$ is a lattice of rank n and $r \in \mathbb{Q}$ is a rational number, such that*

- (L, r) *is a YES instance if $\lambda_1(L) \leq r$,*
- (L, r) *is a NO instance if $\lambda_1(L) > \gamma \cdot r$.*

Definition 2 (GAPCVP$_\gamma$). (L, t, r) *is an instance of GAPCVP$_\gamma$, where $L \subseteq \mathbb{Z}^m$ is a lattice of rank n, $t \in \mathbb{Z}^m$ is a vector and $r \in \mathbb{Q}$ is a rational number, such that*

- (L, t, r) *is a YES instance if $dist(L, t) \leq r$,*
- (L, t, r) *is a NO instance if $dist(L, t) > \gamma \cdot r$.*

Definition 3 (GAPSIVP$_\gamma$). (L, r) *is an instance of GAPSIVP$_\gamma$, where $L \subseteq \mathbb{Z}^m$ is a lattice of rank n and $r \in \mathbb{Q}$ is a rational number, such that*

- (L, r) *is a YES instance if $\lambda_n(L) \leq r$,*
- (L, r) *is a NO instance if $\lambda_n(L) > \gamma \cdot r$.*

Definition 4 (GAPSBP$_\gamma$). (L, r) *is an instance of GAPSBP$_\gamma$, where $L \subseteq \mathbb{Z}^m$ is a lattice of rank n and generated by a basis B and $r \in \mathbb{Q}$ is a rational number, such that*

- (L, r) *is a YES instance if there exists an equivalent basis B' to B such that $g(\mathcal{L}(B')) \leq r$,*
- (L, r) *is a NO instance if for all equivalent basis B' to B has $g(\mathcal{L}(B')) > \gamma \cdot r$.*

Definition 5 (SVP′ [16]). *Given a lattice $B \in \mathbb{Z}^{m \times n}$ and an index $i \in \{1, \ldots, n\}$, find a lattice vector Bx with $x_i \neq 0$ such that $\|Bx\| \leq \gamma min\{\|Bx\| : x_i \neq 0\}$.*

We now propose the promise problem GAPSVP′ associated to the approximate problem SVP′.

Definition 6 (GAPSVP′$_\gamma$). (L, i, r) *is an instance of GAPSVP′$_\gamma$, where $L \subseteq \mathbb{Z}^m$ is a lattice of rank n and generated by a basis B and $r \in \mathbb{Q}$ is a rational number, such that*

- (L, i, r) *is a YES instance if $\lambda_1^{(i)}(L) \leq r$, i.e. there exists a vector $x \in \mathbb{Z}^n$ with $x_i \neq 0$ such that $\|Bx\| \leq r$,*
- (L, i, r) *is a NO instance if $\lambda_1^{(i)}(L) > \gamma \cdot r$, i.e. for all vectors $x \in \mathbb{Z}^n$ with $x_i \neq 0$ such that $\|Bx\| > \gamma \cdot r$.*

where $\lambda_1^{(i)}(L) = \min_{x \in \mathbb{Z}^n} \{\|Bx\| : x_i \neq 0\}$.

The next definition is a new lattice problem proposed in [6] where reductions from SVP, CVP, SIVP, and SMP to GSVP are given.

Definition 7 (GSVP). *Given a lattice $L \subseteq \mathbb{Z}^m$ and a linear subspace $M \subset span(L)$, the goal is to find a vector $v \in L \backslash M$ such that $\|v\| \leq \gamma \cdot dist(0, L \backslash M)$.* We set

$$\lambda_M(L) = min\{r \in \mathbb{R} | \exists\ v \in L \backslash M, \|v\| \leq r\}$$

and call this the subspace avoiding minimum (SAM).

It is clear that SVP is a special case of GSVP when $M = \{0\}$, we have $\lambda_M(L) = \lambda_1(L)$. So, there is a trivial reduction from SVP$_\gamma$ to GSVP$_\gamma$.

3   The Transference Theorems for GAPSAM

In this section, we first propose the promise problem (GAPSAM) associated to GSVP and present new transference theorems for GAPSAM.

3.1   The Variants of Cai's Transference Theorems

Definition 8 (GAPSAM$_\gamma$). (L, M, r) *is an instance of GAPSAM$_\gamma$, where* $L \subseteq \mathbb{Z}^m$ *is a lattice of rank* n, M *is a linear subspace of* $span(L)$, $r \in \mathbb{Q}$ *is a rational number, such that*

- (L, M, r) *is a YES instance if* $\lambda_M(L) \leq r$,
- (L, M, r) *is a NO instance if* $\lambda_M(L) > \gamma \cdot r$.

Banaszcyk [4], Cai [10], and Regev [17] proved that the following theorem.

Theorem 1. *For any rank-n lattice* L, *its dual lattice is* L^*, *there exist constants* c, d *such that*

1. $\lambda_1(L) \cdot \lambda_n(L^*) \leq c \cdot n$.
2. $1 \leq \lambda_1(L) \cdot g(L^*) \leq d \cdot n$.
3. $1 \leq \lambda_1(L) \cdot \lambda_1(L^*) \leq n$.

We also need the following lemma.

Lemma 1 [16] . There is a polynomial time algorithm that on input a lattice basis $B = [b_1, b_2, \ldots, b_n] \in \mathbb{Q}^{m \times n}$ and a linear subspace S, outputs a new basis $\tilde{B} = [\tilde{b}_1, \ldots, \tilde{b}_d]$ for $\mathcal{L}(B)$ such that $\mathcal{L}(\tilde{b}_1, \ldots, \tilde{b}_d) = S \cap \mathcal{L}(B)$, where d is the dimension of $S \cap span(B)$.

Combining Lemma 1 with Theorem 1, we immediately obtain the following theorem about $\lambda_M(L)$. The first two parts in the following theorem are variants of Cai's result [10]. We prove this independently with a simple method.

Theorem 2. *For any rank-l lattice* L *and a subspace* $M \subset span(L)$, *there exist constants* $c > 0$, $d > 0$ *such that*

1. $1 \leq \lambda_M(L) \cdot \lambda_n(L_1^*) \leq c \cdot n$.
2. $1 \leq \lambda_M(L) \cdot g(L_1^*) \leq d \cdot n$.
3. $1 \leq \lambda_M(L) \cdot \lambda_1(L_1^*) \leq n$.

where L_1^* *is the dual of saturated sublattice* L_1 *with rank* n *of* L.

Proof. Assume the lattice L is generated by a basis $B \in \mathbb{Z}^{m \times l}$. Because M is a subspace of $span(L)$, $rank(M) < rank(span(L))$. Note that, by the properties of subspaces, there must exists a subspace V such that

$$V \oplus M = span(L).$$

Run the algorithm from Lemma 1 on the lattice L and the subspace V to obtain a lattice basis $\widetilde{B} = [\tilde{b}_1, \ldots, \tilde{b}_n] \in \mathbb{Z}^{m \times n}$ for L, such that $\mathcal{L}(\tilde{b}_1, \ldots, \tilde{b}_n) = V \cap L$, where $n = dim(V \cap span(L))$.

Clearly, the two bases B and $\widetilde{B}$ are equivalent, that is, $\widetilde{B} = BU$ for some unimodular matrix U. Let $\mathcal{L}(\tilde{b}_1, \ldots, \tilde{b}_n) = L_1$. Using Theorem 1 for a lattice L_1 of rank n, we obtain the inequality:

$$\lambda_1(L_1) \cdot \lambda_n(L_1^*) \leq c \cdot n.$$

Furthermore, we need to prove that $1 \leq \lambda_1(L_1) \cdot \lambda_n(L_1^*)$. Let $v \in L_1$ be a vector such that $\|v\| = \lambda_1(L_1)$. By definition of $\lambda_n(L_1^*)$, there exist n linearly independent vectors $x_1, \ldots, x_n$ in L_1^* such that $\|x_i\| \leq \lambda_n(L_1^*)$. We clearly see that not all of them are orthogonal to v. Hence, there exists an i such that $\langle x_i, v \rangle \neq 0$. Since $x_i \in L_1^*$ there must be $\langle x_i, v \rangle \in \mathbb{Z}$. We have $1 \leq \langle x_i, v \rangle \leq \|x_i\| \cdot \|v\| \leq \lambda_n(L_1^*) \cdot \lambda_1(L_1)$. Then,

$$\lambda_1(L_1) \cdot \lambda_n(L_1^*) \geq 1.$$

Because $\lambda_1(L_1)$ is the shortest non-zero vector of the saturated sublattice $L_1 \subset L$ generated by $L \cap V$ and $\lambda_M(L)$ is the shortest non-zero vector of the lattice $L \backslash M$, we have $\lambda_M(L) \leq \lambda_1(L_1)$. Therefore

$$1 \leq \lambda_M(L) \cdot \lambda_n(L_1^*) \leq c \cdot n.$$

The proofs of 2 and 3 similar. For the lattice L_1, we have $1 \leq \lambda_1(L_1) \cdot g(L_1^*) \leq d \cdot n$ and $1 \leq \lambda_1(L_1) \cdot \lambda_1(L_1^*) \leq d \cdot n$. Because $\lambda_M(L) \leq \lambda_1(L_1)$, the results follow. This completes the proof.

Since $\lambda_1(L) \leq \lambda_M(L)$, we obtain the following corollary.

Corollary 1. *For any rank-l lattice L and a subspace $M \subset span(L)$, there exist constants c, d such that*

1. $1 \leq \lambda_1(L) \cdot \lambda_n(L_1^*) \leq c \cdot n.$
2. $1 \leq \lambda_1(L) \cdot g(L_1^*) \leq d \cdot n.$
3. $1 \leq \lambda_1(L) \cdot \lambda_1(L_1^*) \leq n.$

where L_1^* is the dual of saturated sublattice L_1 with rank n of L.

This corollary reflects the relationships between the shortest lattice vector of L and the nth successive minimum, the shortest basis, and the first successive minimum of the dual of a saturated sublattice L_1. That is, it connects the lattice with the dual lattice of a saturated sublattice.

Part 1 of Theorem 2 immediately implies reductions between GAPSIVP and GAPSAM.

Theorem 3. *There are the following cook reductions between problem GAPSIVP and GAPSAM:*

– The problem GAPSAM$_{cn}$ can be reduced to GAPSIVP$_1$;
– The problem GAPSIVP$_{cn}$ can be reduced to GAPSAM$_1$,

where c is a constant.

Proof. Let $(\boldsymbol{L}, \boldsymbol{M}, r)$ be an instance of GAPSAM$_{cn}$, where $\boldsymbol{L} \subseteq \mathbb{Z}^m$ is a lattice of rank l, and let $\boldsymbol{M} \subset span(\boldsymbol{L})$ be a subspace of $\boldsymbol{L}$. Note that $(\boldsymbol{L}, \boldsymbol{M}, r)$ is a YES instance if $\lambda_M(\boldsymbol{L}) \leq r$, whereas $(\boldsymbol{L}, \boldsymbol{M}, r)$ is a NO instance if $\lambda_M(\boldsymbol{L}) > cnr$.

From the proof of Theorem 2, we can obtain a lattice $\boldsymbol{L}_1$ of rank n with the dual $\boldsymbol{L}_1^*$. By Theorem 2, if $\lambda_M(\boldsymbol{L}) \leq r$ then $\lambda_n(\boldsymbol{L}_1^*) \geq 1/\lambda_M(\boldsymbol{L}) > 1/r$, if $\lambda_M(\boldsymbol{L}) > cnr$ then $\lambda_n(\boldsymbol{L}_1^*) \leq cn/\lambda_M(\boldsymbol{L}) < cn/cnr < 1/r$.

The reduction calls a GAPSIVP$_1$ oracle on $(\boldsymbol{L}_1^*, 1/r)$, which allows GAPSAM$_{cn}$ to be solved. Indeed, if the GAPSIVP$_1$ oracle on $(\boldsymbol{L}_1^*, 1/r)$ answers YES, then $(\boldsymbol{L}, \boldsymbol{M}, r)$ is a NO instance of GAPSAM$_{cn}$. On the other hand, if GAPSIVP$_1$ oracle on $(\boldsymbol{L}_1^*, 1/r)$ answers NO, then $(\boldsymbol{L}, \boldsymbol{M}, r)$ is a YES instance of GAPSAM$_{cn}$.

The second reduction follows by a similar method.

Using Theorem 3, we can also show the non-approximability result for GAPSAM, namely that there exists a constant c such that GAPSAM$_{cn} \in coNP$.

Corollary 2. *GAPSAM$_{cn} \in coNP$ for some constant c.*

Proof. Assume that $(\boldsymbol{L}, \boldsymbol{M}, r)$ is an instance of GAPSAM$_{cn}$. Then $(\boldsymbol{L}, \boldsymbol{M}, r)$ is a YES instance if $\lambda_M(\boldsymbol{L}) \leq r$, and $(\boldsymbol{L}, \boldsymbol{M}, r)$ is a NO instance if $\lambda_M(\boldsymbol{L}) > cnr$. Hence, we need to prove that if $(\boldsymbol{L}, \boldsymbol{M}, r)$ is a YES instance then there is no witness that the verifier accepts, and that if $(\boldsymbol{L}, \boldsymbol{M}, r)$ is a NO instance then there is a witness that the verifier accepts.

Indeed, using Theorem 3, when $(\boldsymbol{L}, \boldsymbol{M}, r)$ is a YES instance of GAPSAM$_{cn}$ we have $\lambda_n(\boldsymbol{L}_1^*) > 1/r$, and when $(\boldsymbol{L}, \boldsymbol{M}, r)$ is a NO instance we have $\lambda_n(\boldsymbol{L}_1^*) \leq 1/r$.

We then obtain n vectors $\boldsymbol{v}_1, \boldsymbol{v}_2, \ldots, \boldsymbol{v}_n$ non-deterministically, and check that they are linearly independent in $\boldsymbol{L}_1^*$ and that each length at most $1/r$. Hence, there exist n vectors for which we accept a NO instance of GAPSAM$_{cn}$.

3.2　Relationships Between GAPSAM and Other Lattice Problems

In this section, we give polynomial time reductions between promise problems of GAPSVP, GAPSBP and GAPSAM.

Theorem 4. *There are polynomial time Karp reductions between GAPSVP and GAPSAM.*

– GAPSVP$_n$ is reducible to GAPSAM$_1$.
– GAPSAM$_n$ is reducible to GAPSVP$_1$.

Proof. Let $(\boldsymbol{L}_1^*, r)$ be an instance of GAPSVP$_n$, where $\boldsymbol{L}_1^* \subset \mathbb{Z}^m$ is a lattice. $\boldsymbol{b}_1^*, \ldots, \boldsymbol{b}_n^*$ be a basis of the lattice $\boldsymbol{L}_1^*$, and let $\boldsymbol{L}_1$ be the dual lattice of $\boldsymbol{L}_1^*$. We may assume that $(\boldsymbol{b}_1, \ldots, \boldsymbol{b}_n)$ is a basis of $\boldsymbol{L}_1$, so there must exist a lattice

L of rank l such that $(b_1, \ldots, b_n)$ is a basis of $L \cap span(b_1, \ldots, b_n)$, that is, $L_1 = L \cap span(L_1)$. Thus L has a basis $b_1, \ldots, b_n, b_{n+1}, \ldots, b_l$.

Set $V = span(b_1, \ldots, b_n)$. Then V is a subspace of $span(L)$ and L_1 is a saturated sublattice of L. Define the orthogonal projection

$$\pi : span(L) \longrightarrow span(b_1, \ldots, b_n)^{\perp}$$

as following, for all $b \in span(L)$,

$$\pi(b) = b - \sum_{i=1}^{n} \frac{\langle b, \tilde{b}_i \rangle}{\langle \tilde{b}_i, \tilde{b}_i \rangle} \tilde{b}_i$$

where $\tilde{b}_i$ is the Gram-Schmidt orthogonal vector of b_i, $i = 1, \ldots, n$. $\pi(L)$ is a lattice of rank $l - n$ with basis $[\pi(b_{n+1}), \ldots, \pi(b_l)]$, where $b_{n+1}, \ldots, b_l \in L$. Then, we see that $b_1, \ldots, b_n, b_{n+1}, \ldots, b_l$ is a basis of the lattice L. In the linear span of lattice L, we can find a subspace M such that $V \oplus M = span(L)$.

The output of the reduction is $(L, M, 1/r)$. We next show this reduction is correct.

Assume that (L_1^*, r) is a YES instance of GAPSVP$_n$, such that $\lambda_1(L_1^*) \leq r$. From the Theorem 2, $1 \leq \lambda_M(L) \cdot \lambda_1(L_1^*) \leq n$. We have $\lambda_M(L) \geq 1/r$. Then, $(L, M, 1/r)$ is a NO instance of GAPSAM$_\gamma$.

Now assume that (L_1^*, r) is a NO instance of GAPSVP$_n$, so that $\lambda_1(L_1^*) > nr$. By Theorem 2, we have $\lambda_M(L) < 1/r$. It follows that $(L, M, 1/r)$ is a YES instance of GAPSAM$_\gamma$.

The proof of the second part is similar.

Using Theorem 2, we obtain the following corollary.

Corollary 3. *There are approximate reductions between GAPSBP and GAPSAM, for some constant d.*

- *GAPSAM$_{dn}$ can be reduced to GAPSBP$_1$.*
- *GAPSBP$_{dn}$ can be reduced to GAPSAM$_1$.*

4   The Rank and Approximation Preserving Reductions

In this section, we will establish the rank and approximation preserving reduction between GAPSAM and other lattice problems.

Theorem 5. *For any approximation factor γ, there is a deterministic polynomial time rank-preserving reduction from GAPSVP$_\gamma$ to GAPSAM$_\gamma$.*

Proof. Let (L, r) be an instance of GAPSVP$_\gamma$, and define GAPSAM$_\gamma$ instance (L, M, r), where $M = \{0\} \subseteq span(L)$. If we computer a shortest non-zero lattice vector in L, we compute a shortest lattice vector in $L \backslash M$, i.e., $\lambda_M(L) = \lambda_1(L)$. So there is a trivial reduction from GAPSVP$_\gamma$ to GAPSAM$_\gamma$.

In the following, we will give a deterministic polynomial time rank-preserving reduction from GAPSAM to GAPCVP by an intermediate problem GAPSVP$'$.

Theorem 6. *For any approximation factor γ, there is a deterministic polynomial time rank-preserving reduction from GAPSAM$_\gamma$ to GAPSVP$'_\gamma$.*

Proof. Let (L, M, r) be an instance of GAPSAM$_\gamma$, where $L \subseteq \mathbb{Z}^m$ is a lattice of rank n and L is generated by a basis $B = (b_1, \ldots, b_n)$, and let $M \subset span(L)$ be a subspace. Using the algorithm from Lemma 1, the algorithm that on input a lattice L and a subspace M, outputs a new basis $\widetilde{B} = [\tilde{b}_1, \ldots, \tilde{b}_n]$ for L such that $M \cap L = \mathcal{L}(\tilde{b}_1, \ldots, \tilde{b}_d)$, where d is the dimension of $M \cap span(L)$, then $M = span(\tilde{b}_1, \ldots, \tilde{b}_d)$. We have $L = \mathcal{L}(B) = \mathcal{L}(\widetilde{B})$, for any lattice vector in L can be represented by the integral combinations of n linearly independent vectors $\tilde{b}_1, \ldots, \tilde{b}_n$. Hence, on input an GAPSAM$_\gamma$ instance (L, M, r), the reduction outputs the GAPSVP$'_\gamma$ instance (L, i, r) where $i \in \{d+1, \ldots, n\}$. We prove that the reduction is correct.

First assume that (L, M, r) is a YES instance of GAPSAM$_\gamma$, $\lambda_M(L) \leq r$, i.e., there exists a vector $x = (x_1, \ldots, x_d, x_{d+1}, \ldots, x_n) \in \mathbb{Z}^n$ with $x_i \neq 0$, $i \in \{d+1, \ldots, n\}$ such that

$$\|\widetilde{B}x\| = \|x_1\tilde{b}_1 + \ldots + x_d\tilde{b}_d + x_{d+1}\tilde{b}_{d+1} + \ldots + x_n\tilde{b}_n\| \leq r.$$

For any vector $x' = (x'_1, \ldots, x'_d, x'_{d+1}, \ldots, x'_n) \in \mathbb{Z}^n$ with $x'_i \neq 0$, $i \in \{d+1, \ldots, n\}$, we have

$$\lambda_1^{(i)}(L) = \min_{x' \in \mathbb{Z}^n, x'_i \neq 0} \{\|\widetilde{B}x'\|\} \leq \|\widetilde{B}x\| \leq r.$$

This prove that (L, i, r) is a YES instance.

Now assume that (L, M, r) is a NO instance, $\lambda_M(L) > \gamma \cdot r$, i.e., for all vectors $x = (x_1, \ldots, x_d, x_{d+1}, \ldots, x_n) \in \mathbb{Z}^n$ with $x_i \neq 0$, $i \in \{d+1, \ldots, n\}$ such that $\|\widetilde{B}x\| > \gamma \cdot r$. First assume for contradiction that (L, i, r) is not a NO instance, i.e., there exists a vector $x' = (x'_1, \ldots, x'_d, x'_{d+1}, \ldots, x'_n) \in \mathbb{Z}^n$ with $x'_i \neq 0$, $i \in \{d+1, \ldots, n\}$, hence, $\|\widetilde{B}x'\| \leq \gamma \cdot r$. Since (L, M, r) is a NO instance of GAPSAM$_\gamma$, we have $\|\widetilde{B}x'\| > \gamma \cdot r$, contradicting the fact that (L, i, r) is not a NO instance of GAPSVP$'_\gamma$. Then, this proved that (L, i, r) is a NO instance.

Theorem 7. *For any approximation factor γ, there is a deterministic polynomial time rank-preserving reduction from GAPSVP$'_\gamma$ to GAPCVP$_\gamma$.*

Proof. Let (L, i, r) be an instance of GAPSVP$'_\gamma$, where $L \subseteq \mathbb{Z}^m$ is a lattice of rank n and L is generated by a basis $B = (b_1, \ldots, b_n)$. We construct instances of GAPCVP$_\gamma$ as follows. The ides is to use the reduction from GCVP$_\gamma$ (Generalized Closest Vector Problem) to CVP$_\gamma$ of [16]. The jth instance consists of a lattice $L^{(j)} = \mathcal{L}(B^{(j)}) = \mathcal{L}(b_1, \ldots, 2^{j+1}b_i, \ldots, b_n)$ and the target vector $t^{(j)} = 2^j b_i$, $j = 0, 1, \ldots, \lfloor \log_2 A \rfloor$ (A is sufficiently large and the bound can be determined (see [16] (Theorem 3.2)). We use these instances of GAPCVP$_\gamma$

corresponding queries to the GAPCVP$_\gamma$ oracle. By call on all these instances $(L^{(j)}, t^{(j)})$, the GAPCVP$_\gamma$ oracle return the shortest difference vectors. Since r is given in GAPSVP$'_\gamma$ instance (L, i, r), and return YES if and only if at least one of the oracle calls is answered by YES. For example, the jth call on input $(L^{(j)}, t^{(j)})$, the shortest of the vector $B^{(j)}x - t^{(j)} \in L$ is returned where $x = (x_1, x_2, \ldots, x_i, \ldots, x_n) \in \mathbb{Z}^n$ and

$$\|B^{(j)}x - t^{(j)}\| = \|x_1 b_1 + x_2 b_2 + \ldots + x_i \cdot 2^{j+1} b_i + \ldots + x_n b_n - 2^j b_i\|$$
$$= \|x_1 b_1 + x_2 b_2 + \ldots + 2^j (2x_i - 1) b_i + \ldots + x_n b_n\|$$
$$\leq \gamma.$$

Since $x_i \in \mathbb{Z}^n$, we have $2^j (2x_i - 1) \neq 0$. There exists a vector $x' = (x_1, x_2, \ldots, x'_i, \ldots, x_n) \in \mathbb{Z}^n$ with $x'_i = 2^j (2x_i - 1) \neq 0$ for some $i \in \{1, \ldots, n\}$ such that $\|B^{(j)}x - t^{(j)}\| = \|Bx'\| \leq r$. Then, (L, i, r) is a YES instance of GAPSVP$'_\gamma$. And selecting j is the hight power of 2 such that 2^j divides x_i. The reduction outputs the GAPCVP$_\gamma$ instance $(L^{(j)}, t^{(j)}, r)$.

We want to prove that if (L, i, r) is a YES instance then $(L^{(j)}, t^{(j)}, r)$ is a YES instance for some $j = 1, \ldots, n$, while if (L, i, r) is a NO instance then $(L^{(j)}, t^{(j)}, r)$ is a NO instance for all $j = 1, \ldots, n$.

First assume (L, i, r) is a YES instance, $\lambda_1^{(i)}(L) \leq r$, i.e., there exists a vector $x = (x_1, x_2, \ldots, x_i, \ldots, x_n) \in \mathbb{Z}^n$ with $x_i \neq 0$, $i \in \{1, \ldots, n\}$ such that $\|Bx\| \leq r$. Let j be the hight power of 2 such that 2^j divides x_i. Since x_i is nonzero, we define $x_i = 2^j (2a - 1)$ for some integer a. We obtain the vector x' by replacing the ith entry x_i with a, i.e., $x' = (x_1, x_2, \ldots, a, \ldots, x_n) \in \mathbb{Z}^n$. Then,

$$dist(L^{(j)}, t^{(j)}) \leq \|B^{(j)}x' - t^{(j)}\|$$
$$= \|x_1 b_1 + x_2 b_2 + \ldots + a \cdot 2^{j+1} b_i + \ldots + x_n b_n - 2^j b_i\|$$
$$= \|x_1 b_1 + x_2 b_2 + \ldots + \cdot 2^j (2a - 1) b_i + \ldots + x_n b_n\|$$
$$= \|Bx\| \leq r.$$

This proves that $(L^{(j)}, t^{(j)}, r)$ is a YES instance.

Now assume that (L, i, r) is a NO instance, $\lambda_1^{(i)}(L) > \gamma \cdot r$, i.e., for any vector $x = (x_1, x_2, \ldots, x_i, \ldots, x_n) \in \mathbb{Z}^n$ with $x_i \neq 0$, $i \in \{1, \ldots, n\}$ such that $\|Bx\| > \gamma \cdot r$. For some j,

$$dist(L^{(j)}, t^{(j)}) = \min_{x \in \mathbb{Z}^n} \|B^{(j)}x - t^{(j)}\|$$
$$= \min_{x \in \mathbb{Z}^n} \|x_1 b_1 + x_2 b_2 + \ldots + x_i \cdot 2^{j+1} b_i + \ldots + x_n b_n - 2^j b_i\|$$
$$= \min_{x \in \mathbb{Z}^n} \|x_1 b_1 + x_2 b_2 + \ldots + 2^j (2x_i - 1) b_i + \ldots + x_n b_n\|$$
$$> \gamma \cdot r.$$

This proves that $(L^{(j)}, t^{(j)}, r)$ is a NO instance.

Combining the two theorem we get the following corollary.

Corollary 4. *For any approximation factor γ, there is a deterministic polynomial time rank-preserving reduction from GAPSAM$_\gamma$ to GAPCVP$_\gamma$.*

5   Conclusions

In this paper, we propose the promise problem associated with GSVP, namely GAPSAM. We present variants of Cai's transference theorems for GAPSAM. From the relationship, we prove that $GAPSAM_{cn}$ lies in $coNP$, where c is a constant. We also give the relationships between the shortest vector of a lattice, the nth successive minima, shortest basis, and the shortest vector of the dual of a saturated sublattice. Using these new relations, we reduce some lattice problems to GAPSAM. We also reduce GAPSAM to GAPCVP under a deterministic polynomial time rank-preserving reduction.

References

1. Ajtai, M.: The shortest vector problem in l2 is NP-hard for randomized reductions. In: 30th ACM Symposium on Theory of Computing, pp. 10–19 (1998)
2. Ajtai, M., Kumar, R., Sivakumar, D.: A sieve algorithm for the shortest lattice vector problem. In: Proceedings of the 33th ACM Symposium on Theory of Computing, pp. 601–610 (2001)
3. Aharonov, D., Regev, O.: Lattice problems in NP intersect coNP. J. ACM **52**(5), 749–765 (2005). Preliminary version in FOCS04
4. Banaszczyk, W.: New bounds in some transference theorems in the geometry of numbers. Math. Ann. **296**, 625–635 (1993)
5. Blömer, J., Naewe, S.: Sampling methods for shortest vectors, closest vectors and successive minima. Theor. Comput. Sci. **410**, 1648–1665 (2009)
6. Blömer, J., Naewe, S.: Sampling methods for shortest vectors, closest vectors and successive minima. In: Arge, L., Cachin, C., Jurdziński, T., Tarlecki, A. (eds.) ICALP 2007. LNCS, vol. 4596, pp. 65–77. Springer, Heidelberg (2007)
7. Blöer, J., Seifert, J.P.: On the complexity of computing short linearly independent vectors and short bases in a lattice. In: Thirty-First Annual ACM Symposium on Theory of Computing, pp. 711–720. ACM (1999)
8. Boppana, R., Håstad, J., Zachos, S.: Does co-NP have short interactive proofs? Inf. Process. Lett. **25**, 127–132 (1987)
9. Cai, J.Y.: A New Transference Theorem and Applications to Ajtais Connection Factor, Electronic Colloquium on Computational Complexity, TR, pp. 98–05 (1998)
10. Cai, J.Y.: A new transference theorem in the geometry of numbers and new bounds for Ajtais connection factor. Discrete Appl. Math. **126**, 9–31 (2003)
11. Goldreich, O., Goldwasser, S.: On the limits of nonapproximability of lattice problems. J. Comput. Syst. Sci. **60**(3), 540–563 (2000)
12. Guruswami, V., Micciancio, D., Regev, O.: The complexity of the covering radius problem on lattices and codes. Comput. Complexity **14**(2), 90–121 (2005). Preliminary version in CCC 2004
13. Haviv, I., Regev, O.: Tensor-based hardness of the shortest vector problem to within almost polynomial factors. Theory Comput. **8**, 513–531 (2012)
14. Khot, S.: Hardness of approximating the shortest vector problem in lattices. J. ACM **52**(5), 789–808 (2005)
15. Lgarias, C., Lenstra, H., Schnorr, C.P.: Korkin-Zolotarev bases and successive minima of a lattice and its reciprocial lattice. Combinatorica **10**, 333–348 (1990)

16. Micciancio, D.: Efficient reductions among lattice problems. In: 19th Annual ACM-SIAM Symposium on Discrete Algorithms, SODA 2008, pp. 84–93. Society for Industrial and Applied Mathematics (2008)
17. Regev, O.: Lecture Note on Lattices in Computer Science. Lecture 8: Dual Lattice (2004)

Secret Key Extraction with Quantization Randomness Using Hadamard Matrix on QuaDRiGa Channel

Xuanxuan Wang[1], Lihuan Jiang[2], Lars Thiele[2], and Yongming Wang[1]([⊠])

[1] Institute of Information Engineering, Chinese Academy of Sciences, Beijing, China
wangyongming@iie.ac.cn
[2] Fraunhofer Institute for Telecommunications, Heinrich Hertz Institute, Berlin, Germany

Abstract. The existing scheme of secret key extraction based on the channel properties can be implemented in the three steps: quantization, information reconciliation and privacy amplification. Despite the tremendous researches of quantization and information reconciliation techniques, there is little consideration about the risk of information reconstruction by the unauthorized node due to the high correlation of subsequent quantization bits, which is unavoidably leaked on the public channel between quantization and information reconciliation. In this paper, we propose an improved scheme of secret key extraction with quantization randomness using Hadamard matrix on QuaDRiGa channel. Simulation results show that with this kind of quantization randomness, the correlation between the subsequent quantization bits can be significantly decreased, which can reduce the possibility of information reconstruction by the unauthorized node, and the improved scheme can increase the randomness of the final secret key bits as compared with the existing ones.

Keywords: Quantization randomness · Hadamard matrix · Correlation · Secret key extraction

1 Introduction

In recent years, how to make a great use of the randomness of the wireless channel for secret key extraction between two wireless nodes has been increasingly paid much attention to. Different from traditional security methods, which mainly rely on the cryptography encryption technology and mathematical tools with a large cost of computing complexity and focus on the upper communication protocol, the principle of secret key extraction from the randomness of the wireless channel is the uncorrelation between the channels lying in a pair of two communication nodes and other nodes [1]. The underlying randomness results from temporal and spatial variation in the wireless channel, which is a natural and perfect resource for secret key extraction to keep the information security in physical

© Springer International Publishing Switzerland 2016
S. Qing et al. (Eds.): ICICS 2015, LNCS 9543, pp. 50–61, 2016.
DOI: 10.1007/978-3-319-29814-6_5

layer (PHY). So, secret key extraction based on the underlying randomness appears a promising alternative of the existing security methods, especially for the devices with limited resource.

The essential idea of PHY-based secret key extraction is that two legitimate wireless devices measure the reciprocal properties of a common wireless channel on the basis of public information exchanged over the channel. This means that the measurements for two intended node are theoretically identical. However, the time-varying feature of wireless channel results in a non-ideal consistency of PHY-based measurements. In order to obtain the independent channel measurements, we perform the process during the coherence time period according to [2], during which the channel impulse response is considered to be unchanged. That is to say, we can get the high correlation between the sampled channel measurements and increase the measurements consistency.

The basic scheme of secret key extraction based on the channel measurements in coherence time can be implemented in three steps [3–5]: quantization, information reconciliation and privacy amplification. The quantization techniques on common measurements can be used to quantize the observations measured from the public channel and get an initial bit stream between two legitimate nodes, respectively. Due to the channel measurements done in coherence time, it has high correlation between subsequent bits in the initial quantization bit stream. Information reconciliation techniques tackle the mismatch quantization bits generated at two legitimate nodes and correct them through the initial quantized sequence exchanged over the public channel. Finally, in privacy amplification the two legitimate nodes apply a deterministic function to generate the secret key bits.

Most of the previous work mainly focuses on the development and analysis of quantization techniques [3,6,7] and information reconciliation techniques [8,9]. But ignores the possibility of information reconstruction by the unintended device through the high correlation of the initial subsequent quantization bits. Due to the broadcast nature of a common channel, it seems that the information leakage is unavoidable when the initial quantization bits exchange over the public channel for information reconciliation, which is an advantage for the unauthorized node to reconstruct and predict the information.

To deal with this issue, we propose an improved scheme of secret key extraction in this paper. The quantization bits are randomized with Hadamard matrix before being transmitted on a common channel for information reconciliation, which can reduce the correlation in the subsequent quantized bit stream. We carry out the operation on the QuaDRiGa channel. Simulation results show that this scheme can decrease the correlation of the subsequent quantized bit stream, as well as the possibility of information reconstruction by the unintended node, and can also improve the randomness of the final secrete key bits in comparison with the existing ones.

The rest of the paper is organized as follows. Section 2 describes the basic system model and the adversarial model. Section 3 details the improved scheme with Hadamard matrix. In Sect. 4, we present and discuss the numerical results. Finally, Sect. 5 concludes the paper.

2 A Basic Model

2.1 System Model

The general model of PHY-based secret key extraction discussed in this paper is a basic three-terminal system shown in Fig. 1, which consists of a legitimate transmitter (called Alice), an intended (legitimate) receiver (called Bob), and an unauthorized receiver (called Eve). In this security model, Alice and Bob try their best to establish a shared key based on the reciprocal measurements of the wireless channel. Eve, an eavesdropper, targets the derivation of the pairwise key generated by Alice and Bob.

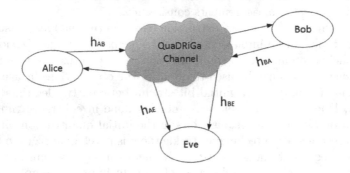

Fig. 1. System model

The particular properties of the wireless channel used for secret key extraction can be the parameters of the wireless channel, such as delay spread, amplitude, phase, Receive Signal Strength (RSS) and so on. Two legitimate nodes Alice and Bob measure the randomness and reciprocity of the wireless channel gains in coherence time, denoted by h_{AB} and h_{BA}, and follow the general three-step scheme of secret key extraction to obtain the shared key bits. In this scheme, the basic steps are as following:

Quantization: the existing quantization approaches aim to convert consecutive channel measurements into discrete random bits based on various thresholds setting. In general, it can be classified into two categories: lossy quantization and lossless quantization. The former is achieved at the cost of probabilistically dropping bits to maintain the high bit entropy, and the latter generates quantized data for the whole input stream so as to produce a high generation rate output.

Information Reconciliation: this is a reconciled process to deal with the discrepancy in the initial quantization bit stream, which mainly focuses on various error correct codes, such as LDPC code.

Privacy Amplification: privacy amplification is used to generate a final secret key bits. Alice and Bob use the same means (e.g., hash function) to generate a secret key bit stream by choosing a longer input randomly and fixing the output in a smaller length randomly. The random input and output in privacy amplification can make the final secret key bits strong.

The unauthorized party Eve can observe the channel measurements h_{AE} and h_{BE}. To Eve, how to perceive the related channel coefficient is subject to the relative distance from the two legitimate nodes in spatial dimension. The shorter the relative distance is, the higher the correlation is between h_{AE} and h_{AB} or h_{BE} and h_{BA} and the more possibility there is for Eve to extract the transmitted data exactly.

In this model, we choose the Quasi Deterministic Radio Channel Generator (QuaDRiGa) [10] as the channel model so as to achieve a better performance evaluation. The QuaDRiGa channel models wireless channel propagation in three dimensions (3D) over time (4D). Based on the collection of features created in Spatial Channel Model (SCM) and WINNER channel models, the QuaDRiGa channel provides features to enable quasi-deterministic multi-link tracking of user (receiver) movements in different propagation environments, which can evaluate a more realistic environment and play a great importance to the research on physical layer security. The QuaDRiGa channel follows a geometry-based stochastic channel model and creates an arbitrary double directional radio channel. The key impacts of the QuaDRiGa are: (i) to split MT trajectory into segments based on the geo-correlation of Large Scale Parameters (LSPs) and realize the continuous time evolution; (ii) to insert three dimensional antenna dependently; (iii) to support variable speed of the terminal by interpolation of channel coefficients.

2.2   Adversarial Model

In our adversary model, we assume Eve can sense all the process of the communication between Alice and Bob. Eve can try his best to measure the channels between Alice or Bob and himself at the same time when Alice and Bob measure the channel between themselves for secret key extraction. We also assume Eve has the same calculation capability and knows the same scheme of channel estimation as Alice and Bob. There is no limitation on Eve's position from Alice and Bob. That is to say, Eve can choose the optimum position to estimate the correlated coefficients of the wireless channel between Alice and Bob by himself and then achieve their shared key successfully. We assume Eve is a passive attacker, who can neither obstruct the common channel between Alice and Bob nor modify any exchanged message transmitted on the common channel.

3   Methodology of Quantization Randomness

As highlighted before, the high correlation between subsequent bits in the initial quantized bit stream is a great advantage for Eve to recreate and predicate the secret key bits. So, it is very important to reduce the correlation between a bit and the subsequent bit in the initial quantization bit stream. In the following, we will present an improved scheme based on Hadamard matrix to randomize the quantization bits so as to weaken the correlation.

3.1 Hadamard Matrix

The Hadamard matrix is a symmetric matrix. Due to the symmetric property it has been poured into the applications, such as data encryption, randomness measures and so on [11]. The Hadamard matrix $\mathbf{H_m}$ can be achieved through the Hadamard transform. We define the 1×1 Hadamard transform H_0 by the identity $H_0 = 1$, then the Hadamard matrix $\mathbf{H_m}$ is:

$$\mathbf{H_m} = \frac{1}{\sqrt{2}} \begin{pmatrix} \mathbf{H_{m-1}} & \mathbf{H_{m-1}} \\ \mathbf{H_{m-1}} & -\mathbf{H_{m-1}} \end{pmatrix} = \mathbf{H_1} \otimes \mathbf{H_{m-1}} \tag{1}$$

where m is the order of Hadamard matrix and $m > 0$.

The Hadamard matrix, $\mathbf{H_m}$, is a square matrix of order $m = 1, 2$ or $4k$, where k is a positive integer. The elements of $\mathbf{H_m}$ are either $+1$ or -1 and $\mathbf{H_m} \cdot \mathbf{H_m^T} = n\mathbf{I_m}$, where $\mathbf{H_m^T}$ is the transpose of $\mathbf{H_m}$ and $\mathbf{I_m}$ is the identity matrix of order m.

3.2 Random and Random_inverse

In this section, we detail the improved scheme of random and random_inverse for the quantization bits with Hadamard matrix based on [12]. Here we only consider the non-binary matrix to random the quantization bits based on the Hadamard matrix, so we carry out modulo operations on the negative values in the Hadamard matrix in order to make the negative values into the non-negative ones. We specify each negative number replaced with the corresponding modulo number. For example, with the operation of modulo 7, the elements -1 in the Hadamard matrix are replaced with 6 so as to make the elements in the matrix non-binary. In order to simplify the calculation, we only perform prime modulo operations that is because non-prime number can be divisible with numbers other than 1 and itself.

Figure 2 illustrates the process of randomizing the quantization bits with Hadamard matrix, which is composed of the following four steps:

1. choose an arbitrary prime number n and divide the quantization bits S into several bit groups, where the number of bits in each group is equal to n.
2. convert each group of binary bits into the corresponding decimal values D.
3. segment the decimal sequence and perform multiplication with Hadamard matrix. The decimal sequence D is broken down into chunks D', the size of which is equal to 2^n. Multiply each group of decimal subsequence D' with the corresponding Hadamard matrix $\mathbf{H}$ to get D''. Here, the Hadamard matrix $\mathbf{H}$ is a $2^n \times 2^n$ modified matrix of the form modulo $(2^n - 1)$ in order to change the negative values in the matrix into the non-negative ones. Then perform the operation of modulo $(2^n - 1)$ on each resultant decimal subsequence D'' to reduce the complexity of the calculation result.

4. combine each resultant multiplied decimal subsequence D'' and convert them into the corresponding binary sequence S'.

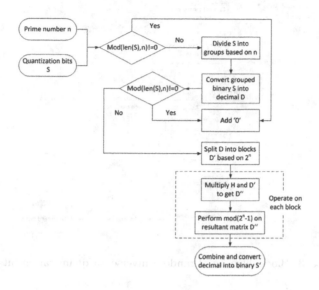

Fig. 2. Block diagram of random for quantization bits

Note that the '0' appending operation in (1) and (3) may be required in order to meet the requirement for the length of each bit block.

Figure 3 shows the process of random inverse for the quantization bits with the Hadamard matrix. We choose the resultant binary sequence S' obtained in the randomness process and the prime number n as the input. Here n is the same as that in the randomness process.

1. split the input binary sequence S' into groups, where the number of bits in each group is equal to n, and convert them into corresponding decimal values D_1.
2. divide the input decimal sequence D_1 into blocks D_1', whose length is equal to 2^n.
3. calculate the modular multiplicative inverse of D_1' with respect to modulo $(2^n - 1)$ to get D_1'' and multiply each resultant subsequence D_1'' with the matrix $\mathbf{H}^{-1}$ on each block. Here the matrix $\mathbf{H}^{-1}$ is the inverse of the Hadamard matrix $\mathbf{H}$, which is a $2^n \times 2^n$ modified matrix of the form modulo $(2^n - 1)$.
4. combine each resultant decimal subsequence D_1''.
5. convert the combined decimal sequence into the corresponding binary sequence S.

Note that the '0' dropping in (4) and (5) may be required if there is consecutive 0' at the end of the sequence.

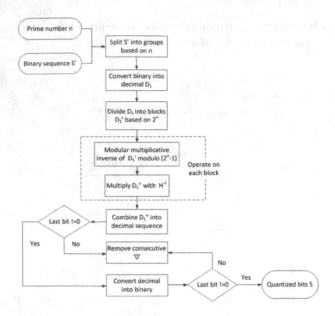

Fig. 3. Block diagram of random_inverse for quantization bits

3.3   Secret Key Extraction with Quantization Randomness

Figure 4 illustrates the process of secret key extraction with quantization randomness based on Hadamard matrix. In this paper, we take the Alice as the leader to perform the information exchange with Bob. We take the RSS measurements from the QuaDRiGa channel as the target and apply the multiple bits quantization scheme as proposed in [3]. In order to reduce the correlation between subsequent quantization bits, we first random the quantization bits collected from RSS measurements by Alice rather than directly transmit them over the common channel to Bob in information reconciliation. Different from the highly correlated bit stream obtained by Bob in [3], a bit sequence with less correlation between subsequent bits is received. We choose the LDPC code as the information reconciliation scheme to deal with the asymmetry lying in the two randomized quantization bit streams. This is an iterative scheme and LDPC encode is carried out in small blocks. So it is important for Bob to perform the LDPC decode and random_inverse for the received sequence once the randomized quantization bit stream is obtained. Finally, we choose the most popular methods, hash function, to fix the size and obtain a small length output from the long bit stream in privacy amplification.

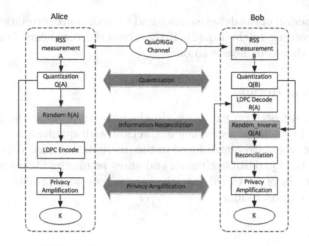

Fig. 4. Flowchart of extracting secret key with quantization randomness

4   Numerical Results

4.1   Performance Evaluation

We choose the autocorrelation function to identify the correlation of the subsequent bits in a bit stream. Given the data sequence $X_1, X_2, X_3, \ldots, X_N$ at times $t_1, t_2, t_3, \ldots, t_N$, the kth autocorrelation (lag k) is defined as:

$$r_k = \frac{\sum_{i=1}^{N-k} \left(X_i - \overline{X}\right) \left(X_{i+k} - \overline{X}\right)}{\sum_{i=1}^{N} \left(X_i - \overline{X}\right)^2} \tag{2}$$

where $\overline{X}$ is the mean of the data sequence X_i, $i = 1, 2, \ldots, N$.

The result of Eq. (2) is a correlation coefficient, which represents the correlation between values at different times t_i and t_{i+k} in the same variable. If the data values are random, such autocorrelation coefficients should be near zero for any time-lag separations. If they are not random, then one or more of the autocorrelation coefficients will be significantly non-zero.

Guaranteeing the randomness of the final secret key is essential for physical layer security because Alice and Bob are intended to rely on the secret keys for information encryption [13]. Since we have assumed Eve can sense all the process of the communication between Alice and Bob and has the same calculation ability as them, any bad randomness behavior of the final secret key can result in the low complexity of cracking the key for Eve. In order to evaluate the randomness of the secret key bits, we focus on the following equation [11]:

$$R = 1 - \frac{1}{n-1} \sum_{k=1}^{n-1} \left(|r_k|\right) \tag{3}$$

where n is the period of the data sequence and r_k is the autocorrelation coefficient figured out according to the Eq. (2). If the given data sequence is random, the randomness R should be nearer to one.

4.2   Simulation Results

In this section, we perform extensive simulations to evaluate the performance of the improved scheme of secret key extraction with quantization randomness based on Hadamard matrix introduced in the previous sections. We carry out the simulations on the QuaDRiGa channel and show results by means of exemplary implementation. In order to validate the scheme, we also present our executed analysis on simulation results.

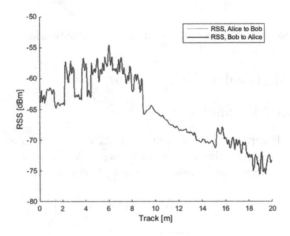

Fig. 5. The RSS measurements between Alice and Bob

Figure 5 illustrates the RSS measurements at Alice (red) and Bob (blue) vs. track based on the QuaDRiGa channel. It can be seen that, the two measurements between Alice and Bob have a great similarity. That is to say, because of the broadcast nature of the wireless communication channel, Eve can easily wiretap any shared RSS measurements between Alice and Bob by choosing his optimum position as a passive attacker.

Figure 6 shows the comparison of the correlation between a bit and the subsequent bit in a quantized RSS bit stream without (a) and with (b) randomness with Hadamard matrix. It can been seen that in Fig. 6(a), the quantization bit stream exhibits a highly-correlated connection between subsequent bits, where the correlation coefficient r lies between 0.9 and 1. From the security perspective, the highly-correlated quantized RSS bits can supply an advantage for Eve to eavesdrop and reconstruct the message due to the broadcast nature of the common channel and the unavoidable information leakage during the information reconciliation. Consequently, Eve can make use of the correlation to easily

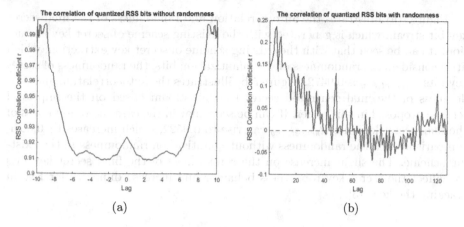

Fig. 6. Comparison of the correlation of quantized RSS bits without (a) and with (b) randomness

deduce the considerable amount of the legitimate node's key, which is a great threat for secret key generation.

Figure 6(b) illustrates the correlation coefficients decrease to less than 0.25 and even some values are less than 0, which are lower than those showed in Fig. 6(a). With the Hadamard matrix to randomize the quantization bit stream, the subsequent bits of the initial quantization bit stream have less correlation. So, little possibility is supplied for Eve to reconstruct the secret key bits when this randomized quantization bit stream is transmitted over the public channel for information reconciliation.

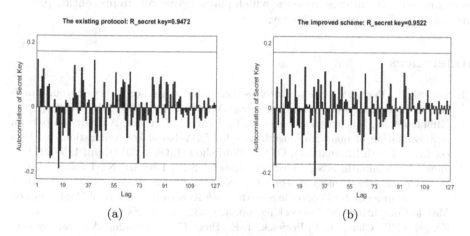

Fig. 7. Comparison of the autocorrelation and randomness of secret key extraction with the existing protocol (a) and the improved scheme (b)

Figure 7(a) illustrates the autocorrelation and randomness of the final secret key bit stream which is generated with the existing scheme of secret key extraction. It can be seen that with the existing scheme of secret key extraction, which little considers the randomness of the quantization bits, the randomness of secret key bits R_{secret_key} is 0.9472. Figure 7(b) illustrates the autocorrelation and randomness of the final generated secret key bit stream based on the improved scheme proposed in this paper. It can be seen that in the case the randomness of the final secret key bits R_{secret_key} can rise to 0.9522, which increases by 0.05 in comparison with the randomness without quantization randomness in the existing scheme. The slight increase on the randomness of the final secret key bits can affect the secret key robustness behavior and increase difficulty for Eve in cracking the key [13].

5   Conclusion

It has the high correlation between subsequent quantized RSS bit stream. Due to the openness feature of the common channel, the highly-correlated quantization bit stream is unavoidably leaked when it is exchanged over the public channel for information reconciliation, which is a perfect source of secret key reconstruction for the unintended node.

Based on RSS measurements from the QuaDRiGa channel model, we present an improved scheme of secret key extraction with quantization randomness using Hadamard matrix. Our simulation results show that the improved scheme with Hadamard matrix significantly decreases the correlation between adjacent quantization bits, reduces the possibility of secret information reconstruction by the unauthorized party, and can increase the randomness of the final secret key bits as compared with the existing ones, which plays a great role in preventing passive attacker Eve from cracking the key.

References

1. Sayeed, A., Perrig, A.: Secure wireless communications: secret keys through multipath. In: Speech and Signal Processing, Acoustics, pp. 3013–3016 (2008)
2. Guillaume, R., Mueller, A., Zenger, C.T., Paar, C., Czylwik, A.: Fair comparison and evaluation of quantization schemes for PHY-based key generation. In: Proceedings of 18th International OFDM Workshop (InOWo 2014), pp. 1–5 (2014)
3. Jana, S., Premnath, S.N., Clark, M., Kasera, S.K., Patwari, N., Krishnamurthy, S.V.: On the effectiveness of secret key extraction from wireless signal strength in real environments. In: Proceedings of the 15th Annual International Conference on Mobile Computing and Networking, pp. 321–332. ACM (2009)
4. Zenger, C.T., Chur, M.-J., Posielek, J.-F., Paar, C., G. Wunder: A novel key generating architecture for wireless low-resource devices. In: International Workshop on Secure Internet of Things (SIoT), pp. 26–34. IEEE (2014)
5. Bloch, M., Barros, J.: Physical-Layer Security: from Information Theory to Security Engineering. Cambridge University Press, Cambridge (2011)

6. Tope, M., McEachen, J.C.: Unconditionally secure communications over fading channels. In: Military Communications Conference, MILCOM 2001. Communications for Network-Centric Operations: Creating the Information Force, vol. 1, pp. 54–58. IEEE (2001)
7. Mathur, S., Trappe, W., Mandayam, N., Ye, C., Reznik, A.: Radio- telepathy: extracting a secret key from an unauthenticated wireless channel. In: Proceedings of the 14th ACM International Conference on Mobile Computing and Networking, pp. 128–139. ACM (2008)
8. Bloch, M., Thangaraj, A., McLaughlin, S.W., Merolla, J.-M.: LDPC-based secret key agreement over the Gaussian wiretap channel. In: IEEE International Symposium on Information Theory, pp. 1179–1183. IEEE (2006)
9. Etesami, J., Henkel, W., Wakeel, A.: LDPC code construction for wireless physical-layer key reconciliation. In: First IEEE International Conference on Communications in China (ICCC 2012). Beijing (2012)
10. http://www.hhi.fraunhofer.de/departments/wireless-communications-and-net works/research-areas/system-level-analysis-and-concepts/quadriga.html
11. Ella, V.S.: Randomization using quasigroups, hadamard and number theoretic transforms (2012). arXiv preprint arXiv:1202.0223
12. Reddy, R.S.: Encryption of binary and non-binary data using chained hadamard transforms (2010). arXiv preprint arXiv:1012.4452
13. http://cs.nyu.edu/dodis/randomness-in-crypto/random1.pdf

Practical Lattice-Based Fault Attack and Countermeasure on SM2 Signature Algorithm

Weiqiong Cao[1][✉], Jingyi Feng[1], Shaofeng Zhu[1], Hua Chen[1],
Wenling Wu[1], Xucang Han[2], and Xiaoguang Zheng[2]

[1] Trusted Computing and Information Assurance Laboratory, Institute of Software,
Chinese Academy of Sciences, Beijing 100190, People's Republic of China
{caowq,fengjingyi,zhushaofeng,chenhua,wwl}@tca.iscas.ac.cn
[2] Beijing Key Laboratory of RFID Chip Test Technology,
CEC Huada Electronic Design Co., Ltd,
Beijing 102209, People's Republic of China
{hanxc,zhengxg}@hed.com.cn

Abstract. We present a practical lattice-based fault attack against SM2 signature algorithm in a smart card. This seems to be the first combination of the lattice attack presented in SAC'2013 and fault attack against SM2 in practice. We successfully utilize the laser fault attack to skip the instructions of nonces being written into RAM, so that the nonces in signatures share partial same bits from each other. Next, we build the model of lattice attack and recover the private key. The experimental results show we only need 3 faulty signatures to mount lattice attack successfully in about 32 μs. Moreover, we propose a new countermeasure for SM2 signature algorithm to resist lattice-based fault attack by destroying the condition of lattice attack rather than thwarting fault attack. It is proved the countermeasure can guarantee the ability to resist lattice attack, even if some information of the nonces is leaked.

Keywords: Fault attack · Lattice attack · Countermeasure · SM2

1 Introduction

Elliptic curve cryptosystem (ECC) has been used widely in cryptographic devices such as smart card. For the implementation of ECC in device, we must analyze not only its mathematic security but also the ability against physical attacks, such as fault attack (FA). So far, there have been many results about FA against ECC [1–3], especially against elliptic curve digital signature algorithm (ECDSA) [4–6]. Among them, lattice-based fault attack (LFA) is one of the most effective attacks. It combines both fault attack (FA) and lattice attack (LA). Firstly, some information about the nonce k in signature is revealed by FA. Next, with the leakage information of k, LA can disclose the private key d_A. LAs against (EC) DSA-like signature algorithm are mainly classified into three

© Springer International Publishing Switzerland 2016
S. Qing et al. (Eds.): ICICS 2015, LNCS 9543, pp. 62–70, 2016.
DOI: 10.1007/978-3-319-29814-6_6

types. The first type [7–9] is based on knowing parts of the nonce k. The second type [10] is based on the fact that there exist a few same blocks in each nonce k. The last type [11] is based on the condition that some different nonces in signatures share partial same bits from each other. Nevertheless, it seems only the first type of LA combined with FA is applied successfully on ECDSA-like signature algorithm in practice [4,6,12]. There seems to be no FA combined with the other two types of LA in practice. It is worthy to do further research about the kind of FA and the corresponding countermeasures on ECDSA-like signature, such as SM2 signature algorithm.

SM2 signature algorithm (hereafter SM2) is a signature algorithm standard based on elliptic curve published by Chinese Government [13], and has been extensively used in cryptographic device in finance. The first type of LA based on knowing parts of k against SM2 has been introduced in INSCRYPT'2014 [9].

Our Contributions. A practical LFA against SM2 is presented based on the condition of LA that there are some bits shared between different nonces, and the attack is mounted in a smart card successfully. It seems that it is the first time to combine FA and the last type of LA (sharing some bits between nonces) against SM2 in practice. We first utilize practical laser FA to make the instructions of writing nonces into RAM skipped deliberately, so that the nonces in SM2 share partial same bits. Next, based on the faulty results of the above FA, we build the model of LA proposed in SAC'2013 [11] and recover the private key d_A successfully. At last, we propose a new countermeasure for SM2 to resist LFA by destroying the condition of LA directly. We also prove its security against LFA. Even if some information of the nonce k is leaked, the countermeasure still guarantees the ability to resist LA.

The remainder of the paper is organized as follows: Sect. 2 gives a brief introduction of SM2 and the basic theory of lattice. In Sect. 3, the practical LFA against SM2 is described. In Sect. 4, the countermeasure to resist LFA is presented. Finally, the conclusion is given in Sect. 5.

2 Preliminaries

2.1 SM2 Signature Algorithm

For simplicity, we only analyze the elliptic curve $E(a, b)$ in prime finite field F_p defined by the Weierstrass equation $y^2 = x^3 + ax + b \bmod p$, where $a, b \in F_p$ and $4a^3 + 27b^2 \neq 0 \bmod p$. The set of points on $E(a, b)$ and the infinity point $\mathcal{O}$ constitute an additive group $E(F_p)$. The scalar multiplication (SM) $Q = kG$ is the most important operation in $E(F_p)$, where $G, Q \in E(F_p)$ and $k \in \mathbb{Z}$. The detailed introduction about SM on $E(F_p)$ can be found in [14].

In SM2, the curve parameters a, b, p and the base point $G \in E(F_p)$ with order n are all given. The private key d_A is randomly selected in interval $[1, n-1]$ and the corresponding public key P_A satisfies $P_A = d_A G$.

Signature: sign message M with private key d_A.

1. Compute $e = SHA(Z_A\|M)$, where $SHA(.)$ is the hash algorithm SM3 and Z_A is the public user information;
2. Select $k \in [1, n-1]$ randomly;
3. Compute $Q(x_1, y_1) = kG$;
4. Compute $r = e + x_1 \bmod n$. If $r = 0$ or $r + k = n$ then goto step 2;
5. Compute $s = (1 + d_A)^{-1}(k - rd_A) \bmod n$. If $s = 0$ then goto step 2;
6. Return results (r, s).

Verification: verify (M', r', s') with public key P_A.

1. If r' or $s' \notin [1, n-1]$ then return false;
2. Compute $e' = SHA(Z_A\|M')$;
3. Compute $t = r' + s' \bmod n$. If $t = 0$ then return false;
4. Compute $(x_1', y_1') = s'G + tP_A$;
5. Compute $R = e' + x_1' \bmod n$. If $R = r'$ then return true, else return false.

2.2 Lattice Attack Basis

Suppose that there exist the vectors $\boldsymbol{b}_1, \boldsymbol{b}_2, \ldots, \boldsymbol{b}_N \in \mathbb{Z}^n$ which are all linearly independent from each other. Let $L = \{\sum_{i=1}^{N} x_i \boldsymbol{b}_i | x_1, \ldots, x_N \in \mathbb{Z}\}$, then L is the called **integer lattice** generated by the $\boldsymbol{b}_i$'s, where the vector set $B = \{\boldsymbol{b}_1, \ldots, \boldsymbol{b}_N\}$ is a basis of L. Let matrix $A = (\boldsymbol{b}_1, \ldots, \boldsymbol{b}_N)^T$, then for any vector $w \in L$, there exists $\boldsymbol{x} = (x_1, \ldots, x_N) \in \mathbb{Z}^n$ satisfying $w = \boldsymbol{x}A$.

The closest vector problem (CVP): given a basis B of L and a vector $\boldsymbol{u} \in \mathbb{Z}^n$, find a lattice vector $\boldsymbol{v} \in L$ satisfying $\|\boldsymbol{v} - \boldsymbol{u}\| = \lambda(L, \boldsymbol{u})$, where $\lambda(L, \boldsymbol{u})$ is the closest distance between L and $\boldsymbol{u}$. CVP can be solved in polynomial time by the combination of LLL algorithm [15] and Babai's Nearest Plane algorithm [16]. Moreover, as presented in [7,16], it has been proved, as long as the unknown lattice vector $\boldsymbol{v} \in L$ and any nonzero vector $\boldsymbol{u} \in \mathbb{Z}^n$ satisfy $\|\boldsymbol{v} - \boldsymbol{u}\|^2 \leq c_1 c_2 \Delta(A)^{2/N}$, then $\boldsymbol{v}$ can be determined uniquely in polynomial time as a CVP. Here $c_1 \approx 1$, $1 < c_2 \leq N$, and $\Delta(A)$ is the determinant of matrix A.

3 Lattice-Based Fault Attack on SM2

In this section, we will introduce the procedure of the lattice-based fault attack against SM2. First, during implementing signatures repeatedly, we will mount laser fault attack (FA) on the smart card to obtain some shared bits between different nonces. Next, based on the faulty signatures derived from FA, we can build the model of the last type of lattice attack (LA) and recover the private key d_A by some known LA tools.

3.1 Experimental Condition

In the experiment, SM2 is implemented in a smart card and there are no countermeasures. The CPU frequency is 14 MHz and the bus width is 32 bits. The implementation of SM2 is based on hardware and software with a key length of 256 bits. As shown in Fig. 1, CPU implements the instructions of SM2 algorithm in EEPROM, with the help of coprocessor which supports the operations of modular addition, reduction and multiplication of big number. The random number generator is responsible for generating random numbers and sending them to RAM. In addition, as shown in Fig. 2, we use the laser attack platform of Riscure Company in experiments. Finally, the LA is performed in a computer with Inter Core i7-3770 at 3.4 GHz.

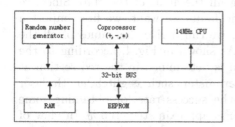

Fig. 1. The construction of smart card chip

Fig. 2. The laser attack platform for FA

3.2 Fault Attack Against SM2

Actually, during the execution of SM2 in the chip, at the moment when the nonces are written into RAM through BUS, there will be obvious peak value appearing in the power consumption curve. As shown in Fig. 3, the part of power consumption curve in red box is easy to be distinguished, which indicates two operations, generating the random numbers and storing them into RAM.

For a 256-bit nonce k with big endian storage pattern, only 32 bits of k are generated every time, so it needs to generate 8 times. After each 32-bit random number is generated, it is transferred into RAM through 32-bit BUS, so we can mount laser FA at the above appropriate time. We use laser attack platform to induce forcibly some faults at the time that the random numbers will be written into RAM, so that the written instructions are skipped. As a result, the new generated random numbers are not written into RAM successfully, and the corresponding block of k remains unchanged as the last one stored in the RAM which is the block of nonce in the last signature or the initial value in RAM.

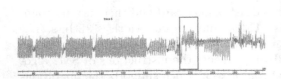

Fig. 3. The power consumption curve when the random numbers are generated and transferred (Color figure online)

Fig. 4. The right position in EEP-ROM for laser fault attack (Color figure online)

This implies that there exist some bits shared between different nonces although they are still unknown.

In addition, in order to determine the right position for attack in the chip, we use the laser attacker platform to scan all the areas of the chip. Since we can not judge whether the nonces own the faults we want, we first import a known private key into the chip. Thereby, we can derive the values of all the nonces from the faulty signature results. As shown in Fig. 4, according to the derived values of nonces, the right position is determined in the red section at the edge of EEPROM. Given the proper parameters such as glitch length, laser intensity, laser duration time and so on, the success rate for obtaining some shared bits between nonces at the position is approximately 100%. In view of the big endian storage pattern of k, we find out that the shared bits are the most significant bits (MSBs) of nonces and the number l of shared bits is a multiple of 32. After that, we import an unknown private key for real experiments. Based on the determined injection position and time, the fault attack can be mounted against many signatures uninterruptedly. Finally, we obtain 50 continuous faulty signature results $(r_i, s_i)(i = 0, \ldots, N)$.

3.3   Model of Lattice Attack Against SM2

As mentioned before, we have $N+1(N = 49)$ faulty signature results $(r_i, s_i)(i = 0, \ldots, N)$. Knowing that at least l MSBs of all the nonces are same, we can build the model of LA as presented in [11]. Let k_i and a represent respectively the nonce in the i-th signature and the shared l MSBs of all the nonces, then $k_i = a2^{m-l} + b_i(i = 0, \ldots, N)$ and $0 < a < 2^l$. Here $m(m = 256)$ is the key length of SM2 and b_i is the rest of k_i satisfying $0 < b_i < 2^{m-l}$. For $i = 0, \ldots, N$, substitute $k_i = a2^{m-l} + b_i$ into step 5 in SM2 signature, and obtain $N + 1$ equations. Then subtract the 0-th equation from the other equations respectively, and obtain the following equations.

$$(s_i + r_i - s_0 - r_0)d_A - (s_0 - s_i) = b_i - b_0 \bmod n(i = 1, \ldots, N) \qquad (1)$$

Since $0 < b_i, b_0 < 2^{m-l}$, apparently $0 < |b_i - b_0| < 2^{m-l}$. Let $\Delta b_i = |b_i - b_0|$, $\Delta t_i = (s_i + r_i - s_0 - r_0) \bmod n$ and $\Delta u_i = (s_0 - s_i) \bmod n$, then the above equations are written as

$$0 < |\Delta t_i d_A - \Delta u_i + n h_i| = \Delta b_i < 2^{m-l} (i = 1, \ldots, N). \qquad (2)$$

Where $h_i \in \mathbb{Z}$ is the smallest integer which makes the above equations true.

Let matrix $A = \begin{pmatrix} 1 & 2^l \Delta t_1 & \cdots & 2^l \Delta t_N \\ 0 & 2^l n & \cdots & 0 \\ \vdots & \vdots & \ddots & \vdots \\ 0 & 0 & \cdots & 2^l n \end{pmatrix}$, then all the row vectors $\boldsymbol{b}_0, \ldots, \boldsymbol{b}_N$

of A generate a lattice L, where $A = (\boldsymbol{b}_0, \ldots, \boldsymbol{b}_N)^T$. For $\boldsymbol{x} = (d_A, h_1, \ldots, h_N) \in \mathbb{Z}^{N+1}$, $\boldsymbol{v} = \boldsymbol{x}A = (d_A, d_A 2^l \Delta t_1 + h_1 2^l n, \ldots, d_A 2^l \Delta t_N + h_N 2^l n)$ is a nonzero lattice vector in L. Let vector $\boldsymbol{u} = (0, 2^l \Delta u_1, \ldots, 2^l \Delta u_N) \in \mathbb{Z}^{N+1}$, then the above inequations can be rewritten as $\|\boldsymbol{v} - \boldsymbol{u}\| \leq 2^m \sqrt{N+1}$. As mentioned in Sect. 2, if $2^m \sqrt{N+1} \leq \sqrt{c_1 c_2} (2^{lN} n^N)^{1/(N+1)} (2^{m-1} < n < 2^m)$, i.e., $N > m/(l-1)$, then vector $\boldsymbol{v}$ can be determined uniquely by solving CVP [7], where $c_1 = N+1$ and $c_2 = 1$. Naturally, the private key d_A can be recovered from $\boldsymbol{v}$.

3.4   Attack Results

In the attack experiments, we set the length $l = 32i(i = 1, \ldots, 7)$ of the shared MSBs and the number $N = 50 - t(t = 0, \ldots, 49 - 256/l)$ of signatures by increasing the values of i and t in turn. After each setting, based on fplll-4.0 Lattice Reduction Library [17], we perform $51 - N$ attacks, where the N signatures in the i-th attack are selected from i-th signature to $(i + N - 1)$-th signature. If only one of the attacks can obtain the key d_A that meets $P_A = d_A G$, we think the lattice attack is successful.

The experimental results show that the lattice attack is still successful when $l = 192(i = 6)$ and $N = 3(t = 47)$, and the average time for each attack is about $32 \mu s$. It implies that there are 192 MSBs shared between the nonces and we only need 3 signatures to disclose d_A successfully. Moreover, there are 20 successful cases in the 48 attacks with success rate 41%.

4   Countermeasure to Resist Lattice-Based Fault Attack

In this section, a new countermeasure to resist LFA is proposed for SM2. It destroys directly the conditions of LA rather than purely preventing FA. Therefore, even though the FA has made the nonces known partially or sharing some bits, the LA still cannot be mounted.

4.1   SM2 with Countermeasure

Signature with Countermeasure: sign message M with keys d_A and P_A.

1. Compute $e = SHA(Z_A\|M)$;
2. Select $k, w \in [1, n-1]$ randomly;

3. Compute $Q(x_1, y_1) = kG + wP_A$;
4. Compute $r = e + x_1 \bmod n$. If $r = 0$ or $r + k = n$ then goto step 2;
5. Compute $s = (1 + d_A)^{-1}(k + (w - r)d_A) \bmod n$. If $s = 0$ then goto step 2;
6. Return results (r, s).

In the SM2 with countermeasure above, there are two nonces k and w generated with same length, and the public key P_A is employed for signature. The nonce k is actually added with the mask wd_A. Moreover, the verification without any modification can be passed successfully.

4.2   Provable Security Against Lattice Attack

As mentioned above, the condition of the LA based on knowing parts of nonce k is strongest. Hence, it is sufficient to only analyze the security of our countermeasure against the strongest LA. Obviously, the result of analysis can be also applied similarly to our proposed attack.

As shown in SM2 Signature with countermeasure, it is assumed that we obtain $N(N > m/(l-1))$ signature results $(r_i, s_i)(i = 1, \ldots, N)$, and both the l MSBs a_i of nonce k_i and the l MSBs c_i of nonce w_i are known in the i-signature. Here m is the key length of SM2. Let b_i, d_i represent the remaining unknown values of k_i, w_i respectively, then $k_i = a_i 2^{m-l} + b_i$ and $w_i = c_i 2^{m-l} + d_i$. Where $a_i, c_i < 2^l$ and $b_i, d_i < 2^{m-l}$. Let $t_i = (s_i - c_i 2^{m-l} + r_i) \bmod n$ and $u_i = (a_i 2^{m-l} - s_i) \bmod n$, then we have the following equations.

$$t_i d_A - u_i + h_i n = b_i + d_i d_A (i = 1, \ldots, N) \tag{3}$$

where h_i is the smallest integer which makes the above equations true.

Similarly, we can construct a lattice L by matrix $A = \begin{pmatrix} \beta & t_1 & \cdots & t_N \\ 0 & n & \cdots & 0 \\ \vdots & \vdots & \ddots & \vdots \\ 0 & 0 & \cdots & n \end{pmatrix}$, where

β is any nonzero real number. Let vector $\boldsymbol{u} = (0, u_1, u_2, \ldots, u_N) \in \mathbb{Z}^{N+1}$ and lattice vector $\boldsymbol{v} = \boldsymbol{x}A = (\beta d_A, d_A t_1 + h_1 n, \ldots, d_A t_N + h_N n)$, where $\boldsymbol{x} = (d_A, h_1, h_2, \ldots, h_N) \in \mathbb{Z}^{N+1}$, then we have the following equation

$$||\boldsymbol{v} - \boldsymbol{u}||^2 = (\beta d_A)^2 + \sum_{i=1}^{N} (b_i + d_i d_A)^2. \tag{4}$$

It is known that d_A is a random number less than $n(2^{m-1} < n < 2^m)$. The probability is $\frac{1}{2^{d+1}}$ when $\log_2 d_A = m - d$, where d is non-negative integer. Therefore, $\log_2 d_A$ is slightly smaller than or equal to $\log_2 n$. In other words, d is very small in general. In addition, $\log_2 d_i$ is much greater than d in practical FA, otherwise d_i and d_A can be directly obtained from exhaustive search attack rather than LA. Thereby, the inequation $\log_2 n - \log_2 d_A \ll \log_2 d_i$ holds, namely, $n \ll d_i d_A < n^2/2^l$. Therefore, the following inequation holds.

$$||\boldsymbol{v} - \boldsymbol{u}||^2 \gg (N+1)(n^{2N}\beta^2 d_A^2)^{1/(N+1)} > (N+1)\Delta(A)^{2/(N+1)} \tag{5}$$

As described in Sect. 2, the above inequation does not satisfy the condition of CVP, so v can not be determined. Apparently, it is also impossible to recover d_A. The conditions of LA are destroyed completely. In addition, if the known bits in the nonces are the least significant bits or contiguous blocks in the middle, the same conclusion can be proved by the similar way as above.

5   Conclusion

In this paper, we introduce a lattice-based fault attack (LFA) against SM2 in a smart card. The attack is based on the condition of lattice attack (LA) that there are some bits shared between different nonces. First, the instructions of writing nonces into RAM are skipped by practical laser fault attack (FA), so that some bits between the nonces in SM2 remain unchanged. Then we combine the results of FA with the model of LA to recover the private key d_A successfully. The experimental results show that 3 faulty signatures are needed to recover d_A with average time $32\,\mu s$ and success rate $42\,\%$. In addition, we also propose a countermeasure for SM2 to resist LFA by destroying the condition of LA from algorithm level. It is proved in theory that the countermeasure is sufficient to resist LFA. Moreover, the similar attack and countermeasure can also be applied to ECDSA.

Acknowledgments. We thank the anonymous referees for their careful reading and insightful comments. This work is supported by the National Science and Technology Major Project (No. 2014ZX01032401-001) and the National Basic Research Program of China (No. 2013CB338002).

References

1. Biehl, I., Meyer, B., Müller, V.: Differential fault attacks on elliptic curve cryptosystems. In: Bellare, M. (ed.) CRYPTO 2000. LNCS, vol. 1880, pp. 131–146. Springer, Heidelberg (2000)
2. Ciet, M., Joye, M.: Elliptic curve cryptosystems in the presence of permanent and transient faults. Des. Codes Cryptogr. **36**(1), 33–43 (2005)
3. Blömer, J., Otto, M., Seifert, J.-P.: Sign change fault attacks on elliptic curve cryptosystems. In: Breveglieri, L., Koren, I., Naccache, D., Seifert, J.-P. (eds.) FDTC 2006. LNCS, vol. 4236, pp. 36–52. Springer, Heidelberg (2006)
4. Schmidt, J., Medwed, M.: A fault attack on ECDSA. In: 2009 Workshop on Fault Diagnosis and Tolerance in Cryptography (FDTC), pp. 93–99. IEEE (2009)
5. Barenghi, A., Bertoni, G., Palomba, A., Susella, R.: A novel fault attack against ECDSA. In: 2011 IEEE International Symposium on Hardware-Oriented Security and Trust (HOST), pp. 161–166. IEEE (2011)
6. Nguyen, P.Q., Tibouchi, M.: Lattice-based fault attacks on signatures. Fault Analysis in Cryptography. ISC, pp. 201–220. Springer, Berlin (2012)
7. Howgrave-Graham, N., Smart, N.P.: Lattice attacks on digital signature schemes. Des. Codes Cryptogr. **23**(3), 283–290 (2001)

8. Nguyen, P.Q., Shparlinski, I.E.: The insecurity of the elliptic curve digital signature algorithm with partially known nonces. Des. Codes Cryptogr. **30**(2), 201–217 (2003)
9. Liu, M., Chen, J., Li, H.: Partially known nonces and fault injection attacks on SM2 signature algorithm. In: Lin, D., Xu, S., Yung, M. (eds.) Inscrypt 2013. LNCS, vol. 8567, pp. 343–358. Springer, Heidelberg (2014)
10. Leadbitter, P.J., Page, D.L., Smart, N.P.: Attacking DSA under a repeated bits assumption. In: Joye, M., Quisquater, J.-J. (eds.) CHES 2004. LNCS, vol. 3156, pp. 428–440. Springer, Heidelberg (2004)
11. Faugère, J.-C., Goyet, C., Renault, G.: Attacking (EC)DSA given only an implicit hint. In: Knudsen, L.R., Wu, H. (eds.) SAC 2012. LNCS, vol. 7707, pp. 252–274. Springer, Heidelberg (2013)
12. Naccache, D., Nguyên, P.Q., Tunstall, M., Whelan, C.: Experimenting with faults, lattices and the DSA. In: Vaudenay, S. (ed.) PKC 2005. LNCS, vol. 3386, pp. 16–28. Springer, Heidelberg (2005)
13. Office State Commercial Cryptgraphy Administration: Public key cryptographic algorithm SM2 based on elliptic curves (in Chinese) (2010). http://www.oscca.gov.cn/UpFile/2010122214822692.pdf
14. Hankerson, D., Menezes, A.J., Vanstone, S.: Guide to Elliptic Curve Cryptography. SPC. Springer, New York (2006)
15. Lenstra, A.K., Lenstra, H.W., Lovász, L.: Factoring polynomials with rational coefficients. Mathematische Annalen **261**(4), 515–534 (1982)
16. Babai, L.: On lovász' lattice reduction and the nearest lattice point problem. Combinatorica **6**(1), 1–13 (1986)
17. Stehlé, D., Albrecht, M., Cadé, D.: fplll-4.0 Lattice Reduction Library (2012). https://github.com/dstehle/fplll

The Security of Polynomial Information of Diffie-Hellman Key

Yao Wang[1,2,3] and Kewei Lv[1,2(✉)]

[1] State Key Laboratory of Information Security, Institute of Information
Engineering, Chinese Academy of Sciences, Beijing 100093, China
{wangyao,lvkewei}@iie.ac.cn
[2] Data Assurance Communication Security Research Center,
Chinese Academy of Sciences, Beijing 100093, China
[3] University of Chinese Academy Sciences, Beijing 100049, China

Abstract. In this paper, we study the relations between the security
of Diffie-Hellman (DH) key and the leakage of polynomial information
of it again. Given a fixed sparse polynomial $F(X)$ and an oracle, which
returns value of polynomial of DH key i.e., $F(g^{xy})$ when called by g^x and
g^y, we obtain a probabilistic algorithm to recover the key. It is an extension of Shparlinski's result in 2004. This shows that finding polynomial
information of DH key is as difficult as the whole key again. Furthermore,
we study a variant of DH problem given 2 and g^y to compute 2^y and the
n-DH problem with this method respectively, and obtain similar results.

Keywords: Diffie-Hellman key · m-sparse polynomial · Polynomial
information · n-DH problem

1 Introduction

In 1976, Diffie and Hellman proposed a practical method to agree on a secret key
over an insecure channel called Diffie-Hellman (DH) key exchange protocol. Let
$g \in F_p^*$ be an element of multiplicative order t. In DH key exchange protocol over
F_p^*, two parties calculate g^a, g^b respectively, where $a, b \in [0, t - 1]$ and exchange
them to form their common key $K = g^{ab}$. The element K has the same bit
length n as p and n is chosen to make this protocol secure. Since then, many
new cryptosystems have been proposed based on DH protocol.

In general, after the key exchange protocol is finished, both parties need to
switch to a private key cryptosystem. For practicality and speed, they may wish
to use a block cipher and therefore need to derive a much shorter bit string
from K. A natural way would be to use a block of bits from g^{ab}. So when we
analyze the security of DH key, bit security is an important aspect. Boneh and
Venkatesan proved that a part (32 bits) of the most significant bits (MSB) is as
secure as the whole (1024 bits) key. They showed that finding $n^{1/2}$ MSB of K
is as difficult as the whole key in [2,3]. A detailed survey of several other results
of this type of problem has been given in [4].

© Springer International Publishing Switzerland 2016
S. Qing et al. (Eds.): ICICS 2015, LNCS 9543, pp. 71–81, 2016.
DOI: 10.1007/978-3-319-29814-6_7

Verheul [5] studies another aspect of DH key. Assume $q = p^t$ *and* $\gamma \in F_q$ is a generator of a group. If $g(x) = \sum_{i=0}^{t} a_i x^i$ is an irreducible polynomial of degree t in $F_p[X]$, then we can describe the extension field F_q as $F_p[x]/g(x)$, i.e., each element f in F_q can be uniquely written modulo $g(x)$, as a polynomial of degree $< t$. In this setting, for any i less than t, let f_i denote the i-th coefficient of an element f. There exists a function that would be a linear mapping from F_q onto F_p and its value is the coefficient f_i. [5] proves that this function can be expressed as $F(X) = \Sigma_{i=1}^{m} c_i X^{e_i} (c_i \in F_q)$ and c_i can be easily determined. [5] also studies the security of polynomial information of DH key and proves that finding coefficients f_i (i.e., polynomial information $F(\gamma^{xy})$) of DH key γ^{xy} is as difficult as the whole key.

As an application of [5,6] gives a variant of DH scheme. In this variant, both parties send each other the minimal polynomials of γ^x, γ^y rather than the element themselves and the exchanged key is some coefficient of non-constant term of the minimal polynomial of γ^{xy}. This coefficient can be expressed as $F(\gamma^{xy})$ and the polynomial F must have a very large degree, such that it is unfeasible to find γ^{xy} by solving the equation $F(\gamma^{xy}) = A$. [5,6] proves that if we are given an oracle which for each pair (γ^x, γ^y) returns $F(\gamma^{xy})$, then one can construct a polynomial time algorithm to recover γ^{xy}. This shows that the variant are at least as secure as the original DH scheme over a multiplicative group of F_q. So the security of polynomial information of DH key is closely related to the security of DH key.

Shparlinski's result [1] is a generalization of [5,6]. It studies the security of polynomial transformations of DH key. Indeed, this polynomial transformation is a value of given polynomial function of the key. And [1] also extends [5] to the unreliable oracle case, that is, the oracle returns correct result only for a certain very small fraction of inputs and an error message for other inputs. Then an algorithm is given making expected number of calls of the oracle, to return γ^{xy}. It is deterministic when correct answers could be obtained from oracle. But it requires that the error answers of oracle could be identified. Moreover, in [1], only one part of the input to oracle is random and the other is fixed.

Here we improve the oracle and algorithm in [1] to get a probabilistic algorithm to recover DH key. In this improvement, not only the error from oracle could be not identified, but also both parts of inputs are random. In our algorithm, we use the Chebyshev inequality to identify error answers of the oracle. And for the two parts random inputs (γ^x, γ^y) of the oracle, we use the Markov inequality to find a good y which makes us have a sufficient advantage in receiving correct answers from the oracle taking over x only. Thus we can solve a nonsingular system of linear equations to recover DH key. As corollaries, we study two special cases. Finally, we use the same method to study variants of DH problem, i.e., given 2 and g^y trying to recover the key 2^y and the n-DH problem.

2 Preliminaries

In order to show our algorithms, we need an estimate on the number of zeros of polynomials from [1] and two important inequalities. Let F_q be a finite field of q elements and F_p^* be a multiplicative subgroup of F_q, where p is a prime.

Lemma 1 ([1]). *For* $m \geq 2$, *elements* $a_1, a_2, \ldots, a_m \in F_q^*$ *and integers* $e_1, \ldots, e_m$, *an element* $\theta \in F_q$ *of multiplicative order* t. *We denote by* W *the number of solutions of the equation* $\sum_{i=1}^m a_i \theta^{e_i u} = 0, u \in [0, t-1]$. *Then* $W \leq 3t^{1-1/(m-1)} D^{1/(m-1)}$, *where* $D = min_{1 \leq i \leq m} max_{j \neq i} gcd(e_j - e_i, t)$.

Let $E(\xi)$ be the expected value of a random variable ξ and $D(\xi)$ be the variance value of ξ. So $E_\xi[g(\xi)]$ denotes the expected value of a random variable $g(\xi)$, where the function g only depends on the distribution of ξ.

Theorem 1 *(Markov). For a positive* c *and a random variable* ξ *upper bounded by* M, $Pr[\xi \geq E(\xi)/c] \geq M^{-1}(1 - 1/c)E(\xi)$.

Theorem 2 *(Chebyshev). For an arbitrary positive* δ, $Pr[|\xi - E(\xi)| \geq \delta] \leq D(\xi)/\delta^2$.

3 The Security of Polynomial Information of DH Key

Let γ be an element in F_q of multiplicative order t. We consider an m-sparse polynomial $F(X) = \sum_{i=1}^m c_i X^{e_i} \in F_q[X]$, where $c_1, \ldots, c_m \in F_q^*$ and $e_1, \ldots, e_m$ are pairwise distinct modulo t.

3.1 The Polynomial Information from an Imperfect Oracle

Let $0 < \varepsilon \leq 1$. Assume there exists an oracle $O_{F,\varepsilon}$ satisfying that, given values of (γ^x, γ^y) to the oracle, it returns correct values of $F(\gamma^{xy})$ for at least εt^2 pairs $(x, y) \in [0, t-1]^2$ and returns a random element of F_p^* for other pairs of $(x, y) \in [0, t-1]^2$. The case $\varepsilon = 1$ is a noise-free oracle which had been considered in [5]. So the following discussion only involves in the case of $\varepsilon < 1$.

Here we try to construct a nonsingular system of linear equations using polynomial information from the oracle. We firstly study how to select the coefficient matrix of this equation system.

Given $\theta \in F_p^*$, for a vector $\vec{u} = (u_1, u_2, \ldots, u_m)$, we say that $\vec{u}$ is good if $det(\theta^{e_i u_j})_{i,j \neq 1}^m \neq 0$. We set $U = \{\vec{u} \mid \vec{u} \text{ is good}\}$. Here we estimate the possibility of finding a good $\vec{u}$.

Assume that for some $k(2 \leq k \leq m)$, we have already found $k-1$ elements $u_1, u_2, \ldots, u_{k-1} \in [0, t-1]$ with

$$det(\theta^{e_i u_j})_{i,j \neq 1}^{k-1} \neq 0 \tag{1}$$

We select element $u_k \in [0, t-1]$ until

$$det(\theta^{e_i u_j})_{i,j \neq 1}^k \neq 0 \tag{2}$$

We know that if the determinant (2) vanishes then u_k is a solution of equation

$$\triangle_1^{e_k u_k} + \cdots + \triangle_k^{e_1 u_k} = 0 \tag{3}$$

where, by (1), $\triangle_1 = det(\theta^{e_i u_j})_{i,j}^{k-1} \neq 0$.

Applying Lemma 1, the number of elements $u_k \in [0, t-1]$ satisfying (3) is at most $3t^{1-1/(k-1)}$. So the probability of finding $u_k \in [0, t-1]$ which satisfy (2) is at least $1 - 3t^{-1/(k-1)}$. If we select $u_1, u_2, .., u_m \in [0, t-1]$ uniformly and independently at random to get the vector $\overrightarrow{u} = (u_1, u_2, \ldots, u_m)$, then $Pr[\overrightarrow{u} \in U] \geq \prod_{i=2}^{m}(1 - 3t^{-\frac{1}{i-1}})$.

Since both parts of inputs to this oracle are random, for input (γ^x, γ^y) of oracle, using idea of [1], we hope that we could choose a set of good y with a high probability such that, for each good y, we have a sufficient advantage in receiving correct answers from the oracle taking over x only. Then we can query oracle by randomizing the γ^x-component, fixing a good y. Thus, we can obtain a probabilistic algorithm to recover γ^{xy} with a high probability.

Let ε_y be the average success probability of $O_{F,\varepsilon}$, taken over random x for a given y. Thus, $E_y[\varepsilon_y] = \varepsilon$. For $k = \lceil \log \frac{2}{\varepsilon} \rceil$, we say that y is j-good if $\varepsilon_y \in [2^{-j}, 2^{-j+1})$, $j = 1, 2, \ldots, k$. Let $S_j = \{y | y \text{ is } j\text{-good}\}$ (thus we ignore any y satisfying $\varepsilon_y < \varepsilon/2$). By Theorem 1, for $c = 2, M = 1, Pr[\varepsilon_y \geq \frac{\varepsilon}{2}] \geq \frac{\varepsilon}{2}$.

If all j satisfy $Pr[(y+v) \in S_j] < \frac{\varepsilon \cdot 2^{j-2}}{k}$, then

$$\frac{\varepsilon}{2} \leq \sum_{j=1}^{k} 2^{-j+1} Pr[(y+v) \in S_j] < \sum_{j=1}^{k} 2^{-j+1} \cdot \frac{\varepsilon \cdot 2^{j-2}}{k} = \frac{\varepsilon}{2},$$

which is a contradiction. So there must exist j such that $Pr[(y+v) \in S_j] \geq \frac{\varepsilon \cdot 2^{j-2}}{k}$. It means that we could find a suitable v such that $y + v$ is j-good.

Now we present a probabilistic algorithm (Algorithm 1) to look for a suitable v.

Algorithm 1. On input (t, γ^y, B), given oracle $O_{F,\varepsilon}$, output (v, ε_{y+v}).

1: Choose a random $v \in [0, t-1]$ and set $count := 0$;
2: For a sufficiently large integer $B = poly(k)$, choose $r_1, r_2, \ldots, r_B$ randomly. Using $(\gamma^{r_i}, \gamma^{y+v})$ to call the oracle, it returns A_i, $i = 1, 2, .., B$;
3: For every r_i, compute $\gamma^{r_i(y+v)}$ and if $\gamma^{r_i(y+v)}$ equals A_i, set $count = count + 1$;
4: Compute the approximate value of $\varepsilon_{y+v} = \frac{count}{B}$. If $\varepsilon_{y+v} \geq \frac{\varepsilon}{2}$, outputs (v, ε_{y+v}), else aborts.

In Algorithm 1, for every r_i, we can compute correct values of $\gamma^{r_i(y+v)}$ to determine whether the output A_i of the oracle in step 2 is correct. So in step 4, we can get an approximate value of ε_{y+v} for some v. Because $k = \lceil \log \frac{2}{\varepsilon} \rceil$, we know that if y is j-good, that is, $\varepsilon_{y+v} \in [2^{-j}, 2^{-j+1})$, the value of ε_{y+v} must satisfy $\varepsilon_{y+v} \geq \frac{\varepsilon}{2}$. Thus if Algorithm 1 finds a suitable v satisfying $\varepsilon_{y+v} \geq \frac{\varepsilon}{2}$, we can get j and $y + v \in S_j$ with the probability of at least $\frac{\varepsilon}{2}$.

Based on Algorithm 1, we get Algorithm 2 which can output DH key by calling oracle $O_{F,\varepsilon}$.

Algorithm 2. On input $(t, \delta, \gamma, \gamma^x, \gamma^y)$, for $0 < \delta < 1$, given oracle $O_{F,\varepsilon}$, output γ^{xy}.

1: Run Algorithm 1 to find some $v \in [0, t-1]$ which satisfies $y + v \in S_j$ and compute $\theta = \gamma^{y+v}$;
2: Find some $\overrightarrow{u} = (u_1, u_2, \ldots, u_m)$ satisfying $\overrightarrow{u} \in U$;
3: For every component $u_j (j = 1, 2, \ldots, m)$ of $\overrightarrow{u}$, using $(\gamma^{x+u_j}, \gamma^{y+v})$ to call the oracle, it returns A_j;
4: Solve the system of equations $\sum_{i=1}^{m} c_i (\theta^{x+u_j})^{e_i} = A_j, j = 1, 2, \ldots, m$ to get a candidate value of γ^{xy};
5: Choose some n satisfying $n \geq \frac{1 - 2^{-jm}}{2^{jm}\delta^2(1-\varepsilon)}$. Repeat steps 2,3,4 n times to get a list $\mathcal{L}$ of candidate values of γ^{xy}. If some γ^{xy} appears $z(z \leq (2^{-jm} + \delta)n)$ times in the list $\mathcal{L}$ and $|\frac{z}{n} - 2^{-jm}| \leq \delta$, output this γ^{xy}. Otherwise, choose another n to redo this step.

Theorem 3. *Let t be a prime, $m \geq 2$ and an m-sparse polynomial $F(X) = \sum_{i=1}^{m} c_i X^{e_i} \in F_q[X]$, where $c_1, \ldots, c_m \in F_q^*$ and $e_1, \ldots, e_m$ are pairwise distinct modulo t. Given an oracle $O_{F,\varepsilon}$, Algorithm 2 can output DH key with a probability at least $\frac{\varepsilon}{2} \cdot (1 - \frac{1}{n\delta^2 \cdot 2^{jm}}) \cdot (1 - 3t^{-\frac{1}{m-1}})^{m-1}$ in time polynomial in (mn, B) by making $mn + B$ calls to the oracle. In particular, if $t \geq (\frac{3}{1 - 2^{-\frac{1}{m-1}}})^{m-1}$ and $\delta \geq (\frac{1}{n \cdot 2^{jm}})^{\frac{1}{2}}$, DH key could be found with a probability of at least $\frac{\varepsilon}{4}$.*

Proof. After running steps 1, 2, 3 of Algorithm 2, we can get a nonsingular system of linear equations

$$(\theta^{e_i u_j})_{i,j=1}^{m} \cdot \begin{pmatrix} c_1 \theta^{x e_1} \\ \vdots \\ c_m \theta^{x e_m} \end{pmatrix} = \begin{pmatrix} A_1 \\ \vdots \\ A_m \end{pmatrix}$$

Because the coefficient matrix is non-singular, we can solve the system of equations to get the values of $(c_1 \theta^{x e_1}, \ldots, c_m \theta^{x e_m})$. Because $m \geq 2$ and $e_1, \ldots, e_m$ are pairwise distinct modulo t, at least one of $e_1, \ldots, e_m$ is relatively prime to t. So we can find an integer $f_i \in [0, t-1]$ satisfying $e_i f_i \equiv 1 \pmod{t}$ and compute $\theta^x = (\theta^{x e_i})^{f_i}$, that is, $(\gamma^{y+v})^x$. Thus we can get a candidate value of γ^{xy} from $(\gamma^{y+v})^x = \gamma^{xy} \cdot \gamma^{xv}$.

Then we estimate the probability of which step 5 outputs a correct value of DH key. When we use $(\gamma^{x+u_i}, \gamma^{y+v})$ to call the oracle, it returns the correct value of $F(\gamma^{(x+u_i)(y+v)})$ with probability at least 2^{-j}. So after repeating steps 2, 3, 4 one time, we can get the correct γ^{xy} with probability at least 2^{-jm}. From Theorem 2, with the increasing number of repetitions n in step 5, the value of $\frac{z}{n}$ infinitely close to 2^{-jm}. Thus the value of δ should be chosen as small as possible, but at this time, the value of n will be very big. In order to keep the efficiency of the algorithm, one should make a trade-off in choosing the value of $\delta \in (0, 1)$. Here by Theorem 2, we know that the output of step 5 is correct with the probability of $Pr[|\frac{z}{n} - 2^{-jm}| \leq \delta] \geq 1 - \frac{2^{-jm}(1 - 2^{-jm})}{n\delta^2}$.

The success of the Algorithm 2 means that steps 1, 2, 5 run successfully. So the successful probability of Algorithm 2 is:

$$Pr[Algorithm\ 2\ succeeds] \geq \frac{\varepsilon}{2} \cdot (1 - \frac{2^{-jm}(1 - 2^{-jm})}{n\delta^2}) \cdot \prod_{i=2}^{m}(1 - 3t^{-\frac{1}{i-1}})$$

$$\geq \frac{\varepsilon}{2} \cdot (1 - \frac{1}{n\delta^2 \cdot 2^{jm}}) \cdot (1 - 3t^{-\frac{1}{m-1}})^{m-1}$$

Obviously, Algorithm 1 run in polynomial time $poly(B)$ and steps 2, 3, 4, 5 of Algorithm 2 are done in polynomial time $poly(mn)$. So Algorithm 2 is done in time polynomial in (mn, B). When Algorithm 2 succeeds, we run the step 1 one time with B calls to the oracle and repeat step 2, 3, 4 n times with mn calls. Thus, we make the totally number of $mn + B$ calls to the oracle.

If $t \geq (\frac{3}{1-2^{-\frac{1}{m-1}}})^{m-1}$, we know $\prod_{i=2}^{m}(1 - 3t^{-\frac{1}{i-1}}) \geq \frac{1}{2}$. In order to output DH key with a probability at least $\frac{\varepsilon}{4}$, one can choose the value of δ at least $(\frac{1}{n \cdot 2^{jm}})^{\frac{1}{2}}$. This completes the proof.

3.2   Further Discussions on Another Two Cases

From Sect. 3.1, we can get two special cases. In these cases, we give two algorithms which can recover DH key by calling two special oracles respectively.

Assume that there is a special oracle $\tilde{O}_{F,\varepsilon}$ satisfying that, for every $x \in [0, t-1]$, when we use (γ^x, γ^y) to make a call of the oracle, it returns the correct value of $F(\gamma^{xy})$ for at least εt values of $y \in [0, t-1]$ and returns a random element of F_p^* for other values of $y \in [0, t-1]$. Here the error output from oracle $\tilde{O}_{F,\varepsilon}$ could not be identified.

We give Algorithm 3 to recover DH key by calling oracle $\tilde{O}_{F,\varepsilon}$.

Algorithm 3. On input $(t, \delta, \gamma, \varepsilon, \gamma^x, \gamma^y)$, for $0 < \delta < 1$, given oracle $\tilde{O}_{F,\varepsilon}$, output γ^{xy}.

1: Set $\theta = \gamma^x$. Find some $\vec{u} = (u_1, u_2, \ldots, u_m)$ satisfying $\vec{u} \in U$;
2: For every component $u_j (j = 1, 2, \ldots, m)$ of $\vec{u}$, using $(\gamma^x, \gamma^{y+u_j})$ to call the oracle, it returns A_j;
3: Solve the system of equations $\sum_{i=1}^{m} c_i(\theta^{y+u_j})^{e_i} = A_j, j = 1, 2, \ldots, m$ to get a candidate value of γ^{xy};
4: Choose some n satisfying $n \geq \frac{\varepsilon^m(1-\varepsilon^m)}{(1-\varepsilon)\delta^2}$. Repeat steps 1, 2, 3 n times to get a list $\mathcal{L}$ of candidate values of γ^{xy}. If some γ^{xy} appears $z(z \leq (\varepsilon^m + \delta)n)$ times in the list $\mathcal{L}$ and $|\frac{z}{n} - \varepsilon^m| \leq \delta$, output this γ^{xy}. Otherwise, choose another n to redo this step.

Theorem 4. *Let t be a prime, $m \geq 2$ and an m-sparse polynomial $F(X) = \sum_{i=1}^{m} c_i X^{e_i} \in F_q[X]$, where $c_1, \ldots, c_m \in F_q^*$ and $e_1, \ldots, e_m$ are pairwise distinct modulo t. Given an oracle $\tilde{O}_{F,\varepsilon}$, Algorithm 3 can output DH key with a probability of at least $(1 - \frac{\varepsilon^m}{n\delta^2}) \cdot (1 - 3t^{-\frac{1}{m-1}})^{m-1}$ in time polynomial in mn by making mn calls to the oracle.*

Proof. The proof is similar to Theorem 3, except that the probability of success is different. Using $(\gamma^x, \gamma^{y+u_j})$ to call the oracle, it returns the correct value of $F(\gamma^{x(y+u_j)})$ with probability at least ε. So after repeating steps 1, 2, 3 one time, we can get the correct γ^{xy} with probability at least ε^m. By Theorem 2, for some $0 < \delta < 1$, the output of step 4 is correct with the probability of $Pr[|\frac{z}{n} - \varepsilon^m| \leq \delta] \geq 1 - \frac{\varepsilon^m(1-\varepsilon^m)}{n\delta^2}$.

The success of Algorithm 3 means that steps 1, 4 run successfully. So the successful probability of Algorithm 3 is:

$$Pr[Algorithm\ 3\ succeeds] \geq (1 - \frac{\varepsilon^m(1-\varepsilon^m)}{n\delta^2}) \cdot \prod_{i=2}^{m}(1 - 3t^{-\frac{1}{i-1}})$$

$$\geq (1 - \frac{\varepsilon^m}{n\delta^2}) \cdot (1 - 3t^{-\frac{1}{m-1}})^{m-1}$$

Obviously, when the Algorithm 3 succeeds, we repeat step 1, 2, 3 n times. Thus, we make the totally number of mn calls to the oracle.

Assume that there is another special oracle $\hat{O}_{F,\varepsilon}$ satisfying that, given values of (γ^x, γ^y) to the oracle, it returns correct values of $F(\gamma^{xy})$ for at least εt^2 pairs $(x, y) \in [0, t-1]^2$ and returns an error message for other pairs of $(x, y) \in [0, t-1]^2$. The oracle $\hat{O}_{F,\varepsilon}$ makes two parts of inputs randomize instead of only one part in [1].

Here we give Algorithm 4 to recover DH key by calling oracle $\hat{O}_{F,\varepsilon}$.

Algorithm 4. On input $(t, \gamma, \gamma^x, \gamma^y)$, given oracle $\hat{O}_{F,\varepsilon}$, output γ^{xy}.

1: Run Algorithm 1 with the oracle $\hat{O}_{F,\varepsilon}$ to find some $v \in [0, t-1]$ satisfying $y + v \in S_j$ and compute $\theta = \gamma^{y+v}$;
2: Find some $\vec{u} = (u_1, u_2, \ldots, u_m)$ satisfying $\vec{u} \in U$. For every component $u_j(j = 1, 2, \ldots, m)$ of $\vec{u}$, computing γ^{x+u_j}. Use $(\gamma^{x+u_j}, \gamma^{y+v})$ to call the oracle, it returns value of $F(\gamma^{(x+u_j)(y+v)}) = A_j$.
3: Solve the system of equations $\sum_{i=1}^{m} c_i(\theta^{x+u_j})^{e_i} = A_j, j = 1, 2, \ldots, m$ to get the value of γ^{xy}, output this γ^{xy}.

Theorem 5. *Let t be a prime, $m \geq 2$ and an m-sparse polynomial $F(X) = \sum_{i=1}^{m} c_i X^{e_i} \in F_q[X]$, where $c_1, \ldots, c_m \in F_q^*$ and $e_1, \ldots, e_m$ are pairwise distinct modulo t. Given an oracle $\hat{O}_{F,\varepsilon}$, Algorithm 4 can output DH key with a probability of at least $\frac{\varepsilon}{2^{jm+1}} \cdot (1 - 3t^{-\frac{1}{m-1}})^{m-1}$ in time polynomial in (m, B) by making $m + B$ calls to the oracle.*

Proof. The proof is similar to Theorem 3 except for the probability of success. The success of Algorithm 4 means that steps 1, 2 run successfully. Step 2 can find a suitable u_j such that oracle returns the correct values of $F(\gamma^{(x+u_j)(y+v)})$ and $det(\theta^{e_i u_j})_{i,j=1}^{m} \neq 0$. So step 2 runs successfully with probability of at least $(2^{-j})^m \prod_{i=2}^{m}(1 - 3t^{-\frac{1}{i-1}})$.

Thus, the successful probability of Algorithm 4 is:

$$Pr[Algorithm\ 4\ succeeds] \geq \frac{\varepsilon}{2} \cdot (2^{-j})^m \cdot \prod_{i=2}^{m}(1 - 3t^{-\frac{1}{i-1}})$$

$$\geq \frac{\varepsilon}{2^{jm+1}} \cdot (1 - 3t^{-\frac{1}{m-1}})^{m-1}$$

When Algorithm 4 succeeds, we run the step 1 one time with B calls to the oracle and the step 2 one time with m calls. Thus, we make the totally number of $m + B$ calls to the oracle.

Algorithms 2–4 all show that finding polynomial information of DH key is as difficult as the whole key.

4   Some Variants of DH Problem and Their Polynomial Information Security

In this section, we present some variants of DH problem, such as, $DH_g(2, g^y)$, the n-DH problem and Multiple DH problem. For these variants, we give algorithms and theorems with the similar method to Sect. 3 respectively. All theorems show that finding polynomial information of DH key of these variants is also as difficult as the whole key.

4.1   DH Problem $DH_g(2, g^y)$

In [2], there is a new variant of the DH key exchange protocol. Say Alice and Bob wish to perform secret key over p. Alice picks a random number x in the range $[1, p - 1]$ such that $gcd(x, p - 1) = 1$, computes $g = 2^x (mod\ p)$ and sends g to Bob. Bob picks a random number y in $[1, p - 1]$ and sends g^y to Alice. The key they agree on is $\alpha = 2^y (mod\ p)$. Clearly Bob can compute this value. Alice can compute this value since $2^y = g^{yx^{-1}} (mod\ p)$. So this variant of DH can be described as knowing 2 and g^y to recover the key 2^y, denoted $DH_g(2, g^y)$. There is an oracle $O_{F,\varepsilon}$ whose definition is the same as Sect. 3.1.

Corollary 1. *Given the oracle $O_{F,\varepsilon}$, 2^y can be recovered from $(2, g^y)$ running Algorithm 2.*

Proof. We use $(2, g^y)$ as the inputs of the oracle $O_{F,\varepsilon}$. Then running Algorithm 2 given input $(p, \delta, g, 2, g^y)$, we can get the value of 2^y.

4.2   The n-DH Problem

In [7], Cash, Kiltz and Shoup proposed a new computational problem and named it the twin Diffie-Hellman (twin DH) problem with the meaning that given a random triple of the form $(\gamma^{x_1}, \gamma^{x_2}, \gamma^y) \in F_q^3$, compute $\gamma^{x_1 y}$ and $\gamma^{x_2 y}$. [8] presented a modification of the twin DH problem by extending the number of the (ordinary) DH instances from 2 to an arbitrary integer n, and name it the n-DH problem. The n-DH problem is that given a random $n+1$ tuple of the form $(\gamma^{x_1}, \ldots, \gamma^{x_n}, \gamma^y) \in F_q^{n+1}$, compute $(\gamma^{x_1 y}, \ldots, \gamma^{x_n y})$.

Assume that there is a n-DH oracle $O_{F,\varepsilon}^n$ satisfying that, for every $x_i \in [0, t-1]$, $i = 1, 2, .., n$, given the values of (γ^{x_i}, γ^y), it returns correct $F(\gamma^{x_i y})$ for at least εt values of $y \in [0, t-1]$ and returns an error message for other values of $y \in [0, t-1]$.

Here we can construct an algorithm using similar method to recover n-DH key by calling oracle $O_{F,\varepsilon}^n$.

Algorithm 5. On input $(t, \gamma, \gamma^{x_1}, \ldots, \gamma^{x_n}, \gamma^y)$, given oracle $O_{F,\varepsilon}^n$, output $(\gamma^{x_1 y}, \ldots, \gamma^{x_n y})$.

1: Set $\theta = \gamma^{x_1}$. Find some $\overrightarrow{u} = (u_1, u_2, \ldots, u_m)$ satisfying $\overrightarrow{u} \in U$. For every component u_j of $\overrightarrow{u}$, using (θ, γ^{y+u_j}) to call the oracle, it returns value of $F(\theta^{y+u_j}) = A_j$. Solve the system of equations $\sum_{i=1}^m c_i (\theta^{y+u_j})^{e_i} = A_j, j = 1, 2, \ldots, m$ to get the value of $\gamma^{x_1 y}$;

2: Replace θ with γ^{x_2} and repeat step 1, we can get the value of $\gamma^{x_2 y}$;

3: Repeatedly calculate as step 2 until getting all values of $\gamma^{x_i y}$, then output values of $(\gamma^{x_1 y}, \ldots, \gamma^{x_n y})$.

Theorem 6. Let t be a prime, $m \geq 2$ and an m-sparse polynomial $F(X) = \sum_{i=1}^m c_i X^{e_i} \in F_q[X]$, where $c_1, \ldots, c_m \in F_q^*$ and $e_1, \ldots, e_m$ are pairwise distinct modulo t. Given the oracle $O_{F,\varepsilon}^n$, Algorithm 5 can output n-DH key with a probability of at least $\varepsilon^{mn} \cdot (1 - 3t^{-\frac{1}{m-1}})^{(m-1)n}$ in time polynomial in mn by making mn calls to the oracle.

Proof. It can easily imply from Theorem 5 that there exists an algorithm one can get value of $\gamma^{x_1 y}$ with a probability of at least $\varepsilon^m \cdot (1 - 3t^{-\frac{1}{m-1}})^{(m-1)}$. Algorithm 5 is n repeats of Algorithm 4, so it can output the value of n-DH key with a probability of at least $\varepsilon^{mn} \cdot (1 - 3t^{-\frac{1}{m-1}})^{(m-1)n}$.

4.3 Multiple DH Problem

Based on Sect. 4.2, we define another variant of DH problem. It can be described as knowing $\gamma^{x_1}, \gamma^{x_2}, \ldots, \gamma^{x_n}$ to recover the key $\gamma^{\prod_{i=1}^n x_i}$.

Assume that there is a Multiple DH oracle $O_{F,\varepsilon}^M$ satisfying that, for every $x_1, x_2, \ldots, x_n \in [0, t-1]$, given values of $(\gamma^{x_1}, \gamma^{x_2}, \ldots, \gamma^{x_n})$, it returns correct $F(\gamma^{\prod_{i=1}^n x_i})$ for at least εt values of $x_n \in [0, t-1]$ and returns an error message for other values of $x_n \in [0, t-1]$.

Here we can construct a recursion algorithm using similar method to Sect. 3 to recover Multiple DH key by calling oracle $O_{F,\varepsilon}^M$.

Algorithm 6. On input $(t, \gamma, \gamma^{x_1}, \ldots, \gamma^{x_n})$, given oracle $O_{F,\varepsilon}^M$, output $\gamma^{\prod_{i=1}^n x_i}$

1: Find some $\overrightarrow{u} = (u_1, u_2, \ldots, u_m)$ satisfying $\overrightarrow{u} \in U$. Set $\theta_1 = \gamma^{x_1}, \theta_2 = \gamma^{x_2}$. For every component u_j of $\overrightarrow{u}$, using $(\gamma, \ldots, \gamma, \theta_1, \theta_2 \cdot \gamma^{u_j})$ to call the oracle, it returns value of $F(\theta_1^{x_2+u_j}) = A_j$. Solve the system of equations $\sum_{i=1}^m c_i (\theta_1^{x_2+u_j})^{e_i} = A_j, j = 1, 2, \ldots, m$ to get the value of $\gamma^{x_1 x_2}$;

2: Replace θ_1, θ_2 with $\gamma^{x_1 x_2}, \gamma^{x_3}$ and repeat step 1, we can get the value of $\gamma^{x_1 x_2 x_3}$;

3: Recursively calculate as step 2 until getting the value of $\gamma^{\prod_{i=1}^n x_i}$, then output this value of $\gamma^{\prod_{i=1}^n x_i}$.

Theorem 7. *Let t be a prime, $m \geq 2$ and an m-sparse polynomial $F(X) = \sum_{i=1}^m c_i X^{e_i} \in F_q[X]$, where $c_1, \ldots, c_m \in F_q^*$ and $e_1, \ldots, e_m$ are pairwise distinct modulo t. Given the oracle $O_{F,\varepsilon}^M$, Algorithm 6 which given $(\gamma^{x_1}, \gamma^{x_2}, \ldots, \gamma^{x_n})$ makes the expected number of at most $2m\varepsilon^{-1}(n-1)$ calls of the oracle, it returns the value of $\gamma^{\prod_{i=1}^n x_i}$.*

Proof. Theorem 5 has proved that there exists an algorithm one can get value of $\gamma^{x_1 x_2}$. We can easily know it needs the expected number of at most $2m\varepsilon^{-1}$ calls of the oracle. Algorithm 6 is $n-1$ recursions of Algorithm 4, so it can output the value of $\gamma^{\prod_{i=1}^n x_i}$ by the expected number of at most $2m\varepsilon^{-1}(n-1)$ calls of the oracle.

5   Conclusion

In this paper, we study the relations between security of DH key and its polynomial information, and give several algorithms to recover DH key γ^{xy} for different DH problems. These algorithms construct systems of equations to recover DH key by making polynomial number of calls to oracle to find polynomial information of DH key with a certain probability. And all these algorithms imply that finding polynomial information of DH key is as difficult as the whole key.

References

1. Shparlinski, I.E.: Security of polynomial transformations of the Diffie-Hellman key. Finite Fields Appl. **10**(1), 123–131 (2004)
2. Boneh, D., Venkatesan, R.: Hardness of computing the most significant bits of secret keys in Diffie-Hellman and related schemes. In: Koblitz, N. (ed.) CRYPTO 1996. LNCS, vol. 1109, pp. 129–142. Springer, Heidelberg (1996)
3. Vasco, M.I.G., Shparlinski, I.E.: On the security of Diffie-Hellman bits. In: Proceedings of the Workshop on Cryptography and Computer Number Theory, Singapore, 1999, pp. 257–268. Birkhauser, Basel (2001)
4. Vasco, M.I.G., Naslund, M.: A survey of hard core functions. In: Proceedings of the Workshop on Cryptography and Computational Number Theory, Singapore, 1999, pp. 227–256. Birkhauser, Basel (2001)
5. Verheul, E.R.: Certificates of recoverability with scalable recovery agent security. In: Imai, H., Zheng, Y. (eds.) PKC 2000. LNCS, vol. 1751, pp. 258–275. Springer, Heidelberg (2000)
6. Brouwer, A.E., Pellikaan, R., Verheul, E.R.: Doing more with fewer bits. In: Lam, K.-Y., Okamoto, E., Xing, C. (eds.) ASIACRYPT 1999. LNCS, vol. 1716, pp. 321–332. Springer, Heidelberg (1999)

7. Cash, D.M., Kiltz, E., Shoup, V.: The twin Diffie-Hellman problem and applications. In: Smart, N.P. (ed.) EUROCRYPT 2008. LNCS, vol. 4965, pp. 127–145. Springer, Heidelberg (2008)
8. Chen, L., Chen, Y.: The n-Diffie-Hellman problem and its applications. In: Lai, X., Zhou, J., Li, H. (eds.) ISC 2011. LNCS, vol. 7001, pp. 119–134. Springer, Heidelberg (2011)

How to Vote Privately Using Bitcoin

Zhichao Zhao$^{(\boxtimes)}$ and T.-H. Hubert Chan

The University of Hong Kong, Pokfulam, Hong Kong
zczhao@cs.hku.hk

Abstract. Bitcoin is the first decentralized crypto-currency that is currently by far the most popular one in use. The bitcoin transaction syntax is expressive enough to setup digital contracts whose fund transfer can be enforced automatically.

In this paper, we design protocols for the bitcoin voting problem, in which there are n voters, each of which wishes to fund exactly one of two candidates A and B. The winning candidate is determined by majority voting, while the privacy of individual vote is preserved. Moreover, the decision is irrevocable in the sense that once the outcome is revealed, the winning candidate is guaranteed to have the funding from all n voters. As in previous works, each voter is incentivized to follow the protocol by being required to put a deposit in the system, which will be used as compensation if he deviates from the protocol. Our solution is similar to previous protocols used for lottery, but needs an additional phase to distribute secret random numbers via zero-knowledge-proofs. Moreover, we have resolved a security issue in previous protocols that could prevent compensation from being paid.

1 Introduction

Private e-voting is a special case of secure multi-party (MPC) computation [9] which allows a group of people to jointly make a decision such that individual opinion can be kept private. However, the MPC framework only guarantees that the outcome is received by everyone, whose privacy is also protected. When the decision is financially related, it is not obvious how to ensure that the outcome is respected. For instance, a dishonest party may simply run away with his money.

Bitcoin [15] provides new tools for tackling this problem. Although it was originally intended for money transfer, surprisingly it can also be used to enforce a contract such that money transfer is guaranteed once the outcome is known, without the need of a trusted third party.

Our Problem. We study the *bitcoin voting problem*. There are n voters $P_1, \ldots, P_n$, each of which wishes to fund exactly one of two candidates A and B with 1Ƀ[1]. The winning candidate is determined by majority voting (assuming n is odd) and receives the total prize nɃ. The voting protocol should satisfy the following basic properties:

This research is partially funded by a grant from Hong Kong RGC under the contract HKU719312E.

[1] We use the latex code from [3] to generate the bitcoin symbol Ƀ.

© Springer International Publishing Switzerland 2016
S. Qing et al. (Eds.): ICICS 2015, LNCS 9543, pp. 82–96, 2016.
DOI: 10.1007/978-3-319-29814-6_8

- *Privacy and Verifiability.* Only the number of votes received by each candidate is known, while individual votes are kept private.
- *Irrevocability.* Once the final outcome of the voting is revealed, the winner is guaranteed to receive the total sum $n\mathcal{B}$.

In order to incentivize voters to follow the protocol, each voter needs extra bitcoins as deposit, which will be refunded if he follows the protocol, but will be used as compensation if he deviates from the protocol. The candidates A and B also need to participate in the protocol to collect the prize, however they do not need to own bitcoins initially.

Our Approach. In voting, each voter P_i has a private vote $O_i \in \{0,1\}$ (0, 1 stands for A, B respectively), and the sum $\sum_i O_i$ reveals the winning candidate, where the O_i's must be kept private. Our voting protocol consists of two parts:

- *Vote Commitment.* The n voters generate n random numbers R_i's summing to 0 (mod N) using a distributed protocol, where R_i is kept secret and commitments to R_i and the *masked vote* $\widehat{O}_i = R_i + O_i$ are public known, together with a zero-knowledge proof which proves the values are generated correctly. By using zero-knowledge proofs we enforce the voters to obey the protocol.
- *Vote Casting.* This part of the protocol utilizes the bitcoin system for the voters to reveal their $\widehat{O}_i$'s, which also guarantees that the winner can receive the prize and any voter that does not reveal his masked vote is penalized. In Sect. 3.2, we use the *claim-or-refund* technique as in [8] to design a protocol in which the voters reveal their masked votes sequentially. As a result, this protocol takes $\Theta(n)$ rounds and $\Theta(n^2)$ bytes in the bitcoin network. In Sect. 3.3, improved upon the previous section, we use the idea of a *joint transaction* as in [4,13] to reveal the masked votes, where only constant number of rounds and $O(n)$ bytes in the bitcoin network are used.

Previous Security Issue and Our Fix. In vote casting, we use a similar idea as that of [4]. As pointed out in [4], the way timed-commitment is used presents a serious security flaw because the compensation is paid with a transaction depending on the hash of a (unconfirmed) joint transaction. In the protocol described in [4], an adversarial party could create an alternate joint transaction with a different hash by resigning it. The details are discussed in Sect. 3.3 of our full paper [16]. The cause of this issue is that the joint transaction is signed by each voter individually, who has the ability to produce a different signature. We resolve this issue by using a threshold signature scheme [10] in which a valid signature can only be produced by all voters together, which prevents the previous attack.

Our Constribution. In this paper, we propose a protocol that solves the bitcoin voting problem.

- We design a vote commitment scheme that hides individual votes in random numbers, where verifiability and privacy are guaranteed by using zero-knowledge proofs. This part can be used independent of the bitcoin network.

– We design vote casting schemes that place transactions in the bitcoin network in a carefully designed way. Such that any adversaries deviating from the protocol will be punished.
– We point out a security issue from previous protocol, which we fix by using threshold signature schemes.

The rest of the paper is organized as follows: In Sect. 2, we define Bitcoin and related cryptographic primitives. In Sect. 3, we present our protocol, which contains vote commitment and vote casting. In Sect. 4, we discuss implementation details and the performance of our protocols.

1.1 Other Related Work

The bitcoin protocol [15] has inspired many lines of research since its introduction in 2008. Some researchers have worked on identifying the protocol's weakness [5]. Other researchers have designed new crypto-currency with more features. For instance, zero-knowledge proofs and accumulators have been used to improve the currency's anonymity [6,14]. In [6], a new system is designed such that the *proof-of-work* to mine new coins is achieved by storage consumption, as opposed to computation power in bitcoin.

Another line of research, including this paper, is to design protocols that are compatible with the existing bitcoin system. Since bitcoin is still by far the most popular crypto-currency, protocols that can be deployed in the current bitcoin system have the most practical impact. For instance, a lottery protocol [4] was proposed, in which a group of gamblers transfer all their money to a randomly selected winner. General secure multi-party computation protocols [8,13] were also considered, in which bitcoin provides a way to penalize dishonest users.

Basic functionalities has been implemented in the bitcoin system that can serve as building blocks for more complicated protocols. In [8], the *claim-or-refund* mechanism is designed to enforce the promise made by party P that he will pay party Q a certain amount, provided that Q (publicly) reveals a certain secret before a certain time. As utilized in this paper, this mechanism allows a protocol in which parties reveal their secrets sequentially such that the first party that deviates from the protocol has to compensate the parties that have already revealed their secrets.

In [4], the *timed-commitment* mechanism is designed to enforce the promise made by party P that he will pay party Q a certain amount, unless he (publicly) reveals a certain secret before a certain time. In [13], the timed-commitment mechanism is extended for multiple-parties to reveal their secrets together. However, as mentioned in [4], their implementation of the timed-commitment mechanism has a security issue such that an adversary could prevent the compensation from being paid even when a party does not reveal his secret before the deadline.

2 Preliminaries

Bitcoin. We use the same terminology for Bitcoin [15] as in [4]. Bitcoin consists of a block of *transactions* known as the *blockchain*, which is maintained and synchronized at each peer. New transactions are packed into block and linked at the end of the blockchain at a fixed time interval. Each transaction contains multiple *inputs*, *outputs* and an optional *locktime*, and is indexed by its hash called txid.

Validation of Transactions. An output of a transaction specify a program indicating how the coin (unspent output) can be redeemed. Each input must refer to an unspent output which is specified by its txid and the output index. The input contains an input-script which servers as parameters of the referred output (as a program). For the transaction to validate, the referred output (as a program) must evaluates to true on all the inputs, all referred outputs must be unspent, and the current time must be no earlier than the locktime.

For a detailed description of the Bitcoin network, please see our full paper [16].

Zero-Knowledge Proof. We utilize the zero-knowledge Succinct Non-interactive ARgument of Knowledge (zk-SNARKs) [7]. Zero-knowledge proof allows a party to convince others that he knows a secret witness w such that $C(x, w) = 1$, where x is known by all parties. E.g., "I know an w such that $\mathsf{sha256}(w) = x$". The use of zk-SNARKs is to guarantee that the voters cannot deviate from the protocol. We use the definition for zk-SNARKs from [7]. Informally, zk-SNARKs is a triple of (randomized) algorithms (G, P, V), where G is the key generator which runs only once universally and outputs the key-pairs (pk, vk), $P(pk, x, w)$ is the prover and $V(vk, x, \pi)$ is the verifier.

We informally summarize the properties satisfied by zk-SNARKs.

- *Completeness.* Prover P can produce a proof that is accepted by V.
- *Soundness and Proof of Knowledge.* No polynomial-time adversary can fake a proof for x, without knowing its witness w.
- *Efficiency.* The algorithms runs in time polynomial in the sizes of their inputs and the given security parameter.
- *Zero-knowledge.* The proof leaks no information other than the statement itself.

Commitment Schemes. Commitment schemes allow one party to hide to a secret value which is opened in a later phase to another party, where the other party is convinced that the opened value is the original one. As it turns out, the Bitcoin protocol is restricted to certain operations, which limits the choice of commitment schemes. In Sect. 2.3 of our full paper [16], we give the formal definition and discuss commitment schemes that is compatible with the Bitcoin protocol.

Security Model. In this paper, we assume that the blockchain is unique (no branching) and one block is grown at a fixed time interval known as *round*. The only ways to interact with the blockchain are submitting transactions and reading transaction histories. No one can affect the blockchain by other "non-standard" ways. We assume that the blockchain is always publicly accessible. However, we do not assume such access is private. At the time a transaction is submitted, it is publicly known. A submitted transaction may or may not appear on the blockchain, depending on its validity. If a transaction is valid, it will be *confirmed* one round later, otherwise it will be *rejected*. If conflicting transactions are submitted in the same round, only one of them will be confirmed. Hence, if an adversary is able to create a different input-script for a (newly submitted) unconfirmed transaction. He could submit another transaction with the modified input-script within the same round. In such case, either transaction could appear in the final blockchain.

A type of attack called signature *malleability* needs to be considered. Briefly, it means creating a valid signature from an existing one, without the corresponding plain text. Many protocols [4,13] suffers from this attack especially when a joint transaction is concerned. For a detailed discussion of malleability attack, please see our full paper [16]. We tackle this issue by using a threshold signature scheme, which we describe in details through the protocols.

Peers (voters and candidates) need to communicate in the protocol. We assume there exists a secure private channel between any pair of participants. We also assume there exists a public broadcast channel among all participants.

3   Our Protocols

We present our protocol for bitcoin voting. Apart from a (universal) one-time setup using zk-SNARKs [7], our protocol works in a peer-to-peer fashion without a centralized server. Suppose N is the least power of 2 that is greater than the number n of voters. We use $\mathbb{Z}_N$ to denote the group of integers modulo N. We choose N to be a power of 2 to simplify the implementation of modulo arithmetic.

On a high level, our protocol consists of two components.

- **Vote Commitment.** In this phase, each voter P_i has a private vote $O_i \in \{0,1\}$, where 0 indicates candidate A and 1 indicates candidate B. Each voter P_i receives a secret random number R_i, which is constructed in a distributed fashion such that $\sum_j R_j = 0$.
  At the end of this phase, each voter P_i makes commitment C_i to R_i, and commitment $\widehat{C}_i$ to his masked vote $\widehat{O}_i := O_i + R_i$. The commitments C_i and $\widehat{C}_i$ are broadcast publicly, while the underlying values and opening keys remain secret.
  Every participant convinces others that he follows the protocol using zero-knowledge proofs. In particular, everyone is convinced that $\sum_i R_i = 0$ and $\widehat{O}_i - O_i \in \{0,1\}$ with respect to the commitments. This part is described in Sect. 3.1.
- **Vote Casting.** In this phase, the votes are cast using transactions in the bitcoin protocol, which are responsible for revealing the outcome and guaranteeing money transfer to the winning candidate. After each voter P_i reveals his masked vote $\widehat{O}_i$, the outcome $\sum_i \widehat{O}_i$ (the number of votes supporting B) is known, and the winning candidate is guaranteed to receive $n\mathbb{B}$.
  Moreover, parties that deviate from the protocol are penalized. We have two versions for vote casting, which have different consequences for the penalty and the funding outcome for the candidates when a voter deviates from the protocol.

(a) The first version is based on the lottery protocol in [8] using a *claim-or-refund* functionality. The voters reveal their masked votes in the order: $P_1, P_2, \ldots, P_n$. If voter P_i is the first to deviate from the protocol, he pays a penalty to each voter that has already revealed his masked vote. Everyone else gets his deposit back, and the protocol terminates while neither candidate A nor B gets any money.

(b) The second version is an improvement over other protocols [4,13] using *joint transaction* to incentivize fair computation via the bitcoin system. Each voter P_i places $(1 + d)Ƀ$ into the bitcoin system, where $1Ƀ$ is for paying the winning candidate and $dƀ$ is for deposit. If a voter reveals his masked vote $\widehat{O}_i$, he can get back the deposit $dƀ$. For each voter that does not reveal his masked vote within some time period, his deposit $dƀ$ will be used as compensation. For instance, with $d = 2n$, the deposit can be shared between the candidates A and B.

The two versions are described in Sects. 3.2 and 3.3, respectively.

3.1 Vote Commitment

Recall that we wish to uniformly generate random numbers R_i's that sum to 0 such that for each i, only voter P_i receives R_i. Moreover, the commitments to R_i and $\widehat{O}_i = (R_i + O_i)$ are public.

We first give a high level idea of the procedure. Imagine that there is an $n \times n$ matrix $[r_{ij}]$ whose entries contain elements from $\mathbb{Z}_N$. The protocol can be described in terms of the matrix as follows.

1. For each i, voter P_i generates the i-th row whose sum $\sum_j r_{ij}$ is zero. This is done by generating $n - 1$ random numbers and derive the last.
2. For each i and j, voter P_i sends r_{ij} to P_j via the secret channel.
3. For each i, voter P_i knows the i-th column. Hence, he computes and commits to both $R_i := \sum_j r_{ji}$ and the masked vote $\widehat{O}_i := O_i + R_i$.

The trick here is that commitment schemes and zero-knowledge proofs are used to ensure that every party follows the protocol, while maintaining the secrecy of the random numbers. For a step-by-step description of the algorithm please see Fig. 2.

Security Analysis. The security of the vote commitment protocol follows readily from the security of commitment schemes [11] and zero-knowledge proofs from zk-SNARKs [7]. Observe that as long as at least one party generate his random numbers uniformly at random, the resulting R_i's will still be uniform. Hence no private information is leaked by revealing $\widehat{O}_i$'s. Using commitment schemes and zero-knowledge-proofs, each P_i commits to both R_i and the masked vote $\widehat{O}_i := R_i + O_i$, and convinces everyone that $\widehat{O}_i - R_i \in \{0, 1\}$, while keeping them secret.

3.2 Vote Casting via Claim-or-Refund

This version of the vote casting protocol is based on the lottery protocol in [8] that makes use of bitcoin transactions to guarantee money transfer. The protocol is not symmetric among the voters, and the voters are supposed to reveal their masked votes in the order: $P_1, P_2, \ldots, P_n$. In order to participate in the protocol, for $i \in [n-1]$, voter P_i needs to place $(i+1)\cancel{B}$ into the system, and voter P_n needs to place $(3n-1)\cancel{B}$ into the system. This protocol requires a linear number of bitcoin rounds, as opposed to constant number of rounds in the protocol that is given in Sect. 3.3. The protocol in this section guarantees the following:

- If every voter reveals his masked vote, the net effect is that each voter pays $1\cancel{B}$ to the winning candidate.
- If voter P_i is the first that does not reveal his masked vote, the net effect is that he pays $1\cancel{B}$ to each voter that has already revealed his masked vote. Neither candidate receives any money in this case.

We make use of the claim-or-refund (COR) functionality which is first introduced in [8]. It can be used for "conditionally transfer of coins". Briefly, COR protocol between two parties X and Y guarantees that, after a deposit phase, either X reveals some secret (predetermined by X and Y) to Y, or Y is compensated after some time interval. We assume the readers are familiar with it and the description is omitted from here.

Vote Casting via COR. We show how the vote casting protocol can be implemented with a sequence of COR instances in Figs. 5 and 6. The idea is similar to that in [13]. For n voters, there are $2n$ COR instances. The deposit transactions of the COR instances are placed in the reversed order as the claim transactions are broadcast to reveal the masked votes.

Correctness. The correctness of the protocol is analyzed in the same way as [13]. The voters are supposed to reveal their masked votes in the order: $P_1, P_2, \ldots, P_n$. At the moment just after voters $P_1, P_2, \ldots, P_i$ have revealed their masked votes in the corresponding claim transactions, the net effect is that P_{i+1} has paid each of the previous voters $1\cancel{B}$. Hence, if P_{i+1} does not reveal his masked vote, eventually all outstanding COR instances will expire and the protocol terminates.

On the other hand, if everyone follows the protocol, then at the end all the masked votes can be summed up to determine the winner, who can collect $n\cancel{B}$ from P_n.

3.3   Vote Casting via Joint Transaction

The protocol in Sect. 3.2 requires a linear number of bitcoin rounds. In this section, we give an alternative protocol that only needs constant number of bitcoin rounds. Also, our protocol has the advantage of small total transaction size. The total size of the transactions in the protocol is $\Theta(n)$ bytes, instead of $\Theta(n^2)$ from previous protocol.

Loosely speaking, we achieve this by locking all bitcoins involved in a transaction that is jointly signed by all voters. The protocol is symmetric among the n voters. In the protocol, each voter P_i needs $(1+d)\cancel{B}$, of which $1\cancel{B}$ is to be paid to the winning candidate if everyone reveals his masked vote and the remaining

$d\mathcal{B}$ is for deposit that will be used for compensation if P_i does not reveal his masked vote. The *timed-commitment* technique in [4] can be used to handle the deposit and compensation.

The protocol guarantees the following:

- If a voter reveals his masked vote, he can get back the deposit $d\mathcal{B}$.
- If every voter reveals his masked vote, the sum $\sum_i \widehat{O}_i$ determines the winner who receives $n\mathcal{B}$.
- If at least one voter does not reveal his masked vote, the $n\mathcal{B}$ originally intended for the winner will be locked. For each voter that does not reveal his masked vote, his deposit will be used for compensation. Here are several options:
  - (a) For $d = 2n$, the deposit can be shared between candidates A and B. We shall concentrate on this option in this section.
  - (b) For $d = n$, the deposit can be distributed among all voters in a similar way.

There is a potential problem in the "joint transactions" described in [4,13]. We fix this problem by using threshold signature schemes. The detail of the problem is discussed in our full paper [16].

Description of Vote Casting Protocol.

Key Setup. We use the threshold signature scheme [10] for ECDSA. The n voters jointly generate a group address such that voter P_i learns the group public key $\widehat{\mathsf{pk}}$ and his share $\widehat{\mathsf{sk}}_i$ of the private key. No party knows the underlying secret key $\widehat{\mathsf{sk}}$, which could be reconstructed from all parties' secret shares. Each party also has his own bitcoin address, whose key pairs are denoted by $(\mathsf{pk}_i, \mathsf{sk}_i)$.

Coin Lock. Eventually, the n voters will sign some transaction JOIN together, whose inputs are contributed by the n voters. We introduce a protocol that locks the contribution from each voter in a state such that only with all voters' permission can it be redeemed. This ensures that only one version of the JOIN transaction can use these coins later. On the other hand, if the protocol ends prematurely and the JOIN transaction is not created successfully, we wish to let each voter P_i get back his contribution with the transaction BACK$_i$. The coin lock protocol is described in Fig. 3.

Joint Transaction. In the next step, the n voters shall jointly sign a transaction JOIN using the threshold signature scheme, each with his private key share $\widehat{\mathsf{sk}}_i$. The JOIN transaction has n inputs referring to the LOCK$_i$'s, each of which contributes $(1+d)\mathcal{B}$. It has $(n+1)$ outputs, of which out-prize delivers $n\mathcal{B}$ to the winning candidate, while each out-deposit$_i$ of the remaining n outputs handles the deposit $d\mathcal{B}$ of each voter.

Using the timed-commitment technique as in [4], the output out-deposit$_i$ can be redeemed by a transaction that either (1) reveals the masked vote $\widehat{O}_i$ and is signed with the key associated with P_i, or (2) is signed with the group key. Hence, before JOIN takes effect (by appearing in the blockchain), a transaction PAY$_i$

with some timelock that can redeem out-deposit$_i$ needs to be created and signed using the threshold signature scheme, in case P_i does not reveal his masked vote and his deposit is used for compensation. The details are in Fig. 4.

Outcome Revealing Phase. After JOIN appears on the blockchain, each voter P_i can collect his deposit $d\mathcal{B}$ (from the output out-deposit$_i$) by submitting a CLAIM$_i$ transaction that provides the opening key $\widehat{K}_i$ to reveal his masked vote $\widehat{O}_i$. If all voters have submitted their transactions CLAIM$_i$'s, the winning candidate is determined and can redeem $n\mathcal{B}$ from out-prize with his signature.

On the other hand, if some voter i does not reveal his masked vote, then the $n\mathcal{B}$ from out-prize cannot be accessed anymore. However, since PAY$_i$ is publicly known, after time t_2, the $d\mathcal{B}$ from out-deposit$_i$ can be redeemed by PAY$_i$ as compensation.

Correctness. After the coin lock protocol, all the transactions LOCK$_i$'s remain secret, while their hashes and the BACK$_i$'s are publicly known. Observe that before the transaction JOIN appears on the blockchain, any voter can terminate the whole protocol without losing any money by submitting BACK$_i$ to the bitcoin system. On the other hand, once JOIN has appeared on the block chain, no voter can terminate the protocol without either revealing his masked vote or losing his deposit $d\mathcal{B}$.

4 Experiment

We describe our implementation of the proposed protocols below.

Vote Commitment. We have implemented vote commitment protocol Sect. 3.1. For zk-SNAKRs [7], we choose snarkfront [12]. We translated the required relation into circuits. We run the program using a computer with 4G RAM and Intel Core i5-3570 CPU. The key generator typically takes 5 times longer than the time to generate proofs. However, since it only needs to be run once universally, we omit its running time here as it is not a performance concern. In Fig. 1, we report the time to generate proofs for different number of users. We consider three kinds of proofs: (1) to prove n numbers sum to 0, (2) to prove n numbers sum to the $(n+1)$-st number, (3) to prove the subtraction of a number from another is either 0 or 1.

In zk-SNARKs, the time for verification is only linear in the size of the input (and the security parameter). Typically, it takes less than 0.1 s.

Vote Casting. As a proof of concept, we have executed the protocols in bitcoin (testnet) network [2]. We use bitcoinj Java library to create and send the transactions.

Below we present txid of the transactions. There are 9 voters in our protocol. One may read the full transaction data on chain.so website.

For the protocol using claim-or-refund in Sect. 3.2, we first create a transaction with multiple outputs, each of which acts as the source address of each claim-or-refund transaction. The source of each claim-or-refund transaction can be found with index $0 - 17$ at:

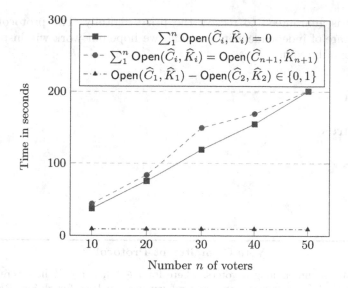

Fig. 1. Performance of zk-SNARKs

https://chain.so/tx/BTCTEST/d3f62d6dfd9722699938a3d7457e23ba786a3e
8d14615d128847ad7ca56b7a1a _{d3f62d6dfd9722699938a3d7457e23ba786a3e8d14615d128847ad7ca56b7a1a.}

All following transactions can be found following the outputs. Another execution in which an adversary terminated the protocol and was punished is here:

https://chain.so/tx/BTCTEST/8d4031dfa71bf9b1a296b6f67c3cb1d801e899
d4ff7d1ee6dd6751622032b60f _{8d4031dfa71bf9b1a296b6f67c3cb1d801e899d4ff7d1ee6dd6751622032b60f.}

For the protocol using joint transaction in Sect. 3.3, the JOIN transaction of a successful execution is here:

https://chain.so/tx/BTCTEST/ca42f58d2a7eadc4360029ea31e6f2224c9b7f4
7c18ef985a9b477ac869822c7 _{ca42f58d2a7eadc4360029ea31e6f2224c9b7f47c18ef985a9b477ac869822c7.}

All claim transactions can be found by following the outputs.

A JOIN transaction of an unsuccessful (terminated by adversary) execution is here:

https://chain.so/tx/BTCTEST/6506857a75b1f25b930a923e6bd8274cbccb42
339425e21f29cf5ba2ce389738

_{6506857a75b1f25b930a923e6bd8274cbccb42339425e21f29cf5ba2ce389738.}

All CLAIM$_i$ and PAY$_i$ transactions can be found by following the outputs.

5 Conclusion

We present protocols that solve the bitcoin voting problem and run directly on the current bitcoin network. Our protocols consist of two phases. The first phase generates a masked vote for each voter. We guarantee that the generated masks are publicly verifiable by the use of zero-knowledge proofs. The second phase takes the masked votes and put transactions on the blockchain, so that the winner is guaranteed to receive the prize digitally. The protocols of the two phases are of independent interest and we hope our work will inspire other applications of bitcoin.

Appendix

A   Figures

Vote Commitment Protocol

This protocol runs among n voters, where for $i \in [n]$, party P_i has secret vote $O_i \in \{0, 1\}$. We assume the proving and verification keys for zk-SNARKs are already generated and distributed to all voters. For each $i \in [n]$, the procedure for P_i is as follows.

1. Generate n secret random numbers $r_{ij} \in \mathbb{Z}_N$, for $j \in [n]$, such that they sum to 0.
   For $j \in [n]$, commit $(c_{ij}, k_{ij}) \leftarrow \mathsf{Commit}(r_{ij})$, where k_{ij} is the opening key to the commitment c_{ij}.
2. Generate zero-knowledge proofs that shows $\sum_j r_{i,j} = 0$. Specifically, the circuit C takes two components. The input component is the n commitments, while the witness component is the n corresponding opening keys. The circuit C evaluates to 1 if the opened values sum to 0.
   Broadcast the commitments and zero-knowledge proofs to all voters.
3. Receive commitments and verify the zero-knowledge proofs from all other parties generated in Step 2.
4. For all $j \in [n] \setminus \{i\}$, send to P_j the opening key k_{ij}.
   For $j \in [n] \setminus \{i\}$, wait for the opening key k_{ji} from P_j, and check that $r_{ji} = \mathsf{Open}(c_{ji}, k_{ji}) \neq \bot$.
5. Compute $R_i \leftarrow \sum_j r_{ji}$ and $\widehat{O}_i \leftarrow R_i + O_i$, and commit $(C_i, K_i) \leftarrow \mathsf{Commit}(R_i)$ and $(\widehat{C}_i, \widehat{K}_i) \leftarrow \mathsf{Commit}(\widehat{O}_i)$, where $K_i, \widehat{K}_i$ are the opening keys. Broadcast the commitment C_i and $\widehat{C}_i$ publicly.
6. Generate and broadcast publicly the zero-knowledge proofs for the following:
   (a) "$R_i = \sum_j r_{ji}$". This is similar to Step 2.
   (b) "The committed value in $\widehat{C}_i$ minus that in C_i is either 0 or 1." The input part of the circuit is the two commitments C_i and $\widehat{C}_i$, and the witness part is their opening keys. The circuit evaluates to 1 if the opened values differ by 0 or 1 as required.
7. Receive and verify all proofs from other parties generated in Step 6. The protocol terminates.

Fig. 2. Vote commitment protocol

Coin Lock Protocol

Each voter locks $(1 + d)\cancel{B}$ into the system, where $1\cancel{B}$ is to fund the winner, and $d\cancel{B}$ is for deposit; here, we set $d := 2n$. Each voter P_i does the following:

1. P_i creates a (secret) transaction LOCK_i. Its input is $(1 + d)\cancel{B}$ owned by P_i, and its output is the address of the group public key $\widehat{\mathsf{pk}}$.
   P_i also creates a simplified transaction BACK_i that transfers the money from LOCK_i back to an address pk_i owned by P_i. Note that $\mathsf{hash}(\mathsf{LOCK}_i)$ is embedded in BACK_i, but LOCK_i remains secret.
   P_i broadcasts (simplified) BACK_i to all other voters.
2. On receiving BACK_j for $j \in [n] \setminus \{i\}$, P_i checks that the hash value referred to by its input is not $\mathsf{hash}(\mathsf{LOCK}_i)$. At this point, P_i has only contributed coins to $\widehat{\mathsf{pk}}$ through the transaction LOCK_i, and hence, he can sign anything else using $\widehat{\mathsf{sk}}_i$ without losing money.
3. For each $j \in [n]$, P_i participates in the threshold signature scheme to sign BACK_j using his secret key share $\widehat{\mathsf{sk}}_i$.
4. On receiving the correct signature for BACK_i, P_i is ready to submit LOCK_i to the bitcoin network later.

Fig. 3. Coin lock protocol

Joint Transaction Protocol

Assume that the Coin Lock Protocol has been run, and each P_i has created the (secret) transaction LOCK_i, whose hash is publicly known. Suppose $t_1 < t_2$ are times far enough in the future. Each voter runs the following protocol.

1. Each voter generates the same simplified transaction JOIN as follows.
   - It has n inputs, each of which refers to LOCK_i that contributes $(1+d)\mathcal{B}$.
   - It has $n+1$ outputs:
     out-deposit$_i$, $i \in [n]$: each has value $d\mathcal{B}$, and requires either (1) the opening key $\widehat{K}_i$ (revealing $\widehat{O}_i$) and a signature verifiable with P_i's public key pk_i, or (2) a valid signature verifiable with the group's public key $\widehat{\mathsf{pk}}$.
     out-prize: has value $n\mathcal{B}$, and requires all opening keys $\widehat{K}_i$'s (revealing the masked votes $\widehat{O}_i$'s) and a signature from the winning candidate (which can be determined from the sum $\sum_i \widehat{O}_i$).
2. The voters jointly sign JOIN using the threshold signature scheme, each with his private key share $\widehat{\mathsf{sk}}_i$. Observe that JOIN has n inputs, each of which requires its own group signature. (See [1] for details.) The signed JOIN is ready to be submitted.
3. Each voter generates, for each $i \in [n]$, the same simplified transaction PAY_i with timelock t_2 whose input refers to out-deposit$_i$. The output handles the compensation $d\mathcal{B}$ if voter P_i does not reveal his masked vote by time t_2. For instance, with $d = 2n$, the compensation can be shared between candidates A and B. The n voters jointly sign PAY_i using the threshold signature scheme.
4. Each voter P_i verifies that the above steps have been completed, and submit LOCK_i to the bitcoin system.
5. After all LOCK_i's have appeared on the blockchain, JOIN is submitted to the blockchain.
6. As long as JOIN has not appeared on the blockchain, say by time t_1, any voter P_i can terminate the whole protocol by submitting BACK_i to get back $(1+d)\mathcal{B}$.

Fig. 4. Joint transaction

Vote Casting: Deposit Phase

Assume that the commitments $\widehat{C}_i$'s to the masked votes $\widehat{O}_i$'s are publicly known, and each P_i knows the opening key $\widehat{K}_i$ for $\widehat{C}_i$. Assuming that n is odd, the winner is B if $\sum_i \widehat{O}_i > \frac{n}{2}$.

Assume that the times $\tau_1 < \tau_2 < \ldots < \tau_n < \tau_{n+1}$ are spaced sufficiently wide apart, for they will be used as locktimes.

The protocol runs as follows.

1. P_n submits the deposit transactions of the following COR instances to the bitcoin network:

$$P_n \xrightarrow[n, \tau_{n+1}]{\widehat{O}_1, \ldots, \widehat{O}_n : A \text{ wins}} A$$

$$P_n \xrightarrow[n, \tau_{n+1}]{\widehat{O}_1, \ldots, \widehat{O}_n : B \text{ wins}} B$$

2. Simultaneously for each $i \neq n$, P_i verifies that the deposit transactions broadcast in the previous step are on the block chain, and broadcasts the deposit transaction of the following COR instance to the bitcoin system:

$$P_i \xrightarrow[2, \tau_n]{\widehat{O}_1, \ldots, \widehat{O}_n} P_n$$

3. Sequentially for i from n down to 2:

   P_i verifies that all deposit transactions broadcast previously have appeared in the blockchain, and broadcasts the deposit transaction of the following COR instance to the bitcoin system:

$$P_i \xrightarrow[i-1, \tau_{i-1}]{\widehat{O}_1, \ldots, \widehat{O}_{i-1}} P_{i-1}$$

Fig. 5. Deposit phase of vote casting

Vote Casting: Claim/Refund Phase

- For $i \neq n$, if before time τ_i, all previous secrets $\widehat{O}_1, \ldots, \widehat{O}_{i-1}$ are revealed, then P_i reveals his secret $\widehat{O}_i$ and use the claim transaction to receive $i\mbox{\ss}$ from P_{i+1}.
- If before time τ_n, all secrets $\widehat{O}_i$ for $i \neq n$ are revealed, P_n reveals his secret $\widehat{O}_n$ and use the claim transactions to receive $2\mbox{\ss}$ from each P_i for $i \neq n$.
- If before time τ_{n+1} all secrets are revealed, the winner is determined and he can use the corresponding claim transaction to receive $n\mbox{\ss}$ from P_n.
- At any time when the locktime of a COR instance has passed, the sender can immediately use the corresponding refund transaction to get his amount back.

Fig. 6. Vote casting: claim/refund Phase

References

1. Checksig - bitcoin wiki. https://en.bitcoin.it/wiki/OP_CHECKSIG (2015). Accessed 10 May 2015
2. Testnet - bitcoin wiki. https://en.bitcoin.it/wiki/Testnet (2015). Accessed 10 May 2015
3. Andrychowicz, M., Dziembowski, S., Malinowski, D., Mazurek, L.: How to deal with malleability of bitcoin transactions (2013). CoRR, abs/1312.3230
4. Andrychowicz, M., Dziembowski, S., Malinowski, D., Mazurek, L.: Secure multiparty computations on bitcoin. In: IEEE Symposium on Security and Privacy, SP, pp. 443–458. Berkeley, 18–21 May 2014
5. Barber, S., Boyen, X., Shi, E., Uzun, E.: Bitter to better — how to make bitcoin a better currency. In: Keromytis, A.D. (ed.) FC 2012. LNCS, vol. 7397, pp. 399–414. Springer, Heidelberg (2012)
6. Ben-Sasson, E., Chiesa, A., Garman, C., Green, M., Miers, I., Tromer, E., Virza, M.: Zerocash: decentralized anonymous payments from bitcoin. In: IEEE Symposium on Security and Privacy, SP, pp. 459–474. Berkeley, 18–21 May 2014
7. Ben-Sasson, E., Chiesa, A., Genkin, D., Tromer, E., Virza, M.: SNARKs for C: verifying program executions succinctly and in zero knowledge. In: Canetti, R., Garay, J.A. (eds.) CRYPTO 2013, Part II. LNCS, vol. 8043, pp. 90–108. Springer, Heidelberg (2013)
8. Bentov, I., Kumaresan, R.: How to use bitcoin to design fair protocols. In: Garay, J.A., Gennaro, R. (eds.) CRYPTO 2014, Part II. LNCS, vol. 8617, pp. 421–439. Springer, Heidelberg (2014)
9. Chaum, D., Crépeau, C., Damgård, I.: Multiparty unconditionally secure protocols (extended abstract). In: Proceedings of the 20th Annual ACM Symposium on Theory of Computing, pp. 11–19. Chicago, 2–4 May 1988
10. Goldfeder, S., Gennaro, R., Kalodner, H., Bonneau, J., Kroll, J.A., Felten, E.W., Narayanan, A.: Securing bitcoin wallets via a new DSA/ECDSA threshold signature scheme (2015). http://www.cs.princeton.edu/stevenag/threshold_sigs.pdf
11. Goldreich, O.: Foundations of Cryptography, vol. 1. Cambridge University Press, New York (2006)
12. Carlsson, J.: Snarkfront: a c++ embedded domain specific language for zero knowledge proofs. https://github.com/jancarlsson/snarkfront
13. Kumaresan, R., Bentov, I.: How to use bitcoin to incentivize correct computations. In: Proceedings of the ACM SIGSAC Conference on Computer and Communications Security, pp. 30–41. Scottsdale, 3–7 Nov 2014
14. Miers, I., Garman, C., Green, M., Rubin, A.D.: Zerocoin: anonymous distributed e-cash from bitcoin. In: IEEE Symposium on Security and Privacy, SP, pp. 397–411. Berkeley, 19–22 May 2013
15. Nakamoto, S.: Bitcoin: a peer-to-peer electronic cash system (2008). http://bitcoin.org/bitcoin.pdf
16. Zhao, Z., Hubert Chan, T-H.: How to vote privately using bitcoin. Cryptology ePrint Archive, Report 2015/1007 (2015). http://eprint.iacr.org/

Multidimensional Zero-Correlation Linear Cryptanalysis on 23-Round LBlock-s

Hong Xu[1,2]($\boxtimes$), Ping Jia[1], Geshi Huang[2], and Xuejia Lai[2]

[1] Zhengzhou Information Science and Technology Institute, Zhengzhou, China
xuhong0504@163.com
[2] Shanghai Jiao Tong University, Shanghai, China

Abstract. LBlock-s is the kernel block cipher of the authentication encryption algorithm LAC submitted to CAESAR competition. The LBlock-s algorithm is almost the same as LBlock except that the former adopts an improved key schedule algorithm with better diffusion property. Using the shifting relation of certain subkeys derived by the new key schedule algorithm, we present a multidimensional zero-correlation linear cryptanalysis on 23-round LBlock-s. The time complexity of the attack is about $2^{75.4}$ 23-round encryptions, where $2^{62.3}$ known plaintexts are used and 60 subkey bits are guessed, which is three bits less than that of LBlock. Our research showed that the improved key schedule algorithm did not enhance their ability to protect against zero-correlation linear cryptanalysis, and it is better to use the irregular bit-shifting to disturb the shifting relation between subkeys.

Keywords: LBlock · LBlock-s · Multidimensional zero-correlation linear cryptanalysis · Key schedule

1 Introduction

With the development of communication and electronic applications, the limited-resource devices such as RFID tags and sensor nodes have been used in many aspects of our life. Traditional block cipher is not suitable for this extremely constrained environment. Therefore, research on designing and analyzing lightweight block ciphers has become a hot topic. LBlock [1] is such a kind of a lightweight block cipher presented by Wu et al. in ACNS 2011. It employs a variant Feistel structure and consists of 32 rounds. The round function is composed with S-boxes, nibble-wise permutation and bit rotation, and the key schedule algorithm is similar to that of PRESENT [2], one of the lightweight block cipher standards.

The LBlock algorithm has attracted a lot of attention because of its simplicity, efficiency and low cost. In 2012, Liu and Karakoc et al. [3,4] presented an impossible differential cryptanalysis on 21 and 22-round LBlock, Minier and Liu et al. [5,6] presented a related impossible differential attack on 22-round LBlock, and Sasaki et al. [7] presented an integral attack on 22-round LBlock. Later, Wang et al. [8] studied the security of LBlock against biclique cryptanalysis and

© Springer International Publishing Switzerland 2016
S. Qing et al. (Eds.): ICICS 2015, LNCS 9543, pp. 97–108, 2016.
DOI: 10.1007/978-3-319-29814-6_9

found the diffusion of the original key schedule algorithm was not enough. They also presented an improved key schedule algorithm and used it in lightweight block cipher LBlock-s, the kernel block cipher of the authentication encryption algorithm LAC [9] submitted to CAESAR competition [10]. Up to now, little research has been done on the cryptanalysis of LBlock-s or the property of the improved key schedule algorithm.

Linear cryptanalysis [11,12] is one of the most prominent cryptanalysis methods against block ciphers. In 2011 and 2012, Bogdanov *et al.* [13–15] proposed the method of zero-correlation linear cryptanalysis and used it in the cryptanalysis of many block ciphers such as AES, CLEFIA, TEA and XTEA etc. Deferent with linear cryptanalysis which uses linear approximations with correlation far from zero, the zero-correlation linear cryptanalysis used linear approximations with correlation zero to reduce the key space. For block cipher with Feistel-structure, Soleimany and Nyberg proposed the matrix method [16] to automatic search for longest linear approximations with correlation zero, and found 64 classes of zero-correlation linear approximations for 14-round LBlock. Based on this, they also proposed a general zero-correlation linear cryptanalysis on 22-round LBlock-type block cipher without using the property of the key schedule algorithm. Later in ACISP 2014, Wang *et al.* [17] further presented an improved multidimensional zero-correlation linear cryptanalysis on 23-round LBlock using the special property of the key schedule algorithm, the time complexity was about 2^{76} 23-round encryptions, 2^{62} known plaintexts were used, and totally 63 subkey bits were guessed.

In this paper, we will further evaluate the security of LBlock-s against zero-correlation linear cryptanalysis. From a deeply research on the new improved key schedule algorithm we find that there still exists some simple shifting relations between some subkeys of neighboring rounds. Using these properties, by selecting proper zero-correlation linear approximations, we can also present a multidimensional zero-correlation linear cryptanalysis on 23-round LBlock-s. The time complexity of the attack is about $2^{75.4}$ 23-round encryptions, where $2^{62.3}$ known plaintexts are used, and 60 subkey bits are guessed, which is three bits less than that of LBlock. The results showed that the improved key schedule algorithm did not enhance their ability to protect against zero-correlation linear cryptanalysis, and it was better to use the irregular bit-shifting to disturb the shifting relation between subkeys.

The remainder of this paper is organized as follows. Section 2 presents a brief description of LBlock-s. Section 3 introduces the definition of zero-correlation linear approximation and presents the basic methods of multidimensional zero-correlation linear cryptanalysis. Section 4 presents the multidimensional zero-correlation linear cryptanalysis on 23-round LBlock-s. Finally, Sect. 5 concludes this paper.

2   A Brief Description of LBlock-s

2.1   Notation

Throughout this paper we use the following notations:
- P, C : the 64-bit plaintext and the 64-bit ciphertext;

- K_r : the r-th round subkey;
- X_r: the left half of the r-th round input;
- X_0 : the right half of the first round input;
- $Y|Z$: the concatenation of Y and Z;
- Y_i^j : the j-th 4-bit word of Y_i (where $0 \leq j \leq 7$, and the leftmost index is 7);
- $Y \lll i$: left rotation of Y by i bits;
- $[i]_2$: binary form of an integer i.

2.2 Overview of LBlock-s

LBlock-s is the kernel block cipher of the authentication encryption algorithm LAC submitted to CAESAR competition. Similar to LBlock, the general structure of LBlock-s is a variant of Feistel Network, which is depicted in Fig. 1. The number of iterative rounds is 32.

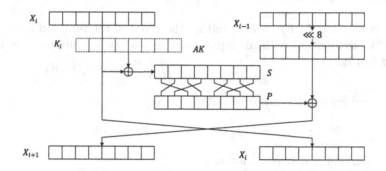

Fig. 1. Round function of LBlock-s block cipher

The round function of LBlock-s includes three basic functions: round subkey addition AK, confusion function S and diffusion function P. The nonlinear layer S consists of 8 identical 4-bit S-boxes in parallel (8 different S-boxes are used in LBlock, see reference [1]). The diffusion function P is defined as a permutation of eight 4-bit nibbles.

Encryption Algorithm. Let $P = (X_1, X_0)$ be a 64-bit plaintext. For $i = 1, 2, \ldots, 32$, do

$$X_{i+1} = P(S(X_i \oplus K_i)) \oplus (X_{i-1} \lll 8)$$

Then the 64-bit ciphertext C is (X_{32}, X_{33}).

The decryption process is the inverse of the encryption process, that is, input 64-bit ciphertext (X_{32}, X_{33}), and output 64-bit plaintext $P = (X_1, X_0)$.

Key Schedule Algorithm. The 80-bit master key K is stored in a key register and denoted as $K = k_{79}k_{78} \ldots k_0$. Output the leftmost 32 bits of register K as subkey K_1.

For $i = 1, 2, \ldots, 31$, update the key register K as follows:

1. $K \lll 24$
2. $[k_{55}k_{54}k_{53}k_{52}] = S[k_{79}k_{78}k_{77}k_{76}] \oplus [k_{55}k_{54}k_{53}k_{52}]$
   $[k_{31}k_{30}k_{29}k_{28}] = S[k_{75}k_{74}k_{73}k_{72}] \oplus [k_{31}k_{30}k_{29}k_{28}]$
   $[k_{67}k_{66}k_{65}k_{64}] = [k_{71}k_{70}k_{69}k_{68}] \oplus [k_{67}k_{66}k_{65}k_{64}]$
   $[k_{51}k_{50}k_{49}k_{48}] = [k_{11}k_{10}k_9k_8] \oplus [k_{51}k_{50}k_{49}k_{48}]$
3. $[k_{54}k_{53}k_{52}k_{51}k_{50}] = [k_{54}k_{53}k_{52}k_{51}k_{50}] \oplus [i]_2$
4. Output the leftmost 32 bits of current content of register K as round subkey K_{i+1}.

The original key schedule of LBlock used the shift $K \lll 29$, and only two nibbles are updated using two S-boxes (see reference [1] or appendix), so the diffusion is not enough as shown by Wang et al. in [8]. Thus in the design of LBlock-s, this improved key schedule was adopted.

3 Zero-Correlation Linear Approximation

Consider a function $f : F_2^n \to F_2^m$, and let the input of the function be $x \in F_2^n$. A linear approximation with an input mask u and an output mask v is the following function:

$$x \to u \cdot x \oplus v \cdot f(x).$$

The linear approximation has probability

$$p(u;v) = Pr_{x \in F_2^n}(u \cdot x \oplus v \cdot f(x) = 0),$$

and its correlation is defined as follows:

$$c_f(u;v) = 2p(u;v) - 1.$$

In linear cryptanalysis we are interested in the linear approximation with correlation far from zero. The number of known plaintexts needed in the linear cryptanalysis is inversely proportional to the squared correlation. Zero-correlation linear cryptanalysis uses linear approximations such that the correlation is equal to zero for all keys. Particularly for multidimensional zero-correlation linear cryptanalysis, if $2^m - 1$ zero-correlation approximations of dimension m is used, then by reference [15] the number of required distinct plaintexts is about $2^{n+2-m/2}$. Next we will review the process of multidimensional zero-correlation linear cryptanalysis in more detail.

For most ciphers, a large number of zero-correlation approximations are available. To remove the statistical independence for multiple zero-correlation linear approximations, the zero-correlation linear approximations available are treated as a linear space spanned by m different zero-correlation linear approximations such that all $l = 2^m - 1$ non-zero linear combinations of them have zero correlation [15]. Thus we can describe a cipher E as a cascade of three parts: $E = E_2 \circ E_1 \circ E_0$, and assume there exists m independent linear approximations (u_i, w_i) for E_1 such that all $l = 2^m - 1$ nonzero linear combinations of them have correlation zero. The E_0 and E_2 are the encryption function added before or after E_1.

For each key candidate, the adversary encrypts the plaintexts for the beginning rounds E_0 and obtain some parts of data x, and decrypts the corresponding ciphertexts for the final rounds E_2 and obtain some parts of data y, then obtain a m-tuple

$$z = (z_1, \ldots, z_m), \text{where } z_i = \langle u_i, x \rangle + \langle w_i, y \rangle,$$

by evaluating the m linear approximations for a plaintext-ciphertext pair.

For each $z \in F_2^n$, the attacker allocates a counter $V[z]$ and initializes it to value zero. Then for each distinct plaintext, the attacker computes the corresponding data in F_2^m and increments the counter $V[z]$ of this data value by one. Then the attacker computes the statistic T:

$$T = \sum_{z=0}^{2^m-1} \frac{(V(z) - N2^{-m})^2}{N2^{-m}(1 - 2^{-m})} = \frac{N2^m}{1 - 2^{-m}} \sum_{z=0}^{2^m-1} \left(\frac{V(z)}{N} - \frac{1}{2^m} \right)^2$$

The value T for right key guess follows a χ^2-distribution with mean $\mu_0 = l \cdot (2^n - N)/(2^n - 1)$ and variance $\sigma_0^2 = 2l(\frac{2^n-N}{2^n-1})^2$ while for the wrong key guess the distribution is a χ^2-distribution with mean $\mu_1 = l$, and variance $\sigma_1^2 = 2l$. Denote the type-I error probability (the probability to wrongfully discard the right key, that is, the success probability) with α and the type-II error probability (the probability to wrongfully accept a random key as the right key) with β. We consider the decision threshold $\tau = \mu_0 + \sigma_0 z_{1-\alpha} = \mu_1 - \sigma_1 z_{1-\beta}$, then the number of known plaintexts N should be about

$$N = \frac{2^n(z_{1-\alpha} + z_{1-\beta})}{\sqrt{l/2} + z_{1-\alpha}}$$

where $z_p = \Phi^{-1}(p)$ for $0 < p < 1$ and Φ is the cumulative function of the standard normal distribution.

4   Multidimensional Zero-Correlation Linear Cryptanalysis on 23-round LBlock-s

Using the miss-in-the-middle technique, Soleimany and Nyberg proposed the matrix method [16] to automatic search for the longest linear approximations with correlation zero, and found 64 classes of zero-correlation linear approximations with the form $(\Gamma_a, 0) \rightarrow_{14r} (0, \Gamma_b)$ for 14-round LBlock, where Γ_a, Γ_b contains exactly one nonzero nibble. Based on this, they also proposed a general zero-correlation linear cryptanalysis on 22-round LBlock-type block cipher without using the property of the key schedule algorithm. Recently, Wang et al. [17] further presented an improved multidimensional zero-correlation linear cryptanalysis on 23-round LBlock using the special property of the key schedule algorithm, the time complexity was about 2^{76} 23-round encryptions, where 2^{62} known plaintexts were used, and totally 63 subkey bits were guessed.

Since the general structure of LBlock-s is the same as LBlock, it also has such 14-round zero-correlation linear approximations of the form $(\Gamma_a, 0) \rightarrow_{14r} (0, \Gamma_b)$ for 14-round LBlock, where Γ_a, Γ_b run through all $l = 2^8 - 1$ nonzero values, they form a linear space spanned by 8 different zero-correlation linear approximations such that all $l = 2^8 - 1$ non-zero linear combinations of them have zero correlation. When used directly to present a multidimensional zero-correlation linear cryptanalysis on 23-round LBlock-s, 76 bits of subkey will be guessed and the total time complexity will be greater than exhaustive search. So we must try to find some dependence between subkey bits and use them to reduce the time complexity. Fortunately, by careful discussion we really find some dependence between subkey bits, for example, we have

$$K_i^0 = K_{i+1}^6, K_i^1 = K_{i+1}^7.$$

Using these relations, by selecting proper zero-correlation linear approximations, we can present a multidimensional zero-correlation linear cryptanalysis on 23-round LBlock-s.

Let E_1 be the encryption function of 14-round LBlock-s with zero-correlation linear approximations of the form $(\Gamma_a, 0) \rightarrow_{14r} (0, \Gamma_b)$, we add r_{in} rounds before E_1 and r_{out} rounds after E_1, then obtain a $(r_{in} + 14 + r_{out})$-round encryption function $E = E_2 \circ E_1 \circ E_0$. Let $Site_{in}$ and $Site_{out}$ be the position of nonzero nibbles of Γ_a and Γ_b, where $0 \leq Site_{in}, Site_{out} \leq 7$.

In order to fully use the dependence of subkey bits to reduce the complexity, we use the improved multidimensional zero-correlation linear cryptanalysis method proposed by Wang et al. in [17] and search for linear approximations and (r_{in}, r_{out}) with least number of guessed keys. The least number of guessed keys is 60, where $r_{in} = 5$, $r_{out} = 4$, and the corresponding choices for $(Site_{in}, Site_{out})$ are as follows:

$$(Site_{in}, Site_{out}) \in \{(6,6), (6,4), (6,2), (6,0)\}.$$

We select $(Site_{in}, Site_{out}) = (6,6)$ to give an attack on 23-round LBlock-s, that is, we use the linear approximations of the form $(0u000000, 00000000) \rightarrow_{14r} (00000000, 0w000000)$. As $r_{in} = 5$, and $r_{out} = 4$, we put the 14-round zero-correlation linear approximations in round 6 to 19 and attack LBlock-s from round 1 to 23 (Fig. 2).

After collecting sufficient plaintext-ciphertext pairs, we guess corresponding subkeys for the first five rounds and the last four rounds to evaluate the statistic T. Using the dependence of subkeys bits and using the partial compression technique we can reduce the time complexity significantly and present an efficient zero-correlation linear attack on 23-round LBlock-s.

As shown in Fig. 2, the nibble X_6^6 is affected by 48 bits of plaintext (X_1, X_0) and 48 bits of round keys and the expression can be shown as:

$$\begin{aligned}
X_6^6 =& X_0^0 \oplus S(X_1^0 \oplus K_1^0) \oplus S(X_1^3 \oplus S(X_0^5 \oplus S(X_1^6 \oplus K_1^6) \oplus K_2^7) \oplus K_3^5) \oplus \\
& S(X_1^0 \oplus S(X_0^6 \oplus S(X_1^1 \oplus K_1^1) \oplus K_2^0) \oplus S(X_0^1 \oplus S(X_1^2 \oplus K_1^2) \oplus \\
& S(X_1^5 \oplus S(X_0^4 \oplus S(X_1^4 \oplus K_1^4) \oplus K_2^6) \oplus K_3^7) \oplus K_4^5) \oplus K_5^4)
\end{aligned}$$

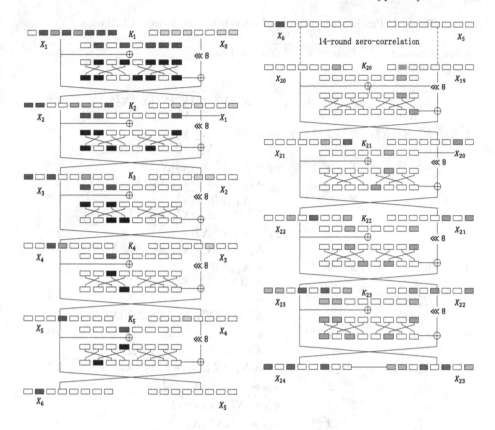

Fig. 2. Attack on 23-round LBlock-s

Similarly, the nibble X_{19}^6 is affected by 32 bits of ciphertext (X_{23}, X_{24}) and 28 bits of round keys and the expression can be shown as:

$$X_{19}^6 = X_{23}^2 \oplus S(X_{24}^2 \oplus S(X_{23}^0 \oplus K_{23}^0) \oplus K_{22}^0) \oplus S(X_{24}^5 \oplus S(X_{23}^7 \oplus K_{23}^7) \oplus$$
$$S(X_{23}^4 \oplus S(X_{24}^7 \oplus S(X_{23}^6 \oplus K_{23}^6) \oplus K_{22}^5) \oplus K_{21}^2) \oplus K_{20}^1)$$

After analyzing the key schedule of LBlock-s, we find the following relations in the round keys:

$$K_2^7 = K_1^1, K_2^6 = K_1^0, K_5^4 = K_1^0 \oplus K_1^1, K_{23}^6 = K_{22}^0.$$

Thus the number of bits need to be guessed can be reduced from 76 to 60.

Assuming that N known plaintexts are used, the partial encryption and decryption using the partial-compression technique are proceeded as in Table 1.

The second column in Table 1 stands for the subkey nibbles that have to be guessed in each step, and the third column denotes the time complexity of corresponding step measured in S-box access. In each step, we save the values of the Obtained States during the encryption and decryption process. For each

Table 1. Partial encryption and decryption on 23-round LBlock-s

Steps	Guessed subkeys	Time (S-box accesses)	Obtained States	Size
1	$K_1^{1,4,6}, K_2^6,$ $K_2^7(K_1^1)$	$N \cdot 2^{16} \cdot 5$	$x_1 = X_0^0\|X_1^0\|X_3^5\|X_2^0\|X_0^1\|X_1^2\|X_3^7\|$ $X_{23}^2\|X_{24}^2\|X_{23}^0\|X_{24}^5\|X_{23}^7\|X_{23}^4\|X_{24}^7\|X_{23}^6$	2^{60}
2	$K_2^0, K_1^0(K_2^6)$	$2^{60} \cdot 2^{16+4} \cdot 2$	$x_2 = X_2^2\|X_3^5\|X_3^2\|X_0^1\|X_1^2\|X_3^7\|$ $X_{23}^2\|X_{24}^2\|X_{23}^0\|X_{24}^5\|X_{23}^7\|X_{23}^4\|X_{24}^7\|X_{23}^6$	2^{56}
3	K_1^2	$2^{56} \cdot 2^{20+4}$	$x_3 = X_2^2\|X_3^5\|X_3^2\|X_2^3\|X_3^7\|$ $X_{23}^2\|X_{24}^2\|X_{23}^0\|X_{24}^5\|X_{23}^7\|X_{23}^4\|X_{24}^7\|X_{23}^6$	2^{52}
4	K_3^5	$2^{52} \cdot 2^{24+4}$	$x_4 = X_4^4\|X_3^2\|X_3^2\|X_3^7\|$ $X_{23}^2\|X_{24}^2\|X_{23}^0\|X_{24}^5\|X_{23}^7\|X_{23}^4\|X_{24}^7\|X_{23}^6$	2^{48}
5	K_3^7	$2^{48} \cdot 2^{28+4}$	$x_5 = X_4^4\|X_3^2\|X_4^5\|$ $X_{23}^2\|X_{24}^2\|X_{23}^0\|X_{24}^5\|X_{23}^7\|X_{23}^4\|X_{24}^7\|X_{23}^6$	2^{44}
6	K_4^5	$2^{44} \cdot 2^{32+4}$	$x_6 = X_4^4\|X_5^4\|$ $X_{23}^2\|X_{24}^2\|X_{23}^0\|X_{24}^5\|X_{23}^7\|X_{23}^4\|X_{24}^7\|X_{23}^6$	2^{40}
7	$K_5^4(K_1^0 \oplus$ $K_1^1)$	$2^{40} \cdot 2^{36+0}$	$x_7 = X_6^6\|$ $X_{23}^2\|X_{24}^2\|X_{23}^0\|X_{24}^5\|X_{23}^7\|X_{23}^4\|X_{24}^7\|X_{23}^6$	2^{36}
8	K_{23}^0	$2^{36} \cdot 2^{36+4}$	$x_8 =$ $X_6^6\|X_{23}^2\|X_{22}^0\|X_{24}^5\|X_{23}^7\|X_{23}^4\|X_{24}^7\|X_{23}^6$	2^{32}
9	$K_{22}^0(K_{23}^6)$	$2^{32} \cdot 2^{40+4} \cdot 2$	$x_9 = X_6^6\|X_{21}^0\|X_{24}^5\|X_{23}^7\|X_{23}^4\|X_{22}^5$	2^{24}
10	K_{22}^5	$2^{24} \cdot 2^{44+4}$	$x_{10} = X_6^6\|X_{21}^0\|X_{24}^5\|X_{23}^7\|X_{21}^2$	2^{20}
11	K_{23}^7	$2^{20} \cdot 2^{48+4}$	$x_{11} = X_6^6\|X_{21}^0\|X_{22}^3\|X_{21}^2$	2^{16}
12	K_{21}^2	$2^{16} \cdot 2^{52+4}$	$x_{12} = X_6^6\|X_{21}^0\|X_{20}^1$	2^{12}
13	K_{20}^1	$2^{12} \cdot 2^{56+4}$	$x_{13} = X_6^6\|X_{19}^6$	2^8

possible value of $x_i(1 \leq i \leq 13)$, the counter $N_i[x_i]$ will record how many plaintext-ciphertext pairs can produce the corresponding intermediate state x_i. The counter size for each x_i is shown in the last column.

To be clear, we explain some steps in Table 1 in detail.

Step 1. We allocate the 60-bit counter $N_1[x_1]$ and initialize it to zero. We then guess 16-bit keys and partially encrypt N plaintexts to compute x_1, and increment the corresponding counter.

Since $K_2^7 = K_1^1$, we only need to guess 16 bits of subkeys $K_1^{1,4,6}, K_2^6$. As shown in Fig. 2, the nibble X_6^6 is affected by 42 bits of plaintext (X_1, X_0). They are represented by

$$x_0 = X_0^0\|X_1^0\|X_1^3\|X_0^5\|X_1^6\|X_0^6\|X_1^1\|X_0^1\|X_1^2\|X_1^5\|X_0^4\|X_1^4\|$$
$$X_{23}^2\|X_{24}^2\|X_{23}^0\|X_{24}^5\|X_{23}^7\|X_{23}^4\|X_{24}^7\|X_{23}^6$$

Since the following three equations

$$X_2^0 = X_0^6 \oplus S(X_1^1 \oplus K_1^1),$$

$$X_3^5 = X_1^3 \oplus S(X_0^5 \oplus S(X_1^6 \oplus K_1^6) \oplus K_2^7),$$
$$X_3^7 = X_1^5 \oplus S(X_0^4 \oplus S(X_1^4 \oplus K_1^4) \oplus K_2^6)$$

are true for LBlock-s, then the 80-bit x_0 can be reduced to 60-bit x_1 :

$$x_1 = X_0^0|X_1^0|X_3^5|X_2^0|X_0^1|X_1^2|X_3^7|X_{23}^2|X_{24}^2|X_{23}^0|X_{24}^5|X_{23}^7|X_{23}^4|X_{24}^7|X_{23}^6$$

after guessing 16 bits subkeys $K_1^{1,4,6}, K_2^6$. Update the expressions of X_6^6 as follows:

$$X_6^6 = X_0^0 \oplus S(X_1^0 \oplus K_1^0) \oplus S(X_3^5 \oplus K_3^5) \oplus S(X_1^0 \oplus S(X_2^0 \oplus K_2^0) \oplus$$
$$S(X_0^1 \oplus S(X_1^2 \oplus K_1^2) \oplus S(X_3^7 \oplus K_3^7) \oplus K_4^5) \oplus K_5^4)$$

Step 2. We allocate the 56-bit counter $N_2[x_2]$ and initialize it to zero. We then guess 4-bit subkeys K_2^0 and partially encrypt x_0 to compute x_1 and add the corresponding $N_1[x_1]$ to $N_2[x_2]$.

Since the subkey $K_1^0 = K_2^6$ is known, and the following two equations

$$X_2^2 = X_0^0 \oplus S(X_1^0 \oplus K_1^0),$$
$$X_3^3 = X_1^0 \oplus S(X_2^0 \oplus K_2^0)$$

are true for LBlock-s, then the 60-bit x_1 can be reduced to 56-bit x_2 :

$$x_2 = X_2^2|X_3^5|X_3^2|X_0^1|X_1^2|X_3^7|X_{23}^2|X_{24}^2|X_{23}^0|X_{23}^5|X_{23}^7|X_{24}^4|X_{24}^7|X_{23}^6$$

after guessing 4 bits subkeys. Update the expressions of X_6^6 as follows:

$$X_6^6 = X_2^2 \oplus S(X_3^5 \oplus K_3^5) \oplus S(X_3^2 \oplus S(X_0^1 \oplus S(X_1^2 \oplus K_1^2) \oplus S(X_3^7 \oplus K_3^7) \oplus K_4^5) \oplus K_5^4)$$

The following steps are similar to the above two steps, and we do not explain in details. The cost of step 1 to step 13 in the process of partial computation is about 2^{83} S-box access, which is about $2^{83} \cdot 1/8 \cdot 1/23 \approx 2^{75.4}$ 23-round LBlock-s encryptions.

Next we will discuss in detail the data complexity and total time complexity of the attack.

As $(0u000000, 00000000) \rightarrow_{14r} (00000000, 0w000000)$ is the selected zero-correlation linear approximations, where $u, w \in F_2^4$. When u, w run through all $l = 2^8 - 1$ nonzero values, they form a linear space of dimension 8, so we can choose 8 independent linear masks with $(u_i, w_i) \in \{(1,0), (2,0), (4,0), (8,0), (0,1), (0,2), (0,4), (0,8)\}$, and calculate the 8-bit tuple

$$z = (z_1, \ldots, z_8), \text{where } z_i = \langle u_i, X_6^6 \rangle + \langle w_i, X_{19}^6 \rangle.$$

Then evaluate the statics $T_k = \frac{N2^8}{1-2^{-8}} \sum_{z=0}^{2^8-1} (\frac{V(z)}{N} - \frac{1}{2^8})^2$ and make decision for each guessing key k.

Similar as in [17], let the type-I error probability $\alpha = 2^{-2.7} \approx 0.154$ and the type-II error probability $\beta = 2^{-9} \approx 0.002$, then $z_{1-\alpha} \approx 1, z_{1-\beta} \approx 2.88$. Since $n = 64$ and $l = 2^8 - 1 = 255$, then from $N = \frac{2^n(z_{1-\alpha}+z_{1-\beta})}{\sqrt{l/2+z_{1-\alpha}}}$ we know the data complexity N is about $2^{62.3}$, and the decision threshold is $\tau = \mu_0 + \sigma_0 z_{1-\alpha}$.

To recover the secret key, the following steps are performed:

1. Allocate a counter $V[z]$ for 8-bit z.
2. For 2^8 values of x_{13} :
   (a) Evaluate all eight basis zero-correlation masks on x_{13} and get z.
   (b) Update the counter $V[z]$ by $V[z] = V[z] + N_{13}[x_{13}]$.
3. For each guessing key k, compute $T_k = \frac{N2^8}{1-2^{-8}} \sum_{z=0}^{2^8-1} (\frac{V(z)}{N} - \frac{1}{2^8})^2$.
4. If $T_k < \tau$, then the guessed subkey values are possible right subkey candidates.
5. Do exhaustive search for all right candidates.

Complexity. The cost of step 1 to step 13 in the process of partial computation is about $2^{75.4}$ 23-round LBlock-s encryptions. Since the type-II error probability $\beta = 2^{-9}$), the number of remaining key candidates is about $2^{80} \cdot \beta = 2^{71}$. Thus the total time complexity is $2^{75.4} + 2^{71} \approx 2^{75.4}$ 23-round LBlock-s encryptions. The data complexity is $2^{62.3}$ known plaintexts, and the memory requirements are about 2^{60} bytes.

5   Conclusions

The security of LBlock-s against multidimensional zero-correlation linear cryptanalysis is evaluated. By choosing proper zero-correlation linear approximations, we present a multidimensional zero-correlation linear cryptanalysis on 23-round LBlock-s using the shifting relation of certain subkeys derived by the new key schedule algorithm. The complexity is almost as that of LBlock. Our research showed that the improved key schedule algorithm did not enhance their ability to protect against zero-correlation linear cryptanalysis, and it is better to use the irregular bit-shifting to disturb the shifting relation between subkeys.

Acknowledgements. We thank the anonymous reviewers for their careful reading of our paper and helpful comments. This research was supported by the National Natural Science Foundation of China (Nos. 61100200, 61170235, 61309017, 61472251) and China Postdoctoral Science Foundation (No. 2014T70417).

Appendix. Key Schedule of LBlock

The 80-bit master key K is stored in a key register and denoted as $K = k_{79}k_{78} \ldots k_0$. Output the leftmost 32 bits of register K as subkey K_1.
    For $i = 1, 2, \ldots, 31$, update the key register K as follows:

1. $K \lll 29$
2. $[k_{79}k_{78}k_{77}k_{76}] = S_8[k_{79}k_{78}k_{77}k_{76}]$
   $[k_{75}k_{74}k_{73}k_{72}] = S_9[k_{75}k_{74}k_{73}k_{72}]$
3. $[k_{50}k_{49}k_{48}k_{47}k_{46}] = [k_{50}k_{49}k_{48}k_{47}k_{46}] \oplus [i]_2$
4. Output the leftmost 32 bits of current content of register K as round subkey K_{i+1}.

References

1. Wu, W., Zhang, L.: LBlock: a lightweight block cipher. In: Lopez, J., Tsudik, G. (eds.) ACNS 2011. LNCS, vol. 6715, pp. 327–344. Springer, Heidelberg (2011)
2. Bogdanov, A.A., Knudsen, L.R., Leander, G., Paar, C., Poschmann, A., Robshaw, M., Seurin, Y., Vikkelsoe, C.: PRESENT: an ultra-lightweight block cipher. In: Paillier, P., Verbauwhede, I. (eds.) CHES 2007. LNCS, vol. 4727, pp. 450–466. Springer, Heidelberg (2007)
3. Liu, Y., Gu, D., Liu, Z., Li, W.: Impossible differential attacks on reduced-round LBlock. In: Ryan, M.D., Smyth, B., Wang, G. (eds.) ISPEC 2012. LNCS, vol. 7232, pp. 97–108. Springer, Heidelberg (2012)
4. Karakoç, F., Demirci, H., Harmancı, A.E.: Impossible differential cryptanalysis of reduced-round LBlock. In: Askoxylakis, I., Pöhls, H.C., Posegga, J. (eds.) WISTP 2012. LNCS, vol. 7322, pp. 179–188. Springer, Heidelberg (2012)
5. Minier, M., Naya-Plasencia, M.: A related key impossible differential attack against 22 rounds of the lightweight block cipher LBlock. Inf. Process. Lett. **112**, 624–629 (2012)
6. Liu, S., Gong, Z., Wang, L.: Improved related-key differential attacks on reduced-round LBlock. In: Chim, T.W., Yuen, T.H. (eds.) ICICS 2012. LNCS, vol. 7618, pp. 58–69. Springer, Heidelberg (2012)
7. Sasaki, Y., Wang, L.: Comprehensive study of integral analysis on 22-round LBlock. In: Kwon, T., Lee, M.-K., Kwon, D. (eds.) ICISC 2012. LNCS, vol. 7839, pp. 156–169. Springer, Heidelberg (2013)
8. Wang, Y., Wu, W., Yu, X., Zhang, L.: Security on LBlock against Biclique cryptanalysis. In: Lee, D.H., Yung, M. (eds.) WISA 2012. LNCS, vol. 7690, pp. 1–14. Springer, Heidelberg (2012)
9. Zhang, L., Wu, W., Wang, Y.: LAC: a lightweight authenticated encryption cipher. In: Submission to CAESAR, version 1, 15 March 2014. http://competitions.cr.yp.to/round1/lacv1.pdf
10. CAESAR: Competition for Authenticated Encryption: Security, Applicability, and Robustness, January 2013–December 2017. http://competitions.cr.yp.to/caesar.html
11. Matsui, M.: Linear cryptanalysis method for DES cipher. In: Helleseth, T. (ed.) EUROCRYPT 1993. LNCS, vol. 765, pp. 386–397. Springer, Heidelberg (1994)
12. Nyberg, K.: Linear approximation of block ciphers. In: De Santis, A. (ed.) EUROCRYPT 1994. LNCS, vol. 950, pp. 439–444. Springer, Heidelberg (1995)
13. Bogdanov, A., Rijmen, V.: Linear hulls with correlation zero and linear cryptanalysis of block ciphers. Des. Codes Cryptogr. **70**(3), 369–383 (2014). https://eprint.iacr.org/2011/123
14. Bogdanov, A., Wang, M.: Zero correlation linear cryptanalysis with reduced data complexity. In: Canteaut, A. (ed.) FSE 2012. LNCS, vol. 7549, pp. 29–48. Springer, Heidelberg (2012)
15. Bogdanov, A., Leander, G., Nyberg, K., Wang, M.: Integral and multidimensional linear distinguishers with correlation zero. In: Wang, X., Sako, K. (eds.) ASIACRYPT 2012. LNCS, vol. 7658, pp. 244–261. Springer, Heidelberg (2012)
16. Soleimany, H., Nyberg, K.: Zero-correlation linear cryptanalysis of reduced-round LBlock. Des. Codes Cryptogr. **73**(2), 683–698 (2014). https://eprint.iacr.org/2012/570
17. Wang, Y., Wu, W.: Improved multidimensional zero-correlation linear cryptanalysis and applications to LBlock and TWINE. In: Susilo, W., Mu, Y. (eds.) ACISP 2014. LNCS, vol. 8544, pp. 1–16. Springer, Heidelberg (2014)

18. Sun, S., Hu, L., Wang, P., Qiao, K., Ma, X., Song, L.: Automatic security evaluation and (related-key) differential characteristic search: application to SIMON, PRESENT, LBlock, DES(L) and other bit-oriented block ciphers. In: Sarkar, P., Iwata, T. (eds.) ASIACRYPT 2014. LNCS, vol. 8873, pp. 158–178. Springer, Heidelberg (2014)
19. Boura, C., Naya-Plasencia, M., Suder, V.: Scrutinizing and improving impossible differential attacks: applications to CLEFIA, Camellia, LBlock and SIMON. In: Sarkar, P., Iwata, T. (eds.) ASIACRYPT 2014. LNCS, vol. 8873, pp. 179–199. Springer, Heidelberg (2014)

Traceable CP-ABE on Prime Order Groups: Fully Secure and Fully Collusion-Resistant Blackbox Traceable

Zhen Liu$^{(\boxtimes)}$ and Duncan S. Wong

Security and Data Sciences, ASTRI, Hong Kong SAR, China
zhenliu7-c@my.cityu.edu.hk, duncanwong@astri.org

Abstract. In Ciphertext-Policy Attribute-Based Encryption (CP-ABE), access policies associated with the ciphertexts are generally role-based and the attributes satisfying the policies are generally *shared* by multiple users. If a malicious user, with his attributes shared with multiple other users, created a decryption blackbox for sale, this malicious user could be difficult to identify from the blackbox. Hence in practice, a useful CP-ABE scheme should have some tracing mechanism to identify this 'traitor' from the blackbox. In this paper, we propose the first CP-ABE scheme which simultaneously achieves (1) fully collusion-resistant blackbox traceability in the standard model, (2) full security in the standard model, and (3) on prime order groups. When compared with the latest fully collusion-resistant blackbox traceable CP-ABE schemes, this new scheme achieves the same efficiency level, enjoying the sub-linear overhead of $O(\sqrt{N})$, where N is the number of users in the system. This new scheme is highly expressive and can take any monotonic access structures as ciphertext policies.

Keywords: Traceable · Ciphertext-policy Attribute Based Encryption · Prime order groups

1 Introduction

In a Ciphertext-Policy Attribute-Based Encryption (CP-ABE) [1,7] system, each user possesses a set of attributes and a private key which is generated according to his attributes, and the encrypting party does not need to know or specify the exact identities of the targeted receivers, instead, the encrypting party can define an *access policy* over role-based/descriptive *attributes* to encrypt a message, so that only the users whose attributes satisfy the access policy can decrypt the ciphertext. For example, a school secretary, say Alice, may encrypt some messages using "(Mathematics AND (PhD Student OR Alumni))", which is an *access policy* defined over descriptive *attributes*, say "Mathematics", "PhD Student", and "Alumni", so that only PhD students and alumni in the Department of Mathematics have access to the messages. Due to the high flexibility and expressivity of the access policy, CP-ABE has promising applications related to access

© Springer International Publishing Switzerland 2016
S. Qing et al. (Eds.): ICICS 2015, LNCS 9543, pp. 109–124, 2016.
DOI: 10.1007/978-3-319-29814-6_10

control, such as secure cloud storage access and sharing, and has attracted great attention in the research community. Among the CP-ABE schemes recently proposed, [1,2,6,8,10,11,19–21], progress has been made on the schemes' security, access policy expressivity, and efficiency. While the schemes with practical security and expressivity (i.e. full security against adaptive adversaries in the standard model and high expressivity of supporting any monotone access structures) have been proposed in [10,11,19], the traceability of traitors which intentionally expose their decryption keys has been becoming an important concern related to the applicability of CP-ABE. Specifically, due to the nature of CP-ABE, access policies associated with the ciphertexts do not have to contain the exact identities of the eligible receivers. Instead, access policies are role-based and the attributes (and the corresponding decryption privilege) are generally *shared* by multiple users. As a result, a malicious user, with his attributes shared with multiple other users, might have an intention to leak the corresponding decryption key or some decryption privilege in the form of a decryption blackbox/device in which the decryption key is embedded, for example, for financial gain or for some other incentives, as there is little risk of getting caught. While all the aforementioned CP-ABE schemes lack the traitor tracing functionality, recently a handful of traceable CP-ABE schemes have been proposed in [3,13,14].

In the aforementioned non-traceable CP-ABE schemes, an easy and attractive way for a malicious user to make money is to sell a well-formed decryption key where the corresponding attribute set does not contain his identity-related attributes. For example, a malicious user with attributes {Bob, PhD, Mathematics} may build and sell a new decryption key with attributes {PhD, Mathematics}, and does not worry getting caught, since many other users share the attributes {PhD, Mathematics}. Liu et al. [14] proposed a whitebox traceable CP-ABE scheme that can deter users from such malicious behaviours, i.e., given a well-formed decryption key as input, a tracing algorithm can find out the malicious user who created the key from his/her original key. To avoid the whitebox traceability, instead of selling a well-formed decryption key, a more sophisticated malicious user may build and sell a decryption device/blackbox while keeping the embedded decryption key and algorithm hidden. Liu et al. [13] proposed a blackbox traceable CP-ABE scheme that can deter users from these more practical attacks, i.e., given a decryption blackbox/device, while the decryption key and even the decryption algorithm could be hidden, the tracing algorithm, which treats the decryption blackbox as an oracle, can still find out the malicious user whose key must have been used in constructing the decryption blackbox. Liu et al. proved that the CP-ABE scheme in [13] is fully secure in the standard model and fully collusion-resistant blackbox traceable in the standard model, where *fully collusion-resistant blackbox traceability* means that the number of colluding users in constructing a decryption blackbox is not limited and can be arbitrary. In addition, the scheme in [13] is highly expressive (i.e. supporting any monotonic access structures), and as a fully collusion-resistant blackbox traceable CP-ABE scheme, it achieves the most efficient level to date, i.e. the overhead for the fully collusion-resistant blackbox traceability is in $O(\sqrt{N})$, where N is the number of users in the system. However, the scheme in [13] is based on composite order groups with order being the product of three large primes, and this severely limits its applicability. Liu and Wong [15] proposed a fully collusion-resistant blackbox traceable CP-ABE scheme on prime order groups, but achieves only selective security, where the adversary is required to declare his attacking target before seeing the system public key. Another recent blackbox traceable CP-ABE scheme is due to Deng et al. [3], which is only *t-collusion-resistant* traceable, where the number of colluding users is limited, i.e., less than a parameter t. In addition, the scheme in [3] is only selectively secure and the security is proven in the random oracle model.

1.1   Our Results

In this paper, we propose a new CP-ABE scheme that is fully secure in the standard model, fully collusion-resistant blackbox traceable in the standard model, and highly expressive (i.e. supporting any monotonic access structures). On the efficiency, as a fully collusion-resistant blackbox traceable CP-ABE scheme, this new scheme also achieves the most efficient level to date, i.e. the overhead for the fully collusion-resistant blackbox traceability is in $O(\sqrt{N})$. When compared with the CP-ABE scheme in [13], the advantage of this new scheme is that this scheme is constructed on prime order groups. Note that this implies this new scheme has better security and performance than the scheme in [13], although both of them are fully secure in the standard model and have overhead in $O(\sqrt{N})$. More specifically, as it has been shown (e.g. in [5,9]), the constructions on composite order groups will result in significant loss of efficiency and the security will rely on some non-standard assumptions (e.g. the Subgroup Decision Assumptions) and an additional assumption that the group order is hard to factor. To the best of our knowledge, this is the first CP-ABE scheme that is fully collusion-resistant blackbox traceable, fully secure, and constructed on prime order groups.

Related Work. In [13] Liu et al. defined a 'functional' CP-ABE that has the same functionality as the conventional CP-ABE (i.e. having all the appealing properties of the conventional CP-ABE), except that each user is assigned and identified by a unique index, which will enable the traceability of traitors. Liu et al. also defined the security and the fully collusion-resistant blackbox traceability for such a 'functional' CP-ABE. Furthermore, Liu et al. defined a new primitive called Augmented CP-ABE (AugCP-ABE) and formalized its security using message-hiding and index-hiding games. Then Liu et al. proved that *an AugCP-ABE scheme with message-hiding and index-hiding properties can be directly transferred to a secure CP-ABE with fully collusion-resistant blackbox traceability.* With such a framework, Liu et al. obtained a fully secure and fully collusion-resistant blackbox traceable CP-ABE scheme by constructing an AugCP-ABE scheme with message-hiding and index-hiding properties. It will be tempting to obtain a prime order construction by applying the existing general tools of converting constructions from composite order groups to prime order groups, e.g. [4,9], to the composite order group construction of [13]. However, as the traceability is a new feature of CP-ABE and these tools focus on the conventional security (i.e. hiding the messages), it is not clear whether these tools are applicable to the traceable CP-ABE of [13].

Outline. In this paper, we also follow the framework in [13]. In particular, in Sect. 2 we review the definitions and security models of AugCP-ABE, then in Sect. 3 we propose our AugCP-ABE construction on prime order groups and prove that our AugCP-ABE construction is message-hiding and index-hiding in the standard model. As a result, we obtain a fully secure and fully collusion-resistant blackbox traceable CP-ABE scheme on prime order groups.

2   Augmented CP-ABE Definitions

In this section, we review the definitions of Augmented CP-ABE, which is proposed by Liu et al. [13] as a primitive that help constructing fully collusion-resistant blackbox traceable CP-ABE.

2.1   Definitions and Security Models

Given a positive integer n, let $[n]$ be the set $\{1, 2, \ldots, n\}$. An Augmented CP-ABE (AugCP-ABE) system consists of the following four algorithms:

$\mathsf{Setup}_\mathsf{A}(\lambda, \mathcal{U}, N) \to (\mathsf{PP}, \mathsf{MSK})$. The algorithm takes as input a security parameter λ, the attribute universe $\mathcal{U}$, and the number of users N in the system, then runs in polynomial time in λ, and outputs the public parameter PP and a master secret key MSK.

$\mathsf{KeyGen}_\mathsf{A}(\mathsf{PP}, \mathsf{MSK}, S) \to \mathsf{SK}_{k,S}$. The algorithm takes as input PP, MSK, and an attribute set S, and outputs a private key $\mathsf{SK}_{k,S}$, which is assigned and identified by a unique index $k \in [N]$.

$\mathsf{Encrypt}_\mathsf{A}(\mathsf{PP}, M, \mathbb{A}, \bar{k}) \to CT$. The algorithm takes as input PP, a message M, an access policy $\mathbb{A}$ over $\mathcal{U}$, and an index $\bar{k} \in [N+1]$, and outputs a ciphertext CT. $\mathbb{A}$ **is included in** CT, **but the value of** $\bar{k}$ **is not.**

$\mathsf{Decrypt}_\mathsf{A}(\mathsf{PP}, CT, \mathsf{SK}_{k,S}) \to M$ or $\bot$. The algorithm takes as input PP, a ciphertext CT, and a private key $\mathsf{SK}_{k,S}$. If S satisfies the ciphertext access policy, the algorithm outputs a message M, otherwise it outputs $\bot$ indicating the failure of decryption.

Correctness. For any attribute set $S \subseteq \mathcal{U}$, $k \in [N]$, access policy $\mathbb{A}$ over $\mathcal{U}$, $\bar{k} \in [N+1]$, and message M, suppose $(\mathsf{PP}, \mathsf{MSK}) \leftarrow \mathsf{Setup}_\mathsf{A}(\lambda, \mathcal{U}, \mathcal{K})$, $\mathsf{SK}_{k,S} \leftarrow \mathsf{KeyGen}_\mathsf{A}(\mathsf{PP}, \mathsf{MSK}, S)$, $CT \leftarrow \mathsf{Encrypt}_\mathsf{A}(\mathsf{PP}, M, \mathbb{A}, \bar{k})$. If $(S$ satisfies $\mathbb{A}) \wedge (k \geq \bar{k})$ then $\mathsf{Decrypt}_\mathsf{A}(\mathsf{PP}, CT, \mathsf{SK}_{k,S}) = M$.

Security. The security of AugCP-ABE is defined by the following three games, where the first two are for message-hiding, and the third one is for the index-hiding property. It is worth noticing that, as pointed in [13], in the three games: (1) the adversary is allowed to specify the index of the private key when it makes key queries for the attribute sets of its choice, i.e., for $t = 1$ to Q, the adversary submits (index, attribute set) pair (k_t, S_{k_t}) to query a private key for attribute set S_{k_t}, where $Q \le N$, $k_t \in [N]$, and $k_t \ne k_{t'}$ $\forall 1 \le t \ne t' \le Q$ (this is to guarantee that each user/key can be *uniquely* identified by an index); and (2) for $k_t \ne k_{t'}$ we do not require $S_{k_t} \ne S_{k_{t'}}$, i.e., different users/keys may have the same attribute set.

In the following **message-hiding game** between a challenger and an adversary $\mathcal{A}$, $\bar{k} = 1$ (the first game, $\mathsf{Game}_{\mathsf{MH}_1}^{\mathsf{A}}$) or $\bar{k} = N+1$ (the second game, $\mathsf{Game}_{\mathsf{MH}_{N+1}}^{\mathsf{A}}$).

Setup. The challenger runs $\mathsf{Setup}_\mathsf{A}(\lambda, \mathcal{U}, N)$ and gives the public parameter PP to $\mathcal{A}$.

Phase 1. For $t = 1$ to Q_1, $\mathcal{A}$ adaptively submits (index, attribute set) pair (k_t, S_{k_t}), and the challenger responds with a private key $\mathsf{SK}_{k_t, S_{k_t}}$.

Challenge. $\mathcal{A}$ submits two equal-length messages M_0, M_1 and an access policy $\mathbb{A}^*$. The challenger flips a random coin $b \in \{0, 1\}$, and sends $CT \leftarrow \mathsf{Encrypt}_\mathsf{A}(\mathsf{PP}, M_b, \mathbb{A}^*, \bar{k})$ to $\mathcal{A}$.

Phase 2. For $t = Q_1 + 1$ to Q, $\mathcal{A}$ adaptively submits (index, attribute set) pair (k_t, S_{k_t}), and the challenger responds with a private key $\mathsf{SK}_{k_t, S_{k_t}}$.

Guess. $\mathcal{A}$ outputs a guess $b' \in \{0, 1\}$ for b.

$\mathsf{Game}_{\mathsf{MH}_1}^{\mathsf{A}}$. In the Challenge phase the challenger sends $CT \leftarrow \mathsf{Encrypt}_\mathsf{A}(\mathsf{PP}, M_b, \mathbb{A}^*, 1)$ to $\mathcal{A}$. $\mathcal{A}$ wins the game if $b' = b$ under the **restriction** that $\mathbb{A}^*$ cannot be satisfied by any of the queried attribute sets $S_{k_1}, \ldots, S_{k_Q}$. The advantage of $\mathcal{A}$ is defined as $\mathsf{MH}_1^{\mathsf{A}}\mathsf{Adv}_\mathcal{A} = |\Pr[b' = b] - \frac{1}{2}|$.

$\mathsf{Game}_{\mathsf{MH}_{N+1}}^{\mathsf{A}}$. In the Challenge phase the challenger sends $CT \leftarrow \mathsf{Encrypt}_\mathsf{A}(\mathsf{PP}, M_b, \mathbb{A}^*, N+1)$ to $\mathcal{A}$. $\mathcal{A}$ wins the game if $b' = b$. The advantage of $\mathcal{A}$ is defined as $\mathsf{MH}_{N+1}^{\mathsf{A}}\mathsf{Adv}_\mathcal{A} = |\Pr[b' = b] - \frac{1}{2}|$.

Definition 1. *A N-user AugCP-ABE system is message-hiding if for all probabilistic polynomial time (PPT) adversaries $\mathcal{A}$ the advantages $\mathsf{MH}_1^{\mathsf{A}}\mathsf{Adv}_\mathcal{A}$ and $\mathsf{MH}_{N+1}^{\mathsf{A}}\mathsf{Adv}_\mathcal{A}$ are negligible in λ.*

$\mathsf{Game}_{\mathsf{IH}}^{\mathsf{A}}$. In the third game, **index-hiding game**, for any non-empty attribute set $S^* \subseteq \mathcal{U}$, we define **the strictest access policy** as $\mathbb{A}_{S^*} = \bigwedge_{x \in S^*} x$, and require that an adversary cannot distinguish between an encryption using $(\mathbb{A}_{S^*}, \bar{k})$ and $(\mathbb{A}_{S^*}, \bar{k} + 1)$ without a private decryption key $\mathsf{SK}_{\bar{k}, S_{\bar{k}}}$ such that $S_{\bar{k}} \supseteq S^*$. The game takes as input a parameter $\bar{k} \in [N]$ which is given to both the challenger and the adversary $\mathcal{A}$. The game proceeds as follows:

Setup. The challenger runs $\mathsf{Setup}_\mathsf{A}(\lambda, \mathcal{U}, N)$ and gives the public parameter PP to $\mathcal{A}$.

Key Query. For $t = 1$ to Q, $\mathcal{A}$ adaptively submits (index, attribute set) pair (k_t, S_{k_t}), and the challenger responds with a private key $\mathsf{SK}_{k_t, S_{k_t}}$.

Challenge. $\mathcal{A}$ submits a message M and a non-empty attribute set S^*. The challenger flips a random coin $b \in \{0, 1\}$, and sends $CT \leftarrow \mathsf{Encrypt}_\mathsf{A}(\mathsf{PP}, M, \mathbb{A}_{S^*}, \bar{k} + b)$ to $\mathcal{A}$.

Guess. $\mathcal{A}$ outputs a guess $b' \in \{0, 1\}$ for b.

$\mathcal{A}$ wins the game if $b' = b$ under the **restriction** that none of the queried pairs $\{(k_t, S_{k_t})\}_{1 \le t \le Q}$ can satisfy $(k_t = \bar{k}) \wedge (S_{k_t}$ satisfies $\mathbb{A}_{S^*})$, i.e. $(k_t = \bar{k}) \wedge (S_{k_t} \supseteq S^*)$. The advantage of $\mathcal{A}$ is defined as $\mathsf{IH}^\mathsf{A}\mathsf{Adv}_\mathcal{A}[\bar{k}] = |\Pr[b' = b] - \frac{1}{2}|$.

Definition 2. *A N-user AugCP-ABE system is index-hiding if for all PPT adversaries $\mathcal{A}$ the advantages $\mathsf{IH}^\mathsf{A}\mathsf{Adv}_\mathcal{A}[\bar{k}]$ for $\bar{k} = 1, \ldots, N$ are negligible in λ.*

2.2   The Reduction of Traceable CP-ABE to Augmented CP-ABE

Let $\Sigma_\mathsf{A} = (\mathsf{Setup}_\mathsf{A}, \mathsf{KeyGen}_\mathsf{A}, \mathsf{Encrypt}_\mathsf{A}, \mathsf{Decrypt}_\mathsf{A})$ be an Augmented CP-ABE, define $\mathsf{Encrypt}(\mathsf{PP}, M, \mathbb{A}) = \mathsf{Encrypt}_\mathsf{A}(\mathsf{PP}, M, \mathbb{A}, 1)$, and let $\Sigma = (\mathsf{Setup}_\mathsf{A}, \mathsf{KeyGen}_\mathsf{A}, \mathsf{Encrypt}, \mathsf{Decrypt}_\mathsf{A})$. It is apparent that Σ is a 'functional' CP-ABE that has the same functionality as the conventional CP-ABE, except that the number of users in the system is predefined and each user is assigned a unique index. As shown in [13], with the Trace algorithm in [13, Sect. 3.2], Σ achieves fully collusion-resistant blackbox traceability against key-like decryption blackbox [1].

Theorem 1. *[13, Theorem 1] If Σ_A is message-hiding and index-hiding, then Σ is secure, and using the Trace algorithm, Σ is traceable against key-like decryption blackbox.*

3   An Augmented CP-ABE Construction on Prime Order Groups

Now we construct an AugCP-ABE scheme on prime order groups, and prove that this AugCP-ABE scheme is message-hiding and index-hiding in the standard model. Combined with the results in Sect. 2.2, we obtain a CP-ABE scheme that is fully collusion-resistant blackbox traceable in the standard model, fully secure in the standard model, and on prime order groups.

3.1   Preliminaries

Before proposing our AugCP-ABE scheme, we first review some preliminaries.

---

[1] Roughly speaking, a key-like decryption blackbox $\mathcal{D}$ is described by a non-empty attribute set $S_\mathcal{D}$ and a non-negligible probability value ϵ, and for any access policy $\mathbb{A}$, if it is satisfied by $S_\mathcal{D}$, this blackbox $\mathcal{D}$ can decrypt the ciphertexts associated with $\mathbb{A}$ with probability at least ϵ. Please refer to [13] for more formal details.

Bilinear Groups. Let $\mathcal{G}$ be a group generator, which takes a security parameter λ and outputs $(p, \mathbb{G}, \mathbb{G}_T, e)$ where p is a prime, $\mathbb{G}$ and $\mathbb{G}_T$ are cyclic groups of order p, and $e : \mathbb{G} \times \mathbb{G} \to \mathbb{G}_T$ is a map such that: (1) (Bilinear) $\forall g, h \in \mathbb{G}, a, b \in \mathbb{Z}_p, e(g^a, h^b) = e(g, h)^{ab}$, (2) (Non-Degenerate) $\exists g \in \mathbb{G}$ such that $e(g, g)$ has order p in $\mathbb{G}_T$. We refer to $\mathbb{G}$ as the *source group* and $\mathbb{G}_T$ as the *target group*. We assume that group operations in $\mathbb{G}$ and $\mathbb{G}_T$ as well as the bilinear map e are efficiently computable, and the description of $\mathbb{G}$ and $\mathbb{G}_T$ includes a generator of $\mathbb{G}$ and $\mathbb{G}_T$ respectively.

Complexity Assumptions. We will base the message-hiding property of our AugCP-ABE scheme on the Decisional Linear Assumption (DLIN), the Decisional 3-Party Diffie-Hellman Assumption (D3DH) and the Source Group q-Parallel BDHE Assumption, and will base the index-hiding property of our AugCP-ABE scheme on the DLIN assumption and the D3DH assumption. Note that the DLIN assumption and the D3DH assumption are standard and generally accepted assumptions, and the Source Group q-Parallel BDHE Assumption is introduced and proved by Lewko and Waters in [12]. Please refer to the full version [16, Appendix A] for the details of the three assumptions.

Dual Pairing Vector Spaces. Our construction will use dual pairing vector spaces, a tool introduced by Okamoto and Takashima [17–19] and developed by Lewko [9] and Lewko and Waters [12]. Let $\boldsymbol{v} = (v_1, \ldots, v_n)$ be a vector over $\mathbb{Z}_p$, the notation $g^{\boldsymbol{v}}$ denotes a tuple of group elements as $g^{\boldsymbol{v}} := (g^{v_1}, \ldots, g^{v_n})$. Furthermore, for any $a \in \mathbb{Z}_p$ and $\boldsymbol{v} = (v_1, \ldots, v_n), \boldsymbol{w} = (w_1, \ldots, w_n) \in \mathbb{Z}_p^n$, define $(g^{\boldsymbol{v}})^a := g^{a\boldsymbol{v}} = (g^{av_1}, \ldots, g^{av_n}), g^{\boldsymbol{v}} g^{\boldsymbol{w}} := g^{\boldsymbol{v}+\boldsymbol{w}} = (g^{v_1+w_1}, \ldots, g^{v_n+w_n})$, and define a bilinear map e_n on n-tuples of $\mathbb{G}$ as $e_n(g^{\boldsymbol{v}}, g^{\boldsymbol{w}}) := \prod_{i=1}^n e(g^{v_i}, g^{w_i}) = e(g, g)^{(\boldsymbol{v} \cdot \boldsymbol{w})}$, where the dot/inner product $\boldsymbol{v} \cdot \boldsymbol{w}$ is computed modulo p.

For a fixed (constant) dimension n, we say two bases $\mathbb{B} := (\boldsymbol{b}_1, \ldots, \boldsymbol{b}_n)$ and $\mathbb{B}^* := (\boldsymbol{b}_1^*, \ldots, \boldsymbol{b}_n^*)$ of $\mathbb{Z}_p^n$ are "dual orthonormal" when $\boldsymbol{b}_i \cdot \boldsymbol{b}_j^* \equiv 0 \pmod{p} \ \forall 1 \le i \ne j \le n$ and $\boldsymbol{b}_i \cdot \boldsymbol{b}_i^* \equiv \psi \pmod{p} \ \forall 1 \le i \le n$, where ψ is a non-zero element of $\mathbb{Z}_p$. (This is a slight abuse of the terminology "orthonormal", since ψ is not constrained to be 1.) For a generator $g \in \mathbb{G}$, we note that $e_n(g^{\boldsymbol{b}_i}, g^{\boldsymbol{b}_j^*}) = 1$ whenever $i \ne j$, where 1 here denotes the identity element in $\mathbb{G}_T$. Let $Dual(\mathbb{Z}_p^n, \psi)$ denote the set of pairs of dual orthonormal bases of dimension n with dot products $\boldsymbol{b}_i \cdot \boldsymbol{b}_i^* = \psi$, and $(\mathbb{B}, \mathbb{B}^*) \xleftarrow{R} Dual(\mathbb{Z}_p^n, \psi)$ denote choosing a random pair of bases from this set. As our AugCP-ABE construction will use dual pairing vector spaces, the security proof will use a lemma and a Subspace Assumption, which are introduced and proved by Lewko and Waters [12], in the setting of dual pairing vector spaces. Please refer to the full version [16, Appendix A.1] for the details of this lemma and the Subspace Assumption. Here we would like to stress that *the Subspace Assumption is implied by DLIN assumption*.

To construct our AugCP-ABE scheme, we further define a new notation. In particular, for any $\boldsymbol{v} = (v_1, \ldots, v_n) \in \mathbb{Z}_p^n, \boldsymbol{v}' = (v_1', \ldots, v_{n'}') \in \mathbb{Z}_p^{n'}$, we define

$$(g^{\boldsymbol{v}})^{\boldsymbol{v}'} := ((g^{\boldsymbol{v}})^{v_1'}, \ldots, (g^{\boldsymbol{v}})^{v_{n'}'}) = (g^{v_1' v_1}, \ldots, g^{v_1' v_n}, \ldots, g^{v_{n'}' v_1}, \ldots, g^{v_{n'}' v_n}) \in \mathbb{G}^{nn'}.$$

Note that for any $v, w \in \mathbb{Z}_p^n, v', w' \in \mathbb{Z}_p^{n'}$, we have

$$e_{nn'}((g^v)^{v'}, (g^w)^{w'}) = \prod_{j=1}^{n'} \prod_{i=1}^{n} e(g^{v'_j v_i}, g^{w'_j w_i}) = e(g, g)^{(v \cdot w)(v' \cdot w')}.$$

Linear Secret-Sharing Schemes (LSSS). As of previous work, we use linear secret-sharing schemes (LSSS) to express the access policies. An LSSS is a share-generating matrix A whose rows are labeled by attributes via a function ρ. An attribute set S satisfies the LSSS access matrix (A, ρ) if the rows labeled by the attributes in S have the *linear reconstruction* property, namely, there exist constants $\{\omega_i | \rho(i) \in S\}$ such that, for any valid shares $\{\lambda_i\}$ of a secret s, we have $\sum_{\rho(i) \in S} \omega_i \lambda_i = s$. Please refer to the full version [16, Appendix D] for the formal definitions of access structures and LSSS.

Notations. Suppose the number of users N in the system equals n^2 for some n^2. We arrange the users in a $n \times n$ matrix and uniquely assign a tuple (i, j) where $1 \leq i, j \leq n$, to each user. A user at position (i, j) of the matrix has index $k = (i - 1) * n + j$. For simplicity, we directly use (i, j) as the index where $(i, j) \geq (\bar{i}, \bar{j})$ means that $((i > \bar{i}) \vee (i = \bar{i} \wedge j \geq \bar{j}))$. The use of pairwise notation (i, j) is purely a notational convenience, as $k = (i - 1) * n + j$ defines a bijection between $\{(i, j) | 1 \leq i, j \leq n\}$ and $\{1, \ldots, N\}$. We conflate the notation and consider the attribute universe to be $[\mathcal{U}] = \{1, 2 \ldots, \mathcal{U}\}$, so $\mathcal{U}$ servers both as a description of the attribute universe and as a count of the total number of attributes. Given a bilinear group order p, one can randomly choose $r_x, r_y, r_z \in \mathbb{Z}_p$, and set $\chi_1 = (r_x, 0, r_z)$, $\chi_2 = (0, r_y, r_z)$, $\chi_3 = \chi_1 \times \chi_2 = (-r_y r_z, -r_x r_z, r_x r_y)$. Let $span\{\chi_1, \chi_2\}$ be the subspace spanned by χ_1 and χ_2, i.e. $span\{\chi_1, \chi_2\} = \{\nu_1 \chi_1 + \nu_2 \chi_2 | \nu_1, \nu_2 \in \mathbb{Z}_p\}$. We can see that χ_3 is orthogonal to the subspace $span\{\chi_1, \chi_2\}$ and that $\mathbb{Z}_p^3 = span\{\chi_1, \chi_2, \chi_3\} = \{\nu_1 \chi_1 + \nu_2 \chi_2 + \nu_3 \chi_3 | \nu_1, \nu_2, \nu_3 \in \mathbb{Z}_p\}$. For any $v \in span\{\chi_1, \chi_2\}$, we have $(\chi_3 \cdot v) = 0$, and for random $v \in \mathbb{Z}_p^3$, $(\chi_3 \cdot v) \neq 0$ happens with overwhelming probability.

3.2 AugCP-ABE Construction

$\mathsf{Setup}_A(\lambda, \mathcal{U}, N = n^2) \rightarrow (\mathsf{PP}, \mathsf{MSK})$. The algorithm chooses a bilinear group $\mathbb{G}$ of order p and two generators $g, h \in \mathbb{G}$. It randomly chooses $(\mathbb{B}, \mathbb{B}^*), (\mathbb{B}_0, \mathbb{B}_0^*) \in Dual(\mathbb{Z}_p^3, \psi)$ and $(\mathbb{B}_1, \mathbb{B}_1^*), \ldots, (\mathbb{B}_{\mathcal{U}}, \mathbb{B}_{\mathcal{U}}^*) \in Dual(\mathbb{Z}_p^6, \psi)$. We let $b_j, b_j^* (1 \leq j \leq 3)$ denote the basis vectors belonging to $(\mathbb{B}, \mathbb{B}^*)$, $b_{0,j}, b_{0,j}^* (1 \leq j \leq 3)$ denote the basis vectors belonging to $(\mathbb{B}_0, \mathbb{B}_0^*)$, and $b_{x,j}, b_{x,j}^* (1 \leq j \leq 6)$ denote the basis vectors belonging to $(\mathbb{B}_x, \mathbb{B}_x^*)$ for each $x \in [\mathcal{U}]$. The algorithm also chooses random exponents $\alpha_1, \alpha_2 \in \mathbb{Z}_p$, $\{r_i, z_i, \alpha_{i,1}, \alpha_{i,2} \in$

---

[2] If the number of users is not a square, we add some "dummy" users to pad to the next square.

$\mathbb{Z}_p\}_{i \in [n]}$, $\{c_{j,1}, c_{j,2}, y_j \in \mathbb{Z}_p\}_{j \in [n]}$. The public parameter PP is set to

$$
\begin{aligned}
\mathsf{PP} = \Big(& (p, \mathbb{G}, \mathbb{G}_T, e), \ g, h, \ g^{\boldsymbol{b_1}}, g^{\boldsymbol{b_2}}, h^{\boldsymbol{b_1}}, h^{\boldsymbol{b_2}}, h^{\boldsymbol{b_{0,1}}}, h^{\boldsymbol{b_{0,2}}}, \\
& \{h^{\boldsymbol{b_{x,1}}}, h^{\boldsymbol{b_{x,2}}}, h^{\boldsymbol{b_{x,3}}}, h^{\boldsymbol{b_{x,4}}}\}_{x \in [\mathcal{U}]}, \ F_1 = e(g,h)^{\psi\alpha_1}, \ F_2 = e(g,h)^{\psi\alpha_2}, \\
& \{E_{i,1} = e(g,g)^{\psi\alpha_{i,1}}, \ E_{i,2} = e(g,g)^{\psi\alpha_{i,2}}\}_{i \in [n]}, \\
& \{G_i = g^{r_i(\boldsymbol{b_1}+\boldsymbol{b_2})}, \ Z_i = g^{z_i(\boldsymbol{b_1}+\boldsymbol{b_2})}\}_{i \in [n]}, \\
& \{H_j = g^{c_{j,1}\boldsymbol{b_1^*}+c_{j,2}\boldsymbol{b_2^*}}, \ Y_j = H_j^{y_j}\}_{j \in [n]} \Big).
\end{aligned}
$$

The master secret key is set to

$$
\begin{aligned}
\mathsf{MSK} = \Big(& \boldsymbol{b_1^*}, \boldsymbol{b_2^*}, \ \boldsymbol{b_{0,1}^*}, \boldsymbol{b_{0,2}^*}, \ \{\boldsymbol{b_{x,1}^*}, \boldsymbol{b_{x,2}^*}, \boldsymbol{b_{x,3}^*}, \boldsymbol{b_{x,4}^*}\}_{x \in [\mathcal{U}]}, \\
& \alpha_1, \alpha_2, \ \{r_i, z_i, \ \alpha_{i,1}, \alpha_{i,2}\}_{i \in [n]}, \ \{c_{j,1}, c_{j,2}\}_{j \in [n]} \Big).
\end{aligned}
$$

In addition, a counter $ctr = 0$ is implicitly included in MSK.

$\mathsf{KeyGen}_A(\mathsf{PP}, \mathsf{MSK}, S) \to \mathsf{SK}_{(i,j),S}$. The algorithm first sets $ctr = ctr + 1$ and computes the corresponding index in the form of (i,j) where $1 \le i, j \le n$ and $(i-1) * n + j = ctr$. Then it randomly chooses $\sigma_{i,j,1}, \sigma_{i,j,2}, \delta_{i,j,1}, \delta_{i,j,2} \in \mathbb{Z}_p$, and outputs a private key $\mathsf{SK}_{(i,j),S} =$

$$
\Big\langle (i,j), S, \ \boldsymbol{K}_{i,j} = g^{(\alpha_{i,1}+r_i c_{j,1})\boldsymbol{b_1^*}+(\alpha_{i,2}+r_i c_{j,2})\boldsymbol{b_2^*}} h^{(\sigma_{i,j,1}+\delta_{i,j,1})\boldsymbol{b_1^*}+(\sigma_{i,j,2}+\delta_{i,j,2})\boldsymbol{b_2^*}},
$$

$$
\boldsymbol{K}'_{i,j} = g^{(\alpha_1+\sigma_{i,j,1}+\delta_{i,j,1})\boldsymbol{b_1^*}+(\alpha_2+\sigma_{i,j,2}+\delta_{i,j,2})\boldsymbol{b_2^*}}, \ \boldsymbol{K}''_{i,j} = (\boldsymbol{K}'_{i,j})^{z_i},
$$

$$
\boldsymbol{K}_{i,j,0} = g^{\delta_{i,j,1}\boldsymbol{b_{0,1}^*}+\delta_{i,j,2}\boldsymbol{b_{0,2}^*}}, \ \{\boldsymbol{K}_{i,j,x} = g^{\sigma_{i,j,1}(\boldsymbol{b_{x,1}^*}+\boldsymbol{b_{x,2}^*})+\sigma_{i,j,2}(\boldsymbol{b_{x,3}^*}+\boldsymbol{b_{x,4}^*})}\}_{x \in S} \Big\rangle.
$$

$\mathsf{Encrypt}_A(\mathsf{PP}, M, \mathbb{A} = (A, \rho), (\bar{i}, \bar{j})) \to CT$. A is an $l \times m$ LSSS matrix and ρ maps each row A_k of A to an attribute $\rho(k) \in [\mathcal{U}]$. The algorithm first chooses random $\kappa, \tau, s_1, \ldots, s_n, t_1, \ldots, t_n \in \mathbb{Z}_p$, $\boldsymbol{v_c}, \boldsymbol{w_1}, \ldots, \boldsymbol{w_n} \in \mathbb{Z}_p^3$, $\xi_{1,1}, \xi_{1,2}, \ldots, \xi_{l,1}, \xi_{l,2} \in \mathbb{Z}_p$, $\boldsymbol{u_1}, \boldsymbol{u_2} \in \mathbb{Z}_p^m$. It also chooses random $r_x, r_y, r_z \in \mathbb{Z}_p$, and sets $\boldsymbol{\chi_1} = (r_x, 0, r_z)$, $\boldsymbol{\chi_2} = (0, r_y, r_z)$, $\boldsymbol{\chi_3} = (-r_y r_z, -r_x r_z, r_x r_y)$. Then it randomly chooses $\boldsymbol{v_i} \in \mathbb{Z}_p^3$ for $i = 1, \ldots, \bar{i}$, $\boldsymbol{v_i} \in span\{\boldsymbol{\chi_1}, \boldsymbol{\chi_2}\}$ for $i = \bar{i}+1, \ldots, n$. Let π_1 and π_2 be the first entries of $\boldsymbol{u_1}$ and $\boldsymbol{u_2}$ respectively. The algorithm creates a ciphertext $\langle (A, \rho), \ (\boldsymbol{R}_i, \boldsymbol{R}'_i, \boldsymbol{Q}_i, \boldsymbol{Q}'_i, \boldsymbol{Q}''_i, T_i)_{i=1}^n, \ (C_j, C'_j)_{j=1}^l, \ (\boldsymbol{P}_k)_{k=0}^l \rangle$:

1. For each row $i \in [n]$:
   - if $i < \bar{i}$: choose random $\hat{s}_i \in \mathbb{Z}_p$, then set

$$
\boldsymbol{R}_i = (g^{\boldsymbol{b_1}+\boldsymbol{b_2}})^{\boldsymbol{v_i}}, \quad \boldsymbol{R}'_i = \boldsymbol{R}_i^\kappa, \quad \boldsymbol{Q}_i = g^{s_i(\boldsymbol{b_1}+\boldsymbol{b_2})},
$$

$$
\boldsymbol{Q}'_i = h^{s_i(\boldsymbol{b_1}+\boldsymbol{b_2})} \boldsymbol{Z}_i^{t_i} h^{\pi_1 \boldsymbol{b_1}+\pi_2 \boldsymbol{b_2}}, \quad \boldsymbol{Q}''_i = g^{t_i(\boldsymbol{b_1}+\boldsymbol{b_2})}, \quad T_i = e(g,g)^{\hat{s}_i}.
$$

   - if $i \ge \bar{i}$: set

$$
\boldsymbol{R}_i = (\boldsymbol{G}_i)^{s_i \boldsymbol{v_i}}, \quad \boldsymbol{R}'_i = \boldsymbol{R}_i^\kappa, \quad \boldsymbol{Q}_i = g^{\tau s_i(\boldsymbol{v_i}\cdot\boldsymbol{v_c})(\boldsymbol{b_1}+\boldsymbol{b_2})},
$$

$$
\boldsymbol{Q}'_i = h^{\tau s_i(\boldsymbol{v_i}\cdot\boldsymbol{v_c})(\boldsymbol{b_1}+\boldsymbol{b_2})} \boldsymbol{Z}_i^{t_i} h^{\pi_1 \boldsymbol{b_1}+\pi_2 \boldsymbol{b_2}}, \quad \boldsymbol{Q}''_i = g^{t_i(\boldsymbol{b_1}+\boldsymbol{b_2})},
$$

$$
T_i = M \frac{(E_{i,1}E_{i,2})^{\tau s_i(\boldsymbol{v_i}\cdot\boldsymbol{v_c})}}{(F_1 F_2)^{\tau s_i(\boldsymbol{v_i}\cdot\boldsymbol{v_c})} F_1^{\pi_1} F_2^{\pi_2}}.
$$

2. For each column $j \in [n]$:
   - if $j < \bar{j}$: choose random $\mu_j \in \mathbb{Z}_p$, then set
     $$\boldsymbol{C}_j = (\boldsymbol{H}_j)^{\tau(\boldsymbol{v}_c + \mu_j \boldsymbol{\chi}_3)}(\boldsymbol{Y}_j)^{\kappa \boldsymbol{w}_j}, \quad \boldsymbol{C}'_j = (\boldsymbol{Y}_j)^{\boldsymbol{w}_j}.$$
   - if $j \geq \bar{j}$: set $\boldsymbol{C}_j = (\boldsymbol{H}_j)^{\tau \boldsymbol{v}_c}(\boldsymbol{Y}_j)^{\kappa \boldsymbol{w}_j}, \boldsymbol{C}'_j = (\boldsymbol{Y}_j)^{\boldsymbol{w}_j}.$
3. $\boldsymbol{P}_0 = h^{\pi_1 \boldsymbol{b}_{0,1} + \pi_2 \boldsymbol{b}_{0,2}}$,
   $\{\boldsymbol{P}_k = h^{(A_k \cdot \boldsymbol{u}_1 + \xi_{k,1})\boldsymbol{b}_{\rho(k),1} - \xi_{k,1}\boldsymbol{b}_{\rho(k),2} + (A_k \cdot \boldsymbol{u}_2 + \xi_{k,2})\boldsymbol{b}_{\rho(k),3} - \xi_{k,2}\boldsymbol{b}_{\rho(k),4}}\}_{k \in [l]}.$

$\mathsf{Decrypt_A}(\mathsf{PP}, CT, \mathsf{SK}_{(i,j),S}) \to M$ or $\bot$. If the private key's attribute set S does not satisfy the ciphertext's LSSS (A, ρ), the algorithm outputs $\bot$, otherwise

1. Compute constants $\{\omega_k \in \mathbb{Z}_p | \rho(k) \in S\}$ such that $\sum_{\rho(k) \in S} \omega_k A_k = (1, 0, \ldots, 0)$, then compute $D_P = e_3(\boldsymbol{K}_{i,j,0}, \boldsymbol{P}_0) \prod_{\rho(k) \in S} e_6(\boldsymbol{K}_{i,j,\rho(k)}, \boldsymbol{P}_k)^{\omega_k}$.

2. Compute $D_I = \dfrac{e_3(\boldsymbol{K}_{i,j}, \boldsymbol{Q}_i) \cdot e_3(\boldsymbol{K}''_{i,j}, \boldsymbol{Q}''_i) \cdot e_9(\boldsymbol{R}'_i, \boldsymbol{C}'_j)}{e_3(\boldsymbol{K}'_{i,j}, \boldsymbol{Q}'_i) \cdot e_9(\boldsymbol{R}_i, \boldsymbol{C}_j)}.$

3. Compute $M = T_i/(D_P \cdot D_I)$ as the output message. Assume the ciphertext is generated from message M' and index $(\bar{i}, \bar{j})$, it can be verified that only when $(i > \bar{i})$ or $(i = \bar{i} \wedge j \geq \bar{j})$, $M = M'$ will hold. This follows from the facts that for $i > \bar{i}$, we have $(\boldsymbol{v}_i \cdot \boldsymbol{\chi}_3) = 0$ (since $\boldsymbol{v}_i \in span\{\boldsymbol{\chi}_1, \boldsymbol{\chi}_2\}$), and for $i = \bar{i}$, we have that $(\boldsymbol{v}_i \cdot \boldsymbol{\chi}_3) \neq 0$ happens with overwhelming probability (since $\boldsymbol{v}_i$ is randomly chosen from $\mathbb{Z}_p^3$). The correctness details can be found in the full version [16, Appendix B].

Remarks: We borrow the ideas of [12, Sect. 5] to achieve the full security for prime order group constructions, and borrow the ideas of [13] to achieve fully collusion-resistant blackbox traceability. But the above construction and the later security proof are not trivial combinations of the two schemes. In particular, the public parameter components $g^{\boldsymbol{b}_1}, g^{\boldsymbol{b}_2}, h^{\boldsymbol{b}_1}, h^{\boldsymbol{b}_2}, h^{\boldsymbol{b}_{0,1}}, h^{\boldsymbol{b}_{0,2}}, \{h^{\boldsymbol{b}_{x,1}}, h^{\boldsymbol{b}_{x,2}}, h^{\boldsymbol{b}_{x,3}}, h^{\boldsymbol{b}_{x,4}}\}_{x \in [\mathcal{U}]}, F_1, F_2$, the key components $\boldsymbol{K}'_{i,j}, \boldsymbol{K}_{i,j,0}, \{\boldsymbol{K}_{i,j,x}\}_{x \in S}$, and ciphertext components $\boldsymbol{P}_0, \{\boldsymbol{P}_k\}_{k \in [l]}$ are designed using the ideas of [12, Sect. 5]. To achieve fully collusion-resistant blackbox traceability, $\{E_{i,1}, E_{i,2}, \boldsymbol{G}_i, \boldsymbol{Z}_i\}_{i \in [n]}, \{\boldsymbol{H}_j\}_{j \in [n]}$ are put in the public parameter, and $\boldsymbol{K}_{i,j}, \boldsymbol{K}''_{i,j}$ are introduced into the private key. Note that $\boldsymbol{G}_i$ and $\boldsymbol{H}_j$ will be used to generate ciphertext components $\boldsymbol{R}_i$ and $\boldsymbol{C}_j$ respectively, and $e_9(\boldsymbol{R}_i, \boldsymbol{C}_j)$ will be computed during decryption, so that $\boldsymbol{G}_i$ and $\boldsymbol{H}_j$ must use the basis vectors of a pair of dual orthonormal bases, i.e. $\boldsymbol{G}_i$ uses $(\boldsymbol{b}_1, \boldsymbol{b}_2)$ and $\boldsymbol{H}_j$ uses $(\boldsymbol{b}_1^*, \boldsymbol{b}_2^*)$. This prevents us from trivially using the proof of [12, Sect. 5], because in the construction of [12, Sect. 5], only $\boldsymbol{b}_1, \boldsymbol{b}_2, \boldsymbol{b}_{0,1}, \boldsymbol{b}_{0,2}, \{\boldsymbol{b}_{x,1}, \boldsymbol{b}_{x,2}, \boldsymbol{b}_{x,3}, \boldsymbol{b}_{x,4}\}_{x \in [\mathcal{U}]}$ appear in the exponents of the public parameter components. As an informal evidence, while the AugCP-ABE scheme of [13] reduces its message-hiding property (in $\mathsf{Game}^{\mathsf{A}}_{\mathsf{MH}_1}$) to the security of the CP-ABE scheme of [11], it is impossible to make a similar reduction here, since the public parameter of the above AugCP-ABE construction contains $(\boldsymbol{b}_1^*, \boldsymbol{b}_2^*)$ while the public parameter of [12, Sect. 5] does not contain them. To address this problem, we introduce a new and crucial public parameter component $\boldsymbol{Y}_j = \boldsymbol{H}_j^{y_j}$ which does not have counterpart in the AugCP-ABE scheme of [13] or the CP-ABE scheme in [12, Sect. 5], and we reduce the message-hiding property of our construction directly to the underlying assumptions.

3.3   Security of the AugCP-ABE Construction

The following Theorems 2 and 3 show that our AugCP-ABE construction is message-hiding, and Theorem 4 shows that our AugCP-ABE construction is index-hiding.

Theorem 2. *Suppose the DLIN assumption, the D3DH assumption, and the source group q-parallel BDHE assumption hold. Then no PPT adversary can win* $\mathsf{Game}^{\mathsf{A}}_{\mathsf{MH}_1}$ *with non-negligible advantage.*

Proof. Our message-hiding proof route here is quite similar to the security proof route of the conventional CP-ABE scheme by Lewko and Waters [12, Sect. 5]. But as discussed previously, this is not a trivial work.

We begin by defining our various types of semi-functional keys and ciphertexts. The semi-functional space in the exponent will correspond to the span of b_3, b_3^*, the span of $b_{0,3}, b_{0,3}^*$ and the span of each $b_{x,5}, b_{x,6}, b_{x,5}^*, b_{x,6}^*$.

Semi-functional Keys. To produce a semi-functional key for an attribute set S, one first calls the normal key generation algorithm to produce a normal key consisting of $K_{i,j}, K_{i,j}', K_{i,j}'', K_{i,j,0}, \{K_{i,j,x}\}_{x \in S}$ with index (i, j). One then chooses random value γ. The semi-functional key is

$$K_{i,j}h^{\gamma b_3^*}, \ K_{i,j}'g^{\gamma b_3^*}, \ K_{i,j}''g^{z_i\gamma b_3^*}, \ K_{i,j,0}, \ \{K_{i,j,x}\}_{x \in S}.$$

Semi-functional Ciphertexts. To produce a semi-functional ciphertext for an LSSS matrix (A, ρ) of size $l \times m$, one first calls the normal encryption algorithm to produce a normal ciphertext consisting of $\langle (A, \rho), (R_i, R_i', Q_i, Q_i', Q_i'', T_i)_{i=1}^n, (C_j, C_j')_{j=1}^n, (P_k)_{k=0}^l \rangle$. One then chooses random values $\pi_3, \xi_{k,3}(1 \le k \le l) \in \mathbb{Z}_p$ and a random vector $u_3 \in \mathbb{Z}_p^m$ with first entry equal to π_3. The semi-functional ciphertext is:

$$\langle (A, \rho), (R_i, R_i', Q_i, Q_i'h^{\pi_3 b_3}, Q_i'', T_i)_{i=1}^n, (C_j, C_j')_{j=1}^n,$$
$$P_0 h^{\pi_3 b_{0,3}}, (P_k h^{(A_k \cdot u_3 + \xi_{k,3})b_{\rho(k),5} - \xi_{k,3}b_{\rho(k),6}})_{k=1}^l \rangle.$$

Our proof is obtained via a hybrid argument over a sequence of games:

Game_{real}: The real message-hiding game $\mathsf{Game}^{\mathsf{A}}_{\mathsf{MH}_1}$ as defined in the Sect. 2.1.

Game_t $(0 \le t \le Q)$: Let Q denote the total number of key queries that the attacker makes. For each t from 0 to Q, we define Game_t as follows: In Game_t, the ciphertext given to the attacker is semi-functional, as are the first t keys. The remaining keys are normal.

Game_{final}: In this game, all of the keys given to the attacker are semi-functional, and the ciphertext given to the attacker is a semi-functional encryption of a *random message*.

The outer structure of our hybrid argument will progress as shown in Fig. 1. First, we transition from Game_{real} to Game_0, then to Game_1, next to Game_2, and so on. We ultimately arrive at Game_Q, where the ciphertext and all of the keys given to the attacker are semi-functional. We then transition to Game_{final}, which is defined to be like Game_Q, except that the ciphertext given to the attacker is a semi-functional encryption of a random message. This will complete our proof, since any attacker has a zero advantage in this final game.

The transitions from Game_{real} to Game_0 and from Game_Q to Game_{final} are relatively easy, and can be accomplished directly via computational assumptions. The transitions from Game_{t-1} to Game_t require more intricate arguments. For these steps, we will need to treat **Phase 1** key requests (before the challenge ciphertext) and **Phase 2** key requests (after the challenge ciphertext) differently. We will also need to define two additional types of semi-functional keys:

Nominal Semi-functional Keys. To produce a nominal semi-functional key for an attribute set S, one first calls the normal key generation algorithm to produce a normal key consisting of $K_{i,j}, K'_{i,j}, K''_{i,j}, K_{i,j,0}, \{K_{i,j,x}\}_{x \in S}$ with index (i,j). One then chooses random values $\sigma_{i,j,3}, \delta_{i,j,3} \in \mathbb{Z}_p$. The nominal semi-functional key is:

$$K_{i,j}h^{(\sigma_{i,j,3}+\delta_{i,j,3})b_3^*}, \quad K'_{i,j}g^{(\sigma_{i,j,3}+\delta_{i,j,3})b_3^*}, \quad K''_{i,j}g^{z_i(\sigma_{i,j,3}+\delta_{i,j,3})b_3^*},$$

$$K_{i,j,0}g^{\delta_{i,j,3}b_{0,3}^*}, \quad \{K_{i,j,x}g^{\sigma_{i,j,3}(b_{x,5}^*+b_{x,6}^*)}\}_{x \in S}.$$

We note that a nominal semi-functional key still correctly decrypts a semi-functional ciphertext.

Temporary Semi-functional Keys. A temporary semi-functional key is similar to a nominal semi-functional key, except that the semi-functional component attached to $K'_{i,j}$ will now be randomized (this will prevent correct decryption of a semi-functional ciphertext) and $K_{i,j}$ and $K''_{i,j}$ change accordingly. More formally, to produce a temporary semi-functional key for an attribute set S, one first calls the normal key generation algorithm to produce a normal key consisting of $K_{i,j}, K'_{i,j}, K''_{i,j}, K_{i,j,0}, \{K_{i,j,x}\}_{x \in S}$ with index (i,j). One then chooses random values $\sigma_{i,j,3}, \delta_{i,j,3}, \gamma \in \mathbb{Z}_p$. The temporary semi-functional key is formed as:

$$K_{i,j}h^{\gamma b_3^*}, \quad K'_{i,j}g^{\gamma b_3^*}, \quad K''_{i,j}g^{z_i\gamma b_3^*}, \quad K_{i,j,0}g^{\delta_{i,j,3}b_{0,3}^*}, \quad \{K_{i,j,x}g^{\sigma_{i,j,3}(b_{x,5}^*+b_{x,6}^*)}\}_{x \in S}.$$

For each t from 1 to Q, we define the following additional games:

Game_t^N: This is like Game_t, except that the tth key given to the attacker is a nominal semi-functional key. The first $t-1$ keys are still semi-functional in the original sense, while the remaining keys are normal.

Game_t^T: This is like Game_t, except that the tth key given to the attacker is a temporary semi-functional key. The first $t-1$ keys are still semi-functional in the original sense, while the remaining keys are normal.

In order to transition from Game_{t-1} to Game_t in our hybrid argument, we will transition first from Game_{t-1} to Game_t^N, then to Game_t^T, and finally to

Game_t. The transition from Game_t^N to Game_t^T will require different computational assumptions for Phase 1 and Phase 2 queries (As shown in Fig. 1, we use two lemmas based on different assumptions to obtain the transition).

As shown in Fig. 1, we use a series of lemmas, i.e. Lemmas 4, 5, 6, 7, 8, and 9, to prove the transitions. The details of these lemmas and their proofs can be found in the full version [16, Appendix C.1].

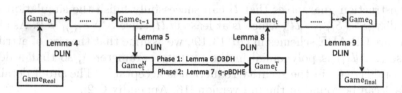

Fig. 1. Lemmas 4, 5, 8, and 9 rely on the subspace assumption, which is implied by the DLIN assumption, Lemma 6 relies on the D3DH assumption, and Lemma 7 relies on the source group q-parallel BDHE assumption.

Theorem 3. *No PPT adversary can win* $\mathsf{Game}_{\mathsf{MH}_{N+1}}^{\mathsf{A}}$ *with non-negligible advantage.*

Proof. The argument for security of $\mathsf{Game}_{\mathsf{MH}_{N+1}}^{\mathsf{A}}$ is very straightforward since an encryption to index $N+1 = (n+1, 1)$ contains no information about the message. The simulator simply runs actual $\mathsf{Setup}_{\mathsf{A}}$ and $\mathsf{KeyGen}_{\mathsf{A}}$ algorithms and encrypts the message M_b by the challenge access policy $\mathbb{A}$ and index $(n + 1, 1)$. Since for all $i = 1$ to n, the values of T_i contain no information about the message, the bit b is perfectly hidden and $\mathsf{MH}_{N+1}^{\mathsf{A}}\mathsf{Adv}_{\mathcal{A}} = 0$.

Theorem 4. *Suppose that the D3DH assumption and the DLIN assumption hold. Then no PPT adversary can win* $\mathsf{Game}_{\mathsf{IH}}^{\mathsf{A}}$ *with non-negligible advantage.*

Proof. Theorem 4 follows Lemmas 1 and 2 below.

Lemma 1. *Suppose that the D3DH assumption holds. Then for $\bar{j} < n$ no PPT adversary can distinguish between an encryption to $(\bar{i}, \bar{j})$ and $(\bar{i}, \bar{j}+1)$ in $\mathsf{Game}_{\mathsf{IH}}^{\mathsf{A}}$ with non-negligible advantage.*

Proof. In $\mathsf{Game}_{\mathsf{IH}}^{\mathsf{A}}$, the adversary $\mathcal{A}$ will behave in one of two different ways:

Case I: In Key Query phase, $\mathcal{A}$ will not submit $((\bar{i}, \bar{j}), S_{(\bar{i},\bar{j})})$ for some attribute set $S_{(\bar{i},\bar{j})}$ to query the corresponding private key. In Challenge phase, $\mathcal{A}$ submits a message M and a non-empty attribute set S^*. There is not any restriction on S^*.

Case II: In Key Query phase, $\mathcal{A}$ will submit $((\bar{i}, \bar{j}), S_{(\bar{i},\bar{j})})$ for some attribute set $S_{(\bar{i},\bar{j})}$ to query the corresponding private key. In Challenge phase, $\mathcal{A}$ submits a message M and a non-empty attribute set S^* with the restriction that the corresponding strictest access policy $\mathbb{A}_{S^*}$ is not satisfied by $S_{(\bar{i},\bar{j})}$ (i.e., $S^* \setminus S_{(\bar{i},\bar{j})} \neq \emptyset$).

The simulation for **Case I** is very similar to that of [5] because the simulator does not need to generate private key indexed $(\bar{i}, \bar{j})$ and there is not any restriction on the attribute set S^*. The **Case II** captures the security that even when a user has a key indexed $(\bar{i}, \bar{j})$ he cannot distinguish between an encryption to $(\mathbb{A}_{S^*}, (\bar{i}, \bar{j}))$ and one to $(\mathbb{A}_{S^*}, (\bar{i}, \bar{j}+1))$ if the corresponding attribute set $S_{(\bar{i}, \bar{j})}$ is not a superset of S^*. With the crucial components $\boldsymbol{Z}_i^{t_i}$ (in $\boldsymbol{Q}_i'$) and $\boldsymbol{Q}_i'' = g^{t_i(b_1+b_2)}$ in the ciphertext, and $\boldsymbol{Y}_j$ in the public parameter, our particular construction guarantees that $\mathcal{B}$ can successfully finish the simulation with probability $|S^* \setminus S_{(\bar{i}, \bar{j})}|/|\mathcal{U}|$, which is at least $1/|\mathcal{U}|$ since $S^* \setminus S_{(\bar{i}, \bar{j})} \neq \emptyset$. As of the fully secure CP-ABE schemes in [10–13,19], we assume that the size of attribute universe (i.e. $|\mathcal{U}|$) is polynomial in the security parameter λ, so that a degradation of $O(1/|\mathcal{U}|)$ in the security reduction is acceptable. The proof details of Lemma 1 can be found in the full version [16, Appendix C.2].

Lemma 2. *Suppose the D3DH assumption and the DLIN assumption hold. Then for any $1 \leq \bar{i} \leq n$ no PPT adversary can distinguish between an encryption to $(\bar{i}, n)$ and $(\bar{i}+1, 1)$ in $\mathsf{Game}_{\mathsf{IH}}^{\mathsf{A}}$ with non-negligible advantage.*

Proof. The proof of this lemma follows from a series of lemmas that establish the indistinguishability of the following games, where "less-than row" implies the corresponding $\boldsymbol{v}_i$ is randomly chosen from $\mathbb{Z}_p^3$ and T_i is a random element (i.e. $T_i = e(g,g)^{s_i}$), "target row" implies the corresponding $\boldsymbol{v}_i$ is randomly chosen from $\mathbb{Z}_p^3$ and T_i is well-formed, and "greater-than row" implies the corresponding $\boldsymbol{v}_i$ is randomly chosen from $span\{\chi_1, \chi_2\}$ and T_i is well-formed.

- H_1: Encrypt to column n, row $\bar{i}$ is the target row, row $\bar{i}+1$ is the greater-than row.
- H_2: Encrypt to column $n+1$, row $\bar{i}$ is the target row, row $\bar{i}+1$ is the greater-than row.
- H_3: Encrypt to column $n+1$, row $\bar{i}$ is the less-than row, row $\bar{i}+1$ is the greater-than row (no target row).
- H_4: Encrypt to column 1, row $\bar{i}$ is the less-than row, row $\bar{i}+1$ is the greater-than row (no target row).
- H_5: Encrypt to column 1, row $\bar{i}$ is the less-than row, row $\bar{i}+1$ is the target row.

It can be observed that game H_1 corresponds to the encryption being done to $(\bar{i}, n)$ and game H_5 corresponds to encryption to $(\bar{i}+1, 1)$. As shown in Fig. 2, we use a series of lemmas, i.e. Lemmas 10, 11, 12, and 13, to prove the indistinguishability of the games H_1 and H_5. The details of these lemmas and their proofs can be found in the full version [16, Appendix C.3].

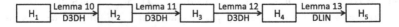

Fig. 2. Lemmas 10, 11, and 12 rely on the D3DH assumption, and Lemma 13 relies on the DLIN assumption.

4   Conclusion

In this paper, we proposed a new Augmented CP-ABE construction on prime order groups, and proved its message-hiding and index-hiding properties in the standard model. This implies the first CP-ABE that simultaneously achieves (1) fully collusion-resistant blackbox traceability in the standard model, (2) full security in the standard model, and (3) on prime order groups. The scheme is highly expressive in supporting any monotonic access structures, and as a fully collusion-resistant blackbox traceable CP-ABE scheme, it achieves the most efficient level to date, with the overhead in $O(\sqrt{N})$ only.

References

1. Bethencourt, J., Sahai, A., Waters, B.: Ciphertext-policy attribute-based encryption. In: IEEE Symposium on Security and Privacy, pp. 321–334 (2007)
2. Cheung, L., Newport, C.C.: Provably secure ciphertext policy ABE. In: ACM Conference on Computer and Communications Security, pp. 456–465 (2007)
3. Deng, H., Wu, Q., Qin, B., Mao, J., Liu, X., Zhang, L., Shi, W.: Who is touching my cloud. In: Kutyłowski, M., Vaidya, J. (eds.) ICAIS 2014, Part I. LNCS, vol. 8712, pp. 362–379. Springer, Heidelberg (2014)
4. Freeman, D.M.: Converting pairing-based cryptosystems from composite-order groups to prime-order groups. In: Gilbert, H. (ed.) EUROCRYPT 2010. LNCS, vol. 6110, pp. 44–61. Springer, Heidelberg (2010)
5. Garg, S., Kumarasubramanian, A., Sahai, A., Waters, B.: Building efficient fully collusion-resilient traitor tracing and revocation schemes. In: ACM Conference on Computer and Communications Security, pp. 121–130 (2010)
6. Goyal, V., Jain, A., Pandey, O., Sahai, A.: Bounded ciphertext policy attribute based encryption. In: Aceto, L., Damgård, I., Goldberg, L.A., Halldórsson, M.M., Ingólfsdóttir, A., Walukiewicz, I. (eds.) ICALP 2008, Part II. LNCS, vol. 5126, pp. 579–591. Springer, Heidelberg (2008)
7. Goyal, V., Pandey, O., Sahai, A., Waters, B.: Attribute-based encryption for fine-grained access control of encrypted data. In: ACM Conference on Computer and Communications Security, pp. 89–98 (2006)
8. Herranz, J., Laguillaumie, F., Ràfols, C.: Constant size ciphertexts in threshold attribute-based encryption. In: Nguyen, P.Q., Pointcheval, D. (eds.) PKC 2010. LNCS, vol. 6056, pp. 19–34. Springer, Heidelberg (2010)
9. Lewko, A.B.: Tools for simulating features of composite order bilinear groups in the prime order setting. In: Pointcheval, D., Johansson, T. (eds.) EUROCRYPT 2012. LNCS, vol. 7237, pp. 318–335. Springer, Heidelberg (2012)
10. Lewko, A.B., Okamoto, T., Sahai, A., Takashima, K., Waters, B.: Fully secure functional encryption: attribute-based encryption and (hierarchical) inner product encryption. In: Gilbert, H. (ed.) EUROCRYPT 2010. LNCS, vol. 6110, pp. 62–91. Springer, Heidelberg (2010)
11. Lewko, A.B., Waters, B.: New proof methods for attribute-based encryption: achieving full security through selective techniques. In: Safavi-Naini, R., Canetti, R. (eds.) CRYPTO 2012. LNCS, vol. 7417, pp. 180–198. Springer, Heidelberg (2012)
12. Lewko, A.B., Waters, B.: New proof methods for attribute-based encryption: achieving full security through selective techniques. IACR Cryptology ePrint Archive 2012: 326 (2012)

13. Liu, Z., Cao, Z., Wong, D.S.: Blackbox traceable CP-ABE: how to catch people leaking their keys by selling decryption devices on ebay. In: ACM Conference on Computer and Communications Security, pp. 475–486 (2013)
14. Liu, Z., Cao, Z., Wong, D.S.: White-box traceable ciphertext-policy attribute-based encryption supporting any monotone access structures. IEEE Trans. Inf. Forensics Secur. 8(1), 76–88 (2013)
15. Liu, Z., Wong, D.S.: Practical attribute based encryption: Traitor tracing, revocation, and large universe. IACR Cryptology ePrint Archive, 2014:616 (2014)
16. Liu, Z., Wong, D.S.: Traceable CP-ABE on prime order groups: Fully secure and fully collusion-resistant blackbox traceable. IACR Cryptology ePrint Archive 2015:850 (2015)
17. Okamoto, T., Takashima, K.: Homomorphic encryption and signatures from vector decomposition. In: Galbraith, S.D., Paterson, K.G. (eds.) Pairing 2008. LNCS, vol. 5209, pp. 57–74. Springer, Heidelberg (2008)
18. Okamoto, T., Takashima, K.: Hierarchical predicate encryption for inner-products. In: Matsui, M. (ed.) ASIACRYPT 2009. LNCS, vol. 5912, pp. 214–231. Springer, Heidelberg (2009)
19. Okamoto, T., Takashima, K.: Fully secure functional encryption with general relations from the decisional linear assumption. In: Rabin, T. (ed.) CRYPTO 2010. LNCS, vol. 6223, pp. 191–208. Springer, Heidelberg (2010)
20. Rouselakis, Y., Waters, B.: Practical constructions and new proof methods for large universe attribute-based encryption. In: ACM Conference on Computer and Communications Security, pp. 463–474 (2013)
21. Waters, B.: Ciphertext-policy attribute-based encryption: an expressive, efficient, and provably secure realization. In: Catalano, D., Fazio, N., Gennaro, R., Nicolosi, A. (eds.) PKC 2011. LNCS, vol. 6571, pp. 53–70. Springer, Heidelberg (2011)

Generic Construction of Audit Logging Schemes with Forward Privacy and Authenticity

Shoichi Hirose[1](✉)

Graduate School of Engineering, University of Fukui, Fukui, Japan
hrs_shch@u-fukui.ac.jp

Abstract. In this paper, audit logging schemes with forward privacy and authenticity are formalized in the symmetric-key setting. Then, two generic audit logging schemes with forward privacy and authenticity are proposed. One consists of an authenticated encryption scheme with associated data. The other consists of a symmetric encryption scheme and a MAC function. Both of them also uses a forward-secure pseudorandom generator to achieve forward security. Finally, the forward privacy and authenticity of the schemes are confirmed in the manner of provable security. The security properties of the proposed schemes are reduced to the standard security properties of the underlying primitives.

Keywords: Audit logging · Forward security · Privacy · Authenticity

1 Introduction

Background and Our Motivation. Audit logging is an important technique to secure the systems. Audit logs record the events on systems to give a view of system activities. Any tampering with records including deletion and reordering should at least be detectable. Audit logs may contain sensitive information to be kept secret from attackers. Cryptographic techniques are useful to guarantee such authenticity and privacy of log files. Once an attacker gets the key, however, he can tamper with the records or decrypt the ciphertexts of sensitive information. To thwart these attacks, forward security is often incorporated in secure audit logging schemes [5,12,18].

Forward security prevents attackers having got the current key, for example, by intrusion from tampering with records or decrypting ciphertexts generated in the past by updating keys. Two settings for updating keys are found in literature of secure audit logging. We will call them time-driven setting and event-driven setting. In the time-driven setting, the time is divided into intervals, and secret keys are updated at the end of every interval. Thus, multiple records may be generated with the same key assigned to an interval. In the event-driven setting, on the other hand, secret keys are updated after every event. Each record is generated with a new secret key.

In spite of the importance of forward-secure audit logging with privacy and authenticity, it has not been provided formal treatment and its security has been discussed informally.

© Springer International Publishing Switzerland 2016
S. Qing et al. (Eds.): ICICS 2015, LNCS 9543, pp. 125–140, 2016.
DOI: 10.1007/978-3-319-29814-6_11

Our Contribution. First, audit logging schemes and their security are formally defined in the symmetric-key setting. The security properties are called forward privacy and forward authenticity. Then, two generic constructions of audit logging schemes with forward privacy and authenticity are presented. One assumes the time-driven setting and is constructed with an AEAD (authenticated encryption with associated data) scheme. The other assumes the event-driven setting and is constructed with a symmetric-key encryption scheme and a MAC function. For the first scheme, as far as the authors know, application of AEAD to secure audit logging has not been discussed before. Both schemes also use a forward-secure pseudorandom generator to get forward security. Finally, it is shown that the proposed schemes are provably secure. The forward privacy and authenticity of the proposed schemes are reduced to the standard security properties of their components.

Related Work. Schneier and Kelsey [18,19] proposed a forward-secure audit logging scheme with privacy and authenticity in the symmetric-key setting. Actually, they also considered a communication protocol between an untrusted machine creating its log files and a trusted machine which stores log files. We will focus on the creation of log files in this paper.

Forward security was first introduced for key exchange protocols [10]. Bellare and Yee [6] formalized forward-secure symmetric-key primitives and their security notions. They treated pseudorandom generators, message authentication schemes, and encryption schemes. They also provided their generic constructions and discussed their security.

Audit logging schemes with authenticity can also be found in literature. Bellare and Yee [5] initiated the study to secure audit logging with cryptographic techniques. Ma and Tsudik [12] introduced the notion of forward-secure sequential aggregate message authentication, which can be used for audit logging with authenticity [13]. They also presented a scheme using a collision-resistant hash function as well as a MAC function. Hirose and Kuwakado [11] formalized the notion and proposed a provably secure scheme without a collision-resistant hash function.

Among the audit logging schemes mentioned above, the Bellare-Yee scheme [5] and the Hirose-Kuwakado scheme [11] assume the time-driven setting for key update. The Schneier-Kelsey scheme [18,19] and the Ma-Tsudik scheme [13], on the other hand, assume the event-driven setting.

Accorsi [1] made a brief survey of secure logging schemes. It also includes the schemes in the public-key setting, which are out of scope of the paper.

Recently, due to the CAESAR project [8], authenticated encryption has been attracting much interest. AEAD is formalized in [15]. Generic composition of an encryption scheme and a MAC function for AEAD is discussed in [3,14].

Waters et al. [20] presented a scheme to construct encrypted audit log searchable with keywords in the public-key setting.

Organization. Section 2 gives notations and definitions of cryptographic primitives used in the proposed schemes. Section 3 presents definitions of audit logging schemes and their forward privacy and authenticity. Section 4 describes the proposed generic constructions. Section 5 shows that the generic constructions are secure if their components are secure. Section 6 concludes the paper.

2 Preliminaries

Notation. For sequences x and y, $x\|y$ represents their concatenation. An empty sequence is denoted by ε.

Let $\boldsymbol{F}(\mathcal{X}, \mathcal{Y})$ be the set of all functions with domain $\mathcal{X}$ and range $\mathcal{Y}$. For keyed function $F : \mathcal{K} \times \mathcal{X} \to \mathcal{Y}$ with key space $\mathcal{K}$, $F(K, \cdot)$ is often denoted by $F_K(\cdot)$.

For set S, let $s \leftarrow S$ denote that an element s is chosen uniformly at random from S. For a pair of elements e_1 and e_2 of a totally ordered set, let $[e_1, e_2] = \{e \mid e_1 \leq e \leq e_2\}$. If e_1 and e_2 are integers, then $[e_1, e_2]$ represents the set of integers from e_1 to e_2 inclusive.

Pseudorandom Generator. A pseudorandom generator (PRG) [7] is a function with its range larger than its domain. Let $G : \mathcal{S} \to \mathcal{S}'$ such that $|\mathcal{S}'| > |\mathcal{S}|$. G is called PRG if it is intractable to distinguish $G(S)$ with $S \leftarrow \mathcal{S}$ and $S' \leftarrow \mathcal{S}'$.

Adversary A against G takes an element of $\mathcal{S}'$ and outputs 0 or 1. The advantage of A is defined by

$$\mathrm{Adv}_G^{\mathrm{prg}}(\mathsf{A}) = \Big| \Pr[\mathsf{A}(G(S)) \Rightarrow 1] - \Pr[\mathsf{A}(S') \Rightarrow 1] \Big|,$$

where $S \leftarrow \mathcal{S}$ and $S' \leftarrow \mathcal{S}'$.

Pseudorandom Function. A pseudorandom function (PRF) [9] is a keyed function. $F : \mathcal{K} \times \mathcal{X} \to \mathcal{Y}$ is called PRF if it is intractable to distinguish F_K with $K \leftarrow \mathcal{K}$ and a function chosen uniformly at random from $\boldsymbol{F}(\mathcal{X}, \mathcal{Y})$.

Adversary A against F is given a function in $\boldsymbol{F}(\mathcal{X}, \mathcal{Y})$ as an oracle. A makes adaptive queries to the oracle, and then outputs 0 or 1. The advantage of A is defined by

$$\mathrm{Adv}_F^{\mathrm{prf}}(\mathsf{A}) = \Big| \Pr\left[\mathsf{A}^{F_K} \Rightarrow 1\right] - \Pr\left[\mathsf{A}^{\rho} \Rightarrow 1\right] \Big|,$$

where $K \leftarrow \mathcal{K}$ and $\rho \leftarrow \boldsymbol{F}(\mathcal{X}, \mathcal{Y})$.

The definition can be extended to adversaries with independent multiple oracles:

$$\mathrm{Adv}_F^{m\text{-}\mathrm{prf}}(\mathsf{A}) = \Big| \Pr\left[\mathsf{A}^{F_{K_1}, \dots, F_{K_m}} \Rightarrow 1\right] - \Pr\left[\mathsf{A}^{\rho_1, \dots, \rho_m} \Rightarrow 1\right] \Big|,$$

where $(K_1, K_2, \dots, K_m) \leftarrow \mathcal{K}^m$ and $(\rho_1, \rho_2, \dots, \rho_m) \leftarrow \boldsymbol{F}(\mathcal{X}, \mathcal{Y})^m$.

Theorem 1 [2]. *For any adversary* A *against* F *with access to* m *oracles, there exists an adversary* A' *against* F *with access to a single oracle such that*

$$\mathrm{Adv}_F^{m\text{-}\mathrm{prf}}(\mathsf{A}) - m \cdot \mathrm{Adv}_F^{\mathrm{prf}}(\mathsf{A}').$$

The run time of A′ *is not larger than the sum of the run time of* A *and the time to compute F for the queries by* A. *The number of the queries by* A′ *is not larger than* $\max\{q_i \mid 1 \leq i \leq m\}$, *where* q_i *is the number of the queries by* A *to its i-th oracle.*

Rogaway and Shrimpton [17] introduced a vector-input PRF. It is a PRF which takes as input a vector of strings as well as a key. They also showed how to construct a vector-input PRF from a regular PRF which takes as input a string as well as a key.

Forward-Secure Pseudorandom Generator. A forward-secure pseudorandom generator (FSPRG) [6] is a stateful generator. A stateful generator is defined by $\mathsf{Gen} = (G, n)$, where $G : \mathcal{S} \rightarrow \mathcal{K} \times \mathcal{S}$ such that $(K_i, S_{i+1}) \leftarrow G(S_i)$ for $1 \leq i \leq n$ and $S_1 \in \mathcal{S}$. It is depicted in Fig. 1.

The security of an FSPRG is formalized as indistinguishability against adaptive attacks with experiment $\mathsf{Exp}_{\mathsf{Gen},\mathsf{A}}^{\mathsf{fsprg}\text{-}b}$ given in Fig. 2. Adversary A works in two phases. First, in the query phase, A gets $K_1, K_2, \ldots, K_{i'}$ for some $i' \leq n$ chosen by A. $K_1, K_2, \ldots, K_{i'}$ are generated by G if $b = 0$, and chosen uniformly at random if $b = 1$. Then, in the try phase, A receives $S_{i'+1}$ and outputs 0 or 1. The advantage of A against Gen is defined by

$$\mathsf{Adv}_{\mathsf{Gen}}^{\mathsf{fsprg}}(\mathsf{A}) = \left| \Pr\left[\mathsf{Exp}_{\mathsf{Gen},\mathsf{A}}^{\mathsf{fsprg}\text{-}0} \Rightarrow 1\right] - \Pr\left[\mathsf{Exp}_{\mathsf{Gen},\mathsf{A}}^{\mathsf{fsprg}\text{-}1} \Rightarrow 1\right] \right|.$$

The following theorem shows that Gen is an FSPRG if G is a PRG.

Theorem 2 [6]. *For any adversary* A *against* Gen, *there exists an adversary* A′ *against G such that*
$$\mathsf{Adv}_{\mathsf{Gen}}^{\mathsf{fsprg}}(\mathsf{A}) \leq 2n \cdot \mathsf{Adv}_G^{\mathsf{prg}}(\mathsf{A}')$$
and the run time of A′ *is about the run time of* $\mathsf{Exp}_{\mathsf{Gen},\mathsf{A}}^{\mathsf{fsprg}\text{-}1}$.

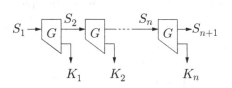

Fig. 1. $\mathsf{Gen} = (G, n)$

```
 1: i ← 1; his ← ε
 2: S₁ ← S
 3: repeat
 4:     (Kᵢ, Sᵢ₊₁) ← G(Sᵢ)
 5:     if b = 1 then
 6:         Kᵢ ← K
 7:     end if
 8:     (phase, his) ← A(query, Kᵢ, his)
 9:     i ← i + 1
10: until (phase = try) ∨ (i > n)
11: b′ ← A(try, Sᵢ, his)
12: return b′
```

Fig. 2. Experiment $\mathsf{Exp}_{\mathsf{Gen},\mathsf{A}}^{\mathsf{fsprg}\text{-}b}$ for $b \in \{0,1\}$

Symmetric-Key Encryption. A symmetric-key encryption scheme is defined by SE $= (E, D)$, where $E : \mathcal{K} \times \mathcal{M} \to \mathcal{C}$ is an encryption algorithm and $D : \mathcal{K} \times \mathcal{C} \to \mathcal{M} \cup \{\bot\}$ is a decryption algorithm. $\mathcal{K}$ is the key space, $\mathcal{M}$ is the message space and $\mathcal{C}$ is the ciphertext space. For any $K \in \mathcal{K}$, if $C \leftarrow E_K(M)$ for some $M \in \mathcal{M}$, then $M \leftarrow D_K(C)$. Otherwise, $\bot \leftarrow D_K(C)$.

The security requirement for a symmetric-key encryption scheme is privacy. It is indistinguishability of the outputs of E from sequences of the same lengths chosen uniformly at random. Adversary A is given either E_K or ϖ as an oracle and makes an adaptive chosen message attack. For any $M \in \mathcal{M}$, ϖ simply produces a sequence of the same lengths as the output of $E_K(M)$ chosen uniformly at random. The advantage of A against SE is defined by

$$\mathrm{Adv}_{\mathsf{SE}}^{\mathrm{priv}}(\mathsf{A}) = \left| \Pr\left[\mathsf{A}^{E_K} \Rightarrow 1\right] - \Pr\left[\mathsf{A}^{\varpi} \Rightarrow 1\right]\right|,$$

where $K \leftarrow \mathcal{K}$.

Authenticated Encryption with Associated Data. We will define nonce-based authenticated encryption with associated data (AEAD) [15,16]. An AEAD scheme is defined by AEAD $=$ (en, de). en $: \mathcal{K} \times \mathcal{N} \times \mathcal{A} \times \mathcal{M} \to \mathcal{C} \times \mathcal{T}$ is an encryption algorithm and de $: \mathcal{K} \times \mathcal{N} \times \mathcal{A} \times \mathcal{C} \times \mathcal{T} \to \mathcal{M} \cup \{\bot\}$ is a decryption algorithm. $\mathcal{K}$ is the key space, $\mathcal{N}$ is the nonce space, $\mathcal{A}$ is the associated-data space, $\mathcal{M}$ is the message space, $\mathcal{C}$ is the ciphertext space, and $\mathcal{T}$ is the tag space. For any $K \in \mathcal{K}$, if $(C, T) \leftarrow \mathsf{en}_K(N, A, M)$ for some $(N, A, M) \in \mathcal{N} \times \mathcal{A} \times \mathcal{M}$, then $M \leftarrow \mathsf{de}_K(N, A, C, T)$. Otherwise, $\bot \leftarrow \mathsf{de}_K(N, A, C, T)$. The security requirements for AEAD is privacy and authenticity. Messages require both privacy and authenticity, while associated data require only authenticity.

The privacy of AEAD is indistinguishability of the outputs of en from sequences of the same lengths chosen uniformly at random. Adversary A is given either en_K or \$ as an oracle and makes an adaptive chosen message attack. For any $(N, A, M) \in \mathcal{N} \times \mathcal{A} \times \mathcal{M}$, \$ simply produces a sequence of the same lengths as the output of $\mathsf{en}_K(N, A, M)$ chosen uniformly at random. The advantage of A against AEAD with respect to privacy is defined by

$$\mathrm{Adv}_{\mathsf{AEAD}}^{\mathrm{priv}}(\mathsf{A}) = \left| \Pr\left[\mathsf{A}^{\mathsf{en}_K} \Rightarrow 1\right] - \Pr\left[\mathsf{A}^{\$} \Rightarrow 1\right]\right|,$$

where $K \leftarrow \mathcal{K}$.

The authenticity of AEAD is formalized by existential unforgeability. Adversary A is given oracle access to en_K and de_K. A is not allowed to use the same sequence for nonce in distinct queries to en_K, nor to ask any reply from en_K to de_K. We say that $\mathsf{A}^{\mathsf{en}_K, \mathsf{de}_K}$ forges if $\mathsf{A}^{\mathsf{en}_K, \mathsf{de}_K}$ asks a query to de_K such that the corresponding reply is not $\bot$. The advantage of A against AEAD with respect to authenticity is defined by

$$\mathrm{Adv}_{\mathsf{AEAD}}^{\mathrm{auth}}(\mathsf{A}) = \Pr\left[\mathsf{A}^{\mathsf{en}_K, \mathsf{de}_K} \text{ forges}\right],$$

where $K \leftarrow \mathcal{K}$.

3   Audit Logging Scheme with Privacy and Authenticity

3.1   Scheme

An audit logging scheme is a stateful scheme defined by $\mathsf{ALG} = (\mathsf{U}, \mathsf{E}, \mathsf{D}, n)$, where $\mathsf{U} : \mathcal{S} \to \mathcal{K} \times \mathcal{S}$ is a key-update algorithm, $\mathsf{E} : \mathcal{K} \times \mathcal{T} \times \mathcal{A} \times \mathcal{M} \to \mathcal{C} \times \mathcal{T}$ is an encryption algorithm, $\mathsf{D} : \mathcal{K}^+ \times \mathcal{T} \times (\mathcal{A} \times \mathcal{C} \times \mathcal{T})^+ \to \mathcal{M}^+ \cup \{\bot\}$ is a decryption algorithm, and n is the number of the stages. The algorithms are described below.

Key Update $(K_i, S_{i+1}) \leftarrow \mathsf{U}(S_i)$ for $1 \leq i \leq n$, where $S_1 \leftarrow \mathcal{S}$.
The key-update algorithm takes as input the secret master key S_i for the i-th stage. It then outputs the secret key K_i for the current stage and the new secret master key S_{i+1} for the next stage.

Encryption $(C_{i,j}, \tau_{i,j}) \leftarrow \mathsf{E}(K_i, \tau_{i,j-1}, A_{i,j}, M_{i,j})$ for $1 \leq i \leq n$ and $j \geq 1$.
In the i-th stage, the encryption algorithm takes encryption key K_i, previous tag $\tau_{i,j-1}$, associated data $A_{i,j}$ and message $M_{i,j}$ as input. $\tau_{i,0}$ is an initial state of the i-th stage. It then outputs ciphertext $C_{i,j}$ for $M_{i,j}$, and tag $\tau_{i,j}$ for $(A_{i,j}, M_{i,j})$. $(A_{i,j}, M_{i,j})$ is called an event. $(A_{i,j}, C_{i,j}, \tau_{i,j})$ is called a record.

Decryption Let $\boldsymbol{R} = (\boldsymbol{R}_1, \boldsymbol{R}_2, \ldots, \boldsymbol{R}_n)$ be the ordered sequence of the records, where $\boldsymbol{R}_i = (R_{i,1}, R_{i,2}, \ldots, R_{i,\sigma_i})$ and $R_{i,j} = (A_{i,j}, C_{i,j}, \tau_{i,j})$ for $1 \leq i \leq n$ and $1 \leq j \leq \sigma_i$. σ_i is the total number of the records in the i-th stage. For $1 \leq i \leq n$ and $1 \leq j \leq \sigma_i$, let (i, j) be a pair of integers such that $(i, j) \leq (i', j')$ if and only if $i < i'$, or $i = i'$ and $j \leq j'$. The decryption algorithm is defined as follows:

$$\alpha \leftarrow \mathsf{D}(\boldsymbol{K}_{[i_1, i_2]}, \tau_{i_1, j_1 - 1}, \boldsymbol{R}_{[(i_1, j_1), (i_2, j_2)]}),$$

where $(1, 1) \leq (i_1, j_1) \leq (i_2, j_2) \leq (n, \sigma_n)$, $\boldsymbol{K}_{[i_1, i_2]}$ is the subsequence of $K_1, K_2, \ldots, K_n$ from K_{i_1} to K_{i_2} inclusive, and $\boldsymbol{R}_{[(i_1, j_1), (i_2, j_2)]}$ is the subsequence of $\boldsymbol{R}$ from the (i_1, j_1)-th record to the (i_2, j_2)-th record inclusive. D outputs $M_{i_1, j_1}, \ldots, M_{i_2, j_2}$ if $\boldsymbol{R}_{[(i_1, j_1), (i_2, j_2)]}$ is valid with respect to $\tau_{i_1, j_1 - 1}$. Otherwise, it outputs $\bot$.

We consider two kinds of settings for key update: time-driven setting and event-driven setting. In the time-driven setting, time is divided into intervals, and the key is updated at the end of each interval. In the event-driven setting, on the other hand, the key is updated after every event. A stage corresponds to an interval in the time-driven setting and to an event in the event-driven setting.

For event $(A_{i,j}, M_{i,j})$, it is assumed that $A_{i,j}$ includes the index i of the current stage. For the time-driven setting, it is assumed that $A_{i,j}$ also includes a flag representing whether the event is the last one in the i-th stage or not. The flag is a countermeasure against truncation attacks [5,13]. A truncation attack simply deletes the tail of a sequence of records and the corresponding tags. Thus, it cannot be detected without any kind of end-marker such as the flag assumed in the scheme.

3.2 Security

The forward privacy and authenticity of $\mathsf{ALG} = (\mathsf{U}, \mathsf{E}, \mathsf{D}, n)$ is defined below. Each of them is defined by an experiment with an adversary. The adversary works in two phases: The first phase is the query phase, and the second phase is the try phase.

Forward Privacy. The forward privacy of ALG is indistinguishability of a ciphertext and a tag in each record from a sequence of the same length chosen uniformly at random. Let $\mathbf{Exp}_{\mathsf{ALG},\mathsf{A}}^{\mathrm{fpriv}\text{-}b}$ be the experiment given in Fig. 3. In the query phase, adversary A makes adaptive queries to its oracle. A should respect the state: A should ask a new query involving the current state (the previous tag). The oracle is either E_{K_i} or $\$_i$. K_i is chosen uniformly at random from $\mathcal{K}$. For each query, $\$_i$ returns a uniformly distributed random sequence of the same length as the sequence returned by E_{K_i}. A is allowed to decide when to break into the system. In the time-driven setting, A is also allowed to control when to proceed to the next stage. If A decides to break into the system during the a-th stage, then A enters into the try phase. In this phase, A receives S_{a+1} and outputs 0 or 1. The advantage of A against ALG with respect to forward privacy is defined by

$$\mathrm{Adv}_{\mathsf{ALG}}^{\mathrm{fpriv}}(\mathsf{A}) = \left| \Pr\left[\mathbf{Exp}_{\mathsf{ALG},\mathsf{A}}^{\mathrm{fpriv}\text{-}0} \Rightarrow 1\right] - \Pr\left[\mathbf{Exp}_{\mathsf{ALG},\mathsf{A}}^{\mathrm{fpriv}\text{-}1} \Rightarrow 1\right] \right|.$$

Forward Authenticity. The forward authenticity of ALG is existential unforgeability against adaptive attacks. Let $\mathbf{Exp}_{\mathsf{ALG},\mathsf{A}}^{\mathrm{fauth}}$ be the experiment given in Fig. 4. In the query phase, A makes adaptive queries to E_{K_i}. A should respect the state. A is allowed to decide when to break into the system. In the time-driven setting, A is also allowed to decide when to proceed to the next stages. If A decides to break into the system during the a-th stage, then A receives S_{a+1} and enters into the try phase. In this phase, A tries to forge. Let $\boldsymbol{R} = (\boldsymbol{R}_1, \boldsymbol{R}_2, \ldots, \boldsymbol{R}_a)$ be the ordered sequence of records obtained in the query phase. For $1 \leq i_1 \leq i_2 \leq a$, let $V(\boldsymbol{R}, i_1, i_2)$ be the set of $(\tau_{i_1, u_1 - 1}, \boldsymbol{R}_{[(i_1, u_1),(i_2, u_2)]})$ such that $1 \leq u_1 \leq \sigma_{i_1}$ and $1 \leq u_2 \leq \sigma_{i_2}$ if $i_1 < i_2$, and $1 \leq u_1 \leq u_2 \leq \sigma_{i_1}$ if $i_1 = i_2$. The forgery $(\tau'_{i_1, j_1 - 1}, \boldsymbol{R}'_{[(i_1, j_1),(i_2, j_2)]})$ is successful if

- $1 \leq i_1 \leq i_2 \leq a$, $(\tau'_{i_1, j_1 - 1}, \boldsymbol{R}'_{[(i_1, j_1),(i_2, j_2)]}) \notin V(\boldsymbol{R}, i_1, i_2)$, and
- the output of $\mathsf{D}(\boldsymbol{K}_{[i_1, i_2]}, \tau'_{i_1, j_1 - 1}, \boldsymbol{R}'_{[(i_1, j_1),(i_2, j_2)]})$ is not $\perp$.

The advantage of A against ALG with respect to authenticity is defined by

$$\mathrm{Adv}_{\mathsf{ALG}}^{\mathrm{fauth}}(\mathsf{A}) = \Pr\left[\mathbf{Exp}_{\mathsf{ALG},\mathsf{A}}^{\mathrm{fauth}} \Rightarrow 1\right].$$

4   Generic Construction

For each of the time-driven setting and the event-driven setting, an audit logging scheme with forward privacy and authenticity is proposed. The FSPRG Gen with PRG $G : \mathcal{S} \to \mathcal{K} \times \mathcal{S}$ is used for key update in both of the settings.

1: $i \leftarrow 1$; $his \leftarrow \varepsilon$
2: $S_1 \twoheadleftarrow \mathcal{S}$
3: **repeat**
4:     $(K_i, S_{i+1}) \leftarrow \mathsf{U}(S_i)$
5:     $(phase, his) \leftarrow \mathsf{A}^{\mathcal{O}_i^b}(\mathbf{query}, his)$
6:     $i \leftarrow i+1$
7: **until** $(phase = \mathbf{try}) \vee (i > n)$
8: $b' \leftarrow \mathsf{A}(\mathbf{try}, S_i, his)$
9: **return** b'

1: $i \leftarrow 1$; $his \leftarrow \varepsilon$
2: $S_1 \twoheadleftarrow \mathcal{S}$
3: **repeat**
4:     $(K_i, S_{i+1}) \leftarrow \mathsf{U}(S_i)$
5:     $(phase, his) \leftarrow \mathsf{A}^{\mathsf{E}_{K_i}}(\mathbf{query}, his)$
6:     $i \leftarrow i+1$
7: **until** $(phase = \mathbf{try}) \vee (i > n)$
8: $forgery \leftarrow \mathsf{A}(\mathbf{try}, S_i, his)$
9: **if** $forgery$ is successful **then**
10:     $d \leftarrow 1$
11: **else**
12:     $d \leftarrow 0$
13: **end if**
14: **return** d

Fig. 3. Experiment $\mathbf{Exp}_{\mathsf{ALG,A}}^{\text{fpriv-}b}$ for $b \in \{0,1\}$. $\mathcal{O}_i^0 = \mathsf{E}_{K_i}$ and $\mathcal{O}_i^1 = \$_i$.

Fig. 4. Experiment $\mathbf{Exp}_{\mathsf{ALG,A}}^{\text{fauth}}$. $forgery = (\tau'_{i_1,j_1-1}, \boldsymbol{R}'_{[(i_1,j_1),(i_2,j_2)]})$.

4.1 Time-Driven Setting

An audit logging scheme in the time-driven setting is composed with an AEAD scheme $\mathsf{AEAD} = (\mathsf{en}, \mathsf{de})$ and the FSPRG $\mathsf{Gen} = (G, n)$. It is called tALG. tALG requires some injective encoding from the tag space to the nonce space of AEAD. In the following, it is assumed for the simplicity of the description that the tag space is included in the nonce space.

Key update $(K_i, S_{i+1}) \leftarrow G(S_i)$ for $1 \leq i \leq n$.
Encryption $(C_{i,j}, \tau_{i,j}) \leftarrow \mathsf{en}_{K_i}(\tau_{i,j-1}, A_{i,j}, M_{i,j})$ for $1 \leq i \leq n$ and $1 \leq j \leq \sigma_i$, where σ_i is the total number of the events in the i-th stage, $\tau_{1,0}$ is an initial constant, and $\tau_{i,0} = \tau_{i-1,\sigma_{i-1}}$ for $i \geq 2$.
Decryption For $(\tau_{i_1,j_1-1}, \boldsymbol{R}_{[(i_1,j_1),(i_2,j_2)]})$, if $\mathsf{de}_{K_i}(\tau_{i,j-1}, A_{i,j}, C_{i,j}, \tau_{i,j}) \neq \bot$ for all $(i,j) \in [(i_1,j_1),(i_2,j_2)]$, then output $\mathsf{de}_{K_i}(\tau_{i,j-1}, A_{i,j}, C_{i,j}, \tau_{i,j})$ for all $(i,j) \in [(i_1,j_1),(i_2,j_2)]$. Otherwise, it outputs $\bot$.

Figure 5 depicts the encryption procedure for a sequence of events.

4.2 Event-Driven Setting

Let $\mathsf{SE} = (E, D)$ be an encryption scheme such that $E : \mathcal{K}_\mathsf{e} \times \mathcal{M} \to \mathcal{C}$ and $D : \mathcal{K}_\mathsf{e} \times \mathcal{C} \to \mathcal{M}$. Let $F : \mathcal{K}_\mathsf{t} \times (\mathcal{T} \times \mathcal{A} \times \mathcal{C}) \to \mathcal{T}$ be a vector-input PRF. For $\mathsf{Gen} = (G, n)$ with $G : \mathcal{S} \to \mathcal{K} \times \mathcal{S}$, let $\mathcal{K} = \mathcal{K}_\mathsf{e} \times \mathcal{K}_\mathsf{t}$.

An audit logging scheme in the event-driven setting is composed with SE, F and Gen. It is an Encrypt-then-MAC scheme [3,4,14]. It is called eALG. In this setting, only a single record is generated in each stage. Thus, in the following description, the index (i,j) of an event or a record is simply replaced with i.

Key update $(K_i, L_i, S_{i+1}) \leftarrow G(S_i)$ for $1 \leq i \leq n$.

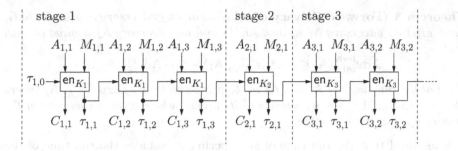

Fig. 5. Encryption of the generic scheme in the time-driven setting

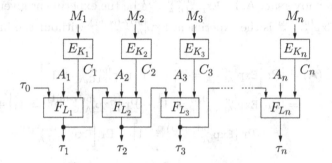

Fig. 6. Encryption of the generic scheme in the event-driven setting

Encryption For a new event (A_i, M_i), $C_i \leftarrow E_{K_i}(M_i)$ and $\tau_i \leftarrow F_{L_i}(\tau_{i-1}, A_i, C_i)$, where $1 \le i \le n$ and τ_0 is an initial constant.

Decryption For $(\tau_{i_1-1}, \boldsymbol{R}_{[i_1, i_2]})$, compute $\tau_i' \leftarrow F_{L_i}(\tau_{i-1}, A_i, C_i)$ for $i_1 \le i \le i_2$. If $\tau_{i_2}' = \tau_{i_2}$, then return $M_i \leftarrow D_{K_i}(C_i)$ for $i_1 \le i \le i_2$. Otherwise, return $\perp$.

Figure 6 depicts the encryption procedure for a sequence of events.

Remark 1. The decryption algorithm only checks the validity of the final tag τ_{i_2}. It does not check the validity of intermediate tags. This allows eALG aggregation of the tags.

5   Provable Security of Generic Construction

The forward privacy and authenticity of the proposed schemes are analyzed in the manner of provable security.

5.1   Time-Driven Setting

The following theorem asserts that tALG satisfies forward privacy if the underlying AEAD scheme satisfies privacy and the function G is a PRG:

Theorem 3 (Forward Privacy of tALG). *For any adversary* A *against* tALG, *there exist an adversary* A_1 *against* AEAD *and an adversary* A_2 *against* G *such that*

$$\text{Adv}_{\text{tALG}}^{\text{fpriv}}(A) \leq n \cdot \text{Adv}_{\text{AEAD}}^{\text{priv}}(A_1) + 2n \cdot \text{Adv}_{G}^{\text{prg}}(A_2).$$

Each of the run times of A_1 *and* A_2 *is about the run time of* $\text{Exp}_{\text{tALG,A}}^{\text{fpriv-0}}$. A_1 *makes at most* $\max\{q_i \,|\, 1 \leq i \leq n\}$ *queries to its oracle, where* q_i *is the number of the queries by* A *in the* i-*th stage.*

It is assumed that the run time of an experiment includes the run time of the adversary and the time required when the oracles of the adversary are simulated.

Proof. For any adversary A, let $\text{Exp}_{\text{tALG,A}}^{\text{fpriv-}(b_0,b_1)}$ be the experiment given in Fig. 7. Notice that $\text{Exp}_{\text{tALG,A}}^{\text{fpriv-}b_0}$ is the experiment $\text{Exp}_{\text{tALG,A}}^{\text{fpriv-}(b_0,b_1)}$ without the lines from 5 to 7. Then,

$$\begin{aligned}
\text{Adv}_{\text{tALG}}^{\text{fpriv}}(A) &= \left| \Pr\left[\text{Exp}_{\text{tALG,A}}^{\text{fpriv-0}} \Rightarrow 1\right] - \Pr\left[\text{Exp}_{\text{tALG,A}}^{\text{fpriv-1}} \Rightarrow 1\right] \right| \\
&= \left| \Pr\left[\text{Exp}_{\text{tALG,A}}^{\text{fpriv-}(0,0)} \Rightarrow 1\right] - \Pr\left[\text{Exp}_{\text{tALG,A}}^{\text{fpriv-}(0,1)} \Rightarrow 1\right] \right| + \\
&\quad \left| \Pr\left[\text{Exp}_{\text{tALG,A}}^{\text{fpriv-}(0,1)} \Rightarrow 1\right] - \Pr\left[\text{Exp}_{\text{tALG,A}}^{\text{fpriv-}(1,1)} \Rightarrow 1\right] \right|. \quad (1)
\end{aligned}$$

For the term in the second line of Eq. (1), let $\text{Exp}_{\text{Gen,A}'}^{\text{fsprg-}b_1}$ be the experiment given in Fig. 8. It is different from $\text{Exp}_{\text{tALG,A}}^{\text{fpriv-}(b_0,b_1)}$ only in the lines 8 and 11. $A'(\text{query}, K_i, his)$ runs A with input (query, his) and simulates en_{K_i} to answer to the queries made by A. $A'(\text{try}, S_i, his)$ simply runs A with input (try, S_i, his). Then, $\text{Exp}_{\text{tALG,A}}^{\text{fpriv-}(0,b_1)}$ is equivalent to $\text{Exp}_{\text{Gen,A}'}^{\text{fsprg-}b_1}$. Thus,

$$\left| \Pr\left[\text{Exp}_{\text{tALG,A}}^{\text{fpriv-}(0,0)} \Rightarrow 1\right] - \Pr\left[\text{Exp}_{\text{tALG,A}}^{\text{fpriv-}(0,1)} \Rightarrow 1\right] \right| = \text{Adv}_{\text{Gen}}^{\text{fsprg}}(A'),$$

where the run time of A' is about the sum of the run time of A and the time to compute en to answer to the queries made by A. From Theorem 2, there exists A_2 such that

$$\text{Adv}_{\text{Gen}}^{\text{fsprg}}(A') \leq 2n \cdot \text{Adv}_{G}^{\text{prg}}(A_2)$$

and the run time of A_2 is about the run time of $\text{Exp}_{\text{tALG,A}}^{\text{fpriv-0}}$.

For the term in the last line of Eq. (1), the hybrid argument is used in the standard way. Adversary A_1 against AEAD is given in Fig. 9. A_1 has oracle $\mathcal{O}$, which is either en with $K \leftarrow \{0,1\}^l$ or \$. Notice that A_1 is equivalent to $\text{Exp}_{\text{tALG,A}}^{\text{fpriv-}(0,1)}$ if $i^* = n$ and $\mathcal{O} = \text{en}_K$, and to $\text{Exp}_{\text{tALG,A}}^{\text{fpriv-}(1,1)}$ if $i^* = 1$ and $\mathcal{O} = \$$. Thus,

$$\begin{aligned}
\text{Adv}_{\text{AEAD}}^{\text{priv}}(A_1) &= \left| \Pr[A_1^{\text{en}_K} \Rightarrow 1] - \Pr\left[A_1^{\$} \Rightarrow 1\right] \right| \\
&= \frac{1}{n} \left| \Pr\left[\text{Exp}_{\text{tALG,A}}^{\text{fpriv-}(0,1)} \Rightarrow 1\right] - \Pr\left[\text{Exp}_{\text{tALG,A}}^{\text{fpriv-}(1,1)} \Rightarrow 1\right] \right|.
\end{aligned}$$

The run time of A_1 is about the run time of $\text{Exp}_{\text{tALG,A}}^{\text{fpriv-0}}$. $\qquad\square$

```
1: i ← 1; his ← ε
2: S₁ ⟵ S
3: repeat
4:      (Kᵢ, Sᵢ₊₁) ← G(Sᵢ)
5:      if b₁ = 1 then
6:          Kᵢ ⟵ K
7:      end if
8:      (phase, his) ← A^{O_i^{b_0}}(query, his)
9:      i ← i + 1
10: until (phase = try) ∨ (i > n)
11: b' ← A(try, Sᵢ, his)
12: return b'
```

```
1: i ← 1; his ← ε
2: S₁ ⟵ S
3: repeat
4:      (Kᵢ, Sᵢ₊₁) ← G(Sᵢ)
5:      if b₁ = 1 then
6:          Kᵢ ⟵ K
7:      end if
8:      (phase, his) ← A'(query, Kᵢ, his)
9:      i ← i + 1
10: until (phase = try) ∨ (i > n)
11: b' ← A'(try, Sᵢ, his)
12: return b'
```

Fig. 7. $\text{Exp}_{\text{tALG,A}}^{\text{fpriv-}(b_0,b_1)}$ for $(b_0, b_1) \in \{0,1\}^2$. $\mathcal{O}_i^0 = \text{en}_{K_i}$ and $\mathcal{O}_i^1 = \$_i$.

Fig. 8. $\text{Exp}_{\text{Gen,A'}}^{\text{fsprg-}b_1}$ for $b_1 \in \{0,1\}$.

```
1: i ← 1; his ← ε; i* ⟵ [1, n]
2: S₁ ⟵ S
3: repeat
4:      (Kᵢ, Sᵢ₊₁) ← G(Sᵢ)
5:      Kᵢ ⟵ K
6:      if i < i* then
7:          (phase, his) ← A^{en_{K_i}}(query, his)
8:      else if i = i* then
9:          (phase, his) ← A^{O}(query, his)
10:     else
11:         (phase, his) ← A^{$_i}(query, his)
12:     end if
13:     i ← i + 1
14: until (phase = try) ∨ (i > n)
15: b' ← A(try, Sᵢ, his)
16: return b'
```

Fig. 9. Adversary A_1. $\mathcal{O}$ is the oracle of A_1. $\mathcal{O}$ is either en_K with $K \leftarrow \mathcal{K}$ or $\$$.

The following theorem asserts that tALG satisfies forward authenticity if the underlying AEAD scheme satisfies both privacy and authenticity and the function G is a PRG:

Theorem 4 (Forward Authenticity of tALG). *Let* A *be any adversary against* tALG. *Suppose that* A *makes at most* σ_i *queries to its encryption oracle during the i-th stage in the query phase and outputs a forgery with at most* μ *records. Then, there exist adversaries* A_1, A_2 *against* AEAD, *and* A_3 *against* G *such that*

$$\text{Adv}_{\text{tALG}}^{\text{fauth}}(A) \leq n \cdot \text{Adv}_{\text{AEAD}}^{\text{auth}}(A_1) + n \cdot \text{Adv}_{\text{AEAD}}^{\text{priv}}(A_2) + 2n \cdot \text{Adv}_{G}^{\text{prg}}(A_3)$$

$$+ \frac{1}{2|\mathcal{T}|} \sum_{i=1}^{n} \sigma_i(\sigma_i - 1).$$

Each of the run times of A_1, A_2 *and* A_3 *is about the run time of* $\mathrm{Exp}_{\mathrm{tALG,A}}^{\mathrm{fauth}}$. A_1 *makes at most* $\max\{\sigma_i \mid 1 \le i \le n\}$ *queries to its encryption oracle and at most* μ *queries to its decryption oracle.* A_2 *makes at most* $\max\{\sigma_i \mid 1 \le i \le n\}$ *queries to its oracle.*

1: $i \leftarrow 1$; $his \leftarrow \varepsilon$
2: $S_1 \twoheadleftarrow \mathcal{S}$
3: **repeat**
4:     $(K_i, S_{i+1}) \leftarrow G(S_i)$
5:     **if** $b = 1$ **then**
6:         $K_i \twoheadleftarrow \mathcal{K}$
7:     **end if**
8:     $(phase, his) \leftarrow \mathsf{A}^{\mathrm{en}_{K_i}}(\mathbf{query}, his)$
9:     $i \leftarrow i + 1$
10: **until** $(phase = \mathbf{try}) \vee (i > n)$
11: $forgery \leftarrow \mathsf{A}(\mathbf{try}, S_i, his)$
12: **if** $forgery$ is successful **then**
13:     $d \leftarrow 1$
14: **else**
15:     $d \leftarrow 0$
16: **end if**
17: **return** d

1: $i \leftarrow 1$; $his \leftarrow \varepsilon$
2: $S_1 \twoheadleftarrow \mathcal{S}$
3: **repeat**
4:     $(K_i, S_{i+1}) \leftarrow G(S_i)$
5:     **if** $b = 1$ **then**
6:         $K_i \twoheadleftarrow \mathcal{K}$
7:     **end if**
8:     $(phase, his) \leftarrow \mathsf{A}'(\mathbf{query}, K_i, his)$
9:     $i \leftarrow i + 1$
10: **until** $(phase = \mathbf{try}) \vee (i > n)$
11: $\mathsf{A}'(\mathbf{try}, S_i, his)$
12:
13:
14:
15:
16:
17: **return** d

Fig. 10. $\mathrm{Exp}_{\mathrm{tALG,A}}^{\mathrm{fauth}\text{-}b}$ for $b \in \{0,1\}$. $forgery = (\tau'_{i_1,j_1-1}, \boldsymbol{R}'_{[(i_1,j_1),(i_2,j_2)]})$.

Fig. 11. $\mathrm{Exp}_{\mathrm{Gen,A}'}^{\mathrm{fsprg}\text{-}b}$ for $b \in \{0,1\}$

Proof. Let $\mathrm{Exp}_{\mathrm{tALG,A}}^{\mathrm{fauth}\text{-}b}$ for $b \in \{0,1\}$ be the experiment given in Fig. 10. Then, $\mathrm{Exp}_{\mathrm{tALG,A}}^{\mathrm{fauth}\text{-}0}$ is equivalent to $\mathrm{Exp}_{\mathrm{tALG,A}}^{\mathrm{fauth}}$. Thus,

$$\mathrm{Adv}_{\mathrm{tALG}}^{\mathrm{fauth}}(\mathsf{A}) = \Pr\left[\mathrm{Exp}_{\mathrm{tALG,A}}^{\mathrm{fauth}\text{-}0} \Rightarrow 1\right].$$

Let $\mathrm{Exp}_{\mathrm{Gen,A}'}^{\mathrm{fsprg}\text{-}b}$ be the experiment given in Fig. 11. $\mathrm{Exp}_{\mathrm{Gen,A}'}^{\mathrm{fsprg}\text{-}b}$ is different from $\mathrm{Exp}_{\mathrm{tALG,A}}^{\mathrm{fauth}\text{-}b}$ in the line 8 and in the lines from 11 to 16. In $\mathrm{Exp}_{\mathrm{Gen,A}'}^{\mathrm{fsprg}\text{-}b}$, $\mathsf{A}'(\mathbf{query}, K_i, his)$ runs A with input $(\mathbf{query}, his)$ and simulates en_{K_i} to answer to the queries made by A. $\mathsf{A}'(\mathbf{try}, S_i, his)$ executes the lines from 11 to 16 of $\mathrm{Exp}_{\mathrm{tALG,A}}^{\mathrm{fauth}\text{-}b}$. Then,

$$\mathrm{Adv}_{\mathrm{Gen}}^{\mathrm{fsprg}}(\mathsf{A}') = \left|\Pr\left[\mathrm{Exp}_{\mathrm{tALG,A}}^{\mathrm{fauth}\text{-}0} \Rightarrow 1\right] - \Pr\left[\mathrm{Exp}_{\mathrm{tALG,A}}^{\mathrm{fauth}\text{-}1} \Rightarrow 1\right]\right|.$$

Thus,

$$\mathrm{Adv}_{\mathrm{tALG}}^{\mathrm{fauth}}(\mathsf{A}) \le \Pr\left[\mathrm{Exp}_{\mathrm{tALG,A}}^{\mathrm{fauth}\text{-}1} \Rightarrow 1\right] + \mathrm{Adv}_{\mathrm{Gen}}^{\mathrm{fsprg}}(\mathsf{A}').$$

The run time of A' is about the sum of the run time of A and time to simulate en_{K_i} and verify whether $(\tau'_{i_1,j_1-1}, \boldsymbol{R}'_{[(i_1,j_1),(i_2,j_2)]})$ is a successful forgery or not. It

```
 1:  i ← 1; his ← ε; i* ← [1, n]
 2:  S₁ ← S
 3:  repeat
 4:      (Kᵢ, Sᵢ₊₁) ← G(Sᵢ)
 5:      Kᵢ ← K
 6:      if i = i* then
 7:          (phase, his) ← Aᵉⁿᴷ(query, his)
 8:      else
 9:          (phase, his) ← Aᵉⁿᴷⁱ(query, his)
10:      end if
11:      i ← i + 1
12:  until (phase = try) ∨ (i > n)
13:  (τ′ᵢ₁,ⱼ₁₋₁, R′[(i₁,j₁),(i₂,j₂)]) ← A(try, Sᵢ, his)
14:  for all j s.t. (i*, j) ∈ [(i₁, j₁), (i₂, j₂)] do
15:      if (τ′ᵢ*,ⱼ₋₁, R′ᵢ*,ⱼ) is new then
16:          Ask (τ′ᵢ*,ⱼ₋₁, R′ᵢ*,ⱼ) to deᴋ
17:      end if
18:  end for
```

Fig. 12. Adversary A_1 against AEAD. $R'_{i^*,j} = (A'_{i^*,j}, C'_{i^*,j}, \tau'_{i^*,j})$. For the line 15, "$(\tau'_{i^*,j-1}, R'_{i^*,j})$ is new" means that $(\tau'_{i^*,j-1}, R'_{i^*,j})$ is not obtained in the query phase.

is at most the run time of $\mathrm{Exp}^{\mathsf{fauth}}_{\mathsf{tALG},A}$. From Theorem 2, there exists an adversary A_3 such that

$$\mathrm{Adv}^{\mathsf{fsprg}}_{\mathsf{Gen}}(A') \leq 2n \cdot \mathrm{Adv}^{\mathsf{prg}}_{G}(A_3),$$

where the run time of A_3 is also about the run time of $\mathrm{Exp}^{\mathsf{fauth}}_{\mathsf{tALG},A}$.

For $\mathrm{Exp}^{\mathsf{fauth}}_{\mathsf{tALG},A}$, if A succeeds in forgery, then A succeeds in forgery for AEAD with some K_i or A finds a collision among tags during some stage in the query phase. Let $\mathtt{forge}_i$ be the event that A succeeds in forgery for AEAD with K_i. Let $\mathtt{collision}$ be the event that A finds a collision among tags in the query phase. Then,

$$\Pr\left[\mathrm{Exp}^{\mathsf{fauth}\text{-}1}_{\mathsf{tALG},A} \Rightarrow 1\right] \leq \Pr\left[\bigvee_{i=1}^{n} \mathtt{forge}_i\right] + \Pr[\mathtt{collision}].$$

Let A_1 be the adversary given in Fig. 12. A_1 has oracle access to en_K and de_K. Then,

$$\Pr\left[\bigvee_{i=1}^{n} \mathtt{forge}_i\right] \leq n \cdot \mathrm{Adv}^{\mathsf{auth}}_{\mathsf{AEAD}}(A_1).$$

The run time of A_1 is about the run time of $\mathrm{Exp}^{\mathsf{fauth}}_{\mathsf{tALG},A}$.

1: $i \leftarrow 1$; $his \leftarrow \varepsilon$	1: $i \leftarrow 1$; $his \leftarrow \varepsilon$; $i^* \twoheadleftarrow [1,n]$
2: $S_1 \twoheadleftarrow \mathcal{S}$	2: $S_1 \twoheadleftarrow \mathcal{S}$
3: **repeat**	3: **repeat**
4: $(K_i, S_{i+1}) \leftarrow G(S_i)$	4: $(K_i, S_{i+1}) \leftarrow G(S_i)$
5: $K_i \twoheadleftarrow \mathcal{K}$	5: $K_i \twoheadleftarrow \mathcal{K}$
6: $(phase, his) \leftarrow \mathsf{A}^{\mathcal{O}_i^b}(query, his)$	6: **if** $i < i^*$ **then**
7:	7: $(phase, his) \leftarrow \mathsf{A}^{\mathrm{en}_{K_i}}(query, his)$
8:	8: **else if** $i = i^*$ **then**
9:	9: $(phase, his) \leftarrow \mathsf{A}^{\mathcal{O}}(query, his)$
10:	10: **else**
11:	11: $(phase, his) \leftarrow \mathsf{A}^{\$_i}(query, his)$
12:	12: **end if**
13: $i \leftarrow i+1$	13: $i \leftarrow i+1$
14: **until** $(phase = \mathsf{try}) \vee (i > n)$	14: **until** $(phase = \mathsf{try}) \vee (i > n)$
15: **if** collision occurs **then**	15: **if** collision occurs **then**
16: $b' \leftarrow 1$	16: $b' \leftarrow 1$
17: **else**	17: **else**
18: $b' \leftarrow 0$	18: $b' \leftarrow 0$
19: **end if**	19: **end if**
20: **return** b'	20: **return** b'

Fig. 13. $\mathrm{Exp}_{\mathrm{tALG,A}}^{\mathrm{fpriv}'\text{-}b}$ for $b \in \{0,1\}$. $\mathcal{O}_i^0 = \mathrm{en}_{K_i}$ and $\mathcal{O}_i^1 = \$_i$.

Fig. 14. Adversary A_2

Let $\mathrm{Exp}_{\mathrm{tALG,A}}^{\mathrm{fpriv}'\text{-}b}$ be an experiment given in Fig. 13. Then,

$$
\begin{aligned}
\Pr[\text{collision}] &= \Pr\left[\mathrm{Exp}_{\mathrm{tALG,A}}^{\mathrm{fpriv}'\text{-}0} \Rightarrow 1\right] \\
&\leq \left|\Pr\left[\mathrm{Exp}_{\mathrm{tALG,A}}^{\mathrm{fpriv}'\text{-}0} \Rightarrow 1\right] - \Pr\left[\mathrm{Exp}_{\mathrm{tALG,A}}^{\mathrm{fpriv}'\text{-}1} \Rightarrow 1\right]\right| + \Pr\left[\mathrm{Exp}_{\mathrm{tALG,A}}^{\mathrm{fpriv}'\text{-}1} \Rightarrow 1\right] \\
&\leq \left|\Pr\left[\mathrm{Exp}_{\mathrm{tALG,A}}^{\mathrm{fpriv}'\text{-}0} \Rightarrow 1\right] - \Pr\left[\mathrm{Exp}_{\mathrm{tALG,A}}^{\mathrm{fpriv}'\text{-}1} \Rightarrow 1\right]\right| + \frac{\sum_{i=1}^{n} \sigma_i(\sigma_i - 1)}{2|\mathcal{T}|}.
\end{aligned}
$$

Let A_2 be an adversary against AEAD given in Fig. 14. A_2 has oracle access to $\mathcal{O}$, which is either en_K with $K \twoheadleftarrow \mathcal{K}$ or $\$$. Notice that A_2 is equivalent to $\mathrm{Exp}_{\mathrm{tALG,A}}^{\mathrm{fpriv}'\text{-}1}$ if $i^* = n$ and $\mathcal{O} = \mathrm{en}_K$, and to $\mathrm{Exp}_{\mathrm{tALG,A}}^{\mathrm{fpriv}'\text{-}0}$ if $i^* = 1$ and $\mathcal{O} = \$$. Then,

$$
\left|\Pr\left[\mathrm{Exp}_{\mathrm{tALG,A}}^{\mathrm{fpriv}'\text{-}0} \Rightarrow 1\right] - \Pr\left[\mathrm{Exp}_{\mathrm{tALG,A}}^{\mathrm{fpriv}'\text{-}1} \Rightarrow 1\right]\right| = n \cdot \mathrm{Adv}_{\mathrm{AEAD}}^{\mathrm{priv}}(\mathsf{A}_2).
$$

The run time of A_2 is at most the run time of $\mathrm{Exp}_{\mathrm{tALG,A}}^{\mathrm{fauth}}$. $\qquad\square$

5.2   Event-Driven Setting

The forward privacy of eALG is reduced to the privacy of encryption function E, the PRF property of keyed function F and the PRG property of function G:

Theorem 5 (Forward Privacy of eALG). *For any adversary* A *against* eALG, *there exist adversaries* A_1 *against* E, A_2 *against* F *and* A_3 *against* G *such that*

$$\mathrm{Adv}_{\mathsf{eALG}}^{\mathrm{fpriv}}(A) \leq n \cdot \mathrm{Adv}_E^{\mathrm{priv}}(A_1) + n \cdot \mathrm{Adv}_F^{\mathrm{prf}}(A_2) + 2n \cdot \mathrm{Adv}_G^{\mathrm{prg}}(A_3).$$

Each of A_1 *and* A_2 *makes at most a single query to its oracle. Each of the run times of* A_1, A_2 *and* A_3 *is about the run time of* $\mathrm{Exp}_{\mathsf{eALG},A}^{\mathrm{fpriv}\text{-}0}$.

The forward authenticity of eALG is reduced to the PRF property of keyed function F and the PRG property of function G:

Theorem 6 (Forward Authenticity of eALG). *Let* A *be any adversary against* eALG. *Then, there exist adversaries* A_1, A_2 *against* AEAD, *and* A_3 *against* G *such that*

$$\mathrm{Adv}_{\mathsf{eALG}}^{\mathrm{fauth}}(A) \leq n \cdot \mathrm{Adv}_F^{\mathrm{prf}}(A_1) + 2n \cdot \mathrm{Adv}_G^{\mathrm{prg}}(A_2) + \frac{n+1}{|T|}.$$

Each of the run times of A_1 *and* A_2 *is about the run time of* $\mathrm{Exp}_{\mathsf{eALG},A}^{\mathrm{fauth}}$. A_1 *makes at most two queries.*

The proofs of Theorems 5 and 6 are omitted due to the page limit.

Remark 2. The security of eALG requires the underlying encryption scheme to be secure only against single-query adversaries. Thus, to construct eALG, we can use naive modes of operations for encryption such as CBC and CTR in textbooks.

6   Conclusion

In this paper, audit logging schemes with forward privacy and secrecy have been formalized first. Then, two generic schemes have been proposed. Finally, it has been proved that the proposed schemes meet the security requirements.

Acknowledgments. The author would like to thank Hidenori Kuwakado for valuable discussions. This work was partially supported by JSPS KAKENHI Grant Number 25330150.

References

1. Accorsi, R.: Safe-keeping digital evidence with secure logging protocols: state of the art and challenges. In: Goebel, O., Ehlert, R., Frings, S., Günther, D., Morgenstern, H., Schadt, D. (eds.) IMF 2009, Fifth International Conference on IT Security Incident Management and IT Forensics, pp. 94–110 (2009)
2. Bellare, M., Canetti, R., Krawczyk, H.: Pseudorandom functions revisited: the cascade construction and its concrete security. In: Proceedings of the 37th IEEE Symposium on Foundations of Computer Science, pp. 514–523 (1996)

3. Bellare, M., Namprempre, C.: Authenticated encryption: relations among notions and analysis of the generic composition paradigm. In: Okamoto, T. (ed.) ASI-ACRYPT 2000. LNCS, vol. 1976, pp. 531–545. Springer, Heidelberg (2000)
4. Bellare, M., Namprempre, C.: Authenticated encryption: relations among notions and analysis of the generic composition paradigm. J. Cryptology **21**(4), 469–491 (2008)
5. Bellare, M., Yee, B.S.: Forward integrity for secure audit logs. Technical report, University of California, San Diego (1997)
6. Bellare, M., Yee, B.S.: Forward-security in private-key cryptography. In: Joye, M. (ed.) CT-RSA 2003. LNCS, vol. 2612, pp. 1–18. Springer, Heidelberg (2003). the full version is IACR Cryptology ePrint Archive: Report 2001/035 at http://eprint.iacr.org/
7. Blum, M., Micali, S.: How to generate cryptographically strong sequences of pseudo-random bits. SIAM J. Comput. **13**(4), 850–864 (1984)
8. CAESAR: Competition for authenticated encryption: security, applicability, and robustness, http://competitions.cr.yp.to/caesar.html
9. Goldreich, O., Goldwasser, S., Micali, S.: How to construct random functions. J. ACM **33**(4), 792–807 (1986)
10. Günther, C.G.: An identity-based key-exchange protocol. In: Quisquater, J.-J., Vandewalle, J. (eds.) EUROCRYPT 1989. LNCS, vol. 434, pp. 29–37. Springer, Heidelberg (1990)
11. Hirose, S., Kuwakado, H.: Forward-secure sequential aggregate message authentication revisited. In: Chow, S.S.M., Liu, J.K., Hui, L.C.K., Yiu, S.M. (eds.) ProvSec 2014. LNCS, vol. 8782, pp. 87–102. Springer, Heidelberg (2014)
12. Ma, D., Tsudik, G.: Extended abstract: forward-secure sequential aggregate authentication. In: IEEE Symposium on Security and Privacy, pp. 86–91. IEEE Computer Society (2007), also published as IACR Cryptology ePrint Archive: Report 2007/052 at http://eprint.iacr.org/
13. Ma, D., Tsudik, G.: A new approach to secure logging. ACM Trans. Storage **5**(1), 2:1–2:21 (2009)
14. Namprempre, C., Rogaway, P., Shrimpton, T.: Reconsidering generic composition. In: Nguyen, P.Q., Oswald, E. (eds.) EUROCRYPT 2014. LNCS, vol. 8441, pp. 257–274. Springer, Heidelberg (2014)
15. Rogaway, P.: Authenticated-encryption with associated-data. In: Atluri, V. (ed.) ACM Conference on Computer and Communications Security, pp. 98–107 (2002)
16. Rogaway, P., Bellare, M., Black, J., Krovetz, T.: OCB: a block-cipher mode of operation for efficient authenticated encryption. In: ACM Conference on Computer and Communications Security, pp. 196–205 (2001)
17. Rogaway, P., Shrimpton, T.: A provable-security treatment of the key-wrap problem. In: Vaudenay, S. (ed.) EUROCRYPT 2006. LNCS, vol. 4004, pp. 373–390. Springer, Heidelberg (2006)
18. Schneier, B., Kelsey, J.: Cryptographic support for secure logs on untrusted machines. In: Rubin, A.D. (ed.) Proceedings of the 7th USENIX Security Symposium. USENIX Association (1998)
19. Schneier, B., Kelsey, J.: Secure audit logs to support computer forensics. ACM Trans. Inf. Syst. Secur. **2**(2), 159–176 (1999)
20. Waters, B.R., Balfanz, D., Durfee, G., Smetters, D.K.: Building an encrypted and searchable audit log. In: Proceedings of the Network and Distributed System Security Symposium, NDSS 2004, The Internet Society (2004)

A Novel Post-processing Method to Improve the Ability of Reconstruction for Video Leaking Signal

Xuejie Ding, Meng Zhang$^{(\boxtimes)}$, Jun Shi, and Weiqing Huang

Institute of Information Engineering,
Chinese Academy of Sciences, Beijing, China
{dingxuejie,zhangmeng,shijun,huangweiqing}@iie.ac.cn

Abstract. The confidential information can be reconstructed by received weak electromagnetic signal from a radiation object, such as a computer display. Usually, the radiation signal is submerged in strong noise and faded in channel, so it is not an easy task to understand the information existed in the signal. In this paper, we propose a new post-processing system to improve the visual quality of reconstruction image in sparse domain. Different from filter and enhancement technologies in image filed, our system focuses on data shrink and repair using the methods in machine learning. It can not only remove the noise interference, but also complement the lost high-frequency and compensate the distortion. Experimental section displays complete procedures and better performance, and it also proves the effectiveness of the novel framework.

Keywords: Electromagnetic radiation · Sparse representation · Data shrink · Data repair

1 Introduction

As the increasing need and wide spread using of information technology equipment (ITE), it has brought a great communication convenience but also the information crisis for human society. One side, people can deal with important information and data easily by ITE, on the other hand, the eavesdroppers can steal the information operated on computer displays by electromagnetic radiation [1–3]. Therefore the information leakage has a strong impact on social and economic activities, and the protection and attack technology for electromagnetic radiation are concerned by military and government of world.

The weak leak signal can be captured and reconstructed to an image or video by eavesdropper's facility [4, 5]. However, understanding this captured data is not an easy job, because the received signal is submerged in strong noise and faded in channel. In order to solve this problem, there are two ways, one is to design a better receiver equipment to improve the received quality, and the other is to add a post-processing part in favor of comprehending the information. Comparing with the first way, adding a post-processing is more flexible. In the past decades, the researchers focused on the post-processing system by means of digital image processing technologies. For example,

© Springer International Publishing Switzerland 2016
S. Qing et al. (Eds.): ICICS 2015, LNCS 9543, pp. 141–151, 2016.
DOI: 10.1007/978-3-319-29814-6_12

the authors in [6] used the adaptive filtering algorithm to improve SNR of the reconstruction images. In report [7], multi-frame average de-noising filter and wavelet transform filter are applied to reconstruct computer video. In order to improve the visual quality of received data, in this paper, we propose a novel post-processing system based on machine learning, which is different from traditional method in image processing filed.

In our framework, the reconstruction image is divided into several blocks, and each block is sparse represented. Then a sparse coefficients set is obtained, which includes the sparse coefficients of each block. We expect to improve the intelligibility of received data by modifying the sparse coefficients set. Firstly, each block is assumed to have a category, and is labeled as background, interference or information. We predict the category for each block using multi-class logistic regression algorithm, then a shrink operation is done on the base of predict result. Secondly, with the purpose of repair the data further, for the blocks labeled as information, the Kernel Density Estimation (KDE) method is imported to estimate their probability density functions, and smooth the sparse coefficients based on the statistical property. It expects to be able to complement the lost high-frequency and compensate the distortion.

The structure of the paper is as follows: the principle of the novel framework is introduced in Sect. 2, and the proposed method is depicted in details in Sect. 3. The experimental results and their analysis are shown in Sect. 4. The conclusion and future work are given at the last part of this paper.

2   The Principle of Novel Method

In this section, we will display the principle of our framework. There are three main parts, they are sparse representation for received data, data processing for sparse coefficients set, and data reconstruction using the new sparse coefficients and original dictionary. The details are shown in Fig. 1.

After the reconstruction image is divided into blocks, each block is sparse represented on the basis of a dictionary which is learned by sparse theory using an abundant training dataset. Then a coefficients set is generated composed by the spare representation of each block.

Then the sparse coefficients set is processed by two steps: (1) Shrink, it means some useless components are removed. It dependents on the multi-class predict model trained by logistic regression algorithm, and each block is predicted to a category, such as background, interference or information. According to the shrink criterion, some block coefficients are set to zeros. (2) Repair, it means some non-zeros data are smoothed. It dependents on the fit model obtained by Kernel Density Estimation (KDE). For the blocks labeled as information, KDE is used to complement the missing part and compensate the distortion.

At last, the data is reconstructed by the new sparse coefficients set and the dictionary. The process can be seen as an inverse transform of sparse representation.

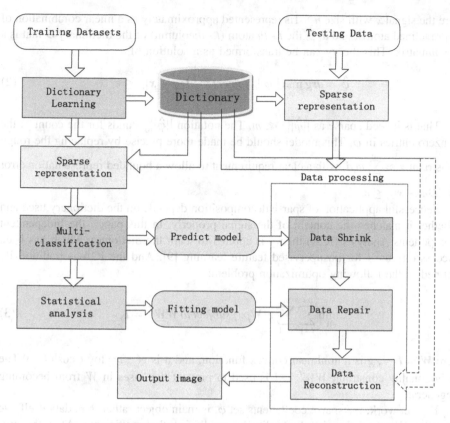

Fig. 1. The principle of our framework

3 The Proposed Method

This section will introduce the details of this novel method. First, the sparse representation theory is presented, it includes the signal decomposition and reconstruction based on this theory. Then the method of shrink is given according to shrink criterion decided by the result of category prediction. At last, KDE is imported to repair the data by smoothing the statistical property.

3.1 Sparse Representation of Received Data

Sparse representation is a powerful decomposition method, it can represent the signal as a linear combination of few elementary components [8]. The sparse representation of a signal is depicted as follows:

$$x \approx \sum_{t=1}^{m} \varphi_t d_t = D\varphi \ \varphi \triangleq (\varphi_1, \varphi_2, \cdots, \varphi_m) \qquad ((1))$$

here the signal x with size $n \times 1$ is represented approximately as a linear combination of m predefined atoms, and d_t is the t - th atom (t - th column) of the dictionary D that is a $n \times m$ matrix. This theory can be transformed as a solution of

$$\hat{\varphi} = arg \min_{\varphi} ||\varphi||_0 \; subject \; to \; ||D\varphi - x||_2 \le \varepsilon \tag{2}$$

That is indeed sparse as $||\hat{\varphi}||_0 \ll m$. The notation $||\hat{\varphi}||_0$ stands for the count of the nonzero entries in φ. This model should be made more precise by replacing the rough constraint $x \approx \sum_{t=1}^{m} \varphi_t d_t$ with a clear requirement to allow a bounded representation error as $||D\varphi - x||_2 \le \varepsilon$.

Successful application of sparse decomposition depends on the dictionary used and whether it matches the content of the signal properly. In this paper, the Independent Components Analysis (ICA) theory is applied to learn the dictionary which has been successfully used for unsupervised feature learning [9]. And the ICA is traditionally defined as the following optimization problem:

$$\min_{W} \sum_{i=1}^{m} \sum_{j=1}^{n} g(W_j x_i) \; subject \; to \; WW^T = I, \tag{3}$$

here $W = D^{-1}$, g is a nonlinear convex function, and it is $g(\cdot) = \log (\cosh (\cdot))$. The orthogonality constraint $WW^T = I$ is used to prevent the bases in W from becoming degenerate.

For our work, the sparse coefficients set φ_t is main object rather than data itself, we expect to improve the signal equality by modifying the coefficients. After the processing for sparse coefficients set, the new data is reconstructed as

$$x_{new} = D\varphi_{new} \tag{4}$$

The process of sparse representation and reconstruction can be seen as a reversible transform.

3.2   Data Shrink

According to their morphology, the sparse representation of each block can be roughly divided into three categories: background component (0 class), noise interference (1 class) and useful information (2 class). In order to extract the useful information, we should remove the noise and interference signal by means of setting their sparse coefficients to zeros. The first step is to predict which category the block is like. In this section, logistic regression algorithm is employed to solve this multi-classifying problem.

The logistic regression model is one of the most useful tools for multi-classifying, and it does so by providing posterior probabilities which will place the data in the appropriate group. It is parameterized by a weight matrix ω and a bias vector b [10, 11]. Classification is done by projecting an input vector onto a set of hyperplanes, each of which corresponds to a class. The distance from the input to a hyperplane reflects the probability that the input is a member of the corresponding class. Mathematically, the probability of an input vector φ_i which belongs to the class $I \in [0, 1, 2]$, can be written as:

$$P(Y = I|\varphi_t, \omega, b) = \frac{e^{\omega_I \varphi_t + b_I}}{\sum_j e^{\omega_j \varphi_t + b_j}} \tag{5}$$

where Y is the notation of the class label. The model's prediction y_{pred} is the class whose probability is maximal, specifically:

$$y_{pred} = \arg\max_I P(Y = I|\varphi_t, \omega, b) \tag{6}$$

In order to learn the optimal model parameters, we should minimize a loss function. In the case of multi-class logistic regression, it is very common to use the negative log-likelihood as the loss function.

This is equivalent to maximize the likelihood of the data set $\Re$ under the model parameterized by θ. Let us first start by defining the likelihood L and the loss l.

$$L(\theta = \{\omega, b\}, \Re) = \sum_{i=0}^{|\Re|} \log(P(Y = y^{(i)}|\varphi_t^{(i)}, \omega, b)) \tag{7}$$

$$l(\theta = \{\omega, b\}, \Re) = - L(\theta = \{\omega, b\}, \Re) \tag{8}$$

And the gradient descent is applied for minimizing arbitrary non-linear functions. Then we set the sparse coefficients to zeros which belongs to the background and the interference, when the probability of background is larger than useful information's. And the shrink criterion is depicted as:

$$\varphi_t = \begin{cases} 0 & if & t \in I[0] \\ 0 & if & t \in I[1] \& P_{I[0]} > P_{I[2]} \\ \varphi_t & else \end{cases} \tag{9}$$

3.3 Data Repair

After the processing of data shrink, we get a more 'clean' sparse coefficients set. However, the non-zero coefficient values are not so smooth in samples. Some of them should be pulled up or down to smooth the representations well. Kernel density estimation (KDE) is a non-parametric way to estimate the probability density function and to make the data more smooth [12, 13] KDE differs from the parametric approach in that kernel density estimation does not force the distribution to take on any pre-defined shape; instead, it lets the data speak for itself.

Let $(\varphi_t^1, \varphi_t^2 \cdots \varphi_t^n)$ be an independent and identically distributed sample with an unknown density. Its kernel density estimator is

$$\hat{f}(\varphi_t) = \frac{1}{nh} \sum_{i=1}^{n} K\left(\frac{(\varphi_t - \varphi_t^i)}{h}\right) \qquad (10)$$

here K is the kernel function. A range of kernel functions are commonly used: gaussian, Epanechnikov, tophat, exponetial and others. And $h > 0$ is a bandwidth parameter which is crucial to dictate the smoothness, controls the tradeoff between bias and variance in the result. A large bandwidth can lead to a very smooth (i.e. high-bias) density distribution, meanwhile, a small bandwidth can lead to an unsmooth (i.e. high-variance) density distribution. However, choosing the optimal bandwidth is not a simple task and is often done by attempting to maximize the asymptotic integrated mean squared error (AMISE).

A simple way to select a bandwidth parameter is to choose a known distribution, such as Gaussian, and assume that its AMISE optimal bandwidth is sufficient for other distributions. The optimal bandwidth for Gaussian kernel is given as

$$h = \left(\frac{4\hat{\sigma}}{3n}\right)^{1/5} \qquad (11)$$

And $\hat{\sigma}$ is the standard deviation of the samples.

4   Experimental Results

In this section, to evaluate the performances of our novel system, we conducted the experiments on 1500 data blocks as the training data at the same receiving condition. And the size of block was 20×20. We used a LCD monitor as a leakage source which resolution is 1024×768. The signal was received by a frequency spectrometer, and it connected to a transmission line with a current clamp. Then the experimental results are displayed according to the steps in our system, at the same time, a kind of no-reference image quality assessment [14] is applied to evaluate the performance of our framework. The original received signals and their reconstruction images are shown in Fig. 2.

In order to classify the different categories of image blocks, we use multi-classifier to distinguish the signal to three categories, they are background (0 class), interference signal (1 class) and useful information (2 class). And the sparse coefficients of some blocks are set to zeros according to the shrink criterion. The processing results are shown in Fig. 3.

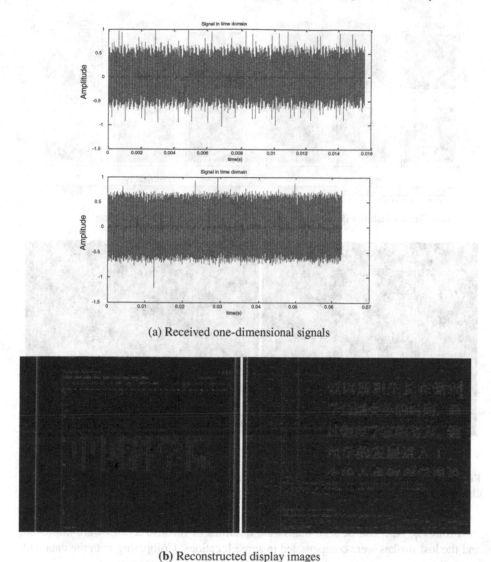

(a) Received one-dimensional signals

(b) Reconstructed display images

Fig. 2. Two received signals and their reconstructed images

The prediction accuracies of data with fewer characters are 89 % and 88.3 % using the two logistic regression methods with L2 and L1 regularizations. And the prediction accuracies of data with more characters are lower as 74.2 % and 74.2 % respectively. It can be found that the error prediction is higher around the edges of character when the character's space is less. According to the principle of our framework, the received signals are repaired further, and the results are shown in Fig. 4.

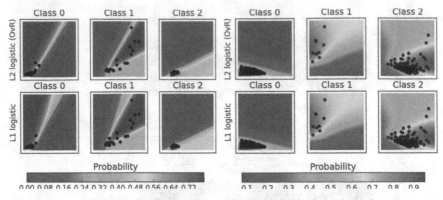

(a) The probability distributions for multi-class using logistic regression

(b) The results after data shrink

Fig. 3. Two kinds logistic regression algorithms are implemented, the two categories (0 class, 1 class) are shrunk by setting sparse coefficients to zeros.

From Fig. 4, it can be seen that visual qualities of reconstructions were improved, and the lost strokes were compensated in some locations. Comparing with the data with more characters, the one with fewer characters had better performance.

In order to measure the effectiveness of our methods objectively, we explored the no–reference evaluation algorithm proposed in [14] to assess the image equality, and the results are given in Table 1.

Table 1 described the non-reference image equality assessment results for the original image and the new image processed by our method respectively. It can be observed that all the scores of new images are great higher than the original ones, such as φ_{data1}, the original score is 17.4439, and the highest score of new image is 63.6877 when the bandwidth is 0.01. This proved that the novel system had a better performance for the weak information recovery.

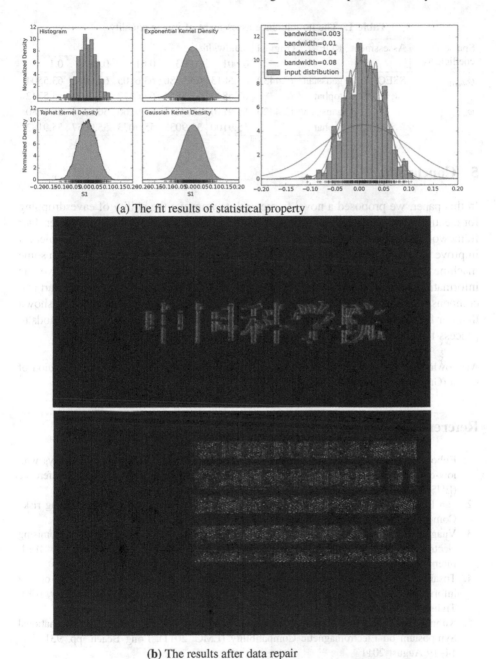

(a) The fit results of statistical property

(b) The results after data repair

Fig. 4. The fit results using different kernel functions are given in the left of (a), and Gaussian Kernel density is chosen, the fit results using different bandwidths are given in the right of (a). The reconstruct images shown in (b) are attained using the bandwidth as 0.01.

Table 1. The no-reference assessment of image equality

Sparse coefficients	Assessment	KDE	Original	bandwidth				
				0.001	0.003	0.01	0.02	0.1
φ_{data1}	SSEQ	gaussian	17.4439	63.5813	63.5786	63.6205	62.9068	63.5504
		tophat		63.5842	63.5854	63.6877	62.9676	63.5742
φ_{data2}		gaussian	12.4420	55.9110	55.9018	55.9260	56.0574	56.6080
		tophat		55.9100	55.9038	55.9073	55.9057	55.9182

5   Conclusion

In this paper, we proposed a novel framework to improve the ability of eavesdropping for electromagnetic leakage by means of making the reconstruction image clearer. Our framework is different from the filter and enhancement technologies in image filed, it improve the visual quality of image by modifying the sparse coefficients based on some machine learning algorithms. It can remove the interference and only reserve the information at the data shrink step. Meanwhile, it can complement the missing part and compensate the distortion at the data repair step. The experimental results had shown that our framework works well. In the future work, we hope to import more methods to process the sparse coefficients and improve the image quality further.

Acknowledgment. This work was supported by the National Natural Science Foundation of China (Grant No.61401460).

References

1. Elibol. F., Sarac, U., Erer, I.: Realistic eavesdropping attacks on computer displays with low-cost and mobile receiver system. In: 20th European Signal Processing Conference (EUSIPCO, 2012), pp:1767–1771 (2012)
2. van Eck, W.: Electromagnetic radiation from video display units: an eavesdropping risk? Comput. Secur. **4**, 269–286 (1985)
3. Vuagnoux, M., Pasini, S.: An improved technique to discover compromising electromagnetic emanations, Electromagnetic Compatibility (EMC), 2010 In: IEEE International Symposium on Digital object Identifier, pp:121–126 (2010)
4. Tosaka, T., Yamanaka, Y., Fukunaga, K.: Method for determining whether or not information is contained in electromagnetic disturbance radiated from a PC display. IEEE Trans. Electromagn. Compat. **53**(2), 318–324 (2011)
5. Kuhn, M.G.: Compromising Emanations of LCD TV Sets. In: IEEE International Symposium on Electromagnetic Compatibility (EMC, 2011), Long Beach, pp. 931–936, 14–19 August 2011
6. Koksaldi, N.E., Olcer, I., Yapanel, U., Sarac, U.: Signal processing applications for information extraction from the radiation of VDUs, National Institute of Electronics & Cryptology, Kocaeli, vol. 41470
7. Tang, Y.: Research on monitoring platform of computer video leaking signal, East China normal university, March 2011

8. Zheng, Z., Yong, X., Jian, Y.: A survey of sparse representation: algorithms and applications. IEEE Access **3**, 490–530 (2015)
9. Yanhui, X., Zhengfeng, Z., Yao, Z.: Kernel reconstruction ICA for sparse representation. IEEE Trans. Networks Learn. Syst. **26**(6), 1222–1232 (2015)
10. Christopher, M.B.: Pattern Recognition and Machine Learning, pp. 205–210. Springer, New York (2006). ISBN: 0-387-31073-8
11. Wenping, Hu, Qian, Yao, et al.: Improved mispronunciation detection with deep neural network trained acoustic models and transfer learning based logistic regression classifiers. Speech Commun. **67**, 154–166 (2015)
12. Gonzalez, R. et al.: Process monitoring using kernel density estimation and Bayesian networking with an industrial case study. ISA Transactions (2015). http://dx.doi.org/10.1016/j.isatra.2015.04.001
13. Silverman, B.W.: Density Estimation for Statistical and Data Analysis, p. 48. Chapman &Hall/CRC, London (1998). http://dx.doi.org/10.1016/j.isatra.2015.04.001. ISBN: 0-412-24620-1
14. Liu, L., Liu, B., Huang, H., Bovik, A.C.: No-reference image quality assessment based on spatial and spectral entropies. Sig. Process. Image Commun. **29**(8), 856–863 (2014)

TMSUI: A Trust Management Scheme of USB Storage Devices for Industrial Control Systems

Bo Yang[1]([⊠]), Yu Qin[1], Yingjun Zhang[1], Weijin Wang[1], and Dengguo Feng[1,2]

[1] Trusted Computing and Information Assurance Laboratory,
Institute of Software, Chinese Academy of Sciences, Beijing, China
{yangbo,qin_yu,zhangyingjun,wangweijin,Feng}@tca.iscas.ac.cn
[2] State Key Laboratory of Computer Science, Institute of Software,
Chinese Academy of Sciences, Beijing, China

Abstract. The security of sensitive data and the safety of control signal are two core issues in industrial control system (ICS). However, the prevalence of USB storage devices brings a great challenge on protecting ICS in those respects. Unfortunately, there is currently no solution specially for ICS to provide a complete defense against communication between untrusted USB storage devices and critical equipment without forbidding normal USB device function. This paper proposes a trust management scheme of USB storage devices for ICS (TMSUI). By fully considering application scenarios, TMSUI is designed based on security chip to flexibly achieve authorizing a certain USB storage device to only access some exact protected terminals in ICS for a particular period of time. The scheme enables administrators to revoke authorized devices. We analyze six security properties of TMSUI. The prototype system is finally implemented. The evaluation results indicate that our scheme meets the security goals with high compatibility and good efficiency.

Keywords: Trust management · USB storage device · Security chip · Industrial control system · Industrial security · TPM/TCM

1 Introduction

The easiness to carry around and the simplicity to access a variety of computers are two significant advantages of USB storage devices. USB flash disk, memory card, mobile HDD, smartphone and many other embedded devices can all be treated as specific forms of USB storage devices. With regard to them, the main functions cover data storage and offline communication between remote terminals. Undoubtedly, the prevalence of USB storage devices benefits the masses, including the engineers who manage and operate the modern ICS. Updating software, uploading and downloading industrial data give the engineers chances to attach USB storage devices to ICS. However, USB storage devices are becoming the dangerous media to potentially threaten the security of ICS.

By the end of June 2014, a total of 549 vulnerabilities of ICS were publicly reported by American Common Vulnerabilities and Exposures (CVE) [23], the

© Springer International Publishing Switzerland 2016
S. Qing et al. (Eds.): ICICS 2015, LNCS 9543, pp. 152–168, 2016.
DOI: 10.1007/978-3-319-29814-6_13

Industrial Control Systems Cyber Emergency Response Team (ICS-CERT) of US Department Homeland Security [26] and China National Vulnerability Database (CNVD) [21]. From the report [25], the number of security incidents of ICS shows a rapid growth trend. These incidents involve several key industry areas. Sadly, many serious malicious codes, including evil scripts and varied malwares such as viruses, worms, spyware and Trojan horses, are able to invade ICS together with USB-based hack tools through USB storage devices [30]. Especially, the exclusive core part of ICS is relatively (or absolutely somewhere) isolated from the external network, which dramatically reduces the risks of attacks via Internet, but therefore, USB storage devices become the more dangerous tools potentially used by attackers to spread malicious codes into ICS. Known as Autorun malwares, some malicious codes exploits operating system (OS) vulnerabilities to replicate via USB drives and automatically activate themselves. Both the notorious Stuxnet, which attacked Iranian nuclear power plant, and the latest Havex, which could shut down the nationwide power grid, try to access ICS originally via USB storage devices [29]. Although the local firewall, anti-virus software and intrusion detection system (IDS) protect ICS from attacks to some extent, 0-day and unknown vulnerabilities of ICS still leave opportunities for attackers. Additionally, in Black Hat USA 2014, BadUSB is presented as a new form of malware that operates from controller chips inside USB devices which can be reprogrammed to spoof various other device types in order to take control of a computer, exfiltrate data, or spy on the user [15].

On the other hand, launching social engineering attacks using USB storage devices is considered to cause more damage than malicious codes themselves in ICS [28]. The unauthorized access behavior of USB storage devices taken by a corrupt engineer, an evil staff member or an infiltrator is able to easily upload malicious codes to ICS or unimpededly steal valuable data from ICS. In fact, the lack of authentication and restriction on USB storage devices and permitting every device to easily access ICS are the reasons that lead to these risky situations. Therefore, building up a trust management scheme of USB storage devices is necessary to keep the hazardous devices away from ICS.

Nevertheless, compared with traditional computer and network systems, ICS architecture has its own characteristics:

- **Isolated.** Not only ICS is partly isolated from external network, but also the different sections inside ICS are isolated from each other to some extent. The network communication between terminals is limited and costly.
- **Complicated.** In order to be well managed, controlled and supervised, ICS is divided to several system or network sections which make it complicated.
- **Stable.** For guaranteeing continuous running with no mistake, ICS architecture and equipment require to remain both reliable and stable, and cannot tolerate large-scale changes.

For these characteristics, applying some existing comprehensive technologies to ICS, for example using Public Key Infrastructure (PKI) to issue certificates to USB devices, is not appropriate because they are inflexible and may further increase ICS's complexity, instability and performance overhead. Likewise, the real-time online solutions such as Online Certificate Status Protocol (OCSP) are hardly applicable for ICS either. Furthermore, the existing access control mechanisms in Windows and Linux do not fulfill the enough fine-grained control over USB devices. To our best knowledge, there is no complete solution specially designed for the architecture of ICS.

Our Contributions. In this paper, we propose TMSUI, a trust management scheme combined with related security rules. The scheme is able to authorize some certain USB storage devices to have limited permission to access specific protected terminals such as engineer stations and supervisory control and data acquisition (SCADA) servers in ICS, while other unauthorized devices are directly ejected by the target terminals. As a result, the use of USB storage devices in ICS is meticulously controllable. Our work is summarized as follows.

- We design TMSUI expressly for ICS without changing its architecture. Based on security chip and digital signature technique, the administrators have the privilege to authorize USB storage devices flexibly and at a fine granular level. Meanwhile, the administrators are held accountable for their respective misconduct. The authorization is time-limited.
- We elaborate an offline whitelist mechanism with no need for each terminal to download and hold a huge whitelist. A lightweight revocation strategy is presented for remediation in case the authorized devices are stolen.
- We analyze six security properties achieved by our TMSUI.
- We implement a prototype system with full functions of TMSUI and the evaluation results show its good effectiveness with high compatibility and low performance overhead.

2   Related Work

There are many studies focusing on security issues of ICS and several approaches are proposed against threats to ICS. The protection measures in SCADA networks provided by access control, firewalls, IDS, protocol vulnerability assessment and cryptography are discussed in [13]. Artificial immune algorithm, which borrows the ideas from the modeling of human immune system, is used in ICS in order to detect and stop the intrusion [7]. Attack tree model [19] is leveraged to evaluate the vulnerabilities of cybersecurity in SCADA system. Infrastructure vulnerability assessment model [12] is conductive to quantify the vulnerabilities in ICS networks. TCG-based integrity measurement architecture [18] provides a method to control the untrusted processes in operating system and establish the trusted execution environment for software in ICS. [9] emphasizes that the application of technology alone will not provide solutions, but human factors can cause the insider threat and even easily destroy the secure environment of ICS. The latest NIST guide to ICS security [14] standardizes both the security technology used in ICS architecture and the ICS-specific security policies that regularize employees' behaviors. However, few publications explicitly mention the defense on the threats from USB storage devices and existing security measures hardly forbid USB storage devices accessing to steal sensitive data from ICS or upload malicious codes to ICS unless prohibiting USB devices completely.

Trusted computing (TC), as one security support technology, aims at constructing a specific integrity measurement mechanism to prevent untrusted codes from executing on the computing platform [36,37]. TC can report on the hash-value of software modules and help platform to build up trust chain. Using TC for x86-based hardware platform, Trusted Computing Group (TCG) proposes Trusted Platform Module (TPM) [31], while China proposes Trusted Cryptography Module (TCM) [22]. Nowadays, the widely used TPM chip is designed according to TPM v1.2 specification [32]. TCG has already released the latest TPM v2.0 specification [33], which absorbs some techniques from TCM including serial algorithms of Standard Commercial Cryptography (SM). TPM has been generally employed to construct trusted execution environment for security-sensitive computers in the similar way of [18]. TPM and TCM are the alternative security chips to build up our TMSUI. The unique endorsement key of the chip fixed on the mainboard is tamper-resistant and can be leveraged to identify the terminal of ICS. The chip's tamper-resistant cryptographic algorithm library crucially maintains the trust relationship between the administrators and the protected terminals.

Apart from system and network security, some research pays attention to the trust management and security issues of USB storage devices. Sinan et al. design and implement a security platform for USB flash disks [11]. The scheme only targets Windows OS and needs to deeply modify the kernel drivers. Moreover, it protects against only some of the known malwares. A method of USB device management in Linux is proposed by [10], which concerns the access control to USB device and defends against the attacks from computers. Some configure policies are given by [17] for Windows to block malwares and hack tools from USB devices. But it is considered vulnerable without concrete security technology. [20] details the forensic evidence for USB devices as a supplementary approach to trace the devices that behave abnormally. Physical information fixed in the firmware of USB device is treated as the identification which is hardly tampered. And recently, IronKey Secure USB devices [24] are recommended to protect against BadUSB malware using signed firmware. Nonetheless, the specially-made devices with high cost are unlikely to be accepted in large scale by enterprises. In general, all of these approaches cannot singly achieve a trust management scheme that is directly applied to the architecture of ICS and imposes fine-grained restrictions on USB storage devices.

3   Overview

This section gives an overview of our design, including the system architecture, our threat model and assumptions, and the design principles.

3.1 System Architecture

On the basis of ICS deployment diagram [28], we abstract general ICS architecture and omit some repeated or irrelevant components according to the USB
storage devices application scenarios. Figure 1 illustrates the system architecture
of our TMSUI. It consists of three sections. The left section belongs to corporate
network which serves for inner-enterprise applications such as ERP system and
top monitoring system. It provides the only interface of the whole enterprise
to access Internet, while some enterprises disable the external access interface
for more security needs. Authorization server (AS) locates this area as one part
of enterprise management systems for administrators to authorize USB storage devices. There can be several ASs with several administrators. The middle
section is part of process control network which optionally contains engineer station, SCADA server and many other control and supervising terminals such as
operation station. Established on general computers, these terminals are responsible for programing industrial controllers, collecting industrial operation data
and automatically altering controllers based on exceptional data. Their security
is so vital that some errors intentionally caused by malicious codes may lead to
faulty operation of controllers and finally cause an accident. Moreover some confidential data on these terminals indeed need good protection from theft through
USB storage devices. Thus, these terminals are our protected objects (PO) and
equipped with security chip. The right section consists in control system network
where some specialized control devices run. These devices involve programmable
logic controller (PLC), programmable automation controller (PAC), remote terminal unit (RTU) and intelligent electronic device (IED). They are the only
components of ICS accessing field devices and rarely attacked directly. The networks in the left and the middle sections adopt general structure of Ethernet,
while the right one often uses filedbus structure or industrial Ethernet with
protocols such as Modbus [27] and Profibus [35].

3.2 Threat Model and Assumptions

We seek to protect the confidentiality and integrity of industrial data on PO and
keep threats from USB storage devices away. More precisely, our core goal is to
forbid unauthorized (untrusted) USB storage devices to access PO. An adversary
is assumed to use arbitrarily extraneous USB storage devices to attempt accessing PO. Malicious codes including malwares and evil scripts can be injected into
these USB devices. The adversary is also able to tamper the physical information of his own USB storage devices with the similar information of the formal
USB devices used inside the ICS. More powerfully, the adversary may randomly
steal an authorized USB storage device to access arbitrary PO[1], and modify its
physical information or format it in order to access his ideal attacking target.

  Our solution does not consider the direct attack itself on network, system,
databases or integrity of our software, which is beyond the protection scope in

---

[1] The adversary has a very low probability in ICS to find and access the right one of
PO that is just his ideal target and could be accessed by the stolen USB device.

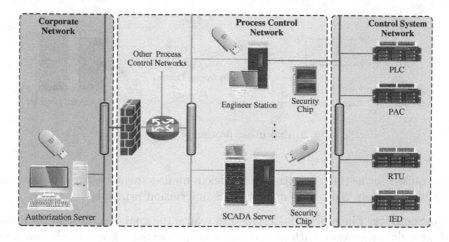

Fig. 1. System architecture of TMSUI.

this paper. The traditional safeguards like IDS, firewall, anti-virus software or isolated execution environment schemes [16,18] could be deployed along with TMSUI. Moreover our technical solution cannot absolutely stop the social engineering attack. For example, it is hard to prevent that a corrupt engineer "steals" his own authorized USB storage device to exactly access the PO which he often operates.

We explicitly lock the permission to change the OS time. It can be achieved by setting the OS and BIOS on terminals.

3.3 Design Principles

We propose TMSUI according to following desired design principles.

Strong Compatibility. The scheme is designed for a majority of ICSs. It executes on general computers with x86 architecture and is suitable for both Windows and GNU/Linux. The scope of USB storage devices covers mainstream devices including USB flash disk, memory card, mobile HDD, smartphone and embedded devices.

Low Cost. The scheme does not change the system architecture of ICS or require other special equipment except for security chip. On the one hand, many manufacturers have already equipped computers with TPM/TCM chips as standard components. On the other hand, it is easy and inexpensive to install an additional security chip into the legacy hardware through inserting chip into its PCI slot.

Centralized and Efficient Management. The scheme guarantees administrators have the privilege to authorize USB storage devices, manage trust relationship and revoke authorization. The administrators are regarded as proficient and faithful employees on the side of ASs. The model of rights allocation and

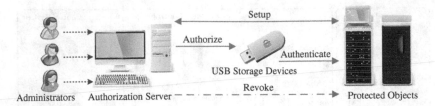

Fig. 2. Execution process of TMSUI.

trust transfer forms the centralized and efficient management, ensures the scheme security and meets the requirement of ICS supervision principle.

High Security. The scheme is designed to realize the goal described in Sect. 3.2 and provide protection with sound security properties. The attacks on the whitelist scheme and USB storage device cannot effectively threaten the security of our PO.

4   Trust Management Scheme

In this section, we detail our scheme. The execution process is first illustrated. Then we specify the phases of TMSUI. The security rules are finally presented.

4.1   Execution Process

The proposed scheme is composed of four phases: Setup, Authorize, Authenticate and Revoke. And there are mainly four kinds of entities participating in the execution process, including administrator, AS, PO and USB storage device. Setup only needs to securely execute at the very first time when the scheme is installed and launched in ICS or some considerable changes take place in ICS. After Setup, Authorize and Authenticate execute repeatedly for normally using USB storage devices. Revoke is a supplementary phase that can execute at any time after Setup. Figure 2 shows the execution process of the proposed scheme. To simplify the description of our TMSUI, we assume only one AS here with several administrators. In practice, another synchronization server could be added for coordinating data sharing among all the ASs.

4.2   Detailed Phases

The scheme takes one USB storage device as example. The physical serial number sn[2] and vendor ID vid of USB storage device could together uniquely identify the USB device [8,34]. The security chip owns a unique endorsement key ek

---

[2] On the market, a few USB storage devices do not have their serial numbers. It is reasonable and feasible to forbid using these devices here. In fact, these devices cannot pass the authentication of PO and will be ejected directly.

bound with the legal and secure identity for everyone of PO in ICS. This key is a pair of asymmetric keys in the form of (epk, esk), in which epk is the public key and esk is the private key. For the sake of security, esk never leaves the security chip. AS has an original database table that records all the legal epk of the security chips with which the enterprise has equipped PO. The information of the security chips could come from the chip manufacturer or be exported by the enterprise using a specific tool. In addition, respective administrator ID number $adminID$ with password $pswd$ for login in the AS is assigned to each administrator. The four phases of our TMSUI are described in detail as follow.

Setup. This phase initializes several keys and transmits original data between AS and PO for future use.

1. AS generates public parameters $param$ based on cryptography rules and randomly chooses a master key seed mks for creating other keys. Particularly, mks must be securely stored in AS. The revocation list $RevokeList$ is also generated by AS even if it is blank now.
2. There could be many administrators participating in the scheme. We take the administrator α for instance. The administrator α uses his ID number and password to login the AS and generates his authorizing key, which is a pair of asymmetric keys (apk_α, ask_α) by a key derivation function (KDF) with inputs of $param$, mks, ctr and $\mathsf{H}(pswd_\alpha)$. ctr is a monotonous counter value that ensures generating an unique key pair. $\mathsf{H}()$ represents a hash function. The generating process runs as

$$pdigest_\alpha \leftarrow \mathsf{H}(pswd_\alpha), \quad (apk_\alpha, ask_\alpha) \leftarrow \mathsf{KDF}(param, mks, ctr, pdigest_\alpha).$$

The private key ask_α represents α's identity in the later phases and becomes the forensic evidence when inside attacks occur. AS automatically generates storage protection key k_α by a pseudorandom number generator (PRNG) and then saves α's authorizing key after encryption action ENC. These two steps are

$$k_\alpha \leftarrow \mathsf{PRNG}(mks, pdigest_\alpha), \quad blob_\alpha \leftarrow \mathsf{ENC}_{k_\alpha}(apk_\alpha, ask_\alpha).$$

Likewise, all the administrators generate their own authorizing keys, storage protection keys and encrypted key blobs in this phase.

3. One of the PO ρ calls the driver of security chip to export the public key epk_ρ, and then sends it with more information, such as its plant area ID, production line ID and its usage, to AS for registering its legal identity. All the PO do this procedure similarly. If using TCM chip, for example, the epk_ρ exporting method is like

$$epk_\rho \leftarrow \mathsf{Tspi\_TCM\_GetPubEndorsementKey}().$$

Tspi_TCM_GetPubEndorsementKey is TCM API for exporting public ek.

4. After receiving epk_ρ, AS queries the original database table for checking the key's legitimacy. Passing the check, AS recodes the related information of ρ bound with its unique epk_ρ into a registration database table. At the end

of Setup, AS sends $param$, $RevokeList$ and all the effective administrators' public authorizing keys (apk) with their respective identifications ($adminID$) back to the successful registrants of PO. PO calls security chip to use its inside storage root key srk to seal each apk and save the ciphertext $EncData$ in the local hard disk:

$$EncData \leftarrow \mathsf{Tspi\_Data\_Seal}_{srk}(apk).$$

Authorize. In this phase, an unauthorized USB storage device is taken to AS. After confirming security of the device, one administrator operates to build up the trust relationship between it and some exact PO for a certain period of time.

1. In the light of the requirements for using USB storage device in ICS, engineers, staff members or operators could ask an administrator α to authorize the device. Plugging into the AS, USB storage device is first scanned and checked for malicious codes and other threats by traditional anti-virus software. Relying on rich experience, the administrator will judge whether the USB storage device is secure enough to be used in ICS.
2. After detection, the physical information of the USB storage device, including sn and vid, is extracted by AS. And then, with the physical information, some additional information such as brand, type, usage and holder are together recorded in a device management database table.
3. The administrator α uses his ID number and password to login the AS. Automatically, AS decrypts his authorizing key using decryption function DEC as

$$pdigest_\alpha \leftarrow \mathsf{H}(pswd_\alpha), \quad k_\alpha \leftarrow \mathsf{PRNG}(mks, pdigest_\alpha),$$

$$(apk_\alpha, ask_\alpha) \leftarrow \mathsf{DEC}_{k_\alpha}(blob_\alpha).$$

4. From the user of the USB storage device, α confirms which terminal of PO the user is going to access. For the selected terminal ρ, the corresponding epk_ρ is obtained from the registration database table. Then, the expiry date exp of authorization for USB storage device is determined by the negotiation between the user and α. The authorization for the device is in the form of a digital signature σ signed by α. The signature is generated at AS by calling function SIG using the private authorizing key of α. The detailed process of generating σ runs as follow.

$$sdigest \leftarrow \mathsf{H}(exp, epk_\rho, sn, vid), \quad \sigma \leftarrow \mathsf{SIG}_{ask_\alpha}(sdigest, param).$$

AS does not sign the data content of the USB storage device, which allows staff to use the authorized device repeatedly and flexibly after this phase. The enough security is guaranteed and controlled by the expiry date.

5. An authorization item is finally created and written into the authorization whitelist saved in a document in the USB storage device. The attribute of the document is set to "readonly" and "hidden" for preventing the whitelist from being modified unintentionally. The pattern of the item is a quadruple form like $(exp, epk_\rho, adminID, \sigma)$. $adminID$ identifies which administrator

---

Algorithm 1. Whitelist Verification Algorithm

Input: I: set of items in whitelist and each *item* contains $(exp, epk, adminID, \sigma)$
clt: current local time; E: set of *EncData*; epk_ρ; *sn*; *vid*; *param*
Output: *result*
1: $result \leftarrow false$
2: **for** *item* $\in I$ and *result* $\neq true$ **do**
3:      $i \leftarrow adminID$
4:      **if** not_expired(exp, clt) and $epk = epk_\rho$ and $EncData_i \in E$ **then**
5:           $sdigest \leftarrow$ Tspi_Hash_GetHashValue(exp, epk_ρ, sn, vid)
6:           $apk \leftarrow$ Tspi_Data_Unseal$_{srk}(EncData_i)$;   Tspi_Key_LoadKey(apk)
7:           $result \leftarrow$ Tspi_Hash_VerifySignature$_{apk}(\sigma, sdigest, param)$
8:      **end if**
9: **end for**
10: **if** $result = false$ **then** eject_USB_storage_device()
11: **end if**
12: **return** *result*

---

issues the authorization item and actually implies which public authorizing key is applicable to verify the signature σ. If the user wants to access several different PO, a few items could be simultaneously created using different *epk*. All the data used for generating items are saved in the registration database table as backup for revocation and forensics.

Authenticate. When a USB storage device is taken to one of PO such as ρ, this phase is triggered on ρ for authenticating whether the device is authorized legitimately and effectively. Some actions will be taken depending on the authentication result.

1. As a USB storage device is plugged into ρ, *sn* and *vid* are firstly extracted similar to the way in Authorize phase. And then, epk_ρ is exported from the security chip as ρ did in Setup phase.
2. Authentication process checks whether the authorization of USB storage device is revoked by AS. ρ tries to match *sn* and *vid* with each item in *RevokeList*. If one item is matched, the USB storage device is immediately ejected and Authenticate phase is terminated.
3. In this step, ρ reads out the whitelist in the USB storage device and uses security chip to check it. Algorithm 1 shows the specific verification algorithm for checking the whitelist. Four TCM APIs are called including Tspi_Hash_GetHashValue for computing the digest, Tspi_Data_Unseal for unsealing public authorizing key, Tspi_Key_LoadKey for loading the key into TCM and Tspi_Hash_VerifySignature for verifying the signature. The returned value *false* indicates the ejection of USB device and the termination of Authenticate phase. Conversely, the value *true* indicates the approval for normal use of USB device on ρ.

Revoke. This phase allows a revocation of some still effective authorizations of the lost USB storage devices. The lightweight strategy acts as a kind of remedial measure.

1. When a staff member notices his authorized USB storage device μ is missing, he would report the situation to one of administrators.
2. After receiving the report, the administrator looks up the corresponding sn_μ and vid_μ in the device management database table relying on the description of the lost USB storage device.
3. The administrator operates AS to make sure that there are really some authorization items of μ within its validity period. Using sn_μ and vid_μ to search in the registration database table, every related items exp is selected out and checked. If there is an unexpired authorization item, the following steps are executed.
4. AS adds sn_μ and vid_μ to *RevokeList*. In the meantime, AS validates every revoked information item again in the current *RevokeList*. The revoked information item is checked whether the corresponding authorization is expired and if it is, the revoked information item is deleted from *RevokeList*. In this way, *RevokeList* is updated into a new version.
5. According to the specific needs, AS could distribute the new updated version of *RevokeList* to all the PO with a certain frequency such as once a month or half a year, which would not cost much network traffic.

4.3   Security Rules

The technical solution of TMSUI could dramatically reduce the threat from externally unknown USB storage devices. However, the authorized devices may be infected later and unwittingly carry malicious codes to access PO. We propose the following security operation rules recommended as a complementary part of TMSUI:

– authorize USB storage devices with the period of validity as short as possible,
– carefully scan USB storage devices every time before authorizing it.

5   Security Analysis

In this section, we give an informal security analysis on TMSUI scheme. The proposed scheme satisfies the following security properties based on the assumptions in Sect. 3.2.

Correctness. TMSUI does not aim at any certain USB-based attacks, but its Authenticate phase theoretically prevents the unauthorized access and the invasion of most malicious codes from USB storage devices, as long as it is not authorized. The security chip uniquely identifies each of PO, and the unite of sn and vid uniquely identifies each of USB storage devices. Consequently, the flexible and specific whitelist scheme achieves our design goal.

Difficulty in Faking. If the adversary tries his best to tamper the physical information of his USB device and employ it to access the ideal target PO, he has to obtain the ideal sn and vid of the corresponding device for the target PO. It is definitely no easier than directly stealing a both authorized and ideal USB device from the inside of ICS, i.e., launching a complete social engineering attack.

Unforgeability. A valid whitelist in USB storage devices can only be created by a legal administrator through Authorize phase. The whitelist is signed using ask which is encrypted and saved only in AS. The whitelist is verified using apk which is protected by security chip in PO. Adversaries hardly forge or tamper a valid whitelist without stealing ask, cracking security chip or breaking cryptographic algorithms. Preventing these attacks is beyond the scope of this paper.

Copy Protection. The adversary may attempt to copy an ideal and legal whitelist from the authorized USB device to his illegal device and then use it furtively in ICS. Nevertheless, the signed whitelist contains the original sn and vid which are not match the illegal device. Therefore, PO would not admit the replicate but unmatched whitelist during Authenticate phase.

Non-repudiation. The administrators cannot deny their authorizing operation on the exact USB storage devices because of the signature associated with their unique $adminID$ and authorizing keys. Once the authorized USB device is stolen or malicious act is revealed, the related user and administrator could be sought out based on the relevant evidence in the registration database.

Revocability. The scheme considers revocation issue and enables revoking the authorization of the authorized USB storage devices. Revoke phase could reduce the threat and loss to a certain extent once the devices are stolen. PO are able to refuse the access of adversaries who try to use the revoked devices.

6   Implementation and Evaluation

This section describes the prototype system and evaluation of TMSUI on it.

The implementation of TMSUI is divided into a server part for AS and a client part for PO. In our prototype system, Windows platform is the target OS. Microsoft Windows device development kit (DDK) is used to develop bottom driver and achieve capturing, deleting and ejecting actions for USB storage devices. The bottom drive could load the public parameters to verify the whitelist in USB devices. We acquire the physical information of USB storage devices by reading some Windows registry entries mainly under the path: HKEY_LOCAL_MACHINE\SYSTEM\CurrentControlSet\services\. This method is generally feasible for different USB protocol standards including 1.1, 2.0 and 3.0. Besides, we accomplish to capture the event of devices' access by means of registering a daemon as system service running in background on both the server side and the client side. MySQL 5.6 is adopted to construct database on the server. In regard to cryptographic algorithms, we employ high-performance SM serials algorithms [22], also supported by TCM chip. We implement or set ENC, DEC, Tspi_Data_Seal and Tspi_Data_Unseal using symmetric cryptographic algorithm SMS4, SIG and Tspi_Hash_VerifySignature using digital signature algorithm SM2, and the hash function using SM3. In the client, these algorithms are directly provided by the security chip. The server of TMSUI totally consists of 3500 lines of C++ code, while the client has 2500 lines. In fact, TMSUI is not merely designed for one OS platform. The technic skills in [10] can help us implement TMSUI also on GNU/Linux system.

To establish the prototype system environment, we use a DELL OptiPlex 990 as AS. It has a 3.3 GHz Intel i3-2120 processor, 4 GB memory and USB 2.0 ports, and runs Windows 7 SP1. For PO, we use two of Lenovo ThinkCentre M8500t equipped with a 3.4 GHz Intel i7-4770 processor, 8 GB memory and USB 3.0 ports. These two PO respectively run Windows XP SP3 and Windows Server 2003 SP2, as well as some industrial control software for simulating an engineer station and a SCADA server. Moreover, we choose TCM 1.1 by Tongfang Micro-electronics Company as the security chip fixed inside the two PO. As PLC, a Honeywell PKS C200 is connected with the two PO for testing the impact of the potential threat from USB storage devices.

Table 1 shows the different kinds of USB storage devices we select to test compatibility of TMSUI on the prototype system. Only two devices cannot be applicable to TMSUI. For Apple device, it is unable to directly access PO without its dedicated driver. And for SD card, it works well when using the same card reader (reader1) to be authorized and authenticated, while it is invalid when using different card reader (reader2) during those two phases. This is because the physical information correlated with SD card is actually from the card reader.

Table 1. Compatibility of TMSUI for USB storage devices

Device	Toshiba 16 GB U-disk	Kingston 32 GB U-disk	WD 2TB mobile HDD	SanDisk 64 GB SD card + reader1
USB standard	2.0	3.0	3.0	2.0
Applicable	✔	✔	✔	✔
Device	Apple iPad mini 16 GB	BeagleBone-Black demo board	Samsung S4 smartphone	SanDisk 64 GB SD card + reader2
USB standard	2.0	2.0	2.0	2.0
Applicable	✘	✔	✔	✘

On the other hand, the executing cases of TMSUI definitely attest that it is impossible to download data from and upload data to PO through an unauthorized USB storage device or a wrongly authorized device. In order to evaluate protective property on defending malicious codes in unauthorized devices,

Table 2. Security of TMSUI for defending malwares in unauthorized devices

Malware	USBC [6]	RavMonE [3]	Stuxnet [5]
Defensible	✔	✔	✔
Malware	Havex [2]	Red Oct. [4]	BadUSB [1]
Defensible	✔	✔	partly

we pick out six typical malwares, including virus, Trojans, worm for ICS and BadUSB, and we save their samples in an unauthorized USB disk to access our POs for the test. Some malware samples are downloaded from public web pages [1,2,5] with source codes, while the others [3,4,6] are selected from our previous collection. By detecting whether POs are invaded by these malwares and whether PLC is disordered, TMSUI's effectiveness is examined. Especially, although Stuxnet only targets Siemens PLC and Havex hunts for SCADA systems using OPC communication standard, we can still identify their invasions on our experimental POs by monitoring their preliminary behaviors such as malicious scanning. Table 2 illustrates the test results. TMSUI is effective to prevent invasion of almost all the test malwares except BadUSB. With regard to BadUSB, defensibility of TMSUI depends on different situations. If a USB device is tampered into a storage device, or it first identifies itself as other devices like USB keyboard or network adapter and then requests reinitialization as a storage device, TMSUI could deny the unauthorized storage device successfully. But if a USB storage device is fully tampered into other kinds of devices, it is hardly recognized by TMSUI. This test result does not violate our security goal which aims at controlling the access in the exact form of USB storage device. Overall, TMSUI fulfills the design principles of compatibility and security.

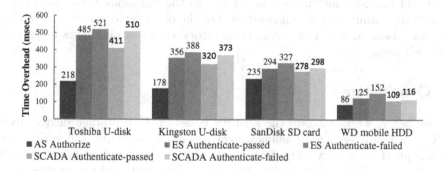

Fig. 3. Time overheads of 4 USB devices executing authorize and authenticate

Furthermore, we evaluate the performance of TMSUI by using four kinds of prevalent USB storage devices in Table 1 to execute Authorize phase and Authenticate phase. The Authenticate is tested on engineer station (ES) and

SCADA server for both passing the authentication and not passing. 10 administrators, 50 authorization items in each USB device and 10 items in *RevokeList* are assumed in the experiment. Every failed authentication result is given after attempting all test branch paths. Figure 3 illustrates the average time overheads of each test case running 20 times. Evidently, all the operations spend less than 600 milliseconds. This does not affect the normal use of USB storage devices and endows TMSUI more security on account of the speediness of ejecting dangerous devices. In practice, the prototype system of TMSUI has been tested in depth and got positive feedback from an automatic control system company and some industrial enterprises.

7 Discussion

In this section, we discuss some practical issues about deploying TMSUI.

Feasibility for Large-Scale ICSs. For large-scale ICSs with many POs, TMSUI operation overheads might overwhelm some absolutely centralized administrators. However, the issue can be solved through a well-designed hierarchy of administrators with the divided rights of jurisdiction. In fact, one or two administrators may only manage a specific region of ICSs, for example just involving a certain manufacturing process. Thus, the number of USB devices used within the region is quite limited for the administrators to focus on handling the TMSUI operations. The hierarchy does not violate the principle of centralization because the USB devices are still under the control of relatively centralized administrators who are also under the higher-level supervision.

Auditability for Administrators. With the help of backup proofs and logs in TMSUI, the administrative hierarchy enables the top-down audits on administrators' behaviors. On the one hand, once any POs are found invaded, the logs could provide clues to correlate them to the malicious USB devices and the corrupt administrators' misconduct. On the other hand, the regular audits may contribute to revealing the administrators' errors or oversights to prevent possible losses.

8 Conclusion

In this paper, we investigate the security issues on USB storage devices used in ICS, and propose a trust management scheme to specially deal with them. With support of security chip, the scheme achieves customizing offline whitelist for authorized USB storage device accessing exactly protected terminals in ICS. The management and control mechanisms prevent data transmission between unknown devices and sensitive terminals. Digital forensic and authorization revocation are enabled. The evaluation on the prototype system shows that our scheme is universal, effective and efficient. Our future work will concern formal proofs related to the security properties of TMSUI, and building trust chain on PO using security chip.

Acknowledgment. We thank the anonymous reviewers for their valuable comments. This work was supported in part by grants from the National Natural Science Foundation of China (No. 91118006, No. 61202414 and No. 61402455) and the National 973 Program of China (No. 2013CB338003).

References

1. BadUSB: http://github.com/adamcaudill/Psychson. Accessed 20 July 2015
2. Havex: https://www.f-secure.com/weblog/archives/00002718.html. Accessed 15 May 2015
3. Mon E.R.: https://en.wikipedia.org/wiki/RavMonE.exe. Accessed 9 June 2015
4. Red Oct.: http://heavy.com/news/2013/01/red-october-virus-cyber-attack/. Accessed 15 May 2015
5. Stuxnet: https://github.com/micrictor/stuxnet. Accessed 10 June 2015
6. USBC: http://www.mu-43.com/threads/20289/. Accessed 9 June 2015
7. Cai, N., Wang, J., Yu, X.: SCADA system security: complexity, history and new developments. In: 6th IEEE International Conference on Industrial Informatics, INDIN, pp. 569–574. IEEE (2008)
8. Carvey, H., Altheide, C.: Tracking USB storage: analysis of windows artifacts generated by USB storage devices. Digital Invest. **2**(2), 94–100 (2005)
9. Colwill, C.: Human factors in information security: the insider threat-who can you trust these days? Inf. Secur. **14**(4), 186–196 (2009). technical report
10. Deroncelé, E.B., Fuentes, A.P., Tejera Hernández, D.C., Cáceres Navarro, H., Fírvida Donestévez, A.A., Febles Parker, M.E.: USB Device Management in GNU/Linux Systems. In: Corral, L., Sillitti, A., Succi, G., Vlasenko, J., Wasserman, A.I. (eds.) OSS 2014. IFIP AICT, vol. 427, pp. 218–225. Springer, Heidelberg (2014)
11. Diwan, S.A., Perumal, S., Fatah, A.J.: Complete security package for USB thumb drive. Comput. Eng. Intell. Syst. **5**(8), 30–37 (2014)
12. Ezell, B.C.: Infrastructure vulnerability assessment model (I-VAM). Risk Anal. **27**(3), 571–583 (2007)
13. Igure, V.M., Laughter, S.A., Williams, R.D.: Security issues in SCADA networks. Comput. Secur. **25**(7), 498–506 (2006)
14. Keith, S., Suzanne, L., Victoria, P., Marshall, A., Adam, H.: Guide to industrial control systems (ICS) security. NIST Spec. Publ. **800**, 82 (2014)
15. Nohl, K., Kribler, S., Lehl, J.: BadUSB-on accessories that turn evil (2014). https://srlabs.de/badusb. Accessed 15 October 2014
16. Owusu, E., Guajardo, J., McCune, J., Newsome, J., Perrig, A., Vasudevan, A.: OASIS: on achieving a sanctuary for integrity and secrecy on untrusted platforms. In: Proceedings of 2013 ACM SIGSAC Conference on Computer & Communications Security, pp. 13–24. ACM (2013)
17. Pham, D.V., Halgamuge, M.N., Syed, A., Mendis, P.: Optimizing windows security features to block malware and hack tools on USB storage devices. In: Progress in Electromagnetics Research Symposium (2010)
18. Sailer, R., Zhang, X., Jaeger, T., Van Doorn, L.: Design and implementation of a TCG-based integrity measurement architecture. In: USENIX Security Symposium, vol. 13 (2004)
19. Ten, C.W., Liu, C.C., Govindarasu, M.: Vulnerability assessment of cybersecurity for SCADA systems using attack trees. In: IEEE Power Engineering Society General Meeting, pp. 1–8. IEEE (2007)

20. Tetmeyer, A., Saiedian, H.: Security threats and mitigating risk for USB devices. IEEE Technol. Soc. Mag. **29**(4), 44–49 (2010)
21. China National Vulnerability Database (CNVD: 2014). http://www.cnvd.org.cn. Accessed 20 September 2014
22. China State Password Administration Committee: Functionality and interface specification of cryptographic support platform for trusted computing (2007). http://www.oscca.gov.cn. Accessed 28 November 2013
23. Common Vulnerabilities and Exposures (CVE: 2014). http://www.cve.mitre.org. Accessed 15 September 2014
24. Imation Corporation: IronKey secure USB devices (2014). http://www.ironkey. com/en-US/solutions/protect-against-badusb.html. Accessed 25 November 2014
25. Industrial Control Systems Cyber Emergency Response Team (ICS-CRET): ICS-CERT monitor for October-December 2013 (2013). https://ics-cert.us-cert. gov/sites/default/files/Monitors/ICS-CERT_Monitor_Oct-Dec2013.pdf. Accessed 10 October 2014
26. Industrial Control Systems Cyber Emergency Response Team (ICS-CRET): ICS-CERT monitor for January-April 2014 (2014). https://ics-cert.us-cert.gov/sites/ default/files/Monitors/ICS-CERT_Monitor_%20Jan-April2014.pdf. Accessed 20 September 2014
27. Modbus: Modbus application protocol specification v1.1b3 (2012). http://www. modbus.org/docs/Modbus_Application_Protocol_V1_1b3.pdf. Accessed 10 November 2014
28. NSFOCUS Information Technology Co., Ltd: Research report on ICS and its security (2013). http://www.nsfocus.com. Accessed 5 February 2014
29. NSFOCUS Information Technology Co., Ltd: 2014 ICS security report (2014). http://vdisk.weibo.com/s/r1DAFAovsYVH. Accessed 28 September 2014
30. NSFOCUS Information Technology Co., Ltd: Research and practice on security of industry control system (2014). http://www.nsfocus.com/report/NSFOCUS_ICS_ Security_Report_20140311.pdf. Accessed 28 July 2014
31. Trusted Computing Group: TCG specification architecture overview, version 1.4 (2007). http://www.trustedcomputinggroup.org/resources/tcg_architecture_ overview_version_14/. Accessed 25 October 2013
32. Trusted Computing Group: TPM main specification version 1.2, revision 116 (2011). http://www.trustedcomputinggroup.org/resources/tpm_main_ specification. Accessed 25 October 2013
33. Trusted Computing Group: Trusted platform module library, family 2.0 (2014). http://www.trustedcomputinggroup.org/resources/tpm_library_specification. Accessed 10 December 2013
34. Thomas, P., Morris, A.: An investigation into the development of an anti-forensic tool to obscure USB flash drive device information on a Windows XP platform. In: Third International Annual Workshop on WDFIA, pp. 60–66. IEEE (2008)
35. Tovar, E., Vasques, F.: Real-time fieldbus communications using profibus networks. IEEE Trans. Industr. Electron. **46**(6), 1241–1251 (1999)
36. Yang, B., Feng, D., Qin, Y.: A lightweight anonymous mobile shopping scheme based on DAA for trusted mobile platform. In: 2014 IEEE 13th International Conference on Trust, Security and Privacy in Computing and Communications (TrustCom), pp. 9–17. IEEE (2014)
37. Yang, B., Yang, K., Qin, Y., Zhang, Z., Feng, D.: DAA-TZ: an efficient DAA scheme for mobile devices using ARM trustZone. In: Conti, M., Schunter, M., Askoxylakis, I. (eds.) TRUST 2015. LNCS, vol. 9229, pp. 209–227. Springer, Heidelberg (2015)

Characterization of the Third Descent Points for the k-error Linear Complexity of 2^n-periodic Binary Sequences

Jianqin Zhou[1,2]($\boxtimes$), Wanquan Liu[1], and Xifeng Wang[2]

[1] Department of Computing, Curtin University, Perth, WA 6102, Australia
zhou9@yahoo.com, w.liu@curtin.edu.au
[2] School of Computer Science, Anhui University of Technology,
Ma'anshan 243032, China
wxf80106@163.com

Abstract. In this paper, a structural approach for determining CELCS (critical error linear complexity spectrum) for the k-error linear complexity distribution of 2^n-periodic binary sequences is developed via the sieve method and Games-Chan algorithm. Accordingly, the third descent point (critical point) distribution of the k-error linear complexity for 2^n-periodic binary sequences is characterized. As a consequence, we derive the complete counting functions on the 5-error linear complexity of 2^n-periodic binary sequences when it is the third descent point. With the structural approach proposed here, one can further characterize other third and fourth descent points of the k-error linear complexity for 2^n-periodic binary sequences.

Keywords: Periodic sequence · Linear complexity · k-error linear complexity · k-error linear complexity distribution

1 Introduction

The linear complexity of a sequence s, denoted as $L(s)$, is defined as the length of the shortest linear feedback shift register (LFSR) that can generate s. As a measure on the linear complexity stability of sequences, the weight complexity and sphere complexity were defined in the monograph by Ding, Xiao and Shan in 1991 [1]. Similarly, Stamp and Martin [7] introduced the k-error linear complexity, which is in essence the same as the sphere complexity. Specifically, suppose that s is a sequence with period N. For any $k(0 \leq k \leq N)$, the k-error linear complexity of s, denoted as $L_k(s)$, is defined as the smallest linear complexity that can be obtained when any k or fewer elements of the sequence are changed within one period.

The CELCS (critical error linear complexity spectrum) is first studied by Etzion et al. [2]. The CELCS of a sequence s consists of the ordered set of points $(k, L_k(s))$ satisfying $L_k(s) > L_{k'}(s)$, for $k' > k$. In fact, they are the points where a decrease occurs for the k-error linear complexity, and thus are

© Springer International Publishing Switzerland 2016
S. Qing et al. (Eds.): ICICS 2015, LNCS 9543, pp. 169–183, 2016.
DOI: 10.1007/978-3-319-29814-6_14

called critical points in [2], hence are called descent points here. In previous research, investigators mainly focus on the first descent points of the k-error linear complexity. There are some results on the second descent points [2,11].

In another research direction, Rueppel [6] derived the number of 2^n-periodic binary sequences with given linear complexity $L, 0 \leq L \leq 2^n$. For $k = 1, 2$, Meidl [5] characterized the complete counting functions on the k-error linear complexity of 2^n-periodic binary sequences with linear complexity 2^n. For $k = 2, 3$, Zhu and Qi [12] further gave the complete counting functions on the k-error linear complexity of 2^n-periodic binary sequences with linear complexity $2^n - 1$. The distribution of 1-error linear complexity of binary sequences with arbitrary prime period was studied by Tan et al. [8]. By using algebraic and combinatorial methods, Fu et al. [4] characterized the 2^n-periodic binary sequences with the 1-error linear complexity and derived the counting function completely for the 1-error linear complexity of 2^n-periodic binary sequences. The complete counting functions for the number of 2^n-periodic binary sequences with the 3-error linear complexity are characterized recently in [9].

In this paper, we present a structural approach for determining CELCS for 2^n-periodic binary sequences based on the idea reported in [9]. Accordingly, the third descent point (critical point) distribution of the k-error linear complexity for 2^n-periodic binary sequences is characterized. As a consequence, we obtain the complete counting functions on the 5-error linear complexity when it is the third descent point of the k-error linear complexity for 2^n-periodic binary sequences. We expect that with the structural approach proposed here, one can further characterize other third and fourth descent points of the k-error linear complexity for 2^n-periodic binary sequences.

In [9], all 2^n-periodic binary sequences with the prescribed 3-error linear complexity are investigated. In contrast, in [11] we only investigated the 2^n-periodic binary sequence with the given 1 and 3-error linear complexity as the first and the second descent points separately. Further in this paper, we will investigate the 2^n-periodic binary sequence with the given 1, 3 and 5-error linear complexity as the first, the second and the third descent points, respectively. In fact, we intend to characterize the 2^n-periodic binary sequence via CELCS and the obtained result here is more accurate.

The rest of this paper is organized as follows. In Sect. 2, we first give an outline about our main approach for determining CELCS for 2^n-periodic binary sequences. Also some preliminary results are presented. In Sect. 3, the third descent point (critical point) distribution of the 5-error linear complexity for 2^n-periodic binary sequences is characterized and also the complete counting functions on the 5-error linear complexity as the third descent point is presented. Concluding remarks are given in Sect. 4.

2   Preliminaries

In this section we first give some preliminary results which will be used in the sequel. At the same time an outline about the proposed structural approach is presented for determining CELCS for the k-error linear complexity distribution of 2^n-periodic binary sequences.

Let $x = (x_1, x_2, \cdots, x_n)$ and $y = (y_1, y_2, \cdots, y_n)$ be vectors over $GF(q)$. Then define $x + y = (x_1 + y_1, x_2 + y_2, \cdots, x_n + y_n)$. When $n = 2m$, we define $Left(x) = (x_1, x_2, \cdots, x_m)$ and $Right(x) = (x_{m+1}, x_{m+2}, \cdots, x_{2m})$.

The Hamming weight of an N-periodic sequence s is defined as the number of nonzero elements per period of s, denoted by $W_H(s)$. Let s^N be one period of s. If $N = 2^n$, s^N is also denoted as $s^{(n)}$. The distance of two elements is defined as the difference of their indexes. Specifically, for an N-periodic sequence $s = \{s_0, s_1, s_2, s_3, \cdots, \}$, the distance of s_i, s_j is $j - i$, where $0 \le i \le j \le N$.

The linear complexity of a 2^n-periodic binary sequence s can be recursively computed by the Games-Chan algorithm [3] as follows.

Algorithm 2.1
Input: A 2^n-periodic binary sequence $s = [Left(s), Right(s)]$, $c = 0$.
Output: $L(s) = c$.
Step 1. If $Left(s) = Right(s)$, then deal with $Left(s)$ recursively. Namely, $L(s) = L(Left(s))$.
Step 2. If $Left(s) \neq Right(s)$, then $c = c + 2^{n-1}$ and deal with $Left(s) \oplus Right(s)$ recursively. Namely, $L(s) = 2^{n-1} + L(Left(s) \oplus Right(s))$.
Step 3. If $s = (a)$, then if $a = 1$ then $c = c + 1$.

The following two lemmas are well known results on 2^n-periodic binary sequences. Please refer to [5,9,12] for details.

Lemma 2.1. Suppose that s is a binary sequence with period $N = 2^n$. Then $L(s) = N$ if and only if the Hamming weight of a period of the sequence is odd.

Lemma 2.2. Let s_1 and s_2 be two binary sequences with period 2^n. If $L(s_1) \neq L(s_2)$, then $L(s_1 + s_2) = \max\{L(s_1), L(s_2)\}$; otherwise if $L(s_1) = L(s_2)$, then $L(s_1 + s_2) < L(s_1)$.

Suppose that the linear complexity of s can decrease when at least k elements of s are changed. By Lemma 2.2, the linear complexity of the binary sequence, in which elements at exactly those k positions are all nonzero, must be $L(s)$. Therefore, for the computation of the k-error linear complexity, we only need to find the binary sequence whose Hamming weight is minimum and its linear complexity is $L(s)$.

Based on Games-Chan algorithm, the following lemma is given in [5].

Lemma 2.3. Suppose that s is a binary sequence with one period $s^{(n)} = \{s_0, s_1, s_2, \cdots, s_{2^n-1}\}$, a mapping φ_n from $F_2^{2^n}$ to $F_2^{2^{n-1}}$ is defined as

$$\varphi_n(s^{(n)}) = \varphi_n((s_0, s_1, s_2, \cdots, s_{2^n-1}))$$
$$= (s_0 + s_{2^{n-1}}, s_1 + s_{2^{n-1}+1}, \cdots, s_{2^{n-1}-1} + s_{2^n-1})$$

Let $W_H(v)$ denote the Hamming weight of a vector v. Then the mapping φ_n has the following properties.

(1) $W_H(\varphi_n(s^{(n)})) \leq W_H(s^{(n)})$;
(2) If $n \geq 2$, then $W_H(\varphi_n(s^{(n)}))$ and $W_H(s^{(n)})$ are either both odd or both even;
(3) The set

$$\varphi_{n+1}^{-1}(s^{(n)}) = \{v \in F_2^{2^{n+1}} | \varphi_{n+1}(v) = s^{(n)}\}$$

of the preimage of $s^{(n)}$ has cardinality 2^{2^n}.

Rueppel [6] presented the following result on the number of sequences with a given linear complexity.

Lemma 2.4. The number $N(L)$ of 2^n-periodic binary sequences with linear complexity $L, 0 \leq L \leq 2^n$, is given by $N(L) = \begin{cases} 1, & L = 0 \\ 2^{L-1}, & 1 \leq L \leq 2^n \end{cases}$

Based on algebraic and combinatorial methods, Fu, Niederreiter and Su [4] characterized the 2^n-periodic binary sequences with the 1-error linear complexity and derived the counting function completely for the 1-error linear complexity of 2^n-periodic binary sequences. Meidl [5] characterized the complete counting functions on the 1-error linear complexity of 2^n-periodic binary sequences with linear complexity 2^n. Zhu and Qi [12] gave the complete counting functions on the 2-error linear complexity of 2^n-periodic binary sequences with linear complexity $2^n - 1$.

In this paper, we will study the k-error linear complexity of 2^n-periodic binary sequences by using the sieve approach and Games-Chan algorithm. The adopted approach is similar to [9] but different from those in [4,5,12]. The proposed structural approach in this paper is based on the following framework. Let $S = \{s|L(s) = c\}, E = \{e|W_H(e) = k\}, SE = \{s + e|s \in S, e \in E\}$, where s is a sequence with linear complexity c and e is sequence with $W_H(e) = k$. With the following sieve method, we aim to sieve sequences $s + e$ with $L_k(s + e) = c$ from SE.

For given linear complexity c, it remains to investigate two cases. One is that $s + u \in SE$, but $L_k(s + u) < c$. This is equivalent to checking if there exists a sequence v such that $L(u + v) = c$. The other is the case that $s + u, t + v \in SE$ and $L_k(s+u) = L_k(t+v) = c$ with $s \neq t$, $u \neq v$, but $s+u = t+v$. It is equivalent to checking if there exists a sequence v such that $L(u + v) = L(s + t) < c$ and if so, check the number of such sequence v, where $W_H(u) = W_H(v) = k$.

3   Counting Functions for 2^n-periodic Binary Sequences with Given 5-error Linear Complexity as the Third Descent Point

Next we derive the counting formula of 2^n-periodic binary sequences with the prescribed 1-error linear complexity as the first descent point, prescribed 3-error linear complexity as the second descent point and the prescribed 5-error linear complexity as the third descent point. To this end, we will use *Cube Theory* recently introduced in [10]. Cube theory and some related results are presented next for completeness.

Suppose that the position difference of two non-zero elements of a sequence s is $(2x+1)2^y$, where x and y are non-negative integers. From Algorithm 2.1, only in the $(n-y)$th step, the sequence length is 2^{y+1}, so the two non-zero elements must be in the left and right half of the sequence respectively, thus they can be removed or reduce to one non-zero element in consequence operation. Therefore we have the following definitions.

Definition 3.1 ([10]). Suppose that the position difference of two non-zero elements of a sequence s is $(2x+1)2^y$, where both x and y are non-negative integers, then the distance between the two elements is defined as 2^y.

Definition 3.2 ([10]). Suppose that s is a binary sequence with period 2^n, and there are 2^m non-zero elements in s, and $0 \le i_1 < i_2 < \cdots < i_m < n$. If $m = 1$, then there are 2 non-zero elements in s and the distance between the two elements is 2^{i_1}, so it is called as a 1-cube. If $m = 2$, then s has 4 non-zero elements which form a rectangle, the lengths of 4 sides are 2^{i_1} and 2^{i_2} respectively, so it is called as a 2-cube. In general, s has 2^{m-1} pairs of non-zero elements, in which there are 2^{m-1} non-zero elements which form a $(m-1)$-cube, the other 2^{m-1} non-zero elements also form a $(m-1)$-cube, and the distance between each pair of elements are all 2^{i_m}, then the sequence s is called as an m-cube, and the linear complexity of s is called as the linear complexity of the cube as well.

Definition 3.3 ([10]). A non-zero element of sequence s is called a vertex. Two vertexes can form an edge. If the distance between the two elements (vertices) is 2^y, then the length of the edge is defined as 2^y.

As demonstrated in [10], the linear complexity of a 2^n-periodic binary sequence with only one cube has the following nice property.

Theorem 3.1. Suppose that s is a binary sequence with period 2^n, and non-zero elements of s form a m-cube, if lengths of edges are $2^{i_1}, 2^{i_2}, \cdots, 2^{i_m}$ ($0 \le i_1 < i_2 < \cdots < i_m < n$) respectively, then $L(s) = 2^n - (2^{i_1} + 2^{i_2} + \cdots + 2^{i_m})$.

Based on Algorithm 2.1, we may have a standard cube decomposition for any binary sequence with period 2^n.

Algorithm 3.1
Input: $s^{(n)}$ is a binary sequence with period 2^n.
Output: A cube decomposition of sequence $s^{(n)}$.
Step 1. Let $s^{(n)} = [Left(s^{(n)}), Right(s^{(n)})]$.
Step 2. If $Left(s^{(n)}) = Right(s^{(n)})$, then we only consider $Left(s^{(n)})$.
Step 3. If $Left(s^{(n)}) \ne Right(s^{(n)})$, then we consider $Left(s^{(n)}) \oplus Right(s^{(n)})$. In this case, some nonzero elements of s may be removed.
Step 4. After above operation, we can obtain one nonzero element. By only restoring the nonzero elements in $Right(s^{(n)})$ removed in Step 2, so that $Left(s^{(n)}) = Right(s^{(n)})$. In this case, we obtain a cube c_1 with linear complexity $L(s^{(n)})$.
Step 5. With $s^{(n)} \oplus c_1$, run Step 1 to Stop 4. We obtain a cube c_2 with linear complexity less than $L(s^{(n)})$.

Step 6. With these nonzero elements left in $s^{(n)}$, run Step 1 to Step 5 recursively we will obtain a series of cubes in the descending order of linear complexity.

Obviously, this is a cube decomposition of sequence $s^{(n)}$, and we define it as **the standard cube decomposition**. One can observe that cube decomposition of a sequence may not be unique in general and **the standard cube decomposition** of a sequence described above is unique.

Suppose that $s^{(n)}$ is a 2^n-periodic binary sequence. We first investigate the relationship among the first descent point, the second descent point and the third descent point of the k-error linear complexity. Second, based on the first descent point, the second descent point and the third descent point, we obtain the complete counting functions of 2^n-periodic binary sequences with given 1-error linear complexity, 3-error linear complexity and 5-error linear complexity as the first descent point, the second descent point and the third descent point separately.

Theorem 3.2. Let $s^{(n)}$ be a 2^n-periodic binary sequence with linear complexity 2^n. Then

(i). Suppose that c_1, c_2 and c_3 are in the standard cube decomposition of sequence $s^{(n)}$. $L_5(s^{(n)}) < L_3(s^{(n)}) < L_1(s^{(n)})$ if and only if c_1 is a 0-cube (only one nonzero element), c_2 and c_3 are two 1-cubes or c_1 is a 0-cube and c_2 is a 2-cube;

(ii). $L_5(s^{(n)}) < L_3(s^{(n)}) < L_1(s^{(n)})$ if and only if $L_1(s^{(n)}) = 2^n - (2^i + 2^j), 0 \leq i < j < n$, $L_3(s^{(n)}) = 2^n - (2^p + 2^q), 0 \leq p < q < n, j < q, p \neq i, j$, or $L_3(s^{(n)}) = 2^n - (2^i + 2^j + 2^r), 0 \leq r < n, r \neq i, j$.

Proof. Based on cube theory, sequence $s^{(n)}$ has a standard cube decomposition. As $L(s^{(n)}) = 2^n$, it is obvious that c_1 is a 0-cube.

First, suppose that c_2 and c_3 are two 1-cubes. Then $L_1(s^{(n)}) = 2^n - (2^i + 2^j)$, where $0 \leq i < j < n, L(c_2) = 2^n - 2^j$ and $L_3(s^{(n)}) = 2^n - (2^p + 2^q)$, where $0 \leq p < q < n, L(c_3) = 2^n - 2^q$ or $L_3(s^{(n)}) = 2^n - (2^i + 2^j + 2^q)$, where $0 \leq q < n, q \neq i, j, L(c_3) = 2^n - 2^q$. Thus $j < q$.

In the case that $L_3(s^{(n)}) = 2^n - (2^p + 2^q)$, we now prove that $p \neq i, j$. Assume that $p = i$, and the distance (based on Definition 3.1) of nonzero elements p_1 and p_4 is 2^i, where p_1 is in c_1 (in the case that p_1 is in c_2, the proof is similar), p_4 is in c_3. As the distance of nonzero elements p_1 and p_2 is also 2^i, so the distance of nonzero elements p_2 and p_4 is 2^{i+1}, thus $L_3(s^{(n)}) = 2^n - (2^{i+1} + 2^q)$ should be true, which contradicts to the fact that $L_3(s^{(n)}) = 2^n - (2^i + 2^q)$.

Assume that $p = j$, similarly one can prove that $L_3(s^{(n)}) = 2^n - (2^{j+1} + 2^q)$, which is not true, or one can prove that $L_3(s^{(n)}) = 2^n - (2^i + 2^j + 2^q)$. In this case, it is obvious that $q \neq i, j$.

Second, suppose that c_2 is a 2-cube and $L(c_2) = 2^n - (2^i + 2^j)$. It is easy to show that $L_1(s^{(n)}) = 2^n - (2^i + 2^j)$ and $L_3(s^{(n)}) = 2^n - (2^i + 2^j + 2^r), 0 \leq r < n, r \neq i, j$. □

Next we investigate the distribution of $L_5(s^{(n)})$.

Theorem 3.3. Let $s^{(n)}$ be a 2^n-periodic binary sequence with linear complexity 2^n and $L_5(s^{(n)}) < L_3(s^{(n)}) < L_1(s^{(n)})$, $L_1(s^{(n)}) = 2^n - (2^i + 2^j), 0 \le i < j < n$.

(i). If $L_3(s^{(n)}) = 2^n - (2^p + 2^q), 0 \le p < q < n, j < q, p \ne i, j$, then $L_5(s^{(n)})$ can be $2^n - (2^{i_1} + 2^{i_2} + \cdots + 2^{i_m}) < 2^n - (2^p + 2^q)$, where $0 \le i_1 < i_2 < \cdots < i_m < n, m > 3$.
For the case of $m = 3$. If $j < p$ or $i < p < j$, $\{i_1, i_2, i_3\} \ne \{i, p, q\}$; if $i > p$, $\{i_1, i_2, i_3\} \ne \{i, p, q\}$ and $\{j, p, q\}$. For the case of $m = 2$, $\{i_1, i_2\}$ can not include i, j, p or q.

(ii). If $L_3(s^{(n)}) = 2^n - (2^i + 2^j + 2^r), 0 \le r < n, r \ne i, j$, then $L_5(s^{(n)})$ can be $2^n - (2^{i_1} + 2^{i_2} + \cdots + 2^{i_m}) < 2^n - (2^p + 2^q)$, where $0 \le i_1 < i_2 < \cdots < i_m < n, m > 3$.
For the case of $m = 3$, $\{i_1, i_2, i_3\}$ can not contain $\{i, j\}$. For the case of $m = 2$, $\{i_1, i_2\}$ can not include i, j or r.

Proof. The following proof is based on the framework: $SE = \{t + e | t \in S, e \in E\}$.

(i). In the case that $L_5(s^{(n)}) = 2^n - (2^{i_1} + 2^{i_2} + \cdots + 2^{i_m}) < 2^n - (2^i + 2^j), m > 3$, let $s^{(n)}$ be a 2^n-periodic binary sequence with linear complexity 2^n, $L_1(s^{(n)}) = 2^n - (2^i + 2^j)$ and $L_3(s^{(n)}) = 2^n - (2^p + 2^q)$.

Let $S = \{t | L(t) = 2^n - (2^{i_1} + 2^{i_2} + \cdots + 2^{i_m})\}, E = \{e | W_H(e) = 5\}, SE = \{t + e | t \in S, e \in E\}$, where t is a sequence with linear complexity $2^n - (2^{i_1} + 2^{i_2} + \cdots + 2^{i_m})$ and e is sequence with $W_H(e) = 5$. With the sieve method, we aim to sieve sequences $t + e$ with $L_5(t + e) = 2^n - (2^{i_1} + 2^{i_2} + \cdots + 2^{i_m})$ from SE.

We investigate the case that $s + u \in SE$, but $L_5(t + u) < 2^n - (2^{i_1} + 2^{i_2} + \cdots + 2^{i_m})$. This is equivalent to checking if there exists a sequence $v \in E$ such that $L(u + v) = 2^n - (2^{i_1} + 2^{i_2} + \cdots + 2^{i_m}), m \ge 4$. As a 4-cube has $2^4 = 16$ nonzero elements and $W_H(u) = W_H(v) = 5$, thus it is impossible that $L(u + v) = 2^n - (2^{i_1} + 2^{i_2} + \cdots + 2^{i_m}), m \ge 4$. Therefore, $L_5(s^{(n)})$ can be $2^n - (2^{i_1} + 2^{i_2} + \cdots + 2^{i_m}) < 2^n - (2^p + 2^q)$.

Second consider the case that $m = 3$ and $i > p$.

Let $s^{(n)}$ be a 2^n-periodic binary sequence with linear complexity 2^n. If $L_1(s^{(n)}) = 2^n - (2^i + 2^j)$ and $L_3(s^{(n)}) = 2^n - (2^p + 2^q)$, then $L_5(s^{(n)}) \ne 2^n - (2^p + 2^i + 2^q)$.

We will prove it by a contradiction. Suppose that $L_5(s^{(n)}) = 2^n - (2^p + 2^i + 2^q)$. Let $S = \{t | L(t) = 2^n - (2^p + 2^i + 2^q)\}, E = \{e | W_H(e) = 5\}, SE = \{t + e | t \in S, e \in E\}$, where t is a sequence with linear complexity $2^n - (2^p + 2^i + 2^q)$ and e is sequence with $W_H(e) = 5$. With the sieve method, we aim to sieve sequences $t + e$ with $L_5(t + e) = 2^n - (2^p + 2^i + 2^q)$ from SE.

We now investigate the case that $s + u \in SE$, but $L_5(t + u) < 2^n - (2^p + 2^i + 2^q)$. This is equivalent to checking if there exists a sequence $v \in E$ such that $L(u + v) = 2^n - (2^p + 2^i + 2^q)$.

For any $u \in E$ such that $L_1(t + u) = 2^n - (2^i + 2^j)$ and $L_3(t + u) = 2^n - (2^p + 2^q)$. It is easy to prove that there exists a sequence $v \in E$ such that $L_1(t + v) = 2^n - (2^i + 2^j)$, $L_3(t + v) = 2^n - (2^p + 2^q)$ and $L(u + v) = 2^n - (2^p + 2^i + 2^q)$. (Refer to Example 3.1 for the illustration of the proof) So $L_5(t + u) < 2^n - (2^p + 2^i + 2^q)$. Therefore $\{i_1, i_2, i_3\} \ne \{i, p, q\}$.

Similarly, let $L(t) = 2^n - (2^p + 2^j + 2^q)$. There exists a sequence $v \in E$ such that $L_1(t + v) = 2^n - (2^i + 2^j)$, $L_3(t + v) = 2^n - (2^p + 2^q)$ and $L(u + v) = 2^n - (2^p + 2^j + 2^q)$. So $L_5(t + u) < 2^n - (2^p + 2^j + 2^q)$. Therefore $\{i_1, i_2, i_3\} \neq \{j, p, q\}$.

In the case that $m = 2$, $\{i_1, i_2\}$ can not contain i, j, p or q. Suppose that $\{i_1, i_2\}$ comprises q and $L = 2^n - (2^w + 2^q)$. As $L = 2^n - (2^w + 2^q) < 2^n - (2^p + 2^q)$, thus $w > p$. For any $u \in E$ such that $L_1(t + u) = 2^n - (2^i + 2^j)$ and $L_3(t + u) = 2^n - (2^p + 2^q)$. It is easy to prove that there exists a sequence $v \in E$ such that $L_1(t + v) = 2^n - (2^i + 2^j)$, $L_3(t + v) = 2^n - (2^p + 2^q)$ and $L(u + v) = 2^n - (2^w + 2^q)$. (Refer to Example 3.2 for the illustration of the proof.) So $L_5(t + u) < 2^n - (2^w + 2^q)$. Therefore $\{i_1, i_2\} \neq \{w, q\}$.

(ii). In the case that $m = 3$ and $r > j$, $\{i_1, i_2, i_3\}$ can not contain $\{i, j\}$.

In the case that $L_3(s^{(n)}) = 2^n - (2^i + 2^j + 2^r)$. Note that c_1 is a 0-cube and c_2 is a 2-cube, $L(c_2) = L_1(s^{(n)}) = 2^n - (2^i + 2^j)$. For any $u \in E$ such that $L_1(t + u) = 2^n - (2^i + 2^j)$ and $L_3(t + u) = 2^n - (2^i + 2^j + 2^r)$. It is easy to prove that there exists a sequence $v \in E$ such that $L_1(t + v) = 2^n - (2^i + 2^j)$, $L_3(t + v) = 2^n - (2^i + 2^j + 2^r)$ and $L(u + v) = 2^n - (2^i + 2^j + 2^w)$. (Refer to Example 3.3 for the illustration of the proof.) So $L_5(t + u) < 2^n - (2^i + 2^j + 2^w)$. Therefore $\{i_1, i_2, i_3\}$ can not contain $\{i, j\}$.

Similarly, for the case of $m = 2$, it is easy to show that $\{i_1, i_2\}$ can not include i, j or r.

This completes the proof.   □

Example 3.1. Let $u = \{1101\ 0100\ 1000\ 0000\}$ with $L_1(u) = 2^4 - (2 + 2^2)$ and $L_3(u) = 2^4 - (1 + 2^3)$. There exists a sequence $v = \{0010\ 0100\ 0111\ 0000\}$ such that $L_1(v) = 2^4 - (2 + 2^2)$, $L_3(v) = 2^4 - (1 + 2^3)$, and $L(u + v) = 2^4 - (2^0 + 2^1 + 2^3)$.

Example 3.2. Suppose that $n = 5, i = 2, j = 3, p = 1, q = 4, w = 2$,
$u^{(5)} = \{1010\ 0010\ 0010\ 0000\ 1000\ 0000\ 0000\ 0000\}$.
Then $L = 2^n - (2^w + 2^q) = 12$. There exists
$v^{(5)} = \{0010\ 1010\ 0010\ 0000\ 0000\ 1000\ 0000\ 0000\}$, such that $L(u^{(5)} + v^{(5)}) = 2^5 - (2^2 + 2^4) = 12$.

Example 3.3. Suppose that $n = 4, i = 0, j = 1, r = 2, w = 3$,
$u^{(4)} = \{1111\ 1000\ 0000\ 0000\}$. Then there exists $v^{(4)} = \{0000\ 1000\ 1111\ 0000\}$, such that $L(u^{(4)} + v^{(4)}) = 2^4 - (1 + 2 + 2^3)$.

We next derive the counting formula of binary sequences with the prescribed 1-error linear complexity, the prescribed 3-error linear complexity and the prescribed 5-error linear complexity.

Theorem 3.4. paginationLet $s^{(n)}$ be a 2^n-periodic binary sequence with linear complexity 2^n.

(1) Suppose that $L_5(s^{(n)}) < L_3(s^{(n)}) < L_1(s^{(n)})$ and $L_1(s^{(n)}) = 2^n - (2^i + 2^j), 0 \leq i < j < n$, $L_3(s^{(n)}) = 2^n - (2^p + 2^q), 0 \leq p < q < n, j < q, p \neq i, j$, and $L_5(s^{(n)}) = 2^n - (2^{i_1} + 2^{i_2} + \cdots + 2^{i_m}) < L_3(s^{(n)})$, where $0 \leq i_1 < i_2 < \cdots < i_m < n, m > 1$. Then the number of 2^n-periodic binary sequences $s^{(n)}$ can be given by

$$\delta \times 2^{5n-q-p-j-i-6} \times 2^{L-1}/(\theta \times \mu \times 2^\epsilon \times 32^{n-i_m-1})$$

where θ is defined in (1) of the following proof, δ, μ and ϵ are defined in the following proof according to $j < p$, $i < p < j$ and $p < i < j$.

If $L_5(s^{(n)}) = 0$, then the number of 2^n-periodic binary sequences $s^{(n)}$ can be given by

$$\gamma \times 2^{5n-q-p-j-i-6}$$

where if $j < p$ then $\gamma = 3$, if $j > p > i$ then $\gamma = 2$ else $\gamma = 1$.

(2) Suppose that $L_5(s^{(n)}) < L_3(s^{(n)}) < L_1(s^{(n)})$ and $L_1(s^{(n)}) = 2^n - (2^i + 2^j), 0 \le i < j < n$, $L_3(s^{(n)}) = 2^n - (2^i + 2^j + 2^r), 0 \le r < n, r \ne i, j$, and $L_5(s^{(n)}) = 2^n - (2^{i_1} + 2^{i_2} + \cdots + 2^{i_m}) < L_3(s^{(n)})$, where $0 \le i_1 < i_2 < \cdots < i_m < n, m > 1$. Then the number of 2^n-periodic binary sequences $s^{(n)}$ can be given by

$$\delta \times 2^{5n-r-2j-i-6} \times 2^{L-1} / (\theta \times 2^\epsilon \times 32^{n-i_m-1})$$

where δ, θ and ϵ are defined in the following proof according to $j < r$, $i < r < j$ and $r < i < j$.

If $L_5(s^{(n)}) = 0$, then the number of 2^n-periodic binary sequences $s^{(n)}$ can be given by

$$\gamma \times 2^{5n-r-2j-i-6}$$

where if $r < i$ then $\gamma = 1/2$ else $\gamma = 1$.

Proof. (1) Let $S = \{t | L(t) = L\}, E = \{e | W_H(e) = 5\}, SE = \{t+e | t \in S, e \in E\}$, where t is a sequence with linear complexity $L = 2^n - (2^{i_1} + 2^{i_2} + \cdots + 2^{i_m}), m > 2$ and e is sequence with $W_H(e) = 5$, $L_1(e) = 2^n - (2^i + 2^j)$ and $L_3(e) = 2^n - (2^p + 2^q)$. With the sieve method, we aim to sieve sequences $t + e$ with $L_5(t + e) = L$ from SE.

By Lemma 2.4, we know that the number of 2^n-periodic binary sequences t with $L(t) = L$ is 2^{L-1}. Now we will compute the number of sequences e with $W_H(e) = 5$, $L_1(e) = 2^n - (2^i + 2^j)$ and $L_3(e) = 2^n - (2^p + 2^q), j < q$.

In the case of $i < j < p < q$. The number of 2^{j+1}-periodic binary sequences $e^{(j+1)}$ with linear complexity $2^{j+1} - 2^j = 2^j$ and $W_H(e^{(j+1)}) = 2$ is 2^j. First one nonzero element is added so that $L_1(e^{(j+1)}) = 2^{j+1} - (2^i + 2^j)$. The number of $e^{(j+1)}$ becomes $2^j \times 2^{j-i}$.

Second one 1-cube with linear complexity $2^{q+1} - 2^q$ is added so that $L_3(e^{(q+1)}) = 2^{q+1} - (2^p + 2^q)$. Note that for $i = 0, j = 1, p = 2, q = 3$, sequence $\{1110\ 0100\}$ is from both $\{1110\ 0000\}$ and $\{1010\ 0100\}$. At the same time from sequence $\{1110\ 0100\}$, we have both $\{1110\ 0100\ 0100\ 0000\}$ and $\{1110\ 0100\ 0000\ 0100\}$ with $L_3(e^{(q+1)}) = 2^{q+1} - (2^p + 2^q)$. So the number of $e^{(q+1)}$ becomes $2^{2j-i} \times (2^3)^{p-j} \times 3 \times (2^4)^{q-p-1} \times 2^3 = 3 \times 2^{4q-p-j-i-1}$.

Finally the number of sequences $e^{(n)}$ with $W_H(e^{(n)}) = 5$, $L_1(e^{(n)}) = 2^n - (2^i + 2^j)$ and $L_3(e^{(n)}) = 2^n - (2^p + 2^q)$ can be given by

$$3 \times 2^{4q-p-j-i-1} \times (2^5)^{n-q-1} = 3 \times 2^{5n-q-p-j-i-6}$$

In the case of $i < p < j < q$. One 1-cube with linear complexity $2^{q+1} - 2^q$ is added so that $L_3(e^{(q+1)}) = 2^{q+1} - (2^p + 2^q)$. The number of $e^{(q+1)}$ becomes $2^{2j-i} \times 2 \times 2^{j-p} \times (2^4)^{q-j-1} \times 2^3 = 2 \times 2^{4q-p-j-i-1}$.

Thus the number of sequences $e^{(n)}$ can be given by

$$2 \times 2^{4q-p-j-i-1} \times (2^5)^{n-q-1} = 2 \times 2^{5n-q-p-j-i-6}$$

In the case of $p < i < j < q$. One 1-cube with linear complexity $2^{q+1} - 2^q$ is added so that $L_3(e^{(q+1)}) = 2^{q+1} - (2^p + 2^q)$. The number of $e^{(q+1)}$ becomes $2^{2j-i} \times 2^{j-p} \times (2^4)^{q-j-1} \times 2^3 = 2^{4q-p-j-i-1}$.

Thus the number of sequences $e^{(n)}$ can be given by

$$2^{4q-p-j-i-1} \times (2^5)^{n-q-1} = 2^{5n-q-p-j-i-6}$$

In general, the number of these $e^{(n)}$ can be given by

$$\gamma \times 2^{5n-q-p-j-i-6}$$

where if $j < p$ then $\gamma = 3$, if $j > p > i$ then $\gamma = 2$ else $\gamma = 1$.

We investigate the case that $s+u, t+v \in SE$ and $L_5(s+u) = L_5(t+v) = L$ with $s \neq t$, $u \neq v$, but $s + u = t + v$. It is equivalent to checking if there exists a sequence v such that $L(u+v) = L(s+t) < L$ and if so, check the number of such sequence v, where $W_H(u) = W_H(v) = 5$. We need to consider the following two cases.

The first case is related to the minimum $i_0 < q$ such that $2^n - (2^{i_0} + 2^q) < L = 2^n - (2^{i_1} + 2^{i_2} + \cdots + 2^{i_m})$, where $q = i_m$. If $p < i, j$, then i_0 can be i or j.

For any $u \in E$, it is easy to show that there exist $2^{q-i_0} - 1$ sequences v, such that $L(u+v) < L$.

Second we consider the case of $i_m < w < n$.

Suppose that $j < p$. For $i_m < w < n$, there exist $31 \times 32^{w-i_m-1}$ sequences v, such that $L(u+v) = 2^n - (2^q + 2^w) < L$ or $L(u+v) = 2^n - (2^p + 2^w) < L$ or $L(u+v) = 2^n - (2^j + 2^w) < L$ or $L(u+v) = 2^n - (2^i + 2^w) < L$ or $L(u+v) = 2^n - 2^w < L$.

Note that for any sequence v with 5 nonzero elements, if we double the period of sequence v, then 2^5 new sequences will be generated. Therefore there exist

$$31 + 31 \times 32 + \cdots + 31 \times 32^{n-i_m-2} = 32^{n-i_m-1} - 1$$

sequences v, such that $L(u+v) < L$.

On the other hand, if $q < i_m$ and only $2^n - (2^q + 2^{i_m}) < L$ then the number of v will be increased by 32^{n-i_m-1}.

If $2^n - (2^p + 2^{i_m}) < L$ and $2^n - (2^j + 2^{i_m}) > L$ then the number of v will be increased by $3 \times 32^{n-i_m-1}$.

If $2^n - (2^j + 2^{i_m}) < L$ and $2^n - (2^i + 2^{i_m}) > L$ then the number of v will be increased by $7 \times 32^{n-i_m-1}$.

If $2^n - (2^i + 2^{i_m}) < L$ then the number of v will be increased by $15 \times 32^{n-i_m-1}$.

It follows that the number of 2^n-periodic binary sequences $s^{(n)}$ with $L(s^{(n)}) = 2^n$, $L_1(s^{(n)}) = 2^n - (2^i + 2^j)$, $L_3(s^{(n)}) = 2^n - (2^p + 2^q)$ and $L_5(s^{(n)}) = L$ can be given by

$$\delta \times 2^{5n-q-p-j-i-6} \times 2^{L-1}/(\theta \times \mu \times 2^\epsilon \times 32^{n-i_m-1})$$

where

$$\text{if } q = i_m \text{ and there exits } i_0 < q \text{ then } \theta = 2^{q-i_0} \text{ else } \theta = 1. \qquad (1)$$

For the case of $j < p$. If $L = 2^n - (2^j + 2^p + 2^q)$ then $\delta = 1$, if $L = 2^n - (2^i + 2^p + 2^q)$ then $\delta = 0$ else $\delta = 3$; if $L > 2^n - (2^i + 2^p + 2^q)$ then $\mu = 2$ else $\mu = 1$; if $q < i_m$ and only $2^n - (2^q + 2^{im}) < L$ then $\epsilon = 1$, if $2^n - (2^p + 2^{im}) < L$ and $2^n - (2^j + 2^{im}) > L$ then $\epsilon = 2$, if $2^n - (2^j + 2^{im}) < L$ and $2^n - (2^i + 2^{im}) > L$ then $\epsilon = 3$, if $2^n - (2^i + 2^{im}) < L$ then $\epsilon = 4$.

For the case of $j > p > i$. If $L = 2^n - (2^j + 2^p + 2^q)$ then $\delta = 1$, if $L = 2^n - (2^i + 2^j + 2^q)$ then $\delta = 1/2$, if $L = 2^n - (2^i + 2^p + 2^q)$ then $\delta = 0$ else $\delta = 2$; if $L > 2^n - (2^i + 2^p + 2^q)$ then $\mu = 2$ else $\mu = 1$; if $q < i_m$ and only $2^n - (2^q + 2^{im}) < L$ then $\epsilon = 1$, if $2^n - (2^j + 2^{im}) < L$ and $2^n - (2^p + 2^{im}) > L$ then $\epsilon = 2$, if $2^n - (2^p + 2^{im}) < L$ and $2^n - (2^i + 2^{im}) > L$ then $\epsilon = 3$, if $2^n - (2^i + 2^{im}) < L$ then $\epsilon = 4$.

For the case of $j > i > p$. If $L = 2^n - (2^j + 2^p + 2^q)$ or $L = 2^n - (2^i + 2^p + 2^q)$ then $\delta = 0$ else $\delta = 1$; if $L > 2^n - (2^i + 2^p + 2^q)$ and $L > 2^n - (2^j + 2^p + 2^q)$ then $\mu = 4$, if only $L > 2^n - (2^j + 2^p + 2^q)$ then $\mu = 2$ else $\mu = 1$; if $q < i_m$ and only $2^n - (2^q + 2^{im}) < L$ then $\epsilon = 1$, if $2^n - (2^j + 2^{im}) < L$ and $2^n - (2^i + 2^{im}) > L$ then $\epsilon = 2$, if $2^n - (2^i + 2^{im}) < L$ and $2^n - (2^p + 2^{im}) > L$ then $\epsilon = 3$, if $2^n - (2^p + 2^{im}) < L$ then $\epsilon = 4$.

(2) First consider the case of $i < j < r$. Suppose that $s^{(i)}$ is a 2^i-periodic binary sequence with linear complexity 2^i and $W_H(s^{(i)}) = 1$, then the number of these $s^{(i)}$ is 2^i.

So the number of 2^{i+1}-periodic binary sequences $s^{(i+1)}$ with linear complexity $2^{i+1} - 2^i = 2^i$ and $W_H(s^{(i+1)}) = 2$ is also 2^i.

For $j > i$, if 2^j-periodic binary sequences $s^{(j)}$ with linear complexity $2^j - 2^i$ and $W_H(s^{(j)}) = 2$, then $2^j - 2^i - (2^{i+1} - 2^i) = 2^{j-1} + 2^{j-2} + \cdots + 2^{i+1}$.

Based on Algorithm 2.1, the number of these $s^{(j)}$ can be given by $(2^2)^{j-i-1} \times 2^i = 2^{2j-i-2}$.

So the number of 2^{j+1}-periodic binary sequences $s^{(j+1)}$ with linear complexity $2^{j+1} - (2^j + 2^i)$ and $W_H(s^{(j+1)}) = 4$ is also 2^{2j-i-2}.

Thus the number of 2^{r+1}-periodic binary sequences $s^{(r+1)}$ with linear complexity $2^{r+1} - (2^r + 2^j + 2^i)$ and $W_H(s^{(r+1)}) = 8$ is $(2^4)^{r-j-1} \times 2^{2j-i-2} = 2^{4r-2j-i-6}$.

There exist 2^4 2-cubes with linear complexity $2^{r+1} - (2^j + 2^i)$ from one 3-cube with linear complexity $2^{r+1} - (2^r + 2^j + 2^i)$. Any pair of one 2-cube with linear complexity $2^{r+1} - (2^j + 2^i)$ and one vertex from the 3-cube comes from exactly two different 2-cubes.

As $u \in E$ such that $L_1(u) = 2^n - (2^i + 2^j)$ and $L_3(u) = 2^n - (2^i + 2^j + 2^r)$. So the number of these u can be given by

$$2^3 \times 2^2 \times (2^5)^{n-r-1} \times 2^{4r-2j-i-6} = 2^{5n-r-2j-i-6}$$

Second consider the case of $r < i < j$.

We know that the number of 2^n periodic binary sequences $s^{(n)}$ with linear complexity $2^n - (2^j + 2^i)$ and $W_H(s^{(n)}) = 4$ is $(2^4)^{n-j-1} \times 2^{2j-i-2} = 2^{4n-2j-i-6}$.

There exit $\frac{2^n}{2^{r+1}}$ locations with the distance 2^r (Definition 3.1) to every vertex in a 2-cube. As $u \in E$ such that $L_1(u) = 2^n - (2^i + 2^j)$ and $L_3(u) = 2^n - (2^i + 2^j + 2^r)$. So the number of these u can be given by

$$\frac{2^n}{2^{r+1}} \times 2^{4n-2j-i-6} = 2^{5n-r-2j-i-7}$$

Third consider the case of $i < r < j$.

We know that the number of 2^n-periodic binary sequences $s^{(n)}$ with linear complexity $2^n - (2^j + 2^i)$ and $W_H(s^{(n)}) = 4$ is $2^{4n-2j-i-6}$.

There exit $\frac{2^n}{2^{r+1}}$ locations with the distance 2^r to every two vertices in a 2-cube. As $u \in E$ such that $L_1(u) = 2^n - (2^i + 2^j)$ and $L_3(u) = 2^n - (2^i + 2^j + 2^r)$. So the number of these u can be given by

$$\frac{2^n}{2^{r+1}} \times 2 \times 2^{4n-2j-i-6} = 2^{5n-r-2j-i-6}$$

We now investigate the case that $s+u, t+v \in SE$ and $L_5(s+u) = L_5(t+v) = L$ with $s \neq t$, $u \neq v$, but $s + u = t + v$. We need to consider the following two cases.

The first case is related to the minimum $i_0 < j$ such that $2^n - (2^{i_0} + 2^i + 2^j) < L = 2^n - (2^{i_1} + 2^{i_2} + \cdots + 2^{i_m})$. Suppose that $j = i_m$ and $r < i$, $i_0 < i$. For any $u \in E$, it is easy to show that there exist $2^{j-i_0-1} - 1$ sequences v, such that $L(u+v) < L$.

(The following example is given to illustrate the above case.

Suppose that $n = 5, i = 3, j = 4, r = 1, i_1 = 0, i_2 = 1, i_3 = 3, i_4 = 4$. So $L = 2^n - (2^{i_1} + 2^{i_2} + 2^{i_3} + 2^{i_4}) = 5$.

If $u^{(5)} = \{1010\ 0000\ 1000\ 0000\ 1000\ 0000\ 1000\ 0000\}$, then $v^{(5)} = \{0010\ 1000\ 0000\ 1000\ 0000\ 1000\ 0000\ 1000\}$.

Thus $L(u^{(5)} + v^{(5)}) = 2^5 - (2^2 + 2^3 + 2^4) = 4, i_0 = 2$.)

Suppose that $j = i_m$ and $i < r < j$, $i < i_0 < j$. For any $u \in E$, it is easy to show that there exist $2^{j-i_0} - 1$ sequences v, such that $L(u+v) < L$.

The second case is related to $i_m < w < n$.

Suppose that $j < r$. For $i_m < w < n$, there exist $31 \times 32^{w-i_m-1}$ sequences v, such that $L(u+v) = 2^n - (2^r + 2^w) < L$ or $L(u+v) = 2^n - (2^i + 2^j + 2^w) < L$ or $L(u+v) = 2^n - (2^j + 2^w) < L$ or $L(u+v) = 2^n - (2^i + 2^w) < L$ or $L(u+v) = 2^n - 2^w < L$.

Note that for any sequence v with 5 nonzero elements, if we double the period of sequence v, then 2^5 new sequences will be generated. Therefore there exist

$$31 + 31 \times 32 + \cdots + 31 \times 32^{n-i_m-2} = 32^{n-i_m-1} - 1$$

sequences v, such that $L(u+v) < L$.

On the other hand, if $r < i_m$ and only $2^n - (2^r + 2^{i_m}) < L$ then the number of v will be increased by 32^{n-i_m-1}.

If $2^n - (2^i + 2^j + 2^{i_m}) < L$ and $2^n - (2^j + 2^{i_m}) > L$ then the number of v will be increased by $3 \times 32^{n-i_m-1}$.

If $2^n - (2^j + 2^{im}) < L$ and $2^n - (2^i + 2^{im}) > L$ then the number of v will be increased by $7 \times 32^{n-im-1}$.

If $2^n - (2^i + 2^{im}) < L$ then the number of v will be increased by $15 \times 32^{n-im-1}$.

It follows that the number of 2^n-periodic binary sequences $s^{(n)}$ with $L(s^{(n)}) = 2^n$, $L_1(s^{(n)}) = 2^n - (2^i + 2^j)$, $L_3(s^{(n)}) = 2^n - (2^i + 2^j + 2^r)$ and $L_5(s^{(n)}) = L$ can be given by

$$\delta \times 2^{5n-r-2j-i-6} \times 2^{L-1}/(\theta \times 2^\epsilon \times 32^{n-im-1})$$

For the case of $j < r$. $\delta = 1, \theta = 1$. If $r < i_m$ and only $2^n - (2^r + 2^{im}) < L$ then $\epsilon = 1$, if $2^n - (2^i + 2^j + 2^{im}) < L$ and $2^n - (2^j + 2^{im}) > L$ then $\epsilon = 2$, if $2^n - (2^j + 2^{im}) < L$ and $2^n - (2^i + 2^{im}) > L$ then $\epsilon = 3$, if $2^n - (2^i + 2^{im}) < L$ then $\epsilon = 4$.

For the case of $i < r < j$. $\delta = 1$. If $j = i_m$ and $i < i_0 < j$ then $\theta = 2^{j-i_0}$ else $\theta = 1$. If $j < i_m$ and only $2^n - (2^i + 2^j + 2^{im}) < L$ then $\epsilon = 1$, if $2^n - (2^j + 2^{im}) < L$ and $2^n - (2^r + 2^{im}) > L$ then $\epsilon = 2$, if $2^n - (2^r + 2^{im}) < L$ and $2^n - (2^i + 2^{im}) > L$ then $\epsilon = 3$, if $2^n - (2^i + 2^{im}) < L$ then $\epsilon = 4$.

For the case of $r < i < j$. $\delta = 1/2$. If $j = i_m$ and $i_0 < i$ then $\theta = 2^{j-i_0-1}$ else $\theta = 1$. If $j < i_m$ and only $2^n - (2^i + 2^j + 2^{im}) < L$ then $\epsilon = 1$, if $2^n - (2^j + 2^{im}) < L$ and $2^n - (2^i + 2^{im}) > L$ then $\epsilon = 2$, if $2^n - (2^i + 2^{im}) < L$ and $2^n - (2^r + 2^{im}) > L$ then $\epsilon = 3$, if $2^n - (2^r + 2^{im}) < L$ then $\epsilon = 4$.

The proof is complete.   □

To further illustrate Theorem 3.4, we give the following two examples, which are verified by a computer program as well.

Example 3.4. Suppose that $n = 5, i = 0, j = 1, p = 2, q = 4, i_1 = 0, i_2 = 1, i_3 = 2, i_4 = 4$. So $L = 2^n - (2^{i_1} + 2^{i_2} + 2^{i_3} + 2^{i_4}) = 9$. As $j < p$ and $q = i_4$, so $\delta = 3, i_0 = 3, \theta = 2^{q-i_0} = 2, \epsilon = 0$. The number of 2^5-periodic binary sequences $s^{(5)}$ with $L(s^{(5)}) = 32$, $L_1(s^{(5)}) = 29$, $L_3(s^{(5)}) = 12$ and $L_5(s^{(5)}) = 9$ can be given by

$$(3 \times 2^{5 \times n-4-2-1-6}) \times 2^{9-1}/(2 \times 32^{5-4-1}) = 3 \times 2^{19}$$

Example 3.5. Suppose that $n = 5, i = 3, j = 4, r = 1, i_1 = 0, i_2 = 1, i_3 = 3, i_4 = 4$. So $L = 2^n - (2^{i_1} + 2^{i_2} + 2^{i_3} + 2^{i_4}) = 5$. As $r < i$ and $j = i_4$, so $i_0 = 2$, $\delta = 1/2, \theta = 2^{j-i_0-1} = 2, \epsilon = 0$. The number of 2^5-periodic binary sequences $s^{(5)}$ with $L(s^{(5)}) = 32$, $L_1(s^{(5)}) = 8$, $L_3(s^{(5)}) = 6$ and $L_5(s^{(5)}) = 5$ can be given by

$$(\frac{1}{2} \times 2^{5 \times n-1-8-3-6}) \times 2^{5-1}/(2 \times 32^{5-4-1}) = 2^9$$

4   Conclusion

A new approach to determining CELCS for the k-error linear complexity distribution of 2^n-periodic binary sequences was developed via the sieve method and Games-Chan algorithm. The third descent point distribution of the 5-error linear complexity for 2^n-periodic binary sequences was characterized completely.

Suppose that $s^{(n)}$ is a 2^n-periodic binary sequence. Let $N_k(L)$ be the number of 2^n-periodic binary sequences $s^{(n)}$ with linear complexity 2^n and the k-error linear complexity L. The complete counting function $N_1(L)$ is obtained in [5]. The complete counting function $N_3(L)$ is obtained in [9]. With an approach different from [9], we now consider a possible way to obtain the complete counting function $N_5(L)$ based on the results in this paper.

Let $N_{i,k}(L)$ be the number of 2^n-periodic binary sequences $s^{(n)}$ with linear complexity 2^n, the i-error linear complexity as the last descent point and the k-error linear complexity being L. Then we can have

$$N_5(L) = N_{1,5}(L) + N_{3,5}(L) + N_{5,5}(L)$$

As the complete counting functions on the 3-error linear complexity of 2^n-periodic binary sequences as the second descent point are obtained in [11]. Combined with the result of Sect. 3, we may have the complete counting function $N_5(L)$. Here we only give two examples to illustrate the counting function.

We further define $N_{3,5}(C1, L)$ as the number of 2^n-periodic binary sequences $s^{(n)}$ with linear complexity 2^n, the 1-error linear complexity $C1$, the 3-error linear complexity as the last descent point and the 5-error linear complexity being L. Define $N_{5,5}(C1, C2, L)$ as the number of 2^n-periodic binary sequences $s^{(n)}$ with linear complexity 2^n, the 1-error linear complexity $C1$, the 3-error linear complexity $C2$ and the 5-error linear complexity L as the third descent point. Now we can have the following examples.

Example 4.1. Let $n = 5, L = 12$. Note that $12 = 32 - (2^2 + 2^4)$. If $L_1(s^{(n)}) = 12$, then $L_5(s^{(n)}) < 12$.

If $L_3(s^{(n)}) = 12$, then $s^{(n)}$ contains one 0-cube (only one nonzero element) and two 1-cubes, thus $L_5(s^{(n)}) < 12$.

In the case of $N_{5,5}(C1, C2, L)$, from Theorem 3.3, i, j, p, q, r can not be 2 or 4. So

$$N_5(17) = N_{5,5}(29, 21, 12) + N_{5,5}(23, 21, 12) + N_{5,5}(22, 21, 12)$$
$$= 16777216 + 2097152 + 1048576$$
$$= 19922944$$

Example 4.2. Let $n = 5, L = 21$. Note that $21 = 32 - (1 + 2 + 2^3)$. If $L_1(s^{(n)}) = 32 - (1 + 2)$ and $L_3(s^{(n)}) = 32 - (1 + 2 + 2^3)$, then $s^{(n)}$ contains one 0-cube (only one nonzero element) and one 2-cube, hence $L_5(s^{(n)}) < 21$. It is similar for $s^{(n)}$ with $L_1(s^{(n)}) = 32 - (1 + 2^3)$ or $L_1(s^{(n)}) = 32 - (2 + 2^3)$.

In the case of $N_{5,5}(C1, C2, L)$, from Theorem 3.3, $\{i, j\} \subset \{0, 1, 3\}$ is impossible, $\{p, q\} \subset \{0, 1, 3\}$ does not hold. Thus

$$N_5(21) = N_{1,5}(21) + N_{3,5}(27, 21) + N_{3,5}(26, 21) + N_{5,5}(27, 25, 21) + N_{5,5}(26, 25, 21)$$
$$= 16777216 + 67108864 + 33554432 + 134217728 + 67108864$$
$$= 16777216 + 33554432 + 134217728 + 134217728$$
$$= 318767104$$

The examples above have been verified by a computer program.

Let $s^{(n)}$ be a 2^n-periodic binary sequence with linear complexity less then 2^n. Suppose that c_1, c_2 and c_3 are in the standard cube decomposition of sequence $s^{(n)}$ and $L(s^{(n)}) = L(c_1)$. $L_6(s^{(n)}) < L_4(s^{(n)}) < L_2(s^{(n)}) < L_{(s^{(n)})}$ if and only if c_1 is one 1-cube and c_2 is one 2-cube or c_1, c_2 and c_3 are three 1-cubes. Similarly, we can compute the number of 2^n-periodic binary sequences $s^{(n)}$ with given $L_{(s^{(n)})}$, $L_2(s^{(n)})$, $L_4(s^{(n)})$ and $L_6(s^{(n)})$. Accordingly, the solution to the complete counting functions of 2^n-periodic binary sequences with the prescribed 6-error linear complexity can be obtained.

The expected value of the k-error linear complexity of 2^n-periodic binary sequences could also be investigated based on our results. We will continue this work in future due to its importance.

References

1. Ding, C.S., Xiao, G.Z., Shan, W.J. (eds.): The Stability Theory of Stream Ciphers. LNCS, vol. 561, pp. 85–88. Springer, Heidelberg (1991)
2. Etzion, T., Kalouptsidis, N., Kolokotronis, N., Limniotis, K., Paterson, K.G.: Properties of the error linear complexity spectrum. IEEE Trans. Inf. Theory **55**(10), 4681–4686 (2009)
3. Games, R.A., Chan, A.H.: A fast algorithm for determining the complexity of a binary sequence with period 2^n. IEEE Trans. Inf. Theory **29**(1), 144–146 (1983)
4. Fu, F.-W., Niederreiter, H., Su, M.: The characterization of 2^n-periodic binary sequences with fixed 1-error linear complexity. In: Gong, G., Helleseth, T., Song, H.-Y., Yang, K. (eds.) SETA 2006. LNCS, vol. 4086, pp. 88–103. Springer, Heidelberg (2006)
5. Meidl, W.: On the stablity of 2^n-periodic binary sequences. IEEE Trans. Inf. Theory **51**(3), 1151–1155 (2005)
6. Rueppel, R.A.: Analysis and Design of Stream Ciphers. Springer, Berlin (1986). chapter 4
7. Stamp, M., Martin, C.F.: An algorithm for the k-error linear complexity of binary sequences with period 2^n. IEEE Trans. Inf. Theory **39**, 1398–1401 (1993)
8. Tan, L., Qi, W.F., Xu, H.: Distribution of one-error linear complexity of binary sequences for arbitrary prime period. J. Syst. Sci. Complex. **25**(6), 1223–1233 (2012)
9. Zhou, J.Q., Liu, W.Q.: The k-error linear complexity distribution for 2^n-periodic binary sequences. Des. Codes Crypt. **73**(1), 55–75 (2014)
10. Zhou, J., Liu, W., Zhou, G.: Cube theory and stable k-error linear complexity for periodic sequences. In: Lin, D., Xu, S., Yung, M. (eds.) Inscrypt 2013. LNCS, vol. 8567, pp. 70–85. Springer, Heidelberg (2014)
11. Zhou, J.Q., Wang, X.F., Liu, W.Q.: Structure Analysis on the k-error Linear Complexity for 2^n-periodic Binary Sequences (2013). http://arxiv.org/abs/1312.6927
12. Zhu, F.X., Qi, W.F.: The 2-error linear complexity of 2^n-periodic binary sequences with linear complexity 2^n-1. J. Electron. (China) **24**(3), 390–395 (2007). http://www.springerlink.com/content/3200vt810p232769/

QRL: A High Performance Quadruple-Rail Logic for Resisting DPA on FPGA Implementations

Chenyang Tu[1,2,3], Jian Zhou[1,2(✉)], Neng Gao[1,2], Zeyi Liu[1,2,3], Yuan Ma[1,2], and Zongbin Liu[1,2]

[1] State Key Laboratory of Information Security,
Institute of Information Engineering, CAS, Beijing, China
{tuchenyang,zhoujian,gaoneng,liuzeyi,mayuan,liuzongbin}@iie.ac.cn
[2] Data Assurance and Communication Security Research Center,
CAS, Beijing, China
[3] University of Chinese Academy of Sciences, Beijing, China

Abstract. Dual-Rail Precharge Logic (DPL) has proven to be an effective countermeasure logic style against Differential Power Analysis (DPA). All previous DPL architectures employ the precharge mechanism to achieve DPA resistance. However, due to its additional precharge phase, an inherent drawback of these DPL architectures lies within its degraded performance (less than 1/2 times compared to the nominal data rate), and hence they are not suitable for applications where high performance is required. In this paper, we present Quadruple-Rail Logic (QRL), a new DPA-hardened approach for cryptographic implementations in FPGA. The main merit of this proposal is that the system throughput can be effectively maintained by removing the precharge phase. By introducing a synchronized and identical quadruple-rail network, strengthened DPA resistance can be achieved. In order to test the robustness of QRL against DPA, we launch DPA on a QRL-based standard AES processor on Xilinx Virtex-5 FPGA. The experimental results show that DPA on QRL AES is failed by analyzing 100,000 power consumption traces, which achieves the competitive DPA resistance level as typical DPL schemes, and gains at least 110 times stronger than the unprotected AES.

Keywords: FPGA · Power analysis · Dual-rail precharge logic (DPL) · High performance · Quadruple-rail

1 Introduction

Since the inspiring work of Kocher et al. [7], Differential Power Analysis (DPA) has been widely considered as a critical threat to the hardware implementations of cryptographic algorithms. The idea of DPA is that the processed data in

C. Tu—This work is supported by a grant from the National High Technology Research and Development Program of China (863 Program, No. 2013AA01A214).

the crypto device inevitably has correlation with the amount of the withdrawn current from the power source. By analyzing the dependencies hidden inside the collected power consumption, some confidential information, typically as the cipher key, can be exploited. FPGA has been one of the most widely used platforms of cryptographic implementations, and it is shown in [10,13] that DPA can be a real and important threat against the FPGA based cryptographic implementations. Moreover, authors of [14] show that the register on FPGA is an important source of power leakage, and the activity of register can be easily distinguished due to the enable signal of registers managed by a control part, which makes register the most common DPA attack element on FPGA.

To defeat DPA, many countermeasures need to be applied at low-level logic layers, *i.e.*, gate level or layout level. This is due to the fact that many significant power leakages come from the physical level rather than the higher algorithmic level. Dual-Rail Precharge Logic (DPL) is one of the typical protection methods aiming at low-level protection. In order to compensate the data-dependent power leakages, two parallel rails corresponding to the true rail and the false rail are generated to work in the evaluation phase and the precharge phase periodically. However, one of the most influential drawbacks of DPL scheme is the significant degradation of the system throughput, since the precharge phase which generates invalid value in the circuit commonly occupies a great portion of the computation time. For instance, the calculation speed of WDDL (a typical DPL scheme) [18] falls to 50 % of the unprotected implementation. In fact, all DPL methods suffer from such a reduction of computational performances. Thus, these countermeasures are not suitable for the high performance environments (*e.g.*, base stations in modern encryption-supported mobile communication systems).

Two possible methods to solve this problem are reducing the precharge phase and eliminating the precharge phase. In [9], a non-regular clock is applied to BCDL, in order to reduce the precharge phase. Unfortunately, the non-regular clock is more complex than the conventional clock scheme, and the speed of BCDL still falls to 75 % of the unprotected implementation. Different from DPL schemes, a new Dual-Rail scheme named HDRL [16] removes the precharge phase, by connecting together the ground voltage current (*i.e.* VSS) of the complementary gate and the supply voltage current (*i.e.* VDD) of the original gate. However, HDRL is not applicable to FPGAs, since the VSS and VDD cannot be properly implemented on Look-Up-Tables (LUTs).

Our Contributions. In this paper, we follow the same general idea about eliminating the precharge phase and take advantage of the strategy of trading space for time, in order to improve the performance of our DPA countermeasure. We propose a new DPA-hardened approach on FPGA based implementations, namely, the Quadruple-Rail Logic (QRL) architecture, which can maintain a high performance that is approximately equal to the unprotected system, while without sacrificing its resistance against DPA attacks. In order to verify the robustness of QRL against DPA, we perform experiments on a QRL-enabled AES implementation based on FPGA. The experimental results show that the

DPA robustness of QRL is as good as a typical DPL scheme WDDL, and is at least 110 times stronger than the unprotected AES implementation.

Organization. In Sect. 2, we briefly introduce the related works of existing DPL solutions. Section 3 discusses the reason for the performance degradation and introduces the details of our new QRL structure. We launch experiments to further demonstrate the strength of QRL against DPA in Sect. 4. Section 5 concludes the paper.

2   Related Work

DPL is one of the most typical logic-level countermeasures against DPA. The operation of the DPL logic is defined by two main concepts. First, DPL has two parallel rails, namely, the dual-rail which consists of the original (True/T) rail and the complementary (False/F) rail as a counterpart of the T rail. Therefore, the signals in DPL are represented with a pair of values which are generated by the T rail and the F rail respectively. Second, the dual rails work simultaneously in complementary behaviors. More precisely, the T rail and the F rail work in the evaluation and the precharge phase periodically. In each evaluation period, the value $a_{(T)}$ in T rail and $a_{(F)}$ in F rail compensate with each other (*i.e.*, $[a_{(T)} : a_{(F)}]$ is always in state of $[1 : 0]$ or $[0 : 1]$). In each precharge period, the pair of values $[a_{(T)} : a_{(F)}]$ is reset to a fix state (typically $[0 : 0]$). In a sequel, the circuit system theoretically provides constant power consumption regardless of the processed data if DPL can be properly realized. The theoretical foundations for security of dual-rail logic and some efficient techniques for building such logic circuits is introduced by [6].

Many architectures have been introduced for achieving a secure and low-cost DPL realization. Wave Dynamic Differential Logic (WDDL) was proposed in [18], where a logic wave of values '0' is propagated through all the gate of the combinatorial logic chain. To optimize and improve DPL, several techniques have been previously proposed. Some techniques focus on the problem about identical routing, such as MDPL (Mask DPL)[11], DWDDL (Double WDDL) [19], and routing repair methods [4]. Others pay attention to the Early Propagation Effect (EPE) [15]. For instance, DRSL [2], STTL [12], BCDL [9], DPL-noEE [1], and PADPL [3], take different tactics to overcome the EPE problem.

According to the effect of the precharge mechanism, one of the most influential drawbacks of DPL schemes is its significant decrease of the performance. In [9], authors prove that among several schemes (WDDL, MDPL, STTL, DRSL, Seclib, IWDDL and basic BCDL), all schemes provide a low calculation speed which is less than 50 %. The performance of PADPL is also less than half of the unprotected implementation. In [3] and [4], two PADPL instances respectively provide 25 % and 41.7 % evaluation time during each clock cycle.

To improve the performance of DPL schemes, two solutions are usually employed: the first is to reduce the precharge phase and the second is to eliminate the precharge phase. The first idea can be achieved by using a non-regular clock, which leads to a shorter clock cycle in each precharge phase. In [9], compared with the basic BCDL, the accelerated BCDL can achieve a higher speed up to 1.3–1.5 times. More precisely, the maximum frequency of the accelerated BCDL is 50.64 MHz, rising up to 70 % of unprotected implementation (71.88 MHz of unprotected implementation). Unlike the DPL architectures, a Dual-Rail scheme called HDRL [16] improves the calculation speed by following the second idea. HDRL is designed based on the hypothesis that the VSS current drawn by a gate is indistinguishable for different inputs. The complementary pair of gates consists of two identical gates where the VDD of the gate in F rail is connected with the VSS of the gate in T rail. Through this scheme, the precharge phase is unnecessary and HDRL can achieve a higher calculation speed that is approximately equal to the unprotected system. HDRL is the first approach to eliminate the precharge phase, although the source current drawn by the circuit is not considered in HDRL, and the result is based on simulation tools rather than practical experiments [8].

However, compared with the unprotected implementation, both ideas have some drawbacks. Although the non-regular clock provides a less precharge time, the performance degradation still exists. Another drawback of the non-regular clock is that it may be limited by the clock system in ASIC or FPGA. Furthermore, even if HDRL is a good method to remove the precharge phase, it is not suitable for FPGA platform, where the VSS and VDD of LUT are restricted. Therefore, how to increase the performance of DPL-like approaches remains an open problem, and it is still the main bottleneck to apply these countermeasure in high performance environments, especially in FPGA.

3   Quadruple-Rail Logic

Although HDRL is not suitable for FPGA platform, it does imply that the DPL structure without the precharge mechanism is a promising approach to achieve higher performance. Based on the general idea, we propose a logic style named Quadruple-Rail Logic (QRL), which follows the strategy of trading space for time to highly improve the performance while still maintaining strong DPA resistance.

3.1   The Low Performance and Precharge Mechanism

Although the DPL schemes mentioned in Sect. 2 provide resistance against generic side-channel analyses, they are not able to provide satisfying performances compared with the unprotected implementation. For instance, in the case of WDDL, supposing the signal sequence of $a_{(T)}$ to be "1,0,0,1,1", the corresponding time sequence is shown in Fig. 1. WDDL takes 10 clocks to accomplish such operation while only 5 clocks are required in the unprotected one. The main cause of this efficiency reduction is the typical two-phase protocol (precharge and evaluation). In most cases, the precharge phase has roughly the same duration as the evaluation phase, it must last long enough for the signal '0' to propagate through the longest combinatorial logic chain.

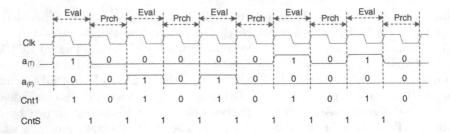

Fig. 1. The time sequence of WDDL

However, the precharge mechanism plays an important role in DPL, where the precharge phase is inserted between two adjacent evaluation phases to forcibly reset the whole system, except for the values stored in the precharge state, as shown in Fig. 1. Let $CntS$ and $Cnt1$ be the number of switches between every two adjacent states and value '1' in each state respectively. It is obvious that all values of $CntS$ are 1 in both phases. At the same time, $Cnt1$ keeps 1 in each evaluation phase and 0 in each precharge phase. This operation ensures that each complementary signal pair $[a_{(T)} : a_{(F)}]$ is able to provide constant values in both phases, and only one bit switch in each phase. Thus, this scheme effectively mitigates the variations of the power leakages, but at the expense of occupying half of the duty cycle of the evaluation phase. Briefly speaking, DPL provides a dual-rail complementary scheme in circuit: the first one is the value complement through the dual-rail mechanism, and the second one is the switch complement through the precharge mechanism.

3.2 QRL Architecture

As mentioned above, the DPL circuit is based on 2 principles: the value complement and the switch complement, while sacrificing its performance due to the precharge phase. To improve the performance, the precharge duty cycle must be decreased. Compared to the solution of reducing the precharge phase, removing the precharge phase is a more thoroughgoing solution. Following the solution of removing the precharge phase, we will conceive our new scheme, which adheres to the 2 principles in DPL circuit. Thus, the new scheme should follow the three principles:

- **Value Complement.** Maintain each state of the complementary signal pair which has half and only half bits to '1'.
- **Switch Complement.** Maintain two adjacent states of the complementary signal pair which have half and only half bits switch. In other words, the new scheme ensures that the complementary signal pair has half and only half bits switch in each clock cycle.
- **No precharge.** The precharge phase is fully removed.

In QRL, a quadruple-rail network which consists of four rails replaces the single rail in the unprotected implementation. The four rails in QRL are defined as follows:

- Original (True/T) rail: the value $a_{(T)}$ in the T rail is the original value in the unprotected single rail circuit.
- Complementary (False/F) rail: the value $a_{(F)}$ in the F rail is the complementary value of $a_{(T)}$ as the case of DPL, i.e., $a_{(F)} = \overline{a_{(T)}}$.
- Switch complementary (SC) rail: the value $a_{(SC)}$ in the SC rail is generated by $a_{(T)}$ and the last state of $a_{(T)}$. When $a_{(T)}$ is switched in two adjacent states, $a_{(SC)}$ would keep its state. On the contrary, $a_{(SC)}$ would be switched. To sum up, the switch complementary rail ensures that the signal pair $[a_{(T)} : a_{(SC)}]$ has one and only one switch in each clock cycle. Let $a_{(v)}^L$ and $a_{(v)}^P$ denote the last and the current state of the value $a_{(v)}$. The value $a_{(SC)}^P$ is described by:

$$a_{(T)}^L \oplus a_{(T)}^P = \overline{a_{(SC)}^L \oplus a_{(SC)}^P}$$
$$a_{(SC)}^P = a_{(T)}^L \oplus a_{(T)}^P \oplus \overline{a_{(SC)}^L}. \tag{1}$$

- Double complementary (DC) rail: the value $a_{(DC)}$ in the DC rail is the complementary value of $a_{(SC)}$. The DC rail is not only the value complement of the SC rail, but also ensures that the signal pair $[a_{(F)} : a_{(DC)}]$ has one and only one bit switch in each clock cycle. Similarly, the value $a_{(DC)}^P$ is described by:

$$a_{(DC)}^P = a_{(F)}^L \oplus a_{(F)}^P \oplus \overline{a_{(DC)}^L}. \tag{2}$$

We use the consecutive switching states of QRL in five clock cycles as an example to further clarify QRL. Suppose all signals are reset (typically value '0' to $a_{(T)}$ and $a_{(SC)}$, and value '1' to $a_{(F)}$ and $a_{(DC)}$ in this instance) before evaluation, and the state sequence of $a_{(T)}$ is "1,0,0,1,1". Due to the definition of each rails, the state sequences of $a_{(F)}$, $a_{(SC)}$, and $a_{(DC)}$ are "0,1,1,0,0", "0,0,1,1,0", and "1,1,0,0,1" respectively, as shown in Fig. 2. Let $CntS$ and $Cnt1$ be the number of switches between every two adjacent states and value '1' in each state respectively. It is obvious that all values of $CntS$ and $Cnt1$ are 2. It means that the complementary signal quartet $[a_{(T)} : a_{(F)} : a_{(SC)} : a_{(DC)}]$ is able to provide only two bits to '1' and only two bits switch in each clock cycle. Therefore, QRL meets the three principles, and improves the computational performance.

Based on the aforementioned theoretical elaboration, we discuss the practical implementation of QRL. Firstly, we show how to implement the basic component, namely, the QRL-enabled compound register system. Then we explain how to complete the whole QRL system.

3.3   QRL Register Exemplar

As mentioned above, a quadruple-rail network with four rails is employed in QRL instead of the single rail in the unprotected implementation. Thus, a compound

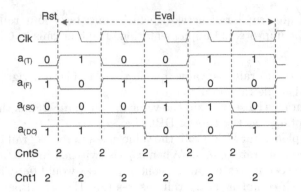

Fig. 2. The time sequence of QRL

register system which consists of four registers replace the originally single register. Let T-reg, F-reg, SC-reg, and DC-reg be four standard registers of the compound register system. Let u_{in} and u_{out} denote the input and output of u-reg respectively. According to Eqs. 1 and 2, the relationship between these registers is as follows:

$$SC_{out} = T_{in} \oplus T_{out} \oplus \overline{SC_{in}}$$
$$= T_{in} \oplus T_{out} \oplus DC_{in}. \tag{3}$$

$$DC_{out} = F_{in} \oplus F_{out} \oplus \overline{DC_{in}}$$
$$= F_{in} \oplus F_{out} \oplus SC_{in}. \tag{4}$$

The compound register system follows the three principles, and QRL is capable of protecting a single standard register by a compound register system, as shown in Fig. 3.

3.4   Generalized QRL

Although the register can be easily protected by QRL, similar protection manner can not be applied to LUT, the basic calculation component in FPGA, mainly due to the fact that the last state of LUT cannot be stored. As a result, it is impossible to make the LUTs on SC and DC rails meet the Switch Complement principle. Therefore, a different strategy of implementing QRL on LUT must be developed.

Considering the instance of QRL sequence '1,0,0,1,1' as shown in Fig. 2, there is an interesting fact that $a_{(SC)}$ is equal to $a_{(T)}$ in the second and the fourth clock cycles, and it is equal to $a_{(F)}$ in the first, the third, and the fifth clock cycles. Since we have $a_{(F)}^L = a_{(T)}^L$, and according to Eq. 3, $a_{(SC)}^P$ can be described as follows:

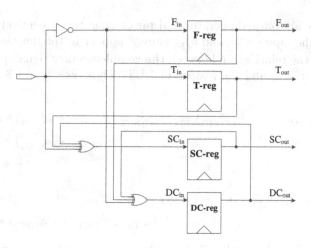

Fig. 3. The compound register system used in QRL

$$a_{(SC)}^P = \overline{a_{(SC)}^L} \oplus a_{(T)}^L \oplus a_{(T)}^P = \begin{cases} \overline{a_{(T)}^P}, & when \ a_{(SC)}^L = a_{(T)}^L, \\ a_{(T)}^P, & when \ a_{(SC)}^L = a_{(F)}^L. \end{cases} \quad (5)$$

Therefore, $a_{(SC)}$ is determined by the reset value of QRL. Two cases need to be discussed about the reset value:

- **Reset the complementary signal quartet** $[a_{(T)} : a_{(F)} : a_{(SC)} : a_{(DC)}]$ **which meet that** $a_{(SC)} = a_{(T)}$, $a_{(F)} = \overline{a_{(T)}}$, **and** $a_{(DC)} = \overline{a_{(SC)}}$. According to Eq. 5, in such situation, $a_{(SC)} = a_{(T)}$ in each even clock cycle, and $a_{(SC)} = a_{(F)}$ in each odd clock cycle. The relationship of $a_{(DC)}$ is similar.
- **Reset the complementary signal quartet** $[a_{(T)} : a_{(F)} : a_{(SC)} : a_{(DC)}]$ **which meet that** $a_{(SC)} = \overline{a_{(T)}}$, $a_{(F)} = \overline{a_{(T)}}$, **and** $a_{(DC)} = \overline{a_{(SC)}}$. As similar as the first case, in such situation, $a_{(SC)} = a_{(F)}$ in each even clock cycle, and $a_{(SC)} = a_{(T)}$ in each odd clock cycle. The relationship of $a_{(DC)}$ is similar.

For the sake of simplicity, the reset value of QRL follows the second case. Thus, the functions of LUTs on SC and DC rails can be established by a control signal Par which indicates the parity of the number of clock cycle. Let $f_v()$ and $a_{(v)}^i$ denote the function of LUT on v rail and the i-th input of such LUT respectively. The i-input functions of LUTs on SC and DC rails are defined as follows:

$$f_{SC}(a_{(SC)}^1, a_{(SC)}^2, \cdots, a_{(SC)}^i) = f_T(a_{(T)}^1, a_{(T)}^2, \cdots, a_{(T)}^i) * Par + f_F(a_{(F)}^1, a_{(F)}^2, \cdots, a_{(F)}^i) * \overline{Par}. \quad (6)$$

$$f_{DC}(a_{(DC)}^1, a_{(DC)}^2, \cdots, a_{(DC)}^i) = f_F(a_{(F)}^1, a_{(F)}^2, \cdots, a_{(F)}^i) * Par + f_T(a_{(T)}^1, a_{(T)}^2, \cdots, a_{(T)}^i) * \overline{Par}. \quad (7)$$

where $*$ and $+$ are bit-and operator and bit-or operator respectively.

However, the inputs $a^i_{(T)}$ and $a^i_{(F)}$ cannot appear in the function $f_{SC}()$ and $f_{DC}()$, due to the relationship between the complementary signal quartet $[a_{(T)} : a_{(F)} : a_{(SC)} : a_{(DC)}]$ and the feature of LUT. Thus, Eqs. 6 and 7 are replaced by:

$$f_{SC}(a^1_{(SC)}, a^2_{(SC)}, \cdots, a^i_{(SC)}) = f_T(a^1_{(SC)}, a^2_{(SC)}, \cdots, a^i_{(SC)}) * Par + f_F(a^1_{(SC)}, a^2_{(SC)}, \cdots, a^i_{(SC)}) * \overline{Par}. \quad (8)$$

$$f_{DC}(a^1_{(DC)}, a^2_{(DC)}, \cdots, a^i_{(DC)}) = f_F(a^1_{(DC)}, a^2_{(DC)}, \cdots, a^i_{(DC)}) * Par + f_T(a^1_{(DC)}, a^2_{(DC)}, \cdots, a^i_{(DC)}) * \overline{Par}. \quad (9)$$

To ensure all LUTs on all rails have the same number of inputs, LUTs on T and F rails must have an additional control signal En which indicates the state of the whole system (in work state or not). The i-input functions of LUTs on T and F rails are defined by:

$$f_T(a^1_{(T)}, a^2_{(T)}, \cdots, a^i_{(T)}) = f_T(a^1_{(T)}, a^2_{(T)}, \cdots, a^i_{(T)}) * En + f_F(a^1_{(T)}, a^2_{(T)}, \cdots, a^i_{(T)}) * \overline{En}. \quad (10)$$

$$f_F(a^1_{(F)}, a^2_{(F)}, \cdots, a^i_{(F)}) = f_F(a^1_{(F)}, a^2_{(F)}, \cdots, a^i_{(F)}) * En + f_T(a^1_{(F)}, a^2_{(F)}, \cdots, a^i_{(F)}) * \overline{En}. \quad (11)$$

When the whole system is in work state, $i.e.$ $En = 1$, the functions of LUTs on T and F rails remain unchanged, all rails work as expected. When the whole system is not in work state, $i.e.$ $En = 0$, the sensitive data is not in the system, thus it has no effect on the security of whole system. As a result, the control signal is embedded inside the LUT equations by using an extra LUT input. In other words, 6-input LUT utilization for the task logic is equivalent to that of a 5-input LUT in QRL.

Taking each rail which consists of register and LUT into consideration, the compound register system should be replaced with four standard registers. The inputs of registers are generated by LUTs on each rails, and the outputs of registers become inputs of subsequent LUTs on corresponding rails. Therefore, the generalized QRL scheme consists of two parts. The first part is the compound register system, which stores the input data (e.g., plaintext and key) from the top module, in order to generate the complementary signal quartet $[a_{(T)} : a_{(F)} : a_{(SC)} : a_{(DC)}]$. The second part is the four divided rails, which consist of registers and LUTs , in order to complete the compensation of the quadruple-rail network. More precisely, the generalized QRL scheme can be completed only by the second part, when the input data from the top module meets the requirement of the complementary signal quartet.

Moreover, QRL can be potentially applied to other non-FPGA platforms, although it is designed directly for FPGA scenarios. LUT, which is the special component in FPGA, can be implemented by standard CMOS cells. For instance, ASIC platform, which has more design freedom to designers than FPGA, can generate a QRL circuit by standard CMOS cells. Consequently, QRL is not only suitable for FPGA, but also portable to other platforms.

4 Implementation and Security Evaluation

In order to evaluate the robustness, area cost and performance of QRL, we implemented AES-128 with three different structures, an unprotected AES-128, a WDDL AES-128 and a QRL AES-128 on a Xilinx Virtex-5 XC5VLX50 FPGA, where the clock frequency is 2 MHz.

4.1 Implementation

To implement QRL, we used a strategy based on an automated "copy-paste" and "conflict-repair" method as mentioned in [5, 17], which can reduce the design complexity and provide more balanced routing on FPGAs. Firstly, we split the initial AES-128 design into two functional modules, one functional module *Cont* to supply clock signal, to control I/O and to be the top package, the other called *Enc* to preform AES algorithm. It is obvious that only the security-sensitive *Enc* needs to be transformed into QRL style. Then, the original rail in *Enc* is generated with 5-input LUTs, and other three rails are created by the "copy-paste" execution. In this case, it would hardly be possible to repair the routing conflicts between four rails with an interleaved placement way, so we adopt the separate placement of each rail in QRL. Next, we insert the control signals *Par* and *En* into corresponding LUTs, and recode the Boolean functions of these LUTs. Afterwards, all wires are routed and repaired by the "re-route" execution in the FPGA editor. Finally, the netlist is exported to the FPGA editor to generate the bitstream.

4.2 Security Evaluation and Attack Results

Pearson Correlation Coefficient based Power Analysis (CPA) is applied during the security analysis, for evaluating the security level of the QRL against differential power attacks. In order to make fair comparisons, we launch similar attacks to an unprotected implementation and a WDDL implementation. The power traces are captured using a LeCroy WaveRunner 610Zi digital oscilloscope at a sampling rate of 2.5 GS/s. The attack point is the registers which store the S-box outputs from each computation rounds, and the transitions of those registers will leak the information about AES sub-keys. Hamming distance model is used in our experiments due to the power consumption property of register on the Virtex-5 FPGA.

The experiment results show that the right hypotheses of all AES sub-keys at last round can be differentiated from the wrong hypotheses by analyzing merely less than 900 traces in the CPA attack to the unprotected one. Comparatively, we are unable to reveal even one of these sub-keys of either WDDL or QRL AES, when the number of power traces reaches 100,000. To further illustrate the result, we choose the first sub-key as an instance. The tendency of the relationship between the each hypothesis correlation coefficient and the number of power traces in the unprotected case is shown in Fig. 4, and the number of measurements to disclosure (MTD) is 837. On the contrary, in the cases of WDDL and QRL, the right key is not yet revealed when the trace number increases to 100,000, as seen in Figs. 5 and 6. More precisely, the rank of the right key in each structure is shown in Table 1.

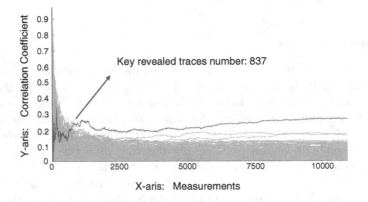

Fig. 4. Tendency of experimental attacks to unprotected structure

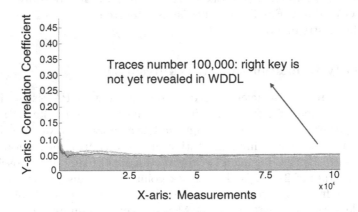

Fig. 5. Tendency of experimental attacks to WDDL

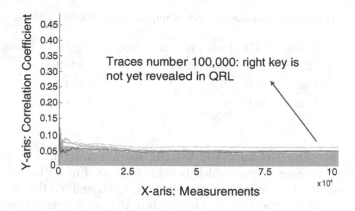

Fig. 6. Tendency of experimental attacks to QRL

Table 1. Rank of right key in unprotected, WDDL, QRL structures.

	Rank
Unprotected	1
WDDL	3
QRL	12

According to Table 1, it is obvious that both WDDL and QRL have the tendencies that the right keys may be revealed by significantly increasing the number of power traces, although the right keys do not lead to the highest coefficient. In this case, their ranks in all key guesses list seem small, and the right keys in WDDL and QRL can be revealed by the analysis based on the 3rd-order success rate and the 12th-order success rate respectively. The primary cause is the unbalanced routing repairs which are generated by commercial FPGA design tools, and it is more severe in the case of QRL, which should be keep the balanced routing signal quartet. However, even if QRL suffers more serious unbalanced routing that may lead to glitches, the rank of the right key in QRL is larger than that of WDDL, which implies that the security of QRL is a little better than that of WDDL. Consequently, QRL gains an increase factor of robustness against DPA at least 110 times compared to the unprotected one, and its DPA resistance level is comparable to WDDL.

4.3 Cost and Performance Evaluation

We estimate several indicators, in terms of register occupation, LUT occupation, duty cycle of evaluation phase and the maximum throughput for each design. The results are illustrated in Table 2.

Compared with the unprotected structure, both register occupations of QRL and WDDL are increased by 768. The increased area of QRL comes from the registers to store the 128-bit round-key and 128-bit intermediate state of each

Table 2. Cost and performance of AES in unprotected, WDDL, QRL structures.

	Register	LUT	Duty cycle of evaluation	Maximum throughput
Unprotected	737	1346	100 %	1.89 Gbps
WDDL	1505	5153	50 %	0.91 Gbps
QRL	1505	5428	100 %	1.78 Gbps

round in F, SC, and DC rails. For WDDL, the increased area is due to the "Master-Slave" register system which is commonly used in DPL architectures. The total number of occupied registers in both QRL and WDDL is less than 4 times of the unprotected one, due to the fact that some control components do not require transformation, such as the control registers in $Cont$. In the perspective of LUT, both the quadruple-rail network with four complementary rails and the 5 inputs of LUT (the last input is used by Par or En) contribute to the increased area of QRL. However, the results show that the LUT occupation of QRL just rises up to 105 % of WDDL (5428 LUTs of QRL compared to 5153 LUTs of WDDL). This is because of the restriction to the usage of limited gates as the AND and OR logic in WDDL. More precisely, we can constraint 2 compound 2-input gates to one SLICE, since there are 4 LUTs in each Virtex-5 SLICE. According to the result, we find that the cost of QRL is a little more than WDDL.

Next, we discuss the performance for each design. Due to the removal of the precharge phase, the duty cycle of evaluation phase in QRL is equal to the unprotected one, which is 2 times higher than WDDL (100 % in QRL compared to 50 % in WDDL). Thus, the maximum throughput of QRL is theoretically equal to the unprotected one, and rises up to 94 % of the unprotected one in practical evaluations (1.78 Gbps of QRL compared to 1.89 Gbps of the unprotected case), which is much higher than WDDL (0.91 Gbps of WDDL). Moreover, in order to further evaluate the performance, we compare QRL to the accelerated BCDL[1], which has the highest performance among the existing DPL schemes for FPGA. According to [9], the duty cycle of evaluation phase and the maximum throughput of the accelerated BCDL rise up to 75 % and 53 % of the unprotected implementation respectively. It is obvious that QRL has a higher performance than the accelerated BCDL. The result implies that the more efficient solution for improving performance is to eliminate the precharge phase rather than to reduce it.

5   Conclusion

In this paper, we proposed QRL as a new countermeasure against DPA on FPGAs. Based on the strategy of trading space for time, by adopting the quadruple-rail network, we can remove the precharge phase in previous DPL

---

[1] The data of the speed-optimized BCDL is derived from [9].

architectures in order to concurrently achieve high performance and high DPA resistance. Due to the elimination of the precharge phase, QRL provides the performance at a high level that is equal to the unprotected system, which is roughly 2 times higher than other DPL-based countermeasures. At the same time, the high resistance against DPA is not sacrificed. As shown in our experiments, a QRL implementation of AES-128 on FPGA offers the competitive DPA resistance level as WDDL, at least 110 times stronger than the unprotected implementation. Thus, QRL is suitable for some high performance scenarios where the security enhancement is as well desired. The techniques to minimize the glitches and unbalanced routing signal quartet among each rail in QRL will be specially emphasized in the future work.

References

1. Bhasin, S., Guilley, S., Flament, F., Selmane, N., Danger, J.-L.: Countering early evaluation: an approach towards robust dual-rail precharge logic. In: WESS 2010, p. 6. ACM (2010)
2. Chen, Z., Zhou, Y.: Dual-rail random switching logic: a countermeasure to reduce side channel leakage. In: Goubin, L., Matsui, M. (eds.) CHES 2006. LNCS, vol. 4249, pp. 242–254. Springer, Heidelberg (2006)
3. He, W., de la Torre, E., Riesgo, T.: A precharge-absorbed DPL logic for reducing early propagation effects on FPGA implementations. In: 6th IEEE International Conference on ReConFigurable Computing and FPGAs, Cancun (2011)
4. He, W., de la Torre, E., Riesgo, T.: An interleaved EPE-immune PA-DPL structure for resisting concentrated EM side channel attacks on FPGA implementation. In: Schindler, W., Huss, S.A. (eds.) COSADE 2012. LNCS, vol. 7275, pp. 39–53. Springer, Heidelberg (2012)
5. He, W., Otero, A., de la Torre, E., Riesgo, T.: Automatic generation of identical routing pairs for FPGA implemented DPL logic. In: ReConFig 2012, pp. 1–6. IEEE (2012)
6. Ishai, Y., Sahai, A., Wagner, D.: Private circuits: securing hardware against probing attacks. In: Boneh, D. (ed.) CRYPTO 2003. LNCS, vol. 2729, pp. 463–481. Springer, Heidelberg (2003)
7. Kocher, P.C., Jaffe, J., Jun, B.: Differential power analysis. In: Wiener, M. (ed.) CRYPTO 1999. LNCS, vol. 1666, pp. 388–397. Springer, Heidelberg (1999)
8. Marzouqi, H., Mahmoud, A., Khaled, S.: Review of gate-level differential power analysis and fault analysis countermeasures. Inf. Secur. 8, 51–66 (2014). IET
9. Nassar, M., Bhasin, S., Danger, J.-L., Duc, G., Guilley, S.: BCDL: a High speed balanced DPL for FPGA with global precharge and no early evaluation. In: Proceedings of Design, Automation and Test in Europe, pp. 849–854. IEEE Computer Society, Dresden (2010)
10. Örs, S.B., Oswald, E., Preneel, B.: Power-analysis attacks on an FPGA – first experimental results. In: Walter, C.D., Koç, Ç.K., Paar, C. (eds.) CHES 2003. LNCS, vol. 2779, pp. 35–50. Springer, Heidelberg (2003)
11. Popp, T., Mangard, S.: Masked dual-rail pre-charge logic: DPA-resistance without routing constraints. In: Rao, J.R., Sunar, B. (eds.) CHES 2005. LNCS, vol. 3659, pp. 172–186. Springer, Heidelberg (2005)

12. Soares, R., Calazans, N., Lomne, V., Maurine, P., Torres, L., Robert, M.: Evaluating the robustness of secure triple track logic through prototyping. In: Proceedings of the 21st Symposium on Integrated Circuits and System Design (SBCCI08), Gramado, Brazil, pp. 193–198. ACM, New York (2008)

13. Standaert, F.-X., Örs, S.B., Preneel, B.: Power analysis of an FPGA implementation of rijndael: is pipelining a DPA countermeasure? In: Joye, M., Quisquater, J.-J. (eds.) CHES 2004. LNCS, vol. 3156, pp. 30–44. Springer, Heidelberg (2004)

14. Standaert, F.-X., van Oldeneel tot Oldenzeel, L., Samyde, D., Quisquater, J.-J.: Power analysis of FPGAs: how practical is the attack? In: Cheung, P.Y.K., Constantinides, G.A. (eds.) FPL 2003. LNCS, vol. 2778, pp. 701–711. Springer, Heidelberg (2003)

15. Suzuki, D., Saeki, M.: Security evaluation of DPA countermeasures using dual-rail pre-charge logic style. In: Goubin, L., Matsui, M. (eds.) CHES 2006. LNCS, vol. 4249, pp. 255–269. Springer, Heidelberg (2006)

16. Tanimura, K., Dutt, N.: HDRL: homogeneous dual-rail logic for DPA attack resistive secure circuit design. IEEE Embed. Syst. Lett. 4(3), 57–60 (2012)

17. Tu, C., He, W., Gao, N., de la Torre, E., Liu, Z., Liu, L.: A progressive dual-rail routing repair approach for FPGA implementation of crypto algorithm. In: Huang, X., Zhou, J. (eds.) ISPEC 2014. LNCS, vol. 8434, pp. 217–231. Springer, Heidelberg (2014)

18. Tiri, K., Verbauwhede, I.: A logic level design methodology for a secure DPA resistant ASIC or FPGA implementation. In: DATE 2004, Vol. 1, pp. 246–251. IEEE Computer Society, Los Alamitos (2004)

19. Yu, P., Schaumont, P.: Secure FPGA circuits using controlled placement and routing. In: Hardware/Software Codesign and System Synthesis - CODES+ISSS 2007, pp. 45–50. ACM, New York (2007)

Strategy of Relations Collection in Factoring RSA Modulus

Haibo Yu[1](✉) and Guoqiang Bai[2,3]

[1] Department of Computer Science and Technology,
Tsinghua University, Beijing, China
yhb13@mails.tsinghua.edu.cn
[2] Institute of Microelectronics, Tsinghua University, Beijing, China
baigq@mail.tsinghua.edu.cn
[3] Tsinghua National Laboratory for Information Science and Technology,
Beijing 100084, China

Abstract. In this paper, we propose a new strategy of relations collection in factoring RSA modulus. The strategy has absolute advantage at computation efficiency with a highly parallel structure, and the reports have higher probability of being relations, since the strategy only considers small and medium primes in factor base without large primes. Besides, it is worth noting that the proposed algorithm used in strategy, only involves a multiplication, which can speed up relations collection step. Furthermore, we propose an architecture for multiplier that is based on our algorithm. Due to the inherent characters of the algorithm, our proposed architecture can perform with less registers, which makes for VLSI area optimization. Additionally, the comparison results with the published achievements show that our strategy could be a good choice for relations collection in factoring RSA modulus.

Keywords: General number field sieve · Relations collection · Prime factors · Highly parallel structure · Multiplication

1 Introduction

General Number Field Sieve (GNFS) [1,2] is the asymptotically fastest factorization algorithm so far [1], which is a threat to public-key cryptography (PKC) relied on the hardness of factoring large numbers, RSA included.

In its main step, relations collection step, pairs of integers called *relations* being collected, is dominant expensively and theoretically in GNFS, which is usually performed by sieving technology.

Many sieving methods used in GNFS have been proposed. Line sieving [1] was firstly proposed in 1993, which was applied to 423-bit factorization [3]. In the same year, Pollard described a more efficient implementation on the basis of line sieving, called lattice sieving [2], which was the main idea of the majority of the published approaches, such as 768-bit RSA modulus factorization [4]. In the following year, 1994, a combination of lattice sieving and trial division [5] was

© Springer International Publishing Switzerland 2016
S. Qing et al. (Eds.): ICICS 2015, LNCS 9543, pp. 199–211, 2016.
DOI: 10.1007/978-3-319-29814-6_16

adopted to speed up sieving step and collect triple and quadruple large prime relations. Most recently, a higher efficiency was obtained by using so-called continued fractions and lattice sieving in 2005, where a large parallel computers were employed to speed up sieving step. [6] suggests that PC-based implementation of GNFS for 1024-bit composites is prohibitive and ASICs design for the computationally expensive steps of GNFS is attractive. Researchers therefore have presented a couple of different hardware designs to realize sieving, such as TWINKLE [6], TWIRL [7], SHARK [8] and CAIRN2 [3].

Generally speaking, the reports from sieving or lattice sieving, have low probability to be relations. Besides, large primes are always allowed to improve speed of sieving, which results in larger sieving region and more workload. Thus in this paper, we propose a new strategy of relations collection in factoring RSA modulus. The main contributions of the paper are detailed below.

Firstly, we propose a new module of relations collection in factoring large integers, in which a highly parallel structure is adopted to decrease computation time. Besides, the module only considers small and medium primes in factor base, the reports from our module therefore are more likely to be relations.

Secondly, we present a algorithm used in relations collection module. For a fixed prime, the investigated algorithm computes a estimated value with a precomputed value, in order to tell whether input data is a integer multiple of the prime. And it is worth noting that the proposed algorithm only involves a multiplication, which can speed up relations collection step and be beneficial to hardware implementation. Moreover, adequate parameters can be chosen to guarantee the feasibility of the proposed algorithm, and meanwhile, maintain the concision of algorithm.

A third contribution is the architecture for a multiplier that is based on our algorithm. Multiplication is the core part of the proposed algorithm, which is also the only time-consuming operation in algorithm. The running time of multiplication is mainly depends on the size of input data, and is not strongly dependent in the size of the factor given. Due to the inherent characters of the algorithm, our proposed architecture can perform with less registers, which makes for VLSI area optimization.

The organization of this paper is given as follows: relevant definitions are described in Sect. 2, which do a brief look back at the relevant mathematical background. In Sect. 3, the proposed module of relations collection in factoring RSA modulus is presented, and the investigated algorithm used in strategy is introduced in Sect. 4, being the core part of the paper. The architecture of multiplier based on the proposed algorithm is presented in Sect. 5. Some comparison results are given in Sect. 6, which shows that the proposed strategy could be a good choice of relations collection. Finally, Sect. 7 concludes the paper.

2   Preliminaries

Relations Collection Step. The entire factorization begins with polynomial selection. Two irreducible polynomial f_r, $f_a \in \mathbb{Z}[x]$, degree d_r and d_a, respectively, and an integer e, satisfy the condition $f_r(e) \equiv f_a(e) \equiv 0 \pmod{N}$. In general, f_r and f_a are called *rational* and *algebraic* polynomials, with smoothness bounds B_r and B_a, respectively. A pair of coprime integers (a, b) with $b > 0$ is referred to as *relations*, such that $b^{d_r} f_r(a/b)$ is B_r-smooth and $b^{d_a} f_a(a/b)$ is B_a-smooth, where an integer is B-smooth if all its prime factors are at most B, as usual. A combination of *sieving*, collection of a large passel of promising relations (called *candidates*), and *cofactorization*, identification whether it really being a relation or not, is usually adopted in the relations collection step.

3   The Proposed Module of Relations Collection

Finding sufficiently many relations, namely sieving, is the major work of GNFS, which is normally about 90 % of the total computational time [9]. A primary reason for the popularity of line sieving or lattice sieving is less division operations, which is one of the computationally expensive algorithms.

In both sieve and lattice sieve, large primes are always allowed to speed up sieving step. However, they make it harder to decide whether enough relations have been found, as the criterion [1] of the number of relations needed is no longer adequate. It is worth noting that few candidates can survive in cofactorization and become relations needed in following steps. For instance, only 0.027522 % and 0.0006789 % candidates can survive in [9] and [10], respectively.

In this section, a new module of relations collection is proposed. The module only considers the small and medium primes in factor base without large primes. Besides, we try to find the expression of integer's standard factorization, in order to tell whether it being B_r-smooth or B_a-smooth. As a consequence, the candidates from the proposed module are more likely to be relations, which can decrease the workload of relations collection to a great extent.

Let a set of odd primes $\{p_1, p_2, \cdots, p_i, \cdots, p_k\}$ be factor base and N be input data for smoothness test, such that $N = b^{d_r} f_r(a/b)$ or $b^{d_a} f_a(a/b)$ for rational or algebraic side. The whole structure consists of k isolated units in parallel, shown in Fig. 1, where k is the number of primes in factor base and F_i is one-bit output signal (if N is an integer multiple of p_i, $F_i = 1$; otherwise, $F_i = 0$). Moreover, we assume that most of the work is spent in the first splitting and subsequent splittings are negligible, thus power of primes is not considered.

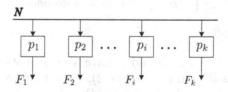

Fig. 1. High-level schema of the proposed relations collection module

All basic units run in parallel as soon as input data N arrives, and output F_i, $1 \le i \le k$, tells whether N is a smooth integer. The most straightforward way, finding all prime factors in factor base of integer N, is adopted, which can decrease the influence of large primes. Besides, with synchronous parallel triggered structure, the proposed module has absolute advantage at computation efficiency. For realization of the proposed strategy, the algorithm used in basic units and hardware implementations are of great importance, which will be described in Sects. 4 and 5 in more detail, respectively.

4   Investigated Algorithm

4.1   Basic Definitions

To make the following explanations and descriptions easier, we present some notations used in this paper firstly. An n-bit integer X is denoted in radix 2 representation as $X = (X_{n-1} \cdots X_0)_2$ and $X_{n-1} \neq 0$; X_i refers to the i-th bit of X, $0 \leq i \leq n - 1$; $|X|$ refers to the bit width of X in radix 2. Note that all integers discussed in this paper are represented in radix 2. Known that N is a nonnegative odd integer, after shifting all factors of two, and p is an odd prime. For now, let us assume their bit lengths are m and $m+\gamma$, respectively, i.e. $|p| = m$ and $|N| = m+\gamma$, thus we have $\gamma > 0$, $2^{m-1} \leq p < 2^m$ and $2^{m+\gamma-1} \leq N < 2^{m+\gamma}$.

For given N and p, the intermediate ratio B is defined as:

$$B = \frac{N}{p} 2^{\alpha-\beta} \tag{1}$$

where α and β are two parameters and $\alpha > \beta$.

Lemma 1. *For given N and p, if N is an integer multiple of p, the conclusion holds: $B_{\alpha-\beta-1}, \cdots, B_1, B_0 = 0$ and $B_{\alpha-\beta} = 1$.*

Proof. See the Appendix.   ∎

Lemma 2. *Let $\mu = \left\lfloor \frac{N}{2^{m+\beta}} \left\lfloor \frac{2^{m+\alpha}}{p} \right\rfloor \right\rfloor$ be $(\gamma + \alpha - \beta)$-digit positive integer, with $\beta > \gamma$ and $\alpha > m + \gamma$. Then it holds*

$$\mu = \begin{cases} B - 1, & \text{if } B \text{ is an integer} \\ \lfloor B \rfloor, & \text{if } B \text{ is a decimal} \end{cases} \tag{2}$$

Proof. See the Appendix.   ∎

Based on Lemma 1 and 2, B and μ have a kind of standard binary representations, denoted as B_s and μ_s (see Fig. 2), respectively, when N is an integer multiple of p. Moreover, we also have $\mu_s = B_s - 1$.

As we can see above, choosing adequate parameters α, β and γ is of great importance. First of all, we have $\gamma > 0$, according to the definition of γ. Besides, Lemma 2 shows that $\beta > \gamma$ and $\alpha > m + \gamma$ are necessary. More generally, parameters should meet the requirements of $\alpha > \beta > \gamma > 0$ and $\alpha > m + \gamma$.

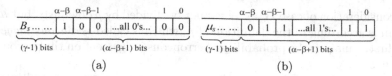

Fig. 2. The standard binary representations (a) the sets of B_s; (b) the sets of μ_s.

4.2 The Main Idea of the Algorithm

Based on Lemma 1, we conclude that $B = B_s$ is a necessary and sufficient condition for N being an integer multiple of p. Thus, the proposed algorithm is developed to test whether B is a standard representation for the purpose of determining the prime factor of an integer.

To avoid computationally expensive divisions, the algorithm uses the input N and a reciprocal of p to compute the intermediate ratio B. Rewrite (1) as

$$B = \frac{N}{2^{m+\beta}} \frac{2^{m+\alpha}}{p}$$

in which $2^{m+\alpha}/p$ is a constant and the value can be precomputed, for a fixed odd prime p. Since $2^{m+\alpha}/p$ is a decimal but not an integer, we use $\left\lfloor \frac{2^{m+\alpha}}{p} \right\rfloor$ to avoid storing floating-point values. Therefore, we focus on $\mu = \left\lfloor \frac{N}{2^{m+\beta}} \left\lfloor \frac{2^{m+\alpha}}{p} \right\rfloor \right\rfloor$, which is a estimated value of B.

If $\mu = \mu_s$, p is possibly a prime factor of N based on Lemmas 1 and 2, for the reason that $\mu = \mu_s$ is just the necessary condition. However, in most of cases μ-value can give correct result about divisibility of N and p. There is only one situation in which μ could not work, namely $B = B_{evil}$ (see Fig. 3).

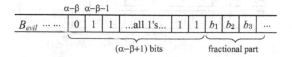

Fig. 3. Binary representation of the sets B_{evil}

With some simplifications, the algorithm computes μ-value, checks whether μ eauls μ_s or not, and outputs $F = 1$ if it does, without consideration of case B_{evil}. (If $F = 0$, p is not a prime factor of N; otherwise, p is very possible a prime factor of N.)

4.3 The Feasibility of the Proposed Algorithm

In this subsection, we show that even if a defect in the idea of testing μ-value only, the algorithm can still produce satisfactory results in relations collection.

In consideration of case B_{evil}, N cannot be divided by p obviously, but $\mu = \mu_s$ still stands according to the definition of μ, which is called *erroneous judgement*. Let us firstly analysis the probability of erroneous judgement on the precondition of $\mu = \mu_s$.

For now, an integer N_p, being less than N and the greatest multiple of p, satisfies $N = d + N_p$, $p|N_p$ and $0 < d < p$. Let rewrite (1) once more as:

$$B = \frac{N}{p} \, 2^{\alpha-\beta} = \frac{d + N_p}{p} \, 2^{\alpha-\beta} = \frac{d}{p} \, 2^{\alpha-\beta} + \frac{N_p}{p} \, 2^{\alpha-\beta}$$

in which $d/p \, 2^{\alpha-\beta}$ and $N/p \, 2^{\alpha-\beta}$ are denoted as B_u and B_v, respectively. For more simple analysis, we assume $\alpha - \beta = 3$ for no reason (this works with other positive integers).

Because of $0 < d < p$, i.e. $0 < d/p < 1$, we have the conclusion that $d/p = b_1 2^{-1} + b_2 2^{-2} + b_3 2^{-3} + \cdots$, shown in Fig. 4.

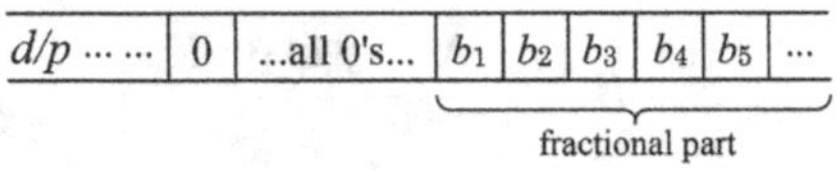

$d/p \cdots \cdots$	0	...all 0's...	b_1	b_2	b_3	b_4	b_5	$\cdots$

fractional part

Fig. 4. Binary representation of the sets d/p

It is always true that N_p/p is an integer since N_p is an integer multiple of p. Besides B_v is obtained by left shifting $\alpha - \beta$ bits of N_p/p (3 bits, based on assumption above), which means $B_{v(\alpha-\beta-1)}, B_{v(\alpha-\beta-2)}, \cdots, B_{v0} = 0$. Similarly, after left shifting $\alpha - \beta$ bits of d/p, we obtain B_u in binary representation. To clarify the properties of the sets of B_v and B_u, we give Fig. 5.

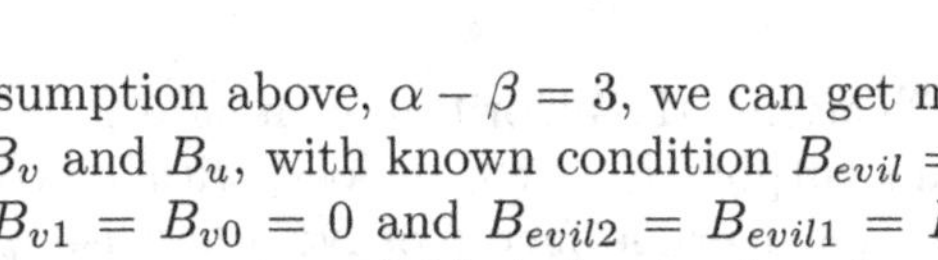

$B_v \cdots \cdots$	0/1	... 0/1 ...	0/1	0	0	0			
$B_u \cdots \cdots$	0	...all 0's...	0	b_1	b_2	b_3	b_4	b_5	$\cdots$

$(\alpha-\beta+1)$ bits   fractional part

Fig. 5. Binary representation of the sets B_v and B_u with $\alpha - \beta = 3$

Based on the assumption above, $\alpha - \beta = 3$, we can get more detailed binary representations of B_v and B_u, with known condition $B_{evil} = B_u + B_v$. Because of the fact $B_{v2} = B_{v1} = B_{v0} = 0$ and $B_{evil2} = B_{evil1} = B_{evil0} = 1$, we have $b_1 = b_2 = b_3 = 1$. The range value of d/p is hence given by

$$2^{-1} + 2^{-2} + 2^{-3} < \frac{d}{p} < 1 \tag{3}$$

Furthermore, it is easy to obtain that $B_{v3} = 0$ (that is $B_{v(\alpha-\beta)} = 0$). On the basis of relation between B_v and N_p/p, the last significant bit of N_p/p

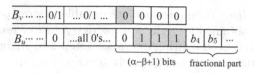

Fig. 6. Detailed binary representation of the sets B_v and B_u with $\alpha - \beta = 3$

equals to $B_{v(\alpha-\beta)}$, which give the conclusion that N_p/p is even. A more specific representations of B_v and B_u are indicated in Fig. 6.

Since N_p is a arbitrary integer that is multiple of p, it is reasonable to suppose that the probability of any N_p/p being even is $1/2$. Moreover, generally assuming $\alpha - \beta = w$, the range value of d/p is given by

$$2^{-1} + 2^{-2} + \cdots + 2^{-w} < \frac{d}{p} < 1$$

The probability of erroneous judgement is obtained as follows:

$$P = \frac{1}{2}\left[1 - \left(1 - \frac{1}{2^w}\right)\right] = \frac{1}{2^{w+1}} \tag{4}$$

As it can be observed, if we want to minimize the probability of erroneous judgement we must guarantee the difference between α and β being large enough. For instance, for $\alpha - \beta = 15$, the probability of judgement result being true is $99.9985\,\%$ on the precondition of $\mu = \mu_s$. Higher success probability therefore owes to larger difference between α and β.

Finally, the proposed algorithm is given in Algorithm 1. The main idea of the algorithm is computing a estimated μ-value to approach B-value in order to decrease computational complexity. The algorithm computes $\mu = \left\lfloor \frac{N}{2^{m+\beta}} \left\lfloor \frac{2^{m+\alpha}}{p} \right\rfloor \right\rfloor$ for an input N and a precomputed reciprocal of p. If $\mu \neq \mu_s$, we have that p is not a prime factor of N; otherwise, it is highly possible to get that p is a prime factor of N.

Algorithm 1. The proposed algorithm

Input: p, with $|p| = m$; N, with $|N| = m + \gamma$; precomputing $P_{re} = \left\lfloor \frac{2^{m+\alpha}}{p} \right\rfloor$;

Output: F, being the state of divisibility relation;

1: $temp \Leftarrow N \cdot P_{re}$;
2: $\mu \Leftarrow \left\lfloor \frac{temp}{2^{m+\beta}} \right\rfloor$;
3: **if** $\mu \neq \mu_s$ **then**
4:     $F \Leftarrow 0$;
5: **else**
6:     $F \Leftarrow 1$;
7: **end if**
8: **return** F;

In Algorithm 1, $temp$ is an intermediate variable to store product of N times P_{re}, and μ-value is obtained by right shifting $m + \beta$ bits of $temp$. Since $m + \beta$ is a constant, we do not need shifting operation (step 2 in Algorithm 1), but just compare fixed partial bits of $temp$, namely $temp[m + \alpha : m + \beta]$, with μ_s. As a consequence, the critical path only contains one multiplication.

In relations collection of GNFS, it is worth noting that input data N has similar bit width for different pairs in sieving region. Therefore, parameters in basic units are not much different from each other. Let m_{max} and γ_{max} denote as the maximum bit width of prime and the maximum distance between $|N|$ and $|p|$. Based on assumptions above and parameters conditions, we assume $\alpha = m_{max} + \gamma_{max} + 1$, recorded as α_{max}. Note that a larger α-value means wider binary multiplier, thus we choose $\alpha_{max} = m_{max} + \gamma_{max} + 1$. Moreover, β is determined according to the desired success probability, denoted as β_{max}. It is obvious that α_{max} and β_{maxe} satisfy all basic units' requirements.

5 Hardware Implementation and Synthesis Results

The effectiveness of the proposed strategy lies in an efficient area-time hardware implementation. In particular, the multiplier plays a crucial role, which is also the concern of hardware implementation. To optimize the multiplier, one obviously needs to minimize the latency and/or maximize the throughput [11]. Of course, speed is not the only criterion of interest. VLSI area and cost also influence and limit the designs. Because of the amount of primes in factor base, we focus on the less area design of multipliers. Therefore, a economical design, using as few registers as possible, is proposed in this section.

It is obvious that one of the operands, i.e. P_{re}, being fixed and precomputed, is a constant, which can be wrote in ROM or FLASH during manufacture of the ASICs. Besides, to save register resources, the multiplier receives the input data N in synchronous serial mode from lower to higher bits. Consequently, one-bit register is required to store input bit of N and no register is needed for P_{re}.

A conventional binary multiplier produces an output whose number of bit is sum of the input operands. However, due to the inherent characters of the proposed algorithm, the minimum $m + \beta$ bits of the product is unnecessary and can be discarded for multiplier optimization in terms of area. Under assumption above ($\alpha = m + \gamma + 1$), we have bit widths of P_{re} and $temp$ are $\alpha + 1$ and $m + \gamma + \alpha + 2$, respectively. Figure 7 gives a more direct comprehension of the product $temp$, in which shadow areas are essential bits to compare with μ_s.

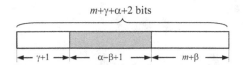

Fig. 7. Schematic diagram of the product $temp$'s component

For instance, setting $m = 24$, $\gamma = 96$, $\alpha = 121$ and $\beta = 100$, we have $|temp| = m + \gamma + \alpha + 2 = 243$ and the minimum 124 bits of $temp$ are useless. Therefore, we propose a specific multiplier design based on above phenomenon, which can save up to 50 % register resources.

The following notation is used in our discussion of multiplication design:

(a) X Multiplicand $X_{k-1}X_{k-2}\cdots X_1 X_0$
(b) Y Multiplier $Y_{s-1}Y_{s-2}\cdots Y_1 Y_0$
(c) MP Product $MP_{k+s-1}MP_{k+s-2}\cdots MP_1 MP_0$

The cumulative product MP is stored in shift register. Because we assume N (regarded as the multiplier) is received in serial mode, the next bit of the multiplier Y (being the role of N) to be considered is always available at a one-bit register and is used to select 0 or X for the addition. Multiplication can be done by adding a successive number (0 or X) to cumulative partial product (initialized to 0) and shifting the cumulative partial product by one bit.

In order to introduce our approach with the help of an example, let us consider $Y = (1011)_2$ and $X = (1101)_2$. Figure 8 depicts the detail of shift register in the multiplication.

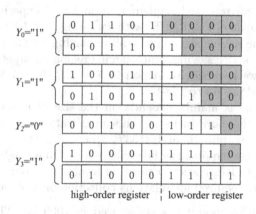

high-order register ¦ low-order register

Fig. 8. Behavior of shift register in the 4×4 multiplication

Note that the cumulative partial product and initialed "0" (shadow areas bits) share the same register, keeping the total number of bits at $k + s + 1$. When all initialed "0" (s bits in total) shift from register, the multiplication is done. Besides, results of accumulation are only assigned to high-order register, and lower bits of the cumulative partial product is stored in low-order register with initialed "0". If what we need is only the maximum 5 bits of the full product, the high-order register is adequate to store cumulative partial product without the use of low-order register.

For the proposed algorithm, the last $m + \beta$ bits of full product are useless. Besides, it is obvious that $m + \beta > m + \gamma$, where $m + \gamma$ is the bit width of N (called multiplier in multiplication). With less-registers multiplier, $\alpha + 2$ bits wide is adequate for register *temp*, instead of $m + \gamma + \alpha + 2$. Thus there are almost $(\alpha + 2)$-bit registers are used, without consideration of control portion.

Since the optimization goal of the multiplier design is minimum area, there are some limitations of speed of multiplication. Because of serial input and bit-at-a-time, the running time mainly depends on the size of N.

The proposed algorithm has been described by Verilog HDL and then synthesized with Synopsys Design Compiler 2013. The design library for compiling is SMIC 130 nm CMOS cell library. For $\gamma = 24$ and $m + \gamma = 128$, total area is 1680 gates; and for $\gamma = 31$ and $m + \gamma = 140$, total area is 1830 gates, in which area is measured by the number of NAND gate with two inputs.

6   Estimates of Factoring

A significant improvement in the design of the relations collection module has a great impact on the entire large integer factorization. In this section, we briefly estimate the costs and running time of a special hardware as ASICs. This special hardware could be produced as single ICs, ready for the use in large circuits.

423-Bit. In 2007, [3] reported implementational and experimental results of dedicated sieving device "CAIRN 2" with factoring a 423-bit integer. 30 days were required for the sieving step, in which line sieving (or the pipelined sieving) was used instead of lattice sieving. Since sieving region parameters $H_a = 2.3 \cdot 10^9$ and $H_b = 3 \cdot 10^4$, we have sieving region is $S = 2H_aH_b = 1.38 \cdot 10^{14}$. Besides, relations found are up to 128-bit.

The running time is mainly depends on the size of input data N for the proposed strategy, therefore including the initialization and postprocessing, a input integer requires approximately $133T$, where T is the system clock cycle. The proposed strategy requires the following effort. On a single 2.2 GHz (as the same frequency as [3]) IC, relations collection would take about 98 days. In other words, 19.6 days are required for relations collection on five chips in parallel.

768-Bit. 768-bit RSA modulus was factored in 2009 [4]. The most cumbersome step, sieving, took almost two years on many hundreds of 2.2 GHz AMD Opteron processors. Input integers were up to 2^{140} and 2^{110} for algebraic and rational smoothness tests, respectively. Moreover, $2 \cdot 10^{18}$ coprime pairs should be considered based on sieving experiments.

With the same operation frequency, we assume $140T$ is required for an input data (or a coprime pair) on average, based on the proposed less-registers multipliers. For one single chip, $2 \cdot 10^{18}$ inputs can be handled within 4027 years.

The estimable result above is limited by VLSI area. Now, let us consider the situation with the optimization goal being speed and throughput. Based on many achievements of fast multipliers, multiplication on the critical path can be performed in one clock cycle with pipeline design. Thus we assume one input pair can be handle in three clock cycles (initialization, multiplication and postprocessing in total). Holding the conditions above, relations collection would take 86.56 years (in other words, 90 chips could handle the problem of relations collection within one year). A good trade-off between speed and area is necessary because of many limitations in real systems.

1024-Bit. Factoring 1024-bit RSA modulus would be about a thousand times harder than 768-bit [4], and it is still a challenge for factorization [12]. SHARK [8] was a parallelized lattice sieving device for factoring 1024-bit numbers, which consisted of 2300 identical isolated machines sieving in parallel at a clock frequency of 1 GHz. Cost estimates of SHARK were as following. One machine took 20 seconds per special q, one year was therefore necessary for 2300 machines to handle $3.7 \cdot 10^9$ special q.

There are $5.36 \cdot 10^8$ input data for each special q and each input data in sieving region is at most 125-bit. We assume $130T$ is required for each input data at 1 GHz. If the optimization goal is less area, running time of relations collection is 8188 years with one chip, which means 8188 identical chips in parallel can finish the work within one year. On the other hand, if we pursue high speed, with $3T$ for one input data, one chip can perform within 189 years (189 chips can in parallel can handle relations collection within one year) at 1 GHz.

Summary of Comparison. Note that all estimates mentioned above are given under the same workload with associated work. Since the reports from the proposed relations collection module are highly possible to be relations, compared with sieving or lattice sieving, the proposed strategy can result in smaller sieving region and less workload, with the same amount of relations. Comparison results presented above shows that our strategy could be a good choice for relations collection in factoring RSA modulus.

7   Conclusion

This work presents a new strategy of relations collection in factoring RSA modulus. The motivation is to speed up relations collection step with highly parallel structure. The aim is also to decrease the sieving region and workload since the proposed strategy only considers small and medium primes in factor base. The investigated algorithm used in strategy only involves a multiplication, which is suitable for high-speed applications. And the architecture based on the proposed algorithm perform multiplication with less area. Additionally, we estimate the costs of factoring 423-bit, 768-bit and 1024-bit, respectively, and compare them with the published results. The comparison results show that our strategy could be a good choice for relations collection in factorization. Moreover, the reports from relation collection module, based on the proposed strategy, have higher probability of being relations needed in following steps. Our strategy therefore can decrease the whole workload and computational time to a great extent.

Acknowledgment. This work was supported by the National Natural Science Foundation of China (Grants 61472208 and U1135004), and by the National Key Basic Research Program of China (Grant 2013CB338004) The authors would like to thank the editor and reviewers for their comments.

A   Proof of Lemmas

Proof of Lemma 1. If N is divisible by p, then $A = B/2^{\alpha-\beta}$ is a positive integer, which leads to the least $\alpha - \beta$ significant bits of B are fixed to be all 0's. Therefore we have $B_{\alpha-\beta-1}, \cdots, B_1, B_0 = 0$.

On the other hand, let us suppose $B_{\alpha-\beta} = 0$. Because A is obtained by right shifting $(\alpha-\beta)$ bits of B in binary representation, we have $A_0 = B_{\alpha-\beta} = 0$, which means A is even. Since $N = p \cdot A$, we can get that N is an even number, which contradicts with the known condition. According to the proof by contradiction, this shows that $B_{\alpha-\beta} = 1$, while the other $\gamma - 1$ bits can be randomly chosen. ■

Proof of Lemma 2. Given parameter $\varepsilon = \frac{N}{2^{m+\beta}} \left\lfloor \frac{2^{m+\alpha}}{p} \right\rfloor$, we may write:

$$\varepsilon - 1 < \mu \leq \varepsilon \tag{A-1}$$

$$\frac{N}{2^{m+\beta}} \left(\frac{2^{m+\alpha}}{p} - 1 \right) < \varepsilon < \frac{N}{2^{m+\beta}} \frac{2^{m+\alpha}}{p} \tag{A-2}$$

Since $2^{m+\alpha}$ cannot be divided by p, it is always true that $\left\lfloor \frac{2^{m+\alpha}}{p} \right\rfloor < \frac{2^{m+\alpha}}{p}$, which implies ε is strictly less than B. As $N < 2^{m+\gamma}$, let us rewrite (A-2):

$$B - 2^{\gamma-\beta} < \varepsilon < B \tag{A-3}$$

According to (A-1) and (A-3), we have $B - 1 - 2^{\gamma-\beta} < \mu < B$. The B-value must satisfy the one of the following two cases.

Case 1—B is an integer: If $0 < 2^{\gamma-\beta} < 1$ $(\beta > \gamma)$, we have $\mu = B - 1 = \lfloor B - 1 \rfloor$, thus (2) is satisfied, as it can be observed in Fig. 9(a).

Case 2—B is not an integer: If the fractional part of B is greater than $2^{\gamma-\beta}$, we have $B - 1 - 2^{\gamma-\beta} > \lfloor B - 1 \rfloor$. That is $\mu = \lfloor B \rfloor$, as shown in Fig. 9(b). By the definition of $B = 2^{\alpha-\beta}N/p$, the minimum fractional part of B is $2^{-m+\alpha-\beta}$, as a consequence $2^{\gamma-\beta} < 2^{-m+\alpha-\beta}$ $(\alpha > m + \gamma)$ is required.

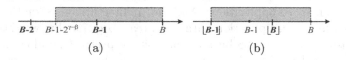

(a)   (b)

Fig. 9. The value range of μ (a) for B being an integer; (b) for B being a decimal.

Just as a slight clarification, the short thick lines give the position of integers; the dash lines stand for the open intervals; and the shadow areas indicate the value range of μ in Fig. 9. ■

References

1. Bernstein, D.J., Lenstra, A.K.: A general number field sieve implementation. In: Lenstra, A.K., Lenstra, H.W. (eds.) The Development of the Number Field Sieve. Lecture Notes in Mathematics, vol. 1554, pp. 103–126. Springer, Heidelberg (1993)
2. Pollard, J.M.: The lattice sieve. In: Lenstra, A.K., Lenstra, H.W. (eds.) The Development of the Number Field Sieve. Lecture Notes in Mathematics, vol. 1554, pp. 43–49. Springer, Heidelberg (1993)
3. Izu, T., Kogure, J., Shimoyama, T.: CAIRN 2: an FPGA implementation of the sieving step in the number field sieve method. In: Paillier, P., Verbauwhede, I. (eds.) CHES 2007. LNCS, vol. 4727, pp. 364–377. Springer, Heidelberg (2007)
4. Kleinjung, T., Aoki, K., Franke, J., Lenstra, A.K., Thomé, E., Bos, J.W., Gaudry, P., Kruppa, A., Montgomery, P.L., Osvik, D.A., te Riele, H., Timofeev, A., Zimmermann, P.: Factorization of a 768-bit RSA modulus. In: Rabin, T. (ed.) CRYPTO 2010. LNCS, vol. 6223, pp. 333–350. Springer, Heidelberg (2010)
5. Golliver, R.A., Lenstra, A.K., McCurley, K.S.: Lattice sieving and trial division. In: Huang, M.-D.A., Adleman, L.M. (eds.) ANTS 1994. LNCS, vol. 877, pp. 18–27. Springer, Heidelberg (1994)
6. Shamir, A.: Factoring large numbers with the TWINKLE device. In: Koç, Ç.K., Paar, C. (eds.) CHES 1999. LNCS, vol. 1717, pp. 2–12. Springer, Heidelberg (1999)
7. Shamir, A., Tromer, E.: Factoring large numbers with the TWIRL device. In: Boneh, D. (ed.) CRYPTO 2003. LNCS, vol. 2729, pp. 1–26. Springer, Heidelberg (2003)
8. Franke, J., Kleinjung, T., Paar, C., Pelzl, J., Priplata, C., Stahlke, C.: SHARK: a realizable special hardware sieving device for factoring 1024-bit integers. In: Rao, J.R., Sunar, B. (eds.) CHES 2005. LNCS, vol. 3659, pp. 119–130. Springer, Heidelberg (2005)
9. Miele, A., Bos, J.W., Kleinjung, T., Lenstra, A.K.: Cofactorization on graphics processing units. In: Batina, L., Robshaw, M. (eds.) CHES 2014. LNCS, vol. 8731, pp. 335–352. Springer, Heidelberg (2014)
10. Kleinjung, T.: Cofactorisation strategies for the number field sieve and an estimate for the sieving step for factoring 1024 bit integers. In: Proceedings of SHARCS, vol. 6 (2006)
11. Behrooz, P.: Computer Arithmetic: Algorithms and Hardware Designs, vol. 19. Oxford University Press, Oxford (2000)
12. Lenstra, A.K., Tromer, E., Shamir, A., Kortsmit, W., Dodson, B., Hughes, J., Leyland, P.: Factoring estimates for a 1024-bit RSA modulus. In: Laih, C.-S. (ed.) ASIACRYPT 2003. LNCS, vol. 2894, pp. 55–74. Springer, Heidelberg (2003)

Ultra High-Performance ASIC Implementation of SM2 with SPA Resistance

Dan Zhang[1] and Guoqiang Bai[1,2(✉)]

[1] Institute of Microelectronics, Tsinghua University, Beijing, China
zhangdan105603630163.com
[2] Tsinghua National Laboratory for Information Science and Technology,
Beijing, China
baigq@mail.tsinghua.edu.cn

Abstract. To ensure secure information exchange, demand for hardware implementation of elliptic curve cryptography (ECC) is increasing rapidly in recent years. In this paper, we propose an ASIC design for ECC over SCA-256 prime field, delivering both high performance and great SPA resistance. For algorithm selection, we integrate calculation simplification into the classic algorithm, Montgomery Powering Ladder (MPL). Based on the deduction of Fast NIST Reduction, we innovatively achieve the configurable modular multiplication module and then the isochronous point addition and double units. Pipeline architecture, execution order optimization and modular design are all applied to improved performance. Evaluated by CMOS standard cell library of $0.13\,\mu m$, this ECC processor costs only $208\,\mu s$ and $6.8\,\mu J$ for one scalar multiplication and runs at high frequency of $228\,MHz$ with area of $156\,k$ gates. Compared to related works, it is much more advantageous in not only area-time product but also SPA resistant protection.

Keywords: ECC · SM2 · SPA · MPL · Mersenne prime

1 Introduction

With the explosive growth of demand for secure information exchange, efficient public-key cryptography is becoming more and more indispensable. Compared to traditional achievable schemes such as RSA and Diffie-Hellman, elliptic curve cryptography (ECC) has become the more attractive alternative. In December 2010, Chinese State Cryptography Administration published the national public-key cryptography based on ECC in [1], short for SM2. The same series of national cryptographic algorithms also include hash function and symmetric cipher, known as SM3 and SM4. These algorithms have got accepted and vigorously promoted by the government, possessing a spacious application foreground. SM2 is ECC defined over a pseudo-Mersenne prime field of 256 bits, which is represented by SCA-256 in the following discussion. Facing such a bright application prospect, ASIC implementation of SM2 has become very valuable, but study on this aspect is far form sufficient. So we decide to do some research to fill this gap

© Springer International Publishing Switzerland 2016
S. Qing et al. (Eds.): ICICS 2015, LNCS 9543, pp. 212–219, 2016.
DOI: 10.1007/978-3-319-29814-6_17

as much as we can. In this paper, both analysis and implementation of SM2 are conducted in a meticulous and deep going way, while defensive measures for SPA are also under consideration. Then we propose a high-performance implementation of SM2 with SPA resistance, using an innovative isochronous architecture of MPL with mathematical optimization.

The remainder of this paper proceeds as follows. Section 2 briefly presents the background knowledge of ECC and SM2. Section 3 introduces Our SM2 architecture in detail. The implementation performance as well as comparison with previous works are given in Sect. 4, followed by a comprehensive conclusion.

2   Mathematical Background

A non-supersingular elliptic curve over $GF(p)$ is usually expressed as the Weierstrass equation in Eq. 1:

$$E : y^2 = x^3 + ax + b \tag{1}$$

where $a, b \in GF(p)$, $4a^3 + 27b^2 \neq 0 \pmod{p}$. All the solutions $(x, y) \in GF(p) * GF(p)$ that fulfill this equation make up the curve, together with the point P_∞ at infinity. To form an abelian group, ECC arithmetic defines the operation addition of two points over this curve in Eq. 2, which distinguishes the case for equal and unequal ones. Let $P = (x_1, y_1), Q = (x_2, y_2) \in E$, then $R(x_3, y_3) = P + Q \in E$. If $P \neq Q$, we have the point addition formulas, otherwise we have point double formulas.

$$x_3 = \lambda^2 - x_1 - x_2$$
$$y_3 = -y_1 - (x_3 - x_1)\lambda$$

where

$$\lambda = \begin{cases} \frac{3x_1^2 + a}{2y_1} & (x_1, y_1) = (x_2, y_2) \\ \frac{y_1 - y_2}{x_1 - x_2} & otherwise. \end{cases} \tag{2}$$

The main operation that dominates the execution time of ECC is point multiplication (PM), also called scalar multiplication. It is defined as $kP = \sum_1^k P = P + P + \cdots + P$, where P is a point on elliptic curve and k is a random integer. It is computed by a series of point addition (PA) and point double (PD), further decomposed into a certain number of finite field operations. The design level of point multiplication determines the final performance of SM2. To achieve high-performance implementation of PM is our core subject in this paper.

Compared with international standard ECC algorithm, SM2 adopts the unique prime field, called SCA-256. It is also improved in some aspects, such as the procedures of encryption, the structure of data to be signed and so on, which enhances its applicability and safety in commercial environment. The parameters of SM2 are clearly specified in [1]. Among them, the most important one is the selected pseudo-Mersenne prime field: $p_{SCA-256} = 2^{256} - 2^{224} - 2^{96} + 2^{32} - 1$.

3   Proposed ECC Processor

In this section, we firstly choose the main algorithm of point multiplication based on a complete consideration. Then the succeeding units are achieved and optimized from the bottom up, with the entire architecture presented at last.

3.1   Optimization for Point Multiplication

Since proposed, SPA has proved to be the most common threat for cryptographic devices. Resistant strategies mainly concentrates on algorithm level, grouped into three methods: double-and-add always (DAA) algorithm, normalization algorithm and Montgomery powering ladder. The first one used in [2] makes a simple change to traditional LR-DA. It performs both PA and PD operation in each iteration, resisting SPA by average 50 % PA operation overhead. But it gives great opportunity to C-fault analysis [3] attack. [4] normalized PA and PD. Addition formulas on the elliptic curve were rewritten so that the same formula apply equally to add two different or same points. As the third method, MPL was first proposed in [5], shown as Algorithm 1.

Algorithm 1. MPL Point Multiplication

Input: integer k and point P, l = bit length of k
1: **Initial:** $Q_1 = 2P, Q_0 = P, i = l - 2$
2: **While** $i \geq 0$, **do:**
3:     If $k_i = 0$ then $Q_1 = Q_0 + Q_1$, $Q_0 = 2Q_0$
4:     else $k_i = 1$ then $Q_0 = Q_0 + Q_1$, $Q_1 = 2Q_1$
5:     $i = i - 1$
6: **end While**
Output: $kP = \sum_1^k P = Q_0$

By maintaining the relation of $Q_1 = Q_0 + P(x_p, y_p)$, PA and PD are executed without any redundant operation. What's more, the sum of two points whose difference is fixed can be computed without the y-coordinate, reducing both computation effort and storage space. Brier and Joye [4] deduced the mathematic simplification formula of PA and PD for MPL over prime field in projective coordinate, shown as Eqs. 3 and 4. This optimization can save all storage space for y-coordinate and the efforts of computing them, resulting in higher efficiency. They also recovered the y-coordinate of result kP, shown as Eq. 5.

$$\begin{cases} X(Q_0 + Q_1) = -4bZ_0Z_1(X_0Z_1 + X_1Z_0) + (X_0X_1 + aZ_0Z_1)^2 \\ Z(Q_0 + Q_1) = x_p \cdot (X_1Z_0 - X_0Z_1)^2 \end{cases} \tag{3}$$

$$\begin{cases} X(2Q_1) = (X_1^2 - aZ_1^2)^2 - 8bX_1Z_1^3 \\ Z(2Q_1) = 4Z_1(X_1^3 + aX_1Z_1^2 + bZ_1^3) \end{cases} \tag{4}$$

$$y = (2y_p)^{-1}[2b + (a + x_px_1)(x_p + x_1) - x_0(x_p - x_1)^2] \tag{5}$$

Since x-coordinates of both Q_0 and Q_1 are needed for the final result, we convert them to affine coordinate system using the Eq. 6 as follow. By this special design highlight, once MPL scalar multiplication need no more modular inversion than usual algorithm.

$$Z_{inv} = \frac{1}{Z_0 Z_1} \implies x_0 = Z_{inv} Z_1 X_0, \quad x_1 = Z_{inv} Z_0 X_1 \tag{6}$$

The computation amount of once kP in different algorithms are compared in Table 1. It is obvious that MPL with simplification offers better SPA resistance with lower consumption. And it's the only one that can execute PA and PD in parallel. Without redundant operations and y-coordinate, it can also resist C safe-error and M safe-error fault attacks. So our implementation uses it as our main algorithm.

Table 1. Calculation cost of different algorithm

Algorithm	PA	PD	Trans	kP
LR-DA	(L/2)*12M	L*8M	I+2M	14LM+2M+I
LR-DAA	L*12M	L*8M	I+2M	20LM+2M+I
Normalization	(L/2)*16M	L*16M	I+2M	24LM+2M+I
MPL	L*9M	L*9M	I+10M	18LM+10M+I

[a]L for bit length of k, M for modular multiplication, I for modular inversion

3.2 Optimization for Finite Field Arithmetic

Modular multiplication (MM) is made up of regular multiplication and modular divider. For the pseudo-Mersenne prime of SM2, we adopt the Fast Reduction Scheme in [6], whose execution cycles can be precisely controlled according to the number of adders. Then by matching appropriate number of adders to multipliers and introducing pipelined structure, we achieve configurable MM modules. For one MM module with M's N-bit multiplier and one $2N$-bit adder, the number of execution cycles of a 256-bit MM will be $(\frac{256}{N})^2 * \frac{1}{M} + 1$, called as a unit of cycles. For modular inversion, we adopt the fast radix-4 unified division algorithm in [7]. For modular addition and subtraction, we design a combination module which can execute both and costing only one cycle. By these optimization, all the finite field operation units achieve high hardware utilization and fast speed, which will greatly improve the overall performance.

3.3 Optimization for Point Addition and Point Double

Since the final performance of MPL algorithm largely depends on the implementation effect of point arithmetic layer, then optimization for PA and PD become

what matters the most. The computation steps of them have been defined as
Eqs. 3 and 4. As we can know from last section, modular multiplication and addition/subtraction are performed by corresponding units respectively. And time
consumption needed for the later is far less than the former. So on the premise of
saving area as much as possible, performing addition/subtraction in fully parallel with multiplication would be the most efficient case undoubtedly. But it's not
easy. There are at least three issues that ought to be considered. Firstly, data
dependencies in PA and PD formulas are very complicated. Secondly, due to our
two-pipelined architecture, it needs two units of cycles before the modular multiplication result can be used after data incoming, which also brings difficulty to
operation scheduling. Finally, in order to save storage space, we want to reduce
intermediate data as much as possible. All the three make stringent requests on
the design of execution order. After a lot of careful thought and analysis, we
have found the optimal scheduling scheme fortunately. The optimization results
for point doubling is shown in Table 2 while addition in Table 3.

Table 2. Point double execution order

T	Multiply	Modular	Register
U	$Z_1 * Z_1$		
U	$X_1 * X_1$	$mod(Z_1^2)$	
U	$Z_1^2 * b$	$mod(X_1^2)$	$T_2 = Z_1^2$
U	$X_1 * Z_1$	$mod(bZ_1^2)$	$T_1 = X_1^2$
U	$T_2 * bZ_1^2$	$mod(X_1Z_1)$	$T_1 = T_1 - 3T_2$
U	$T_1 * X_1Z_1$	$mod(bZ_1^4)$	$T_2 = 2T_2, T_1 = T_1 + 3T_2$
U	$T_2 * X_1Z_1$	$mod(X_1Z_1(X_1^2 - 3Z_1^2))$	$T_2 = bZ_1^4$
U	$T_1 * T_1$	$mod(2X_1Z_1^3)$	$Z = 4(T_2 + T_1)$
U	$2X_1Z_1^3 * 4b$	$mod((X_1^2 + 3Z_1^2)^2)$	
U		$mod(8bX_1Z_1^3)$	$T_1 = (X_1^2 + 3Z_1^2)^2$
C			$T_2 = (8bX_1Z_1^3)$
C			$X = T_1 - T_2$

[a]T for time axis, U for one unit of cycles, C for one cycle

In this optimal schedule, we keep multipliers busy all the time and hide
the execution time of adders in parallel with them. Since PA and PD need
almost the same computation load of multiplication, we assign each of them
one MM unit with multiplier scale of 64-bit. Then we encapsulate PA and PD
into two synchronous modules, at the same time they share only one modular
addition/subtraction unit to perform all the operation other than MM. Base on
the above optimization, our PA and PD units achieve superior performance and
hit the design expectation successfully.

Table 3. Point addition execution order

T	Multiply	Modular	Register
U	$X_1 * Z_2$		
U	$X_2 * Z_1$	$mod(X_1 Z_2)$	
U	$Z_1^* Z_2$	$mod(X_2 * Z_1)$	$T_1 = X_1 Z_2$
U	$X_1^* X_2$	$mod(Z_1 * Z_2)$	$T_1 = T_1 + T_2$
U	$Z_1 Z_2 * T_1$	$mod(X_1 X_2)$	$T_1 = T_1 - 2T_2$
U	$T_1 * T_1$	$mod(Z_1 Z_2(X_1 Z_2 + X_2 Z_1))$	$T_1 = X_1 X_2$
U	$Lmod * 4b$	$mod((X_1 Z_2 - X_2 Z_1)^2)$	$T_1 = T_1 + 3T_2$
U	$Lmod * x$	$mod(4bZ_1 Z_2(X_1 Z_2 + X_2 Z_1))$	
U	$T_1 * T_1$	$mod(x(X_1 Z_2 - X_2 Z_1)^2)$	$T_2 = Lmod$
U		$mod(X_1 X_2 + 3Z_1 Z_2)^2)$	$Z = Lmod$
C			$T_1 = (X_1^2 + 3Z_1^2)^2$
C			$X = T_1 - T_2$

^{a}T for time axis, U for one unit of cycles, C for one cycle
^{b}Lmod means the modular result of last round

3.4 SM2 Architecture

The whole architecture is composed of three modules. Storage module is made up of register heap and store logic. It efficiently performs the storage and communication of all the data in ECC algorithm. PA and PD share one modular addition/subtraction unit, forming the arithmetic module. Main Control module serves as the commander, guiding the other two to execute PM efficiently.

Table 4. Performance comparison

	Ours	[8]	[7]	[9]	[10]
Prime field	SCA-256	256-bit	256-bit	256-bit	256-bit
Library	0.13 m	90 nm	90 nm	0.13 m	0.13 m
Freq(MHz)	228	185	250	137.7	556
Gate counts	156 k	540 k	122 k	120 k	122 k
Cycle	47.5 k	22.3 k	193 k	340 k	562 k
Time(μs)	208	120	770	2680	1010
kP/s	4.80 k	8.33 k	1.30 k	0.37 k	0.99 k
AT$^\alpha$	1	2.88	4.18	9.91	3.79
Resistance	SPA FA	SPA	No	No	No

^{a}AT=area-time   product=Gate
counts*Time*0.13 μs/Technology

4   Comparison and Conclusion

This architecture has been verified in Verilog-HDL and evaluated in $0.13\,\mu m$ CMOS standard cell library. Results are shown in Table 4, compared with the previously published results over 256-bit prime field. While absolutely fair comparison can't be promised due to different backgrounds, area-time product provides the most objective assessment standards. And in this comparison, our architecture offers the best AT product.

In a word, this paper proposes a high-performance ASIC implementation of point multiplication for SM2. For the field operation level, modular addition/subtraction and inversion are designed into efficient modules that fit the whole architecture very well. As for the most important modular multiplication, we adopt Fast Reduction scheme and achieve a configurable modular multiplication with pipelined architecture. For the addition level, execution order of PA and PD are elaborately planned, bringing ultra high hardware efficiency. For the algorithm level, MPL algorithm with computation simplification brings both efficiency and security. Synthesize results show that this processor only needs $208\,\mu s$ and $6.8\,\mu J$ to achieve a 256-bit point multiplication at $228\,MHz$, and it can effective resist SPA. Compare with related works, this architecture offers not only the superior area-time product but also great security. However, our performance comes at a costly price of flexibility. In our future work, we will focus on the extended application of isochronous and configurable architecture of ECC, hoping to achieve more instructive and flexible implementation.

Acknowledgment. This work was supported by the National Natural Science Foundation of China (Grants U1135004 and 61472208) and National Key Basic Research Program of China (Grant 2013CB338004).

References

1. State Cryptography Administration of China. Public Key Cryptographic Algorithm SM2 Based on Elliptic Curves (2010). http://www.oscca.gov.cn/News/201012/News_1198.htm
2. Lee, J.-W., Chung, S.-C., Chang, H.-C., Lee, C.-Y.: Efficient power-analysis-resistant dual-field elliptic curve cryptographic processor using heterogeneous dual-processing-element architecture. IEEE Trans. Very Large Scale Integr. (VLSI) Syst. **22**(1), 49–61 (2014)
3. Junfeng Fan, X., Guo, E.D., Mulder, P.S., Preneel, B., Verbauwhede, I.: State-of-the-art of secure ECC implementations: a survey on known side-channel attacks and countermeasures. In: IEEE International Symposium on Hardware-Oriented Security and Trust (HOST), pp. 76–87. IEEE (2010)
4. Brier, E., Joye, M.: Weierstraß elliptic curves and side-channel attacks. In: Naccache, D., Paillier, P. (eds.) PKC 2002. LNCS, vol. 2274, pp. 335–345. Springer, Heidelberg (2002)
5. Montgomery, P.L.: Speeding the pollard and elliptic curve methods of factorization. Math. Comput. **48**(177), 243–264 (1987)

6. Hankerson, D., Vanstone, S., Menezes, A.J.: Guide to Elliptic Curve Cryptography. Springer Professional Computing. Springer, New York (2004)
7. Chen, Y.-L., Lee, J.-W., Liu, P.-C., Chang, H.-C., Lee, C.-Y.: A dual-field elliptic curve cryptographic processor with a radix-4 unified division unit. In: IEEE International Symposium on Circuits and Systems (ISCAS), pp. 713–716. IEEE (2011)
8. Chung, S.-C., Lee, J.-W., Chang, H.-C., Lee, C.-Y.: A high-performance elliptic curve cryptographic processor over GF (p) with SPA resistance. In: IEEE International Symposium on Circuits and Systems (ISCAS), pp. 1456–1459. IEEE (2012)
9. Satoh, A., Takano, K.: A scalable dual-field elliptic curve cryptographic processor. IEEE Trans. Comput. **52**(4), 449–460 (2003)
10. Chen, G., Bai, G., Chen, H.: A high-performance elliptic curve cryptographic processor for general curves over GF (p) based on a systolic arithmetic unit. IEEE Trans. Circuits Syst. II Express Briefs **54**(5), 412–416 (2007)

Multi-input Functional Encryption and Its Application in Outsourcing Computation

Peili Li[1,2,3], Haixia Xu[1,2]([✉]), and Yuanyuan Ji[1,2,3]

[1] State Key Laboratory of Information Security,
Institute of Information Engineering of Chinese Academy of Sciences, Beijing, China
{plli,hxxu}@is.ac.cn, jiyuanyuan@iie.ac.cn
[2] Data Assurance and Communication Security Research Center
of Chinese Academy of Sciences, Beijing, China
[3] University of Chinese Academy Sciences, Beijing, China

Abstract. We study functional encryption and its application in outsourcing computation. Functional encryption is a new primitive first defined by Boneh, Sahai and Waters: given an encryption of a message x and a decryption key sk_f for a function f, anyone can obtain $f(x)$ but cannot learn anything else about x. In multi-input functional encryption, the secret key sk_f corresponds to an n-ary function f and takes multiple ciphertexts as its input. Prior works on multi-input functional encryption are based on indistinguishability obfuscation which is either rely on a polynomial set of assumptions or an exponential number of assumptions. In this paper, we construct a multi-input functional encryption scheme without obfuscation. And we show its application in outsourcing computation and construct a multi-client outsourcing computation scheme that is publicly verifiable.

Keywords: Functional encryption · Outsourcing computation · Multi-input · Multi-client · Privacy · Public verification

1 Introduction

Traditional public key encryption has been used to secure the communication channel between two parties, the sender and receiver. It has two features: (1) The ciphertexts are sent through the channel, and the party who has the secret key can recover the plain message. (2) The secret key holder can decrypt and know the entire plaintext, but those who do not have the secret key can learn nothing at all ("black and white" property) [4]. Traditional public key encryption scheme can help a user to share its data over an insecure network. However, with the development of the internet and cloud services, this "black and white" notion encryption is inefficient for many applications. For example, an outside server which acts as a spam filter should be able to determine if an encrypted email is spam or not without learning anything else about the email's content; the encrypted data which is stored in the cloud may be used in different ways by different users. To solve these problems, functional encryption is studied in recent

© Springer International Publishing Switzerland 2016
S. Qing et al. (Eds.): ICICS 2015, LNCS 9543, pp. 220–235, 2016.
DOI: 10.1007/978-3-319-29814-6_18

years. The notion of functional encryption was first defined by Boneh et al. [4]. In functional encryption, the owner of the master secret key can generate the secret key sk_f for any function f in a family F. Given the ciphertext CT of message x, the user who holds the secret key sk_f can do the decryption to obtain $f(x)$ but does not know anything else about x.

It is natural to extend the notion of functional encryption to multi-input functional encryption which is a very general tool for computing on encrypted data. Let f be a n-ary function $(n \geq 1)$. In multi-input functional encryption, given n ciphertexts $CT_1, CT_2, \cdots, CT_n$ of underlying messages $x_1, x_2, \cdots, x_n$ and a secret key sk_f corresponding to function f, the user can obtain $f(x_1, x_2, \cdots, x_n)$ but can not learn anything else about the messages $x_1, x_2, \cdots, x_n$. Multi-input functional encryption has many applications, for example it can be used in multi-client outsourcing computation, computing over encrypted data stream, running on SQL queries on encrypted database and so on [11].

Functional encryption is a suitable tool in designing outsourcing computation scheme [13]. With the development of cloud computing, there are many cloud service providers offer attractive services, client would like to outsource its computation task to service provider and pay the service charge. Multi-client outsourcing computation can be described as following [6]: n computational weak clients each has its input x_i wish to outsource the computation of $f(x_1, \cdots, x_n)$ to an untrusted server. A secure outsourcing scheme should make sure that the clients' inputs are keeping private from the server and the clients can verify the correctness of the computation result returned from the. In this paper, we mainly study multi-input functional encryption and show its application in multi-client outsourcing computation.

1.1   Related Work

The notion of functional encryption was first formalized by Boneh et al. [4]. Early works are known only for restricted functions such as inner product function or a variant of it [1,5,15,21]. These works do not show how to extend the scheme beyond inner products. Sahai and Seyalioglu [20] first proposed a single key query functional encryption for general functions, and [14] extended it and designed a q key bounded functional encryption scheme, which allows the adversary to make q secret key queries for functions. Because of the non-succinctness of the ciphertext size in [14,20]'s work. [13] designed a single key query functional encryption scheme with succinct ciphertext. In the same year, [7] proposed functional encryption supporting unbounded key queries using indistinguishability obfuscation. And it only satisfies selective security. Using puncturable technique, [8,23] designed adaptively secure functional encryption for general functions respectively.

Multi-input Functional Encryption. The study on multi-input functional encryption was done by Goldwasser et al. [11]. They gave constructions of multi-input functional encryption based on indistinguishability obfuscation [7] and differing-inputs obfuscation [2]. Similar to the idea of [7], in [11]'s work n parties first use the two-key encryption technique [17] to encrypt its inputs. Using the property of indistinguishability obfuscation, they hide the verification, decryption and function-computation process in an obfuscation circuit. The obfuscation circuit here is the secret key sk_f corresponding to f. Thus the user who holds sk_f can get the computation result $f(x_1, \cdots, x_n)$ and learn nothing else about $x_1, \cdots, x_n$. Their scheme satisfies selective indistinguishable security and q bounded selective simulation security. While in [11]'s construction, its privacy property relies on a completely honest party. For there must be a party who generates the master secret key (MSK) which contains the secret key of the two-key encryption scheme. If the party who holds the master secret key is dishonest, it can easily get the input of other parties by just decrypting the corresponding ciphertexts. And the indistinguishability obfuscation it based on is still either rely on a polynomial set of assumptions or an exponential number of assumptions, but with an exponential loss in the security reduction [10]. In our work, we aim to design a multi-input functional encryption scheme that avoids using obfuscation and can keep privacy of the parties' inputs from each other without relying on a completely honest party.

Multi-client Outsourcing Computation. There are limited works in this area. [6] constructed a multi-client outsourcing scheme using proxy-OT technique. In its scheme only the client who has the secret key can do the verification and get the computation result. [19,22] also designed multi-client outsourcing computation schemes by using two non-collude servers, while their scheme do not verify the correctness of the computation result. The verification process is essential in achieving secure and correct outsourcing scheme. In some cases, other parties may also need to verify the correctness of the computation result. This leads to the study of public verification which means that using the public verify key any other party can verify the correctness of the result returned by the untrusted server. In this paper, we consider the scenery that n clients outsource their computation task to one server. We use multi-input functional encryption scheme to construct multi-client outsourcing computation scheme that satisfies public verification. This idea comes from the works about functional encryption [12,13], however in their outsourcing schemes, the clients need to execute functional encryption scheme twice in order to do the verification.

1.2   Our Contribution

Our thought mainly comes from Goldwasser et al.'s work [13]. We design a multi-input functional encryption scheme and apply it to design a multi-client outsourcing scheme. The main contributions of our constructions are as follows:

- Based on [13]'s work, we design a multi-input functional encryption scheme using multikey fully homomorphic encryption, and our construction does not need to use obfuscation.
- Compared with [11]'s work, the privacy property of the parties' inputs holds and does not rely on a completely honest party.

– Using multi-input functional encryption we construct a multi-client outsourcing scheme that satisfies public verification. We use a new verify-method to achieve public verification and does not need to run the functional encryption scheme twice.

1.3 Technique Outline

In the rest of this paper, we denote FE the functional encryption. Our work is mainly based on the FE construction of [13]. We briefly introduce [13]'s idea and show how to transfer it to a multi-input FE scheme.

In [13]'s work, a message x's encryption $Enc(x)$ is computed using fully homomorphic encryption (FHE), the decryptor can do homomorphic evaluation on the encrypted data and get $Enc(f(x))$. While in functional encryption the decryptor finally obtains $f(x)$ but can not learn anything else about x. The decryption process is done by using Yao's garbled circuit which hides the secret key sk in the circuit and takes input $Enc(f(x))$. But how to choose the corresponding labels of $Enc(f(x))$ when begin to compute the garbled circuit? To solve this problem it uses two-outcome attribute based encryption scheme as its tool.

The idea of [13] is ingenious, however it only considered one-input functional encryption. Based on its work, we design a multi-input functional encryption scheme using multikey fully homomorphic encryption scheme(MFHE) [16]. In our construction, each party holds its key pair (hpk_i, hsk_i) generated from the multikey FHE. In order to decrypt $Enc(f(x_1, \cdots, x_n))$, the parties first compute the decryption key $hsk = hsk_1 \cdot hsk_2 \cdots hsk_n$ and then one of these parties produces a garbled circuit of $MFHE.Dec(hsk, \cdot)$. In order to avoid interaction among the parties, we use the non-interactive MPC method(NIMPC) recently introduced by [3]. Use NIMPC, the parties can non-interactively generate the decrypt key $hsk = hsk_1 \cdot hsk_2 \cdots hsk_n$.

How to apply it to multi-client outsourcing computation scheme?

The notion of functional encryption is a little similar with outsourcing computation. The clients in outsourcing computation act like the encryptors, and the server acts like the decryptor. In multi-client outsourcing scheme, the server needs to return the result $f(x_1, x_2, \cdots, x_n)$ to the clients. In addition to this process, the clients need to verify the correctness of the computation result. In [12]'s work, they followed the approach of Parno et al. [18] and described how to achieve public verifiable multi-client outsourcing computation scheme. In their design, the clients should first generate two pairs of master secret keys and public keys and run FE scheme twice. Instead of using [18]'s public verify method, we use a new method to do public verification. Using the garbled circuit's output labels which are corresponding to the computation result $f(x)$, we design a public verify method similar to [18] but do not need to run FE scheme twice.

2   Preliminaries

We denote k the security parameter, $negl(\cdot)$ a negligible function and ppt the probabilistic polynomial time. ABE_2 denotes the two-outcome attribute based encryption, MFHE denotes the multikey homomorphic encryption(or Multikey FHE) for short, NIMPC denotes non-interactive multiparty computation and MIFE means the multi-input functional encryption.

2.1 Multikey Fully Homomorphic Encryption

Definition 1 (Multikey C-homomorphic encryption). *[16] let C be a class of circuits. A multikey C-homomorphic encryption consisting four algorithms $(KeyGen, Enc, Dec, Eval)_N$ for all integers $N > 0$ satisfies the followings:*

1. *$KeyGen(1^k) \rightarrow (pk_i, sk_i, ek_i)$: input the security parameter k, output a public key pk_i, a secret key sk_i and a evaluation key ek_i ($i \in [N]$).*
2. *$Enc(pk_i, x) \rightarrow c$: input the public key pk_i and message x_i, output a ciphertext c_i.*
3. *$Eval(C, (c_1', pk_1', ek_1'), \cdots, (c_t', pk_t', ek_t')) \rightarrow c^*$: given a circuit C and t cipher-texts (c_i', pk_i', ek_i'), outputs a ciphertext c^*. Here the t keys $\{pk_1', \cdots, pk_t'\}$ is a subset of $\{pk_1, \cdots, pk_N\}$.*
4. *$Dec(sk_1, \cdots, sk_N, c^*) \rightarrow x^*$: given N secret keys $sk_1, \cdots, sk_N$ and a cipher-text c^*, outputs a message x^*.*

Correctness. *let $c^* = Eval(C, (c_1', pk_1', ek_1'), \cdots, (c_t', pk_t', ek_t'))$, where $c_i' = Enc(pk_i', x_i')$. Then $Dec(sk_1, \cdots, sk_N, c^*) = C(x_1', \cdots, x_t')$.*

Compactness. *Let $c^* = Eval(C, (c_1', pk_1', ek_1'), \cdots, (c_t', pk_t', ek_t'))$. There exist a polynomial P such that $|c^*| \leqslant P(k, n)$.*

Multikey FHE. *An encryption scheme consisting algorithms $(KeyGen, Enc, Dec, Eval)_{N>0}$ is multikey fully homomorphic if it is C-homomorphic for the class of all circuits.*

If the underlying encryption scheme is semantically secure, then the multikey FHE holds semantically secure in the presence of the evaluation key ek [16].

López-Alt et al. [16] designed a multikey FHE scheme, and in their scheme the decryption of a multi-key ciphertext requires a multiplication by the product of all keys that were involved in the generation of the ciphertext.

2.2 Garbled Circuit

Definition 2 (Garbling scheme). *C_n is the set of circuit taking as input n bits. A garbling scheme for a family of circuits $C = \{C_n\}_{n \in N}$, is a tuple of ppt algorithms $Gb=(Gb.Garble, Gb.Enc, Gb.Eval)$ such that*

1. *$Gb.Garble(1^k, C)$ takes as input the security parameter k and a circuit $C \in C_n$ for some n, and outputs the garbled circuit Γ and a secret key sk.*
2. *$Gb.Enc(sk, x)$ takes as input the secret key sk and data $x \in \{0,1\}^n$ and outputs an encoding c.*
3. *$Gb.Eval(\Gamma, c)$ takes as input a garbled circuit Γ, an encoding c and outputs a value y .*

Correctness. For any polynomial $n(\cdot)$, for all sufficiently large security parameters k, for $n = n(k)$, for all circuits $C \in \mathcal{C}_n$ and all $x \in \{0,1\}^n$, $Pr[(\Gamma, sk) \leftarrow Gb.Garble(1^k, C); c \leftarrow Gb.Enc(sk, x); y \leftarrow Gb.Eval(\Gamma, c) : C(x) = y] = 1 - negl(k)$.

Efficiency. There exists a universal polynomial $p = p(k, n)$ (p is the same for all classes of circuits C) such that for all input sizes n, security parameters k, for all boolean circuits C of with n bits of input, for all $x \in \{0,1\}^n$, $Pr[(\Gamma, sk) \leftarrow Gb.Garble(1^k, C) : |sk| \leqslant p(k, n)$ and $runtime(Gb.Enc(sk, x)) \leqslant p(k, n)] = 1$.

Input and Circuit Private. If there exist a ppt simulator Sim_{Garble}, such that for every ppt adversaries A and D, for all sufficiently large security parameters k, the following equation holds. Then the garbled scheme Gb for a family of circuits $\{\mathcal{C}_n\}_{n \in N}$ is input and circuit private.
$$|Pr[(x, C, \alpha) \leftarrow A(1^k); (\Gamma, sk) \leftarrow Gb.Garble(1^k, C); c \leftarrow Gb.Enc(sk, x) : D(\alpha, x, C, \Gamma, c)] - Pr[(x, C, \alpha) \leftarrow A(1^k); (\tilde{\Gamma}, \tilde{c}) \leftarrow Sim_{Garble}(1^k, C(x), 1^{|C|}, 1^{|x|}) : D(\alpha, x, C, \tilde{\Gamma}, \tilde{c})]| = negl(k)$$

2.3   Two-Outcome Attribute-Based Encryption

Definition 3 (Two-outcome   Attribute-based   Encryption). *A two-outcome attribute-based encryption scheme (ABE_2) for a class of predicates $P = \{P_n\}_{n \in N}$ represented as boolean circuits with n input bits and one output bit and an associated message space M is a tuple of algorithms ($ABE_2.Setup$, $ABE_2.KeyGen$, $ABE_2.Enc$, $ABE_2.Dec$) as follows:*

1. *$ABE_2.Setup(1^k)$: Takes a security parameter k as input and outputs a master public key mpk and a master secret key msk.*
2. *$ABE_2.KeyGen(msk, P)$: Given a master secret key msk and a predicate $P \in P_n$ for some n, outputs a key sk_P corresponding to P.*
3. *$ABE_2.Enc(mpk, x, m_0, m_1)$: Takes as input the public key mpk, an attribute $x \in \{0,1\}^n$ for some n, and two messages $m_0, m_1 \in M$, outputs a ciphertext c.*
4. *$ABE_2.Dec(sk_P, c)$: Takes as input a secret key sk_P for a predicate P and a ciphertext c and outputs $m^* \in M$.*

Correctness. We say that the ABE_2 scheme is correct if for any polynomial $n(\cdot)$, for every sufficiently large security parameter k, if $n = n(k)$, for all predicates $P \in P_N$, attributes $x \in \{0,1\}^n$, and messages $m_0, m_1 \in M$:

$$Pr \left| \begin{array}{l} (mpk, msk) \leftarrow ABE_2.Setup(1^k); \\ sk_P \leftarrow ABE_2.KeyGen(msk, P); \\ c \leftarrow ABE_2.Enc(mpk, x, m_0, m_1); \\ m^* \leftarrow ABE_2.Dec(sk_P, c); \\ m^* = m_{P(x)} \end{array} \right| = 1 - negl(k)$$

The space $\{0,1\}^n$ is referred to as the attribute space (with an attribute size of n) and M is referred to as the message space.

Security. We say that the ABE_2 scheme is secure if for all PPT adversary $\mathcal{A}$, and for every sufficiently large security parameter k, the following experiment holds that:

$$Pr|Exp_{ABE_2,\mathcal{A}}(1^k) = 1| \leq 1/2 + negl(k).$$

$$Exp_{ABE_2,\mathcal{A}}(1^k):$$

1. $(mpk, msk) \leftarrow ABE_2.Setup(1^k)$
2. $(P, st_1) \leftarrow A_1(mpk)$
3. $sk_P \leftarrow ABE_2.KeyGen(msk, P)$
4. $(M, M_0, M_1, x, st_2) \leftarrow A_2(st_1, sk_P)$
5. *Choose a bit b at random, let*

$$c = \begin{cases} ABE_2.Enc(mpk, x, M, M_b), if P(x) = 0, \\ ABE_2.Enc(mpk, x, M_b, M), otherwise, \end{cases}$$

6. $b' \leftarrow A_3(st_2, c)$, if $b = b'$, $\exists n$ such that, for all $P \in \mathcal{P}_n$, messages $M, M_0, M_1 \in \mathcal{M}$, $|M_0| = |M_1|$, $x \in \{0,1\}^n$, output 1, else output 0.

2.4   Multi-input Functional Encryption

Definition 4 (Multi-input Functional Encryption). *A multi-input functional encryption scheme(MIFE) for a class of functions $\mathcal{F} = \{\mathcal{F}\}_{n \in N}$ consists of four algorithms (MIFE.Setup, MIFE.Enc, MIFE.KeyGen, MIFE.Dec). We describe them as following:*

1. *MIFE.Setup$(1^k, n)$: takes the secure parameter k and function's arity n as input, outputs a master secret key MSK and a master public key MPK.*
2. *MIFE.Enc$(MPK, x_1, \cdots, x_n)$: takes input public key MPK and messages $x_1, \cdots, x_n$, here x_i is the data corresponding to party i. Using MPK each party encrypts its data x_i and outputs a ciphertext c_i. The algorithm finally output a ciphertext CT related to the ciphertexts $(c_1, \cdots, c_n)$.*
3. *MIFE.KeyGen(MSK, f): takes input the master secret key MSK and an n-ary function f, outputs a key sk_f.*
4. *MIFE.Dec(sk_f, CT): takes ciphertext CT and secret key sk_f as its input and output a value y.*

Correctness. We say that a multi-input functional encryption scheme is correct if for all $f \in \mathcal{F}$ and all $(x_1, \cdots, x_n) \in X_k^n$, the following holds:

$$Pr \begin{bmatrix} (MSK, MPK) \leftarrow MIFE.Setup(1^k); sk_f \leftarrow MIFE.KeyGen(MSK, f); \\ MIFE.Dec(sk_f, MIFE.Enc(x_1, \cdots, x_n)) \neq f(x_1, \cdots, x_n) \end{bmatrix} = negl(k)$$

Full-SIM-Security. *A multi-input functional encryption scheme scheme is (single-key) full-SIM-secure if for every ppt adversary $A = (A_1, A_2)$ there exist a ppt simulator S such that the following two experiments are computational indistinguishable.*

Experiment $REAL_A^{MIFE}(1^k)$:   Experiment $IDEAL_{A,S}^{MIFE}(1^k)$:

$$(MPK, MSK) \leftarrow MIFE.Setup(1^k)$$

$$(f, st_1) \leftarrow A_1(MPK)$$

$$sk_f \leftarrow MIFE.KeyGen(MSK, f)$$

$$(X, st_2) \leftarrow A_2(st_1, sk_f)$$

$c \leftarrow MIFE.Enc(MPK, X)$ $\tilde{c} \leftarrow S(MPK, sk_f, f, f(X), 1^{|X|})$

Output (st_2, c) Output $(st_2, \tilde{c})$

Here X represents a vector of n messages $(x_1, \cdots, x_n)$

2.5 Multi-client Outsourcing Computation Scheme

As far as we know, multi-client outsourcing computation scheme was first considered by choi et al. [6]. There are n clients each has their corresponding input x_i want to outsource the computation of $f(x_1, \cdots, x_n)$ to a server. Here we consider the public verification case where any other clients can verify the correctness of the computation result using the public verify key.

Definition 5 (Multi-client Outsourcing Computation Scheme). *A $n-$ party multi-client outsourcing computation scheme consists four algorithms (KeyGen, ProbGen, Compute, Verify):*

1. *KeyGen$(1^k, f) \to (SK, PK)$: On input the security parameter k and a function $f \in F$, it outputs a secret key SK, a public key PK.*
2. *ProbGen$(PK, SK, x_1, \cdots, x_n) \to (\sigma_X, VK_X)$: Each client uses the public key PK computes the encoding of its input x_i denote by σ_{x_i}. Finally the algorithm output a verification key VK_X and an encoding σ_X related to $\sigma_{x_i}(i = 1, \cdots, n)$.*
3. *Compute$(PK, \sigma_X) \to Z$: This algorithm takes input the public key PK, and the encoding σ_X, output a result Z.*
4. *Verify$(PK, VK_X, Z) \to (y, reject)$: Using the public messages PK, public verify message VK_X, the algorithm verifies the correctness of Z. If the verification passes, the corresponding result y can be recovered after the verification. Otherwise reject*

Correctness. *A multi-client outsourcing computation scheme is correct if for any function* $f \in F$ *and any* $(SK, PK) \leftarrow KeyGen(1^k, f)$, *any* $(x_1, \cdots, x_n) \in Dom(F)$, *if* $(\sigma_X, VK_X) \leftarrow ProbGen(PK, SK, x_1, \cdots, x_n)$ *and* $Z \leftarrow Compute(PK, \sigma_X)$, *then* $y = f(x_1, \cdots, x_n) \leftarrow Verify(PK.VK_X, Z)$ *holds with all but negligible probability.*

Security. *A multi-client outsourcing scheme is secure if the probability that there exist a ppt adversary that can make the clients accept an incorrect computation result is negligible. We describe it via the experiment below:*

> *Experiment* $EXP_{\mathcal{A}}^{Ver}(S, f, k)$
> $(SK, PK) \leftarrow$ **KeyGen**$(1^k, f)$
> *For* $i = 1$ *to* q:
> $X_i \leftarrow \mathcal{A}(PK, \sigma_{X,1}, VK_{X,1}, \ldots, \sigma_{X,i-1}, VK_{X,i-1})$
> $(\sigma_{X,i}; VK_{X,i}) \leftarrow$ **ProbGen**(PK, SK, X_i)
> $X^* \leftarrow \mathcal{A}(PK, \sigma_{X,1}, VK_{X,1}, \ldots, \sigma_{X,q}, VK_{X,q})$
> $(\sigma_{X^*}, VK_{X^*}) \leftarrow$ **ProbGen**(PK, SK, X^*)
> $Z^* \leftarrow \mathcal{A}(PK, \sigma_{X,1}, VK_{X,1}, \ldots, \sigma_{X,q}, VK_{X,q}, \sigma_{X^*}, VK_{X^*})$
> $y^* \leftarrow$ **Verify**(PK, VK_{X^*}, Z^*)
> *Output 1 if* $y^* \notin \{f(X^*), \bot\}$ *and 0 otherwise.*

We say that a multi-client outsourcing scheme is secure if Prob[EXP $_{\mathcal{A}}^{Ver}(S, f, \lambda) = 1]$ *is negligible.*

Privacy. Based on indistinguishability arguments we define input privacy which guarantees that no information about the inputs is leaked [9]. We describe the Experiment EXP$_{\mathcal{A}}^{Priv}$ as follow.

> Experiment EXP$_{\mathcal{A}}^{Priv}[S, f, n, \lambda]$
> $(PK, SK, EK) \leftarrow$ **KeyGen**$(1^\lambda, f)$;
> $(X_0, X_1) \leftarrow \mathcal{A}^{\textbf{ProbGen}_{SK}(\cdot)}(PK)$;
> $(\sigma_0, VK_{X_0}) \leftarrow$ **ProbGen**$_{SK}(X_0)$;
> $(\sigma_1, VK_{X_1}) \leftarrow$ **ProbGen**$_{SK}(X_1)$;
> $b \leftarrow \{0, 1\}$;
> $b^* \leftarrow \mathcal{A}^{\textbf{ProbGen}_{SK}(\cdot)}(PK, X_0, X_1, \sigma_b)$;
> if $b^* = b$, output $'1'$, else $'0'$;

We define the advantage of an adversary $\mathcal{A}$ in the above experiment as:
ADV$_{\mathcal{A}}^{Priv}[S, f, n, \lambda] = |\text{Prob}[\text{EXP}_{\mathcal{A}}^{Priv}[S, f, n, \lambda] = 1] - \frac{1}{2}|$.

A multi-client outsourcing computation scheme is private against the server if for any ppt adversary $\mathcal{A}$ it holds that ADV$_{\mathcal{A}}^{Priv}[S, f, n, \lambda]$ is negligible.

3 Our Construction

3.1 Multi-input Functional Encryption

In this section, we construct a multi-input functional encryption scheme without obfuscation and the inputs are keeping private from each other. For simplicity, we construct MIFE for functions outputting one bit. We use three building blocks:

two-outcome attribute-based encryption scheme, multikey fully homomorphic encryption scheme and Yao's garbled circuit. Let $\mathbf{c}$ be a vector of n ciphertexts $\mathbf{c} = (c_1, \cdots, c_n)$. Let $\text{MFHE.Eval}_f^i(hpk, \mathbf{c})$ be the predicate function that computes the i-th output bit of $\text{MFHE.Eval}_f(hpk, \mathbf{c})$. Let λ be the length of the ciphertexts in MFHE scheme.

In our construction, we use the non-interactive multiparty computation(denote NIMPC) [3] as our tool to help the parties cooperatively compute the decryption key $hsk = hsk_1 \cdot hsk_2 \cdots hsk_n$. In [3]'s NIMPC construction, its process can be divided into offline and online stage. In its offline stage the parties generate correlated randomness; in the online stage, the parties encode their messages respectively and then compute on the encodings to get the final computation result but cannot learn anything else about each others' message.

Now we are ready to give our multi-input FE scheme. The construction of multi-input FE is described as follows:

1. $\text{MIFE.Setup}(1^k)$: Run two-outcome ABE scheme λ times: $(mpk_i, msk_i) \leftarrow \text{ABE}_2.\text{Setup}(1^k)$ for $i \in [\lambda]$. Run the offline stage of NIMPC to generate correlated randomness, denote R. The master public key $MPK = (mpk_1, \cdots, mpk_\lambda)$, the master secret key $MSK = (msk_1, \cdots, msk_\lambda, R)$.
2. $\text{MIFE.Enc}(MPK, x_1, \cdots, x_n)$: let n be the number of inputs. x_i corresponds to the input of party i. The encryption algorithm proceeds as follows:
   (a) Each party generates a fresh key pair $(hpk_i, hsk_i) \leftarrow \text{MFHE.KeyGen}(1^k)$. Each party encrypts its input x_i by computing $c_i \leftarrow \text{MFHE.Enc}(hpk_i, x_i)$. let $\mathbf{c} = (c_1, \cdots, c_n)$.
   (b) The n parties run the online stage of NIMPC protocol to secure compute $hsk = hsk_1 \cdot hsk_2 \cdots hsk_n$. Then one party (suppose the first party) produces a garbled circuit Γ for the MFHE decryption algorithm $\text{MFHE.Dec}(hsk, \cdot)$ together with 2λ input labels L_i^b for $i \in [\lambda]$, $b \in \{0, 1\}$.
   (c) The party who generates the garbled circuit Γ computes the encryption of $\mathbf{c} = (c_1, \cdots, c_n)$ using $\text{ABE}_2.\text{Enc}$ algorithm: $CT_i = \text{ABE}_2.\text{Enc}(mpk_i, (hpk, \mathbf{c}), L_i^0, L_i^1)$ for i in $[\lambda]$.
   (d) Output the ciphertext $CT = (CT_1, \cdots, CT_\lambda, \Gamma)$.
3. $\text{MIFE.KeyGen}(MSK, f)$: As we have mentioned that $\text{MFHE.Eval}_f^i(hpk, \mathbf{c})$ is the predicate function that computes the i-th output bit of $\text{MFHE.Eval}_f(hpk, \mathbf{c})$. Here $hpk = (hpk_1, \cdots, hpk_n)$ and $\mathbf{c}$ consists n MFHE ciphertexts.
   (a) Run the key generation algorithm of ABE_2 for function MFHE.Eval_f^i under different master secret keys: $sk_f^i = \text{ABE}_2.\text{KeyGen}(msk_i, \text{MFHE.Eval}_f^i)$.
   (b) Output $sk_f = (sk_f^1, \cdots, sk_f^\lambda)$ the secret key for function f.
4. $\text{MIFE.Dec}(sk_f, CT)$:
   (a) Run ABE_2 decryption algorithm on ciphertext CT, obtain the labels $L_i^{d_i} \leftarrow \text{ABE}_2.\text{Dec}(sk_f^i, CT_i)$ for $i \in [\lambda]$.
   (b) Run the garbled circuit Γ on the labels $L_i^{d_i}$ to compute the function result: $\text{Gb.Eval}(\Gamma, L_1^{d_1}, \cdots, L_\lambda^{d_\lambda}) = \text{MFHE.Dec}(hsk, d_1 d_2 \cdots d_\lambda) = f(x_1, \cdots, x_n)$.

Intuition. Each party i's secret key hsk_i is keeping private from other parties. Every time the garbled circuit Γ has been regenerated.

3.2 Correctness and Security Proof

Correctness. In the decryption process, according to the correctness of ABE_2 scheme, d_i is the i-th output bit of $MFHE.Eval_f(hpk, \mathbf{c})$. Next the labels $L_i^{d_i}$ are the inputs to the Garbled circuit corresponding to the value of $MFHE.Eval_f(hpk, \mathbf{c})$. For the garbled circuit is the decrypting algorithm of MFHE, denote by $MFHE.Dec(hsk, \cdot)$. Here the decrypt key hsk is computed by the NIMPC algorithm. Thus by the correctness of the NIMPC scheme and the garbled circuit, the output of the garbled circuit is the correct plain message corresponding to $MFHE.Eval_f(hpk, \mathbf{c})$. Finally by the correctness of the Multikey FHE scheme, this plain message is $f(x_1, \cdots, x_n)$. The correctness of the Multi-input FE scheme holds.

Theorem 1. *Assuming the underlying ABE_2 scheme is fully secure, the Multikey FHE scheme is IND-CPA secure, Yao's garbled circuit is input and circuit private, the resulting MIFE scheme is fully secure.*

Security Proof:
We construct a ppt simulator S that receives inputs $(MPK, sk_f, f, f(x_1, \cdots, x_n), 1^n)$ and must output $\tilde{c}$ such that the real and ideal experiments are computational indistinguishable. Simulator S on input $(MPK, sk_f, f, f(x_1, \cdots, x_n), 1^n)$:

1. Choose n key pairs $(hpk_i, hsk_i) \leftarrow MFHE.KeyGen(1^k)$ for $i = 1, \cdots, n$. Encrypt n inputs 0^λ(λ zero bits), we denote the ciphertexts $\hat{0} = (\hat{0}_1 \leftarrow MFHE.Enc(hpk_1, 0^\lambda), \cdots, \hat{0}_n \leftarrow MFHE.Enc(hpk_n, 0^\lambda))$. Compute $hsk = hsk_1 \cdot hsk_2 \cdots hsk_n$.
2. Let Sim_{Garble} be the simulator for Yao's garbled circuit corresponding to $FHE.Dec(hsk, \cdot)$. Run Sim_{Garble} to produce a simulated garbled circuit Γ for the multikey FHE decryption algorithm $MFHE.Dec(hsk, \cdot) : \{0, 1\}^\lambda \rightarrow \{0, 1\}$ together with the simulated encoding consisting of λ labels L_i for $i = 1, \cdots, \lambda$. Namely: $(\hat{\Gamma}, \{\hat{L}_i\}_{i=1}^\lambda) \leftarrow Sim_{Garble}(1^k, f(x_1, \cdots, x_n), 1^{|MFHE.Dec(hsk, \cdot)|}, 1^\lambda)$.
3. Produce encryption $\hat{c}_1, \cdots, \hat{c}_\lambda$ under the ABE_2 scheme by computing the equation below:
$$\hat{c}_i \leftarrow ABE_2.Enc(mpk_i, (hpk, \hat{0}), \hat{L}_i, \hat{L}_i)$$
where the simulator S uses each simulated labels $\hat{L}_i$ twice.
4. Output $\hat{c} = (\hat{c}_1, \cdots, \hat{c}_\lambda, \hat{\Gamma})$.

Next we define a sequence of game experiments to prove the security of our multi-input FE scheme.
Game 0 is the output of the real experiment $Exp_{MIFE, \mathcal{A}}^{H_0} = Exp_{MIFE, \mathcal{A}}^{real}$.
Game 1 is the same as game 0, except that, let $d_i = MFHE.Eval_f^i(hpk, \mathbf{c})$, include L^{d_i} twice in the ABE_2 encryption, namely:

$\hat{c}_i^{(1)} \leftarrow \text{ABE}_2.\text{Enc}(mpk_i, (hpk, \mathbf{c}), L_i^{d_i}, L_i^{d_i})$ and $\hat{c}^{(1)} = (\hat{c}_1^{(1)}, \cdots, \hat{c}_\lambda^{(1)}, \Gamma)$.
Game 2 is the same as game 1 except that the Garbled circuit is generated
by the Sim_{Garble} algorithm. $(\hat{\Gamma}, \{\hat{L}_i\}_{i=1}^\lambda) \leftarrow \text{Sim}_{Garble}(1^k, f(x_1, \cdots, x_n),$
$1^{|MFHE.Dec(hsk,\cdot)|}, 1^\lambda)$.
Game 3 is the output of the ideal experiment $\text{Exp}_{MIFE,\mathcal{A}}^{H_3} = \text{Exp}_{MIFE,\mathcal{A},S}^{ideal}$.

Lemma 1. Assuming the underlying ABE_2 scheme is fully secure, Game 0 and
Game 1 is above is computationally indistinguishable.
Proof: In Game 0 and Game 1 there are λ ABE_2 encryptions, each with a pair of
independent ABE_2 keys. The computational indistinguishability property with
λ encryptions can be hold if these two games are computationally indistinguishable with only one of these encryptions. This property has been proved in [13]'s
work. The difference between Game 0 and Game 1 is that in Game 0 the ABE_2
encryption algorithm encrypts $(L_i^{d_i}, L_i^{1-d_i})$, while in Game 1, the ABE_2 encryption algorithm encrypts $(L_i^{d_i}, L_i^{d_i})$, here $d_i = \text{MFHE.Eval}_f^i(hpk, \mathbf{c})$. If there exist
a ppt algorithm $\mathcal{A}$ that can distinguish these two experiments with different
encodings, then there exist a ppt algorithm $\mathcal{B}$ that can use $\mathcal{A}$'s ability to break
the security of the ABE_2 scheme.

Lemma 2. Assuming the garbled circuit is input and circuit private, Game 1
and Game 2 are computationally indistinguishable.
Proof: The only difference between Game 1 and Game 2 is the generation method
of the garbled circuit. In Game 1, $(\Gamma^*, \{L_i^*\}_{i=1}^\lambda)$ is the output of the real garbled
circuit. while in Game 2, $(\Gamma^*, \{L_i^*\}_{i=1}^\lambda)$ is the output of Sim_{Garble}. If there exist
a ppt algorithm $\mathcal{A}$ that can distinguish Game 1 and Game 2, then these exist a
ppt algorithm $\mathcal{B}$ that can distinguish these two cases how the $(\Gamma^*, \{L_i^*\}_{i=1}^\lambda)$ are
generated.

Lemma 3. Assuming the Multikey FHE scheme is IND-CPA secure, Game 2
and Game 3 are computationally indistinguishable.
Proof: The difference between Game 2 and Game 3 is that the ciphertext $\mathbf{c}$
is computed in different ways. In Game 2 the ciphertext $\mathbf{c}$ is the encryption
of the real messages $x_1, \cdots, x_n$, while in Game 3 the ciphertext $\mathbf{c}$ is a vec-
tor of n ciphertexts of 0^λ. $\mathbf{c} = \hat{0} = (\hat{0}_1 \leftarrow \text{MFHE.Enc}(hpk_1, 0^\lambda), \cdots, \hat{0}_n \leftarrow$
$\text{MFHE.Enc}(hpk_n, 0^\lambda))$. If there exist a ppt algorithm that can distinguish these
two games, then there exist a ppt algorithm that can break the IND-CPA security of the Multikey FHE scheme.

Our lemmas show that there is no PPT adversary $\mathcal{A}$ can distinguish one game
from the next one with non-negligible probability, thus Game 0 corresponds to
the real experiment is indistinguishable from Game 3 corresponds to the ideal
experiment. The security property holds.   □

4 Multi-client Outsourcing Computation Scheme

As we have described, multi-input functional encryption can be used as a tool
in multi-client outsourcing scheme to achieve public verification. This idea has
been showed in [12]'s work. Their public verify method comes from Parno et al.'s

work [18] and needs to run two times of the MIFE scheme. In our multi-client outsourcing scheme we use the output label of the garbled circuit to do the verification. Our thought mainly comes from Gennaro et al.'s work [9], for they used the garbled circuit's output-wire label to map to the computation result.

The multi-input functional encryption(MIFE*) used in our outsourcing computation scheme is the same as the multi-input functional encryption(MIFE) constructed in Sect. 3 except that the value of the garbled circuit's output-wire is the label of the computation result instead of the computation result. For simplicity, we consider the functions with one bit output.

We describe our construction of multi-client outsourcing computation scheme below:

1. $KeyGen(1^k, f) \to (SK, PK)$: Run MIFE*.Setup$(1^k)$ algorithm and get MSK and MPK. Run MIFE*.KeyGen(1^k) algorithm to obtain the decryption key sk_f corresponding to function f. Let $PK = (MPK, sk_f)$, $SK = MSK$.
2. $ProbGen(PK, SK, x_1, \cdots, x_n) \to (\sigma_X, VK_X)$: Run the MIFE*.Enc$(\cdot)$ algorithm, obtain the ciphertexts $\sigma_X = (CT_1, \cdots, CT_\lambda)$ and a garbled circuit Γ. Here the garbled circuit Γ's outputs are the labels (L_y^0, L_y^1) which encode the computation result. Using a one-way function $g(\cdot)$, the client who generates the garbled circuit compute $vk_0 = g(L_y^0)$ and $vk_1 = g(L_y^1)$. Let the public verify message $VK_X = (vk_0, vk_1)$.
3. $Compute(PK, \sigma_X) \to Z$: This algorithm takes input the public key PK, the encodings $\sigma_X = (CT_1, \cdots, CT_\lambda, \Gamma)$, runs MIFE*.Dec$(\cdot) \to L_y^b$ and outputs $Z = L_y^b$.
4. $Verify(PK, VK_X, Z) \to (y, reject)$: Input the public messages PK, VK_X and the returned result Z. The clients verify whether the equation $g(Z) = vk_0$ or $g(Z) = vk_1$ holds. If the former holds, then $f(x) = 0$, if the latter holds, $f(x) = 1$. Otherwise, output $\perp$.

Our scheme can be easily generalized to outsource functions with larger outputs by providing more pairs of the public verify messages in the ProbGen stage.

4.1   Correctness and Security Proof

Correctness. We can easily see that the above multi-client outsourcing scheme is correct. In our multi-client outsourcing scheme, we use the multi-input functional encryption scheme designed in Sect. 3. By the correctness of the multi-input functional encryption scheme, the Verify algorithm can correctly decrypt the ciphertext returned by the worker and get the correct label corresponding to the output $f(x_1, \cdots, x_n)$, and then map the label to the output bit $f(x_1, \cdots, x_n)$.

Theorem 2. *If the underlying multi-input FE scheme is secure and the garbled circuit is circuit and input private, then the scheme designed above is a private and secure multi-client outsourcing scheme.*

Proof: Our proof is divided into two parts. First we talk about the privacy of the outsourced data, and later we proof the unforgeability of the scheme.

The privacy property is guaranteed by the security of the multi-input functional encryption. If the MIFE scheme is secure, then the worker can only get the computation result but can not learn anything else about the outsourced data.

Next we show the unforgeability of the scheme. By contradiction, we assume that there exist a ppt adversary $\mathcal{A}$ that makes the experiment $\text{EXP}_{\mathcal{A}}^{Ver}(S, f, \lambda)$ output 1 with non-negligible probability. Which means that the adversary $\mathcal{A}$ can produce the encoding Z^* that makes the Verify algorithm outputs $y^* \notin \{f(x^*), \bot\}$ with non-negligible probability. For $y^* \notin \{f(x^*), \bot\}$ and it has passed the Verify algorithm, which imply that the adversary gains the other output label that doesn't corresponding to the real output $f(x^*)$, which contradicts the privacy of the garbled circuit.   □

5 Conclusion

In this work, we construct a multi-input functional encryption scheme that can keep privacy of the parties' inputs from each other and does not need to use obfuscation. We also show its application in outsourced computation and design a publicly verifiable multi-client outsourcing scheme using a new verify-method. Our schemes are proved to be correct and secure. We want to point out that our multi-input FE scheme uses the non-interactive MPC protocol to help the parties compute the product of their secret keys. Thus designing an efficient non-interactive MPC protocol can improve the efficiency of the functional encryption and the outsourced computation scheme as well. Another interesting direction in this area is to design multi-input functional encryption with unbounded key queries without obfuscation.

Acknowledgement. This work is supported by the National Natural Science Foundation of China (No. 61379140), the National Basic Research Program of China (973 Program) (No. 2013CB338001). The authors would like to thank anonymous reviewers for their helpful comments and suggestions.

References

1. Agrawal, S., Freeman, D.M., Vaikuntanathan, V.: Functional encryption for inner product predicates from learning with errors. In: Lee, D.H., Wang, X. (eds.) ASIACRYPT 2011. LNCS, vol. 7073, pp. 21–40. Springer, Heidelberg (2011)
2. Ananth, P., Boneh, D., Garg, S., Sahai, A., Zhandry, M.: Differing-inputs obfuscation and applications. In: IACR Cryptology ePrint Archive 2013:689 (2013)
3. Beimel, A., Gabizon, A., Ishai, Y., Kushilevitz, E., Meldgaard, S., Paskin-Cherniavsky, A.: Non-Interactive secure multiparty computation. In: Garay, J.A., Gennaro, R. (eds.) CRYPTO 2014, Part II. LNCS, vol. 8617, pp. 387–404. Springer, Heidelberg (2014)

4. Boneh, D., Sahai, A., Waters, B.: Functional encryption: definitions and challenges. In: Ishai, Y. (ed.) TCC 2011. LNCS, vol. 6597, pp. 253–273. Springer, Heidelberg (2011)
5. Boneh, D., Waters, B.: Conjunctive, subset, and range queries on encrypted data. In: Vadhan, S.P. (ed.) TCC 2007. LNCS, vol. 4392, pp. 535–554. Springer, Heidelberg (2007)
6. Choi, S.G., Katz, J., Kumaresan, R., Cid, C.: Multi-client non-interactive verifiable computation. In: Sahai, A. (ed.) TCC 2013. LNCS, vol. 7785, pp. 499–518. Springer, Heidelberg (2013)
7. Garg, S., Gentry, C., Halevi, S., Raykova, M., Sahai, A., Waters, B.: Candidate indistinguishability obfuscation and functional encryption for all circuits. In: IEEE 54th Annual Symposium on Foundations of Computer Science (FOCS), pp. 40–49. IEEE (2013)
8. Garg, S., Gentry, C., Halevi, S., Zhandry, M.: Fully secure functional encryption without obfuscation. Technical report, Cryptology ePrint Archive, Report /666 (2014)
9. Gennaro, R., Gentry, C., Parno, B.: Non-interactive verifiable computing: outsourcing computation to untrusted workers. In: Rabin, T. (ed.) CRYPTO 2010. LNCS, vol. 6223, pp. 465–482. Springer, Heidelberg (2010)
10. Gentry, C., Lewko, A.B., Sahai, A., Waters, B.: Indistinguishability obfuscation from the multilinear subgroup elimination assumption. IACR Cryptology ePrint Archive, 2014:309 (2014)
11. Goldwasser, S., et al.: Multi-input functional encryption. In: Nguyen, P.Q., Oswald, E. (eds.) EUROCRYPT 2014. LNCS, vol. 8441, pp. 578–602. Springer, Heidelberg (2014)
12. Goldwasser, S., Goyal, V., Jain, A., Sahai, A.: Multi-input functional encryption. In: IACR Cryptology ePrint Archive 2013:727 (2013)
13. Goldwasser, S., Kalai, Y., Popa, R.A., Vaikuntanathan, V., Zeldovich, N.: Reusable garbled circuits and succinct functional encryption. In: Proceedings of the Forty-Fifth Annual ACM Symposium on Theory of Computing, pp. 555–564. ACM (2013)
14. Gorbunov, S., Vaikuntanathan, V., Wee, H.: Functional encryption with bounded collusions via multi-party computation. In: Safavi-Naini, R., Canetti, R. (eds.) CRYPTO 2012. LNCS, vol. 7417, pp. 162–179. Springer, Heidelberg (2012)
15. Katz, J., Sahai, A., Waters, B.: Predicate encryption supporting disjunctions, polynomial equations, and inner products. In: Smart, N.P. (ed.) EUROCRYPT 2008. LNCS, vol. 4965, pp. 146–162. Springer, Heidelberg (2008)
16. López-Alt, A., Tromer, E., Vaikuntanathan, V.: On-the-fly multiparty computation on the cloud via multikey fully homomorphic encryption. In Proceedings of the Forty-Fourth Annual ACM Symposium on Theory of Computing, pp. 1219–1234. ACM (2012)
17. Naor, M., Yung, M.: Public-key cryptosystems provably secure against chosen ciphertext attacks. In: Proceedings of the Twenty-Second Annual ACM Symposium on Theory of Computing, pp. 427–437. ACM (1990)
18. Parno, B., Raykova, M., Vaikuntanathan, V.: How to delegate and verify in public: verifiable computation from attribute-based encryption. In: Cramer, R. (ed.) TCC 2012. LNCS, vol. 7194, pp. 422–439. Springer, Heidelberg (2012)
19. Peter, A., Tews, E., Katzenbeisser, S.: Efficiently outsourcing multiparty computation under multiple keys. IEEE Trans. Inf. Forensics Secur. 8(12), 2046–2058 (2013)

20. Sahai, A., Seyalioglu, H.: Worry-free encryption: functional encryption with public keys. In: Proceedings of the 17th ACM Conference on Computer and Communications Security, pp. 463–472. ACM (2010)
21. Shen, E., Shi, E., Waters, B.: Predicate privacy in encryption systems. In: Reingold, O. (ed.) TCC 2009. LNCS, vol. 5444, pp. 457–473. Springer, Heidelberg (2009)
22. Wang, B., Li, M., Chow, S.S.M., Li, H.: Computing encrypted cloud data efficiently under multiple keys. In: IEEE Conference on Communications and Network Security (CNS), pp. 504–513. IEEE (2013)
23. Waters, B.: A punctured programming approach to adaptively secure functional encryption. Technical report, Cryptology ePrint Archive, Report 2014/588 (2014). http://eprint.iacr.org

A Multivariate Encryption Scheme with Rainbow

Takanori Yasuda[1](✉) and Kouichi Sakurai[1,2]

[1] Institute of Systems, Information Technologies and Nanotechnologies,
Fukuoka, Japan
{yasuda,sakurai}@isit.or.jp
[2] Department of Informatics, Kyushu University, Fukuoka, Japan

Abstract. Multivariate Public Key Cryptosystems (MPKC) are a candidate of post-quantum cryptography. The MPKC signature scheme Rainbow is endowed of efficient signature generation and verification, while no major attack has been reported so far. In this paper, we propose a MPKC encryption scheme based on Rainbow. The public key of Rainbow is a surjective polynomial map, whereas the encryption scheme requires an injective polynomial map. We explain how to change the public key of Rainbow to an injective map.

Keywords: Multivariate Public Key Cryptosystem · Rainbow · Square · Post-quantum cryptography

1 Introduction

1.1 Motivation and Background

The foundation of public key cryptography currently consists of RSA and elliptic curve cryptography. However, these two cryptosystems do not have sufficient resistance against quantum computers. Therefore, the current foundation of public key cryptography needs to shift to cryptography preventing attacks coming from quantum computers, which is called post-quantum cryptography [12], and before quantum computers become widely spread. Since 2013, a working group on post-quantum cryptography at NIST is studying the standardization of Post-Quantum cryptography. ETSI is also holding a regular Quantum-Safe-Crypto Workshop. Main candidates for post-quantum cryptography are lattice-based cryptography, code-based cryptography, multivariate public key cryptography, and hash-based cryptography.

1.2 Previous Work and Challenging Issues

The encryption scheme C^* proposed in [29] is considered to be the first MPKC scheme. However, Patarin in [33] showed an efficient attack against C^*. After that, many encryption schemes have been proposed [17, 35, 36]. However, efficient

© Springer International Publishing Switzerland 2016
S. Qing et al. (Eds.): ICICS 2015, LNCS 9543, pp. 236–251, 2016.
DOI: 10.1007/978-3-319-29814-6_19

attacks have been found against most of these schemes [9,13,21,27], and at present, only few MPKC encryption schemes have remained safe. Among them are ZHFE [39], ABC [41] and cubic ABC [14]. Besides safety, it is also important to design a secure MPKC encryption scheme which has efficient encryption and decryption algorithms.

As for signature schemes, SFlash [36], TTS[10] have been proposed, but efficient attacks against these schemes have been found [13,16]. Rainbow [15] is a signature scheme which has efficient signature generation and verification. Its security has been analyzed by several researchers, and so far no major attack against it has been found.

1.3   Contribution

We propose a new encryption scheme which has an efficient decryption algorithm. The proposed scheme is a combination of the encryption scheme "Square" [7] and the signature scheme "Rainbow". Since the decryption in both Square and Rainbow is efficient, it results that the decryption of the proposed scheme is also efficient. Furthermore, we analyze the security of the proposed scheme. We consider existing attacks against Square and existing attacks against Rainbow etc. Based on this security analysis, we estimate the parameters yielding 80-bit, 112-bit and 160-bit security levels. Finally, for these parameters we have implemented the new scheme and measured encryption time and decryption time.

In MPKC, encryption scheme and signature scheme deploy different kinds of multivariate polynomial maps. MPKC signature scheme often uses surjective maps because given an arbitrary message, the corresponding signature has to be generated at least one. On the other hand, MPKC encryption schemes use injective map because if not, the scheme would cause decryption failures. For instance the lattice-based encryption NTRU can cause decryption failures. But NTRU avoids this problem by tuning parameters so that the probability that a decryption failure occurs is minimal. Among MPKC encryption schemes, ABC also has this problem. The original ABC has a non-negligible probability of decryption failure, but it was improved by using almost injective multivariate maps so that the probability is minimized [42].

Our scheme adopts basically the same policy as the improved ABC. The multivariate map associated with our scheme is almost injective. To the end, we thought of two devices: (1) the vinegar variables used in Rainbow are exchanged to variables in the encryption scheme (which in this paper is Square), and (2) the number of equations increases for each layer in Rainbow. About (1), in the decryption of Rainbow, a signer can substitute several values in the vinegar variables. However in the encryption scheme, the decryption result has to coincide in a unique way with the plain text. We make use of the decryption method of Square instead of substituting in vinegar variables, so that the inverse is determined uniquely. The reason why we adopt Square as an encryption scheme in (1) is that it has strong tolerance against the direct attacks [12] and an efficient decryption algorithm. Next, we explain about (2). In the decryption of Rainbow, solving linear equations is required for each layer. The linear equations may be degenerated, in which case the decryption algorithm reselects values in vinegar variables, and reconstruct linear equations. However, since the proposed scheme does not use vinegar variables, we increase the number of equations such that the linear equations are not degenerated. As the number of equations increases, the probability of degeneration becomes indeed lower; thus we can control the probability.

Square requires square root computation during decryption. This computation is executed by some exponentiation algorithms. In the original paper [7], the decryption time takes more than ten times that of the encryption time. We rather adopt the multi-exponentiation technique [32], which has been put into practice in efficient pairing computations [40], GLV [23], GLS [24], so that seeing on single Square, we achieve about 10 times acceleration of the decryption of the original Square.

1.4   Comparison with Related Works

The public key size of the proposed scheme is about 30 times shorter as large as that of ABC. The decryption of the proposed scheme is more efficient than that of ZHFE because ZHFE requires heavy computations like the Berlekamp algorithm for decryption.

The direct attack is an attack which directly computes the plain text from a cipher text and the public key. Gröbner basis computations are often used for this attack. From our experiments for low parameters, we observed that the multivariate system provided by the proposed scheme is *semi-regular* [4]. Since Square has a property that its security against direct attack is strong [11], and Rainbow has a wide range of possible secret keys, we can expect that the security of our scheme against direct attacks is also strong. Therefore, we infer that our scheme also holds the semi-regular property for higher parameters. On the other hand, since ABC does not have the semi-regular property, we have to select a higher number of variables and of equations than those of our scheme.

The multivariate polynomial maps used in our scheme are constructed from those of Square and Rainbow, and additionally, randomly chosen polynomial maps are appended. Adding such polynomials is called *the Plus method* [12], which is used to enhance the security mainly. In fact, due to the Plus method the UOV attack, the UOV-Reconciliation attack and the Rainbow-Band-Separation attack cannot be applied to our scheme. We remark that the Plus method cannot be applied to the original Rainbow neither because in order to find an inverse image of a randomly chosen polynomial map, a searching process is required, therefore, the signature generation of Rainbow loses its good efficiency. On the other hand, in the case of our scheme, since the decryption requires only the decryption of Square and the decryption Rainbow, the inverse computation of the plus part is not necessary.

2   Background

2.1   A Signature Scheme, Rainbow

Ding and Schmidt proposed a signature scheme called Rainbow, which is a multilayer variant of Unbalanced Oil and Vinegar [15]. In this section, we review Rainbow shortly.

First, we set some parameters in order to describe Rainbow with a h-layer structure. Let v_1 and $o_1, \ldots, o_h$ be positive integers. For $k = 2, \ldots, h + 1$, let $v_k = v_1 + o_1 + \cdots + o_{k-1}$. For $k = 1, \ldots, h$, we define two sets of integers, $V_k = \{1, 2, \ldots, v_k\}$, $O_k = \{v_k + 1, \ldots, v_k + o_k\}$. The sets O_i and V_i are used for the indices of the oil and vinegar variables in Rainbow, respectively. We define $n = v_{h+1}$, which is the number of variables used in Rainbow.

Let $K = GF(q)$ be a finite field of order q. For $k = 1, 2, \ldots, h$, a multivariate quadratic map $G_k = (g_{v_k+1}, \ldots, g_{v_k+o_k}) : K^n \to K^{o_k}$ consists of o_k multivariate polynomials: For $l = v_k + 1, \ldots, v_k + o_k$,

$$g_l(x_1, \ldots, x_n) = \sum_{i \in O_k, j \in V_k} \alpha_{i,j}^{(l)} x_i x_j + \sum_{i,j \in V_k, i \leq j} \beta_{i,j}^{(l)} x_i x_j + \sum_{i \in V_{k+1}} \gamma_i^{(l)} x_i + \eta^{(l)}, \quad (1)$$

where $\alpha_{i,j}^{(l)}, \beta_{i,j}^{(l)}, \gamma_i^{(l)}, \eta^{(l)} \in K$ are randomly chosen. We call the variables x_i ($i \in O_k$) and x_j ($i \in V_j$) oil and vinegar variables in the k-th layer, respectively. A multivariate quadratic map G is then defined by the concatenation,

$$G = G_1 \| G_2 \| \cdots \| G_h = (g_{v_1+1}, \ldots, g_n) : K^n \to K^{n-v_1}.$$

Scheme. We describe the key generation, signature generation and verification processes of Rainbow as follows.

Key Generation. A secret key consists of a central map G and two affine transformations $A_1 : K^m \to K^m$ ($m = n - v_1$), $A_2 : K^n \to K^n$. The public key consists of the field K and the composed map $F = A_1 \circ G \circ A_2 : K^n \to K^m$, which is a system of m quadratic polynomials of n variables over K.

Signature Generation. Let $M \in K^m$ be a message. A signer computes $A = A_1^{-1}(M)$, $B = G^{-1}(A)$ and $C = A_2^{-1}(B)$ in that order. The signature of the message is $C \in K^n$. Here, the inverse computation $B = G^{-1}(A)$ for $A = (a_{v_1+1}, \ldots, a_n)$, is executed by the following algorithm.

Step 1. Select $B_0 = (b_1, \ldots, b_{v_1}) \in K^{v_1}$ randomly.
Step 2. For $k = 1$ to h do:
  (4-1) For a subsequence $A_k = (a_{v_k+1}, \ldots, a_{v_k+o_k})$ of A, set up a linear equation with respect to $X_k = (x_{v_k+1}, \ldots, x_{v_k+o_k})$,

$$G_k(B_{k-1}, X_k) = A_k.$$

  (We remark that G_k can be regarded as a map having v_{k+1} variables.)
  (4-2) Solve the above linear equation. If it has an unique solution, denote the solution by D_k. Otherwise, go back to Step 1.

(4-3) Put $B_k = B_{k-1} \| D_k$ (concatenation).
Output $B = B_h$.

Verification. If $F(C) = M$, the signature is accepted, otherwise it is rejected.

Remark 1. The linear equation $G_k(B_{k-1}, X_k) = A_k$ in Step 4-1 has o_k variables and o_k equations. Therefore, solving the equation fails with the probability of q^{-1}. However, since there are many choice for B_0 in Step 1, the signature generation itself does not fail.

Attacks Against Rainbow. In this section, we summarize the necessary information about the known attacks against Rainbow that have been reported in previous papers. Since the scheme which we propose later make uses of structure of Rainbow, we will analyze the effect of these attacks on the proposed scheme. The known relevant attacks against Rainbow are as follows.

(1) Direct attacks [2,46],
(2) UOV attack [26,28],
(3) MinRank attack [5,22],
(4) HighRank attack [18,22,38],
(5) Rainbow-Band-Separation (RBS) attack [18,37],
(6) UOV-Reconciliation (UOV-R) attack [18,37].

The direct attacks try to solve a system of equations $F(X) = M$ from public key F and (fixed) message M [2,46]. By contrast, the goal of the other attacks is to find a part of the secret key. In the case of a UOV attack or HighRank attack, for example, the target Rainbow with parameters $v_1, o_1, \ldots, o_t$ is then reduced into a version of Rainbow with simpler parameters such as $v_1, o_1, \ldots, o_{t-1}$ without o_t. We can then break the original Rainbow with lower complexity. To carry out a reduction we need to find (a part of) a direct sum decomposition of vector space K^n,

$$K^n = K^{v_1} \oplus K^{o_1} \oplus \cdots \oplus K^{o_t}, \tag{2}$$

because expressing K^n in an available basis enables returning the public key to the central map. In fact, if we can decompose $K^n = W \oplus K^{o_t}$ for a certain W that has a coarser decomposition than (2) then the security of Rainbow can be reduced to that of Rainbow with the number of layer one fewer. There are two methods for finding this decomposition:

(1) Find a simultaneous isotropic subspace of K^n.
Let V be a vector space over K, and let Q_1 be a quadratic form on V. We determine that a subspace W of V is *isotropic* (with respect to Q_1) if

$$v_1, v_2 \in W \Rightarrow Q_1(v_1, v_2) := Q_1(v_1 + v_2) - Q_1(v_1) - Q_1(v_2) = 0.$$

In addition, we assume that V is also equipped with quadratic forms $Q_2, \ldots, Q_m$. We determine that a subspace W of V is *simultaneously isotropic* if W is isotropic with respect to all $Q_1, \ldots, Q_m$.

In Rainbow, m quadratic forms on K^n are defined by the quadratic parts of the public polynomials of F. Note that the subspace K^{o_t} appearing in (2) is a simultaneous isotropic subspace of K^n. If we find a simultaneous isotropic subspace, the basis of K^{o_t} is then obtained and the above attack is feasible. The UOV, UOV-R and RBS attacks are classified as being of this type.

(2) Find a quadratic form with the minimum or second maximum rank.
When the quadratic part of the k-th component polynomial of F in Rainbow is expressed as

$$\sum_{i=1}^{n}\sum_{j=i}^{n} a_{ij}^{(k)} x_i x_j,$$

we associate it with a symmetric matrix $P_k = A + A^{\mathrm{T}}$, where $A = (a_{ij}^{(k)})$. We define $\Omega_F = \mathrm{Span}_K\{P_k \mid k = v_1 + 1, \ldots, n\}$, which is a vector space over K spanned by matrices $P_{v_1+1}, \ldots, P_n$. For example, if we find a matrix of rank $v_2 = v_1 + o_1$ in Ω_F, there is a high probability that the image of this matrix coincides with $K^{v_1} \oplus K^{o_1}$ appearing in (2). Therefore, we obtain the decomposition of $K^n = (K^{v_1} \oplus K^{o_1}) \oplus W'$ for some W' that is a coarser decomposition than (2). The MinRank and HighRank attacks are classified as being of this type.

The details of above mentioned six attacks can be found in the literature [37].

3 Our Proposed Scheme

In this section, we propose a MPKC encryption scheme, which is called SRP because it is constructed by combining Square, Rainbow and the Plus method technique. First, we prepare some parameters necessary to construct our scheme:

- $K = GF(q)$: finite field of odd characteristic ($q \equiv 3 \bmod 4$)
- d: degree of extension field $L = GF(q^d)$ over K ($d \equiv 1 \bmod 2$)
- h: number of layers
- $o_1, \ldots, o_h$: number of oil variables in each layer
- r: number determining the probability of decryption success
- s: number of equations added in the Plus method
- l: number of variables reduced in the embedding method
- $\phi : GF(q^d) \to K^d$: linear isomorphism over K

3.1 Key Generation

Let $n = d + o_1 + \cdots + o_h - l$ and $m = d + o_1 + \cdots + o_h + hr + s$. Then, the public key of the proposed scheme is given by a quadratic polynomial map from K^n to K^m. Let $n' = d + o_1 + \cdots + o_h$. Three multivariate quadratic maps G_S, G_R, G_P on $K^{n'}$ are constructed as follows:

(i) Construction of $G_S : K^{n'} \to K^d$.

A multivariate quadratic map $G'_S : K^d \to K^d$ is defined by

$$G'_S : K^d \xrightarrow{\phi^{-1}} GF(q^d) \ni X \to X^2 \in GF(q^d) \xrightarrow{\phi} K^d.$$

G_S is defined as a natural extension of G'_S to $K^{n'}$, i.e.

$$G_S : K^{d+o_1+\cdots+o_h} \xrightarrow{\text{projection}} K^d \xrightarrow{G'_S} K^d.$$

(ii) Construction of $G_R : K^{n'} \to K^{o_1+\cdots+o_h+hr}$.

For each layer $k = 1, \ldots, h$, we construct a multivariate quadratic map $G_{R,k} : K^{n'} \to K^{o_k+r}$ as follows. Let $v_k = d + o_1 + \cdots + o_{k-1}$ and $V_k = \{1, 2, \ldots, v_k\}$, $O_k = \{v_k + 1, \ldots, v_k + o_k\}$. The $o_k + r$ components of $G_{R,k}$ are chosen by the multivariate quadratic polynomials of the form,

$$g(x_1, \ldots, x_{n'}) = \sum_{i \in O_k, j \in V_k} \alpha_{i,j} x_i x_j + \sum_{i,j \in V_k, i \leq j} \beta_{i,j} x_i x_j + \sum_{i \in V_k \cup O_k} \gamma_i x_i + \eta.$$

Here, $\alpha_{i,j}, \beta_{i,j}, \gamma_i, \eta$ are randomly chosen in K for each component of $G_{R,k}$. Then, G_R is defined by the concatenation $G_R = G_{R,1} \| \ldots \| G_{R,h}$.

(iii) Construction of $G_P : K^{n'} \to K^s$.

G_P consist of randomly chosen s multivariate quadratic polynomials of the form,

$$g(x_1, \ldots, x_{n'}) = \sum_{1 \leq i \leq j \leq n'} \alpha_{i,j} x_i x_j + \sum_{1 \leq i \leq n'} \beta_i x_i + \gamma \quad (\alpha_{i,j}, \beta_i, \gamma \in K).$$

Using above (i), (ii), (iii), a polynomial map $G : K^{n'} \to K^m$ is defined by the concatenation $G = G_S \| G_R \| G_P$. Additionally, the following are selected randomly.

(1) affine embedding map $A_1 : K^n \to K^{n'}$,
(2) affine isomorphism $A_2 : K^m \to K^m$.

A multivariate quadratic map F from K^n to K^m is defined by $F = A_2 \circ G \circ A_1$. Then, the secret key consists of G, A_1 and A_2, and the public key consists of F.

3.2   Encryption

We identify a plain text M with an element of K^n. The cipher text C corresponding to M is obtained by the polynomial evaluation,

$$C = F(M) \in K^m.$$

3.3   Decryption

For a cipher text $C = (c_1, \ldots, c_m) \in K^m$, the decryption is executed as follows.

Step 1. Compute $B = (b_1, \ldots, b_m) = A_2^{-1}(C)$.

Step 2. Compute $B_0 = \phi^{-1}(B_S)$ where $B_S = (b_1, \ldots, b_d)$, the vector of the first d-components of B.

Step 3. Compute $R = \pm B_0^{(q^d+1)/4}$ and $D_0 = \phi(R)$.

Step 4. For $k = 1$ to h do:

(4-1) For $B_k = (b_{m_k+1}, \ldots, b_{m_k+o_k+r})$, where $m_k := v_k + (k-1)r$, set up a linear equation with respect to $X_k = (x_{v_k+1}, \ldots, x_{v_k+o_k})$,

$$G_{R,k}(D_{k-1}, X_k) = B_k.$$

(We remark that $G_{R,k}$ can be regarded as a map having v_{k+1} variables.)

(4-2) Solve the above linear equation, and denote the solution by D_k.

Step 4. Put $D = D_0 \| D_1 \| \cdots \| D_h$ (concatenation).

Step 5. Compute $M' = A_1^{-1}(D)$, which is the corresponding plain text.

Remark 2. In Step 3, the computation of the exponentiation $B_0^{(q^d+1)/4}$ is required. The multi-exponentiation technique [32] can be applied to this computation. The concrete algorithm is described in the Appendix A.

3.4   Probability of Decryption Failure

We have to guarantee that the above decryption algorithm recovers the plain text. To the end, it is necessary to show that the public key F is injective. In the case of the original ABC [41], the probability of decryption failure is non-negligible because its public key is not injective. However, ABC has been already improved such that the public key becomes almost injective [42]. Therefore, the probability of decryption failure of the improved ABC can be minimized by choosing a suitable parameter.

The public key of our scheme is also almost injective. More precisely,

Proposition 1. *The probability of F are not injective is equal to hq^{-l-1}.*

This proposition implies that the probability of the decryption failure in our scheme is equal to hq^{-l-1}. The above proposition is shown in the Appendix B.

4   Security Analysis

In this section, we analyze the security of our scheme. The attacks which we have to observe is as follows:

1. Direct attack
2. Differential attack [6]
3. Rank attacks
4. Other attacks against Rainbow (RBS attack, UOV attack, UOV-R attack)

4.1 Direct Attack

The Direct attack is an attack that compute the plain text by solving multi-variate equation system obtained by the cipher text and the public key. Currently, the most efficient direct attack is the gröbner basis computation algorithm [19,20]. For any multivariate polynomial system, the degree of regularity d_{reg} is defined as an invariant [1]. Moreover, the concept of semi-regular (for an overdetermined system) is defined [4]. For $m > n$, let $c_0, c_1, \ldots \in \mathbb{Z}$ be defined by

$$\sum_k c_k z^k = \frac{(1 - x^2)^m}{(1 - z)^n}. \tag{3}$$

If an overdetermined system of n variables and m equations is semi-regular, then the index d of the first non-positive coefficient c_d coincides with d_{reg} [4].

The complexity of the Gröbner basis computation depends on the degree of regularity, in fact, the complexity of F_5 algorithm [4] is described by

$$\mathcal{O}(m \cdot \binom{n + d_{reg} - 1}{d_{reg}}^{\omega}). \tag{4}$$

Here, $2 < \omega < 3$ is a linear algebra constant. Furthermore, the hybrid method that mixes Gröbner basis computation with exhaustive search is proposed, and its complexity is estimated [4].

Table 1 compares the degree of regularity of the proposed scheme with the semi-regular degree by experiment. We use gröbner basis computation algorithm implemented in the software Magma. In this table, we consider only the case that the layer number h is equal to 1. Time (RS) means the computation time for random system with same m and n. The semi-regular degree is computed by using the Hilbert series (3). This table shows that in any cases of the experiments, the degree of regularity of the proposed scheme are equal to the semi-regular degree.

Table 1. Result of experiments of the direct attack using MAGMA

$(q, d, \{o_1, \ldots\}, r, s, l)$	(m, n)	Time	Time (RS)	d_{reg}	semi-regular degree
$(31, 15, 11, 3, 2, 10)$	$(31, 16)$	14 s	14 s	5	5
$(31, 15, 11, 3, 2, 9)$	$(31, 17)$	44 s	42 s	5	5
$(31, 15, 11, 3, 2, 8)$	$(31, 18)$	206 s	204 s	5	5
$(31, 15, 11, 3, 2, 7)$	$(31, 19)$	2311 s	2351 s	6	6
$(31, 15, 10, 3, 2, 6)$	$(30, 19)$	2916 s	2846 s	6	6
$(31, 15, 11, 3, 2, 6)$	$(31, 20)$	9331 s	8840 s	6	6
$(31, 15, 12, 3, 2, 6)$	$(32, 21)$	34080 s	41647 s	6	6
$(31, 15, 11, 3, 2, 5)$	$(31, 21)$	156624 s	168693 s	7	7

4.2   Differential attack

For a function f, its differential is defined by

$$Df(A, X) = f(A + X) - f(A) - f(X) + f(0).$$

If we take the public key F as f and substitute a point of K^n for A, we have a linear map M from K^n to K^m. In the case of the simple Square, by finding another linear map which is commutative with M, recover a multiplication map by an element of $GF(q^d)$ [6]. The point is that the differential attack is effective to the simple Square because all the variables are obtained by the reduction of the variable for the extension field. However, the proposed scheme includes variables in Rainbow other than variables in Square, therefore, the differential attack is not applied to the proposed scheme.

4.3   Rank Attacks

First, consider the HighRank attack against Rainbow. We can assume that l is less than o_h because if l is greater than or equal to o_h, the scheme has an equivalent secret key as a proposed scheme with $h - 1$ and $l - o_h$ instead of h and l.

$$\Omega_F = \mathrm{Span}_K\{P_k \mid k = 1, \ldots, m\}$$

is defined similarly to Sect. 2.1 (Attacks Against Rainbow) from the public key F. The highest rank of a matrix belonging to Ω_F is n. The second highest rank is $d + o_1 + \cdots + o_{h-1}$ with high probability. Since the difference is $o_h - l$, similarly to computing the complexity in the case of Rainbow, the complexity of HighRank attack against the proposed scheme is

$$n^3/6 \cdot q^{o_h - l} \ \mathbf{m}. \tag{5}$$

Here, $\mathbf{m}$ stands for the number of the field multiplication.

Next, consider the MinRank attack. The same attack can be applied to Double-Layer Square [8], and the complexity has been estimated [43]:

$$(n + l)q^{l+1}(2n + l)^3 \ \mathbf{m}. \tag{6}$$

Against the proposed scheme, the MinRank attack has the same complexity.

4.4   Other Attacks against Rainbow

Let $Q = \{q_1, \ldots, q_m\}$ be the set of all the quadratic forms given by the quadratic parts of the components of the public key F for the proposed scheme. As explained in Sect. 2.1 (Attacks Against Rainbow), the UOV attack, the UOV-R attack and the RBS attack all require a simultaneous isotropic space in K^n with respect to Q. If the parameter s for the proposed scheme is equal to zero, that is, the proposed scheme does not have the plus part G_P substantially, then there is a simultaneous isotropic space in K^n. In fact, the subspace

$$A_1^{-1}(V') \quad \text{where} \quad V' = \{(0, \ldots, 0 | \overbrace{*, \ldots, *}^{o_h})\} (\subset K^{n'}),$$

becomes a simultaneous isotropic space with respect to Q because V' is isotropic with respect to any quadratic form obtained by a component of G_S and G_R. However, if $s > 0$ then V' is not isotropic with respect to a quadratic form obtained by a component of G_P because G_P consists of randomly chosen polynomials. Therefore, there is no simultaneous isotropic space in general. Consequently, the UOV attack, the UOV-R attack and the RBS attack cannot be applied to the proposed scheme.

5   Practical Parameters and Implementation

Consider the following parameters.

(A) $(K, d, h, \{o_1, \ldots\}, r, s, l) = (GF(31), 33, 1, \{32\}, 16, 5, 16)$ (80-bit security level)
(B) $(K, d, h, \{o_1, \ldots\}, r, s, l) = (GF(31), 47, 1, \{47\}, 22, 5, 22)$ (112-bit security level)
(C) $(K, d, h, \{o_1, \ldots\}, r, s, l) = (GF(31), 71, 1, \{71\}, 32, 5, 32)$ (160-bit security level)

We have $(n, m) = (49, 86)$ for (A), $(72, 121)$ for (B) and $(110, 179)$ for (C). The security level for each case is estimated based on (5), (6) and the the complexity of the hybrid method [4]. Here, the complexity of the hybrid method is computed under the assumption that the multivariate polynomial system of the proposed scheme is semi-regular. For each parameter, we execute experiment of encryption and decryption for 100 different plain texts. The following table shows the average time of encryption and decryption. The implementation environment is as follows (Table 2).

Table 2. Experimental results of SRP

SRP	(A)	(B)	(C)
Security	80 bit	112 bit	160 bit
Encryption	0.75 ms	2.26 ms	7.82 ms
Decryption	1.06 ms	3.01 ms	9.14 ms
Secret key size	57.1 kB	161.4 kB	528.1 kB
Public key size	69.9 kB	207.0 kB	701.6 kB
Probability of decryption failure	2^{-80}	2^{-112}	2^{-160}

OS Microsoft Windows 7 Professional 64bit
CPU Intel(R) Xeon CPU E31270 @ 3.40GHz
memory 16.0 GB
Compiler Cygwin + gcc version 3.4.4
Language C

6   Conclusion

We propose a MPKC encryption scheme called SRP. Our scheme has an efficient decryption algorithm, in fact, the decryption time is less than twice that of the encryption time according to our experiments. The system of multivariate quadratic equations obtained in our scheme by any cipher text behave as if it was a system of random quadratic equations with respect to direct attacks.

Acknowledgements. This work was commissioned by Strategic Information and Communications R&D Promotion Programme (SCOPE), no. 0159-0016 Ministry of Internal Affairs and Communications, JAPAN. Dr. Xavier Dahan read carefully and proof-read the preliminary version of this paper. The authors would like to thank him.

A   Decryption Algorithm for Square

In Step 3 of the decryption of the proposed scheme, we require the computation

$$B_0^{(q^d+1)/4} \quad (q \equiv 3 \bmod 4, \quad d \equiv 1 \bmod 2).$$

$(q^d + 1)/4$ has q-adic expansion:

$$\frac{q^d+1}{4} = \frac{q+1}{4} + \frac{3q-1}{4} \cdot q + \frac{q-3}{4} \cdot q^2 + \frac{3q-1}{4} \cdot q^3 + \frac{q-3}{4} \cdot p^4$$
$$+ \frac{3q-1}{4} \cdot q^5 + \frac{q-3}{4} \cdot q^6 + \cdots + \frac{3q-1}{4} \cdot q^{d-2} + \frac{q-3}{4} \cdot q^{d-1}.$$

The cost for computing the Frobenius map for any element is very cheap. Therefore, we have an efficient algorithm computing $B_0^{(q^d+1)/4}$ using multi-exponentiation technique [32].

An efficient algorithm computing $B_0^{(q^d+1)/4}$

Step 1. Compute the binary expansion $(d-1)/2 = [b_k, b_{k-1}, \ldots, b_0]_2$.
Step 2. $\beta \leftarrow 1$, $m \leftarrow 0$, $\delta \leftarrow B_0^q$.
Step 3. for $i = 0$ to k do:
        if $i > 0$ then $\delta \leftarrow \delta \cdot \delta^{q^{2^i}}$
        if $b_i = 1$ then $\beta \leftarrow \beta \cdot \delta^{q^m}$, $m \leftarrow m + 2^{i+1}$.
Step 4. $\gamma \leftarrow B_0 \cdot \beta^q$.
Step 5. $\gamma \leftarrow \beta \cdot \gamma$.
Step 6. $\beta \leftarrow \beta^{\frac{q+1}{2}}$.
Step 7. $\gamma \leftarrow \gamma^{\frac{q-3}{4}}$.
Step 8. $\beta \leftarrow \beta \cdot \gamma \cdot B_0$.
result β.

B   Injectivity of G and F

Here, we prove that the maps G and F used in the proposed scheme are almost injective. More precisely,

Proposition 2. *The probability of G and F are not injective is equal to hq^{-l-1}.*

Since F is defined by $A_2 \circ G \circ A_1$ and A_1, A_2 are both injective, if it is shown that G is injective, F becomes also injective. Let us show that G is almost injective. Now, for $B \in K^m$, we can assume that the equation $G(X) = B$ has solutions at least one because any cipher text is given by a certain plain text. Therefore, it is sufficient to show that $G(X) = B$ does not have solutions more than one. From the construction method of G, any solution of $G(X) = B$ has to be obtained by the above decryption algorithm. In the algorithm, the steps which has a possibility to yields solutions more than one are Step 3 and Step 4-2. In Step 4-2, the linear equation $G_k(D_{k-1}, X_k) = B_i$ has o_k variables and $o_k + r$ equations. Since the coefficients of the equation are behaved as random elements, the probability of the linear equation has exactly one solution coincides with the probability that the linear equation is non-degenerate, which is equal to $(1 - q^{-o_k-r})(1 - q^{-o_k-r+1}) \cdots (1 - q^{-r-1})$. In other word, the probability that solutions more than one in Step 4-2 is about q^{-r-1}. In Step 3, clearly there are two candidate for R_0 (or D_0), but one of candidates of D_0 disapears in Step 4-2 for $k = 1$ with the probability of q^{-r-1}. As a consequence, the probability of G is not injective is equal to hq^{-l-1}.

References

1. Bardet, M., Faugére, J.-C., Salvy, B.: On the complexity of gröbner basis computation of semi-regular overdetermined algebraic equations. In: Proceedings of International Conference on Polynomial System Solving (ICPSS), pp. 71–75 (2004)
2. Bernstein, D.J., Buchmann, J., Dahmen, E.: Post Quantum Cryptography. Springer, Heidelberg (2009)
3. Berger, T.P., Cayrel, P.-L., Gaborit, P., Otmani, A.: Reducing key length of the McEliece cryptosystem. In: Preneel, B. (ed.) AFRICACRYPT 2009. LNCS, vol. 5580, pp. 77–97. Springer, Heidelberg (2009)
4. Bettale, L., Faugère, J.-C., Perret, L.: Hybrid approach for solving multivariate systems over finite fields. J. Math. Crypt. 3(3), 177–197 (2010)
5. Billet, O., Gilbert, H.: Cryptanalysis of rainbow. In: De Prisco, R., Yung, M. (eds.) SCN 2006. LNCS, vol. 4116, pp. 336–347. Springer, Heidelberg (2006)
6. Billet, O., Macario-Rat, G.: Cryptanalysis of the square cryptosystems. In: Matsui, M. (ed.) ASIACRYPT 2009. LNCS, vol. 5912, pp. 451–468. Springer, Heidelberg (2009)
7. Clough, C., Baena, J., Ding, J., Yang, B.-Y., Chen, M.: Square, a new multivariate encryption scheme. In: Fischlin, M. (ed.) CT-RSA 2009. LNCS, vol. 5473, pp. 252–264. Springer, Heidelberg (2009)
8. Clough, C.L., Ding, J.: Secure variants of the square encryption scheme. In: Sendrier, N. (ed.) PQCrypto 2010. LNCS, vol. 6061, pp. 153–164. Springer, Heidelberg (2010)

9. Courtois, N.T., Daum, M., Felke, P.: On the security of HFE, HFEv- and Quartz. In: Desmedt, Y.G. (ed.) PKC 2003. LNCS, vol. 2567, pp. 337–350. Springer, Heidelberg (2002)

10. Chen, J.M., Yang, B.-Y.: A more secure and efficacious TTS signature scheme. In: Lim, J.-I., Lee, D.-H. (eds.) ICISC 2003. LNCS, vol. 2971, pp. 320–338. Springer, Heidelberg (2004)

11. Ding, J., Clough, C., Araujo, R.: Inverting square systems algebraically is exponential. Finite Fields Appl. **26**, 32–48 (2014)

12. Ding, J., Gower, J.E., Schmidt, D.S.: Multivariate Public Key Cryptosystems. Advances in Information Security, vol. 25. Springer, New york (2006)

13. Dubois, V., Fouque, P.-A., Shamir, A., Stern, J.: Practical cryptanalysis of SFLASH. In: Menezes, A. (ed.) CRYPTO 2007. LNCS, vol. 4622, pp. 1–12. Springer, Heidelberg (2007)

14. Ding, J., Petzoldt, A., Wang, L.: The cubic simple matrix encryption scheme. In: Mosca, M. (ed.) PQCrypto 2014. LNCS, vol. 8772, pp. 76–87. Springer, Heidelberg (2014)

15. Ding, J., Schmidt, D.: Rainbow, a new multivariable polynomial signature scheme. In: Ioannidis, J., Keromytis, A.D., Yung, M. (eds.) ACNS 2005. LNCS, vol. 3531, pp. 164–175. Springer, Heidelberg (2005)

16. Ding, J., Schmidt, D., Yin, Z.: Cryptanalysis of the new TTS scheme in CHES 2004. Int. J. Inf. Secur. **5**(4), 231–240 (2006)

17. Ding, J., Wolf, C., Yang, B.-Y.: ℓ-invertible cycles for multivariate quadratic (MQ) public key cryptography. In: Okamoto, T., Wang, X. (eds.) PKC 2007. LNCS, vol. 4450, pp. 266–281. Springer, Heidelberg (2007)

18. Ding, J., Yang, B.-Y., Chen, C.-H.O., Chen, M.-S., Cheng, C.-M.: New differential-algebraic attacks and reparametrization of rainbow. In: Bellovin, S.M., Gennaro, R., Keromytis, A.D., Yung, M. (eds.) ACNS 2008. LNCS, vol. 5037, pp. 242–257. Springer, Heidelberg (2008)

19. Faugére, J.-C.: A new efficient algorithm for computing Gröbner basis (F_4). J. Pure Appl. Algebra **139**(1–3), 61–88 (1999)

20. Faugére, J.-C.: A new efficient algorithm for computing Gröbner basis without to zero (F_5). In: Proceedings of the International Symposium on Symbolic and Algebraic Computation, pp. 75–83 (2002)

21. Fouque, P.-A., Macario-Rat, G., Perret, L., Stern, J.: Total break of the ℓ-IC signature scheme. In: Cramer, R. (ed.) PKC 2008. LNCS, vol. 4939, pp. 1–17. Springer, Heidelberg (2008)

22. Goubin, L., Courtois, N.T.: Cryptanalysis of the TTM cryptosystem. In: Okamoto, T. (ed.) ASIACRYPT 2000. LNCS, vol. 1976, pp. 44–57. Springer, Heidelberg (2000)

23. Gallant, R.P., Lambert, R.J., Vanstone, S.A.: Faster point multiplication on elliptic curves with efficient endomorphisms. In: Kilian, J. (ed.) CRYPTO 2001. LNCS, vol. 2139, pp. 190–200. Springer, Heidelberg (2001)

24. Galbraith, S.D., Lin, X., Scott, M.: Endomorphisms for faster elliptic curve cryptography on a large class of curves. J. Crypt. **24**(3), 446–469 (2011)

25. Hoffstein, J., Pipher, J., Silverman, J.H.: NTRU: a ring-based public key cryptosystem. In: Buhler, J.P. (ed.) ANTS 1998. LNCS, vol. 1423, pp. 267–288. Springer, Heidelberg (1998)

26. Kipnis, A., Patarin, J., Goubin, L.: Unbalanced oil and vinegar signature schemes. In: Stern, J. (ed.) EUROCRYPT 1999. LNCS, vol. 1592, pp. 206–222. Springer, Heidelberg (1999)

27. Kipnis, A., Shamir, A.: Cryptanalysis of the HFE public key cryptosystem by relinearization. In: Wiener, M. (ed.) CRYPTO 1999. LNCS, vol. 1666, pp. 19–30. Springer, Heidelberg (1999)
28. Kipnis, A., Shamir, A.: Cryptanalysis of the oil and vinegar signature scheme. In: Krawczyk, H. (ed.) CRYPTO 1998. LNCS, vol. 1462, pp. 257–266. Springer, Heidelberg (1998)
29. Matsumoto, T., Imai, H.: Public quadratic polynomial-tuples for efficient signature-verification and message-encryption. In: Günther, C.G. (ed.) EUROCRYPT 1988. LNCS, vol. 330, pp. 419–453. Springer, Heidelberg (1988)
30. Moh, T.-T.: A fast public key system with signature ans master key functions. In: CrypTEC 1999, pp. 63–69 (1999)
31. Moh, T.-T.: A public key system with signature and master key functions. Commun. Algebra **27**(5), 2207–2222 (1999)
32. Möller, B.: Algorithms for multi-exponentiation. In: Vaudenay, S., Youssef, A.M. (eds.) SAC 2001. LNCS, vol. 2259, pp. 165–180. Springer, Heidelberg (2001)
33. Patarin, J.: Cryptanalysis of the matsumoto and imai public key scheme of Eurocrypt '88. In: Coppersmith, D. (ed.) CRYPTO 1995. LNCS, vol. 963, pp. 248–261. Springer, Heidelberg (1995)
34. Patarin, J.: Hidden fields equations (HFE) and isomorphisms of polynomials (IP): two new families of asymmetric algorithms. In: Maurer, U.M. (ed.) EUROCRYPT 1996. LNCS, vol. 1070, pp. 33–48. Springer, Heidelberg (1996)
35. Patarin, J., Goubin, L., Courtois, N.T.: C_-+^* and HM: variations around two schemes of T. Matsumoto and H. Imai. In: Ohta, K., Pei, D. (eds.) ASIACRYPT 1998. LNCS, vol. 1514, pp. 35–50. Springer, Heidelberg (1998)
36. Patarin, J., Courtois, N.T., Goubin, L.: FLASH, a fast multivariate signature algorithm. In: Naccache, D. (ed.) CT-RSA 2001. LNCS, vol. 2020, p. 298. Springer, Heidelberg (2001)
37. Petzoldt, A., Bulygin, S., Buchmann, J.: Selecting parameters for the rainbow signature scheme. In: Sendrier, N. (ed.) PQCrypto 2010. LNCS, vol. 6061, pp. 218–240. Springer, Heidelberg (2010)
38. Petzoldt, A., Bulygin, S., Buchmann, J.: CyclicRainbow – a multivariate signature scheme with a partially cyclic public key. In: Gong, G., Gupta, K.C. (eds.) INDOCRYPT 2010. LNCS, vol. 6498, pp. 33–48. Springer, Heidelberg (2010)
39. Porras, J., Baena, J., Ding, J.: ZHFE, a new multivariate public key encryption scheme. In: Mosca, M. (ed.) PQCrypto 2014. LNCS, vol. 8772, pp. 229–245. Springer, Heidelberg (2014)
40. Scott, M., Benger, N., Charlemagne, M., Dominguez Perez, L.J., Kachisa, E.J.: On the final exponentiation for calculating pairings on ordinary elliptic curves. In: Shacham, H., Waters, B. (eds.) Pairing 2009. LNCS, vol. 5671, pp. 78–88. Springer, Heidelberg (2009)
41. Tao, C., Diene, A., Tang, S., Ding, J.: Simple matrix scheme for encryption. In: Gaborit, P. (ed.) PQCrypto 2013. LNCS, vol. 7932, pp. 231–242. Springer, Heidelberg (2013)
42. Tao, C., Xiang, H., Petzoldt, A., Ding, J.: Simple matrix - a multivariate public key cryptosystem (MPKC) for encryption. Finite Fields Appl. **35**, 352–368 (2015)
43. Thomae, E., Wolf, C.: Roots of square: cryptanalysis of double-layer square and square+. In: Yang, B.-Y. (ed.) PQCrypto 2011. LNCS, vol. 7071, pp. 83–97. Springer, Heidelberg (2011)
44. Wolf, C., Preneel, B.: Taxonomy of public key schemes based on the problem of multivariate quadratic equations. Cryptology ePrint Archive, Report 2005/077, December 2005. http://eprint.iacr.org/2005/077

45. Yang, B.-Y., Chen, J.-M.: TTS: rank attacks in tame-like multivariate PKCs. Cryptology ePrint Archive, Report 2004/061, November 2004. http://eprint.iacr.org/2004/061

46. Yang, B.-Y., Chen, J.-M.: All in the XL family: theory and practice. In: Park, C., Chee, S. (eds.) ICISC 2004. LNCS, vol. 3506, pp. 67–86. Springer, Heidelberg (2005)

Efficient and Secure Many-to-One Signature Delegation

Rajeev Anand Sahu[1(✉)] and Vishal Saraswat[1]

C.R.Rao Advanced Institute of Mathematics Statistics and Computer Science,
Hyderabad, India
rajeevs.crypto@gmail.com

Abstract. We propose an IBPMS scheme from pairings, which is more efficient in the sense of computation and operation time than the existing schemes. We also prove on random oracle that the propose d scheme is secure against existential forgery on adaptive chosen-message and adaptive-chosen ID attack under the k-CAA assumption. Additionally, our scheme fulfills all the security requirements of a proxy signature scheme. Moreover we do an efficiency analysis and show that our scheme is significantly more efficient than the existing IBPMS schemes in the sense of computation and operation time.

Keywords: Identity-based cryptography · Digital signature · Bilinear pairings · Delegation of signing rights · Proxy multi-signature · k-CAA problem · Provable security

1 Introduction

In a proxy signature scheme, an original signer o can transfer its signing rights to a proxy signer ρ without transferring its private key; and the proxy signer can sign any document on behalf of the original signer. Proxy signature schemes are applicable in distributed systems, grid computing, mobile agent environment etc. where delegation of rights is quite common.

The notion of proxy signature has been around since 1989 due to Gasser *et al.* [3] but the first formal construction of a proxy signature scheme [6] was proposed in 1996. The notion of proxy multi-signature was introduced by Yi et al. [10] in 2000 and then in 2005, Li and Chen [5] proposed the first proxy multi-signature scheme in ID-based setting using bilinear pairings. Since then, many identity (ID)-based proxy multi-signature (IBPMS) schemes have been proposed using bilinear pairings, but most of the schemes are either too much inefficient or insecure, hence cannot be considered for the practical implementation.

We propose here an IBPMS scheme from bilinear pairings. Our scheme is significantly more efficient than the existing IBPMS schemes [1,5,8,9] in the sense of computation and operation time. Moreover, we prove the security of our scheme against existential forgery on adaptive chosen-message and adaptive chosen-ID attacks in random oracle model. Additionally, we also show that the proposed scheme fulfills all the security requirements of a proxy signature scheme listed in [4].

© Springer International Publishing Switzerland 2016
S. Qing et al. (Eds.): ICICS 2015, LNCS 9543, pp. 252–259, 2016.
DOI: 10.1007/978-3-319-29814-6_20

2   Preliminaries

Definition 1. Let G_1 be an additive cyclic group with generator P and G_2 be a multiplicative cyclic group with generator g. Let both the groups are of the same prime order q. A map $e : G_1 \times G_1 \to G_2$ is called a *cryptographic bilinear map* or a *pairing* if it satisfies the following properties:

1. *Bilinearity*: For all $a, b \in \mathbb{Z}_q^*$, $e(aP, bP) = e(P, P)^{ab}$, or equivalently, for all $Q, R, S \in G_1$, $e(Q+R, S) = e(Q, S)e(R, S)$ and $e(Q, R+S) = e(Q, R)e(Q, S)$.
2. *Non-degeneracy*: There exists $Q, R \in G_1$ such that $e(Q, R) \neq 1$. Note that since G_1 and G_2 are groups of prime order, this condition is equivalent to the condition $e(P, P) \neq 1$, which again is equivalent to the condition that $e(P, P)$ is a generator of G_2.
3. *Computability*: There exists an efficient algorithm to compute $e(Q, R) \in G_2$, for any $Q, R \in G_1$.

Definition 2. The *k-CAA Problem* [7] is to compute $\frac{1}{s+e_0}P$, for some $e_0 \in \mathbb{Z}_q^*$ when given $P, sP \in G_1, e_1, e_2, \ldots, e_k \in \mathbb{Z}_q^*$ and $\frac{1}{s+e_1}P, \frac{1}{s+e_2}P, \ldots, \frac{1}{s+e_k}P \in G_1$.

Definition 3. The (t, ϵ) *k-CAA assumption* holds in G_1 if there is no algorithm which takes at most t running time and can solve the k-CAA problem with at least a non-negligible advantage ϵ.

3   Proposed IBPMS Scheme

3.1   Setup

Given a security parameter 1^K, the private key generator (PKG) generates the system's master secret $s \in \mathbb{Z}_q^*$ and the system's public parameters

$$params = (K, q, G_1, G_2, e, H_1, H_2, P, Q),$$

where G_1 is an additive cyclic group of prime order q; G_2 is a multiplicative cyclic group of prime order q; $e : G_1 \times G_1 \to G_2$ is a bilinear map defined as above; $H_1 : \{0, 1\}^* \to \mathbb{Z}_q^*$ and $H_2 : \{0, 1\}^* \times G_1 \to \mathbb{Z}_q^*$ are two cryptographic hash functions; P is a generator of G_1; and $Q := sP \in G_1$ is system's public key.

3.2   Extraction

Given a user's identity ID, the PKG computes its

– public key as: $Q_{\text{ID}} = H_1(\text{ID})$ and
– private key as: $S_{\text{ID}} = \frac{1}{s+H_1(\text{ID})}P$.

Thus, the proxy signer A_0 and the original signers, A_i, $i = 1, \ldots, n$, have their public keys and the corresponding private keys

– $Q_{\text{ID}_{A_i}} = H_1(\text{ID}_{A_i})$ and
– $S_{\text{ID}_{A_i}} = \frac{1}{s+H_1(\text{ID}_{A_i})}P$,

for $i = 0, 1, \ldots, n$.

3.3 Proxy Key Generation

In this phase, all the original signers interact with the proxy signer to delegate their signing rights through a signed warrant. The warrant w includes some specific information about the message like nature of the message, time of delegation, identity information of the original signers and the proxy signer, period of validity, some public keys etc. After the successful interaction, the proxy signer outputs its proxy signing key. The interaction and proxy key generation can be described in the following phases:

Delegation generation:
   Each of the n original signers, A_i, $i = 1, \ldots, n$, and the proxy signer, A_0, interact and do the following:
   - set $I = \sum_{i=0}^{n} H_1(\mathrm{ID}_{A_i}) \in \mathbb{Z}_q^*$ and $J = (n+1)Q + IP \in G_1$;
   - select $x_i \xleftarrow{\$} \mathbb{Z}_q^*$;
   - compute and publish $V_i = e(J, S_{\mathrm{ID}_{A_i}}) \in G_2$, and $W_i = V_i^{x_i} \in G_2$;
   - create a warrant w which includes the identities ID_{A_i} of the proxy and original signers, the values V_i and $V_o = \prod_{i=0}^{n} V_i$, the values W_i and $W_o = \prod_{i=0}^{n} W_i$, the scope of messages to be signed, time of delegation, period of validity etc.;
   - computes $h_o = H_2(w, W_o) \in \mathbb{Z}_q^*$;
   - and $S_i = (x_i + h_o)S_{\mathrm{ID}_{A_i}}$.
   - Finally each original signer sends (w, S_i), $i = 1, \ldots, n$, to the proxy signer as a partial delegation.

Delegation verification:
   On receiving (w, S_i) from each original signer A_i, the proxy signer A_0 obtains W_i and W_o from the warrant, computes $h_o = H_2(w, W_o) \in \mathbb{Z}_q^*$ and validates each partial delegation by checking

$$e(J, S_i) = W_i V_i^{h_o}.$$

If the above equality does not hold for any $1 \leq i \leq n$, the proxy signer terminates the protocol.

Proxy key generation:
   In this phase, the proxy signer computes its proxy secret key to sign the message on behalf of the group of original signers to be

$$S_{pk} = \sum_{i=0}^{n} S_i.$$

3.4 Proxy Multi-signature

To sign a message $m \in \{0, 1\}^*$ under the warrant w on behalf of the group of original signers, the proxy signer does the following:

- selects $y \xleftarrow{\$} \mathbb{Z}_q^*$;
- computes $V_\rho = V_o^y$ and $W_\rho = W_o^y$;
- computes $h_\rho = H_2(m, W_\rho) \in \mathbb{Z}_q^*$
- and $\sigma = (y + h_\rho)S_{pk}$.
- Finally, (σ, V_ρ, W_ρ) is the IBPMS by the proxy signer on behalf of the group of original signers on message m under the warrant w.

3.5 Verification:

On receiving the IBPMS (σ, V_ρ, W_ρ) on message m under the warrant w, a verifier validates it as follows:

- checks if the message m confirms to the warrant w. Stops if not. Continues otherwise.
- checks whether the proxy signer A_0 is authorized or not in the warrant w, by the group of n original signers. Stops if not. Continues otherwise.
- obtains V_o and W_o from the warrant w, computes $h_o = H_2(w, W_o) \in Z_q^*$ and $h_\rho = H_2(m, W_\rho) \in Z_q^*$ and accepts (σ, V_ρ, W_ρ) as a valid IBPMS on message m, if and only if the following equality holds:

$$e(J, \sigma) = W_\rho V_\rho^{h_o} W_o^{h_\rho} V_o^{h_o h_\rho}.$$

4 Analysis of the Proposed Scheme

In this section, we first give the correctness of our scheme then analyze the security of our scheme and show that the proposed scheme satisfies all the security requirements of a proxy signature scheme [4].

4.1 Correctness

Correctness of the delegation verification holds since for all $0 \le i \le n$,

$$e(J, S_i) = e(J, (x_i + h_o)S_{ID_{A_i}}) = e(J, S_{ID_{A_i}})^{x_i + h_o} = V_i^{x_i + h_o} = W_i V_i^{h_o}. \quad (1)$$

Correctness of the IBPMS verification holds since

$$e(J, \sigma) = e(J, (y + h_\rho)S_{pk}) = e\left(J, (y + h_\rho) \sum_{i=0}^{n} S_i\right)$$

$$= \prod_{i=0}^{n} e(J, (y + h_\rho)S_i) = \prod_{i=0}^{n} e(J, S_i)^{y + h_\rho} = \prod_{i=0}^{n} \left(W_i V_i^{h_o}\right)^{y + h_\rho} \quad \text{from (1)}$$

$$= \left(\prod_{i=0}^{n} W_i V_i^{h_o}\right)^{y + h_\rho} = \left(\prod_{i=0}^{n} W_i \prod_{i=0}^{n} V_i^{h_o}\right)^{y + h_\rho}$$

$$= \left(W_o V_o^{h_o}\right)^{y + h_\rho} = W_o^y (V_o^y)^{h_o} W_o^{h_\rho} (V_o^{h_o})^{h_\rho} = W_\rho V_\rho^{h_o} W_o^{h_\rho} V_o^{h_o h_\rho}.$$

4.2 Security Analysis

Theorem 1. *The proposed IBPMS scheme is strongly unforgeable if the k-CAA is intractable in* G_1.

Proof. For security parameter 1^k, the challenger $\mathcal{C}$ runs the setup algorithm and provides $\langle q, G_1, P, sP, (e_1, f_1), \ldots, (e_k, f_k) \rangle$ to $\mathcal{B}$ where G_1 is an additive cyclic group of prime order q; P is a generator of G_1 and $s, e_1, \ldots, e_k \in \mathbb{Z}_q^*$ are randomly chosen elements and $f_i := \frac{1}{s+e_i} P \in G_1$, $i = 1, \ldots, k$. The goal of $\mathcal{B}$ is to solve the k-CAA problem by producing a pair $\left(e_0, \frac{1}{s+e_0} P \right)$ for some $e_0 \in \mathbb{Z}_q^*$, $e_0 \neq e_i$ for all $i = 1, \ldots, n$.

Let $\mathcal{A}$ be a forger algorithm who claims is to break the proposed identity based proxy multi-signature scheme. The adversary $\mathcal{B}$ simulates the challenger and interacts with $\mathcal{A}$. We facilitate the adversary $\mathcal{A}$ to adaptively select the identity ID* on which it wants to forge the signature. Further the adversary can obtain the private keys associated to the identities. The adversary also can access the proxy multi-generation oracles on warrants w' of its choice, and proxy multi-signature oracles on the warrant, messages pair (w', m') of its choice upto polynomial many times.

Setup: For security parameter 1^k, $\mathcal{B}$ generates the system's public parameter *params* $= \langle q, G_1, G_2, e, H_1, H_2, P, Q = sP \rangle$ where G_2 is a multiplicative cyclic group of prime order q; $e : G_1 \times G_1 \rightarrow G_2$ is a bilinear map defined as in Sect. 2; and $H_1 : \{0,1\}^* \rightarrow \mathbb{Z}_q^*$ and $H_2 : \{0,1\}^* \times G_1 \rightarrow \mathbb{Z}_q^*$ are two cryptographic hash functions and provides *params* to $\mathcal{A}$. $\mathcal{B}$ picks a random index $i^* \in [1, k+1]$ and a random $e_0 \in \mathbb{Z}_q^*$. It then resets the values $(e_i, f_i) = (e_i, f_i)$ for $1 \leq i < i^*$, $(e_{i^*}, f_{i^*}) = (e_0, \perp))$ and $(e_i, f_i) = (e_{i-1}, f_{i-1})$ for $i^* < i \leq k+1$.

H_1-queries: To respond to the H_1 hash function queries, $\mathcal{B}$ maintains a list $L_{H_1} = \{\langle \text{ID}, e, f \rangle\}$. When $\mathcal{A}$ requests the H_1 query on some identity $\text{ID}_i \in \{0,1\}^*$, $i \leq k+1$, $\mathcal{B}$ responds as follows:

1. If the query ID_i already appears in the list L_{H_1} in some tuple $\langle \text{ID}_j, e_j, f_j \rangle$, $j < i$, then algorithm $\mathcal{B}$ responds to $\mathcal{A}$ with $H_1(\text{ID}_i) = e_j$.
   So WLOG we assume $\text{ID}_i \neq \text{ID}_j$ for $i \neq j$.
2. Otherwise $\mathcal{B}$ responds to $\mathcal{A}$ with $H_1(\text{ID}_i) = e_i$ and adds the tuple $\langle \text{ID}_i, e_i, f_i \rangle$ to the list L_{H_1}.

H_2-queries: To respond to the H_2 hash function queries, $\mathcal{B}$ maintains a list $L_{H_2} = \{\langle w, U, g \rangle\}$. When $\mathcal{A}$ requests the H_2 query on (w', U') for some $w' \in \{0,1\}^*$ and $U' \in G_1$, $\mathcal{B}$ responds as follows:

1. If the query (w', U') already appears on the list L_{H_2} in some tuple $\langle w', U', g \rangle$ then algorithm $\mathcal{B}$ responds to $\mathcal{A}$ with $H_2(w'\|U') = g$.
2. Otherwise $\mathcal{B}$ picks a random integer $g \in \mathbb{Z}_q^*$ and adds the tuple $\langle w', U', g \rangle$ to the list L_{H_2} and responds to $\mathcal{A}$ with $H_2(w'\|U') = g$.

Extraction Queries: When $\mathcal{A}$ makes a private key query on some identity ID_i, $i \leq k+q$, $\mathcal{B}$ responds as follows:

1. If $i = i^*$, then $\mathcal{B}$ reports failure and terminates. The probability of such failure is $1/(k+1)$.

2. Otherwise $\mathcal{B}$ responds to $\mathcal{A}$ with $S_{\mathrm{ID}_i} = f_i$ and adds the tuple $\langle \mathrm{ID}_i, e_i, f_i \rangle$ to the list L_{H_1}.

Recall that, for $i \neq i^*$, $H(\mathrm{ID}_i) = e_i$ and $f_i = \frac{1}{s+e_i} P$. So, $S_{\mathrm{ID}_i} = \frac{1}{s+H(\mathrm{ID}_i)} P$ is a valid private key of the user with identity ID_i.

Delegation Queries: To respond to the delegation queries, $\mathcal{B}$ maintains a list $L_{del} = \{\langle w, (x_0, S_0), (x_1, S_1), \ldots, (x_n, S_n)\rangle\}$ and responds to identical queries in a consistent fashion. It uses L_{H_1} and L_{H_2} to generate the needed hash values and the secret keys and computes the delegations $\langle w, S_1, \ldots, S_n \rangle$ as in the actual scheme. $\mathcal{B}$ may have to terminate if the identity of one of the original signers is ID_{i^*} and the probability for that event is bounded by $(n+1)/(k+1)$.

Proxy Key Generation Queries: To respond to the proxy key generation queries, $\mathcal{B}$ maintains a list $L_{pkg} = \{\langle w, S \rangle\}$ and responds to identical queries in a consistent fashion. It uses L_{H_1} and L_{H_2} to generate the needed hash values and the secret keys and computes the proxy key $\langle w, S \rangle$ using L_{del} as in the actual scheme. $\mathcal{B}$ may have to terminate if the identity of one of the original signers or the proxy signer is ID_{i^*} and the probability for that event is $(n+1)/(k+1)$.

Proxy Multi-Signature Queries: To respond to the proxy multi-signature queries, $\mathcal{B}$ maintains a list $L_{pms} = \{\langle w, m, y, V, W, \sigma \rangle\}$ and responds to identical queries in a consistent fashion. It uses L_{H_1} and L_{H_2} to generate the needed hash values and the secret keys and computes the delegations $\langle w, m, V, W, \sigma \rangle$ using L_{del} and L_{pkg} as in the actual scheme.

$\mathcal{B}$ may have to terminate if the identity of one of the original signers or the proxy signer is ID_{i^*} and the probability for that event is $(n+1)/(k+1)$.

Output: $\mathcal{A}$ outputs a valid ID-based proxy multi-signature (σ, V_ρ, W_ρ) on a message m under the warrant w by the proxy signer A_0 on behalf of the group of original signers $A_1, \ldots, A_n$ such that

$$e(J, \sigma) = W_\rho V_\rho^{h_o} W_o^{h_\rho} V_o^{h_o h_\rho} \tag{2}$$

where J, V_o, W_o, h_o, h_ρ are defined as in Sect. 3.

If $\mathcal{A}$ does not query any hash function, that is, if responses to any of the hash function query is picked randomly then the probability that verification equality holds is less than $1/q$. Thus, with probability greater than $1 - 1/q$, all the public keys and were computed using H_1-oracle.

For the forgery to be valid, $\mathcal{A}$ must not have queried the private key of at least one of the signers, say A_i, and must not have received (σ, V_ρ, W_ρ) as a response to a proxy key generation query. The probability that the identity of A_i is ID_{i^*} is $1/(k+1)$ and in that case, $H_1(ID_{A_i}) = e$.

Then, using the Eq. (2) and the values returned by the adversary we can reverse compute the secret key $S_{\mathrm{ID}_{A_i}}$ of A_i as in [2]. But by definition, $S_{\mathrm{ID}_{A_i}} = \frac{1}{s+H_1(ID_{A_i})} P = \frac{1}{s+e} P$. Thus $\mathcal{B}$ can then return the pair $(e, S_{\mathrm{ID}_{A_i}})$ to the challenger $\mathcal{C}$ and win the k-CAA game.

Hence the proposed IBPMS scheme is secure.

5 Efficiency Analysis

We compare the total number of bilinear pairings (P), map-to-point hash functions (H), modular exponentiations (E) and pairing-based scalar multiplications (PSM) in Proxy key generation phase, Proxy multi-signature phase and the Verification phase with those of other IBPMS schemes [1,5,8,9] and show that our scheme is computationally more efficient and takes less operation time than the known best IBPMS schemes given in [1,5,8,9] (Table 1).

Table 1. Efficiency comparison

Proxy key generation

Scheme	P	H	E	PSM
Li et al. [5]	$3n$	n	n	$3n+1$
Wang et al. [9]	$3n$	$n+2$	0	$4n$
Shao [8]	$3n$	$n+2$	0	$2n$
Cao et al. [1]	$3n$	$n+2$	0	$2n$
Our scheme	$2n$	0	$2n$	$n+2$

Proxy multi-signature

Scheme	P	H	E	PSM
Li et al. [5]	1	0	1	2
Wang et al. [9]	0	0	0	3
Shao [8]	0	1	0	2
Cao et al. [1]	0	1	0	2
Our scheme	0	0	2	1

Verification

Scheme	P	H	E	PSM
Li et al. [5]	3	$n+1$	2	0
Wang et al. [9]	3	$2n+3$	0	$n+1$
Shao [8]	4	$n+1$	0	0
Cao et al. [1]	4	$n+2$	0	0
Our scheme	1	0	3	0

Overall Time

Scheme	P	H	E	PSM
Li et al. [5]	$3n+4$	$2n+1$	$n+3$	$3n+3$
Wang et al. [9]	$3n+3$	$3n+5$	0	$5n+4$
Shao [8]	$3n+4$	$2n+4$	0	$2n+2$
Cao et al. [1]	$3n+4$	$4n+5$	0	$2n+3$
Our scheme	$2n+1$	0	$2n+5$	$n+3$

References

1. Cao, F., Cao, Z.: A secure identity-based proxy multi-signature scheme. Inf. Sci. **179**(3), 292–302 (2009)
2. Hongzhen, D., Wen, Q.: An efficient identity-based short signature scheme from bilinear pairings. In: ICCIS 2007, pp. 725–729 (2007)
3. Gasser, M., Goldstein, A., Kaufman, C., Lampson, B.: The digital distributed system security architecture. In: NCSC 1989, pp. 305–319 (1989)
4. Lee, B., Kim, H., Kim, K.: Strong proxy signature and its applications. In: Proceedings of SCIS, vol. 1, pp. 603–608 (2001)
5. Li, X., Chen, K.: Id-based multi-proxy signature, proxy multi-signature and multi-proxy multi-signature schemes from bilinear pairings. Appl. Math. Comput. **169**(1), 437–450 (2005)
6. Mambo, M., Usuda, K., Okamoto, E.: Proxy signatures: delegation of the power to sign messages. IEICE Trans. Fundam. Electron. Commun. Comput. Sci. **79**(9), 1338–1354 (1996)
7. Mitsunari, S., Sakai, R., Kasahara, M.: A new traitor tracing. IEICE Trans. Fundam. Electron. Commun. Comput. Sci. **85**(2), 481–484 (2002)

8. Shao, Z.: Improvement of identity-based proxy multi-signature scheme. J. Syst. Softw. **82**(5), 794–800 (2009)
9. Wang, Q., Cao, Z.: Identity based proxy multi-signature. J. Syst. Softw. **80**(7), 1023–1029 (2007)
10. Yi, L., Bai, G., Xiao, G.: Proxy multi-signature scheme: a new type of proxy signature scheme. Electron. Lett. **36**(6), 527–528 (2000)

Fully Secure IBE with Tighter Reduction in Prime Order Bilinear Groups

Jie Zhang[✉], Aijun Ge, Siyu Xiao, and Chuangui Ma

Zhengzhou Information Science and Technology Institute,
Zhengzhou 450002, Henan Province, China
zhangjie902@sina.cn, geaijun@163.com, 564844418@qq.com,
chuanguima@sina.com

Abstract. This paper present an identity-based encryption (IBE) scheme with full security in prime order bilinear groups by using dual pairing vector space. The security of our scheme is based upon decisional linear and three party Diffie-Hellman assumption by adapting the dual system encryption. We obtain a tighter security reduction compared to previous works based on dual system encryption. The loss for security reduction of our scheme is $\mathcal{O}(q_1)$, where q_1 is the number of key queries in Phase 1.

Keywords: Identity-based encryption · Dual system encryption · Dual pairing vector space · Tighter reduction

1 Introduction

Identity-Based Encryption (IBE) was presented by Shamir [1]. In an IBE system, user's public key is his identity. The first practical IBE scheme was presented almost twenty years later by Boneh and Franklin by applying pairing technique in 2001 [2]. Since then, a host of IBE schemes was proposed, starting with the early constructions of selective security [3,4], to more recent constructions of full security [5,6]. The selective security model is a useful intermediary step, but cannot reflect the real situation comprehensively, since the adversary is required to announce the challenge identity before he receives the public parameters.

Dual system encryption [5] is a powerful tool for building fully secure IBE scheme. There are two forms of ciphertext and secret keys in dual system encryption: normal and semi-functional. Classical dual system encryption utilizes a series of games to prove the security. The real security game is followed by a game that the ciphertext becomes semi-functional. After that, the secret keys become semi-functional one after another, ultimately arrive at the final game, every key and ciphertext becomes semi-functional, which proving security becomes apparent. Each transition is reduce to its underlying security: subgroup or statical indistinguishability. Thus, all the previous works based on dual system encryption except [7,8] results in $\mathcal{O}(q)$ loss for security reduction, where q is the total number of key requests.

© Springer International Publishing Switzerland 2016
S. Qing et al. (Eds.): ICICS 2015, LNCS 9543, pp. 260–268, 2016.
DOI: 10.1007/978-3-319-29814-6_21

The IBE of [7,8] employ two different techniques to achieve the tighter reduction. Chen and Wee [7] choosed an appropriate pseudorandom function with security loss L as a building block. And then, they get an IBE with the security loss $\mathcal{O}(L)$ owing to similar algebraic structure between the IBE and pseudorandom function. The IBE of [7] can work both in composite order and prime order groups. The technique of [8] is based on the following fact: when a specific key is changed from normal to semi-functional in Phase 2, the simulator has learned the challenge identity ID^* before defining the semi-functional parameters, so it can program the parameter using ID^*. This is considerably similar to the requirement of selective security, which is called *delayed parameters* in [9]. By using the technique of *delayed parameters*, scheme [8] organized all the challenge keys in Phase 2 into the correlated distribution, and modified them from normal to semi-functional all at once, which results in tighter reduction, $\mathcal{O}(q_1)$.

Although [8] achieves a tighter reduction, it is built on a composite order bilinear group setting. Compared with prime order bilinear groups, composite order bilinear groups are at a disadvantage both in efficiency and security. In the first place, supersingular curves, which most composite order bilinear groups are based upon, is the main obstacle that affects the efficiency of composite order bilinear groups [10,11]. There is one more point that the security of schemes based upon composite order bilinear groups crucially depend on the difficulty of factoring N. In order to guarantee the scheme's security, the system has to increase the size of the underlying groups, which makes condition much worse for calculating speed. Further more, according to the recent results [12,13], discrete logarithms in supersingular curves may be not as hard as we thought. For these reasons, many research [14,15] have examined how to simulate composite order bilinear groups by using prime order bilinear groups.

In this article, we present IBE with tighter security reduction that enjoys $\mathcal{O}(q_1)$ in prime order bilinear groups. Our scheme is fully secure. The security is rely on the decisional linear and three party Diffie-Hellman assumption. Our construction have a similar structure of scheme [8]. We utilize the techniques developed in [15], taking advantage of the dual pairing vector space as a substitute for the subgroups in the composite order bilinear groups. Likewise, we substitute the subspace assumption for the subgroup decision assumption in the security proof. In addition, we take a 2 dimensional matrix to program the parameters in phase 2 of key queries. We embed g^{xy} to the semi-functional space, so as to obtain the target element g^{xyz} in G when combining with r. As we can re-randomize r by multiplying a random values $r' \in \mathbb{Z}_p$ in the prime order setting, we do not need to simulate the additional element u, which is used as a *randomizer* in [8].

Next, we present the preliminaries that includes the security model and definition of IBE, an overview of dual pairing vector space, and complexity assumptions in Sect. 2. Our IBE scheme is presented in Sect. 3. Finally, we conclude in Sect. 4.

2 Preliminaries

2.1 Identity-Based Encryption Definition

Setup$(\lambda) \to PP, MSK$. This algorithm takes as input a security parameter λ, outputs the master key MSK and the public parameters PP.

KeyGen$(MSK, ID) \to SK_{ID}$. This algorithm takes as input an identity $ID \in \{0,1\}^*$, MSK, and returns a private key SK_{ID}.

Encrypt$(PP, ID, M) \to CT$. This algorithm takes as input PP, an identity ID, and a message M, and outputs a ciphertext CT.

Decrypt$(PP, SK_{ID}) \to M$. This algorithm takes as input SK_{ID} and CT. If the identity of the private key and ciphertext is identical, it returns the message M.

2.2 Security Model

Setup. The challenger $\mathcal{B}$ executes the setup algorithm. It gives the public parameters to the adversary $\mathcal{A}$.

Phase 1. When receives a query for private key of identity ID_i that makes by $\mathcal{A}$, $\mathcal{B}$ executes KeyGen algorithm to obtain the private key SK_{ID_i}. It sends SK_{ID_i} to $\mathcal{A}$, where $i = 1, \ldots, q_1$.

Challenge. $\mathcal{A}$ submits an challenge identity ID^* along with two messages M_0 and M_1, where the length of M_0 and M_1 are the same. The only constraint is that $\mathcal{A}$ never queried ID^* in Phase 1. $\mathcal{B}$ randomly encrypts M_b ($b \in \{0,1\}$) and sends it to $\mathcal{A}$.

Phase 2. $\mathcal{A}$ continually queries the private keys of identities $ID_{q_1+1}, \ldots, ID_q$, with the constraint that ID^* can not be queried. $\mathcal{B}$ responds as the same as Phase 1.

Guess. $\mathcal{A}$ outputs a guess b' for b.

The adversary's advantage is defined to be $Pr[b' = b] - 1/2$.

Definition 1. *An Identity-based Encryption scheme is fully secure, if for all polynomial time adversaries, the advantage is negligible in the security game.*

2.3 Dual Pairing Vector Spaces

Dual pairing vector spaces [16] is a useful tool. It works as follows. Given (p, G, G_T, g, g_T, e), G and G_T are cyclic multiplicative groups of order p (where p is a prime), g is a generator of G, $e : G \times G \to G_T$ is an effective computable non-degenerate bilinear pairing, i.e., $e(g^a, g^b) = e(g, g)^{ab}$ and $g_T = e(g, g) \neq 1$.

We let $\boldsymbol{v}$ denote the vector $(v_1, \ldots, v_n) \in \mathbb{Z}_p^n$, and $g^{\boldsymbol{v}} := (g^{v_1}, \ldots, g^{v_n})$. For $\boldsymbol{v}, \boldsymbol{w} \in \mathbb{Z}_p^n$ and $a \in \mathbb{Z}_p$, we let $g^{a\boldsymbol{v}} := (g^{av_1}, \ldots, g^{av_n}), g^{\boldsymbol{v}+\boldsymbol{w}} := (g^{v_1+w_1}, \ldots, g^{v_n+w_n})$.

We define $e(g^{\boldsymbol{v}}, g^{\boldsymbol{w}}) := \prod_{i=1}^{n} e(g^{v_i}, g^{w_i}) = e(g,g)^{\boldsymbol{v} \cdot \boldsymbol{w}}$, where $\boldsymbol{v} \cdot \boldsymbol{w} = v_1 w_1 + \cdots + v_n w_n \pmod{p}$.

The following lemma from [17] is required in our proof of security.

Lemma 1 (Statistical Indistinguishable). *Let* $C := \{(\boldsymbol{x}, \boldsymbol{v}) | \boldsymbol{x} \cdot \boldsymbol{v} \neq 0\} \subset V \times V^*$, *where* V *is a* n-*dimensional vector space, and* V^* *is its dual. For all* $(\boldsymbol{x}, \boldsymbol{v}) \in C$, *for all* $(\boldsymbol{r}, \boldsymbol{w}) \in C, \rho, \tau \leftarrow \mathbb{Z}_p$, *and* $A \xleftarrow{R} \mathbb{Z}_p^{n \times n}$,

$$Pr[\boldsymbol{x}(\rho A^{-1}) = \boldsymbol{r} \wedge \boldsymbol{v}(\tau A^t) = \boldsymbol{w}] = \frac{1}{\#C},$$

where $\#C = (p^n - 1)(p^n - p^{n-1})$.

2.4 Complexity Assumption

Definition 2 (Three Party Diffie-Hellman Assumption). *Given a group generator* $\mathcal{G}$, *we define the following distribution:*

$$\mathbb{G} := (p, G, G_T, e) \xleftarrow{R} \mathcal{G},$$
$$g \xleftarrow{R} G, \tau, x, y, z \xleftarrow{R} \mathbb{Z}_p,$$
$$D := (\mathbb{G}, g, g^x, g^y, g^z).$$

The advantage of algorithm $\mathcal{A}$ *in breaking this assumption is defined as follows:*

$$Adv_{\mathcal{A}}^{3DH}(\lambda) := |Pr[\mathcal{A}(D, g^{xyz}) = 1] - Pr[\mathcal{A}(D, g^{\tau + xyz}) = 1]|.$$

We say that the Three Party Diffie-Hellman Assumption is hard if $Adv_{\mathcal{A}}^{3DH}(\lambda)$ *is negligible.*

Definition 3 (Decisional Linear Assumption). *Given a group generator* $\mathcal{G}$, *we define the following distribution:*

$$\mathbb{G} := (p, G, G_T, e) \xleftarrow{R} \mathcal{G},$$
$$g, f, v \xleftarrow{R} G, c_1, c_2, w \xleftarrow{R} \mathbb{Z}_p,$$
$$D := (\mathbb{G}, g, f, v, f^{c_1}, v^{c_2}).$$

The advantage of algorithm $\mathcal{A}$ *in breaking this assumption is defined as follows:*

$$Adv_{\mathcal{A}}^{DL}(\lambda) := |Pr[\mathcal{A}(D, g^{c_1 + c_2}) = 1] - Pr[\mathcal{A}(D, g^{c_1 + c_2 + w}) = 1]|.$$

We say that the Decisional Linear Assumption is hard if $Adv_{\mathcal{A}}^{DL}(\lambda)$ *is negligible.*

Definition 4 (Subspace Assumption). *Given a group generator* $\mathcal{G}$, *we define the following distribution* $(n \geq 3, k \leq \frac{n}{3})$:

$$\mathbb{G} := (p, G, G_T, e) \xleftarrow{R} \mathcal{G}, \quad (\mathbb{B}, \mathbb{B}^*) \xleftarrow{R} Dual(\mathbb{Z}_p^n),$$

$$g \xleftarrow{R} G, \eta, \beta, \tau_1, \tau_2, \mu_1, \mu_2, \mu_3 \xleftarrow{R} \mathbb{Z}_p,$$

$$U_1 = g^{\mu_1 \boldsymbol{b}_1 + \mu_2 \boldsymbol{b}_{k+1} + \mu_3 \boldsymbol{b}_{2k+1}}, \dots, U_k = g^{\mu_1 \boldsymbol{b}_k + \mu_2 \boldsymbol{b}_{2k} + \mu_3 \boldsymbol{b}_{3k}},$$

$$V_1 = g^{\tau_1 \eta \boldsymbol{b}_1^* + \tau_2 \beta \boldsymbol{b}_{k+1}^*}, \dots, V_k = g^{\tau_1 \eta \boldsymbol{b}_k^* + \tau_2 \beta \boldsymbol{b}_{2k}^*},$$

$$W_1 = g^{\tau_1 \eta \boldsymbol{b}_1^* + \tau_2 \beta \boldsymbol{b}_{k+1}^* + \tau_3 \boldsymbol{b}_{2k+1}^*}, \dots, W_k = g^{\tau_1 \eta \boldsymbol{b}_k^* + \tau_2 \beta \boldsymbol{b}_{2k}^* + \tau_3 \boldsymbol{b}_{3k}^*},$$

$$D := (g^{\boldsymbol{b}_1}, g^{\boldsymbol{b}_2}, \dots, g^{\boldsymbol{b}_{2k}}, g^{\boldsymbol{b}_{3k+1}}, \dots, g^{\boldsymbol{b}_n}, g^{\eta \boldsymbol{b}_1^*}, \dots, g^{\eta \boldsymbol{b}_k^*},$$

$$g^{\beta \boldsymbol{b}_{k+1}^*}, \dots, g^{\beta \boldsymbol{b}_{2k}^*}, g^{\beta \boldsymbol{b}_{2k+1}^*}, \dots, g^{\beta \boldsymbol{b}_n^*}, U_1, U_2, \dots, U_k, \mu_3).$$

The advantage of an algorithm $\mathcal{A}$ in breaking this assumption is defined as follows:

$$Adv_{\mathcal{A}}^{SD}(\lambda) := |Pr[\mathcal{A}(D, V_1, \dots, V_k) = 1] - Pr[\mathcal{A}(D, W_1, \dots, W_k) = 1]|.$$

We say that the Subspace Assumption is hard if $Adv_{\mathcal{A}}^{SD}(\lambda)$ is negligible.

Lemma 2. [15] *If $\mathcal{G}$ satisfies decisional linear assumption, then $\mathcal{G}$ also satisfies the subspace assumption.*

3   Identity-Based Encryption

3.1   Our Construction

Setup$(\lambda) \to PP, MSK$. First, it selects a bilinear group $\mathbf{G}$ of prime order p along with a generetor g. Then, a couple of dual orthonormal bases $(\mathbb{D}, \mathbb{D}^*)$ of dimension 6 is chosen randomly. The elements of $\mathbb{D}$ is denoted by $\boldsymbol{d}_1, \dots, \boldsymbol{d}_6$, and the elements of $\mathbb{D}^*$ is denoted by $\boldsymbol{d}_1^*, \dots, \boldsymbol{d}_6^*$. What's more, $\boldsymbol{d}_i \cdot \boldsymbol{d}_i^* = \psi$, for $i = 1, \dots, 6$. It also chooses two random values $\alpha_1, \alpha_2 \in \mathbb{Z}_p$. It publishes the public parameters:

$$PP := \{\mathbf{G}, p, e(g,g)^{\alpha_1 \psi}, e(g,g)^{\alpha_2 \psi}, g^{\boldsymbol{d}_1}, \dots, g^{\boldsymbol{d}_4}\},$$

and keeps the master secret key:

$$MSK := \{g^{\alpha_1 \boldsymbol{d}_1^*}, g^{\alpha_2 \boldsymbol{d}_3^*}, g^{\boldsymbol{d}_1^*}, \dots, g^{\boldsymbol{d}_4^*}\}.$$

KeyGen$(MSK, ID) \to SK_{ID}$. This algorithm picks random values $r_1, r_2 \in \mathbb{Z}_p$, and computes:

$$SK_{ID} := g^{(\alpha_1 + r_1 ID)\boldsymbol{d}_1^* - r_1 \boldsymbol{d}_2^* + (\alpha_2 + r_2 ID)\boldsymbol{d}_3^* - r_2 \boldsymbol{d}_4^*}.$$

Encrypt$(PP, ID, M) \to CT$. This algorithm picks up two random values $s_1, s_2 \in \mathbb{Z}_p$, and computes as follows:

$$CT := \{C_0 := M \cdot e(g,g)^{\alpha_1 s_1 \psi + \alpha_2 s_2 \psi}, \quad C_1 := g^{s_1 \boldsymbol{d}_1 + s_1 ID \boldsymbol{d}_2 + s_2 \boldsymbol{d}_3 + s_2 ID \boldsymbol{d}_4}\}.$$

Decrypt$(CT, SK_{ID}) \to M$. This algorithm is executed as follows:

$$M := C_0 / e(C_1, SK_{ID}).$$

3.2 Correctness

Observe that

$$e(C_1, SK_{ID}) = e(g,g)^{s_1(\alpha_1 + r_1 ID)\psi - r_1 s_1 ID\psi + s_2(\alpha_2 + r_2 ID)\psi - r_2 s_2 ID\psi}$$
$$= e(g,g)^{\alpha_1 s_1 \psi + \alpha_2 s_2 \psi},$$

Thus,

$$C_0/e(C_1, SK_{ID}) = M \cdot e(g,g)^{\alpha_1 s_1 \psi + \alpha_2 s_2 \psi}/e(g,g)^{\alpha_1 s_1 \psi + \alpha_2 s_2 \psi} = M.$$

3.3 Proof of Security

Theorem 1. *The IBE scheme can be proven fully secure based on the three party Diffie-Hellman and decisional linear assumption. Or rather, for any PPT adversary $\mathcal{A}$, there exist a PPT algorithm $\mathcal{B}$ with the same running time, such that*

$$Adv_{\mathcal{A}}^{IBE}(\lambda) \le (q_1 + 4)Adv_{\mathcal{B}}^{DLin}(\lambda) + Adv_{\mathcal{B}}^{3DH}(\lambda) + q_1/p,$$

where q_1 is the number of quereies in phase 1.

We describe our semi-functional algorithms as follows.

EncryptSF. There are two forms of semi-functional ciphertext. Type-1 semi-functional ciphertext can be generated as follows. The algorithm picks random values $s_1, s_2, s_3 \in \mathbb{Z}_p$. Then:

$$C_0 := M \cdot e(g,g)^{\alpha_1 s_1 \psi + \alpha_2 s_2 \psi}, \quad C_1 := g^{s_1 d_1 + s_1 ID d_2 + s_2 d_3 + s_2 ID d_4 + s_3 d_5 + s_3 ID d_6}.$$

A semi-functional ciphertext of type-2 is as same as type-1 except that the coefficients of d_5, d_6 are two random values. The algorithm picks $s_1, s_2, z_5, z_6 \in \mathbb{Z}_p$ randomly. Then:

$$C_0 := M \cdot e(g,g)^{\alpha_1 s_1 \psi + \alpha_2 s_2 \psi}, \quad C_1 := g^{s_1 d_1 + s_1 ID d_2 + s_2 d_3 + s_2 ID d_4 + z_5 d_5 + z_6 d_6}.$$

KeyGenSF. There are two types of semi-functional keys. Type-1 semi-functional key can be generated as follows. The algorithm picks random values $r_1, r_2, r_3 \in \mathbb{Z}_p$. Then:

$$SK_{ID} := g^{(\alpha_1 + r_1 ID)d_1^* - r_1 d_2^* + (\alpha_2 + r_2 ID)d_3^* - r_2 d_4^* + r_3 ID d_5^* - r_3 d_6^*}.$$

A semi-functional key of type-2 is as same as type-1 except that the coefficients of d_5^*, d_6^* are two random values. The algorithm picks $r_1, r_2, r_5, r_6 \in \mathbb{Z}_p$ randomly. Then:

$$SK_{ID} := g^{(\alpha_1 + r_1 ID)d_1^* - r_1 d_2^* + (\alpha_2 + r_2 ID)d_3^* - r_2 d_4^* + r_5 d_5^* + r_6 d_6^*}.$$

Game Sequenco. We let $Adv_{\mathcal{A}}^{Game_X}$ denote an adversary $\mathcal{A}'s$ advantage in $Game_X$.

- $\mathsf{Game_{Real}}$: the real security game.
- $\mathsf{Game_0}$: there is no difference the with $\mathsf{Game_{Real}}$ except that challenge ciphertext becomes type-1 semi-functional ciphertext.
- $\mathsf{Game_1}$: there is no difference the with $\mathsf{Game_0}$ except that the challenge ciphertext becomes type-2 semi-functional ciphertext.
- $\mathsf{Game_{2,i}}$ for $i = 0,\dots,q_1$: there is no difference the with $\mathsf{Game_1}$ except that the first i keys become type-2 semi-functional keys. We let $\mathsf{Game_{2,0}}$ denote $\mathsf{Game_1}$, and $\mathsf{Game_{2,q_1}}$ denote $\mathsf{Game_2}$.
- $\mathsf{Game_3}$: there is no difference the with $\mathsf{Game_2}$ except that the challenge ciphertext becomes type-1 semi-functional ciphertext.
- $\mathsf{Game_4}$: there is no difference the with $\mathsf{Game_3}$ except that the last q_2 keys are all type-1 semi-functional keys.
- $\mathsf{Game_5}$: there is no difference the with $\mathsf{Game_4}$ except that the last q_2 keys are all type-2 semi-functional keys.
- $\mathsf{Game_{Final}}$: there is no difference the with $\mathsf{Game_5}$ except that we encrypt a random message $M' \in \mathbf{G}_T$ as the challenge ciphertext.

From $\mathsf{Game_1}$ to $\mathsf{Game_{2,q_1}}$, we convert the first q_1 keys from normal to semi-functional type-2 one after another, which requires $\mathcal{O}(q_1)$ steps. However, as to the last q_2 keys, we can modify them from semi-functional type-1 to type-2 all at once. Hence, we can get a tighter reduction, $\mathcal{O}(q_1)$.

Theorem 1 is accomplished in the following lemmas.

Lemma 3. *Suppose that there is an adversary $\mathcal{A}$ can break our scheme in polynomial-time, then we can construct an algorithm $\mathcal{B}$ with the same running time, to break the subspace assumption with $k = 2, n = 6$.*

Lemma 4. *For any adversary $\mathcal{A}$, $Adv_{\mathcal{A}}^{Game_0}(\lambda) = Adv_{\mathcal{A}}^{Game_1}(\lambda)$.*

Lemma 5. *Suppose that there is an adversary $\mathcal{A}$ can break our scheme in polynomial-time, then we can construct an algorithm $\mathcal{B}$ with the same running time, to break the subspace assumption with $k = 2, n = 6$.*

Lemma 6. *For any adversary $\mathcal{A}$, $Adv_{\mathcal{A}}^{Game_2}(\lambda) = Adv_{\mathcal{A}}^{Game_3}(\lambda)$.*

Lemma 7. *Suppose that there is an adversary $\mathcal{A}$ can break our scheme in polynomial-time, then we can construct an algorithm $\mathcal{B}$ with the same running time, to break the subspace assumption with $k = 2, n = 6$.*

Lemma 8. *Suppose that there is an adversary $\mathcal{A}$ can break our scheme in polynomial-time, then we can construct an algorithm $\mathcal{B}$ with the same running time, to break the three party Diffie-Hellman assumption.*

Lemma 9. *Suppose that there is an adversary $\mathcal{A}$ can break our scheme in polynomial-time, then we can construct an algorithm $\mathcal{B}$ with the same running time, to break the subspace assumption with $k = 2, n = 6$.*

The proofs of Lemmas 3–9 are given in full version.

4 Conclusions

We have presented a fully secure IBE with tighter security in prime order bilinear groups. The full security of our scheme has been proven under DLIN and 3-DH assumption by extending dual system encryption over dual pairing vector space. We used the technique of delayed parameters to achieve the tighter reduction. What's more, it would be interesting to apply this technique to obtain more advanced functional encryption [18] such as inner product encryption [19].

Acknowledgment. The authors would like to thank the anonymous reviewers for their critical suggestions that greatly improved the quality of this paper. This work is supported by the National Natural Science Foundation of China (No. 61379150, 61309016, 61502529).

References

1. Shamir, A.: Identity-based cryptosystems and signature schemes. In: Blakely, G.R., Chaum, D. (eds.) CRYPTO 1984. LNCS, vol. 196, pp. 47–53. Springer, Heidelberg (1985)
2. Boneh, D., Franklin, M.: Identity-based encryption from the weil pairing. In: Kilian, J. (ed.) CRYPTO 2001. LNCS, vol. 2139, p. 213. Springer, Heidelberg (2001)
3. Boneh, D., Boyen, X.: Efficient selective-id secure identity-based encryption without random oracles. In: Cachin, C., Camenisch, J.L. (eds.) EUROCRYPT 2004. LNCS, vol. 3027, pp. 223–238. Springer, Heidelberg (2004)
4. Canetti, R., Halevi, S., Katz, J.: A forward-secure public-key encryption scheme. J. Cryptology **20**(3), 265–294 (2007)
5. Waters, B.: Dual system encryption: realizing fully secure IBE and HIBE under simple assumptions. In: Halevi, S. (ed.) CRYPTO 2009. LNCS, vol. 5677, pp. 619–636. Springer, Heidelberg (2009)
6. Waters, B.: Efficient identity-based encryption without random oracles. In: Cramer, R. (ed.) EUROCRYPT 2005. LNCS, vol. 3494, pp. 114–127. Springer, Heidelberg (2005)
7. Chen, J., Wee, H.: Fully, (almost) tightly secure ibe and dual system groups. In: Canetti, R., Garay, J.A. (eds.) CRYPTO 2013, Part II. LNCS, vol. 8043, pp. 435–460. Springer, Heidelberg (2013)
8. Attrapadung, N.: Dual system encryption via doubly selective security: framework, fully secure functional encryption for regular languages, and more. In: Nguyen, P.Q., Oswald, E. (eds.) EUROCRYPT 2014. LNCS, vol. 8441, pp. 557–577. Springer, Heidelberg (2014)
9. Lewko, A., Waters, B.: New proof methods for attribute-based encryption: achieving full security through selective techniques. In: Safavi-Naini, R., Canetti, R. (eds.) CRYPTO 2012. LNCS, vol. 7417, pp. 180–198. Springer, Heidelberg (2012)
10. Aranha, D.F., Beuchat, J.-L., Detrey, J., Estibals, N.: Optimal eta pairing on supersingular genus-2 binary hyperelliptic curves. In: Dunkelman, O. (ed.) CT-RSA 2012. LNCS, vol. 7178, pp. 98–115. Springer, Heidelberg (2012)
11. Aranha, D.F., Karabina, K., Longa, P., Gebotys, C.H., López, J.: Faster explicit formulas for computing pairings over ordinary curves. In: Paterson, K.G. (ed.) EUROCRYPT 2011. LNCS, vol. 6632, pp. 48–68. Springer, Heidelberg (2011)

12. Joux, A.: Faster index calculus for the medium prime case application to 1175-bit and 1425-bit finite fields. In: Johansson, T., Nguyen, P.Q. (eds.) EUROCRYPT 2013. LNCS, vol. 7881, pp. 177–193. Springer, Heidelberg (2013)
13. Adj, G., Menezes, A., Oliveira, T., Rodríguez-Henríquez, F.: Weakness of $\mathbb{F}_{3^{6 \cdot 509}}$ for discrete logarithm cryptography. In: Cao, Z., Zhang, F. (eds.) Pairing 2013. LNCS, vol. 8365, pp. 20–44. Springer, Heidelberg (2014)
14. Freeman, D.M.: Converting pairing-based cryptosystems from composite-order groups to prime-order groups. In: Gilbert, H. (ed.) EUROCRYPT 2010. LNCS, vol. 6110, pp. 44–61. Springer, Heidelberg (2010)
15. Lewko, A.: Tools for simulating features of composite order bilinear groups in the prime order setting. In: Pointcheval, D., Johansson, T. (eds.) EUROCRYPT 2012. LNCS, vol. 7237, pp. 318–335. Springer, Heidelberg (2012)
16. Okamoto, T., Takashima, K.: Hierarchical predicate encryption for inner-products. In: Matsui, M. (ed.) ASIACRYPT 2009. LNCS, vol. 5912, pp. 214–231. Springer, Heidelberg (2009)
17. Lewko, A., Okamoto, T., Sahai, A., Takashima, K., Waters, B.: Fully secure functional encryption: attribute-based encryption and (hierarchical) inner product encryption. In: Gilbert, H. (ed.) EUROCRYPT 2010. LNCS, vol. 6110, pp. 62–91. Springer, Heidelberg (2010)
18. Boneh, D., Sahai, A., Waters, B.: Functional encryption: definitions and challenges. In: Ishai, Y. (ed.) TCC 2011. LNCS, vol. 6597, pp. 253–273. Springer, Heidelberg (2011)
19. Katz, J., Sahai, A., Waters, B.: Predicate encryption supporting disjunctions, polynomial equations, and inner products. In: Smart, N.P. (ed.) EUROCRYPT 2008. LNCS, vol. 4965, pp. 146–162. Springer, Heidelberg (2008)

A Secure Route Optimization Mechanism for Expressive Internet Architecture (XIA) Mobility

Hongwei Meng[1]([✉]), Zhong Chen[1], Ziqian Meng[1], and Chuck Song[2]

[1] School of Electronics Engineering and Computer Science,
Key Laboratory of High Confidence Software
Technologies Ministry of Education, MoE Key Laboratory of Network and
Software Security Assurance, Peking University, Beijing, China
{menghw, zhongchen, markmzq}@pku.edu.cn
[2] Carnegie Mellon University, Pittsburgh, USA
csong@cmu.edu

Abstract. Motivated by the natural features of ID/location decoupling and self-certifying in Expressive Internet Architecture (XIA), we designs a secure mechanism to protect the binding update message for route optimization in XIA mobility. The proposed mechanism protects the vulnerabilities by combining identity authentication and reachability verification. Meanwhile, in order to reduce the signaling overhead in the following movement of the mobile node, we divide the routing optimization procedure into two phases and replace the public-key cryptography with hashing operation to authenticate the subsequent binding update messages. The analysis shows that our protocol is efficient, especially for nodes that move frequently and the movement can be predicted.

Keywords: Future internet architecture · Expressive internet architecture · Mobility · Route optimization · Binding update · Self-certifying

1 Introduction

Mobility support at the network layer enables a mobile node (MN) move from one network to another still maintaining existing connections to its correspondent nodes (CNs). This is a vital feature for any networking protocol given the dramatic increase in the number of portable devices requiring mobile Internet access [1, 2]. Mobile IPv4 and Mobile IPv6 are designed to provide mobility support on top of the existing IP infrastructure [3, 4]. The advantage of Mobile IPv6 over Mobile IPv4 is that data packets can be directly forwarded between the mobile node and its correspondent nodes. This mode is called route optimization (RO). Route optimization provides mobile node the opportunity to eliminate inefficient triangle routing and bidirectional tunneling with its home agent (HA). Route optimization is only permitted after a binding update (BU) message has been sent from the MN to the CN. In a BU message, MN informs the CN of its new address, thereby allows CN to send subsequent packets directly to MN. However, an unauthenticated or malicious binding update message would provide an intruder with an easy means to launch various types of attacks [5, 6].

S. Qing et al. (Eds.): ICICS 2015, LNCS 9543, pp. 269–281, 2016.
DOI: 10.1007/978-3-319-29814-6_22

Therefore, authenticating BU messages is vital for the security of route optimization. Mobile IPv6 uses an authentication mechanism called return routability (RR) to protect the binding update messages. However, it is generally considered that authentication via routing property is a weak mechanism. Because the RR mechanism that is only to verify the MN reachability in both its home address and care-of address without being a security feature. Other works have attempted to solve the security issues in RR, using the Cryptographically Generated Address (CGA) based authentication, such as the CAM [7, 8], CAM-DM [9], CGA-OMIPv6 [10], ERO [11], and CBU [12]. But the drawback is that the CGA based authentication needs the added information transmission, such as the public key and the auxiliary parameters, to verify the ownership of a given address, and also needs the help of home agent taking part into the proof procedure, which is not efficient and somewhat computationally expensive. In fact, IP network couples the host identity and network locator in one IP address which is naturally shortcomings that may not support mobility well [2].

Integrating the mobility and security is becoming a key feature of future Internet, which demands a rework on the Internet essentially designed about 40 years ago with no vast mobility and security support in architectural consideration [19]. Our work is driven by the desire for both security and mobility as architectural underpinnings, to design a secure route optimization scheme support for XIA mobility. XIA is a novel clean-slate architecture based on new designs expected to meet the emerging demands for security, mobility, content distribution and evolving challenges of current Internet [14]. XIA is one of the three projects founded by NSF FIA and FIA Next-Phase programs since 2010 and 2014 respectively [15] (The others are NDN and MobilityFirst). In XIA, new narrow waist can be introduced to enable the network evolvable. Hashing of the public key as the self-certifying identity achieves end-to-end authentication. Directed Acyclic Graphs (DAGs) are used as the routable addresses to improve the routing scalability and content distribution efficiency. Up to now, how to support mobility as well as the route optimization in a secure manner in XIA is not straightforward yet.

In this paper we explore the nature features of XIA and propose a binding update protocol with high security strength support for XIA route optimization. Our protocol makes use of self-certifying identity-based strong authentication technique, and also by taking advantage of early key exchange, the proposed protocol is highly secure and efficient. The rest of the paper is organized as follows: Section 2 gives an overview of XIA, as well as the general mobility support method, and points out the requirements of routing optimization. Section 3 is devoted to our new protocol. Section 4 analyzes the security and efficiency of the proposed protocol. Section 5 is our conclusion.

2   Background and Requirement

2.1   XIA Overview

XIA is novel future Internet architecture with native support for network evolvement by enabling introduces new type of principal [16–18]. Principal can be defined as a type of narrow waist, such as network domain (or autonomous domain), host, service and content. Each principle type is identified with 160bit XIA identifier (XID), including network ID (NID), host ID (HID), service ID (SID) and content ID (CID). NID, HID and SID are hash of the public key of network domain, host and service respectively, while CID is the hash of the content. NID specifies a network address supports global addressing, HID supports unicast host-based communication, SID supports communication with service instance and achieves anycast forwarding, CID allows to retrieve content from anywhere in the network. Combining these XIDs, the address of a host is represented with Directed Acyclic Graph (DAG), and routing is realized via DAG in XIA.

DAGs are highly flexible and allow packets to express intent as well as scoping to realize forwarding. The simplest DAG of a host has only a dummy source ● and the intent as the sink, e.g., a HID in Fig. 1(a). The dummy source represents the conceptual source with no specific meaning. In order to improve the routing scalability in the public Internet, DAG can also be used to implement scoping, as shown in Fig. 1(b). Routers inspect the network address NID until the packet reached the destination network. Upon reaching the destination network identified with NID, routers forward the packet using only HID. This is similar to the IP forwarding, which supporting for the scoping by *network_portion* and *host_portion* of IP addresses. Figure 1(c) is a DAG with fallback path, shown as a dotted line, which pointing to an extra node N. If the HID is unreachable directly, the fallback is used by a router to forward packet to node N. The solid edge has the higher priority than dotted ones (fallback) in DAGs.

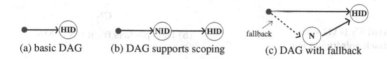

| (a) basic DAG | (b) DAG supports scoping | (c) DAG with fallback |

Fig. 1. DAGs example of a host in XIA

2.2 Mobility Support in XIA

Mobility means that a mobile node moves from one location in the network to another, or its network attachment point changes. In XIA, this implies a change of NID in the MN's DAG. Figure 2 shows MN's DAG before and after moving. Originally, MN locates in NID_1, and its DAG is expressed as $NID_1 \rightarrow HID$. When roaming to another subnet NID_2, MN's DAG becomes $NID_2 \rightarrow HID$. Obviously, after moving to another network, the mobile is no longer reachable at its old location for existing connections.

To solve this, a fallback path pointing to a rendezvous agent (RA) can be added in MN's DAG, which is shown in Fig. 3(a). This means that packets destined to MN will be forwarded to RA first while the router finds no direct routing to MN. RA maintains the current location information of MN, and is responsible for redirecting packets to MN. At the beginning, MN registers its original location (such as NID_1) to RA. When moving to another place, MN informs RA about its new location (such as NID_2) to update RA's binding cache entry (BCE). After that, packets destined to MN's old place

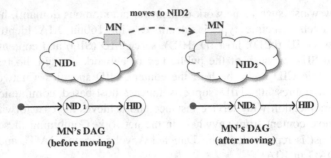

Fig. 2. MN's DAG before and after moving

will be forwarded to RA according to the fallback. While packets arrive via the fallback, RA directs them to MN's latest place according to the corresponding BCE of MN. The traffic flow from CN to MN is shown in Fig. 3(b).

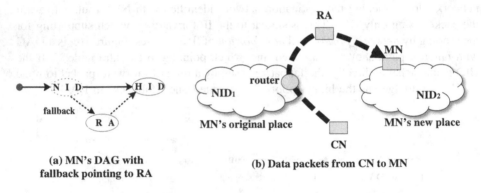

(a) MN's DAG with
fallback pointing to RA

(b) Data packets from CN to MN

Fig. 3. Mobility support with RA

Actually, RA can be seen as a mobile anchor of MN, and plays a role similar to the home agent for MN in Mobile IP. RA also enables solve the double-jump problem, in which two end-points move at the same time. However, there are two important differences. Firstly, unlike Mobile IP where home agent has to be located in a mobile node's home network, RA is not required to share the same NID with MN, and its location can be selected based on considerations of security, bandwidth, disaster recovery, etc., as long as the RA is not itself mobile or inside a mobile network. Secondly, RA directs packets to MN by updating destination DAG's NID in the header. No header in header (or DAG in DAG) and no tunnels are used, unlike IP where IPSec tunnel existing between the home agent and MN's care-of-address.

2.3 Requirements of Security in Route Optimization

Although rendezvous agent in XIA can assure the reachability of packets destined to MN, this will cause the triangle routing problem. A mobile node may notify the new

DAG to its correspondent nodes while moving from one place another, so that sub-sequent packets will be route-optimized and no longer be routed through the mobile node's rendezvous agent. This is called routing optimization. The primary reason for route optimization is to avoid routing all traffic through a rendezvous agent after mobile node moves. Route optimization is achieved by sending binding updates to CNs as soon as mobile node has moved to a new location. However, an unauthenticated or malicious binding update message would provide an intruder with an easy means to launch various types of attack, such as spoofing, man-in-the-middle, connection hijacking, reflection attacks, etc. [5, 6].

In XIA, HID is cryptographically generated, which is hash of host's public key. Such feature allows the mobile node to provide a proof of ownership of its identity and to sign important messages with its private key. XIA's self-certifying property assures the correctness of the mobile node's identity, which makes the spoofing or man-in-the-middle attack against the mobile node much harder. But, it does little to ensure that the mobile node is actually reachable at that network part of the address. A malicious or compromised node could be lying about its own location, which opens the door for attackers to redirect traffic intended to the mobile node to a location of its choice. Attackers can flood a victim with unwanted packets by using the location update to redirect a data stream towards it. If used in combination with distributed correspondent nodes, extra traffic will be burst toward the victim. The victim will suffer terrible distributed denial-of-service (DDoS) attack, which is shown in Fig. 4(a).

Moreover, since public key cryptosystem operations are computationally intensive [10, 11, 13]. A correspondent node communicates with a large number of mobile nodes, such as publicly accessible server, or a correspondent node with constraint computational power, such as smart phone or wearable device, might easily suffer denial-of-service attacks which caused by extra resources consumption on the signature verification of a great number of BU message, which is shown in Fig. 4(b).

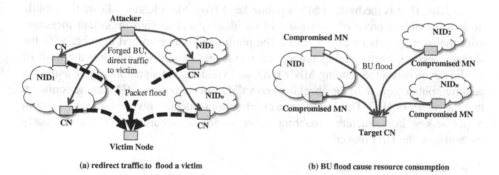

(a) redirect traffic to flood a victim   (b) BU flood cause resource consumption

Fig. 4. Threats in route optimization

For above, we figure out that the main functional requirement for routing opti-mization in XIA is that the mobile node is able to update the correspondent node with its current location. From a security perspective, attackers should not be able to redirect communication flows of legitimate mobile node to themselves or third parties, and attackers should not be able to cause denial-of-service through the potentially expensive computations involved in the route optimization protocol itself.

3 Route Optimization Protocol for XIA Mobility

3.1 Cryptographic Notation

We list below the cryptographic notation used throughout the paper.

$H(m)$: hash of message m

$prf(k, m)$: hash function computing on message m with key k and generates a message authentication code.

$KU_{MN}(m)/KR_{MN}$: public and private key pair of mobile node MN.

$Sig_{MN}(m)$: MN's digital signature on a message m.

$m|n$: concatenation of two messages m and n.

Diffie-Hellman parameters: Let p and g be the public Diffie-Hellman parameters, where p is a large prime and g is a generator of the multiplicative group. To keep our notation compact, we will write g^x mod p simply as g^x. We assume that the values of p and g are agreed upon beforehand by all the parties concerned [12].

3.2 Protocol Design

Basically, the binding update in routing optimization requires the correspondent node to verify the mobile node's ownership of both the identity and the current location. Our protocol employs public key cryptosystems to provide strong security, while keep the reduction of the signaling overhead and the handoff delay in case of MN moves often. The design rationale of the protocol contains following aspects.

1. Identity authentication

In XIA, HID is the hash of MN's public keyKU_{MN}. Such feature allows the mobile node to provide a proof of ownership of its identity and to sign important messages with the owner's private key. Usually, the public key is transmitted together with the signed message. On receiving the signed message, CN verifies whether the hash of public key matches the sending MN's HID, and validates the signature Sig_{MN} using the acquired public key. If all the checking and validation are positive, CN can be confident that the owner of HID. This facilitates a cryptographic identity ownership proof without a public-key infrastructure, enabling other nodes to securely and autonomously authenticate the HID owner.

2. Reachability verification

HID authentication is unable to guarantee that a particular address is actually reachable at a given NID. Reachability verification is for this purpose to prove the reachability of MN at a given location.

3. Two phases exchanges and shared session key authentication

Self-certifying based authentication involves public-key cryptography and is computationally much less efficient than authentication through a shared secret key

[13]. In order to reduce the signaling overhead in the subsequent movements, we divide the routing optimization into two phases. In the first phase, the mobile node uses its private signature key to sign a Diffie-Hellman exponent which is then used to negotiate an initial shared secret key with the correspondent node [10]. This will executes only once. In the second phase, a more effective hashing operation other than asymmetric cryptographic operation is used to form a shared session key K_{BU}, which later used to authenticate the binding update. Authentication using the session key K_{BU} is more efficient in subsequent binding update while MN moves frequently.

3.3 Protocol Operation

The messages exchanged between MN and its correspondent node CN are shown in Fig. 5. The protocol is divided into two separate phases: initial key exchange and subsequent binding update. We show later that the subsequent binding update is much more efficient than the initial key exchange.

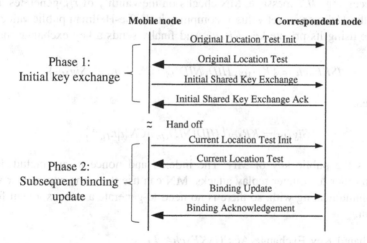

Fig. 5. Message exchange of route optimization in XIA

Phase 1: Initial key exchange.

1. Original Location Test Init (*OLTInit*)

   When sets up communication connection with a correspondent node for the first time, mobile node sends an initial location test request

$$OLTInit = \{HID, NID_{Orig}, CN, r_O\}$$

to correspondent node, and informs the correspondent node both the *HID* and its current NID_{orig}. In this message, *CN* represents the correspondent node's DAG, r_O is a random value used to match the reply message.

2. Original Location Test (*OLT*)

When CN receives *OLTInit* message, it takes the *HID* and NID_{org} of MN as input and generates an original cookie

$$C_O = prf\left(k_{CN}, HID|NID_{Orig}|N_i\right)$$

and replies MN with

$$OLT = \{CN, HID, NID_{Orig}, r_O, C_O, i\}.$$

Each correspondent node has a secret key k_{CN} which does not shared with any other entity. The index i is carried along to allow CN later efficiently finding the nonce value N_i that it used in creating original cookie C_O. This message is used to ensure that the mobile node is reachable at its claimed original address NID_{org}, and is also used for cookies validation before performing computationally expensive public key operation in the following steps.

3. Initial Shared Key Exchange (*ISKExch*)

After receiving *OLT* message, MN checks on the validity of r_O, generates a nonce n_I and a Diffie-Hellman secret value x, computes its Diffie-Hellman public value g^x and its signature using its private key KR_{MN}. And finally sends a key exchange message

$$ISKExch = \left\{KU_{MN}, HID, NID_{Orig}, CN, i, n_I, g^x, Sig_{MN}\right\}$$

to CN, where

$$Sig_{MN} = KR_{MN}\left\{HID|NID_{Orig}|CN|i|n_I|g^x\right\}.$$

KU_{MN} is the public key of MN. The index i and nonce n_I are included in the signature in order to counter replay attacks. MN can use the same exponent x with all CN it is communicating with, so there is no need to generate a new exponent for each protocol run.

4. Initial Shared Key Exchange Ack (*ISKExchAck*)

When CN receives *ISKExch*, it checks the equality of the public key's hash with *HID*, and validates the signature Sig_{MN} using the acquired public key KU_{MN}. If all the checking and validation are positive, CN can be confident that the owner of *HID* and the initial location is authorized and the Diffie-Hellman value g^x is freshly generated by MN. CN next generate its Diffie-Hellman secret value y, its public value g^y, and get the Diffie-Hellman *key* $K_{DH} = g^{xy}$. Then, CN computes the initial shared secret key

$$k_S = prf(k_{DH}, N_i|n_I)$$

and a MAC

$$MAC_S = prf\left(k_S, CN|HID|NID_{Orig}|i|n_I|g^y\right),$$

and sends

$$ISKExchAck = \{CN, HID, NID_{Orig}, i, n_I, g^y, MAC_S)$$

to MN.

The *ISKExchAck* message is received by MN, which first validates the cookies, calculate the Diffie-Hellman public value g^{xy}, and the initial shared secret key $k_S = prf$ (k_{DH}, $N_i|n_I$). The validation of MAC_S is checked by MN and if it is valid, MN creates and stores the initial shared secret key k_S.

As a result of the above initial procedure, the identity of MN has been authenticated and a security association with initial shared secret key k_S has been established in both nodes. The initial shared secret key k_S is used to provide the first part of the session key k_{BU} required in authenticating the subsequent binding update.

Phase 2: Subsequent binding update.

5. Current Location Test Init (*CLTInit*)
   When moving to another place, MN sends

$$CLTInit = \{HID, NID_{Curr}, CN, r_C\}$$

to CN, tells MN's *HID* and current NID_{Curr}. The random values r_C are used to match the responses.

6. Current Location Test (*CLT*)
   In reply, CN creates a nonce N_j and a current test cookie C_C, and sends

$$CLT = \{CN, HID, NID_{Curr}, r_C, C_C, j\}$$

to MN, where $C_C = prf\left(k_{CN}, HID|NID_{Curr}|N_j\right)$. The serial number j indicates CN later find which version of N_j was used to generate the cookie C_C. This message tests that the mobile node is reachable at its claimed current location NID_{Curr}. Moreover, this acknowledgement is used to provide the second part of the session key k_{BU} required in the following binding update message.

7. Binding Update (*BU*)
   When MN receives *CLT*, it hashes the current cookie C_C and initial shared secret key k_S together to form a session key

$$k_{BU} = H(k_S|C_C),$$

which is then used to authenticate the binding message. After obtaining the session key k_{BU}, MN sends the binding update message

$$BU = \{HID, NID_{Curr}, CN, N_{BU}, T_{BU}, j, MAC_{BU}\},$$

to CN, where N_{BU} is a sequence number, timestamp T_{BU} is the creation time of the binding used to detect replay attack, and

$$MAC_{BU} = prf\{k_{BU}, HID|NID_{Curr}|CN|N_{BU}|T_{BU}|j\}$$

is a message authentication code protected by the session key k_{BU}. MAC_{BU} is used to ensure that BU was sent by the same node which received the CLT message and maintained the initial shared secret key with CN. The message contains index j, so that CN knows which nonce value N_j to use to re-compute C_C and session key k_{BU}.

8. Binding Acknowledgment (BA)
   CN receives BU and verifies MAC_{BU}. If MAC_{BU} is verified positive, CN replies MN with a binding acknowledgment message

$$BA = \{CN, HID, NID_{Curr}, N_{BU}, T_{BU}, MAC_{BA}\},$$

where $MAC_{BA} = prf\{k_{BU}, CN|HID|NID_{curr}|N_{BU}|T_{BU}\}$ is a MAC generated using k_{BU} for BA authentication.

After the above-mentioned 8 steps completed, CN updates the binding cache entry for HID with NID_{Curr}, which allows future packets to be directly sent to MN's latest location NID_{Curr}. New procedure starts from step 5 if MN moves again.

4 Protocol Analysis

4.1 Security Analysis

In general, we authenticate identity of MN via self-certifying features, and verify reachability of MN via the routing property. It should be mentioned that while the public key cryptographic operations can provide a protection against unauthenticated signaling, it can expose the involved nodes to denial-of-service attacks since it is computationally expensive. The first two messages $OLTInit/OLT$ are needed in order to guard against resource consumption attacks. In $OLTInit/OLT$, cookies validation is added before performing computationally expensive public key cryptographic operations. The correspondent node will reject any $OLTInit$ message from MN not included in its cache entry. This ensures that at least some communication has taken place before this. The purpose of OLT acknowledgement is also to provide part of the initial shared secret key generates in the initial phase of our mechanism.

We limit the use of public key operation to only the initial key exchange process, in which mobile node and correspondent node are required to perform public key signature/verification only once, in $ISKExch$ and $ISKExchAck$ respectively. After receiving $ISKExch$, if the hash value $H(KU_{MN})$ matches the value of HID and if the signature verification using the public key KU_{MN} is positive, CN will authenticates the identity of MN. This check is critical to detect man-in-the-middle attack. The signature

$$Sig_{MN} = KR_{MN}\{HID|NID_{Orig}|CN|i|n_I|g^x\}$$

serves two purposes. First, it certifies that the Diffie-Hellman value g^x was created by MN, and second, it testifies that NID_{Orig} is a legitimate original address for mobile node.

Diffie-Hellman key exchange allows the two nodes to set up an initial shared secret key and to establish a security association for securing subsequent binding updates more efficient. This test does not need to be repeated upon subsequent movements. It is easy to show that the above protocol performs a strong one-way authentication of MN to CN and provides CN with the confidence that it shares a secret key with MN.

Phase one in our protocol assures the HID of MN is correct, but does little to ensure that the node is actually reachable at the new location. Thus, the *CLTInit/CLT* in phase two is necessary when MN moves to another place. Otherwise malicious mobile node flooding attacks could be launched against the victim. We employ the current test cookie C_C together with initial shared secret key k_S to form the session key $k_{BU} = H(k_S|C_C)$, which then used to authenticate the binding update message. The sequence number and timestamp in all binding updates in the subsequent phase is used to secure against replay and flooding attacks. The mobile node increases this value every time it sends a new message to the correspondent node. The two endpoints will discard any binding messages which not signed with the k_{BU}, correct sequence number and timestamp.

4.2 Efficiency Analysis

Besides the strong security, we concentrate on making the route optimization signaling as efficient as possible. An initial key exchange is performed at first contact between MN and CN. We propose use an initial self-certifying based authentication and Diffie-Hellman key exchange to dynamically create an initial shared secret key. This process may somewhat inefficient. If MN moves to other locations in the future, we use a shared session key to authenticate future BUs to reduce the signal overhead and handoff latency. It is clear that for the cases gain any performance enhancement, the initial key exchange must have completed before movement. Otherwise the delay waiting for public key computations would be long.

For a mobile node moving fast, there is a significant overall reduction of resource consumption, as the public-key cryptographic operations is executed only once at the beginning. Authentication through a shared session key required for every movement is much more efficient than the public-key cryptography.

It is the fact that our protocol is not benefit for the nodes which rarely move. But it is benefit for nodes whose movement can be predicted, such as virtual machine (VM) live migration. Different from devices mobility, VM migration is a specific case, in which the target location and the time migration happens are predictable. The exact time of VM migration can be obtained from the migration instructions by the hypervisor. This gives an opportunity to complete the initial key exchange action in advanced, which will reduce the handoff latency after VM resumes at the target location.

5   Conclusion

The experiences from the future Internet architecture design process highlight the need to consider early the solution of potential security threats created by new technology, such as route optimization in XIA mobility. Although route optimization adds an important means to replace the inefficient triangle routing by allowing an MN to communicate directly with the CN without passing through the rendezvous agent, it provides intruders with an easy way to launch various types of attacks. In this paper, we describe a mechanism to exploit the ID/location decoupling and self-certifying features to authenticate route optimization signaling in XIA. The proposed mechanism protects the vulnerabilities by a combination of identity authentication and reachability verification. In order to minimize the number of computation-expensive operations during every movement, we divide the routing optimization authentication process into two phases. In the first phase, mobile node negotiates an initial shared secret key with the correspondent node using its signature and Diffie-Hellman key exchange, which is executed only once. In the second phase, a more effective hashing operation other than asymmetric cryptographic operation is used to authenticate the future binding update message. The analysis shows that our protocol is efficient, especially in cases that the moving behaviors are frequent or can be predicted in advance.

References

1. Cisco Visual Networking Index: Global Mobile Data Traffic Forecast Update, 2011–2016
2. Zhu, Z., Wakikawa, R., Zhang, L.: A survey of mobility support in the internet, RFC 6301, July, 2011
3. Perkins, C.: IP mobility support for IPv4, RFC 3344 (2002)
4. Johnson, D., Perkins, C., Arkko, J.: Mobility support in IPv6, RFC 3775 (2004)
5. Aura, T., Roe, M.: Designing the mobile IPv6 security protocol. Ann. Telecommun. **61**(3–4), 332–356 (2006)
6. Mankin, A., Patil, B., Harkins, D. et al.: Threat models introduced by mobile IPv6 and requirements for security in mobile IPv6 draft-ietf-mobile-ip-mipv6-scrty-reqts-02, Expired IETF Internet draft, November 2001
7. Shea, G., Roe, M.: Child-Proof Authentication for MIPv6 (CAM), Computer Communications Review, April 2001
8. Aura, T.: Cryptographically Generated Addresses (CGA) RFC 3972, March 2005
9. Roe, M., Aura, T., OShea, G., Arkko, J.: Authentication of Mobile IPv6 Binding Updates and Acknowledgments, draftroe-mobileip-updateauth-02.txt, Expired IETF Intenet draft (2002)
10. Haddad, W., Madour, L., Arkko, J., Dupont, F.: Applying Cryptographically Generated Addresses to Optimize MIPv6 (CGAOMIPv6), draft-haddad-mip6-cga-omipv6-03, Expired IETF Internet draft (2004)
11. Arkko, J., Vogt, C., Haddad, W.: Enhanced Route Optimization for Mobile IPv6, RFC 4866 (2007)
12. Deng, R., Zhou, J., Bao, F.: Defending against redirect attacks in mobile IP. In: Proceedings of the of 9th ACM Conference on Computer and Communications Security (CCS), Washington, pp. 59–67 (2002)

13. Kuang, S., Elz, R., Kamolphiwong, S.: Investigating enhanced route optimization for mobile IPv6. In: 13th Asia-Pacific on Computer Systems Architecture Conference(ACSAC 2008), Hsinchu (2008)
14. XIA Project (2013). http://www.cs.cmu.edu/~xia/
15. NSF Future Internet Architecture Project Next Phase (2014). http://www.nets-fia.net/
16. Naylor, D., Mukerjee, M.K., et al.: XIA: architecting a more trustworthy and evolvable internet. ACM SIGCOMM Comput. Commun. **44**(3), 50–57 (2014)
17. Han, D., Anand, A. et al.: XIA: Efficient Support for Evolvable Internetworking. In: The 9th USENIX Symposium on Networked Systems Design and Implementation (NSDI 2012), San Jose, 25–27 April 2012
18. Anand, A., Dogar, F., Han, D. et al.: XIA: an architecture for an evolvable and trustworthy internet. In: Tenth ACM Workshop on Hot Topics in Networks (HotNets-X), Cambridge, November, 2011
19. Pan, J., Paul, S., Jain, R.: A survey of the research on future internet architectures. IEEE Communications Magazine, July 2011

An Entropy Based Encrypted Traffic Classifier

Mohammad Saiful Islam Mamun$^{(\boxtimes)}$, Ali A. Ghorbani,
and Natalia Stakhanova

Information Security Centre of Excellence (ISCX),
University of New Brunswick, Fredericton, NB, Canada
msi.mamun@unb.ca, ghorbani@unb.ca, natalia.stakhanova@unb.ca

Abstract. This paper proposes an approach of encrypted network traffic classification based on entropy calculation and machine learning technique. Apart from using ordinary Shannon's entropy, we examine entropy after encoding and a weighted average of Shannon binary entropy called BiEntropy. The objective of this paper is to identify any application flows as part of encrypted traffic. To achieve this we (i) calculate entropy-based features from the packet payload: encoded payload or binary payload, *n-length* word of the payload, (ii) employ a Genetic-search feature selection algorithm on the extracted features where fitness function is calculated from True Positive Rate, False Positive Rate and number of selected features, and (iii) propose a data driven supervised machine learning model from Support Vector Machine (SVM) for automatic identification of encrypted traffic. To the best of our knowledge, this is the first attempt to tackle the problem of classifying encrypted traffic using extensive entropy-based features and machine learning techniques.

Keywords: Traffic classification · Entropy · Encoding

1 Introduction

Today's Internet is evolving in scope and complexity. Internet applications adapt rapidly to changing situations. Emerging proprietary protocols (e.g. Skype) serve as obfuscation to bypass network filters, firewalls and NAT restrictions. All these developments significantly obstruct efforts in network analysis and monitoring. Understanding network traffic content (e.g., intrusion detection purposes) becomes increasingly difficult task. Mostly because it requires requires an understanding of network traffic nature or characteristics that can associate traffic flows with the application types. The research studies show that existing traffic classification methods are plagued with problems [1]. Among them the lack of accuracy in classification and unavailability of datasets are prominent.

Techniques based on packet payloads (e.g., [17,20]), usually called Deep Packet Inspection (DPI), provide more accurate result since they classify the traffic based on comparing information included in the packet payload against existing signatures. But these techniques cannot be used in many deployment environments due to privacy concerns [29]. (e.g., imposed legal restrictions of

© Springer International Publishing Switzerland 2016
S. Qing et al. (Eds.): ICICS 2015, LNCS 9543, pp. 282–294, 2016.
DOI: 10.1007/978-3-319-29814-6_23

the organization) or unable to cope with completely encrypted network packets e.g., application is unknown or newly launched (no signatures exists).

Alternatively, techniques based on packet headers [2,3,10,13,14], usually called behavioral statistics focus on general properties of the packet headers/flows (such as packet size, port numbers, inter arrival times, average number of packets in a flow etc.) and aim to match a behavioral pattern to certain applications. However, these models' accuracy were evaluated on the test dataset that might fail when being applied to different point of metric and network environment e.g., network latency jitter, packet loss or fragmentation. Moreover, *time* based features employed by many of these techniques are less likely to remain the same across different networks.

A packet consisting of a sequence of random numbers or a compressed data[1] also yields high entropy level [33]. Therefore, high entropy of a packet alone does not always imply encryption. For instance, a compressed file such as, .gz or .zip shows a high entropy level. In the latter case, the data is actually highly structured and not random [22]. Therefore, observing ordinary entropy alone would not necessarily provide enough information to let the classifier distinguish between encrypted and compressed unencrypted traffic. In this context, we take a look at an alternative set of features.

Apart from encryption, encoding plays a significant role in achieving high-entropy. For example, if we just encode a random bytes into HEX, the resulting string will be twice (each byte encoded to HEX consists of 2 characters) as long as the original random bytes. It sharply increases the randomness and hence entropy. Besides that, many protocols use ASCII encoded plain text for unencrypted payload. If it is converted to HEX values, it looks nearly random. Therefore, HEX-encoded entropy of these payloads is very close to encrypted payload.

Our Contribution: Our DPI-based technique use machine learning (ML) based classifier for filtering out unencrypted traffic. To bypass compressed data, we focus on a binary entropy analysis tool, called Bintropy. Bintropy was introduced as an analysis tool which is a prototype analysis tool to estimate the likelihood of the compressed content [23]. Although the target was to explore trends associated with malware executable files in either compression or encryption state, we discover that features extracting from Bintropy with other reliable features significantly boost the overall performance of the classifier. Note that due to high-entropy output for encrypted traffic, a variant of Bintropy called TBiEn[2] has been used in the experiment.

In order to placate encoded plain text problem, we analyze the influence of the size of the alphabet (n-length) in encoded message on the entropy calculation. At this point, we found that n-length HEX-encoded entropy can distinguish encrypted payloads more correctly where ordinary HEX encoding fails. Since most of the payloads are received in HEX values, we then stress more on a

---

[1] Since the repeated patterns in the uncompressed data are removed the redundancy also disappears making data look random and less predictable.

[2] A logarithmic weighting that gives higher weight to the higher derivatives.

complex possibility that is to check for any other standard encoding scheme e.g., UTF-8.

To decrease training time and improve accuracy and performance of the classifier, we employ feature selection algorithm and choose the best and promising features extracted from different entropy based algorithms. We combine Genetic algorithm with Support Vector Machine (SVM) following the model presented in [34] where authors develop a detection system with optimal features for diagnosing diseases. By using the same model, our aim is to discover traffic patterns for the automatic identification of encrypted traffic from any anonymous network traffic.

Decision trees, in comparison to other classification techniques, produce a set of rules and using C5.0 algorithm can easily be incorporated into real time techniques like traffic classification. As an alternative approach to SVM-based model, we build a decision tree model, namely C5.0 [26] with optimal features and check the feature usage by C5imp function.

Finally, results from Genetic-SVM and C5.0, were cross-checked by employing an unsupervised machine learning algorithm such as K-Means [37]. Cluster analysis is a promising tool to identify traffic classes. We evaluate K-Means as an external validation measure for classifier models using identical features on the same dataset. In [36], authors applied DBSCAN and K-Means clustering algorithms to group Internet traffic using transport layer characteristics. The idea was to use *unsupervised* learning technique to group *unlabelled* training data based on similarity. This approach possesses some practical benefits over learning approaches with labelled training data [36].

The rest of this paper is organized as follows. Related work is discussed in Sect. 2. Section 3 briefly describes the dataset collection and pre-processing for extracting features. While Sect. 4 details employed machine learning algorithms, the experimental results, evaluation and validation methods, conclusions are drawn in Sect. 5.

2 Related Work

In this section, we discuss relevant work based on payloads in traffic classification. Then we focus on some recent work based on entropy in different field of the traffic classification.

DPI or payload based techniques [11,12,16,17] were mainly used for unencrypted traffic because of their error-prone nature to completely encrypted traffic. However, a very recent work on encrypted-traffic based DPI technique in [20] where authors present a classifier based on first-order homogeneous Markov chain to identify encrypted traffic for applications such as Dropbox, Twitter etc. However, if the application protocol do not follow the RFC specifications strictly, use SSL for tunneling only (e.g., Skype, Tor), or behave differently from SSL stacks, this technique fails abruptly. Besides that, the employed periodic update fingerprints need as the application nature changes nature over time.

In [30], an *statistical modelling* based approach has been proposed where the authors define a vector from the number of different *word-values* available in the payload and match the similarity of the vectors with payloads from consecutive packets. After classifying the similarity between network flows they conclude with tracing five applications with 80 % accuracy. A pattern-matching P2P traffic classifier has been proposed in [31] that extracts payload signatures by using temporal correlation of flows and observing network traffic on different links. In [20], authors propose a payload-based method depending on first-order homogeneous Markov chains fingerprints conveyed in TLS sessions. Since application signatures change over time, their fingerprint models need to be updated periodically.

Entropy-based approaches are often used to detect malicious traffic [23–25]. A very few studies have been done for specific encrypted application e.g., Skype [19]. However, we found no research solely devoted to classifying encrypted and unencrypted traffic using entropy. Here we discuss some of the previous work using entropy in the literature.

In Olivian and Goubault-Larrecq [24], proposed an N-truncated entropy range for selected encrypted applications. If a payload's entropy does not satisfy the range, the traffic is deemed as malicious. The study considers consider the payload of the first packet of a connection and compares it with the N-truncated entropy of uniformly distributed payload.

Dorfinger et al. in [19] propose a real-time classifier based on the entropy of the first packet's payload of a flow and compare the result with the entropy of random payload. We found that in some encrypted applications or protocol first packet in a flow is partially encrypted (e.g. Client Hello Message of TLS) or smaller in size that may cause false positive result or unreliable evaluation [20]. Besides that it's an application (skype) specific solution.

In [21], Sun et al. investigated the encrypted web pages based on entropy in a large sample of Web pages using individual object sizes in a page to identify encrypted pages. In [15], authors studied traffic classification from several P2P and non-P2P applications where entropy was used to measure the heterogeneity of network level to characterize traffic samples. Zhang et al. in [18] proposed two high-entropy classifiers to detect bot. In order to avoid falsification, this scheme adds extra tools or mechanisms e.g., BotHunter and flow based cumulative entropy.

In [33], authors use BiEntropy to explore noticeable differences between the encrypted and unencrypted binary files of some real and synthetic spreadsheets (e.g., MS Excel).

Note that almost all of the aforementioned works are based on the measurement of conventional Shannon entropy over the whole packet's payload and for any specific protocol or application. We on the other hand focus on encrypted traffic in general. In compare to previous scheme, we extend our approach in mainly two ways: using different types of entropy measurements and employing it not for a specific protocol, but for any kind of encrypted traffic.

3   Dataset and Preprocessing

When starting a machine learning project the most important piece and hardest to obtain is to get a perfect data set that would have to be heterogeneous enough to emulate real traffic to some extent. To provide a comprehensive evaluation of encrypted traffic, we gathered a large collection of traffic samples representing both encrypted and unencrypted traces.

Capturing background network data in a real life environment is challenging due to two main reasons: privacy concerns of the gathered data and noise such as unwanted packets. Typically, traffic is either collected from a trusted sources or captured in a controlled environment. To address this challenge, our experimental dataset has been generated from combining non-overlapping portion of the several data sources where ground truth was known. Our accumulated dataset combines traffic traces mainly from ISCX 2015 dataset [7], skype traces from [8] and some traces from wireshark [9] samples.

- ISCX 2015 dataset [7] has been created in a controlled testbed environment simulating real applications from a diverse set of application traces and background traffic. To facilitate the labeling process or removing the need of sanitization, when capturing the traffic all unnecessary services and applications were closed. The traffic was captured with wireshark [9] and tcpdump [32], generating a total amount of 5 GB of data (encrypted/unencrypted). Protocols such as HTTPS, HTTP, SMTP, SSH, FTP were chosen to be simulated. However, following protocols were generated readily as a consequence of employing aforementioned protocols: DNS and NetBios. Specific applications were labelled accordingly, for example, Facebook, Twitter, Dropbox traffic as *secure web* or *https* connection. The prepared labelled dataset including full packet payloads, along with the relevant entropy results are publicly available to researchers through our website [7].
- Tstat dataset in [8], a research project testbed data containing only Skype traffic. Traces have been collected and organized with the support of the RECIPE (Robust and Efficient traffic Classification in IP nEtworks) projects.
- Sample captures in Wireshark wiki [9] are some example capture files collected from several application/protocol traces.

Since the dataset includes heterogeneous traffic flows (mixed traffic), experiments on datasets would help assess the accuracy of classification. However, even if the dataset containing *payloads* were collected from homogeneous traffic flows, they must be network independent in compared to their flow/header[3] counterpart.

A detailed description of the different type of captured/collected traffic is given in Table 1. Under Secure web label, we have HTTPS traffic mainly generated while browsing through Firefox and Chrome. Any browser related activities such as voice call using facebook or streaming through Youtube do not belong

---

[3] dependent on network latency, jitter, packet loss etc. that are less likely to remain across heterogeneous network.

Table 1. Number of payloads in the dataset employed

Application	Source	Type	Number of Payloads	Label/Class
HTTPS	ISCX Dataset [7]	Secure web	1814708	Encrypted
Skype	TStat Dataset [8]	VOIP	1945827	Encrypted
DTLS	Wireshark Sample Capture [9]	TLS	6084	Encrypted
LDAP	Wireshark Sample Capture	TLS	73655	Encrypted
SSL	ISCX Dataset	Tunnel	1228889	Encrypted
Youtube	ISCX Dataset	Streaming	194927	Encrypted
HTTP	ISCX Dataset	Weblogs	323158	Unencrypted
DecPhone	Wireshark Sample Capture	VOIP	25868	Unencrypted
Unencrypted Video	ISCX Dataset	Streaming	187196	Unencrypted
DNS	ISCX Dataset	Internet Service	37972	Unencrypted
NetBioS	ISCX Dataset	Network	62224	Unencrypted
SMTP	ISCX Dataset	Mail	4030	Unencrypted
		Total Encrypted payloads	5264090	
		Total Unencrypted payloads	640448	

to this label. The Voice over IP (VOIP) includes traffic generated by voice application such Skype, DecPhone. Streaming data, a continuous and firm stream of data, includes data from Youtube, Vimeo. Unencrypted traffic payloads were collected mainly from 3 type of sources, such as, streaming video, VOIP, and weblogs (HTTP).

jNetPcap [6], an open-source java wrapper for libpcap library native calls, was used to extract payloads from network packet (pcap files). Note application layer payload and transport layer payload were separated. For our experiment, only application layer payloads were considered in order to avoid noises with encrypted payloads. Because in most of the cases, protocols' payload encryption is done in the application layer i.e., SSL, HTTPS etc. For instance, length of application layer payload/transport layer payload (in bytes) for some packets in our experiments were 1133/1338, 3663/4036, 2280/2700 etc. Note that application layer payloads are smaller than that of transport layer.

For training data set we discard any payloads smaller than 20 Bytes (including noise) mainly due to bias such small payloads introduce into the model causing highly unreliable result. Finally, we end up with a large dataset consisting of encrypted payloads from 5264090 packets and unencrypted payloads from 640448 packets as shown in Table 1.

4   Experiment and Results

4.1   Feature Selection

Features for the classifier were chosen from entropy of the entire payloads, n-length Word or sliding window entropy, entropy of the encoded payload, and

Table 2. Entropy Based Features Employed

Encoded payload	Abbreviation	Binary payload	Abbreviation
Entire-file entropy	e_ENC	Entire-file entropy	e_BIN
n-length Word entropy	n_ENC	n-length Word entropy	n_BIN
		Mean of n-length Word Bintropy	$n\_\widehat{BIN}\_m$
		Std. Deviation of n-length Word Bintropy	$n\_\widehat{BIN}\_s$

BiEntropy: a logarithmic weighted average of the Shannon binary entropy. The following three algorithms were considered in calculation of entropy:

1. Entropy of the entire file where conventional Shannon's entropy (in [4]) is used for measurement. In case of a binary file, the entropy is measured in bits where the *symbol* is either 0, or 1. However, in case of a HEX-encoded file, there are 16 distinct symbols: [0–9], [A-F].
2. Entropy of n-length Word (where $n = 2$ to 64) or sliding-window technique [5]. It measures Shannon entropy over a sliding window of all the *word* tokens in a file. For instance, measuring byte entropy over a sliding window (where *word* size or window size $n = 8$) provides entropy value for each byte.
3. Mean and Std. deviation of n-length Word BiEntropy (in [33]) to detect the existence of repetitive pattern. First, calculate all the binary derivatives ($< n$) of a n-length word. If the last derivative is 0, word is *periodic* BiEntropy is 0 and vice versa.

Table 3. Selected Features by Genetic and C5imp

Method	Number of features	Selected Features
GF-SVM	8	e_ENC (HEX), e_BIN, 8_ENC (UTF-8), 8_BIN, 32_$\widehat{BIN}$_m, 32_$\widehat{BIN}$_s 8_$\widehat{BIN}$_s, 16_$\widehat{BIN}$_s
C5imp	10	e_ENC (HEX), e_BIN, 24_$\widehat{BIN}$_m, 12_BIN, 8_BIN, 12_$\widehat{BIN}$_m, 32_$\widehat{BIN}$_m, 8_ENC (UTF-8), 8_$\widehat{BIN}$_s, 4_BIN_m

While (1) and (2) are applied to *encoded* (HEX and UTF-8) payloads, *all* the algorithms are applied to the *binary* payloads as shown in Table 2. Note that all the entropy metrics were transformed by a logarithmic function since it has been observed to greatly increase machine learning accuracy. Resultant entropy were also normalized based on unity-based normalization before applying genetic algorithm.

Feature selection based on Genetic algorithm (in [34]) follows several steps: chromosome coding, initial population or feature chromosome, training Least Square SVM (LSSVM) classifier, fitness function, and terminating condition. For *chromosome coding*, we encode selected feature subset into a binary code[4]

---

[4] where 1 indicates the features to be selected and 0 not.

consisting of the total number of features. Regarding *initial population*, we choose some important features from our initial experiments (e.g., e_ENC (HEX), $32\_\widehat{BIN}\_m$, $8\_\widehat{BIN}\_s$ etc.). LSSVM classifier helps to evaluate initial population (through classification accuracy) and hence the genetic algorithm to decide the effective features finally. The most important step in genetic algorithm is to construct an effective *fitness function* that evaluates a feature's fitness to survive. Chromosomes must be evaluated by fitness function. Our fitness function stems from weighting True Positive Rate (TP), False Positive Rate (FP) and the number of selected features $N(s)$.

$$\text{Fit}(s) = w_t \times \text{TP} + w_f \times \text{FP} + w_s \times \text{N}(s) \tag{1}$$

where w_t, w_f, and w_s be the weight values for TP, FP and $\text{N}(s)$ respectively. In our experiment, we set $w_t = .5, w_f = .3$ and $w_s = .1$ to achieve high TP, low FP, and a small subset of selected features. In each iteration, chromosome with highest fitness value survives by which genetic operator creates new generation. The algorithm *terminates* when the maximum number of iteration takes place.

We start with the features in the Table 2 with varying the value of n. However, considering all possible combinations of features for calculating *detection rate* would require a significant computational cost while dealing with large dataset. That is why, we make several small groups i.e., features based on Bintropy, features based on entire file etc. and run genetic algorithm on each individual group. Apart from Genetic algorithm, we employ C5imp, a variable importance measures for C5.0 models with metric 'splits'[5] with 100 different trials to maximize the C5.0 classifier accuracy.

Table 3 demonstrates the number and labels of important/ optimal features selected by Genetic and C5imp feature selection algorithms. Results show that C5-imp mainly weights on n-length Bintropy based features while both of them consider encoded/binary payload based features.

4.2   Result Discussion

In this section, we discuss the detailed experiments and results of validation on the traced datasets. First, a set of statistical features based on encoding and entropy of the packets' payload has been studied for the experiment. Following the model of Zhao et al. (in [34]) where Genetic algorithm and LSSVM are used to were used to develop a detection model with effective feature selection. We use the same model but to detect encrypted/unencrypted traffic through network.

First, we select optimized number of features for encrypted and unencrypted traffic payload by creating feature chromosomes and evaluating them with the highest classification accuracy. Second, training LSSVM with the training data, that is, support vectors will be created based on training traffic traces. Finally, classifying the traffic data into two class encrypted and unencrypted. Nonetheless, in order to identify an ideal model for encrypted traffic classification and

---

[5] To calculate the percentage of splits associated with each predictor.

compare the robustness of the models with respect to selected features Genetic-LSSVM, LibSVM, and C5.0 algorithms were employed.

This study has employed a LSSVM to distinguish 2 classes (encrypted and unencrypted) of traffic data. Our experiments took place on a Ubuntu platform having configuration Intel core i7 3.6GHz, 32 GB RAM. Feature subset has been selected based on Genetic algorithm and C5imp in terms of ensuring the highest classification accuracy, TP and the lowest FP. The use of top ranked features (8 features out of more than 110 features) for classification give a drastic change in TP and FP values (Table 2). LS-SVMlab toolbox in [35] is used to implement LSSVM and modeling the classifier. LibSVM library available in weka [27] is used to run SVM algorithm with all features. RStudio [28], an integrated development environment (IDE) for R, is used for decision tree based model C5.0.

Table 4 shows the numeric result of the proposed Genetic-LSSVM in comparison to the all features selected SVM model. In fact, proposed model selects the best feature subset and then final results of the classification with the selected features are shown in the table. As the result shows, there is a significant change in both the encrypted and unencrypted class performance using Genetic-LSSSVM, where DR has reached 97 % while it was approx. 87 % using SVM with all possible features. FPR results are also noticeable as it has a 28 % reduction.

In order to compare our model, we apply decision tree and rule based model C5.0 and find 98.1 % accuracy from 10 selected features with minimal error (0.9 %). Note that the accuracy of C5.0 decision tree algorithm depends on the highest Information Gain of the features [26].

High detection rate can be better explained by (i) considering only application layer payloads in case of TCP payloads, (ii) the nature of the type of data, e.g., Skype or HTTPS payloads are huge and might be partially dominating the dataset (iii) dataset is partly biased containing payloads from limited number of applications. Results may fluctuate with much more diverse set of traffic from many applications/protocols.

4.3   Evaluation and Validation

In order to validate the selected features (e.g., word size, encoding scheme etc.), experiments have been done in two steps: (i) using randomly selected plain-text and their corresponding encoded-text and cipher-text, and (ii) using clustering algorithm as an alternative approach to classify traffic and to observe whether cluster analysis can identify encrypted or unencrypted traffic effectively using only the selected features by genetic algorithm. Note that, there is a sharp disparity between the entropies of plain-text and cipher-text. However, Encoded-text's entropy is very close to that of Encrypted-text.

Bintropy based features, that is, a weighted average of the Shannon entropy, show significant differences between the encrypted and unencrypted (but encoded) binary payloads. Especially features from Std. deviation ($32\_\widehat{BIN}\_s$) was promising in most of the case. On the other hand, Encoded-text's entropy, whether from *entire* file or from n-length *word* (e_ENC, 8_ENC), demonstrate keen difference to the encrypted. Nonetheless, our feature selection algorithm chooses HEX encoding for *entire* file and UTF-8 encoding for n-length *word*. Although n-length word entropies (8_ENC and 8_BIN) indicate sharp divergence in this example, for a large file (payloads) difference is not substantial. This experimental procedure has been applied to different size of text files and observed the entropies for the feature set selected by the genetic algorithm and C5imp.

We consider an unsupervised algorithm, namely K-Means to evaluate and compare them with previous used Genetic-LSSVM and C5.0 classification algorithms using the GF-SVM features. It consists of 2 stages: a model generation and a classifier generation. In the former stage, K-Means algorithm clusters training data to produce a set of clusters to be labelled. In the latter stage, this model is used to develop classifier that can label any traffic traces. K-Means clustering evaluated with K initially being 2 exhibits overall accuracy exceeding 96 % with 7 iterations. The overall accuracy was sharply declined to 54 % with 25 iterations when K was 3. This declining continued until we check for K is 10. Accuracy results for DBSCAN clustering is 89.7 % (inc. noise or unclustered 24 instances) with two input parameters: ϵ is 0.3 where at least minPt is 3. The additional 6 clusters found using 3 minPt were typically small clusters containing 3 to 31 instances. However we did not trial with different ϵ and/or minPt that may improve its overall accuracy.

In order to train each of the learning algorithms properly several runs were conducted with different parameter values. It helps to generate accurate model with highest gain and ensures the result is not biased or dominated but from statistically compelling trails.

Table 4. Accuracy using Genetic-LSSVM, traditional LibSVM, C5.0 algorithms

Model	Correctly	FPR		DR	
	Classified instances	Encrypted	Unencrypted	Encrypted	Unencrypted
Genetic-LSSVM	96.639 %	0.034	0.033	0.967	0.966
LibSVM (all features)	86.954 %	0.29	0.31	0.693	0.761
C5.0 (C5imp features)	98.10 %	-	-	-	-
K-Means (GF-SVM features)	95.90 %	-	-	-	-
DBSCAN (GF-SVM features)	89.70 %	-	-	-	-

5   Conclusion

Our primary motivation was to find the solution to detect encrypted traffic from the network traffic depending on entropy-based features. We investigated several interesting characteristics of traffic payloads related to encoding, n-length word of the raw byte distribution and observe the aftermath effect on entropy measurement.

However, we have several shortcomings though. First, although we try to accumulate packets from the popular encrypted protocols, the dataset we worked do not consist of each and every type of encrypted or unencrypted traffic. Aside from these, in some applications, first few payloads are partially encrypted or unencrypted, we could not consider that in this time. That is why, we do believe that still there are some noises in the experiment training dataset. Although our dataset does not contain every kind of encrypted or unencrypted application traces, effectiveness of different combination of entropy features in terms of getting more detection accuracy has been fully studied.

As a future work, we have plan to investigate our proposed model on a wider range of applications and heterogeneous datasets from various networks. We also aim at analyzing protocol's individual signature from entropy and cross-validate its consistency with clustering algorithms. Finally, we plan to apply this approach to reveal signatures for network intrusion detection system. That would make it easy to infer if the encrypted traffic is benign or something that should be investigated further.

Acknowledgements. This work was funded by Atlantic Canada Opportunity Agency (ACOA) through the Atlantic Innovation Fund (AIF) in cooperation with IBM Security division.

References

1. Callado, A., et al.: A Survey on Internet Traffic Identification. IEEE Commun. Surveys Tutorials, **11**(3), 37–52 (2009)
2. Alshammari, R., Nur Zincir-Heywood, A.: Can encrypted traffic be identified without port numbers. Computer networks **55**(6), 1326–1350 (2011)
3. Alshammari, R., Nur Zincir-Heywood, A.: Investigating two different approaches for encrypted traffic classification. Privacy, Security and Trust (2008)
4. Shannon, C.E.: A mathematical theory of communication. Bell Syst. Tech. J. **27**(3), 379–423 (1948)
5. Marsaglia, G., Zaman, A.: Monkey tests for random number generators. Comput. Math. Appl. **26**(9), 1–10 (1993)
6. jNetPcap, Open-source java library. http://jnetpcap.com
7. Datasets: Information Security Center of eXcellence (ISCX). www.unb.ca/research/iscx/dataset/
8. Tstat, Skype Testbed Traces. http://tstat.tlc.polito.it/traces-skype.shtml
9. Wireshark sample captures. http://wiki.wireshark.org/SampleCaptures
10. Schneider, P.: TCP/IP traffic Classification Based on port numbers. Division Of Applied Sciences, Cambridge, **2138** (1996)
11. Karagiannis, T., Papagiannaki, K., Faloutsos, M.: BLINK: multilevel traffic classification in the dark. In: SIGCOMM , Philadelphia, 21–26 August 2005
12. Moore, A.W., Zuev, D.: Internet traffic classification using bayesian analysis techniques. In: SIGMETRIC, Banff, 6–10 June 2005
13. Sen, S., Spatscheck, O., Wang, D.: Accurate, scalable in-network identification of P2P traffic using application signatures. In: WWW2005, USA (2004)
14. Zander, S., Nguyen, T., Armitage, G.: Automated traffic classification and application identification using machine learning. In: LCN, Australia (2005)

15. Gomes, J.V., et al.: Analysis of peer-to-peer traffic using a behavioural method based on entropy. In: Performance, Computing and Communications Conference (2008)
16. Bonfiglio, D., et al.: Revealing skype traffic: when randomness plays with you. In: Proceedings of the ACM SIGCOMM, pp. 37–48. ACM Press, USA (2007)
17. Smith, R., et al.: Deflating the big bang: fast and scalable deep packet inspection. In: ACM SIGCOMM , pp. 207–218. ACM Press, USA (2008)
18. Zhang, H., Papadopoulos, C., Massey, D.: Detecting encrypted botnet traffic. In: Computer Communications Workshops (INFOCOM Workshop). IEEE (2013)
19. Dorfinger, P., et al.: Entropy-based traffic filtering to support real-time Skype detection. In: Proceedings of the 6th International Wireless Communications and Mobile Computing Conference. ACM (2010)
20. Korczynski, M., Duda, A.: Markov chain fingerprinting to classify encrypted traffic. In: INFOCOM, Proceedings IEEE. IEEE (2014)
21. Sun, Q., et al.: Statistical identification of encrypted web browsing traffic. In: IEEE Symposium on Security and Privacy, Proceedings. IEEE (2002)
22. Weber, M., et al.: A toolkit for detecting and analyzing malicious software. In: 18th Annual Proceedings of Computer Security Applications Conference. IEEE (2002)
23. Lyda, R., Hamrock, J.: Using entropy analysis to find encrypted and packed malware. IEEE Secur. Privacy 2, 40–45 (2007)
24. Olivain, J., Goubault-Larrecq, J.: Detecting subverted cryptographic protocols by entropy checking. Laboratoire Specification et Verification, ENS Cachan, France, Research Report LSV-06-13 (2006)
25. Wagner, A., Plattner, B.: Entropy based worm and anomaly detection in fast IP networks. In: WETICE 2005 Proceedings of the 14th IEEE International Workshops on Enabling Technologies: Infrastructure for Collaborative Enterprise, pp. 172–177. IEEE Computer Society, Washington, DC (2005)
26. Quinlan, J.R.: C4.5: Programs for Machine Learning. Morgan Kaufmann Publishers, San Francisco (1993). ISBN=1-55860-238-0
27. Hall, M., et al.: The WEKA data mining software: an update. ACM SIGKDD Explorations Newsletter 11(1), 10–18 (2009)
28. RStudio, an integrated development environment (IDE)for R. http://www.rstudio.com
29. Sicker, D.C., Ohm, P., Grunwald, D.: Legal issues surrounding monitoring during network research, In: Proceeding 7th ACM SIGCOMM conference on Internet measurement, ser. IMC 2007, pp. 141–148. ACM, New York (2007)
30. Chung, J.Y., Park, B., Won, Y.J., Strassner, J., Hong, J.W.: Traffic classification based on flow similarity. In: Nunzi, G., Scoglio, C., Li, X. (eds.) IPOM 2009. LNCS, vol. 5843, pp. 65–77. Springer, Heidelberg (2009)
31. Keralapura, R., Nucci, A., Chuah, C.-N.: Self-learning peer-to-peer traffic classifier. In: Proceedings of 18th Internatonal Conference on Computer Communications and Networks, ICCCN. IEEE (2009)
32. TCPDUMP packet analizer. http://www.tcpdump.org
33. Croll, G.J.: BiEntropy-The Approximate Entropy of a Finite Binary String (2013). arXiv preprint arXiv:1305.0954
34. Zhao, M., et al.: Feature selection and parameter optimization for support vector machines: a new approach based on genetic algorithm with feature chromosomes. Expert Syst. Appl. 38(5), 5197–5204 (2011)
35. LS-SVMlab toolbox. http://www.esat.kuleuven.ac.be/sista/lssvmlab

36. Erman, J., Arlitt, M., Mahanti, A.: Traffic classification using clustering algorithms. In: Proceedings of the SIGCOMM workshop on Mining network data. ACM (2006)
37. Jain, A.K., Dubes, R.C.: Algorithms for Clustering Data. Prentice Hall, Englewood Cliffs (1988)

Modelling and Analysis of Network Security - a Probabilistic Value-passing CCS Approach

Qian Zhang[1,2]([✉]), Ying Jiang[1,2], and Liping Ding[1,3]

[1] Institute of Software, Chinese Academy of Sciences, Beijing, China
zhangq@ios.ac.cn
[2] State Key Laboratory of Computer Science, Beijing, China
[3] National Engineering Research Center for Fundamental Software, Beijing, China

Abstract. In this work, we propose a probabilistic value-passing CCS (Calculus of Communicating System) approach to model and analyze a typical network security scenario with one attacker and one defender. By minimizing this model with respect to probabilistic bisimulation and abstracting it through graph-theoretic methods, two algorithms based on backward induction are designed to compute Nash Equilibrium strategy and Social Optimal strategy respectively. For each algorithm, the correctness is proved and an implementation is realized. Finally, this approach is illustrated by a detailed case study.

Keywords: Network security · Nash equilibrium strategy · Social optimal strategy · Reactive model · Probabilistic value passing CCS

1 Introduction

With the rapid development of Internet, the imminence of how to design an effective network attack-defense strategy is proposed. Nash Equilibrium Strategy (NES) is a relative optimal attack-defense strategy, which means neither the attacker nor the defender is willing to change the current situation. Social Optimal Strategy (SOS) is a global optimal one, which means to minimize the damages caused by the attacker. How to find NES and SOS effectively is far from having been completely solved.

In 1990s, game-theoretic approaches have provided quantitative solutions for NES and SOS [7,10,12,15] in various network security scenarios. *Static game* can model the scenarios in which the attacker and the defender have no idea on the action chosen by the adversary [5]. *Stochastic game* can model the scenarios which involve probabilistic transitions through network states caused by the offensive-defensive actions [6,8,14]. *Markov game* [16] can model the scenarios in which the future offensive-defensive behaviors will impact on the present offensive-defensive action choice [4,17]. *Bayesian game* can model the scenarios with incomplete information set and the attacker and the defender use Bayesian analysis in predicting the outcome [3,9,11].

© Springer International Publishing Switzerland 2016
S. Qing et al. (Eds.): ICICS 2015, LNCS 9543, pp. 295–302, 2016.
DOI: 10.1007/978-3-319-29814-6_24

We are the first, to our knowledge, to present a probabilistic value-passing CCS (PVCCS) approach to model and analyze a typical network security scenario with one attacker and one defender. PVCCS is a common formal language for modelling concurrent systems with precise semantics. A network system is supposed to be composed of three participants: one attacker, one defender and the network environment in which the hardware and software services are under consideration. Our model represents the network as a state transition system. We use processes in PVCCS to represent all possible behaviors of the participants at each state, assign each state with a process depicting all possible offensive-defensive interactions currently. A model is established on the processes transitions and is minimized by probabilistic bisimulation. To increase the reusability, we abstract the minimized model to a finite hierarchical graph, where each strongly connected component can be processed in parallel. Two algorithms based on backward induction are designed to compute NES and SOS respectively. We illustrate the efficiency of our approach by an example introduced in [8].

The major contributions of our work are:

(1) establish a reactive model for PVCCS to model network security;
(2) minimize and abstract the model to reduce the search space and optimize the complexity of the concerned algorithms;
(3) propose two algorithms to find NES and SOS respectively. The novelty lies in combing nontrivially graph-theoretic methods with backward induction, which avails high reusability and makes the backward induction possible in the setting of some infinite paths.

Compared with game-theoretic approaches, our approach features in:

(1) scalability with the fundamental support from probabilistic bisimulation;
(2) filtering the invalid NESs from the results obtained by game-theoretic approach;
(3) high efficiency benefiting from reusability, parallelization, minimized model;
(4) can be extended to a uniform model to analyze various security scenarios.

In the remaining sections, we establish a reactive model for PVCCS and modelling for network security (Sect. 2); present the formal definitions of NES and SOS, as well as the corresponding algorithms (Sect. 3); illustrate our method by a case study (Sect. 4); discuss the conclusion (Sect. 5). Due to lack of space, we omit all proofs for the correctness of the algorithms. Interested readers can refer to the online paper: http://arxiv.org/abs/1507.06769.

2 Modelling Network Security Based on PVCCS

2.1 Reactive Model for PVCCS (PVCCS$_R$)

Syntax: Let $\mathcal{A}$ be a set of channel names ranged over by a, and $\overline{\mathcal{A}}$ be the set of co-names, i.e., $\overline{\mathcal{A}} = \{\overline{a} \mid a \in \mathcal{A}\}$. **Label** $= \mathcal{A} \cup \overline{\mathcal{A}}$. **Var** is a set of value variables ranged over by x and **Val** is a value set ranged over by v. **e** and **b** denote the value expression and the boolean expression respectively. The set of actions, ranged over by α, $\mathbf{Act} = \{a(x) \mid a \in \mathcal{A}\} \cup \{\overline{a}(\mathbf{e}) \mid \overline{a} \in \overline{\mathcal{A}}\} \cup \{\tau\}$, where τ is the silent action. $\mathcal{K}$ and $\mathcal{X}$ are a set of process identifiers and a set of process variables respectively. $R \subseteq \mathcal{A}$, I, J are index sets, and $\alpha_i \neq \alpha_j$ if $i \neq j$. $\sum$ and

$\sum$ are summation notations for processes and real numbers respectively. $\mathbf{Pr}$ is the set of processes in PVCCS_R and is defined inductively as follows:

$$\mathbf{Pr} :: = Nil \mid \sum_{i \in I}\sum_{j \in J}[p_{ij}]\alpha_i.P_{ij} \mid P_1|P_2 \mid P\backslash R \mid \textit{if } \mathbf{b} \textit{ then } P_1 \textit{ else } P_2 \mid A(x)$$

$$\alpha :: = a(x) \mid \overline{a}(\mathbf{e})$$

where $\forall i \in I$, $p_{ij} \in (0,1]$, $\sum_{j \in I} p_{ij} = 1$. The process constant is defined as $A(x) \overset{def}{=}$ P, where P contains no process variables and no free value variables except x.

Likewise the meaning for each process in [2], we just explain $\sum_{i \in I}\sum_{j \in J}[p_{ij}]\alpha_i.P_{ij}$.

It means P_{ij} will be chosen with probability p_{ij} after performing the prefix action α_i. There are two kinds of prefixes: input prefix $a(x)$ and output prefix $\overline{a}(\mathbf{e})$.

Semantics: Table 1 shows the operational semantics of PVCCS_R, where $P \overset{\alpha[p]}{\rightarrow} Q$ describes a transition from P to Q with probability p by performing action α. $P\{\mathbf{e}/x\}$ means substituting $\mathbf{e}$ for every free occurrences of x in P. $chan : \mathbf{Act} \rightarrow \mathcal{A}$, i.e. $chan(a(x)) = chan(\overline{a}(\mathbf{e})) = a$. $\wp$ is the powerset operator and $\mathbf{Pr}/\mathcal{R}$ is a set of equivalence classes induced by the equivalence relation $\mathcal{R}$ over $\mathbf{Pr}$. $\mu : (\mathbf{Pr} \times Act \times \wp(\mathbf{Pr})) \rightarrow [0,1]$ is given by $\forall \alpha \in Act$, $\forall P \in \mathbf{Pr}$, $\forall C \subseteq \mathbf{Pr}$, $\mu(P, \alpha, C) = \dot{\sum}\{p|P \overset{\alpha[p]}{\rightarrow} Q, Q \in C\}$.

Table 1. Operational semantics of PVCCS_R

$$[In]\frac{}{\sum_{i \in I}\sum_{j \in J}[p_{ij}]a(x).P_{ij} \overset{a(\mathbf{e})[p_{ij}]}{\longrightarrow} P_{ij}\{\mathbf{e}/x\}} \qquad [Out]\frac{}{\sum_{i \in I}\sum_{j \in J}[p_{ij}]\overline{a}(\mathbf{e}).P_{ij} \overset{\overline{a}(\mathbf{e})[p_{ij}]}{\longrightarrow} P_{ij}}$$

$$[Res]\frac{P \overset{\alpha[p]}{\rightarrow} P'}{P\backslash R \overset{\alpha[p]}{\rightarrow} P'\backslash R} \;(chan(\alpha) \notin R \cup \overline{R}) \quad [Con]\frac{P\{\mathbf{e}/x\} \overset{\alpha[p]}{\rightarrow} P'}{A(\mathbf{e}) \overset{\alpha[p]}{\rightarrow} P'} \;(A(x) \overset{def}{=} P)$$

$$[Par_l]\frac{P_1 \overset{\alpha[p]}{\rightarrow} P'_1}{P_1|P_2 \overset{\alpha[p]}{\rightarrow} P'_1|P_2} \qquad\qquad [Par_r]\frac{P_2 \overset{\alpha[p]}{\rightarrow} P'_2}{P_1|P_2 \overset{\alpha[p]}{\rightarrow} P_1|P'_2}$$

$$[Com]\frac{P_1 \overset{a(\mathbf{e})[p]}{\rightarrow} P'_1,\; P_2 \overset{\overline{a}(\mathbf{e})[q]}{\rightarrow} P'_2}{P_1|P_2 \overset{\tau[p\cdot q]}{\rightarrow} P'_1|P'_2}$$

$$[If_t]\frac{P_1 \overset{\alpha[p]}{\rightarrow} P'_1}{\textit{if } \mathbf{b} \textit{ then } P_1 \textit{ else } P_2 \overset{\alpha[p]}{\rightarrow} P'_1}(\mathbf{b} = true) \quad [If_f]\frac{P_2 \overset{\alpha[p]}{\rightarrow} P'_2}{\textit{if } \mathbf{b} \textit{ then } P_1 \textit{ else } P_2 \overset{\alpha[p]}{\rightarrow} P'_2}(\mathbf{b} = false)$$

Definition 1. *An equivalence relation $\mathcal{R} \subseteq \mathbf{Pr} \times \mathbf{Pr}$ is a probabilistic bisimulation if $(P,Q) \in \mathcal{R}$ implies: $\forall C \in \mathbf{Pr}/\mathcal{R}$, $\forall \alpha \in Act$, $\mu(P, \alpha, C) = \mu(Q, \alpha, C)$. P and Q are probabilistic bisimilar, written as $P \sim Q$, if there exists a probabilistic bisimulation $\mathcal{R}$ s.t. $P\mathcal{R}Q$.*

2.2 Network Security Model Based on PVCCS$_R$

S is the set of network states, ranged over by s_i; A^a and A^d denote the set of action value for the attacker and the defender; state transition probability is a function $\dot{p} : S \times A^a \times A^d \times S \rightarrow [0,1]$; each transition is weighted by the benefit of the attacker (the damages caused by the attack) and that of the defender (the time for the recovery), which is formalized as a function $\dot{r} : S \times A^a \times A^d \rightarrow \mathbb{R}_1 \times \mathbb{R}_2$, where $\mathbb{R}$ is the real number set.

In our model, $\mathcal{A} = \{Attc, Defd, Tell_a, Tell_d\}$, $\mathbf{Label} = \mathcal{A} \cup \overline{\mathcal{A}} \cup \{\overline{Log}\} \cup \{\overline{Rec}\}$. $\mathbf{Val} = A^a \cup A^d \cup T$, $T \subseteq \mathbb{R} \times \mathbb{R}$. $\mathbf{Act} = Act^a \cup Act^d \cup Act^n$, where Act^a, Act^d and Act^n denote the action sets of the attacker, the defender and the network environment respectively.

$$Act^a = \{\overline{Attc}(u) \mid u \in A^a\} \cup \{Tell_a(x) \mid x \in \mathbf{Var}\}$$

$$Act^d = \{\overline{Defd}(v) \mid v \in A^d\} \cup \{Tell_d(x) \mid x \in \mathbf{Var}\}$$

$$Act^n = \{Attc(x) \mid x \in \mathbf{Var}\} \cup \{Defd(x) \mid x \in \mathbf{Var}\} \cup \{\overline{Tell_a}(x) \mid x \in \mathbf{Var} \cup A^d\}$$

$$\cup \{\overline{Tell_d}(x) \mid x \in \mathbf{Var} \cup A^a\} \cup \{\overline{Log}(x,y) \mid x \in A^a \cup \mathbf{Var}, y \in A^d \cup \mathbf{Var}\}.$$

$$\cup \{\overline{Rec}(\dot{r}(s,u,v)) \mid s \in S, u \in A^a, v \in A^d\}$$

$\overline{Attc}(u)$ (or $\overline{Defd}(v)$) means launching attack u (or defense v); $Attc(x)$ (or $Defd(x)$) means the attack (or defense) works; $\overline{Tell_d}(x)$ (or $\overline{Tell_a}(x)$) means the network environment responses to the attack (or defense); $Tell_a(x)$ (or $Tell_d(x)$) means the attacker (or defender) monitors the network; $\overline{Log}(x,y)$ means a log file is generated to record the attack-defense behaviors; $\overline{Rec}(\dot{r}(s,u,v))$ means recording the benefit of the attacker and the defender caused by this transition.

pA_i, pD_i and pN_i, describing all possible behaviors of the attacker, the defender and the network environment at s_i respectively, are defined as follows:

$$pA_i \overset{def}{=} \sum_{u \in A^a(s_i)} \overline{Attc}(u).Tell_a(y).Nil, \qquad pD_i \overset{def}{=} Tell_d(x). \sum_{v \in A^d(s_i)} \overline{Defd}(v).Nil$$

$$pN_i \overset{def}{=} Attc(x).\overline{Tell_d}(x).Defd(y).\overline{Tell_a}(y).Tr_i(x,y)$$

$$Tr_i(x,y) \overset{def}{=} \sum_{\substack{u \in A^a(s_i) \\ v \in A^d(s_i)}} \overline{Log}(u,v).(if\ (x = u, y = v)\ then$$

$$\sum_{j \in I} [\dot{p}(s_i, u, v, s_j)] \overline{Rec}(\dot{r}(s_i, u, v)).(pA_j \mid pD_j \mid pN_j)\ else\ Nil)$$

The process assigned to each state s_i is defined as

$$G_i \overset{def}{=} (pA_i \mid pD_i \mid pN_i) \backslash R, \ \ R = \{Attc, Defd, Tell_a, Tell_d\}$$

The network state transition system is generated on the processes transitions. Minimize via probabilistic bisimulation and shrink via path contraction [1], we obtain a new labeled directed graph named as ConTS. The vertex set of ConTS, denoted by V, is ranged over by the process G_i. The edge set, denoted by E, is ranged over by e_{ij} if there is a multi-transition from G_i to G_j. Each edge is labeled by the action values transferred, the transition probability and the weight pair of this transition, denoted by $L(e_{ij}) = (L_{Act}(e_{ij}), L_{TranP}(e_{ij}), L_{WeiP}(e_{ij}))$[1]

3   Analyzing Properties as Graph Theory Approach

3.1   NES and SOS

Definition 2. $\forall G_i \in V$, an execution of G_i, denoted by π_i, is a walk starting from G_i and ending with a cycle, on which every vertex's out-degree is 1. $\pi_i[j]$ denotes the subsequence of π_i starting from G_j, where G_j is a vertex on π_i.

Definition 3. The payoff to the attacker (or the defender) on execution π_i, denoted by $PF^a(\pi_i)$ (or $PF^d(\pi_i)$), is the discount sum of $L^a_{WeiP}(e)$ (or $L^d_{WeiP}(e)$) $\forall e$ on π_i. $\beta \in (0,1)$ is a discount factor. The net payoff on π_i is denoted as $PF^S(\pi_i)$, and $PF^S(\pi_i) = PF^a(\pi_i) + PF^d(\pi_i)$.

Definition 4. π_i is a Nash Equilibrium Execution (NEE) of G_i if it satisfies:

$$PF^a(\pi_i) = \max_{e_{ij} \in E(G_i)} \{L^a_{WeiP}(e_{ij}) + \beta \cdot L_{TranP}(e_{ij}) \cdot PF^a(\pi_j)\}$$

$$PF^d(\pi_i) = \max_{e_{ij} \in E(G_i)} \{L^d_{WeiP}(e_{ij}) + \beta \cdot L_{TranP}(e_{ij}) \cdot PF^d(\pi_j)\}$$

where π_j is the NEE of G_j. It is defined coinductively [13].

Definition 5. π_i is a Social Optimal Execution (SOE) of G_i, if it satisfies:

$$PF^S(\pi_i) = \min_{e_{ij} \in E(G_i)} \{L^S_{WeiP}(e_{ij}) + \beta \cdot L_{TranP}(e_{ij}) \cdot PF^S(\pi_j)\}$$

where π_j is the SOE of G_j. It is defined coinductively.

Definition 6. Strategy is a subgraph of ConTS in which the out-degree of each vertex is 1.

Definition 7. Nash Equilibrium Strategy (NES) is a strategy in which every G_i's execution is its NEE.

Definition 8. Social Optimal Strategy (SOS) is a strategy in which every G_i's execution is its SOE.

3.2   Algorithms

Under the same framework, we propose two algorithms to compute NES and SOS respectively. In this section, we just give the outline as follows:

---

[1] In the following paper, superscript a and d are used to distinguish the value for the attacker and the defender respectively. $L^S_{WeiP}(e_{ij}) = L^a_{WeiP}(e_{ij}) + L^d_{WeiP}(e_{ij})$.

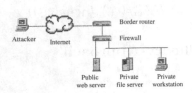

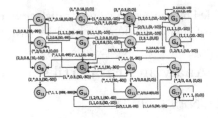

Fig. 1. Example

Fig. 2. ConTS of Example

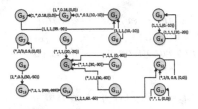

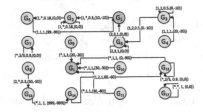

Fig. 3. Nash Equilibrium strategy 1

Fig. 4. Nash Equilibrium strategy 2

(1) Abstract the ConTS into a directed acyclic graph through graph-theoretic methods by viewing each strongly connected component as one cluster. *Leave* denotes the cluster with zero out-degree, and *NonLeave* denotes others;

(2) Find the NES (or SOS) for all *Leaves* firstly. The key point of finding the NES (or SOS) for a *Leave* is to find a cycle in this *Leave* which is a *NEE* (or *SOE*) of every vertex on it;

(3) Compute the NES (or SOS) for *NonLeaves* backward inductively. It is the same as the method in game theory which is used to compute the NES (or SOS) in finite dynamic games [10].

4 Case Study

The details of the example can be found in [8]. It is a local network connected to Internet (see Fig. 1). We assume the firewall is unreliable, so the attacker may steal or damage data stored in private file systems. We instantiate pA_i, pD_i, pN_i and G_i for each s_i and find three pairs of probabilistic bisimilar states. Fig. 2 shows the ConTS. We implement the algorithms by Java on the machine with 3.4GHz Inter(R) Core(TM) i72.99G RAM. Two NESs and one SOS are obtained, shown in Figs. 3, 4 and 5 respectively. Compare with the results obtained in [8] by game-theoretic approach: (1) we filter the third NES obtained in [8] which is invalid, because there has no practical transitions at s_3 and s_6 in this NES; (2) our model is smaller than the game model in [8]. Time consumed to compute NES and SOS by our approach is shown in Table 2.

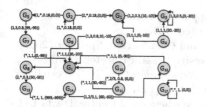

Fig. 5. Social Optimal strategy

Table 2. Time consumed by our approach

ComModel Creation	Nash Equilibrium strategy	Social Optimal strategy
2.8 s	3.7 s	1.4 s

5 Conclusion

We proposed a PVCCS based approach for modeling and analyzing a typical network security scenario with one attacker and one defender. Extension of this method might provide a uniform framework for various network security scenarios. We designed two algorithms for computing Nash Equilibrium strategy and Social Optimal strategy based on backward induction and on graph-theoretic methods. Advantages of these algorithms are also discussed.

Acknowledgments. This work has been partly funded by the French-Chinese project Locali (NSFC 61161130530 and ANR-11-IS02-0002) and by the Chinese National Basic Research Program (973) Grant No. 2014CB34030.

References

1. Diestel, R.: Graph Theory, 3rd edn. Springer-Verlag, New York (2005)
2. van Glabbeek, R., Smolka, S.A., Steffen, B., Tofts, C.M.: Reactive, generative, and stratified models of probabilistic processes. Inf. Comput. **121**(1), 59–80 (1995)
3. Harsanyi, J.C.: Games with incomplete information played by bayesian players, i-iii. Manage. Sci. **14**(3), 159–182 (1967)
4. Jean Tirole, E.M.: Markov perfect equilibrium. J. Econ. Theor. (2001)
5. Jormakka, J., Molsa, J.: Modelling information warfare as a game. J. Inf. Warfare **4**(2), 12–25 (2005)
6. Nguyen, K.C., Alpcan, T., Basar, T.: Stochastic games for security in networks with interdependent nodes. In: Proceedings of International Conference on Game Theory for Networks (2009)
7. Liang, X., Xiao, Y.: Game theory for network security. IEEE Commun. Surv. amp Tutorials **15**(1), 472–486 (2013)
8. Lye, K., Wing, J.: Game strategies in network security. In: Proceedings of the Foundations of Computer Security (2005)
9. Nguyen, K., Alpcan, T., Basar, T.: Stochastic games with incomplete information. In: Proceedings of IEEE International Conference on Communications (ICC) (2009)
10. Osborne, M.J., Rubinstein, A.: A Course in Game Theory. MIT Press, Cambridge (1994)
11. Patcha, A., Park, J.: A game theoretic apporach to modeling intrusion detection in mobile ad hoc networks. In: Proceedings of the 2004 IEEE workshop on Information Assurance and Security (2004)

12. Roy, S., Ellis, C.: A survey of game theory as applied to network security. In: 43rd Hawaii International Conference on System Sciences (2010)
13. Sangiorgi, D.: An Introduction to Bisimulation and Coinduction. Springer (2007)
14. Shapley, L.: Stochastic Games. Princeton University Press, Princeton (1953)
15. Syverson, P.: A different look at secure distributed computation. In: Proceedings 10th IEEE Computer Security Foundations Workshop (1997)
16. Wal, J.V.D.: Stochastic Dynamic Programming. Mathematical Centre Tracts 139. Morgan Kaufmann, Amsterdam (1981)
17. Xiaolin, C., Xiaobin, T., Yong, Z., Hongsheng, X.: A markov game theory-based risk assessment model for network information systems. In: International Conference on Computer Science and Software Engineering (2008)

An Improved NPCUSUM Method with Adaptive Sliding Window to Detect DDoS Attacks

Degang Sun, Kun Yang, Weiqing Huang, Yan Wang[✉], and Bo Hu

Institute of Information Engineering,
Chinese Academy of Sciences (CAS), Beijing, China
{sundegang,yangkun,huangweiqing,wangyan,hubo}@iie.ac.cn

Abstract. DDoS attacks are very difficult to detect, researches have been in the pursuit of highly efficient and flexible DDoS attacks detection methods. For this purpose, we put forward an improved Non-parametric CUSUM method (NPCUSUM), which combined with adaptive sliding windows (ASW), to detect DDoS attacks. In order to evaluate our method, we do experiments on 2000 DARPA Intrusion Detection Scenario Specific Data Set (DARPA 2000 Dataset). The results show that the proposed method improves the detection efficiency and has good flexibility.

Keywords: NPCUSUM · Sliding window · Conditional entropy · DDoS attacks detection · Darpa 2000 dataset

1 Introduction

With the rapid development of Internet, it is an exponential growth on network attacks. Due to the availability of many tools for novices, and the difficulty of tracking attackers, DDoS attacks have become a major threat to Internet [1]. Attackers employ Botnets to launch DDoS attacks for specific targets (Victims), which can lead victims to be paralyzed and cause huge economic losses [2,3].

Currently, there are plenty of detection methods [4–6] against DDoS attacks. Their main idea is almost the same that firstly extracted features which can be used to represent DDoS attacks, then found the abnormalities in network traffic.

In the article [7], the authors proposed to build a database of normal sequences by sliding a window of length n on hosts. However, the size of window is fixed, which does limit the scalability of the algorithm. The authors [8] employed statistical approaches, entropy and Chi-Square Statistic, to detect DDoS attacks. In the paper, the threshold won't be changed, so it is not a smart and wise method. In the article [9], the authors put forward a fast entropy method combined with several sliding windows. But it needs to set the initial thresholds, and it uses the pcap data which means to need much more time on calculation. The authors in the paper [10] proposed a multi-attributes CUSUM

© Springer International Publishing Switzerland 2016
S. Qing et al. (Eds.): ICICS 2015, LNCS 9543, pp. 303–310, 2016.
DOI: 10.1007/978-3-319-29814-6_25

method based on conditional entropy [16,17]. Nevertheless, the thresholds cannot be updated automatically and the size of sliding windows are not variable.

Based on the above reasons, this paper proposes an improved Non-parametric CUSUM method (NPCUSUM) method based on adaptive sliding windows to detect DDoS attacks. The main improvements of the detection method are as follow, (1) calculating conditional entropy based on netflow flow data rather than pcap packets data [13–15], (2) employing an improved NPCUSUM method based on an adaptive sliding window (ASW) to detect DDoS attacks, (3) employing tolerance factor to reduce false positive rate.

In this paper, the adaptive sliding window we designed, which could adjust its size automatically and auto update thresholds without human intervention, according to the network traffic. Our method do not need to set the initial thresholds, it can be auto updated. In order to reduce false positive rate, a tolerance factor does be employed. Only the number of attacks detected beyond the tolerance factor, then produce one alert.

The rest of this paper is organized as follows. In Sect. 2, we present the improved detection algorithm and elaborate each part in detail. In Sect. 3, we show our experiments and analysis the result. Finally, we conclude the paper in Sect. 4 and give the next step of our research.

2   Proposed Detection Algorithm

In this section, we elaborate the proposed detection approach of DDoS attacks. Table 1 lists mainly algorithm's steps, Fig. 1 displays the sketch map of our algorithm, and Table 2 gives some notions.

Table 1. Proposed algroithm' steps

(1) Transform pcap packets data to netflow flows data,
(2) Select features for detection,
(3) Chose interval time and compute the features values,
(4) Compute cumulative sum by the improved NPCUSUM method,
(5) Compare cumulative sum to thresholds and detect attacks,
(6) Updated thresholds and SASW's size.

2.1   Transform Pcap Packets Data to Netflow Flows Data

In order to reduce computation time and achieve good performance in real time, we transform pcap packets data to netflow flows data [18,19]. Generally, Fig. 2 shows a typical output of a NetFlow command line tool-nfdump.

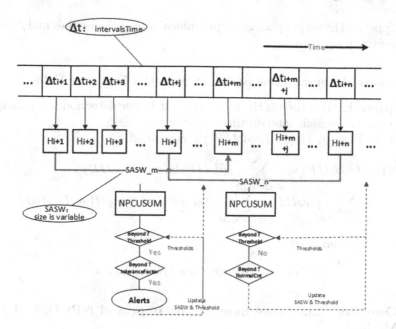

Fig. 1. Proposed algorithm's flowchart

Table 2. Notions

Δt: intervals time. The minimums calculating unit for conditional entropy
Hi: conditional entropy
$SASW$: simple adaptive sliding window. Its size is variable
$\quad$: $SASW\_m$ and $SASW\_n$ represent different SASW's sizes
$NPCUSUM$: Non-parametric CUSUM algorithm
$toleranceFactor$: tolerance factor
$normalCnt$: continuous SASW number of normal level
$Threshold$: estimate whether the flow is a DDoS attack or not

Date flow start	Duration	Proto	Src IP Addr:Port		Dst IP Addr:Port	Packets	Bytes	Flows
2010-09-01 00:00:00.459	0.000	UDP	127.0.0.1:24920	->	192.168.0.1:22126	1	46	1
2010-09-01 00:00:00.363	0.000	UDP	192.168.0.1:22126	->	127.0.0.1:24920	1	80	1

Fig. 2. Netflow's flow data

2.2   Select Features for Detection

In this paper, considering the efficiency of the algorithm, we only chose two features, conditional Entropy ($H(srcIP|dstIP)$) and the number of flows per interval time ($flowCnt$) [11, 12]. We do not choose any ports (source/destination ports) information, because ports usually arc uncertain, and any other information, such as, the number of packets per interval Time (packets), bits per second (bps), packots per second (pps) and Bytes per package (Bpp) information, because they and $flowCnt$ have the same properties.

2.3 Choose Interval Time and Compute the Features Value

In this paper, interval time is the minimize unit in our detection algorithm, and we set 1 s as the default interval time.

Conditional Entropy ($H(srcIP|dstIP)$) is computed,

$$
\begin{aligned}
H(srcIP|dstIP) &= \sum_{dstIP \in \Delta t} p(dstIP)H(srcIP|dstIP) \\
&= -\sum_{dstIP \in \Delta t} p(dstIP) \sum_{srcIP \in \Delta t} p(srcIP|dstIP)logH(srcIP|dstIP)
\end{aligned}
\tag{1}
$$

FlowCnt is computed,

$$
flowCnt = log2(sum(flows)/intervalTime)
\tag{2}
$$

2.4 Compute Cumulative Sum by the Improved NPCUSUM Method

In this paper, we calculate cumulative values between the current SASW and the last normal SASW. ByondnormalLevelSum represents the cumulative sum which beyond averages (normalMeanPre) in the last normal SASW, Lessnormal-LevelPre represents the cumulative sum which less than averages in the last normal SASW.

$$
\begin{aligned}
ByondNormalLevelSum &= sum(\{diffValues|diffValues = currentValues \\
&\quad -normalMeanPre \& diffValues > 0\}) \\
LessNormalLevelSum &= sum(\{diffValues|diffValues = currentValues \\
&\quad -normalMeanPre \& diffValues < 0\})
\end{aligned}
\tag{3}
$$

2.5 Compare Cumulative Sum to Thresholds and Detect Attacks

In traditional methods, they just compare the cumulative sum to thresholds [16,17], which will cause too much alerts, so we introduce tolerance factor-toleranceFactor. Our improved method is to cumulate the number of attacks-AttackCnt. If AttackCnt > toleranceFactor, then produce alerts. In this way it will reduce many alerts. Pseudocode 1 shows our improved idea.

2.6 Updated Thresholds and SASW's Size

In this section, we will update the thresholds and SASW's size. If there is a DDoS attack, we employ the average of three previous thresholds to update the thresholds, and SASW's size substract 1, otherwise, use the previous values. This avoids just use one single threshold to update the new thresholds.

Pseudocode 1. Estimating Improved NPCUSUM

1: **if** ($ByondnormalLevelSum > thresholds \| LessnormalLevelSum < thresholds$)
   then
2:    *warning* : *It is maybe some abnormality, please look out!*
3:    $AttackCnt = AttackCnt + 1$
4:    **if** $AttackCnt > toleranceFactor$ **then**
5:       *alerts* : *Attack is Happened!*
6:    **end if**
7: **else**
8:    *normal values*
9: **end if**

3   Experiment and Analysis

The 2000 DARPA dataset is a typical dataset of DDoS attack traffic, which includes a DDoS attack run by a novice attacker (MIT Lincoln Lab, 2000) [20]. In this section, we do experiments on Darpa 2000 dataset, and analysis the results. The total test time is about 3 h and the initial parameters are as follow, initial threshold is [0,0], intervals time is 1 s, toleranceFactor=4, SASW: [SASWSizeMin,SASWSizeMax]=[3,10].

3.1   Results

In this part, we show the results. Employing formulas (1) and (2), we can compute the conditional entropy ($H(srcIP|DstIP)$) and entropy (flowCnt) at each interval time, which can be seen in Fig. 3, the maximum entropy values represent that there is a DDoS attack.

Figure 4 shows that the thresholds are changed continuously in order to adapt the status of network traffic. At the beginning, the initial threshold is [0,0]. However, when the status of network traffic has changed, the threshold also changed automatically. When DDoS attack has happened at peak points in Fig. 4, thresholds employed the previous values and can still detect the attack.

Figure 5 is cumulative sum at each SASW, which shows that a huge change appeared when DDoS attack happened. And we can compare this value to thresholds. If this value beyond thresholds at toleranceFactor times, then produce alerts.

Figure 6 gives the change of SASW. When there are not DDoS attacks, the SASW will increase, in order to increase cumulative sum, otherwise, the SASW will decrease, because of DDoS attacks happened. At this time, a DDoS attack happened, so SASW has decreased.

Compared with [13], the authors employ many conditional entropy to detect DDoS attacks which spends several hours. But in our paper, we just use $H(srcIP|dstIP)$ and flowCnt to detect, our method spends less time, which is 1993.3560 s – about half hour, to detect DDoS attacks on Darpa 2000 and can automatic adjust parameters to adapt the status of network traffic.

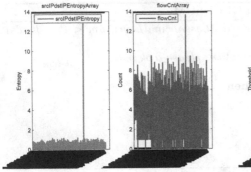

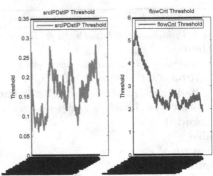

Fig. 3. Entropy

Fig. 4. Threshold

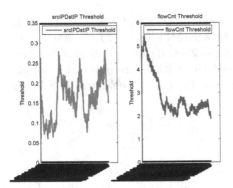

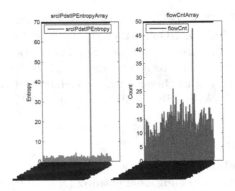

Fig. 5. NPCusum

Fig. 6. SASWSize

Through the experiments, our method can adjust the algorithm's parameters, such as, automatic to learn detection thresholds, dynamic to update detection thresholds and auto-adjust sliding windows size, according to the status of network. Our method improves the detection efficiency and has good flexibility. It can be used in practice for real-time detection.

Notes: Due to lots of values, x-axis can not be seen clearly, so we give the explanation that x-axis represents the start time of each interval or SASW.

4   Conclusion

In this paper, we propose an improved Non-parameter CUSUM method (NPCUSUM) based on an adaptive sliding window to detect DDoS attacks. According to the status of network, it is able to automatically adjust the parameters of NPCUSUM, such as, automatic to learn detection threshold, dynamic to update detection thresholds and automatic to adjust the sliding window size.

In order to evaluate our method, we do experiments on DARPA 2000 Dataset, the results show that its flexible and effective to detect DDoS attacks.

But this method also has several deficiencies, (1) it can't distinguish between Flash Contest and DDoS attacks traffic, (2) it will causes a certain delay. In this paper, we introduce toleranceFactor to reduce the number of alerts. Tolerance-Factor controls the detection sensitivity. It will cause a certain delay. In practice, it is always a tough task for researchers.

In view of the above reasons, we need to constantly improve our method and make it more reasonable and efficient.

References

1. Neustar.biz (2014). http://www.neustar.biz/resources/whitepapers/ddos-protec tion/2014-annual-ddos-attacks-and-impact-report.pdf
2. Kaspersky Report, Statistics on botnet-assisted DDoS attacks in Q1 2015
3. Cloudflare.com (2013). http://blog.cloudflare.com/the-ddos-that-knocked-spamh aus/-offline-and-ho/
4. Bhuyan, M.H., et al.: Detecting distributed denial of service attacks: methods, tools and future directions. Comput. J. **57**(4), 537–556 (2014)
5. Prasad, K.M., Reddy, A.R.M., Rao, K.V.: DoS and DDoS attacks: defense, detection and traceback mechanisms-a survey. Global. J. Comput. Sci. Technol. 14(7) (2014)
6. Murtaza, S.S., Khreich, W., Hamou-Lhadj, A., et al.: A host-based anomaly detectionapproach by representing system calls as states of kernel modules. In: 2013 IEEE 24th International Symposium on Software Reliability Engineering (ISSRE), pp. 431–440. IEEE (2013)
7. Forrest, S., Hofmeyr, S., Somayaji, A., et al.: A sense of self for unix processes. In: 1996 IEEE Symposium on Security and Privacy, pp. 120–128. IEEE (1996)
8. Feinstein, L., Schnackenberg, D., Balupari, R., Kindred, D.: Statistical approaches to DDoS attack detection and response. In: Proceedings of DARPA Information Survivability Conference and Exposition, vol. 1, pp. 303–314. IEEE, April 2003
9. No, G., Ra, I.: Adaptive DDoS detector design using fast entropy computation method. In: 2011 Fifth International Conference on Innovative Mobile and Internet Services in Ubiquitous Computing (IMIS), pp. 86–93. IEEE (2011)
10. Zhao, X.H., Xia, J.B., Guo, W.W., Du, H.H.: Detection DDoS attacks based on multi-dimensional entropy. J. Air Force Eng. Univ. (Natural Science Edition) **3**, 015 (2013)
11. Conditional Entropy. https://en.wikipedia.org/wiki/Conditional_entropy
12. Cover, T.M., Thomas, J.A.: Elements of Information Theory, 1st edn. Wiley, New York (1991). ISBN 0-471-06259-6
13. Bereziski, P., et al.: An entropy-based network anomaly detection method. Entropy **17**(4), 2367–2408 (2015)
14. Thapngam, T., Yu, S., Zhou, W., Makki, S.K.: Distributed Denial of Service (DDoS) detection by traffic pattern analysis. Peer-to-Peer Networking Appl. **7**(4), 346–358 (2014)
15. Bhuyan, M.H., Bhattacharyya, D.K., Kalita, J.K.: An empirical evaluation of information metrics for low-rate and high-rate DDoS attack detection. Pattern Recogn. Lett. **51**, 1–7 (2015)

16. Page, E.S.: Continuous Inspection Scheme. Biometrika 41 (1/2): 100C115(1954). doi:10.1093/biomet/41.1-2.100.JSTOR2333009
17. Bassevilleand, M., Nikiforov, I.V.: Detection of Abrupt Changes: Theory and Application. Prentice-Hall Inc., Upper Saddle River (1993)
18. Cisco. http://www.cisco.com/c/en/us/tech/quality-of-service-qos/netflow/index. html
19. Hofstede, R., Celeda, P.: Flow monitoring explained: from packet capture to data analysis with NetFlow and IPFIX. IEEE Commun. Surv. Tutorials (IEEE Communications Society) 16(4), 28 (2014). doi:10.1109/COMST.2014.2321898
20. Darpa2000. http://www.ll.mit.edu/IST/id/data/2000/LLS_DDOS_1.0.html

Dynamic Hybrid Honeypot System Based Transparent Traffic Redirection Mechanism

Wenjun Fan[1(✉)], Zhihui Du[2], David Fernández[1], and Xinning Hui[2]

[1] Departamento de Ingenierísía de Sistemas Telemáticos,
ETSI Telecomunicación, Universidad Politécnica de Madrid,
28040 Madrid, Spain
efan@dit.upm.es
[2] Tsinghua National Laboratory for Information Science and Technology,
Department of Computer Science and Technology,
Tsinghua University, Beijing 100084, China

Abstract. Honeypots are a type of security tools aimed to capture malicious activity. Related to their data capture function, two main factors are important: scalability and fidelity. A hybrid honeypot is a special honeypot system consisting of frontends and backends that can achieve a good balance between scalability and fidelity, as the frontends can monitor large-scale IP address spaces and the backends can provide fully functional systems to guarantee fidelity. The traffic redirection function is used to bridge the frontends and the backends, allowing to redirect the interesting traffic from the frontends to the backends. In this paper, a dynamic hybrid honeypot system based transparent traffic redirection mechanism is proposed in order to address the identical-fingerprint problem. The experimental results show that this mechanism can keep the traffic redirection stealthy and effective.

Keywords: Traffic redirection · Connection handoff · Hybrid honeypot · Dynamic honeypot

1 Introduction

Numerous computer systems are faced with network attacks every day. Most organizations use different security devices to protect their systems, like firewalls that block traffic aimed to specific destination ports, or intrusion detection system (IDS) that report alerts when the attacks are detected. However, these devices fail to provide traffic capture and analyze capabilities. A honeypot is a system aimed to solve this problem. It is defined as the security system whose value lies in being probed, attacked and compromised [1]. Honeypots have no production value and server-side honeypots even never advertise themselves but passively capture malicious behavior. Thus, the inbound traffic directed to them can be considered unauthorized and suspicious. Honeypots can be roughly classified into two categories in terms of the interaction level: low-interaction honeypot (LIH), which only implements a partial functionality of the complete system they emulate; and high-interaction honeypot (HIH) that provides a fully functional system. LIHs fails to provide fidelity but they can be deployed in large

S. Qing et al. (Eds.): ICICS 2015, LNCS 9543, pp. 311–319, 2016.
DOI: 10.1007/978-3-319-29814-6_26

scale due to its lightweight design. HIHs can guarantee fidelity but they are impractical to be deployed for large address spaces. LIH is less risk than HIH since the adversary can compromise a HIH but not a LIH. Thus, in order to foster strengths and circumvent weakness, hybrid systems made of LIHs and HIHs are proposed.

Hybrid honeypot systems use the LIHs as the frontends [2, 3], replying to attacker connection requests and establishing the TCP connections. Later, if the traffic is interesting enough, the hybrid system will perform a connection handoff and redirect the interesting traffic to the HIH. Due to the fact that most existing traffic redirection approaches only focus on connection handoff but rarely keep the destination fingerprint identical, the existing traffic redirection approaches are only capable to fraud script kiddies and automated attacks, but cannot deceive advanced intruders. In practical terms, a skilled intruder will not only observe the connection state but also check the destination fingerprint. Therefore, it is necessary to apply a transparent traffic redirection mechanism which can keep the connection state and the destination fingerprint for hybrid honeypot systems to capture interesting traffic. The objective of this paper is to design a dynamic hybrid honeypot system based traffic redirection mechanism. In order to achieve this objective two technical challenges have to be addressed: (1) to provide a transparent connection handoff by keeping the connection in the same state after takeover; (2) using dynamic hybrid honeypot system to keep the identical appearance of destination, i.e. IP address and operating system fingerprint.

The paper is organized as follows: in Sect. 2, the related work is reviewed; in Sect. 3, the dynamic hybrid honeypot system is presented; in Sect. 4, several experimental results are demonstrated; in Sect. 5, some conclusions are presented.

2   Related Work

Hybrid honeypot systems [4, 5] using GRE tunnel to connect the frontends and the backends do not show the identical-fingerprint problem, because the backends seem to be directly deployed in the production network. But all traffic is processed with two modes: discard or redirection, due to the use of frontends without interaction capability.

Bailey et al. [2] presented a globally distributed hybrid honeypot architecture which deploys LIHs as the frontend content filters and HIHs to investigate the attack traffic in detail. The system uses a connection handoff mechanism for traffic redirection. In order to avoid saving state for every connection, the connection handoff mechanism takes the decision based on the first payload of any conversation. However, the technical details about the connection handoff mechanisms were not described.

Connection handoff or mobility always needs TCP connection replay between the TCP proxy and the target. Although there are a number of ready-made TCP proxies [6,7], they cannot manipulate or analyze the packets but only redirect them. Similarly, Honeybrid gateway [3] uses the connection replay to implement traffic redirection. Nevertheless, Honeybrid unveiled their technical detail: a TCP replay proxy using libnetfilter_queue [16] to filter traffic. The connection handoff mechanism based on TCP replay is able to provide stealthy redirection for automated malwares. Lin et al. [8] proposed a secure and transparent network environment that allows the automated malwares to attack and propagate but under a stealthy control. Although the TCP/IP stateful traffic replay can facilitate transparent TCP connection handoff, it cannot solve the identical-fingerprint problem.

Some other proposals were trying to address the identical-fingerprint problem for the hybrid honeypot systems. VMI-Honeymon [9] provided a novel solution to clone-routing problem, which is a challenge to create network connectivity to identical HIHs clones without internal in-guest network reconfiguration. Because the network interface in each clone will also remain identical, sharing the same MAC and IP address of the original VM. It will cause MAC and IP collision if the clones are placed on the same network bridge. But in-guest network reconfiguration would inadvertently lead to changing the initial memory state of high-interaction honeypots. Thus, this solution retains the MAC and IP address of the original VM for each clone, and each clone is placed upon a separate network bridge. This solution indirectly addresses the identical-fingerprint problem.

3 System Overview

Reconfiguration is a challenge for most security technologies including honeypot as well. Static honeypot systems lack the capability to reconfigure the decoy on the fly, while dynamic honeypots are able to improve the honeypot deployment according to the specific events [10, 11]. Figure 1 presents an overview of our dynamic hybrid honeypot system architecture which has been proposed by our previous work [12].

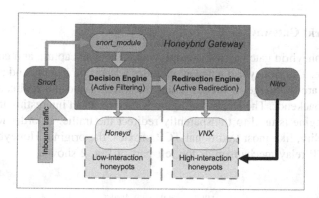

Fig. 1. An overview of the dynamic hybrid honeypot system architecture

We applies several specialized tools as the components for hosting the dynamic hybrid honeypot system but our ideas are not limited to these tools. For the future research, other advanced tools can replace the current tools in the architecture. In this paper, we focus on the honeypot deployment tools and the Honeybrid gateway, while the other detailed descriptions of the architecture can refer to our previous work [12].

3.1   Honeypot Deployment Tools

The system uses Honeyd [13] as the LIHs creation tool, VNX [14] to deploy HIHs and create virtual networks.

Honeyd is a low-interaction virtual honeypot framework, which allows quickly deploying virtual honeypots. It can emulate fingerprints of several operating systems. It also provids a UNIX socket located in/var/run/honeyd.sock to communicate with the inner workings of Honeyd with a script made of Honeyd commands. Thus, using this socket, users can create a client socket to reconfigure the Honeyd based honeypots on the fly, for example, to create and delete any template or even any service.

VNX is employed by our system architecture due to (i) its scalability in creating very complex HIHs; (ii) its ability to automatize the execution of commands inside virtual machines; and (iii), its support for multiple virtualization platforms like KVM, which allows emulating various operating systems under X86 architecture for HIHs. The new version of VNX has developed the capability of dynamic configuration. VNX can automatically reconfigure the scenario through processing an XML syntax based reconfiguration file. One part of the running scenario will be redeployed without impacting on the rest part.

Due to Honeyd and VNX using different configuration languages, we proposed a technology independent honeynet description language (TIHDL) [15] to generally describe and configure the heterogeneous honeynets consisting of Honeyd based LIHs and VNX based HIHs.

3.2   Honeybrid Gateway

The revised Honeybrid gateway [3] is employed as the data capture and control tool in our architecture. The Honeybrid gateway includes a Decision Engine and a Redirection Engine which are in charge of orchestrating the filtering and the redirection between frontends and backends. The Decision Engine is used to select interesting traffic and the Redirection Engine is used to transparently redirect the traffic. In order to implement such functionality, like most traditional TCP proxies, the original Honeybrid gateway applies the TCP relay mechanism as the left part of Fig. 2 shows.

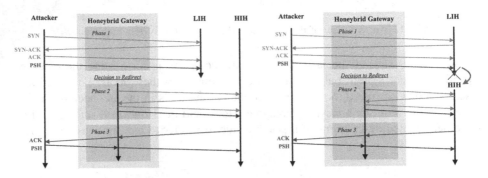

Fig. 2. Illustration of the traffic redirection mechanisms

The main drawback of the original Honeybrid gateway is that it is not able to distinguish the automated attacks from the human manual attacks. More accurately speaking, it neglects the attacks generated by advanced intruders. In the original design, a pair of LIH and HIH use different IP addresses, and the Honeybrid gateway can transparently redirect the traffic from the LIH to the corresponding HIH by connection handoff. It is useful to catch the automated malware but if the attack is from an intelligent adversary, he can easily detect the traffic redirection by simply checking the IP address of final compromised system. If the destination IP address is different from the original target IP address, the adversary can realize that he is accessing a honeypot. We will address this problem by improving transparent traffic redirection between LIH and HIH based on the dynamic hybrid honeypot system. In order to guarantee such functionality, we have to address the following two questions: how to perform connection handoff and how to keep the identical fingerprint.

The answer to the first question is to preserve the presence of states in the communication. This task has been finished in the original Honeybrid gateway. For the second requirement, it is necessary to guarantee the identical IP address and the fingerprint of the pair of LIH and HIH. The right part of Fig. 2 summarizes the revised mechanism involved in the redirection. The Redirection Engine works in three phases:

Phase 1: Incoming packets from the attacker are forwarded to the LIH while being inspected by the Decision Engine;

Phase 2: If the Decision Engine flags the connection as worth redirecting, it sends a signal to the Redirection Engine to switch off the LIH and switch up the corresponding HIH. When the HIH is ready to take over, the Redirection Engine starts replaying the connection to the HIH;

Phase 3: When the connection between the Honeybrid gateway and the HIH is established, packets are proxied between the attacker and the HIH. Thanks to the update of TCP headers of all packets proxied during this phase, the attacker believes it still communicates with the original target from the connection initialized in phase 1.

Therefore, the Honeybrid gateway controls not only the data but also the honeypots. Before it replays the connection, it must switch off the LIH and spin up the corresponding HIH. It is important to notice that while most of the network attacks can be redirected through this mechanism, some specific attack processes are out of the scope of current architecture. These processes include connections based on cryptographic protocols such as SSH or HTTPS. However, in such cases, specific services and IP addresses can be configured to forward directly to the farm of HIHs.

4 Experiments

The transparent traffic redirection mechanism should be evaluated in two ways: firstly, it should be tested if an adversary could fingerprint the redirection; secondly, the performance of redirection mechanism should be verified under heavy traffic.

First of all, for the functional verification we use the telnet service to test the transparent redirection mechanism as Fig. 3 shows.

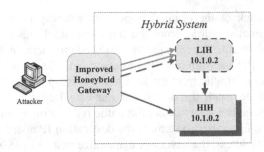

Fig. 3. Testing scenario

The telnet server runs on a HIH. The attacker uses the telnet client to connect a LIH (10.1.0.2), and the Honeybrid gateway can handoff the connection to the HIH. The messages shown on the attacker side are as follows:

```
attacker# telnet 10.1.0.2 23
Trying 10.1.0.2...
Connected to 10.1.0.2.
Escape character is '^]'.
Ubuntu 14.04.2 LTS
HIH login:

HIH#
```

It shows the attacker has connected into the HIH. However, the possible problem is the latency caused by starting a HIH. We tested the duration to start or wake up a VNX based HIH. VNX can deploy KVM based virtual machine and LXC based virtual machine. The delay is very short to start up a LXC based virtual machine (less than 1 s). But the virtual machine based on LXC can only emulate the Linux operation system using the same Linux kernel of the host. Thus, this method lacks of fidelity.

The virtual machine based on KVM can emulate various operating systems. A virtual machine emulated by VNX has five states. They are undefined, defined, running, suspended and hibernated. VNX provides functions that can switch a virtual honeypot from one state to any other state. The average startup latency of KVM based HIH from different states is shown in Table 1. To start up or reboot a KVM based HIH will take 40 s, which could result in time out of connection request. To wake up a hibernated HIH still needs 13 s, so it is not a good choice either. A suspended HIH spins up only within 1.5 s, which has the shortest delay. Therefore, the approach for KVM based HIHs is to start up a group of HIHs and then keep them into suspended state. When the interesting traffic is decided to be redirected, the corresponding suspended HIH should wake up to provide service.

Table 1. Average startup latency from different states

Initial state	Suspended	Hibernated	Defined
Average startup latency (sec)	1.5	13	40

Secondly, for the performance evaluation we use the network bandwidth measurement tool namely Iperf to test the HIH with using Honeybrid and without using Honeybrid. Figure 4 illustrates the bandwidth comparison.

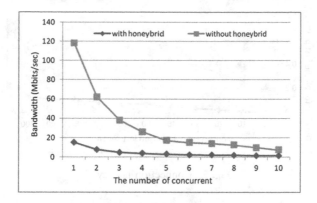

Fig. 4. Bandwidth test by Iperf

The figure shows that the bandwidths under different numbers of parallel TCP connections. It is normal that the more number which the concurrent TCP connections have, the less value that the bandwidth has. Under the function of Honeybrid gateway, the bandwidth of TCP connection between the attacker and HIH is much less than the bandwidth when there is no Honeybrid gateway. It proves that the gateway greatly limits the bandwidth of TCP connection due to its processing on every packet.

We also designed a test based on the SMTP to monitor the latency of the first push packets arriving at the HIH under different rates of incoming connections. An SMTP server (Postfix) was installed in HIHs. An SMTP client script was installed on the remote attacker. The script consists of the following sequence of five SMTP commands:

```
HELO test \n
MAIL FROM: <test@test.test> \n
RCPT TO: <root@localhost> \n
DATA.\n
test.\n
```

The experiment consisted of running the automated SMTP client script at different rates, from a single connection per second up to 100 concurrent connections per second. We just record the duration for all the first push packet of each connection arriving at the backend. The experimental result was shown in Fig. 5.

The first push packet including payload arriving at the backend means the TCP connection between the attacker and HIH has been established. So the timestamp of the first push packet arriving at the network interface of the backend can be used to calculate the duration for establishing TCP connection. The experimental result shows

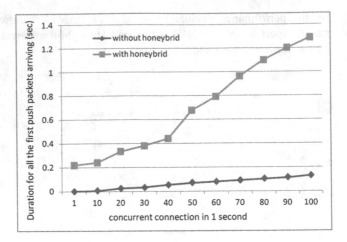

Fig. 5. Connection latency

that the connections with packet processing of Honeybrid gateway can cause much more latency than the normal connections, and the effect will become much more obvious when the number of concurrent connections is increasing.

Therefore, the proposed transparent traffic redirection mechanism is effective. Although there are some approaches to detect honeypots through performance testing, for example, testing the connection latency, the performance reduction caused by the packet processing of Honeybrid gateway is still reasonable.

5 Conclusion and Future Work

In this paper, a novel dynamic hybrid honeypot system based traffic redirection mechanism is proposed in order to solve the identical-fingerprint problem. The proposed system architecture employs several virtualized tools to approach the task. The mechanism uses libnetfilter_queue to process packets and uses the switch between LIHs and HIHs to avoid fingerprint detection. The experimental results show that the mechanism is functional effective and the performance depends on the processing rate of Honeybrid gateway. In the future, firstly we will try to improve the performance of Honeybrid gateway to reduce the risk of being detected. Secondly, we will try to apply this mechanism to some large-scale honeypot systems in order to facilitate resource efficiency as well.

Acknowledgement. This research is supported in part by National Natural Science Foundation of China (No. 61440057, 61272087, 61363019 and 61073008), Beijing Natural Science Foundation (No. 4082016 and 4122039), the Sci-Tech Interdisciplinary Innovation and Cooperation Team Program of the Chinese Academy of Sciences, the Specialized Research Fund for State Key Laboratories. It is also partially funded by the Spanish MICINN (project RECLAMO, Virtual and Collaborative Honeynets based on Trust Management and Autonomous Systems applied to Intrusion Management, with codes TIN2011-28287-C02-01 and TIN2011-28287-C02-02) and the European Commission (FEDER/ERDF).

References

1. Spitzner, L.: The Value of Honeypots, Part One: Definitions and Values of Honeypots, 10 October 2001. http://www.symantec.com/connect/articles/value-honeypots-part-one-definitions-and-values-honeypots
2. Bailey, M., Cooke, E., Watson, D., Jahanian, F., Provos, N.: A hybrid honeypot architecture for scalable network monitoring. Technical Report CSE-TR-499-04, U. Michigan, October 2004
3. Berthier, R., Cukier, M.: Honeybrid: a hybrid honeypot architecture. In: USENIX Security Symposium (2008)
4. Jiang, X., Xu, D.: Collapsar: a VM-based architecture for network attack detention center. In: Proceedings of the USENIX Security Symposium, August 2004
5. Vrable, M., Ma, J., Chen, J., Moore, D., Vandekieft, E., Snoeren, A.C., Voelker, G.M., Savage, S.: Scalability, fidelity, and containment in the Potemkin virtual honeyfarm. In: Proceedings of the Twentieth ACM Symposium on Operating Systems Principles (SOSP 2005), pp. 148–162, New York. ACM Press (2005)
6. Chesneau, B.: tproxy 0.5.4 (2011). https://pypi.python.org/pypi/tproxy/0.5.4
7. Aston, P., Fitzgerald, C.: The Grinder (2013). http://grinder.sourceforge.net/g3/tcpproxy.html
8. Lin, Y.-D., Shih, T.-B., Yu-Sung, W., Lai, Y.-C.: Secure and transparent network traffic replay, redirect, and relay in a dynamic malware analysis environment. Secur. Comm. Netw. **7**(3), 626–640 (2013)
9. Lengyel, T.K., Neumann, J., Maresca, S., Kiayias, A.: Towards hybrid honeynets via virtual machine introspection and cloning. In: Lopez, J., Huang, X., Sandhu, R. (eds.) NSS 2013. LNCS, vol. 7873, pp. 164–177. Springer, Heidelberg (2013)
10. Hung, M.-H., Tsail, C.-L.: Intrusive behavior analysis based on dynamic honeynet and multidimensional hidden markov model. J. C.C.I.T. **40**(1), 29–42 (2011)
11. Hecker, C., Hay, B.: Automated honeynet deployment for dynamic network environment. In: 46th Hawaii International Conference on System Sciences (HICSS), pp. 4880–4889, 7–10 January 2013
12. Fan, W., Fernández, D., Du, Z.: Adaptive and flexible virtual honeynet. In: Proceedings of International Conference on Mobile, Secure and Programmable Networking (MSPN), pp. 1–17, Paris, France, 15-17 June 2015
13. Provos, N.: A virtual honeypot framework. In: Proceedings of the 13th Conference on USENIX Security Symposium (SSYM 2004), vol. 13 (2004)
14. Fernández, D., Cordero, A., Somavilla, J., Rodriguez, J., Corchero, A., Tarrafeta, L., Galan, F.: Distributed virtual scenarios over multi-host Linux environments. In: 5th International DMTF Academic Alliance Workshop on Systems and Virtualization Management (SVM), pp.1–8, 24 October 2011
15. Fan, W., Fernández, D., Villagra, V.: Technology independent honeynet description language. In: Proceedings of 3rd International Conference on Model-Driven Engineering and Software Development (MODELSWARD), pp. 303–311, Angers, Loire Valley, France, 9-11 February 2015
16. Welte, H., Ayuso, P.N.: The netfilter.org "libnetfilter_queue" project (2014). http://www.netfilter.org/projects/libnetfilter_queue/

Leveraging Static Probe Instrumentation for VM-based Anomaly Detection System

Ady Wahyudi Paundu[✉], Takeshi Okuda, Youki Kadobayashi, and Suguru Yamaguchi

Nara Institute of Science and Technology,
8916-5 Takayama, Ikoma, Nara 630-0192, Japan
{ady.paundu.ak9,okuda,youki-k,suguru}@is.naist.jp

Abstract. In this preliminary study, we introduce a framework to predict anomaly behavior from Virtual Machines (VMs) deployed in public IaaS cloud model. Within this framework we propose to use a static probe instrumentation technique inside hypervisor in order to collect monitoring data and a black-box signature based feature selection method using Linear Discriminant Analysis. As a proof of concept, we run several evaluation tests to measure the output quality and computation overhead of our Anomaly Detection System (ADS) using feature selection. The results show that our feature selection technique does not significantly reduce the anomaly prediction quality when compared with full featured ADS and gives a better accuracy when compared to ADS with system-call data. Furthermore, ADS with feature selection method creates lower computing overhead compared to the other two ADS.

Keywords: Anomaly detection system · Virtual Machine · Static probe instrumentation · Cloud security

1 Introduction

One main security threat in virtualization environments of cloud computing is the guest VMs [1]. A VM can be seen as a single point of failure inside a virtualization. To monitor each VM however is not an easy task. In public IaaS there is usually an agreement between a provider and a consumer about privacy that restricts any intervention from hypervisor administrator into the guest internal system. The lack of insider information from guest OS will decrease the quality of information collected from the VM. Hypervisor administrators need to find a method to collect information on the VM's internal operation as clear as possible without guest OS intervention. In this paper, we present a novel, the first to the best of our knowledge using static probe instrumentation inside hypervisor for host-based Virtual Machine monitoring process. This approach applies specifically to Anomaly Detection System (ADS). This technique employs embedded tracepoints inside Virtual Machine Monitor (VMM) to observe VM behavior. To reduce the big dimension of monitoring points inside the hypervisor, we apply

© Springer International Publishing Switzerland 2016
S. Qing et al. (Eds.): ICICS 2015, LNCS 9543, pp. 320–334, 2016.
DOI: 10.1007/978-3-319-29814-6_27

Linear Discriminant Analysis (LDA) technique using system performance aspect of VM. Another main contribution is an empirical evaluation for our framework where we answer questions regarding its feasibility, effectivity, efficiency, scalability, impact and adaptability. We also compare some of these evaluations to two other ADSes which are full-featured static instrumentation ADS and system-call based ADS.

The remainder of this paper is organized as follows. In Sect. 2 we discuss previous related work on anomaly detection in the cloud. We follow this in Sect. 3 by defining our architectural framework for using static-probe instrumentation technique to monitor VM behavior. Then we discuss our empirical evaluation in Sect. 4 to assess the performance of our approach. We use Sect. 5 to discuss some issues in detail, and finally conclude the paper in Sect. 6.

2   Related Work

There have been a lot of papers covering the domain of VM-based anomaly detection system to date. However, most of these researches are focusing on private cloud, where cloud administrator can enforce internal agents inside each VM they monitor. For instance, in some approaches, the author collected VM's internal resources usage information using distributed monitoring system like Ganglia [2,3]. Another example of this intrusive approach is using honeypot-VM kernel sensors to detect intrusions [4]. The most well known method in this subject is Virtual Machine Introspection (VMI) [5]. This approach does not need to employ agents inside the monitored VM, and instead use a wealth of information of VM from Virtual Machine Monitor, like CPU state, memory raw content, I/O state. However, VMI highly depends on certain information from the Operating System (OS) inside the VM to properly interpret the monitored objects that it collected. Such information for example is debugging symbols information file for Windows system or memory offset information file for Linux that have to be copied to the monitoring program residing at the host. All these approaches are not suitable in public cloud where customers are unlikely to allow any intervention within their system.

For monitoring public cloud systems, researchers need to use non-intrusive approaches. One of the options is network-based approach that monitors traffic from and to VM in order to create a model for anomaly detection [6,7]. This method is only able to detect anomaly related to network operation. Another approach is using the fact that from host's point of view, each VM can be seen as a normal user process. Therefore, to monitor the behavior of each VM, a host can collect user process related data, such as CPU usage, memory usage or I/O volume [8,9]. Others attempt to monitor system-call exchange between VM in user-space process and host's kernel-space [10,11]. Although non-intrusive approaches uphold clients privacy and have high attack resistance, they lacks visibility on internal VM operation. This problem is known as semantic gap problem.

In our work, we use static probe instrumentation data of hypervisor to monitor VM's behavior. We argue that this approach can give better visibility into the

VM compared to system-call data or computation resource usage data because it captures its data right inside the hypervisor. To our knowledge, our proposed approach of using this instrumentation technique for VM-based monitoring is a novel approach.

3   Architectural Framework

In this work, the object of our study is public IaaS clous system, so it renders out any monitoring mechanism that requires any interference to guest VM operation. Current external monitoring approach however still cannot give enough visibility because of semantic gap problem. Therefore, we have sought to identify a solution to increase monitoring visibility into the VM, transparently from VM user point of view. Our approach works by instrumenting the hypervisor, which gives us a better access into essential underlying operation of the VM without requiring any guest interruption. Furthermore, our observation points are logically closer to the object compared to previous approaches, and that will ensure a clearer perspective into the VM.

The framework of our approach consists of three main processes, namely data collection, feature extraction and anomaly prediction as depicted in Fig. 1.

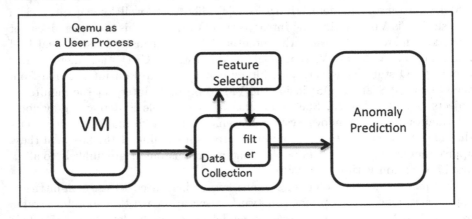

Fig. 1. High level abstraction of architectural framework

3.1   Data Collection Process

In this paper, we propose the collection of monitoring data by using static probe instrumentation inside the hypervisor. A probe is a small piece of code, usually in a form of function call that, when executed, records a certain information, such as its name which constitutes its location within the source code and its parameters value. This information can usually be used to find out the current status and location of the program execution for debugging functions. We put our probe points inside certain VMM's functions and log them every time they are called. Three information could be extracted from these tracepoints. First is their occurrence frequency, second is their arguments value and third is their temporal relation between tracepoints. In this preliminary research on VM monitoring we only use their occurrence frequency (bag of tracepoints).

3.2 Feature Extraction Process

Generally speaking, debugging information from VMM can be huge enough to overwhelm monitoring process. For example, Qemu, one of the most widely used open source VMM, comes with around 1,200 trace points. For real-time anomaly detection, this amount of tracepoints is still very big to observe. Furthermore, from the machine learning point of view, not all of those tracepoints contain significant information. Some of the tracepoints can even act as noises. Therefore, we need to extract just small enough feature without compromising final anomaly prediction quality.

The choice of the proper tracepoints is not easy. The ideal of course is by having a complete understanding on how internal VMM works, which is usually called white-box approach. This clear picture of VMM inner works enables us to identify what functions are related to the processes we want to observe. In this preliminary research, we do not assume any knowledge of VMM internal operation. As a solution, we adopt black-box approach, where we compare each input to its output and tries to figure out their relation. In specific, we decided to use memory, I/O and network process signature as our basic profile. Many well-known and common malicious activities can be directly related to abnormal system performance [12], for instance Denial-of-Service, password dictionary attack and fuzz testing.

The purpose of feature extraction is to select subset of variables that can highly explain the change in memory usage, I/O read-write frequency or network send-receive volume. Hence, we need to use dimension reduction technique that considers class information. For that reason, we use Linear Discriminant Analysis (LDA) technique. LDA seeks to reduce data dimensionality while preserving as much of the class discriminatory information as possible, such that maximizing between-class to within-class covariance. For two class analysis, linear discriminant is defined as the linear function $y = w^T x$ that maximizes criterion function

$$J(w) = \frac{|\widetilde{\mu}_1 - \widetilde{\mu}_2|^2}{\tilde{s}_1^2 + \tilde{s}_2^2}$$

where $\widetilde{\mu}_i$ is mean value for class i and $\tilde{s}_i^2$ is class i's scatter value along w projection. The output of LDA is linear combinations of its variables input.

3.3 Anomaly Prediction Process

In our anomaly prediction process we implement a semi-supervised anomaly detection system. This system introduces only one class model, which is normal profile. Any data input that does not conform to this model will be categorized into new class and considered as an anomaly. This approach is also known as one-class novelty detection system as all the learning data to create the prediction model come from one single class. This approach works better under assumption that a VM in the cloud works for one specific service, for example: web server, application server or mail server. Since this kind of servers create almost homogenous operation, it is easier to provide a sound training dataset.

We use one-class SVM as our prediction engine. This predictor uses several advantageous properties of Support Vector Machine (SVM) where it is more robusts to noise and can easily work with high dimensional data while allowing smooth and flexible nonlinear mappings. Data points that cannot be separated in their original space dimension are mapped to another higher dimension feature space where there is a straight hyperplane that separates one class to another. When the resulted hyperplane is projected back into the original input dimension, it would form some non-linear curve.

3.4 Threat Model and Limitations

In our threat model, we assume that the cloud provider and its infrastructures are trusted. We consider two threat scenarios, either attacks are coming from inside the VM we monitor or the attacks coming from outside, targeting a specific monitored VM.

The approach we present in this paper is a passive approach, since it can only detect anomalies after they happen. However, in the case of long anomaly process, administrator can react upon this information to minimize the impact of malicious anomalies.

As for anomaly detection system in general, our approach cannot distinguish between malicious and non-malicious anomalies. For that purpose, additional steps need to be taken which are beyond the scope of our paper. In our framework, the decision of process maliciousness is decided by manual inspection from the system administrator.

4 Evaluation

Within this section we performed several evaluations on the framework that we described in Sect. 3. There are four research questions that we want to answer in this segment:

1. Feasibility: Can the normal data collected for learning phase converge to a stable model with low false-positives values?
2. Effectiveness: How sensitive is the model created by the training data to distinguish normal to abnormal VM operation?
3. Efficiency and Scalability: What is the cost for a host to monitor the VMs, in term of CPU usage and execution time? Will they scale well over multiple observed VMs?
4. Impact: How much is the monitoring process affecting the performance of the monitored VM?

4.1   General Setup

Hardware Setup. Diagram of our setup is shown in Fig. 2. Host specification was a dual Intel Xeon CPU 1.86 GHz with 8 GB memory and 320 GB hard-disk running Ubuntu 14.04. For the hypervisor we employed the combination of Qemu-KVM. Next, we deployed eight VMs inside the host. The VMs, for better measurements, were all identical with single Qemu Virtual CPU, 1 GB memory and 30 GB harddisk. All of the VMs were using Ubuntu 14.04 operating system and serve Apache-MySQL-PHP (AMP) services.

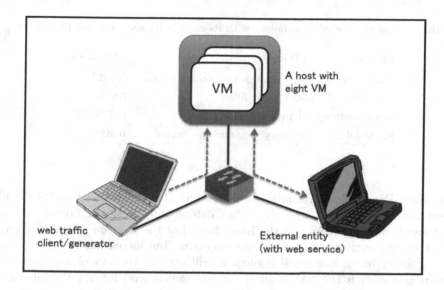

Fig. 2. Hardware setup

Normal Profile. For normal VM operation, we decided to implement a web service. Beside the fact that web service is among the most served function on the internet, it also allowed us to experience multiple normal profiles for our evaluation purpose. To emulate the operation of a web server, we used RUBiS (Rice University Bidding System) application. Using RUBiS, we can emulate a scalable dynamic web server operation.

Data Collection. There were two kinds of data collection in this evaluation process. The first data collection was static probe instrumentation as our suggested approach, while the second was system-call data that will be used as comparison methods to our approach. In the case of static probe instrumentation, we utilized "ust" (user space tracer) backend from LTTng user space tracing (LTTng UST) library. For system-call collection we used "strace" tool. A single data unit was a collection of occurrence frequency of observed features within two seconds.

Feature Selection. We collected five datasets, each with 100 unit data. Those datasets represented the following scenarios: idle, stress-memory, stress-I/O, stress-disk and stress-network. We used "stress" Linux application for generating memory, I/O and disk data while for network we use ping with flood option. Next we paired the idle dataset with each of stress dataset which resulted in four pair scenarios. For each pair we applied Linear Discriminant Analysis to extract tracepoints that best separate each scenario. Table 1 gives the best tracepoint with its associative scenario and its LDA score. All operations within this feature selection process were done using R [13, 14].

Table 1. List of selected tracepoints with its associative scenario and LDA score

idle vs	TP name	LDA score
stress network	tap_send qemu_deliver_packet	0.9913
stress IO	bdrv_aio_flush	0.9869
stress memory	virtqueue_fill	0.5795
stress hd	memory_region_ops_write	0.9992

Anomaly Prediction. Results of one-class SVM are influenced by its ν and γ parameters. ν is a constant > 0 that determines the upper bound on the fraction of training errors and the lower bound of the fraction of support vectors. Over-minimizing ν will reduce training error, but increasing false-positives. On the other hand, not small enough ν will over-fit the model and increase false-negatives. γ is the coefficient (Lagrange multipliers) for our Radial Basis Function kernel. Therefore, as part of the setup, we try to find the best combination of these two paramaters to use throughout our evaluation. Using ν and γ as controlled variables, we try to optimize estimator output by performing grid search. We search within values range $0.01 - 0.1$ with 0.01 step for both ν and γ parameters. We used False Positive as target variable. That is, we search for a combination of ν and γ values that gave the smallest False Positive result. From our normal profile dataset, we randomly prepared five subsets data. The average result from grid search of each subset data gave $\nu = 0.01$ and $\gamma = 0.01$ as our optimal value. For this grid-search process and all anomaly prediction operaton in evaluation section, we use python scripts and scikit-learn [15] library.

4.2   Feasibility with Limited Data

One characteristic of public cloud service is to pay for what is used. Therefore, it is common to see short-lived VMs hosted in the cloud. An anomaly detection system that is able to generate a normal model from smaller input without sacrificing the output quality of the system is preferred. The model created must be able to produce low enough false-positives to be considered effective. For evaluation, we used five-fold cross-validation over 500 units data of normal scenario from selected feature of static probe instrumentation approach. The 500 data were divided into 5 subsets of 100 data. Each subset was then used as evaluation input for anomaly detection model created from increased number of data from the other four subsets. Due to the fact that all the data used in this specific evaluation were normal, an anomaly status would be considered false-positive. Figure 3 shows the average result for false-positive value of 5 subsets, predicted by normal model that was created from different size of training data. It shows that using selected feature data from static probe instrumentation monitoring on normal scenario can create a stable learning model. Furthermore, to achieve at most 5 % false positives, we need at least 100 unit learning data.

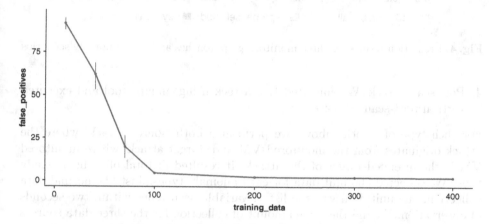

Fig. 3. Percentage of false positives as the number of training data increased

4.3 Effectiveness Against Diverse Attacks

For this evaluation part we emulated several attack scenarios as anomaly data and then observed if the predictor was able to identify them as anomaly or not. There were already many kinds of attacks that have happened in the cloud. However, one of our primary concern in this research is semantic gap information for non-intrusive VM monitoring. Therefore we try to imitate attacks that can represent either processes that extensively use computer resources and can be easily detected without semantic context or processes that in contrary happened in higher layer which makes it very hard to detect. For that reason we utilized these four attacks:

1. Synchronous-packet flood attack. This scenario was emulated using "hping3" tool and targeting port 80.
2. Password brute force attack. Using "ncrack" tool we try to crack an http basic authentication procedure.
3. Slow HTTP attack. We emulated this scenario using "httpslowtest" tool with attack in the body option.

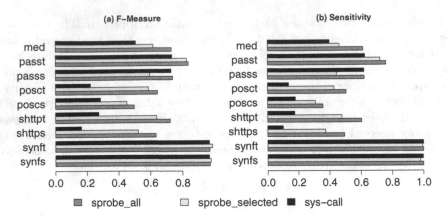

Fig. 4. Prediction results for three monitoring approaches and eight anomaly scenarios

4. Port scan attack. We emulated this attack using "nmap" tool and executed vertical port-scan attack.

For each type of attacks above, we performed both 'source attack' where the attack originates from the monitored VM and 'target attack' where monitored VM is the intended target of the attack. It resulted in total of eight anomaly type. We collected 500 unit data for each anomaly types. Just like normal data collection, one unit data was the list of variable occurrence within two-seconds of observation. We did the same amount of collection for the three data sources (static probe instrumentation using all feature, static probe instrumentation using selected feature and system-call) we want to compare. In total there were 24 scenarios that we evaluated.

To measure effectiveness, we used F-measure metric. F-measure defined as the harmonic-mean of sensitivity and precision.

$$Sensitivity = \frac{TP}{P}; Precision = \frac{TP}{TP+FP}; Fmeasure = \frac{2}{\frac{1}{Precision} + \frac{1}{Sensitivity}}$$

We divided 500 unit data for each scenario into five subsets. We then paired each subset of normal and anomaly, and feed them into one-class SVM outlier predictor. Over the five subsets, we calculated the averages of true-positives (TP), false-positives (FP), true-negatives (TN) and false-negatives (FN). Using these values, we calculated f-measure value of each scenario. We summarize the results of this evaluation in Fig. 4.a.

From Fig. 4.a. we note that, aside from synflood scenario, our static-probe instrumentation approach and system-call approach still give poor prediction values, which are below 90 %. The median of all scenario f-measure value for static-probe using all tracepoints, static-probe using selected tracepoints and system-call monitoring is 73 %, 62 % and 50 % respectively. It is also useful to look in detail to sensitivity value. This metric measure how accurate the system is in detecting real positive data (anomaly data) only. The sensitivity results of this evaluation are given in Fig. 4.b. The median of all scenario sensitivity value for static-probe using all tracepoints, static-probe using selected tracepoints and system-call monitoring is 61 %, 46 % and 40 % respectively. Syn-flood scenario can be easily recognized because it directly affects the volume of send and receive data. However, since slowhttp scenario and portscan scenario do not change transfer rate, prediction is proved more difficult. Due to the fact that our approach works only by monitoring frequency of function-call, it can only detect changes in volume. It cannot however detect changes in sequence pattern for example, which might help increase accuracy. This Fig. 4.b also shows, that in all of scenario test, system-call prediction value was lower than static probe instrumentation prediction.

Prediction Comparison

There are several previous attempts to predict anomaly in IaaS environment without data collection from inside guest VM. Alarifi et al. [11] use bag of system-call data and implement heuristic approach by comparing the frequency table of each system-call to the testing data and calculate their difference. They register sequences of system calls using sliding window technique. For evaluation, they use unmalicious stress test in guest VM to emulate what they called "over-committed migration" attack. They reported that by choosing a window size of 10, they can achieve perfect prediction results, 100 % sensitivity and 0 % fall-out (False Positive Rate). Dean et al. [8] monitored guest VM's behavior through system-level metrics (e.g. CPU usage, memory allocation, network I/O, disk I/O) then applied unsupervised Self-Organizing Maps algorithm to predict anomaly. Injected faults to the guest's VM operation, such as memleak, CPUleak and nethog were used to evaluate the prediction system. As the result of their approach, their ADS can achieve up to 98 % sensitivity and 1.7 % fall-out. Wang et al. [9] proposed a method called EbAT to detect anomaly for utility cloud computing by analyzing metric distributions rather than individual metric threshold. Assesment were conducted by using application faulty and CPU exhaustion. Their results show that their proposed method gave 86 % sensitivity and 4 % fall-out, which is better than threshold-based methods. Doelitzscher et al. [16] tracked user behavior, such as time the VM created or destroyed and the number of running VMs and analyze them using supervised feed-forward neural network. To generate data for evaluation, they created a simulator of cloud environment. The reported result from their approach is 0.01375 % detection error rate. Sha et al. [10] applied Multi-order Markov chain to detect anomaly in cloud server systems. For evaluation purpose, they use system-call information from DARPA's 1998 Intrusion Detection Evaluation data set. In their paper however, there are no specific information on what is the quantified results on their anomaly detection scheme.

All the works mentioned above evaluate their work using anomaly scheme that significantly change the pattern of computing resources usage, such as CPU, memory or I/O. These approaches are indeed useful for detecting volume based attacks. In reality however, many attacks on computer system do not change these resources data, hence are harder to detect. To detect those non-volume based attacks, higher semantic information is needed and for that researchers usually monitor internal operation of observed VMs. Our work were focused on trying to extract clearer semantic information without requiring to interrupt guest VM operation. That is why we choose to evaluate our framework using varied anomaly scenarios, from volume based attack scenarios such as Syncflood attack to non volume based attack such as Slow HTTP attack.

4.4   Efficiency and Scalability

We measured CPU usage and time needed to capture one unit data for certain numbers of VMs using "perf". For scalability evaluation purpose, we used one until eight VMs. The average results over five measurements for static-probe data source and system-call data source are given in Fig. 5.

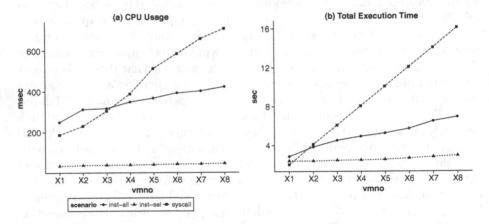

Fig. 5. "perf-stat" result to capture one unit data as the number of VM increased

The figure shows that as the number of VMs increased, the CPU time and the total execution time needed to capture one unit data for each VM increased as well. However, the increase rate of system-call approach is higher than both of static-probe instrumentation methods. From the increase rate we could also see that when we divided the cost, that is task-clock or execution-time, with the number of VMs, then the average cost to capture one unit data per VM using static-probe instrumentation would decrease as the number of VM increased, while relatively constant for system-call method. This is because for static-probe instrumentation methods, data units for all the VMs were collected collectively by one process, which is LTTng. On the other hand, data units for each VM in system-call approach were collected by different independent processes, therefore it created more overhead.

4.5   Performance Impact

We compared CPU and database (MySQL) performance of a VM when it is instrumented and when it is not using sysbench tool from inside one VM. In CPU benchmark, we took note on total execution time to calculate first 2000 prime numbers, while in database benchmark we counted how many transaction can be processed within one minute. Again, in this evaluation, we compared performance of both static instrumentation method, all-feature and selected-feature. Figure 6 presents the averages from ten benchmarking results.

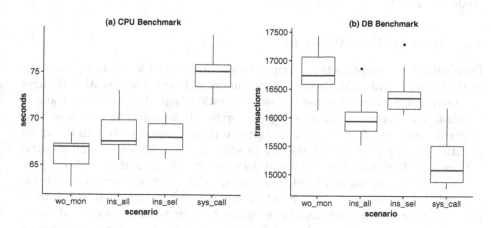

Fig. 6. The impact of monitoring for VM's performance

Both box-plot in Fig. 6 show that the monitoring process, either using static-probe instrumentation or system-call method affects the monitored VM. For CPU benchmark, static-probe instrumentation using all tracepoints, static-probe instrumentation using selected tracepoints and monitoring using system-call added 3.2 %, 2.8 % and 13 % benchmark execution time respectively, while for database benchmark they decrease 4 %, 2 % and 9 % number of database transaction per-minute, respectively. In general, static-probe instrumentation using selected tracepoints gave the least impact on monitored VM, while system-call monitoring on the other hand gave the biggest impact.

5   Discussion

5.1   Windowing to Increase Accuracy

The quality outputs of anomaly prediction as described in Sect. 4.3 are given by evaluating each unit data independently. We argue that by assessing the anomaly status in groups of sequenced data, the accuracy can be increased. This argument comes from an assumption that a change of status from normal to anomaly or reversed from anomaly to normal would not happen in a small space of time, as our data unit describes a VM operation in 2 s. To illustrate this suggestion, consider a sequence of predictor results for an abnormal scenario [... -1 -1 1 -1 -1 -1 -1 1 1 -1 ...]. In our experiment, the sequence might have gave 30 % False Negative value. However, in a system where sequenced data are read collectively, say in a windows of five, the above sequence result will give 0 False Negative because all the windows are dominate by the value -1. The length of sequence to use for ADS had been proposed by several previous research, such as 6 in [17] and 10 in [11]. We argue that these values are unique for each case, so further studies could be taken to decide a proper window size to improve these anomaly prediction results.

5.2   Reducing False Positives

Even with the assumption that a normal scenario within a VM is rarely changed as they usually built with specific service in mind, in real life operation changes are unavoidable. One example for web operation is peak time when there is a significant increase on user using its service. Researchers in [6] show that migration process affects the quality of network anomaly detection in the cloud negatively and they still work on how to solve it. An unknown normal scenario will increase false positives which will decrease overall prediction quality.

We have conducted small side-experiment with peak web scenario and discovered that by using one-class SVM approach, we can simply capture dataset for the new normal scenario and incorporate it to our previous learning dataset. After re-learning process we have 1 % false positives where before re-learning we had 82 % false-positives. Further evaluation using anomaly scenario from Sect. 4.3 shows that the new normal-model after re-learning did not significantly reduce anomaly prediction quality.

5.3   Opportunity for Further Improvements

On Implementation. Our direct concern is on how to implement the feature-selection and collecting learning scenario data for new deployed VM in live operation. Several aspects to consider are many combinations of VM virtual hardware, VM operating system and VM service in real-life, not to mention their life span in the cloud. This opens many new research questions. For example how to find a generic set of initial selected-feature over multiple combination of virtual hardware and operating system? How effective it is to use unsupervised anomaly detection system within this framework? How to deploy an adaptive anomaly prediction method?

On VM's CPU Operation. Qemu+KVM VMM combo gave many advantages for this static-probe instrumentation monitoring approach. The fact that Qemu is an open-source product and it work as user process inside host OS makes instrumentation proses easier. Moreover, since CPU is directly translated to native by KVM, the instrumentation on Qemu does not affect much performance of guest VMs. However it cost us visibility, because CPU operation can hardly be monitored. One simple solution is to concurrently instrument KVM on kernel-space. This however will need another synchronization technique to combine both instrumentations.

6 Conclusion

In this preliminary work, we introduced a framework for anomaly detection system in public IaaS Cloud that use Qemu-KVM hypervisor. For VM monitoring we proposed a novel approach using static probe instrumentation method. In addition, to streamline the features used, we also introduced black-box based feature selection method using Linear Discriminant Analysis. Finally we successfully conducted several empirical evaluations to answer questions regarding its feasibility, effectivity, efficiency, scalability, and impact and also compared some of those evaluations to two other ADSes which are full-featured static probe instrumentation ADS and system-call based ADS.

From our evaluation we found out that our anomaly prediction system still did not provide satisfying prediction quality with just 62 % f-measure value as median for the eight anomaly scenarios that we tested. However, further comparison with static probe instrumentation using all tracepoints and system-call monitoring shows that using static probe instrumentation with selected tracepoints gave overall best solution.

We are very encouraged by these preliminary results and are considering to extend this research in the following ways:

- We would like to investigate further how to increase prediction quality using this static probe instrumentation approach. Due to the logical distance between observation points, which are within hypervisor internal operation, and VMs as the monitored objects are close, we believe there are generic guest VM's operation information that can be recognized using static-probe data within hypervisor. One forward approach that we want to investigate is by utilizing tracepoint's parameters and their temporal relations (sequence pattern).
- Moreover, for future research in this topic, additional study on Qemu-KVM internal operation should be considered. A deeper understanding on how Qemu/KVM works will help to improve anomaly prediction system, for instance to enable researcher to implement more heuristic approaches or correctly choose the right tracepoints.

References

1. Chandramouli, R.: Security recomendations for hypervisor deployment. Draft NIST Special Publication 800 125-A, NIST - National Institute of Standards and Technology (2014)

2. Bhaduri, K., Das, K., Matthews, B.L.: Detecting abnormal machine characteristics in cloud infrastructures. In: ICDMW 2011 Proceedings of the IEEE 11th International Conference on Data Mining Workshops (2011)
3. Vallis, O., Hochenbaum, J., Kejariwal, A.: A novel technique for long term anomaly detection in the cloud. In: 6th USENIX Conference on Hot Topics in Cloud Computing (2014)
4. Asrigo, K., Litty, L., Lie, D.: Using vmm-based sensors to monitor honeypots. In: Proceedings of the 2nd International Conference on Virtual Execution Environments, VEE 2006, pp. 13–23 (2006)
5. Garfinkel, T., Rosenblum, M.: A virtual machine introspection based architecture for intrusion detection. In: The 10th Annual Network and Distributed System Security Symposium (2003)
6. Adamova, K., Schatzmann, D., Plattner, B., Smith, P.: Network anomaly detection in the cloud: the challenge of virtual service migration. In: 2014 IEEE International Conference on Communications (ICC), Proceedings, pp. 3770–3775 (2014)
7. Huang, T., Zhu, Y., Zhang, Q., Zhu, Y., Wang, D., Qiu, M., Liu, L.: An lof-based adaptive anomaly detection scheme for cloud computing. In: IEEE 37th Annual Computer Software and Applications Conference Workshops (COMPSACW) (2013)
8. Dean, D.J., Nguyen, H., Xiaohui, G.: Ubl: unsupervised behavior learning for predicting performance anomalies in virtualized cloud systems. In: ICAC 2012 Proceedings of the 9th International Conference on Autonomic Computing (2012)
9. Wang, C., Viswanathan, K., Choudur, L., Talwar, V., Satterfield, W., Schwann, K.: Statistical techniques for online anomaly detection in data centers. In: IFIP/IEEE International Symposium on Integrated Network Management (2011)
10. Sha, W., Zhu, Y., Chen, M., Huang, T.: Statistical learning for anomaly detection in cloud server systems: a multi-order markov chain framework. IEEE Trans. Cloud Comput. PrePrinted (99) (2015). Doi:10.1109/TCC.2015.2415813
11. Alarifi, S.S., Wolthusen, S.D.: Detecting anomalies in iaas environment through virtual machine host system call analysis. In: The 7th International Conference for Internet Technology and Secured Transactions (ICITST), 2012 (2012)
12. Avritzer, A., Tanikella, R., James, K., Cole, R.G., Weyuker, E.J.: Monitoring for security intrusion using performance signatures. In: WOSP/SIPEW, pp. 93–104 (2010)
13. R Core Team: R: A Language and Environment for Statistical Computing. R Foundation for Statistical Computing, Vienna, Austria (2014)
14. Cerdeira, J.O., Silva, P.D., Cadima, J., Minhoto, M.: Subselect: selecting variable subsets, R package version 0.12-4 (2014)
15. Pedregosa, F., Varoquaux, G., Gramfort, A., Michel, V., Thirion, B., Grisel, O., Blondel, M., Prettenhofer, P., Weiss, R., Dubourg, V., Vanderplas, J., Passos, A., Cournapeau, D., Brucher, M., Perrot, M., Duchesnay, E.: Scikit-learn: machine learning in python. J. Mach. Learn. Res. 12, 2825–2830 (2011)
16. Doelitzscher, F., Knahl, M., Reich, C., Clarke, N.: Anomaly detection in iaas clouds. In: IEEE International Conference on Cloud Computing Technology and Science (2013)
17. Hofmeyr, S.A., Forrest, S., Somayaji, A.: Intrusion detection using sequences of system call. J. Comput. Secur. 6(3), 151–180 (1998)

MB-DDIVR: A Map-Based Dynamic Data Integrity Verification and Recovery Scheme in Cloud Storage

Zizhou Sun[2], Yahui Yang[1(✉)], Qingni Shen[1], Zhonghai Wu[1], and Xiaochen Li[1,2]

[1] School of Software and Microelectronics, Peking University, Beijing, China
{yhyang,qingnishen,wuzhu}@ss.pku.edu.cn
[2] MoE Key Lab of Network and Software Assurance,
Peking University, Beijing, China
sunzz679@pku.edu.cn

Abstract. Outsourcing data to are remote cloud service provider allows organizations or individual users to store more data on the cloud storage than on private computer systems. However, a specific problem encountered in cloud storage is how to ensure user's confidence of the integrity of their outsourced data on cloud. One important approach is Proof of Retrievability (POR) which allows a verifier to check and repair the data stored in the cloud server. However, most of existing PORs can only deal with static data and provide one single recovery method which may lead to inefficiency and inflexibility. To address these cloud storage issues, we propose a map-based dynamic data integrity verification and recovery scheme in cloud storages. We first present two recovery methods with different granularity and introduce a new data structure. Relying on algebraic signature with homomorphism property, our integrity verification is highly efficient. Furthermore, our solution can prevent multiple cloud servers from colluding to fabricate consistent signatures.

Keywords: Cloud storage · Data integrity · Algebraic signature · Dynamic operation · Erasure code

1 Introduction

Since data is increasing exponentially, data owners rapidly increase their demand for cloud storage. Abilities like scalability, reliability, flexibility and security make cloud storage essentially a technology for future. Cloud service providers (CSP) offer users clean and simple distributed file-system interfaces, abstracting away the complexities of direct hardware management.

From the data security's point of view, which is always an concerned aspect of quality of service, however, cloud storage is confronted with new challenging security threats. Firstly, CSP may not be trustworthy, data owners lose direct control over their sensitive data. This problem brings data confidentiality and integrity protection issues. Secondly, cloud storage does not just store static data. The data stored in the cloud may

© Springer International Publishing Switzerland 2016
S. Qing et al. (Eds.): ICICS 2015, LNCS 9543, pp. 335–345, 2016.
DOI: 10.1007/978-3-319-29814-6_28

be frequently modified and updated by users. CSP should have ability to demonstrate users' data is correctly update.

So data integrity and availability are important components of cloud storage, it is imperative for users to verify the integrity of their data and could recover the corrupted data anytime. One solution is the so-called Proof of Retrievability (POR), which was first introduced by Juels and Kaliski [1] and its subsequent versions are [2, 3]. PORs enable the server to demonstrate to the verifier whether the data stored in the servers is intact and available, and enables the clients to recover the data when an error is detected. Atenies et al. [4] introduced a Provable Data Possession (PDP) scheme, in which the user generates some information for a file to be used later for verification purpose through a challenge-response protocol with the cloud server. Based on this scheme, there are different variations of PDP schemes [5–8].

Main Contribution. In this paper, we propose an efficient and secure public auditing and recovering scheme, which also supports the dynamic data operations. Our contributions can be summarized as follows:

(1) To the best of our knowledge, our scheme is the first to support two data recovery methods at different levels of granularity.
(2) We design a data structure called map-based dynamic storage table, which provides better support for dynamic data operation and two different levels of recovery methods.
(3) We propose a solution to protect the security of algebraic signature verification process with little storage overhead against cloud servers colluded to offer fake data signatures and created parity for these signatures.

2   Scheme Overview

2.1   System Model

The system model of the MB-DDIVR scheme is depicted in Fig. 1:

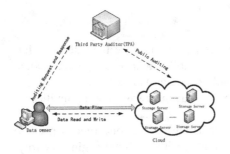

Fig. 1. System model of MB-DDIVR

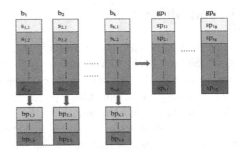

Fig. 2. One group encoding example

User: These entities have data to be stored in the cloud.

Cloud service provider (CSP): The CSP has major resources and expertise in building and managing distributed cloud storage service. The servers are managed and monitored by a CSP.

Third Party Auditor (TPA): This entity is delegated the responsibility to check the servers on behalf of the clients. The TPA is assumed to be trusted

2.2 Thread Model

In this work, we assume the TPA to be curious-but-honest. It performs honestly during the whole auditing procedure but it is curious about the received data. The CSP is not trusted, even though the file data is partially or totally losing, the CSP may try to deceive the user that he holds the correct file. All of storage servers may join up to implement collusion attack, i.e., they may forge the response of integrity challenge to deceive the user and TPA.

2.3 Design Goals

In this paper, we analyze the problem of ensuring the security and dependability for cloud storage and we aim to design efficient mechanisms for data verification, recovery and dynamic operation. We expect to achieve the following goals:

(1) Fast fault localization of data: to effectively and efficiently locate the specific error block when data corruption has been detected.
(2) Fast reparation of data: to use different recovery methods to ensure quick recovery of the data when errors are detected.
(3) Security: to enhance data availability against malicious data modification and server collusion attack.
(4) Support of dynamic data operation: to maintain the same level of storage correctness assurance even if users modify, delete or append their data files in the cloud.

3 Key Solutions on MB-DDIVR

This section presents the principium of our scheme. We start from explaining what two different granularity of recovery methods are, and then present the structure of our map-based dynamic storage table, at last we will show the security of our scheme.

3.1 Recovery Method

To make our recovery method easier to follow, we assume that the user wants to store a file F on the cloud server S which is a finite ordered collection of m blocks: $F = (b_1, b_2, ..., b_m)$ and every b_i is partitioned into n sections (section is the smallest unit of storage) denoted as $b_i = (s_{i1}, s_{i2}, ..., s_{in})$ $(i \in \{1,...,n\})$.

- *Two Levels of Recovery Methods:* We firstly use a dynamic reliability group as an example to illustrate our encoding strategy, which is shown in Fig. 2. Every *k* blocks are grouped into a group which is named *dynamic reliability group*. In each of the group (k + g,g)-erasure code is used to encode group members as *g* parity blocks, which are called *group parity blocks*. For each of F_i, we also use (n + b,b)-erasure code over $GF(2^l)$ to encode $\{f_{ij}\}_{(i \in \{1,...,n\})}$ sections as *b* small parity sections, which are named *block parity sections*.

  As mentioned, our scheme has two data recovery methods at different levels of granularity, there are coarse-grained *intra-group* and fine-grained *intra-block* recovery methods. Group parity blocks are used in intra-group recovery method which has higher fault tolerance but slower rate of recovery, but intra-block recovery method utilizes blocks' parity sections to restore corrupted sections whose feature is fast repair speed but lower data recovery ability.

- *Recovery Scenarios:* To be convenient for explanation, this section only consider the recovery scenario in one single dynamic reliability group. The way to recover multi groups is the same as a single group. When corrupted data is detected, verification function could tell us the number of damaged sections, which is denoted as *d*. The following scenarios are possible:

Scenario A: If $d \leq b$, no matter whether these *d* damaged sections are included in a single block or not, intra-block recovery method, by the knowledge of erasure code, has ability to reconstruct those corrupted blocks. Intra-group recovery method, which has higher fault tolerance, can also recover data successfully in above case, but its rate of recovery is slower than intra-block's. Therefore, we take intra-block recovery method without using intra-group method in this case.

Scenario B: Damaged sections are included in a single block and *d* satisfies the inequality $b < d \leq n$. The *intra-block recovery method* is disable, and intra-group recovery method can play a role to reconstruct the block even this whole block is missed.

Scenario C: If the number of corrupted blocks—in each of which has at least b up to n of broken sections—is up to g, we must first use intra-block recovery method to repair the rest of blocks, and only then use intra-group recovery method to recover above-mentioned block sections.

3.2 Map-Based Dynamic Storage Table

The map-based dynamic storage table (MBDST) is a small dynamic data structure stored on the user(or TPA) side to validate the integrity and consistency of file blocks outsourced to the CSP. It is composed of three sub-tables, which are dynamic group table, block table and section table. An example about the data structure is given in Fig. 3.

As its name indicates, the **group table** is used for managing the information of dynamic reliability group, which consists of three columns. *NoM* is used to show how many original data blocks are in this group. In our scheme the minimum number of blocks that a group contains has been set, if the number of memberships in this group is

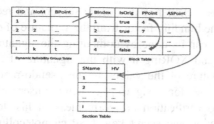

Fig. 3. Map-based dynamic storage table

less than the threshold we will merge a group into another, so we can judge whether this group should be merged or not via *NoM*. *BPoint* is a pointer that points to the block table belonging to this group.

Block table is the virtual table, in other words, the base unit of storage system for blocks and their parity data is section. Each row in a **block table** represents an virtual data block or a parity block, and it has four columns. *BIndex* indicates the logical position of block, and the index is numbered from 1. *IsOrig* is used to mark if this block is an original data block or a parity block. *PPoint* is a point that point to its parity blocks. *ASPoint* points to sections that belonged to this virtual block.

Every virtual block holds a section table, which contains metainformation about each section. There are only two columns: *Sname* and *HV*. *HV* stores the hash value of the block which is used for determining specified corrupted sections.

It is important to note that the verifier keeps only one structure for unlimited number of file sections, i.e., the storage requirement on the verifier side does not depend on the number of file blocks on cloud servers. For k sections of a data file of size $|F|$, the storage requirement on the CSP side is $O(|F|)$, while the verifier's overhead is $O(m + n + k)$ for the whole file (m is the number of dynamic groups, n is the number of blocks).

3.3 Collusion Attack

We apply algebraic signature to verify integrity of data in cloud storage, but that basic verification model may suffer from a drawback: many storage servers may make up signatures as long as they internally consistent. To solve this problem, we developed an improved model that allows a user or TPA to ensure the security of signature verification process with little storage overhead.

We simply blind the original data by pseudo-random stream. Firstly, we design a hash function *H(block_id, user_id, secret_key)*, where block_id identifies a block, user_id varies for each use of the hash function, and secret_key is used to prevent storage servers from deriving the same function. The original data is then XORed with a pseudo-random stream generated by RC4, for example, seeded with a value derived from the above hash function; thus, the value stored for a block section would be $s_{ij} \oplus ps_{ij}$, where s_{ij} is the jth section of the block b_i, and ps_j is the jth value of the pseudo-random stream for b_j.

When the user sends a challenge to storage servers and receives algebraic signatures, he must remove the blinding factor from the signature of encrypted data sections (sig_i, for example). This can be done by computing the signature of the values in the pseudo-random stream and XORing it with the signature of encrypted section data. That is to say, let signature of the values in the pseudo-random stream is ps_i, the signature of original data section is $sig_i \oplus ps_i$. Then the user can utilize the method we mentioned in Sect. 4 to verification the correctness of his data. Because of hardly obtaining the hash function and secret key, CSP cannot colluded to offer fake data signatures, thus our scheme achieves the goal to defense collusion attack.

4   Implementation of MB-DDIVR

We propose a MB-DDIVR scheme allowing the user to update and scale the file outsourced to cloud servers which may be untrusted. Our scheme consists of four algorithms: file distribution preparation, integrity verification, data recovery and dynamic operation. In this section, we will give detailed implements descriptions of these for algorithms in proposed scheme.

4.1   File Distribution Preparation

The preparation operation is to encode files. As mentioned in Sect. 4, firstly we partition F into m distinct blocks $F = (b_1, b_2, ..., b_m)$, then every block b_i continues to be partitioned into n distinct sections $b_i = (s_{i1}, s_{i2}, ..., s_{in})(i \in \{1, ..., m\})$, where $n \leq 2^P - 1$. Next, we group these file blocks into different dynamic reliability groups and compute parity data for dynamic reliability group and blocks. Using erasure code algorithm to generate parity blocks and parity sections for every dynamic reliability group DRG_i and every block, i.e., $(GroupP_{i1}, ..., GroupP_{ig})$ and $(BlockP_{i1}, ..., BlockP_{ik})$, respectively.

We then generate hash for each block section and parity data. Generating secret keys and using pseudo-random stream mentioned in Sect. 4 to blind user's original data sections Σs_{ij} can defense storage servers' collusion attack. At last we should use relevant information to initialize our dynamic map-based storage table. The user only keeps secret keys in local and uploads the file and parity data to the cloud, and dynamic storage table to the TPA respectively.

4.2   Integrity Verification

Algebraic signature interact well with linear error and erasure correcting codes, thus, it may be used to verify that the parity and the data files are coherent without the need to obtain the entire data and parity, and users have no need of saving any validate tags. Specifically, corruption localization is a very important link in integrity verification in storage system. However, many previous schemes do not consider the problem of data error localization. Our scheme exceeds those by combining the integrity verification with error localization.

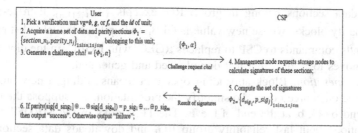

Fig. 4. Protocal of integrity verification

The verification protocol is illustrated in Fig. 4. Like recovery method, our verification method is at different levels of granularity, which are block level verification, group level verification and *file level* verification. We will use b, g and f to represent above verification operations respectively. Our challenging index dataset is $\Phi = \{section\_n_i, parity\_n_j\}_{1 \leq i \leq n, 1 \leq j \leq m}$, where section_$n_i$ indicates the name of the i data section, and parity n_j is the name of the j parity section. The user firstly select which level he want to verify, the index of group or block and the parameter of algebraic signature α, then sends the audition command to the CSP. A user sets a challenging index dataset to the TPA and delegates TPA to carry out the audit. Upon receiving the index dataset, the CSP let each corresponding storage server compute a short signature over the specified blocks and return them to the TPA. After receiving the set of signatures from CSP, the user can easily judge the integrity of data file.

4.3 Dynamic Data Operation

In cloud storage, there are many scenes where data stored in the cloud is dynamic, like log files. Therefore, it is crucial to consider the dynamic cases, where users may perform update, insertion and deletion operation at the block level. However, for users, CSP is untrusted and they do not wish these dynamic operations to be dominated by CSP, but performed by delegated TPA instead. In this section we design dynamic operation to reduce overhead and in practice, this cast is perfectly acceptable to users.

- *Update Operation:* A basic data modification operation refers to replace specified blocks with new ones. Let a file $F = \{b_1, b_2, ..., b_m\}$, suppose the user wants to modify a block b_j with b_j'. He sends the block b_j' to TPA, and delegate the TPA to execute update operation. The TPA gets the reliability group RG_i which contains block b_j, then obtains all block sections belong to group RG_i from CSP. After updating b_j to b_j', and re-encoding group parity blocks and block parity sections, whose new values are GPB_i' and BPS_j', the TPA partitions the new block b_j' into n sections $\{s_{j,i}'\}_{i \in (1,n)}$, and update the table list entry. At last the TPA replaces original data in cloud with new data.
- *Delete Operation:* A delete operation on a file means deleting few file blocks from the file. To delete a specific data block b_j, the TPA gets the reliability group RG_i which contains block b_j, then the user sends download commands to CSP to only

obtain data sections belong to group RG_i excepts $\{s_{j,i}\}_{i \in (1,n)}$, then re-computes group parity blocks, whose new value is GPB_i' and updates the table list entry. The user sends commands to CSP to replaces $RGEC_i$ with $RGEC_i'$ in the cloud storage, and removes local data that just downloaded and generated.

- *Append Operation:* Block appending operation means adding a new block at the end of the outsourced data. To simplify the presentation, we suppose the user want to append block b' at the end of file **F**. The TPA looks in the **MBDST** to get the information about last reliability group RG_i and downloads data sections. If the group RG_i contains too much blocks after adding the block b' (this cloud be judged regarding a threshold), go to (a), or go to (b).

(a) RG_i will be partitioned into two dynamic reliability group RG_i and RG_{i+1}, and b' is merged into group RG_{i+1}. And then calls *GPBGen(RG$_i$)* and *GPBGen(RG$_{i+1}$)* functions to re-encode group parity blocks, whose new values are GPB_i' and GPB_{i+1}'. TPA updates the table list entry, and replace GPB_i with new value, then uploads b' and GPB_{i+1}' to the cloud storage.

(b) b' is merged into group RG_i, TPA re-encodes group parity block GPB_i', then updates the table list entry and replace GPB_i with new value, then uploads b' to the cloud storage.

5   Experiment and Evaluation

We have implemented our scheme in C and JAVA language. We conducted several experiments using the local 32-bit Centos operation system with an Intel Core 2 processor running at 1.86 GHz, 2048 MB of RAM, and run Hadoop 2.7.0. Most PDP and POR schemes who support dynamic data operation are based on an authenticated data structures – Merkle Hash Tree (MHT) [12] (short for MHTPOR-scheme), and we also construct a scheme based on that structure which is used as a reference model for comparing the proposed MB-DDIVR scheme. In [12] the MHT is explained in detail.

In order to compare the performance of the two schemes mentioned above, the stored files are chosen from 200 MB to 800 MB. We set up the size of every data block is 126 MB, and each of them will be partitioned into 6 sections. Every dynamic reliability group contains 3 blocks. One encoded parity block is generated for each of groups and two encoded parity sections are generated for every data block.

5.1   Time Analysis

In this section, we compare the MHTPOR scheme with our proposed scheme in file distribution preparation time and verification time.

- File Distribution Preparation Time
  The experimental results are shown in Table 1. It is can be seen from the result that the computation costs grow with the increase of file size linearly. Note that MHT-scheme need not to generate group encoded blocks, and the run time of our scheme is less than that of the MHT-scheme. That is because the creation of MHT

Table. 1 Preparation Time (second) of the MHT-SCHEME and ours

Preparation Time (second) Of the MHT-SCHEME and ours

File size(MB) / Scheme	200	300	400	500	600	700	800
MHT-scheme	29	42	56	72	99	116	128
MD-DIVR	22	38	48	67	95	107	121

and the operation on it is much more complicated than our designed dynamic storage table.

- Integrity Verification Cost

  In this experiment we select to verification the integrity of whole file. Figure 5(a) the communication cost on the CSP side when audit different size of file. The result shows that the cost is almost constant versus file size, i.e., the file size has no remarkable influence on the CSP's cost. Figure 5(b) also indicates our verification time on TPA side is also almost constant versus file size. That is due to the fact that algebraic signature has feature of homomorphism, and only need XOR operation, which has quick operating speed than regular integrity verification of PORs.

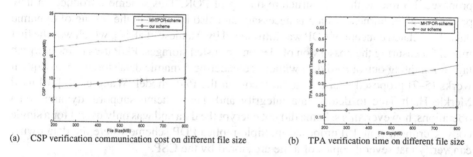

(a) CSP verification communication cost on different file size   (b) TPA verification time on different file size

Fig. 5. Integrity verification cost.

5.2 Recovery Performance Analysis

We will use the experimental 620 MB data file to analyze the performance of our proposed data recovery methods under the same experimental background mentioned above. From the aspect of theoretic analysis, as we discuss in section recovery method in III, the worst-case scenario is the scenario C. In our experiment, each of the two groups misses one block (i.e., six sections, and every section is 21 MB), and each of the rest blocks misses two sections. So the fault tolerance rate in this experimental scheme is (2 * 126 MB + 3 * 2 * 21 MB)/620 MB = 60.9 %.

By contrast, we design the other two recovery methods, and each of them has only one recovery grain: intra-block and intra-group recovery methods. As can be seen in Table 2, the efficiency and capacity of recovery is not high if we use intra-block or

Table. 2 Recovery Performance (%) Comparison

Recovery Performance (%) Comparison

Recovery scenarios Scheme	Scenario A	Scenario B	Scenario C
Only block recovery	8.3	failure	failure
Only group recovery	45.2	45.2	failure
Proposed recovery	8.3	45.2	56.7

intra-group recovery methods alone. We offer flexible and powerful solutions to reconstruct corrupted data, it owns more powerful recovery capability to combine the intra-block and intra-group recovery methods together.

6 Related Works

To check the cloud server, researchers proposed the POR protocol [1–3] that enables the servers to demonstrate to the verifier whether the data stored in the servers is intact and available. But existing POR scheme can only deal with static data. Zheng and Xu [9] proposed 2-3 tree as the data structure on top of POR. This scheme introduced a new property, called fairness, which is necessary and also inherent to the setting of dynamic data. The related concept of PDP was introduced by Ateniese et al. [4], which was the first model for ensuring the possession of files on untrusted storages. PDP uses homomorphic tags for auditing outsourced data without considering dynamic data storage. Subsequent works [5–7] proposed data update protocols in the PDP model. Wang et al. [10] used Merkle Hash Tree to detect data integrity and their scheme supports dynamic data operations, however, this scheme did not encrypt the data and was only useful for a single copy. Curtmola et al. [6] proposed multiple-replica PDP scheme where the data owner can verify that several copies of a file are stored by the CSP.

Algebraic signature was proposed by Schwarz and Miller [11], which detects for sure any change that does not exceed n-symbols for an n-symbol signature. This scheme primarily utilizes one such characteristic homomorphism: taking a signature of parity gives the same result as taking the parity of the signatures. For example, assume that we have an erasure correcting code that calculates k parity containers P_1, ..., P_k from the m data buckets $D_1, D_2, ..., D_m$ as $P_i = \mathcal{P}_i(D_1, D_2, ..., D_m)$. So there is:

$$sig_\alpha(p_i(D_1, D_2, ..., D_m)) = P_i(sig_\alpha(D_1), sig_\alpha(D_2), ..., sig_\alpha(D_m))$$

7 Conclusion

In this paper, we proposed a distributed integrity verification and recovery scheme to ensure users' outsourced data with explicit dynamic data operation support. We utilize erasure coding to guarantee data confidentiality and dependability. To ensure the integrity of data files, an efficient dynamic data integrity checking scheme is constructed based on the principle of algebraic signatures.

Acknowledgment. This work is supported by the National High Technology Research and Development Program ("863" Program) of China under Grant No. 2015AA016009, the National Natural Science Foundation of China under Grant No. 61232005, and the Science and Technology Program of Shen Zhen, China under Grant No. JSGG2014051 6162852628.

References

1. Juels, A., Kaliski, B.S. Jr.: PORs: proofs of retrievability for large files. In: Proceedings of the 14th ACM Conference on Computer and Communications Security. ACM (2007)
2. Shacham, H., Waters, B.: Compact proofs of retrievability. In: Pieprzyk, J. (ed.) ASIACRYPT 2008. LNCS, vol. 5350, pp. 90–107. Springer, Heidelberg (2008)
3. Bowers, K.D., Juels, A., Oprea, A.: Proofs of retrievability: theory and implementation. In: Proceedings of the 2009 ACM Workshop on Cloud Computing Security. ACM (2009)
4. Ateniese, G., Burns, R., Curtmola, R., Herring, J., Kissner, L., Peterson, Z., Song, D.: Provable data possession at untrusted stores. In: Proceedings of the 14th ACM Conference on Computer and Communications Security. ACM (2007)
5. Erway, C.C., Küpçü, A., Papamanthou, C., Tamassia, R.: Dynamic provable data possession. ACM Trans. Inf. Syst. Secur. (TISSEC) **17**(4), 15 (2015)
6. Curtmola, R., Khan, O., Burns, R., Ateniese, G.: MR-PDP: multiple-replica provable data possession. In: The 28th International Conference on Distributed Computing Systems, 2008. ICDCS 2008. IEEE (2008)
7. Hao, Z., Yu, N.: A multiple-replica remote data possession checking protocol with public verifiability. In: Proceedings of 2nd International Symposium Data, Privacy, E-Commerce, pp. 84–89 (2010)
8. Ateniese, G., Di Pietro, R., Mancini, L.V., Tsudik, G.: Scalable and efficient provable data possession. In: Proceedings of the 4th International Conference on Security and Privacy in Communication Networks. ACM (2008)
9. Zheng, Q., Xu, S.: Fair and dynamic proofs of retrievability. In: Proceedings of the First ACM Conference on Data and Application Security and Privacy. ACM (2011)
10. Wang, C., Wang, Q., Ren, K., Lou, W.: Privacy-preserving public auditing for data storage security in cloud computing. In: INFOCOM, 2010 Proceedings IEEE, pp. 1–9. IEEE (2010)
11. Schwarz, T.S.J., Miller, E.L.: Store, forget, and check: using algebraic signatures to check remotely administered storage. In: 26th IEEE International Conference on Distributed Computing Systems, 2006. ICDCS 2006. IEEE (2006)
12. Merkle, R.C.: Protocols for public key crytosystems. In: Proceedings of IEEE Symposium Security and Privacy, p. 122 (1980)

Chameleon: A Lightweight Method for Thwarting Relay Attacks in Near Field Communication

Yafei Ji[1,2,3], Luning Xia[1,2]([✉]), Jingqiang Lin[1,2], Jian Zhou[1,2],
Guozhu Zhang[1,2,3], and Shijie Jia[1,2,3]

[1] State Key Laboratory of Information Security,
Institute of Information Engineering of Chinese Academy of Sciences,
Beijing, China
{jiyafei,xialuning,lingjinqiang,zhoujian,zhangguozhu,
jiashijie}@iie.ac.cn
[2] Data Assurance and Communication Security Research Center
of Chinese Academy of Sciences, Beijing, China
[3] University of Chinese Academy Sciences, Beijing, China

Abstract. Near field communication (NFC) is applied in payment services, setup of high-bandwidth connection and information sharing. Therefore, NFC devices represent an increasing valuable target for adversaries. One of the major threats is relay attack, in which an adversary directly relays messages between a pair of communication peers referred to as initiator and target device. A successful relay attack allows an adversary to temporarily posses a 'virtual' initiator/target and thereby to gain associated benefits. In this paper, we propose a lightweight and automated method featuring role transitions and thus called Chameleon to thwart relay attacks. The principle of the method is: Chameleon exchanges the roles of the two devices after every NFC session in a random manner. The information of exchanged role is included in the messages of every session and encrypted by pre-shared key of the two legitimate devices. In this condition, the adversary cannot decrypt the message and configure themselves to appropriate role during the connection. Consequently, the relayed communication will be interrupted and a transaction is aborted due to uncompleted data packet. This method is implemented in real communication scenario and works well on thwarting relay attack. Our experiments indicate that it is an easy-to-implement and effective defense against relay attacks.

Keywords: Near field communication · Radio frequency identification · Relay attack · Implementation · Role transition · Lightweight · Tradeoff

Y. Ji—This work was partially supported by the National 973 Program of China under award No. 2013CB338001 and the Strategy Pilot Project of Chinese Academy of Sciences under award No. XDA06010702.

S. Qing et al. (Eds.): ICICS 2015, LNCS 9543, pp. 346–355, 2016.
DOI: 10.1007/978-3-319-29814-6_29

1   Introduction

Near field communication (NFC) [1] is a promising and increasingly prevalent short-range wireless technology. Due to its shorter-range of operation and other characteristics, NFC is more suitable than RFID systems in many applications such as access control, payment services, and information sharing. With the release of Android 4.4 in Oct. 2013, Google introduced a new platform, Google Wallet, for NFC-based transactions. In Sept. 2014, Apple also announced support for NFC-powered transactions as part of its Apple Pay program.

With the popularity of NFC application, NFC enabled devices represent an increasing valuable target for adversaries [5,6] and one of the major threats is the relay attack [7]. It is executed by sitting in the middle of two communication parties and simply "relaying" request and response effectively making one invisible to either party. During relay attack, the adversary can employ a proxy-reader and a proxy-token to relay the communication, in either wired or wireless manner, between authenticating reader and token over a distance much longer than intended, which intends to deceive the real reader into believing that real token is in close proximity (while it is not).

To the best of our knowledge, relay attack can hardly been defended by any practical countermeasures. Since the adversary does not need to parse or apprehend the relayed messages, it is well understood that application-layer countermeasures like cryptographic approaches are incompetent at defending against relay attacks. According to [7], relay resistant measures for NFC include enforcing timing constraints [8], distance bounding [9], and additional verification [10–14]. Nevertheless, due to various technical and marketing reasons, effectively counteracting relay attacks is still a very challenging task.

In this paper, we propose a lightweight and automated method featuring role transitions and thus called Chameleon to thwart relay attacks. Chameleon is lightweight as it doesn't involve heavy encryption algorithm like ECC; On the other hand, it is based on software that needn't interact with users and thus is automated. Two NFC devices during communication are configured as initiator and target alternatively, and thus our scheme is named after Chameleon, a type of lizard that can quickly change the color of its skin. The principle of the method is: Chameleon exchanges the roles of the two devices after every NFC session in a random manner. The adversary cannot decipher the messages containing the information of exchanged role and thereby cannot configure themselves to appropriate role during the connection with legitimate devices. Consequently, the relayed communication can be interrupted and a transaction can be aborted due to uncompleted data packet. We also implement Chameleon in a real communication scenario, and the results show that it can work well on defending relay attack.

The remainder of the paper consists of Sect. 2 which provide a brief background summary of NFC and relay attack. Section 3 presents Chameleon, our lightweight solution dedicated for NFC devices to deter relay attack. Evaluation and discussion is presented in Sect. 4. Section 5 discusses related work, and finally concluding remarks are in Sect. 6.

2 Background and Preliminaries

In this section we present a brief overview of NFC characteristics including standard, communication speed, and operation mode, and then introduce the mechanism of relay attack.

NFC Characteristics. NFC is a specification for contactless communication between two devices. It is based on existing Radio Frequency Identification (RFID) technology [4] by allowing two-way communication between endpoints.It is accredited with standard ISO/IEC 18092 [2]. According to this standard,NFC devices operate at 13.56 MHz and are required to be compatible with ISO/IEC 14443 and FeliCa. This standard specifies the interface and protocol for simple wireless communications between close-coupled devices that communicate with transfer rates of 106, 212, 424 kbps. In 2012, NFC also earned a further international accredited standard ISO/IEC 21481 [3].

NFC devices are defined to work in two roles: initiator and target. Initiator generate RF filed and start the NFCIP-1 communication; target responds to initiator command either using load modulation scheme or using modulation of self generate RF field. NFC devices can communicate in either active mode or passive mode. In active mode both initiator and target devices provide their own power supply and create a magnetic field to transfer data between each other. They do this in half duplex, deactivating their RF field until no other devices is transmitting. In passive mode, initiator is the only device that generates an RF signal; the target device answers by modulating the existing field for which the initiator device listens out, and then processes therefore transfers the data.

Relay Attack. Relay attacks exist already for RFID systems and have been perfect to work with regular NFC devices (e.g. phone) by just installing specific pieces of software. Figure 1 shows schematic diagram of relay attack.

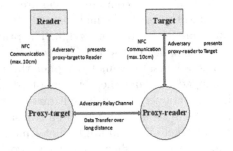

Fig. 1. Schematic diagram of NFC Relay attack setup

In order to execute a relay attack, an adversary needs two devices to act as proxies to relay communication, in either wired or wireless manner, between authenticating reader and target over a distance much longer than intended.

The two devices are connected via suitable communication channel such as Bluetooth to relay information over a greater distance. One proxy device interfaces with the NFC target device of a victim functioning as a proxy-reader. It forwards all messages over the high speed link to the second proxy device imitating a NFC target to interface with the actual NFC reader. The target assumes that it is communicating with the actual reader and responds accordingly. The response is then relayed back to the proxy-target, which will transmit the messages to the reader. The intention of the attacker is to ensure that the reader is unable to distinguish between the real target and the proxy. If he succeeds the reader will assume that the target is in close proximity and grant access to the attack.

Relay attack has serious security implication as it can bypass any application layer security protocol, even if such protocols were based on strong cryptographic principles. It doesn't matter what application layer protocol or security algorithms are used, and the attacker even requires no prior knowledge about the relayed data. If the overarching protocol contains security vulnerability the attacker could also modify the relayed data in real time which is often referred to as "active" relay.

3   Chameleon

According to the principle of NFC, we propose a lightweight and automated method featuring role transitions and thus called Chameleon to thwart relay attacks. In this section the detail of Chameleon is described in the following three parts: security goal and assumption, Chameleon protocol and Chameleon characteristics.

Security Goal and Assumption. The main security goal of Chameleon is to block the communication established by adversary while do not influence normal communication. To achieve this goal we should better disrupt the relayed communication thoroughly or force the adversary to miss at least one data packet. During the communication,two real NFC devices convert their role between initiator and target randomly. The two real devices should reach an agreement on the role transition that indicates which role each device will use for next session. The agreement is unpredictable by adversary while it is manipulated by the two real devices.For the purpose of confidentiality, consistency and integrity of data, the real devices are assumed to pre-share a secret key.

To execute the Chameleon method there are also some assumptions must be proposed. The feature of the Chameleon is role transition and unpredictable by adversary. Unpredictability can be obtained by random number generated by randomizer. Moreover, confidentiality, consistency and integrity of data are considered, the two communicating devices should have a pre-shared secret key and symmetry encryption algorithm such as AES can be applied.

Chameleon Protocol. According to the ISO/IEC 18092 the two NFC devices intending to communicate should first configure themselves as initiator or target respectively, and then the they can pair with each other. The standard also indicates that only initiator and target device can communicate while two initiator or two target devices cannot because the two devices with identical role are impossible to pair successfully. In other words, each device needs to determine the role of the counterpart, otherwise, it cannot configure to appropriate role and therefore pairing will fail. The characteristic of this method is to configure the device before transmitting message. For example, device A is configured as initiator to transmit first data packet to B, and then the role of device A and B may be changed before next session. The role of the two devices may be configured in two possible ways: first, device A and B can continue transmit next data packet with original role; second, the two devices exchange role, which means if A is initiator at first and then it should be configured as target to transmit next packet. Device A and B choose one of the two way randomly, and thus proxy devices may unable to receive messages from real devices as they cannot configure to an appropriate role.

The two legitimate devices should reach an agreement of role transition in order to communicate successfully. We use additional four control bytes C1, C2, ID1 and ID2 to indicate the information of role transition. All of the messages including the agreement are encrypted by pre-shared key. The coding structure of control byte C1 is shown is Table 1. MI represents whether all of the data packets are already transmitted. If MI is set to ONE, it indicates there are still some data packets should be transmitted while ZERO means data packets are transmitted completely. E1 represents which role will be used for transmitting next packet. If E1 is set to ZERO it means to use current role while ONE means the two devices exchange their roles. If E1 is set to ONE, a new ID with ID1 and ID2 should be set for the new target devices so that new initiator can find new target device with it. Control byte C2 is equal with data length modulo packet size, which indicates the data length in last packet.

Table 1. Coding structure of control byte C1

Bit	Bit7-Bit2	Bit1	Bit0
Function	Reserved	E1	MI

Chameleon Characteristics. The main characteristic of the Chameleon is that a pair of NFC devices negotiate and exchange their role randomly in communication. The messages including role information are encrypted by pre-shared key, and therefore the adversary is unable to determine the role of each device. As a result, the proxy devices may not be configured to an appropriate role to pair with legitimate devices and thus pairing would fail. On the other hand, communication or transaction could be aborted once data packet missing is detected.

4 Evaluations and Discussion

In this section, efficiency of the Chameleon on communication and thwarting relay attack is evaluated, and further discussion as well as the experiment results is also presented.

4.1 Experiment

We develop and test a relay attack of our own in order to better understand the level of difficulty an attacker might face in doing the same, as well as to see the strengths and weaknesses of the attack. Then, the Chameleon is applied to thwart the attack.

Attack Setup. We use NFC development board C and D to act as proxy devices to relay communication between A and B. The main component of the development board is PN532 and its associated circuit. The PN532 is a highly integrated transmission module for contactless communication at 13.56 MHz including micro-controller functionality based on an 80C51 core. The transmission module utilizes a modulation and demodulation concept completely integrated for different kinds of contactless communication methods and protocol at 13.56 MHz Two blue modules are used to establish relay channel between C and D. Microcontrollers STM32F407 from STMicroelectronics are served as "relay centers" to control proxy devices and Bluetooth modules.

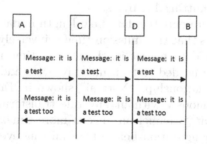

Fig. 2. Schematic diagram of the implemented relay attack

In this experiment device C worked as proxy-target is presented to legitimate device A while D worked as proxy-initiator is presented to legitimate device B. We manage to launch the relay attack between A and B. Figure 2 shows schematic diagram of the implemented relay attack. Adversary presents proxy device C to legitimate device A to trigger NFC communication. Proxy device C interacts with D via Bluetooth modules which act as relay channel. Proxy device D simply relays all messages received over the relay channel. Message "it is a test" is successfully relayed between two distant NFC-enabled devices.

Defense Result. From the above relay attack experiment, we can find that the proxy device can receive message from legitimate devices once it is configured to an appropriate role. In other words, adversary must know which legitimate device is initiator and which one is legitimate target, otherwise, they may not implement a successful relay attack. Figure 3 shows the result of using Chameleon to thwart relay attack.

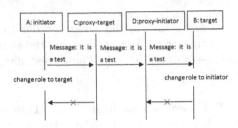

Fig. 3. Thwarting relay attack using Chameleon

When the Chameleon is not applied during the communication, the message "it is a test" can be relayed successfully from legitimate device A to B. However, the attack is thwarted once the Chameleon is executed. The proxy devices fail to pair with legitimate devices and thereby the communication is aborted. In order to measure the effect of this method on message interactions, we set up another experiment to quantify the time for transmitting 1 K bytes. Table 2 shows the required time for transmitting 1 K bytes.

Data packet size represents the data field length in data exchange command of PN532. Table 2 shows that transmission time is inversely proportional to data packet size. The larger data packet is, the shorter time is needed. It can also be found that the time needed to transmit 1 K bytes and the data packet size is generally in linear relationship. "Normal" shown in Table 2 means to transmit data packet continuously without any role transformation. It can also be found from Table 2 that "Chameleon" needs more time to transmit 1 K data due to continuously configuration before transmitting every data packet. However, with the increase of packet size, the time difference between "Normal" and "Chameleon" decrease gradually. This method, to some extent, can defense or reduce the possibility of successful relay attack.

Table 2. Time measurements of 1 K bytes transmitted in different packet size (Unit:second)

Packet size	16 bytes	32 bytes	48 bytes	96 bytes	128 bytes
Normal	13.971226	6.992128	4.816253	2.44235	1.393672
Chameleon	21.363692	10.472058	7.290481	4.15893	2.584200

4.2 Analysis

The legitimate devices act as initiator or target reaching an agreement on the role before communication. As all the messages including the agreement are encrypted by the pre-shared key of the two devices, adversary is unable to precisely determine the role of each legitimate device which result the connection fail. This countermeasure can effectively defense against the relay attack implemented by using off-the-shelf NFC enabled devices. It can be found from the experiment and Table 2 that the "Chameleon" require reasonable overhead. Compared with "Normal" transmission, "Chameleon" spends much more time to transmit 1 K bytes due to re-configuration. The successful rate of the attack is related with data packet number N and equal to $\left(\frac{1}{2}\right)^{N-1}$. In our future work, in order to reduce the time for configuration and therefore to improve communication efficiency, we can use the "Chameleon" method every few data packets instead of each packet.

As mentioned above, our investigation is focused on the relay attack implemented by off-the-shelf devices. However, the Chameleon is invalid to the relay attacks that executed by custom-built devices. For example, adversary can relay in both ways by using custom-built device to listen on both sides and just replay the messages to the right side. This is one drawback of the Chameleon , and we leave this challenge as our future work. In addition to the Chameleon, some assistant facilities can be added to enhance security. For example, monitor can be installed around a door. In this condition, the adversary will give up attacking if he fails to unlock a door in five seconds. Moreover, once adversary fails to relay entire data during communication for several times, the communication will be locked for a while or even be aborted which will trigger a warning signal sent to control center.

5 Related Works

In recent years, more and more attentions have been paid to NFC and many works have been published. Some researchers considered that NFC is more secure than other wireless technologies [1,6]. In Reference [6], NFC is considered the de facto standard for radio communication and the dominator of the contactless payment market. On the other hand, Reference [1] draw a conclusion that NFC exhibits higher security than Bluetooth and ZigBee. Nevertheless, this very lengthy survey on NFC, as well as References [4] and [5], hardly covers the relay attack.

Although NFC is believed to be more secure than RFID, both technologies are subject to relay attacks. In an overview on relay attack [7], the authors raise the concern that even though relay attacks pose a serious security threat, they are often not considered a major risk (like eavesdropping or skimming); examples include certain academic surveys [4,5]. Francis et al. demonstrate the first successful attack in [15] with unmodified NFC-enabled mobile phones running application written with publicly available APIs. Likewise, a software-based relay attack to Google Wallet, a well-known mobile payment system, is presented in [16]. Furthermore, in [17] sophisticated relay attacks are demonstrated using smart phones and improved using custom-made proxy device.

Research efforts to make system relay-resistant are categorized into three types: time-out constraint [8], distance bounding [9], and the use of additional (i.e., external) verification procedures [10–12]. As to detecting relay attacks, there could be other approaches. For example, Ref [13] addresses relay attacks through ambient condition measurement and proposes an authentication protocol. Like Ref [10–12] the proposal is also appliance-based, as specific sensors are required. Another proposal considering environment measurement is in Ref [18]. In Ref [19], NFC's resiliency against relay attacks is evaluated via a formal verification technique for analyzing protocols and systems.

These schemes [8–13] are appliance-based, which may not comply with commodity devices generally available from the market. Moreover, as summarized in [7], countermeasures mentioned above may result in significant increased system cost (e.g., modificate both reader and token), complicate the process (e.g., require user interaction), and/or need strong computation ability (e.g., implement ECC). These observations motivate us to pursue a lightweight and automated solution. This solution needn't additional hardware so as to reduce cost and it also doesn't require a large amount of computation.

6 Conclusion

We propose a lightweight and automated method featuring role transitions and thus called Chameleon to thwart relay attacks. The principle of the method is: Chameleon exchanges the roles of the two devices after every NFC session in a random manner unpredictable by the adversary. The information for exchanged role is included in the messages of every session and encrypted by pre-shared key of the two legitimate devices. The adversary unable to decipher the message and therefore may not configure themselves to the right role during the connection with legitimate devices. As a consequence, the communication may be interrupted and a transaction may be aborted due to uncompleted data packet. This method is implemented in real communication scenario and can work well on thwarting relay attack. Our proposal exhibits an intrinsic tradeoff between security and efficiency, and experiments indicate that it is an easy-to-implement and effectual defense against relay attacks.

References

1. Coskun, V., Ozdenizci, B., Ok, K.: A survey on near field communication (NFC) technology. Wireless Pers. Commun. **71**(3), 2259–2294 (2013)
2. ISO, IEC 18092:2013, Near Field Communication Interface and Protocol (NFCIP-1), March 2013
3. ISO/IEC 21481:2012, Near Field Communication Interface and Protocol (NFCIP-2), June 2012

4. Roberts, C.M.: Radio frequency identification (RFID). Comput. Secur. **25**(1), 18–26 (2006)
5. Haselsteiner, E., Breitfuß, K.: Security in near field communication (NFC): strengths and weaknesses. In: proceedings of 2nd Workshop on RFID Security (RFIDSec 2006), p. 11, July 2006
6. Nelson, D., Qiao, M., Carpenter, A.: Security of the near field communication protocol: an overview. J. Comput. Sci. Coll. **29**(2), 94–104 (2013)
7. Hancke, G.P., Mayes, K.E., Markantonakis, K.: Confidence in smart token proximity: relay attacks revisited. Comput. Secur. **28**(7), 615–627 (2009)
8. Reid, J., Nieto, J.M.G., Tang, T., Senadji, B.: DetectingRelay attacks with timing-based protocols. In: Proceedings of 2nd ACM Symposium on Information, Computer and Communication Security (ASIACCS 2007), pp. 204–213, March 2007
9. Drimer, S., Murdoch, S.J.: Keep your enemies close: distance bounding against smartcard relay attacks. In: proceedings of 16th USENIXSecuritySymposium (USENIX Sec 2007), pp. 87–1C102, August 2007
10. Kang, S., Kim, J., Hong, M.: Button-based method for the prevention of nearfield communication relay attacks. Int. J. Commun. Syst. **28**(10), 1628–1639 (2015)
11. Malek, B., Miri, A.: Chaotic masking for securing RFID systems against relay attacks. Secur. Commun. Netw. **6**, 1496–1508 (2013)
12. Čagalj, M., Perković, T., Bugarić, M., Li, S.: Fortune cookies, smartphones: weakly unrelayable channels to counter relay attacks. Pervasive Mobile Comput. **20**, 64–81 (2015)
13. Urien, P., Piamuthu, S.: Elliptic curve-based RFID/NFC authentication with temperature sensor input for relay attacks. Decis. Support Syst. **59**, 28–36 (2014)
14. Stajano, F., Wong, F.-L., Christianson, B.: Multichannel protocols to prevent relay attacks. In: Sion, R. (ed.) FC 2010. LNCS, vol. 6052, pp. 4–19. Springer, Heidelberg (2010)
15. Francis, L., Hancke, G., Mayesc, K.: A practical generic relay attack on contactless transactions by using NFC mobile phones. Int. J. RFID Secur. Crypt. (IJRFIDSC) **2**(1–4), 92–106 (2013)
16. Roland, M., Langer, J., Scharinger, J.: Applying relay attacks to Google Wallet. In: Proceedings of 5th International Workshop on Near Field Communication (NFC 2013), p. 6, February 2013
17. Korak, T., Hutter, M.: On the power of active relay attacks using custom-made proxies. In: Proceedings of 8th Annual IEEE International Conference on RFID (IEEE RFID 2014), pp. 126–133, April 2014
18. Kim, G.-H., Lee, K.-H., Kim, S.-S., Kim, J.-M.: Vehicle relay attack avoidance methods using RF signal strength. Commun. Netw. **5**, 573–577 (2013)
19. Alexiou, N., Basagiannis, S., Petridou, S.: Security analysis of NFC relay attacks using probabilistic model checking. In: proceedings of 10th International Wireless Communications and Mobile Computing Conference (IWCMC 2014), pp. 524–529, August 2014

A Solution of Code Authentication on Android

Xue Zhang[1,2] and Rui Zhang[1(✉)]

[1] State Key Laboratory of Information Security,
Institute of Information Engineering, Chinese Academy of Sciences,
Beijing, China
{zhangxue,r-zhang}@iie.ac.cn
[2] University of Chinese Academy of Sciences, Beijing, China

Abstract. With the popularity of Android operating system, the Android platform has become one of the major targets of attackers. One of the main threats is code-tampering and repackaging attack against Android APPs. By tampering Android APPs, an attacker is able to complete copyright theft, malicious code injection and other actions. Confronted with this situation, numerous researchers have proposed many protection and detection strategies. But all of these strategies are a kind of passive defenses. A trust mechanism in Android is in demand to defense code-tampering in active. In this paper, we propose a new strategy to actively defense code-tampering and repackaging attacks. We make a thorough analysis of the signature verification mechanism via Android source code, and add certificate authentication mechanism in Android, which improves the security of Android system greatly. With this mechanism, Android can easily recognize repackaged APPs before installing, users can also quickly find the developers who take responsibility for the APPs, as a result, the attackers will be less motivated to tamper APP and upload it to the marketplace.

Keywords: Android · Trust-management · Authentication framework · Code-tampering and repackaging · Certificate authentication · PKI

1 Introduction

With the popularity of Android operating system, a number of third-party alternative marketplaces have been created to host thousands of APPs. Among them, we find a common practice of repackaging legitimate APPs and distributing repackaged ones via third-party marketplaces. By tampering Android APPs, an attacker is able to complete copyright theft, malicious code injection and other actions. In the study of Zhou and Jiang [5], 1083 of 1260 malware samples (or 86.0 %) are repackaged versions of legitimate APPs with malicious payloads.

Confronted with serious code-tampering issues for Android APPs, researchers have proposed a series of protection and detection strategies. Code obfuscation, such as Proguard [2] and DexGuard [1], increases the difficulty to analyze application code statically by removing unused code and obscuring parts of code symbols information. But attackers still can find new methods to analyze the APP

© Springer International Publishing Switzerland 2016
S. Qing et al. (Eds.): ICICS 2015, LNCS 9543, pp. 356–362, 2016.
DOI: 10.1007/978-3-319-29814-6_30

code deeply and tamper the code. Watermarking technology [4] is to inject watermark information into Android applications and can find the piracy problems by extracting watermark dynamically during the execution of the applications. But this method can only prevent misbehaviors during execution that can not avoid malware while installing. Besides, some techniques detect the repackaged APPs in a large scale of APPs through extracting different APP characteristics such as code fuzzy hashes , feature hashes, program dependence grap, and feature view graph. Though detecting methods can find out the repackaged APPs with a high probability, implementing of these method is not prevalent, nowadays the third-part marketplaces do not detecting the APPs using such complicated method. So all the methods above are passive defenses. In this paper, we propose a new strategy to actively defense code-tampering and repackaging attacks.

2   Preliminary

In this section, we briefly review the certificate verification mechanism on Android systems. Lei and Zhang provided a thorough analysis of the signature verification mechanism in Android [3].

2.1   Application Signature Generation Process

We use UnsignedApp.apk to present the unsigned APP, and SignedApp.apk presents the signed APP. After signing the APP by the self-issued certificate (certificate of the developer is issued by himself), we compare the compression file of SignedApp.apk with that of UnsignedApp.apk, find that a directory named /META-INF will be added to the SignedApp.apk. This directory contains three files: MANIFEST.MF, CERT.RSA, and CERT.SF. The specific signature generation process is shown in Fig. 1, including 5 steps.

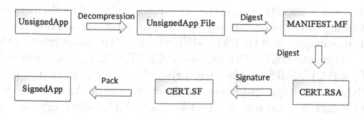

Fig. 1. Signature generation process

- Decompress: decompress UnsignedApp.apk;
- Compute the digest: compute the digest of each file in UnsignedApp.apk separately including the configuration file (AndroidManifest.XML), the program's implementation code (classes.dex), the resource file (/res) etc. and write the results to the MANIFEST.MF file;
- Compute the digest again: compute the digest of each item in MANIFEST.MF file separately and write the results to the CERT.SF file;

– Compute the signature: sign the CERT.SF file by the self-issued certificate. Pack the signature and the certificate into PKCS7 format and write it to the CERT.RSA file;
– Package: Put the three files (MANIFEST.MF, CERT.SF, and CERT.RSA) produced by step 2, step 3, step 4 into a directory named /META-INF, and pack it with the original UnsignedApp.apk file into a package (SignedApp.apk).

2.2 Application Signature Verifying Process

When we install an APP, it will first trigger the PackageInstaller.apk whose path in Android source code is /packages/apps/PackageInstaller, and show the permissions to the user, once the user click the confirm button, it will call the PackageManager service to complete the verification process. The verification process was completed by three moves:

1. Decompress the APP and count its digest, compare it with MANIFEST.MF, this procedure complete by VerifierEntry.verify().
2. Compute the MANIFEST.MF's digest and compare it with CERT.SF, this procedure is completed by JarVerifier.verify().
3. Verify the CERT.RSA's signature using the certificate. This is completed by JarUtils.verifySignature().the certificate is issued by the developer himself.

The signature verifying process is the reverse process of the signature generation process, which make sure the data produced during the signature generation process is not changed by attacker.

3 Analysis

This section will illustrate why certificate authentication mechanism is important for avoiding code-tampering and repackaging attack. Analyzing the signature generation process, we find that MANIFEST.MF is the fingerprint of the whole APP package except /META-INF directory. CERT.SF is the fingerprint of MANIFEST.MF, and CERT.RSA is the fingerprint of CERT.SF. In signature verifying process, these three steps make sure the integrity of the APP, If someone tamper the APP code but do not change the /META-INF directory, the APP will be judged as signature failure. Because it's digest will not coincident with that in MANIFEST.MF. But these steps do not guaranty certificate authentication of the APP. Assuming that someone change the APP code and substitute all the files in /META-INF directory (sign it with another certificate), The tampered APP will be judged as benign one. When the developer pack the APP, developer will sign the APP with the certificate issued by themselves, and the Android verifying process do not care about who issue the certificate. If the attack tampers the APP code and signs the APP again with his own certificate(tamper the source code of the APP and change the whole /META-INF directory), Android cannot realize the APP has been repacked. So the root cause of the repackaging attack is the lack of certificate authentication mechanism. Thus we build an authentic CA who issues certificates to the developers, developers sign the APPs with the authentic certificates. So once the APP has something wrong, we can find the developer who can make responsibility to the trouble.

From the analysis above, we realize that the lack of certificate authentication give code-tampering the opportunity to apply misbehaviors on Android. So we need to look into the Android source code in order to find a method to add certificate authentication mechanism in Android.

4   Design Details

To build the certificate authentication mechanism in Android we need certificate management architecture to issue authentic certificates to developers and manage the certificates revocation. The certificate management architecture is composed by Certificate management base system, TF card, and secure marketplace as shown in Fig. 2. CA system is the certificate center whose main responsibility is issuing the certificates to the users or APP developers. TF card is used to securely storing the root certificate and user's certificates(avoid from tampering by the attackers). secure marketplace is an open store for the users to download applications. Developers upload their signed APPs to marketplace, then the users download the signed APPs from it and verify them with certificate authentication mechanism in Android with the aid of root certificate in TF card. To verify the certificate's validation, the users also need to synchronize the CRL list from CA system.

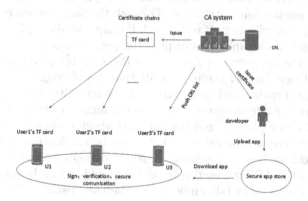

Fig. 2. Certificate management architecture

4.1   Certificate Issue

CA issue the certificates to the developers or to the users (store the root certificate in TF card). The developer's certificates is issued in a form of certificate chains. A typical certificate chain validation process would use cryptography to check the signature relationships between all certificates in the chain. A certificate chain can contain intermediary certificates, so the system would start by validating if the APP's certificate was signed by another certificate median in the chain. Then validate whether certificate median was signed by the next one, and so on, until reaching the trusted root certificate.

To guaranty the root certificate not be tampered by the attacker in Android, we use the safe TF card to store root certificate, the users have no permission to modify the TF card but can read the certificate from it. If the user's TF card is lost, the user should lock the TF card at once, request revocation to CA and change a new TF card. Once CA receive the revocation request, it will add the certificate to the CRL list and push the list to the end users.

4.2   APP Upload and Download

The APP developer signs the APP with the his authentic certificate and upload it to the secure marketplace. Then the user download the APP form the secure marketplace, verify it with certificate authentication mechanism. User can verify the certificate with the root certificate, and then verify the integrity of the APP. If the APP still have misbehavior, we can easily find the developer and give him corresponding punishment.

4.3   Certificate Authentication in Android

We make a thorough analysis of the signature verification mechanism in Android, via statically analyzing Android source code and dynamically monitoring during the process of application installation. Through the analysis, we find that when the user install an application, it will launch PackageInstaller.apk, the main function of PackageInstaller.apk is to display the permissions required by APP to the users. But the integrity and signature of the APP is not verified in PackageInstaller.apk. Once the user confirm installation, it will trigger PackageManager service to begin copying and completing APP's integrity and signature verification. Since now Android system lacks the certification authentication mechanism, we need find a place to add the authentication module to Android source code. We don't have to change the APP integrity verification in PackageManager service because beside certification authentication we also need to guaranty the integrity of the APP. So we finally decide to add the authentication module at beginning of PackageInstaller.apk. When the user install APP, it will launch PackageInstaller.apk and begin the certificate authentication procedure at once. If the certificate is authentic, PackageInstaller.apk will continue the rest process. Otherwise it will abort the installation application and warn the user that the APP is not authentic. The interaction in certificate authentication procedure can be described in Fig. 3.

The certification authentication consists of the following steps:

– Read the certificate chain of the APP which we will install;
– Read the root certificate form the TF card;

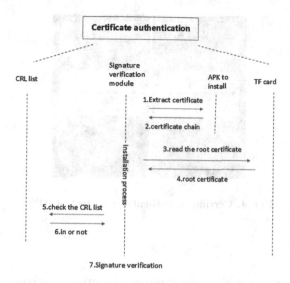

Fig. 3. Certificate authentication process

- Verify the certificate chain;
- Affirm the certificate is not in the CRL list;

To verify the certificate authentication procedure, we conduct an experiment in simulated scenarios. The experiment environment is base on HW Ascend P6. First we use the APP's cert (which is issued by CA) to sign the unsigned APP. Second we store the signed APP in android SD card (emulating the App download procedure). Our authentication procedure is to extract the certificate chain from APP, verify it with the root certificate and assure its validation (if the certificate is in CRL list). The novelty of our strategy is that we use root certificate that safety stored in TF card to verity the validation of the certificate. So we can easily find the developer who can take responsibility of the APP.

We use JarFile object to store entries in APP, scan the entries to find the certificate of the APP. We use getCertificates() function to extract the certificate chain out from JarFile object. Since we extract out a chain, that mean the signature relationships between all certificates is correct. Otherwise, we will get an error.

So next we only need to verity if the root node of the chain is the root certificate that stored in TF card. Finally we verify if the certificate is in CRL. If the APP pass all the verifications, Android recognize it as authenticated. As shown in Fig. 4, if we use a self-issued certificate or other unauthentic certificate sign the APK, the APK will be recognized as an unsafe APK. Only if we use an authentic certificate issued by root certificate to sign the APP, the APP can be recognized as a safe APP. After passing certificate authentication process, the APP continue verify the integrity and complete the installation as usual.

Fig. 4. Certificate authentication test of APP

5   Conclusion

In this paper, we proposal a new strategy to actively defense code-tampering and repackaging attacks. When installing an APP, one first checks the certificate authentication, then checks the rightness of the APP's integrity. Thus, the repackaged APP will be easily recognized if the APP is tampered. In our strategy, the APP is signed by developer's certificate and the developer's certificate is signed by the trusted CA. If the APP passes certificate authentication but still has something wrong, one can easily find the malicious developer. If the attacker changes the APP code and signs it with unauthentic certificates, the repacked APP will not pass the certificate authentication. Therefore, our strategy can avoid code-tampering and repackaging attack from the root cause.

Acknowledgement. This work was partially supported by the Strategic Priority Research Program of the Chinese Academy of Sciences under Grant No. XDA06010703 and XDA06010701, National Natural Science Foundation of China (No. 61472416, 61272478 and 61170282), and National Key Scientific and Technological Project (No. 2014ZX01032401-001).

References

1. Dexguard. http://www.saikoa.com/dexguard
2. Proguard. http://proguard.sourceforge.net
3. Lei, L., Zhang, Z., Wang, Y., Wang, L.: Studying the implementation and security of the signature authentication mechanism in android. Netinfo. Secur. **8**, 25 (2012)
4. Zhou, W., Zhang, X., Jiang, X.: Appink: watermarking android apps for repackaging deterrence. In: Proceedings of the 8th ACM SIGSAC Symposium on Information, Computer and Communications Security, pp. 1–12. ACM (2013)
5. Zhou, Y., Jiang, X.: Dissecting android malware: characterization and evolution. In: IEEE Symposium on Security and Privacy (SP), pp. 95–109. IEEE (2012)

Verifiable Proxy Re-encryption
from Indistinguishability Obfuscation

Muhua Liu[1], Ying Wu[1], Jinyong Chang[1], Rui Xue[1(✉)], and Wei Guo[2]

[1] State Key Laboratory of Information Security,
Institute of Information Engineering, Chinese Academy of Sciences,
Beijing 100093, China
{liumuhua,wuying,changjinyong,xuerui}@iie.ac.cn
[2] Information Center, Guangdong Power Grid Company Limited,
Guangzhou 510000, Guangdong, China
guowei@gdxx.csg.cn

Abstract. Proxy re-encryption scheme allows a semi-trusted proxy to re-encrypt ciphertexts of a client into ciphertexts of a receiver. However, the proxy might not as honest or reliable as supposed in practice.

Ohata et al. [16] recently introduced a new functionality for proxy re-encryption with verifiability of the re-encryption soundness. However, careful inspection reveals that the construction in their work can not resist against normal collusion attack. Specifically, if the proxy and the receiver collude, the master key of the client will be leaked. We consider this as a serious weakness. Moreover, the storage of keys for a receiver in that work will increase linearly with the number of clients.

In this paper, we present a novel generic scheme for verifiable proxy re-encryption from indistinguishability obfuscation. It can ensure the security of master secret key even when the proxy and the receiver collude. In addition, our scheme possesses the advantage that any receiver's key storage will remain constant, no matter how many clients he deals with. Furthermore, the re-encryption mechanism in our construction is very succinct in that the size of re-encrypted ciphertext relies only on the size of the encrypted message and the security parameter, compared to that in [16], which relies on the size of the original ciphertext and the receiver's public key as well.

Keywords: Verifiability · Indistinguishability obfuscation · Proxy re-encryption

1 Introduction

There are many applications that require to covert encrypted messages of one client, per a proxy, into ciphertexts of a receiver, such as secure file systems, outsourced filtering of encrypted spam [1]. Blaze et al. [3] proposed the notion of atomic proxy cryptography, which allows a semi-trusted proxy to convert a ciphertext of a client into a ciphertext of a receiver without seeing the underlying plaintext and the secret key of either the client or the receiver.

© Springer International Publishing Switzerland 2016
S. Qing et al. (Eds.): ICICS 2015, LNCS 9543, pp. 363–378, 2016.
DOI: 10.1007/978-3-319-29814-6_31

In the ordinary proxy re-encryption schemes, the proxy is modeled as a semi-trusted party, who will perform the re-encryption algorithm honestly. But, in some real scenarios, the proxy is not as honest or reliable as it might be. Considering the following scenario, for example, a client stores a large encrypted data CT in the cloud. When he wants to share his encrypted data with a receiver, he will give his transformation key TK to a cloud proxy. Then, the proxy may convert CT into a re-encrypted ciphertext CT_{out} that can be decrypted under the receiver's secret key. However, the proxy may make mistakes for various reasons like a faulty implementation of the re-encryption algorithm, or returning a random result even for saving computation time. Therefore, a proxy re-encryption protocol that allows the receiver to make verification of the correctness of the re-encrypted ciphertexts is much expected.

Ohata et al. [16] recently proposed a verifiable proxy re-encryption protocol. In the protocol, the receiver is enhanced with the function to verify whether a received ciphertext is correctly transformed from an original ciphertext by a proxy, and thus can detect illegal actives of the proxy. The scheme achieves re-encryption verifiability by adding a re-encryption verifiable algorithm, which takes two ciphertexts CT and CT_{out}, a secret key sk_R of a receiver, and a public key pk of a client as input, and allows to check the faithfulness of the transformation of CT_{out}.

The idea of the construction is as follows: the client splits his secret key sk into two shares sk_1 and sk_2 by a threshold public key encryption scheme [5], and sends the original ciphertext CT and sk_1 to the proxy, and $\phi = \mathsf{Enc}_{pk_R}(sk_2)$ to the receiver. Then the proxy re-encrypts the ciphertext CT by $\mu_1 = \mathsf{Dec}_{sk_1}(CT)$ and $CT_{out} = \mathsf{Enc}_{pk_R}(\mu_1 \parallel CT)$. After getting the ciphertexts ϕ and CT_{out}, the receiver computes $\mu_1 \parallel CT = \mathsf{Dec}_{sk_R}(CT_{out})$ and $\mu_2 = \mathsf{Dec}_{sk_2}(CT)$, and outputs a plaintext m by the combining algorithm of the threshold public key encryption scheme. In order to achieve proxy re-encryption with re-encryption verifiability, their scheme complies with the following properties: When re-encrypting CT into CT_{out}, CT is somehow embedded into CT_{out} in such a way that when the receiver decrypts CT_{out}, the embedded ciphertext CT can be extracted. In re-encryption verification, the receiver checks whether an extracted ciphertext CT equals to the given candidate CT'.

In the above scheme, if the proxy and the receiver collude together, the two shares sk_1 and sk_2 can be obtained that could further recover the secret key of the client. Another drawback in their scheme is that the receiver has to store each secret key sk_2 to decrypt the received ciphertexts of one client. When the receiver deals with a couple of clients, the key storage of the receiver grows linearly with the number of clients. In addition, the size of the re-encrypted ciphertext in their construction not only relies on the size of the encrypted message and the security parameter, but also relies on the size of the original ciphertext and the receiver's public key. That is not preferred when a large amount of messages need to be processed.

In this paper, we present a novel verifiable proxy re-encryption scheme that makes up the drawbacks as above. We focus on the unidirectional non-interactive verifiable proxy re-encryption scheme. Here is our desired properties for a verifiable proxy re-encryption scheme:

- **Verifiability:** A malicious proxy can not persuade a receiver to accept a wrong re-encrypted ciphertext.
- **Weak Master Secret Key Security:** An adversary can not get the master secret key even if the proxy and the receiver collude. In our scheme, we just consider the adversary which only gets one transformation key. We call this as weak master secret key security. One motivation [1], to consider this stems from some proxy re-encryption schemes define two or more types of ciphertext, some of which may only be decrypted using the master secret key. A scheme which provides the master key security will protect those ciphertexts.
- **Key Optimality:** The size of the receiver's key storage remains constant, regardless of how many clients from which he receives ciphertext.
- **Succinct:** The size of the re-encrypted ciphertext just relies on the size of the encrypted message and the security parameter.
- **Efficiency:** The time complexity of the verifiable algorithm should be smaller than the transformation algorithm. Otherwise, the receiver can complete the transformation process by himself.

The starting idea for our construction is to pick a standard public-key encryption key pair (pk_1, sk_1) and a symmetric encryption scheme in the setup step of the verifiable proxy re-encryption scheme. Choosing a random string K_1 as the secret key of symmetric encryption scheme, an encryption of a message m will simply be an encryption of K_1 using the public key pk_1 and an encryption of m using the symmetric key K_1. Specifically, our approach is built on the key encapsulated mechanism. We compress the random string K_1 to a shorter string using a hash function, and then, use the output of the hash function to check the correctness of the re-encrypted ciphertext. However, the hash value will leak some entropy of the session key which is no longer uniform. Hence, we apply a key extractor to extract a nearly uniform symmetric key K_{SE}, which will replace the random string K_1 as the symmetric encryption key. To verify the integrity of the symmetric encrypted ciphertext, we compute a hash value on the concatenation of the symmetric encrypted ciphertext and the hash value of K_1, and use the second hash value as the verifiable key. The transformation key TK is an obfuscation of a circuit $\mathcal{G}$ which has the master secret key sk_1 hardwired in its description. It takes a original ciphertext as input, and outputs a re-encrypted ciphertext CT_{out}. While this solution would work if the obfuscator achieves the black box obfuscation definition [2], there is no reason to believe that an indistinguishability obfuscator would necessarily hide sk_1.

Recall that the indistinguishability chosen plaintext attack (CPA) security definition requires that the adversary will not be able to distinguish an encryption of m_0 from an encryption of m_1. A natural first step would be to have two public key pk_1 and pk_2, and require the encryption of random string K_1 to consist of encryption of K_1 under both public keys. Then, we encrypt the message m by using the extracted key from the random string K_1, and get the ciphertext

(CT_1, CT_2, CT_3), where CT_1 and CT_2 are the ciphertexts of the random string K_1, and CT_3 is the ciphertext of the message m. However, in this case, the original decryptor (i.e., client) cannot generate a proof on his own that the ciphertexts CT_1 and CT_2 encrypt the same message to provide to the obfuscator transformation circuit. Thus, we must require the encryptor to generate a proof π, which must hide K_1. A solution is to have the encryptor generate a non-interactive witness indistinguishable proof. One statement is that the ciphertexts CT_1 and CT_2 are encryptions of the same message, the other statement is a commitment to $CT_1 \parallel CT_2$. After getting the ciphertext $CT = (CT_1, CT_2, CT_3, \pi)$, the obfuscated circuit firstly check the proof π, if it checks out, it would use secret key sk_1 for decryption and computation.

Note that the encryption algorithm of our construction is not efficient compared with Ohata's work [16], because of using the tool of NIWI. Our scheme just achieves the CPA security. To construct a scheme which satisfies the CCA security is our future work.

1.1 Related Works

Mambo and Okamoto [14] proposed the notion of proxy encryption, which delegates the ability of decryption through an interaction. Blaze et al. [3] proposed the first bidirectional proxy re-encryption scheme based on the ElGamal encryption scheme. Their construction is CPA secure under the Decisional Diffie-Hellman assumption. However, their scheme is not master secret key secure, and if the proxy and the receiver collude, they can recover client's secret key.

Ivan and Dodis [11] proposed an unidirectional non-interactive proxy encryption for ElGamal encryption scheme by sharing the client's secret to two participants. Their construction also can not achieve the master secret key security and key optimality. Ateniese et al. [1] proposed an unidirectional proxy re-encryption scheme based on bilinear maps. Their construction is weak master secret key secure, efficient, and chosen-plaintext secure under the Bilinear Diffie-Hellman assumption.

Canetti and Hohenberger [4] described a bidirectional construction of proxy re-encryption providing chosen-ciphertext security. Libert and Vergnaud [13] presented the first unidirectional proxy re-encryption schemes with replayable chosen-ciphertext security in the standard model. Shao and Cao [18] proposed the first CCA-secure proxy re-encryption without pairings. But their construction is secure in the random oracle model. Subsequently, Matsuda et al. [15] improved Shao's [18] result and constructed a bidirectional chosen-ciphertext security proxy re-encryption scheme without bilinear maps in the standard model. But later, Weng et al. [19] pointed out that Matsuda's [15] scheme is not chosen-ciphertext secure. Hohenberger et al. [9] proposed a novel proxy re-encryption scheme based on the obfuscation, but their security is weak since the adversary is only allowed to black-box access to re-encryption oracle. Hanaoka et al. [8] presented the first generic construction of chosen-ciphertext secure unidirectional proxy re-encryption scheme based on threshold public key encryption [5]. Isshiki et al. [10] proposed a proxy re-encryption scheme in a stronger security model extended from Hanaoka's scheme [8]. Recently, Kirshanova [12] proposed a new unidirectional proxy scheme based on the hardness of the LWE problem. Their scheme is provably CCA-1 secure in the selective model. However, none of these work considered the re-encryption verifiability. Ohata et al. [16] firstly introduced this property, but their construction can not resist the attack of collusion. In this work, we give a novel construction which has some better properties than the construction of Ohata et al. [16].

1.2 Organization

The rest of this paper is organized as follows. We start by giving the definitions for verifiable proxy re-encryption in Sect. 2. Next, in Sect. 3, we recall the definitions for various cryptographic primitives used in our construction. We then present our construction for verifiable proxy re-encryption scheme in Sect. 4. Finally, we give the conclusion of this work in Sect. 5.

Basic Notation. In what follows we will denote with $\lambda \in \mathbb{N}$ a security parameter. We say $\mathrm{negl}(\lambda)$ is negligible if $|\mathrm{negl}(\lambda)| < 1/\mathrm{poly}(\lambda)$ holds for all polynomials $\mathrm{poly}(\lambda)$ and all sufficiently large λ. Denote PPT as probabilistic polynomial time. "$x \parallel y$" denotes a concatenation of x and y. We write $x \xleftarrow{R} X$ for sampling x from the set X uniformly at random.

2 Verifiable Proxy Re-encryption

In this section, we give the definition of verifiable proxy re-encryption which is different from the definition of Ohata's [16]. Because our verifiable algorithm needs additional information to verify the correctness of the re-encrypted ciphertext, we adopt a new definition. We start by presenting the syntax for verifiable proxy re-encryption and then proceed to give the security definitions.

Syntax. Denote PKE_R as the receiver's encryption system, and the key pairs (pk_R, sk_R) as the receiver's key. A verifiable proxy re-encryption $\mathcal{VPRE}$ consists of five algorithms (Setup, Enc, KeyGen, Trans, Dec):

- Setup(1^λ) $\rightarrow$ (mpk, msk): The setup algorithm takes as input a security parameter λ and outputs the master public key mpk and the master secret key msk.
- Enc(mpk, m) $\rightarrow$ (CT, VK): The encryption algorithm takes as input the master public key mpk and a message $m \in \mathcal{M}$, and outputs a ciphertext CT and a verifiable key VK.
- KeyGen(pk_R, msk) $\rightarrow$ TK: The transformation key generation algorithm takes as input the master secret key msk and the receiver's public key pk_R, and outputs a transformation key TK.
- Trans(CT, TK) $\rightarrow$ CT_{out}: The ciphertext transformation algorithm takes as input a ciphertext CT and a transformation key TK, and outputs a re-encrypted ciphertext CT_{out}.

- Dec(VK, sk_R, CT_{out}) → m or ⊥: The decryption algorithm takes as input the verifiable key VK, the ciphertext CT_{out}, and the receiver's secret key sk_R, and outputs a message m or ⊥, where ⊥ indicates that the transformation ciphertext is invalid.

Definition 1 (*Correctness*). *A verifiable proxy re-encryption scheme $\mathcal{VPRE}$ is correct if the ciphertext generated by the encryption algorithm allows an honest worker to output a transformation ciphertext that will be decrypted as the original message. More formally, for any $m \in \mathcal{M}$, any $(mpk, msk) \leftarrow$ Setup(1^λ), $(CT, VK) \leftarrow$ Enc(mpk, m), and any $TK \leftarrow$ KeyGen(pk_R, msk), if $CT_{out} \leftarrow$ Trans(CT, TK), then $m \leftarrow$ Dec(sk_R, VK, CT_{out}) holds with all but negligible probability.*

CPA Security Experiment. We adopt the chosen plaintext attack (CPA) security for the verifiable proxy re-encryption scheme. The game is described as follows:

Setup: A challenger firstly generates the honest receiver's key pairs $(sk_{R_i}, pk_{R_i}) \leftarrow$ PKE$_{R_i}$.Setup(1^λ) for $i = i, \ldots, \ell$, and sets $PK = \{pk_{R_i}\}_{i=1}^\ell$. Then, the challenger runs the Setup(1^λ) to generate a master public key mpk and a master secret key msk. It gives the master public key mpk and the public key set $PK = \{pk_{R_i}\}_{i=1}^\ell$ to the adversary $\mathcal{A}$.

Phase 1: Proceeding adaptively, the adversary can repeatedly make the transformation key generation queries:

- The adversary $\mathcal{A}$ submits the pk_{R_i} to the challenger.
- If $pk_{R_i} \notin \{pk_{R_i}\}_{i=1}^\ell$, then the challenger outputs ⊥. Else, the challenger runs the KeyGen(pk_{R_i}, msk) to generate the transformation key TK_i, and sends TK_i to the adversary.

Challenge: $\mathcal{A}$ submits two equal-length messages m_0 and m_1 to the challenger. The challenger randomly picks a bit $b \in \{0, 1\}$, and runs Enc(mpk, m_b) to obtain a challenge ciphertext CT^* and a verification key VK^* of the message m_b. It returns (CT^*, VK^*) to the adversary.

Phase 2: This phase is the same as Phase 1.

Guess: $\mathcal{A}$ outputs a guess b'.

Definition 2 (*CPA security*). *A $\mathcal{VPRE}$ scheme is CPA secure if for any PPT adversary $\mathcal{A}$,*

$$\text{Adv}_{\mathcal{VPRE}, \mathcal{A}}^{CPA}(\lambda) := \left| \Pr[b' = b] - \frac{1}{2} \right| \leq \text{negl}(\lambda).$$

Weak Master Secret Key Security. We require that the adversary can not get the master secret key even if the proxy and the receiver collude. A $\mathcal{VPRE}$

scheme is weak master secret key secure if the adversary can not learn the master secret key of the client, even when he is given the transformation key and the receiver's secret key. The adversary is allowed to query the transformation key generation oracle only once. The game is described as follows:

Setup: A challenger runs the Setup(1^λ) to generate a master public key mpk and a master secret key msk, and sends the master public key mpk to the the the adversary $\mathcal{A}$.

Query: The adversary can make the transformation key generation query one time:

- $\mathcal{A}$ runs $(pk_R, sk_R) \leftarrow$ PKE$_R$.Setup(1^λ), and submits the public key pk_R to the challenger.
- The challenger runs the KeyGen(msk, pk_R) to generate a transformation key TK, and sends TK to $\mathcal{A}$.

Challenge: $\mathcal{A}$ outputs a secret key α. The adversary succeeds if and only if $\alpha = msk$.

Definition 3 (Weak Master Secret Key Security). *A $\mathcal{VPRE}$ scheme is weak master secret key secure if for any PPT adversary $\mathcal{A}$,*

$$\mathrm{Adv}_{\mathcal{VPRE},\mathcal{A}}^{MKS}(\lambda) := \Pr[\alpha = msk] \leq \mathrm{negl}(\lambda).$$

Verifiability. A $\mathcal{VPRE}$ scheme is verifiable security if a malicious server can not persuade the receiver to accept an incorrect transformation ciphertext, even when he is allowed to query the transformation key generation oracle and the decryption oracle. The game is described as follows:

Setup: First, the challenger generates the honest receiver's key pairs $(sk_{R_i}, pk_{R_i}) \leftarrow$ PKE$_{R_i}$.Setup(1^λ) for $i = 1, \ldots, \ell$, and sets $PK = \{pk_{R_i}\}_{i=1}^\ell$. Then, the challenger runs $(mpk, msk) \leftarrow$ Setup(1^λ), and sends the master public key mpk and the public key set $PK = \{pk_{R_i}\}_{i=1}^\ell$ to the adversary $\mathcal{A}$.

Phase 1: Proceeding adaptively, the adversary can repeatedly make the transformation key generation queries:

- The adversary $\mathcal{A}$ submits the pk_{R_i} to the challenger.
- If $pk_{R_i} \notin \{pk_{R_i}\}_{i=1}^\ell$, then the challenger outputs $\perp$. Otherwise, the challenger runs the KeyGen(pk_{R_i}, msk) to generate the transformation key TK_i, and sends TK_i to the adversary.

Phase 2: The adversary can repeatedly query the decryption oracle:

- The adversary $\mathcal{A}$ submits the (VK, CT_{out}, TK_i) to the challenger. The challenger finds the corresponding secret key sk_{R_i}, and computes m or $\perp \leftarrow$ Dec(sk_{R_i}, VK, CT_{out}), and returns the result to $\mathcal{A}$.

Challenge: The adversary $\mathcal{A}$ submits a message m to the challenger. The challenger obtains a challenge ciphertext CT^* and a verification key VK^* of the message m. It returns (CT^*, VK^*) to the adversary.

Phase 3: This phase is the same as Phase 1.

Phase 4: This phase is the same as Phase 2.

Verify: The adversary $\mathcal{A}$ outputs a transformation ciphertext (CT^*_{out}, pk_{R_j}). The challenger finds the corresponding sk_{R_j}, and computes $m' \leftarrow \mathsf{Dec}(sk_{R_j}, VK^*, CT^*_{out})$. If $m' \neq m$ and $m' \neq \perp$, then the adversary $\mathcal{A}$ succeeds, and the game outputs 1.

Definition 4 (Verifiability). *A $\mathcal{VPRE}$ scheme is verifiable security if for any $m \in \mathcal{M}$, and for any PPT adversary $\mathcal{A}$,*

$$\mathrm{Adv}^{Verify}_{\mathcal{VPRE},\mathcal{A}}(\lambda) := \Pr[Game\ outputs\ 1] \leq \mathrm{negl}(\lambda).$$

Definition 5 (Efficiency). *A $\mathcal{VPRE}$ scheme is efficient if for any $(CT, VK) \leftarrow \mathsf{PKE.Enc}(mpk, m)$, and $TK \leftarrow \mathsf{KeyGen}(msk, pk_R)$, the time required to verify the correctness of transformation ciphertext is $o(T)$, where T is the time required to compute $CT_{out} \leftarrow \mathsf{Trans}(CT, TK)$.*

3   Preliminaries

In this section, we present definitions for various cryptographic primitives that we will use in our construction. We assume familiarity with standard semantically secure public-key encryption, standard semantically secure symmetric encryption, and omit their formal definition from this section. For reasons of space, we give the definition of non-interactive witness indistinguishable proofs and commitment schemes in Appendix A. We recall the notions of indistinguishability obfuscation, puncturable pseudorandom functions, and randomness extractor.

3.1   Indistinguishability Obfuscation

We present the formal definition following the syntax of Garg et al. [7]

Definition 6 (Indistinguishability Obfuscation (iO)). *A uniform PPT machine iO is called an indistinguishability obfuscator for a circuit class $\{\mathcal{C}_\lambda\}$ if the following holds:*

- *(Correctness): For all security parameters $\lambda \in \mathbb{N}$, $C \in \mathcal{C}_\lambda$, and inputs x, we have that*
$$\Pr[C'(x) = C(x) : C' \leftarrow i\mathcal{O}(\lambda, C)] = 1.$$

- **(Indistinguishability):** For any (not necessarily uniform) PPT distinguisher (Samp, $\mathcal{D}$), there exists a negligible function negl such that the following holds: if $\Pr[\forall x,\ C_0(x) = C_1(x); (C_0, C_1, \sigma) \leftarrow \mathsf{Samp}(1^\lambda)] \geq 1 - \mathrm{negl}(\lambda)$, then:

$$| \Pr[\mathcal{D}(\sigma, i\mathcal{O}(\lambda, C_0)) = 1 : (C_0, C_1, \sigma) \leftarrow \mathsf{Samp}(1^\lambda)]$$
$$- \Pr[\mathcal{D}(\sigma, i\mathcal{O}(\lambda, C_1)) = 1 : (C_0, C_1, \sigma) \leftarrow \mathsf{Samp}(1^\lambda)]| \leq \mathrm{negl}(\lambda).$$

Recently, Garg et al. [7] gave the first candidate construction for an indistinguishability obfuscator $i\mathcal{O}$ for the circuit class P/poly.

3.2 Puncturable Pseudorandom Functions

In our construction, we will use the puncturable PRFs, which are PRFs that can be defined on all bit strings of a certain length, except for any polynomial-size set of inputs. Below we recall their definition, as given by Sahai and Waters [17]:

Definition 7. *A puncturable family of PRFs F is given by a triple of Turing machines* Key, Puncture, Eval, *and a pair of computable functions $n(\cdot)$ and $m(\cdot)$, satisfying the following conditions:*

- **(Functionality Preserved Under Puncturing).** *For every PPT adversary $\mathcal{A}$ such that $\mathcal{A}(1^\lambda)$ outputs a set $S \subseteq \{0,1\}^{n(\lambda)}$, then for all $x \in \{0,1\}^{n(\lambda)}$ where $x \notin S$, we have that:*

$$\Pr[\mathsf{Eval}(K, x) = \mathsf{Eval}(K_S, x) : K \leftarrow \mathsf{Key}(1^\lambda), K_S = \mathsf{Puncture}(K, S)] = 1.$$

- **(Pseudorandom at Punctured Points).** *For every PPT adversary $(\mathcal{A}_1, \mathcal{A}_2)$ such that $\mathcal{A}_1(1^\lambda)$ outputs a set $S \subseteq \{0,1\}^{n(\lambda)}$ and $x \in S$, consider an experiment where $K \leftarrow \mathsf{Key}(1^\lambda)$ and $K_S = \mathsf{Puncture}(K, S)$. Then we have*

$$| \Pr[\mathcal{A}_2(K_S, x, \mathsf{Eval}(K, x)) = 1] - \Pr[\mathcal{A}_2(K_S, x, U_{m(\lambda)}) = 1]| \leq \mathrm{negl}(\lambda),$$

where $U_{m(\lambda)}$ denotes the uniform distribution over $m(\lambda)$ bits.

3.3 Randomness Extractor

For a discrete distribution X over Σ, we denote its min-entropy by $\mathbf{H}_\infty(X) = -\log(\max_{\sigma \in \Sigma} \Pr[X = \sigma])$. The average min-entropy of X conditioned on Y is defined as $\tilde{\mathbf{H}}_\infty(X|Y) = -\log(E_{y \leftarrow Y}[2^{-\mathbf{H}_\infty(X|Y=y)}])$.

We recall a useful lemma that will be used in our proof.

Lemma 1 *[6]. Let X, Y and Z be random variables. If Y has at most 2^r possible values, then $\tilde{\mathbf{H}}_\infty(X|(Y,Z)) \geq \tilde{\mathbf{H}}_\infty(X|Z) - r$.*

Definition 8 (Randomness Extractor). *An efficient function* $\mathsf{Ext} : \mathcal{X} \times \{0,1\}^t \to \mathcal{Y}$ *is an average-case* (k, ϵ)*-strong extractor if for all random variables* (X, Z) *such that* $X \in \mathcal{X}$ *and* $\tilde{\mathbf{H}}_\infty(X|Z) \geq k$, *we have* $\Delta((Z, s, \mathsf{Ext}(X, s)), (Z, s, U_\mathcal{Y})) \leq \epsilon$, *where* $s \xleftarrow{R} \{0,1\}^t, U_\mathcal{Y} \xleftarrow{R} \mathcal{Y}$, *and* $\Delta(\cdot, \cdot)$ *denotes the statistical distance between two distributions.*

By the leftover hash lemma [6], any family of pairwise independent hash functions $\mathcal{H} := \{h : \mathcal{X} \to \mathcal{Y}\}$ is an average case $(\tilde{\mathbf{H}}_\infty(X|Z), \epsilon)$-strong extractor if $\tilde{\mathbf{H}}_\infty(X|Z) \geq \log|\mathcal{Y}| + 2\log(1/\epsilon)$.

4 Construction

In this section we present our construction of the verifiable proxy re-encryption scheme. Our construction relies on the following components: A public key scheme $\mathsf{PKE} = (\mathsf{PKE.KeyGen}, \mathsf{PKE.Enc}, \mathsf{PKE.Dec})$. A symmetric encryption scheme $\mathsf{SE} = (\mathsf{SE.Enc}, \mathsf{SE.Dec})$ with key space $\{0,1\}^{\ell_{\mathsf{SE}}}$. Two collision-resistant hash functions: $H_0 : \mathcal{K} \to \{0,1\}^{\ell_{H_0}}$, $H_1 : \{0,1\}^* \to \{0,1\}^{\ell_{H_1}}$. A family of pairwise independent hash functions $\mathcal{H}$ from $\mathcal{K}$ to $\{0,1\}^{\ell_{\mathsf{SE}}}$. The above parameters satisfy the following condition: $0 < \ell_{\mathsf{SE}} \leq (\log|\mathcal{K}| - \ell_{H_0}) - 2\log(1/\epsilon)$, where ϵ is a negligible value in λ. Let $len_c = len_c(1^\lambda)$ denote the length of ciphertexts in $(\mathsf{PKE.Setup}, \mathsf{PKE.Enc}, \mathsf{PKE.Dec})$. We will use a parameter $len = 2 \cdot len_c$ in the description of our scheme.

Let $(\mathsf{NIWI.Setup}, \mathsf{NIWI.Prove}, \mathsf{NIWI.Verify})$ be a NIWI proof system. Let Com be a perfectly binding commitment scheme. Let $i\mathcal{O}$ be an indistinguishability obfuscator for all efficiently computable circuits. Let $(\mathsf{Key}, \mathsf{Puncture}, \mathsf{Eval})$ be a puncturable family of PRF. We now proceed to describe our scheme $\mathcal{VPRE} = (\mathsf{Setup}, \mathsf{Enc}, \mathsf{KeyGen}, \mathsf{Trans}, \mathsf{Dec})$.

– $\mathsf{Setup}(1^\lambda) \to (mpk, msk)$:
  1. sample two key pairs for the public key encryption scheme $(sk_1, pk_1) \leftarrow \mathsf{PKE.KeyGen}(1^\lambda)$, and $(sk_2, pk_2) \leftarrow \mathsf{PKE.KeyGen}(1^\lambda)$,
  2. compute a CRS $crs \leftarrow \mathsf{NIWI.Setup}(1^\lambda)$ for the NIWI proof system,
  3. choose an extractor $h \in \mathcal{H}$, two hash functions H_0 and H_1, and a symmetric encryption scheme SE,
  4. compute a commitment $C \leftarrow \mathsf{Com}(0^{len})$,
  5. set the master public key to be $mpk = (pk_1, pk_2, h, H_0, H_1, crs, C, \mathsf{SE})$, and the master secret key to be $msk = sk_1$.
– $\mathsf{Enc}(m, mpk) \to (CT, VK)$:
  1. choose a random key K_1, and compute a hash evaluation $\mathsf{Tag} = H_0(K_1)$ of K_1, and an extraction evaluation $K_{\mathsf{SE}} = h(K_1)$,
  2. compute ciphertexts $CT_1 \leftarrow \mathsf{PKE.Enc}(pk_1, K_1; r_1)$, and $CT_2 \leftarrow \mathsf{PKE.Enc}(pk_2, K_1; r_2)$ under the public key encryption scheme, and a ciphertext $CT_3 \leftarrow \mathsf{SE.Enc}(K_{\mathsf{SE}}, m)$ under the symmetric encryption scheme, where r_1 and r_2 are chosen randomly,
  3. compute a NIWI proof $\pi \leftarrow \mathsf{NIWI.Prove}(crs, y, w)$ for the NP statement $y = (CT_1, CT_2, C, pk_1, pk_2)$:

- either CT_1 and CT_2 are encryptions of the same message, or
- C is a commitment to $CT_1 \parallel CT_2$.

A witness $w_{real} = (K_1, r_1, r_2)$ for the first part of the statement, referred to as the real witness, includes the randomness key K_1 and the randomness r_1 and r_2 used to compute the ciphertexts CT_1 and CT_2, respectively. A witness $w_{trap} = s$ for the second part of the statement, referred to as the trapdoor witness, includes the randomness s used to compute C.

4. compute $VK = H_1(\mathsf{Tag} \parallel CT_3)$, and output the ciphertext $CT = (CT_1, CT_2, CT_3, \pi)$ and the verifiable key VK.

- KeyGen$(pk_R, msk) \to TK$:
    1. choose a fresh PRF key $K \leftarrow \mathsf{Key}(1^\lambda)$,
    2. compute the transformation key $TK \leftarrow i\mathcal{O}(\mathcal{G})$, where the circuit $\mathcal{G}$ is described in Fig. 1. Note that $\mathcal{G}$ has the receiver's public key pk_R, the master secret key sk_1, the public key mpk and the PRF key K hardwired in it.

- Trans$(CT, TK) \to CT_{out}$:
    1. on input CT and a transformation key TK, the transformation algorithm computes and outputs $CT_{out} = \mathcal{G}(CT)$.

- Dec$(VK, sk_R, CT_{out}) \to m$ or $\perp$:
    1. parse the transformed ciphertext as $CT_{out} = (C_1, C_2)$ and a verifiable key $VK = H_1(\mathsf{Tag} \parallel CT_3)$,
    2. recover a random key K_1 from $\mathsf{PKE}_R.\mathsf{Dec}(sk_R, C_1)$,
    3. compute $\mathsf{Tag} = H_0(K_1)$, if $H_1(\mathsf{Tag} \parallel C_2) \neq VK$, return $\perp$, otherwise, compute $K_{\mathsf{SE}} = h(K_1)$ and return $m = \mathsf{SE}.\mathsf{Dec}(K_{\mathsf{SE}}, C_2)$.

Input: Ciphertext CT
Constants: mpk, sk_1, K, pk_R

1. Parse $CT = (CT_1, CT_2, CT_3, \pi)$.
2. If NIWI.Verify$(crs, y, \pi) = 0$, then output $\perp$ and stop, otherwise continue to the next step. Here $y = (CT_1, CT_2, C, pk_1, pk_2)$ is the statement corresponding to π.
3. Compute $K_1 \leftarrow \mathsf{PKE}.\mathsf{Dec}(sk_1, CT_1)$.
4. Compute $r \leftarrow \mathsf{Eval}(K, CT_1 \parallel CT_2)$.
5. Compute $C_1 \leftarrow \mathsf{PKE}_U.\mathsf{Enc}(pk_R, K_1; r)$ by using the receiver's encryption algorithm, set $C_2 = CT_3$, and output $CT_{out} = (C_1, C_2)$.

Fig. 1. Functionality $\mathcal{G}$

One thing we emphasize is that the transformed ciphertexts in our scheme are succinct in that their size only depends on the message size and security parameter. However, the size of re-encrypted ciphertext depends on the size of original ciphertext and the receiver's public key as well in Ohata's construction [16].

Theorem 1. *The above verifiable proxy re-encryption is CPA secure if it is instantiated with a secure punctured PRF, a CPA secure public key encryption, a CPA secure symmetric encryption, a perfect binding commitment, and indistinguishability secure obfuscator.*

Here we show the intuition of the proof. Suppose the ciphertext $(CT_0 = (CT_{1,0}, CT_{2,0}, CT_{3,0}, \pi_0), VK_0)$ encrypts the message m_0, and the ciphertext $(CT_1 = (CT_{1,1}, CT_{2,1}, CT_{3,1}, \pi_1), VK_1)$ encrypts the message m_1. We need to prove that the two ciphertexts are computational indistinguishable. In one of our hybrid experiments, we need to move from an obfuscation that on input $CT = (CT_{1,0}, CT_{2,0}, CT_{3,0}, \pi_0)$ would yield the output $((\mathsf{Enc}(pk_R, K_1; r)), C_2)$ to another obfuscation that on the same input would yield the output $((\mathsf{Enc}(pk_R, K_2; r)))$, where the random string r is generated by a pseudorandom function. However, the adversary may not be able to perform such a transformation, since our construction is based on indistinguishability obfuscation, which only guarantees that the obfuscation of circuit that implement identical functions are indistinguishable. Hence, this hybrid change would not be indistinguishable because of $\mathsf{Enc}(pk_R, K_1; r) \neq \mathsf{Enc}(pk_R, K_2; r)$. In order to solve this problem, we introduce five new values that can change the nature of the circuit that we are obfuscating to disable all ciphertexts except for the five ciphertexts. The detailed proof of the theorem is given in the full version of the paper.

Theorem 2. *Suppose that H_0 and H_1 are collision-resistant hash functions, Then, the proxy re-encryption scheme is verifiable security.*

Proof. Given an adversary $\mathcal{A}$ against the verifiable security, we construct an efficient adversary $\mathcal{B}$ to break the collision-resistance of the underlying hash functions H_0 or H_1. Given two challenge hash functions (H_0^*, H_1^*), the adversary $\mathcal{B}$ simulates the verifiability game described as follows.

$\mathcal{B}$ generates honest receiver's key pairs $(sk_{R_i}, pk_{R_i}) \leftarrow \mathsf{PKE}_{R_i}.\mathsf{Setup}(1^\lambda)$ for $i = 1, \ldots, \ell$, and sets $PK = \{pk_{R_i}\}_{i=1}^\ell$. Then, the adversary $\mathcal{B}$ generates the public parameter mpk and the master secret key msk as $\mathsf{Setup}(1^\lambda)$, except for hash function H_0^* and H_1^*, and sends the master public key mpk and the public key set PK to the adversary. Note that, the adversary $\mathcal{B}$ knows the master secret key msk and the receiver's secret key set $SK = \{sk_{R_i}\}_{i=1}^\ell$. Therefore, it can answer the query of the transformation key generation oracle and the decryption oracle. For a challenge message $m \in \mathcal{M}$ submitted by $\mathcal{A}$, the adversary $\mathcal{B}$ invokes $\mathsf{Enc}(mpk, m)$ to obtain a ciphertext $CT^* = (CT_1^*, CT_2^*, CT_3^*, \pi^*)$ of a random string $K_1^* \in \mathcal{K}$. It then computes $\mathsf{Tag} = H_0^*(K_1^*)$ and $VK^* = H_1^*(\mathsf{Tag} \parallel CT_3)$, and sends (CT^*, VK^*) to the adversary $\mathcal{A}$. The adversary $\mathcal{A}$ outputs $CT_{out} = (C_1, C_2)$. $\mathcal{B}$ computes the random string $K_1' \leftarrow \mathsf{PKE}_R.\mathsf{Dec}(sk_R, C_1)$ and $\mathsf{Tag}' = H_0^*(K_1')$. We observe that $\mathcal{A}$ succeeds if and only if $m' \notin \{m, \perp\}$ and $H_1^*(\mathsf{Tag}' \parallel C_2) = VK^*$. If $\mathcal{A}$ succeeds, we consider the following two cases:

Case 1. $(\mathsf{Tag}' \parallel C_2) \neq (\mathsf{Tag} \parallel CT_3)$. If this case occurs, $\mathcal{B}$ immediately obtains a collision of the hash function H_1^*.

Case 2. $(\mathsf{Tag}' \parallel C_2) = (\mathsf{Tag} \parallel CT_3)$, but $K_1^* \neq K_1'$. Because $H_0^*(K_1^*) = \mathsf{Tag} = \mathsf{Tag}' = H_0^*(K_1')$, $\mathcal{B}$ obtains a collision of the hash function H_0^*.

Therefore, the adversary $\mathcal{B}$ is able to break the security of collision-resistant hash functions. This completes the proof.

Theorem 3. *If an adversary $\mathcal{A}$ can break the weak master secret key security with probability ϵ, then, there exists a PPT adversary $\mathcal{B}$, who attacks on the indistinguishability obfuscation, such that $Adv_{i\mathcal{O},\mathcal{B}}^{Obf}(1^\lambda) = \epsilon$.*

Proof. Since the distinguisher $\mathcal{B}$ of obfuscator $i\mathcal{O}$ consists of two parts: Samp and $\mathcal{D}$, we respectively construct them as follows.

The algorithm $\mathsf{Samp}(\cdot)$ takes 1^λ as input. Then randomly choose a PRF key $K \leftarrow \mathsf{Key}(1^\lambda)$ and a random key K_1, sample two key pairs $(pk_1, sk_1) \leftarrow$ PKE.KeyGen(1^λ) and $(pk_2, sk_2) \leftarrow$ PKE.KeyGen(1^λ), compute a CRS $crs \leftarrow$ NIWI.Setup(1^λ) for the NIWI proof system, an extractor $h \in \mathcal{H}$, two hash functions H_0 and H_1, and a symmetric encryption scheme SE, compute a commitment $C \leftarrow \mathsf{Com}(0^{len})$, two ciphertexts $CT_1^* =$ PKE.Enc(pk_1, K_1) and $CT_2^* =$ PKE.Enc(pk_2, K_1), a punctured key $K' \leftarrow$ Puncture$(K, CT_1^* \| CT_2^*)$, and a random string $r^* \leftarrow$ Eval$(K, CT_1^* \| CT_2^*)$, and return $mpk = (pk_1, pk_2, h, H_0, H_1, crs, C, \mathsf{SE})$ to $\mathcal{A}$. When $\mathcal{A}$ makes the transformation key generation query, it sets $\mathcal{G}_0 = \mathcal{G}$ which is a circuit in our construction with (mpk, pk_R, sk_1, K) hardwired in it. It computes $C^* =$ PKE.Enc$(pk_R, K_1; r^*)$, and constructs the circuit $\mathcal{G}_1$ which is described in Fig. 2, and has $(mpk, pk_R, sk_2, K', CT_1^* \| CT_2^*, C^*)$ hardwired in it. Finally, it outputs the two challenge circuits $(\mathcal{G}_0, \mathcal{G}_1)$.

Input: Ciphertext CT
Constants: $mpk, sk_2, K', pk_R, CT_1^* \| CT_2^*, C^*$

1. Parse $CT = (CT_1, CT_2, CT_3, \pi)$.
2. If NIWI.Verify$(crs, y, \pi) = 0$, then output $\perp$ and stop, otherwise continue to the next step. Here $y = (CT_1, CT_2, C, pk_1, pk_2)$ is the statement corresponding to π.
3. If $CT_1 \| CT_2 = CT_1^* \| CT_2^*$, output $CT_{out} = (C_1 = C^*, C_2 = CT_3)$ and stop.
4. Compute $K_1 \leftarrow$ PKE.Dec(sk_2, CT_2).
5. Compute $r \leftarrow$ Eval$(K', CT_1 \| CT_2)$.
6. Compute $C_1 \leftarrow$ PKE$_R$.Enc$(pk_R, K_1; r)$ by using the user's encryption algorithm, set $C_2 = CT_3$, and output $CT_{out} = (C_1, C_2)$.

Fig. 2. Functionality $\mathcal{G}_1$

The sub-distinguisher $\mathcal{D}$ takes as input $TK_b = i\mathcal{O}(\lambda, \mathcal{G}_b)$, where b is the challenge bit for $\mathcal{D}$. It sends TK_b to the adversary $\mathcal{A}$, and receives a secret key sk. If $sk = sk_1$, output $b = 0$, otherwise output $b = 1$.

Now, we prove that the two circuits $\mathcal{G}_0$ and $\mathcal{G}_1$ are equivalent on functionality. First, for any input $CT = (CT_1, CT_2, CT_3, \pi)$, $\mathcal{G}_0$ outputs $\perp$ if and only if $\mathcal{G}_1$ outputs $\perp$. Note that both $\mathcal{G}_0$ and $\mathcal{G}_1$ output $\perp$ if and only if the proof π does not verify, i.e., $\text{NIWI.Verify}(crs, y, \pi) = 0$, where $y = (CT_1, CT_2, pk_1, pk_2, \pi)$. Next, we prove that both $\mathcal{G}_0$ and $\mathcal{G}_1$ have the same functionality for all valid inputs. We consider two cases: $CT_1 \parallel CT_2 \neq CT_1^* \parallel CT_2^*$ and $CT_1 \parallel CT_2 = CT_1^* \parallel CT_2^*$. For the first case, by the first property of puncturable PRF, it follows that $\text{Eval}(K, CT_1 \parallel CT_2) = \text{Eval}(K', CT_1 \parallel CT_2) = r$. Since NIWI is statistical soundness, both $\mathcal{G}_0$ and $\mathcal{G}_1$ can get K_1 by decrypting CT_1 and CT_2 respectively, and output $(C_1 = \text{PKE}_R.\text{Enc}(pk_R, K_1; r), C_2 = CT_3)$ at the same time. In the second case, $\mathcal{G}_0$ computes $\text{Eval}(K, CT_1^* \parallel CT_2^*) = r$, then decrypts $K_1 \leftarrow \text{PKE.Dec}(sk_1, CT_1^*)$ by using the secret key sk_1, and outputs $C_1 = \text{PKE}_U\text{Enc}(pk_R, K_1; r)$. On the other hand, because $CT_1^* \parallel CT_2^* = CT_1 \parallel CT_2$, $\mathcal{G}_1$ outputs the hardwired value C^*. Note that $C_1 = C^*$ and $C_2 = CT_3$ dose not be changed, we can get that $\mathcal{G}_0(CT) = \mathcal{G}_1(CT)$.

Therefore, we have $\text{Adv}_{\mathcal{VPRE}, \mathcal{A}}^{MKS}(\lambda) = \text{Adv}_{i\mathcal{O}, \mathcal{B}}^{Obf}(1^\lambda) = \epsilon$.

Efficiency. Our verifiable proxy re-encryption is efficient. Compared with the transformation algorithm, the verifiable algorithm only introduces a hash value which is the verification key, and two hash value computations in the final decryption algorithm.

5 Conclusion

In this work, we construct a verifiable proxy re-encryption scheme from indistinguishability obfuscation. It can ensure the security of master secret key even when the proxy and the receiver collude. In addition, the key storage of the receiver will remain constant, no matter how many clients he deals with. Furthermore, the size of re-encrypted ciphertexts in our scheme only depends on the message size and security parameter.

Acknowledgment. This work is supported by the "Strategic Priority Research Program" of the Chinese Academy of Sciences, Grants No. XDA06010701, National Natural Science Foundation of China (No. 61402471, 61472414, 61170280), and IIE's Cryptography Research Project.

A Preliminaries (Cont.)

A.1 Non-interactive Witness Indistinguishable Proofs

In this section, we present the definition for non-interactive witness-indistinguishable (NIWI) proofs. We emphasize that we are interested in proof systems, i.e., where the soundness guarantee holds against computationally unbounded cheating provers.

Definition 9. *(NIWI). A non-interactive witness-indistinguishable proof system for a language L with a PPT relation R is a tuple of algorithms* (NIWI.Setup, NIWI.Prove, NIWI.Verify) *such that the following properties hold:*

- **(Perfect Completeness).** For every $(x, w) \in R$, it holds that

$$\Pr[\mathsf{NIWI.Verify}(crs, x, \mathsf{NIWI.Prove}(crs, x, w)) = 1] = 1$$

where $crs \leftarrow \mathsf{NIWI.Setup}(1^\lambda)$, and the probability is taken over the coins of $\mathsf{NIWI.Setup}$, $\mathsf{NIWI.Prove}$ and $\mathsf{NIWI.Verify}$.

- **(Statistical Soundness).** For every adversary $\mathcal{A}$, it holds that

$$\Pr\left[\mathsf{NIWI.Verify}(crs, x, \pi) = 1 \wedge x \notin L \;\middle|\; \begin{array}{l} crs \leftarrow \mathsf{NIWI.Setup}(1^\lambda); \\ (x, \pi) \leftarrow \mathcal{A}(crs) \end{array}\right] = \mathrm{negl}(1^\lambda).$$

- **(Witness Indistinguishability).** For any triplet (x, w_0, w_1) such that $(x, w_0) \in R$ and $(x, w_1) \in R$, the distributions $\{crs, \mathsf{NIWI.Prove}(crs, x, w_0)\}$ and $\{crs, \mathsf{NIWI.Prove}(crs, x, w_1)\}$ are computationally indistinguishable, where $crs \leftarrow \mathsf{NIWI.Setup}(1^\lambda)$.

A.2   Commitment Schemes

A commitment scheme Com is a PPT algorithm that takes as input a string x and a randomness r and outputs $c \leftarrow \mathsf{Com}(x; r)$. A perfectly binding commitment scheme must satisfy the following properties:

- **(Perfectly Binding).** This property states that two different strings cannot have the same commitment. More formally, $\forall x_1 \neq x_2$ and r_1, r_2, $\mathsf{Com}(x_1; r_1) \neq \mathsf{Com}(x_2; r_2)$.
- **(Computational Hiding).** For all strings x_0 and x_1 (of the same length), for all PPT adversaries $\mathcal{A}$, we have that:

$$|\Pr[\mathcal{A}_1(\mathsf{Com}(x_0))] = 1 - \Pr[\mathcal{A}_1(\mathsf{Com}(x_1)) = 1]| \leq \mathrm{negl}(\lambda).$$

References

1. Ateniese, G., Fu, K., Green, M., Hohenberger, S.: Improved proxy re-encryption schemes with applications to secure distributed storage. ACM Trans. Inf. Syst. Secur. **9**(1), 1–30 (2006)
2. Barak, B., Goldreich, O., Impagliazzo, R., Rudich, S., Sahai, A., Vadhan, S.P., Yang, K.: On the (im)possibility of obfuscating programs. In: Kilian, J. (ed.) CRYPTO 2001. LNCS, vol. 2139, pp. 1–18. Springer, Heidelberg (2001)
3. Blaze, M., Bleumer, G., Strauss, M.J.: Divertible protocols and atomic proxy cryptography. In: Nyberg, K. (ed.) EUROCRYPT 1998. LNCS, vol. 1403, pp. 127–144. Springer, Heidelberg (1998)
4. Canetti, R., Hohenberger, S.: Chosen-ciphertext secure proxy re-encryption. In: Proceedings of the 2007 ACM Conference on Computer and Communications Security, CCS 2007, pp. 185–194. Alexandria, 28–31 October 2007
5. Desmedt, Y.G., Frankel, Y.: Threshold cryptosystems. In: Brassard, G. (ed.) CRYPTO 1989. LNCS, vol. 435, pp. 307–315. Springer, Heidelberg (1990)
6. Dodis, Y., Ostrovsky, R., Reyzin, L., Smith, A.: Fuzzy extractors: how to generate strong keys from biometrics and other noisy data. SIAM J. Comput. **38**(1), 97–139 (2008)

7. Garg, S., Gentry, C., Halevi, S., Raykova, M., Sahai, A., Waters, B.: Candidate indistinguishability obfuscation and functional encryption for all circuits. In: 54th Annual IEEE Symposium on Foundations of Computer Science, FOCS 2013, pp. 40–49. Berkeley, 26–29 October 2013

8. Hanaoka, G., Kawai, Y., Kunihiro, N., Matsuda, T., Weng, J., Zhang, R., Zhao, Y.: Generic construction of chosen ciphertext secure proxy re-encryption. In: Dunkelman, O. (ed.) CT-RSA 2012. LNCS, vol. 7178, pp. 349–364. Springer, Heidelberg (2012)

9. Hohenberger, S., Rothblum, G.N., Shelat, A., Vaikuntanathan, V.: Securely obfuscating re-encryption. J. Cryptol. **24**(4), 694–719 (2011)

10. Isshiki, T., Nguyen, M.H., Tanaka, K.: Proxy re-encryption in a stronger security model extended from CT-RSA2012. In: Dawson, E. (ed.) CT-RSA 2013. LNCS, vol. 7779, pp. 277–292. Springer, Heidelberg (2013)

11. Ivan, A., Dodis, Y.: Proxy cryptography revisited. In: Proceedings of the Network and Distributed System Security Symposium, NDSS 2003. San Diego (2003)

12. Kirshanova, E.: Proxy re-encryption from lattices. In: Krawczyk, H. (ed.) PKC 2014. LNCS, vol. 8383, pp. 77–94. Springer, Heidelberg (2014)

13. Libert, B., Vergnaud, D.: Unidirectional chosen-ciphertext secure proxy re-encryption. In: Cramer, R. (ed.) PKC 2008. LNCS, vol. 4939, pp. 360–379. Springer, Heidelberg (2008)

14. Mambo, M., Okamoto, E.: Proxy cryptosystems: delegation of the power to decrypt ciphertexts (special section on cryptography and information security). IEICE Trans. Fundam. Electron. Commun. Comput. Sci. **80**(1), 54–63 (1997)

15. Matsuda, T., Nishimaki, R., Tanaka, K.: CCA proxy re-encryption without bilinear maps in the standard model. In: Nguyen, P.Q., Pointcheval, D. (eds.) PKC 2010. LNCS, vol. 6056, pp. 261–278. Springer, Heidelberg (2010)

16. Ohata, S., Kawai, Y., Matsuda, T., Hanaoka, G., Matsuura, K.: Re-encryption verifiability: how to detect malicious activities of a proxy in proxy re-encryption. In: Nyberg, K. (ed.) CT-RSA 2015. LNCS, vol. 9048, pp. 410–428. Springer, Heidelberg (2015)

17. Sahai, A., Waters, B.: How to use indistinguishability obfuscation: deniable encryption, and more. In: Symposium on Theory of Computing, STOC 2014, pp. 475–484. New York, May 31–June 03 2014

18. Shao, J., Cao, Z.: CCA-secure proxy re-encryption without pairings. In: Jarecki, S., Tsudik, G. (eds.) PKC 2009. LNCS, vol. 5443, pp. 357–376. Springer, Heidelberg (2009)

19. Weng, J., Zhao, Y., Hanaoka, G.: On the security of a bidirectional proxy re-encryption scheme from PKC 2010. In: Catalano, D., Fazio, N., Gennaro, R., Nicolosi, A. (eds.) PKC 2011. LNCS, vol. 6571, pp. 284–295. Springer, Heidelberg (2011)

Higher-Order Masking Schemes for Simon

Jiehui Tang[1,2], Yongbin Zhou[1(✉)], Hailong Zhang[1], and Shuang Qiu[1,2]

[1] State Key Laboratory of Information Security,
Institute of Information Engineering, Chinese Academy of Sciences,
No. 89A Mingzhuang Rd, Beijing 100093, China
{tangjiehui,zhouyongbin,zhanghailong,qiushuang}@iie.ac.cn
[2] University of Chinese Academy of Sciences,
No. 19A Yuquan Road, Beijing 100049, China

Abstract. Simon is a highly optimized lightweight block cipher designed by the U.S. National Security Agency (NSA) and it is considered a promising candidate for resource-constrained embedded applications. Previous analysis results show that its unprotected implementations are vulnerable to side-channel attack (SCA). Thus, for its implementations on embedded platforms, protection against side-channel attacks must be taken into account. Up to now, several masking schemes were presented for Simon. However, those schemes just provide resistance against the first-order SCA and can be broken in practice by second-order or higher-order SCA. In order to deal with those attacks, higher-order masking is needed. The existing higher-order masking schemes were mainly designed for block ciphers based on s-box, invalid for Simon. Therefore it is necessary to design higher-order masking schemes for Simon. In this paper, we present two higher-order boolean masking schemes for the software implementations of Simon. The first is based on the famous ISW scheme proposed at Crypto 2003, and the second is based on the design principle similar to the masking scheme proposed by Coron et al. at FSE 2013. The two proposals are proven to achieve d^{th}-order SCA security in the probing model and they are shown to have a reasonable implementation cost on 8-bit AVR platforms by the evaluation of implementation efficiency.

Keywords: Simon · Side Channel Attack · Higher-Order Boolean Masking

1 Introduction

Simon is a block cipher recently proposed by the U.S. National Security Agency (NSA) as a lightweight alternative to the widely-used AES [18]. Benefited from immense optimizations in its round function, Simon performs well on both hardware and software platforms. Meanwhile, with the addition of its supporting various block sizes, Simon is considered a very promising candidate for resources-constrained embedded applications. However, when actually implemented on

© Springer International Publishing Switzerland 2016
S. Qing et al. (Eds.): ICICS 2015, LNCS 9543, pp. 379–392, 2016.
DOI: 10.1007/978-3-319-29814-6_32

practical embedded platforms, protection against side-channel attacks must be taken into account.

Side-channel attacks (SCA) can recover sensitive information (e.g. key) of cryptographic devices by exploiting physical leakages (e.g. execution time [3], power consumption [4]) during the execution of cryptographic algorithms. This kind of attacks work because the observed physical leakages depend on the manipulated data. If the manipulated data is sensitive, the leaking information about them enables key-recovery attacks. Typically, the adversary calculates the hypothetical leakage based on a power model and a key hypothesis, then compares it with the actual leakage to determine if the key hypothesis is correct. A SCA attack that exploits the leakage related to one intermediate variable is called the first-order SCA, and an attack that exploits the combined leakage resulting from two or more intermediate variables is called second-order or higher-order SCA.

Indeed, the unprotected implementations of SIMON have been shown to be vulnerable to side-channel attacks, see [21, 22]. An especially popular and widely used SCA countermeasure is masking, as introduced in [5]. It consists in randomizing all intermediate variables with random numbers. When a sensitive variable x is masked by $x' = x \oplus r$, the manipulation on x is finished by processing the masked variable x' and the mask r separately. This countermeasure makes the processed data independent of the sensitive data, thus secure against the first-order SCA. Masking schemes of SIMON have been proposed in [21, 24]. The masking scheme in [24] is designed to achieve the requirements for being a threshold implementation and it is provably secure against the first-order SCA. However, if implemented on software, this scheme can be broken in practice by the three-order SCA, which exploits the combined leakage related to three shares. The masking scheme in [21] handles the non-linear transformation of SIMON by partially unmasking the input and using the input mask to re-mask the output after the transformation. The above process is performed in a single look-up table operation so that no leaking about any sensitive data occurs. The security of this scheme depends on its realization and it can provide resistance against some common first-order SCA. However, this scheme is breakable in practice by the second-order SCA, which combines leakage information coming from two intermediate values with the same mask. In conclusion, those masking schemes just provide resistance against the first-order SCA and can be broken in practice by the second-order or higher-order SCA. Therefore, to counteract those attacks, higher-order masking must be used.

The higher-order masking is a generalization of the first-order case. It randomly splits every variable x into d+1 shares by letting $x = x_0 \oplus \ldots \oplus x_d$ as in a secret-sharing scheme [1]. Then, the shares $x_i's$ are processed separately in such a way that the combined leakage about any tuple of d shares is independent from the sensitive variable x. In the past several years, a number of higher-order masking schemes have been proposed for block ciphers, and those schemes can be roughly divided into three categories: randomized computation based, randomized table based and mask conversion based. Randomized computation based schemes are the most popular one, which includes the famous hardware-oriented ISW schemes [6], the software-oriented RP schemes [12] and their successors [13,17,19]. Those schemes mainly target block ciphers based on s-box (e.g. AES, PRESENT [10]). The two remaining types are less popular, mainly described in [20,23]. In addition, randomized table based schemes are suitable for the block ciphers using look-up table and mask conversion based schemes are dedicated for the block ciphers which combines boolean operations with arithmetic operations (ARX-based block ciphers like HIGHT [9], KTANTAN [11]). SIMON has neither s-box and look-up table nor any arithmetic operations, thus being beyond the protection scope of existing higher-order masking schemes. Therefore, it is very important to design higher-order masking schemes for SIMON.

In this paper, we design two higher-order boolean masking schemes for the software implementations of SIMON. The first scheme deals with inapplicability of the ISW scheme [6] on software and we propose a partition based method to solve it by exploiting the bit-oriented structure of SIMON. The second scheme is based on the design principle similar to Coron-Prouff-Rivain-Roche's scheme [19]. Compared with Coron-Prouff-Rivain-Roche's scheme, our scheme requires less random bits. The security proof of the two proposals is given in this paper and they are proven to be secure against d^{th}-order SCA when using $n > d$ shares. In addition, their implementation performance on 8-bit AVR platforms is evaluated and the evaluation results show that the two schemes have a reasonable implementation cost. For example, the second-order masked implementations of the two schemes are just 12.6 and 7.4 times slower than the unprotected case respectively and a small amount of additional memory usage is required.

The rest of this paper is organized as follows. Section 2 briefly introduces some background knowledge. Sections 3 and 4 describe the two proposed masking schemes and their security analyses. Section 5 gives the implementation performance and Sect. 6 concludes the whole paper.

2 Preliminaries

2.1 SIMON

SIMON is a block cipher based on the Feistel structure. SIMON supports blocks with 32, 48, 64, 96 and 128 bits. For each input size, it has a set of allowable key sizes ranging from 64 bits to 256 bits. Following the principles of Feistel structure, the input is split into two words. The corresponding key is also split into two to four words, which are used in the first round of SIMON. The number of rounds in SIMON ranges from 32 to 72, depending on the block and key sizes. For example, SIMON 64/128 has a block size of 64 bits and a key size of 128 bits. It generates a ciphertext after 44 rounds.

Given a round key k, the round function is defined on two n-bit input words x and y as:

$$R_k(x, y) = (y \oplus h(x) \oplus (x \lll 2) \oplus k, \ x), \tag{1}$$

where $h(x) = (x \lll 1)\&(x \lll 8)$ is a non-linear operation. For the sake of clarification, $R_k(x, y)$ is represented by the left part of its output in the rest of paper. The key schedule algorithm of SIMON is an entirely linear operation.

2.2   Higher-Order Boolean Masking

Higher-order boolean masking is to protect cryptographic implementations against higher-order SCA. It randomly splits every sensitive variable x entering into the computation into d+1 variables $x_0, x_1, \ldots, x_d$, satisfying the following equation:

$$x_0 \oplus x_1 \oplus \ldots \oplus x_d = x. \tag{2}$$

When a dth-order masking is involved in protecting a block cipher implementation, a dth-order masking scheme should be designed to enable computation on (d+1) boolean shares. As described in [12], when keeping the correctness of the computation, the dth-order masking scheme must achieve d^{th}-order SCA security, which is defined as follows.

Definition 1. *A (software implementation of) masking scheme is said to achieve d^{th}-order SCA security if every tuple of d or less intermediate variables is independent of any sensitive variable.*

Moreover, in [12], Rivain and Prouff introduce a method to prove the dth-order security of masking schemes. For an elementary masking scheme, proving its security applies similar technique as zero-knowledge proofs [2]. One shall show that the distribution of every d-tuple of intermediate variables can be perfectly simulated without knowing any sensitive variables. For a complex masking scheme (usually consisting of several elementary masking schemes), one should show that every involved elementary masking scheme achieves d^{th}-order SCA security, and then the security of the complex masking scheme should be demonstrated. In this paper, we follow the above security definition and method of proof because they seems well suitable for proving the security of our masking schemes.

2.3   Higher-Order Boolean Masking of SIMON

The key schedule algorithm of SIMON is a linear operation and the encryption of SIMON consists of the repetition of r rounds of an identical transformation. Therefore, designing a higher-order boolean masking scheme for SIMON lies in masking the round function of SIMON. The round function of SIMON makes use of three n-bit operations: xor ($\oplus$), AND ($\&$) and circular shift ($\lll$). Among those, xor and circular shift operations are linear (easy to mask) and AND is a non-linear operation (hard to mask). Therefore, the AND operation, more precisely, the non-linear transformation $h(x) = (x \lll 1)\&(x \lll 8)$ is the main difficulty of masking the round function of SIMON. If we assume that the non-linear transformation h(x) is protected by a masking algorithm, denoted as SecH$(x_0, \ldots, x_d)$, then the masking scheme for the round function of SIMON can be described in Algorithm 1. It is clear that the security of the Algorithm 1 depends on the

Algorithm 1. SecR-Masking Scheme for the Round Function of SIMON

Input: shares $(x_i)_i$, $(y_i)_i$, $(k_i)_i$ such that $\bigoplus x_i = x, \bigoplus y_i = y, \bigoplus k_i = k$
Output: shares $(c_i)_i$ such that $\bigoplus c_i = R_k(x, y)$
1: $(c_0, \ldots, c_d) \leftarrow SecH(x_0, \ldots, x_d)$;
2: $(z_0, \ldots, z_d) \leftarrow ((x_0 \lll 2), \ldots, (x_d \lll 2))$;
3: $(c_0, \ldots, c_d) \leftarrow (c_0 \oplus z_0, \ldots, c_d \oplus z_d)$;
4: $(c_0, \ldots, c_d) \leftarrow (c_0 \oplus y_0, \ldots, c_d \oplus y_d)$;
5: $(c_0, \ldots, c_d) \leftarrow (c_0 \oplus k_0, \ldots, c_d \oplus k_d)$;
6: return $(c_0, \ldots, c_d)$.

security of SecH. In the following two sections, we will describe two masking schemes for the non-linear transformation h(x) and prove their security in the probing model.

3 The First Scheme: Partition Based Masking Scheme

In this section, we introduce the first higher-order boolean masking scheme for the non-linear transformation h(x). This scheme is based on the ISW scheme [6]. We firstly recall the ISW scheme and then describe our scheme. The proof of security and implementation tricks of this scheme are also given in this section.

3.1 Description

Ishai-Sahai-Wagner's Scheme. Ishai-Sahai-Wagner's (ISW) scheme is a higher-order boolean masking scheme tailored to the boolean circuit. The core construction of this scheme is a masking algorithm for the binary AND operation. Let a, b be binary values from F_2 and let $(a_i)_i$, $(b_i)_i$ be the (d+1) shares of a and b respectively. The algorithm securely computes a sharing $(c_i)_i$ of $c = a\&b$ from $(a_i)_i$ and $(b_i)_i$ as follows:

1. For each $0 \le i < j \le d$, generate a random bit $r_{i,j}$;
2. For each $0 \le i < j \le d$, compute $r_{j,i} = (r_{i,j} \oplus a_i \& b_j) \oplus a_j \& b_i$;
3. For each $0 \le i \le d$, compute $c_i = a_i \& b_i \oplus \bigoplus_{j \ne i} r_{i,j}$.

This scheme is sound and can achieve $(\frac{d}{2})^{th}$-order SCA security (proved in [6]). Furthermore, in [12], it is shown that this scheme is actually d^{th}-order secure if the input shares $(a_i)_{i \ge 1}$ and $(b_i)_{i \ge 1}$ are mutually independent. It is noteworthy that the ISW scheme is theoretical, and if implemented on practical platforms, it will suffer a prohibitive overhead (see [7,12]).

Partition Based Masking Scheme. Since the non-linear transformation h(x) is bit-oriented, it is straightforward to apply the ISW scheme to protect the computation of h(x). However, this approach is impractical in software platform because it needs a lot of bit operations.

In this paper, we propose a partition based masking scheme to improve the implementation efficiency. Before describing this method, some notations are defined. For n-bit x, the ith bit of x is denoted as x_i and the bitset of x is $\{x_0, \ldots, x_{n-1}\}$. The index set $\{0, \ldots, n-1\}$ is represented as [0,n-1] and for a subset I of index set, $x|_I$ is defined as $\{x_i\}_{i \in I}$. Now let us describe our method. Firstly, we extend the ISW scheme to the multi-bit case and we denote the extended scheme for n-bit AND as $SecAnd(n, \ldots, \ldots)$. Secondly, we divide the bit set of h(x) into a partition and the partition must satisfy an additional condition that for every subset S in the partition, each bit of x is required to be used at most once to calculate the S. Thirdly, we use $SecAnd(n, \ldots, \ldots)$ to securely compute each subset S in the partition. Taking SIMON32/64 as an example, x has a size of 16 bits and we get a partition of the bitset of y=h(x) as depicted in Table 1. Then the computation of each subset in the partition is protected by the $SecAnd(n, \ldots, \ldots)$. Note that for n-bit y, a partition of its bitset can be represented a partition of the index set [0,n-1]. In the following, for clarification, we use the partition of the index set instead of the partition of the bitset.

Table 1. A example of partition for 16-bit y.

Name of subsets	The elements in subset
S_0	$\{y_0, y_2, y_4, y_6, y_8, y_{10}, y_{12}, y_{14}\}$
S_1	$\{y_1, y_3, y_5, y_7, y_9, y_{11}, y_{13}, y_{15}\}$

For SIMON supporting a word size of n bits, if a partition of the index set [0,n-1] is obtained, then the partition based masking scheme can be described in Algorithm 2.

Algorithm 2. $SecH_1$-Partition based Masking Scheme

Input: shares $(x^i)_i$ such that $\bigoplus x^i = x$
Output: shares $(y^i)_i$ such that $\bigoplus y^i = h(x)$
1: for $j = 1$ to t
2:    $(y^0|_{I_j}, \ldots, y^d|_{I_j}) \leftarrow SecAnd(n_i, (x^0|_{I_j+1}, \ldots, x^d|_{I_j+1}), (x^0|_{I_j+8}, \ldots, x^d|_{I_j+8}))$
3: End for
4: return $(y^0, \ldots, y^d)$

---

where t is the number of subset in the used partition and I_j represents the jth subset. The difference between our method and the ISW scheme is that the latter is bit-oriented, while the former is bitset-oriented. In the following, we will show that our method is suitable for realization on software platforms.

3.2 Security Analysis

Before proving the security of our scheme, we need to introduce two lemmas (proven in [12]) as follows.

Lemma 1. *A masking scheme achieves d^{th}-order SCA security if and only if the distribution of every d-tuple of its intermediate variables can be perfectly simulated from at most d shares of each of its input (d+1)-families.*

Lemma 2. *If a masking scheme T achieves d^{th}-order SCA security then the distribution of t ($t \leq d$) intermediate variable of T can be perfectly simulated from at most t shares of every input (d+1)-families of T.*

The following theorem states the security of our scheme.

Theorem 1. *The partition based masking scheme (Algorithm 2) is correct and can achieve d^{th}-order SCA security.*

Proof. The correctness of this scheme can be directly derived from that of the ISW scheme and we focus on its security proof. Firstly, due to the property of each subset in the partition, the input shares of $SecAnd(n_i, \ldots, \ldots)$ in Algorithm 2 are mutually independent. Therefore, each $SecAnd(n_i, \ldots, \ldots)$ achieves d^{th}-order security (as proven in [12]). Secondly, given any a d-tuple $v = (v_1, \ldots, v_d)$ of Algorithm 2, by Lemma 2, perfectly simulating the c_i intermediates from the ith $SecAnd(n_i, \ldots, \ldots)$ requires at most c_i shares of each of the involved inputs. Thus, perfectly simulating the distribution of the whole d-tuple v requires at most $\sum_{i=1}^{t} c_i = d$ shares of each of the involved inputs. Therefore, by the Lemma 1, Algorithm 2 achieves d^{th}-order SCA security.

3.3 Implementation Aspect

In order to efficiently implement Algorithm 2 on software platforms, we should choose such a partition that the size of each bit subset in it is equal to the size of word of target platform. E.g. for 8-bit platforms, the size of each bit subset should be 8. And for 8-bit platforms, we provide a simple method to obtain such a partition. We rewrite n=m*8 (m bytes), then we define the partition by constructing the jth subset as $y|_{I_j} := \{y_j, y_{j+m}, \ldots, y_{j+7m}\}(0 \leq j < m)$. The correctness of this method can be easily verified.

4   The Second Scheme: Linearity Based Masking Scheme

In this section, we introduce the second higher-order boolean masking scheme for the non-linear transformation h(x). This scheme is based on the design principle similar to Coron-Prouff-Rivain-Roche's scheme [19]. Therefore, we firstly recall Coron-Prouff-Rivain-Roche's scheme, then describe our scheme. The security analysis and the comparison with Coron-Prouff-Rivain-Roche's scheme are also given in this section.

4.1 Description

Coron-Prouff-Rivain-Roche's Scheme. In [19], Coron et al. propose a masking scheme for the field multiplication of the form $x \odot g(x)$, where $\odot$ represents the multiplication over F_{2^n} and g(x) is a F_2-linear function. Alogrithm 3 describes this masking scheme. The construction of Algorithm 3 is based on the F_2-linearity of function g. If we define $f(x, y) = (x \odot g(y)) \oplus (g(x) \odot y)$, the F_2-linearity of function g implies the F_2-bilinearity of f(x,y). Namely, for any $x, y, r \in F_{2^n}$, we have $f(x, y) = f(x, y \oplus r) \oplus f(x, r) = f(x \oplus r, y) \oplus f(r, y)$. Based on the F_2-bilinearity of f(x,y), another random values $r'_{i,j}$ can be introduced to securely process the $r_{j,i} = r_{i,j} \oplus f(x_i, x_j)$ (line 8 in Algorithm 3) as follows.

Algorithm 3. Coron-Prouff-Rivain-Roche's Scheme for the Field Multiplication $y = x \odot g(x)$

Input: shares $(x_i)_i$ such that $\oplus_i x_i = x$
Output: shares $(c_i)_i$ such that $\oplus_i c_i = x \odot g(x)$
1: for $i = 0$ to d
2:    for $j = i + 1$ to d
3:       $r_{i,j} \leftarrow rand(), r'_{i,j} \leftarrow rand()$
4:       $t \leftarrow r_{i,j} \oplus (x_i \odot g(r'_{i,j}))$
5:       $t \leftarrow t \oplus (r'_{i,j} \odot g(x_i))$
6:       $t \leftarrow t \oplus (x_i \odot g(x_j \oplus r'_{i,j}))$
7:       $t \leftarrow t \oplus ((x_j \oplus r'_{i,j}) \odot g(x_i))$
8:       $r_{j,i} \leftarrow t$
9:    end for
10: end for
11: for $i = 0$ to d do
12:    $c_i \leftarrow x_i \odot g(x_j)$
13:    for $j = 0$ to d,$j \neq i$ do $c_i \leftarrow c_i \oplus r_{i,j}$
14: return $(c_0, c_1, \ldots, c_d)$

$$r_{j,i} = (r_{i,j} \oplus f(x_i, r'_{i,j} \oplus x_j)) \oplus f(x_i, r'_{i,j}) \tag{3}$$

The brackets in Eq. 3 specify the order in which the operations are performed. In addition, as show in [19], Algorithm 3 is sound and d^{th}-order secure. In the rest of paper, for simplicity, we denote CPRR scheme as Coron-Prouff-Rivain-Roche's scheme.

Linearity Based Masking Scheme. CPRR scheme is designed for the field multiplication, thus invalid for the computation of h(x). In this part, firstly we observe the F_2-linearity related to the non-linear transformation h(x) and design a masking scheme for h(x) based on the CPRR scheme. The explanation about the masking algorithm is described as follows.

If we define $g_1(x) = (x \lll 1)$ and $g_2(x) = (x \lll 8)$, h(x) can be rewritten as $h(x) = g_1(x)\&g_2(x)$, where function $g_1(x)$ and $g_2(x)$ are F_2-linear. Then we define $F(x,y) = (g_1(x)\&g_2(y)) \oplus (g_2(x)\&g_1(y))$. It can be checked that the F_2-bilinearity of $F(x,y)$ holds. The F_2-bilinearity of $F(x,y)$ enables us to apply exactly the same steps as the CRPP scheme to securely compute the $h(x)$ except that the operation $\odot$ is replaced by $\&$.

Moreover, we show that the number of random bits required by the CRPP scheme can be reduced in half (from $d(d + 1)$ to $d(d + 1)/2$). Observing the Eq. 3, if the $f(x_i, r'_{i,j} \oplus x_j))$ and $f(x_i, r'_{i,j})$ are processed separately, the random value $r_{i,j}$ is redundant. Based on the above observation, we design the optimized masking scheme for $h(x)$ and it is summarized in Algorithm 4.

Algorithm 4. $SecH_2$-Linearity based Masking Scheme

Input: shares $(x_i)_i$ such that $\oplus x_i = x$
Output: shares $(y_i)_i$ such that $\oplus y_i = h(x)$
1: for $i = 0$ to d
2:    for $j = i + 1$ to d
3:      $r_{i,j} \leftarrow rand()$
4:      $t_{i,j} \leftarrow g_1(x_i \oplus r_{i,j})\&g_2(x_j)$
5:      $t_{i,j} \leftarrow t_{i,j} \oplus (g_2(x_i \oplus r_{i,j})\&g_1(x_j))$
6:      $t_{j,i} \leftarrow g_1(r_{i,j})\&g_2(x_j)$
7:      $t_{j,i} \leftarrow t_{j,i} \oplus (g_2(r_{i,j})\&g_1(x_j))$
8:    End for
9: End for
10: for $i = 0$ to d
11: $y_i = g_1(x_i)\&g_2(x_i)$
12:    for $j = 0$ to $d, j \neq i$ do $y_i = y_i \oplus t_{i,j}$
13: return $(y_0, y_1, \ldots, y_d)$

4.2   Security Analysis

Theorem 2. *The linearity based masking scheme (Algorithm 4) is correct and can achieve d^{th}-order SCA security.*

Proof. Our proof consists of two parts: correctness proof and security proof. Firstly, we can get the following two equations from the Algorithm 4.

$$t_{i,j} = f(x_i \oplus r_{i,j}, x_j) \quad t_{j,i} = f(r_{i,j}, x_j) \tag{4}$$

Then, based on the Eq. 4 and the F_2-bilinearity of $F(x,y)$, we have

$$\bigoplus_{i=0}^{d} y_i = (\bigoplus_{i=0}^{d}(x_i \lll 1))\&(\bigoplus_{i=0}^{d}(x_i \lll 8)) = h(x) \tag{5}$$

Therefore, the correctness of Algorithm 4 is proven.

Our security proof sketch is similar to that of CPRR scheme [19] and consists of two stages. This first stage is to construct a strict subset I of indices in [0,d]

The second stage is to design a simulator to perfectly simulate the distribution of the d-tuple v from $x|_I = (x_i)_{i \in I}$. By Lemma 1, this will prove the dth-order security as long as the cardinality of I is strictly smaller than d+1. The details of the proof are given in appendix A. Note that the construction of I and the simulator in our proof are different from that for CPRR scheme.

4.3   Comparison with CPRR Scheme

The design principle of our scheme is similar to CPRR scheme, but the construction is totally different. Specifically, the random values $r_{i,j}$ (line 3 in Algorithm 3) are removed in our scheme. In addition, the $f(x_i \oplus r_{i,j}, x_j)$ and $f(r_{i,j}, x_j)$ are stored in two different variables in our scheme. Those changes result in significant efficiency improvement as illustrated in Table 2.

Table 2. Complexity comparison between our optimized scheme and CPRR scheme regarding the total number of operations

	CPRR scheme [19]	Our scheme
#Random bits	nd(d+1)	$\frac{nd(d+1)}{2}$
#XOR	$4d^2 + 4d$	$3d^2 + 3d$
#*(Non-linear binary operation)	$2d^2 + 3d + 1$	$2d^2 + 3d + 1$

From the Table 2 we can see that the number of random bits required by our scheme reduces in half and the number of other operations remain reduced or unchanged. In addition, the implementation tricks (optimization based look-up table) for CPRR scheme are also suitable for our scheme when the size of x is small (e.g. smaller than 10).

5   Implementation Result

To evaluate the implementation efficiency of our two proposals, we have implemented the masked SIMON64/128 round function for $d \in \{1, 2, 3\}$ on a 8-bit AVR micorcontroller in assembly language. Table 3 lists the implementation performance[1] of each masking scheme. It can be seen that for the second-order case, our two implementations are just 12.6 and 7.4 times slower than the unprotected implementation respectively. Those numerical values mean our masking schemes can be used practically in the embedded system. Furthermore, we find that the second scheme is better than the first regarding all aspects of implementation performance. This is mainly due to the fact that two additional bit permutations are used in the implementations of the latter.

In addition, we compare the implementation efficiency of our optimized scheme (Algorithm 4) in this paper with that of CPRR scheme [19]. We have

---

[1] We use the Atmel Studio 6.2 as the integrated development environment(IDE) and those performance indicators are measured by this IDE.

Table 3. The summary of implementation datas for a masked implementation of the SIMON 64/128 round function with masking order $d \in \{1, 2, 3\}$.

Masking order	Scheme name	Execution time (clock cycles)	Flash (bytes)	SRAM (bytes)
0	No masking	87	528	12
1	The first scheme[Algorithm 2]	686	1462	48
	The second scheme[Algorithm 4]	**353**	**838**	**32**
2	The first scheme[Algorithm 2]	1092	2244	72
	The second scheme[Algorithm 4]	**646**	**1376**	**48**
3	The first scheme[Algorithm 2]	1526	2976	96
	The second scheme[Algorithm 4]	**1026**	**2050**	**64**

Table 4. Execution time (in clock cycles) for a masked implementation of the non-linear trans-formation (h(x)) of SIMON 64/128 w.r.t masking order d.

Masking order	Scheme name	Execution time (clock cycles)
1	CRPP scheme [19]	3363
	Our scheme[Algorithm 4]	**1773**
2	CRPP scheme [19]	9910
	Our scheme[Algoritm 4]	**5140**
3	CRPP scheme [19]	19708
	Our scheme[Algorithm 4]	**10168**

implemented the masked non-linear transformation (h(x)) of SIMON64/128 for $d \in \{1, 2, 3\}$. In order to make the results more practical, we include the step of generating random numbers in the masked implementation and the pseudo-random function (rand()) in the standard C library is used. The execution times (in clock cycles) are reported in Table 4. As expected, our optimized scheme outperforms CPRR scheme and has a timing gain of at least 47 % and 48 % for the first-order and second-order cases respectively.

6   Conclusion

In this paper, we present two d^{th}-order boolean masking schemes for the software implementations of SIMON and prove the dth-order SCA security of those two schemes. Our implementation results show that the proposed two schemes have a comparable implementation cost. In addition, we also compare the optimized scheme (the second scheme) in this paper with CPRR scheme with regard to implementation efficiency and the results confirm that our scheme executes the algorithmic computation in a more efficient manner.

Acknowledgments. This work was supported in part by National Natural Science Foundation of China (Nos. 61472416, 61272478 and 61170282), National Key Scientific and Technological Project (No.2014ZX01032401-001), Strategic Priority Research Program of the Chinese Academy of Sciences (Nos. XDA06010701 and XDA06010703).

A: Security Proof for the Second Masking Scheme (Algorithm 4)

Similar to what has been done in [20], the proof here consists of two stages: construction of the indices subset I and construction of a simulator.

Observing the execution of Algorithm 4, it can be checked that every intermediate variable necessarily belongs to one of the following four categories:

1. x_i, $g_1(x_i)$, $g_2(x_i)$ and $g_1(x_i)\&g_2(x_i)$.
2. $r_{i,j}$, $g_1(r_{i,j})$, $g_2(r_{i,j})$, $x_i \oplus r_{i,j}$, $g_1(x_i \oplus r_{i,j})$ and $g_2(x_i \oplus r_{i,j})$.
3. $g_1(x_i \oplus r_{i,j})\&g_2(x_j)$, $g_1(x_j)\&g_2(x_i \oplus r_{i,j})$, $g_1(r_{i,j})\&g_2(x_j)$, $g_1(x_j)\&g_2(r_{i,j})$, $t_{i,j}$ and $t_{j,i}$.
4. $y_{i,j0} = g_1(x_i)\&g_2(x_i) \oplus \bigoplus_{j=0}^{j0} t_{i,j}$ with $j \neq i$.

Note that for category 2 and 3, we use the notations $r_{i,j}$ only for fresh random values (i.e. the $r_{i,j}$ is always such that $i < j$).

The construction of I. For any given d-tuple $v = (v_1, \ldots, v_d)$, we construct I as follows. Initially, I is empty. Firstly, for every v_h in category 1 or 4, we add i to I. Then, for the v_h in category 2, we add j to I if i is already in I and we add i to I otherwise. Finally, for the remaining v_h (in category 3), we add i to I if j is already in I and we add j to I otherwise.

The definition of simulator. Note that each intermediate v_h add at most one index to I, thus, the cardinality of I can be at most d. In the following, we show how to perfectly simulate the d-tuple v using only the $x|_I$. Firstly, for every $r_{i,j}$ entering in the computation of any v_h, we assign a fresh random values (as done in the step 3 of Algorithm 4). Then we simulate each intermediate variable v_h as follows.

1. if v_h is in category 1, then $i \in I$ and v_h is directly computed from x_i.
2. if v_h is in category 2, then $i \in I$ and v_h is directly computed from x_i and $r_{i,j}$.
3. if v_h is in category 3, then $j \in I$ and two possible cases occur:
   - if $i \in I$, then v_h can be directly computed from $x_i, x_j, r_{i,j}$.
   - if $i \notin I$, then $r_{i,j}$ does not enter in the expression of any other v_h (otherwise i would be in I), and $x_i \oplus r_{i,j}$ or $r_{i,j}$ is randomly distributed and mutually independent of the variables in $\{v_1, v_2, \ldots, v_d\} \setminus \{v_h\}$. Hence $x_i \oplus r_{i,j}$ or $r_{i,j}$ can be assigned to a fresh random value (and $r_{i,j}$ does not need to be assigned to a random value at the beginning of the simulation). Then, v_h can be computed from x_j and $(x_i \oplus r_{i,j}$ or $r_{i,j})$.
4. if $v_h = y_{i,j0}$ is in category 4, then $i \in I$ and the firm term $g_1(x_i) * g_2(x_i)$ is hence directly computed from x_i. Then, every element $t_{i,j}(i \neq j)$ in the sum $\bigoplus_{j=0}^{j0} t_{i,j}$ is assigned as follows:

- If $j < i$, then $t_{i,j} = (g_1(x_i) * g_2(r_{j,i})) \oplus (g_2(x_i) * g_1(r_{j,i}))$ (as done in Steps 6 and 7 in Algorithm 1). Hence, $t_{i,j}$ can be directly computed from x_i and $r_{j,i}$.
- If $i < j$, then $t_{i,j} = (g_1(x_i \oplus r_{i,j}) * g_2(x_j)) \oplus (g_2(x_i \oplus r_{i,j}) * g_1(x_j))$ and two possible cases occur:
  - – if $j \in I$, then $t_{i,j}$ can be directly assigned from x_i, x_j and $r_{i,j}$.
  - – if $j \notin I$, then $r_{i,j}$ does not enter in the expression of any other v_h in category 2 or 3 (otherwise would be in I), and $(x_i \oplus r_{i,j})$ is randomly distributed. Hence, $(x_i \oplus r_{i,j})$ can be assigned to a fresh random value and $t_{i,j}$ can be computed from x_j and $(x_i \oplus r_{i,j})$. Someone may doubt that $r_{i,j}$ may enter in the express of other $y_{i,j1}(j < j1)$ in category 4. However it does not affect the proof because $y_{i,j0}$ and $y_{i,j1}$ use the same intermediate variables $t_{i,j}$ and they do not mutually conflict.

References

1. Shamir, A.: How to share a secret. Commun. ACM **22**(11), 612–613 (1979)
2. Goldwasser, S., Micali, S., Rackoff, C.: The knowledge complexity of interactive proof systems. Siam J. Comput. **18**(1), 291–304 (1985)
3. Kocher, P.C.: Timing attacks on implementations of Diffie-Hellman, RSA, DSS, and other systems. In: Koblitz, N. (ed.) CRYPTO 1996. LNCS, vol. 1109, pp. 104–113. Springer, Heidelberg (1996)
4. Kocher, P.C., Jaffe, J., Jun, B.: Differential power analysis. In: Wiener, M. (ed.) CRYPTO 1999. LNCS, vol. 1666, pp. 388–397. Springer, Heidelberg (1999)
5. Chari, S., Jutla, C.S., Rao, J.R., Rohatgi, P.: Towards sound approaches to counteract power-analysis attacks. In: Wiener, M. (ed.) CRYPTO 1999. LNCS, vol. 1666, pp. 398–412. Springer, Heidelberg (1999)
6. Ishai, Y., Sahai, A., Wagner, D.: Private circuits: securing hardware against probing attacks. In: Boneh, D. (ed.) CRYPTO 2003. LNCS, vol. 2729, pp. 463–481. Springer, Heidelberg (2003)
7. Canright, D.: A very compact S-Box for AES. In: Rao, J.R., Sunar, B. (eds.) CHES 2005. LNCS, vol. 3659, pp. 441–455. Springer, Heidelberg (2005)
8. Nikova, S., Rechberger, C., Rijmen, V.: Threshold implementations against side-channel attacks and glitches. In: Ning, P., Qing, S., Li, N. (eds.) ICICS 2006. LNCS, vol. 4307, pp. 529–545. Springer, Heidelberg (2006)
9. Hong, D., et al.: HIGHT: a new block cipher suitable for low-resource device. In: Goubin, L., Matsui, M. (eds.) CHES 2006. LNCS, vol. 4249, pp. 46–59. Springer, Heidelberg (2006)
10. Bogdanov, A.A., Knudsen, L.R., Leander, G., Paar, C., Poschmann, A., Robshaw, M., Seurin, Y., Vikkelsoe, C.: PRESENT: an ultra-lightweight block cipher. In: Paillier, P., Verbauwhede, I. (eds.) CHES 2007. LNCS, vol. 4727, pp. 450–466. Springer, Heidelberg (2007)
11. De Cannière, C., Dunkelman, O., Knežević, M.: KATAN and KTANTAN — a family of small and efficient hardware-oriented block ciphers. In: Clavier, C., Gaj, K. (eds.) CHES 2009. LNCS, vol. 5747, pp. 272–288. Springer, Heidelberg (2009)
12. Rivain, M., Prouff, E.: Provably secure higher-order masking of AES. In: Mangard, S., Standaert, F.-X. (eds.) CHES 2010. LNCS, vol. 6225, pp. 413–427. Springer, Heidelberg (2010)

13. Kim, H.S., Hong, S., Lim, J.: A fast and provably secure higher-order masking of AES S-Box. In: Preneel, B., Takagi, T. (eds.) CHES 2011. LNCS, vol. 6917, pp. 95–107. Springer, Heidelberg (2011)

14. Genelle, L., Prouff, E., Quisquater, M.: Thwarting higher-order side channel analysis with additive and multiplicative maskings. In: Preneel, B., Takagi, T. (eds.) CHES 2011. LNCS, vol. 6917, pp. 240–255. Springer, Heidelberg (2011)

15. Genelle, L., Prouff, E., Quisquater, M.: Montgomery's trick and fast implementation of masked AES. In: Nitaj, A., Pointcheval, D. (eds.) AFRICACRYPT 2011. LNCS, vol. 6737, pp. 153–169. Springer, Heidelberg (2011)

16. Reparaz, O., Gierlichs, B., Verbauwhede, I.: Selecting time samples for multivariate DPA attacks. In: Prouff, E., Schaumont, P. (eds.) CHES 2012. LNCS, vol. 7428, pp. 155–174. Springer, Heidelberg (2012)

17. Carlet, C., Goubin, L., Prouff, E., Quisquater, M., Rivain, M.: Higher-order masking schemes for S-Boxes. In: Canteaut, A. (ed.) FSE 2012. LNCS, vol. 7549, pp. 366–384. Springer, Heidelberg (2012)

18. Ray, B., Douglas, S., Jason, S., Stefan, T.-C., Bryan, W., Louis, W.: The SIMON and SPECK Families of Lightweight Block Ciphers. Cryptology ePrint Archive, Report. /404 (2013). http://eprint.iacr.org/

19. Coron, J.-S., Prouff, E., Rivain, M., Roche, T.: Higher-order side channel security and mask refreshing. In: Moriai, S. (ed.) FSE 2013. LNCS, vol. 8424, pp. 410–424. Springer, Heidelberg (2014)

20. Coron, J.-S.: Higher order masking of look-up tables. In: Nguyen, P.Q., Oswald, E. (eds.) EUROCRYPT 2014. LNCS, vol. 8441, pp. 441–458. Springer, Heidelberg (2014)

21. Bhasin, S., Graba, T., Danger, J.L., Najm, Z.: A look into SIMON from a side-channel perspective. In: 2014 IEEE International Symposium on Hardware-Oriented Security and Trust, pp. 56–59. IEEE Press, Arlington (2014)

22. Shanmugam, D., Selvam, R., Annadurai, S.: Differential power analysis attack on SIMON and LED block ciphers. In: Chakraborty, R.S., Matyas, V., Schaumont, P. (eds.) SPACE 2014. LNCS, vol. 8804, pp. 110–125. Springer, Heidelberg (2014)

23. Coron, J.-S., Großschädl, J., Vadnala, P.K.: Secure conversion between boolean and arithmetic masking of any order. In: Batina, L., Robshaw, M. (eds.) CHES 2014. LNCS, vol. 8731, pp. 188–205. Springer, Heidelberg (2014)

24. Shahverdi, A., Taha, M., Eisenbarth, T.: Silent SIMON: A Threshold Implementation under 100 Slices. Cryptology ePrint Archive, Report 2015/172 (2015). http://eprint.iacr.org/

An ORAM Scheme with Improved Worst-Case Computational Overhead

Nairen Cao[1], Xiaoqi Yu[1], Yufang Yang[2], Linru Zhang[3], and SiuMing Yiu[1]($\boxtimes$)

[1] The University of Hong Kong, Hong Kong, China
caonr@pku.edu.cn, {xqyu,smyiu}@cs.hku.hk
[2] Tsinghua University, Beijing, China
yfyang12@mails.tsinghua.edu.cn
[3] Sun Yat-sen University, Guangzhou, China
zhanglr3@mail2.sysu.edu.cn

Abstract. We construct a statistically secure ORAM with computational overhead of $O(\log^2 N \log\log N)$. Moreover, when accessing continuous blocks, our scheme can achieve an amortized complexity $O(\log N \log\log N)$, which almost matches the theoretical lower bound of the ORAM problem. Our construction is based on a tree-based construction [16]. The technical novelty comes from the idea of combining $O(\log N)$ blocks into a big block together with a more aggressive and efficient "flush" operation, which is the bottleneck of existing ORAM schemes. All in all, we can achieve better amortized overhead in our new scheme.

1 Introduction

ORAM (oblivious random access memory) was first studied in [4,11,14] by Goldreich and Ostrovsky *et al.* aiming at protecting software privacy against reverse-engineering by hiding the memory access pattern. Recently, researchers (e.g. [12]) also gave examples on the possibility of revealing trading transactions if data access pattern is not protected. Due to advancement of cloud technologies, more and more users host their data in a third-party cloud system (out-sourcing). The privacy problem of access pattern becomes one of the key concerns in these applications.

It is obvious that hiding the access pattern would increase the computational overhead for accessing the data. Many schemes evolve in recent years aiming at achieving better results in efficiency (e.g. [5–8,12,18]). Improvements involving techniques such as using Cuckoo hash functions [1] and randomised Shell sort have also been proposed. However, the complexity of these techniques hingers the practicality of the schemes in real applications. Luckily a breakthrough, which significantly simplifies the ORAM structure, was proposed in [16] by using a binary tree layout. Our scheme also follows its structure of storage. In fact, this tree-based structure triggers several important results in this area (e.g. [3,10,15,17]).

Roughly speaking, in a tree-based ORAM structure, we rely on a linear structure called position map which maps the indexes of data items to the indexes of

© Springer International Publishing Switzerland 2016
S. Qing et al. (Eds.): ICICS 2015, LNCS 9543, pp. 393–405, 2016.
DOI: 10.1007/978-3-319-29814-6_33

tree leaves [16] so that the corresponding path (from root to a particular leaf) can be retrieved to obtain the data item. The security of the approach lies on two facts. First, the server has no idea which node contains the data item as all nodes will be retrieved and some contain dummy values which are not distinguishable from the server point of view. Also, which path corresponds to which data item is also unknown to the server. Second, after each access of a path, the retrieved data items will be randomly assigned to another path of the tree to increase the difficulty of the server to identify the data item. This operation is usually referred as the "flush" operation. This flush operation is usually the bottleneck of the schemes. Moreover, since the position map is important, some schemes assume that this map is stored in the client side. However, this extra space for storing the map would mean a storage requirement of $N \log N$ bits which would be a big burden to the client. The situation will be worse if N, the number of data block (the basic item for operations) is huge (e.g. in a big data application) and the size of the index $\log(N)$ may not be considered as a constant. On the other hand, the position map cannot be stored in plaintext in the server side, otherwise the access pattern privacy may be comprised since server can learn some information of the logical and physical positions such as which path a particular data item is stored. Existing solutions try to make use of the technique of recursive ORAM to store the position map also in the server side, i.e., the position map is also stored in smaller ORAM structures layer by layer in the server side. This, however, affects the block size, for example, a block size of $\omega \log(N)$ is required in [16]. Consequently, the large block size will lead to large overhead of $O(\log^3 N)$, which is one element to bring up the complexity of this problem. To explore a solution that can achieve better efficiency without comprising security requirements is of great significance to apply ORAM to practical situations and better utilise the tree structures in this problem. To our knowledge, it seems that the best results of existing solutions sore both the data items and the position map in the server side to provide a scheme with worst-case overhead complexity of $\varnothing(log^3 N)$. In our work, we propose an improved structure and a more aggressive and efficient flush algorithm, which is the key step in *PathORAM* related structures [16], that can achieve better performance.

ORAM Recursive and Problems. The recursive ORAM idea in PathO-ram [16] is to outsource the position map to a smaller ORAM. We have $ORAM_0, ORAM_1, \ldots$ to represent the ORAM structures. The size of latter ORAM is smaller than the previous one which is the trick for the success of the recursive ORAM idea. Intuitively, the "smaller" idea comes from larger block size. Particularly, they set block size as $O(\log N)$ with constant ≥ 2. Obviously, this setting will result in heavy overhead and bandwidth of the scheme.

While in work [2], Chung *et al.* claim that the number of recursion rounds is $O(\log N)$ in order to reduce the position map to constant, involving the process of a Markov chain-like procedure [9]. However, due to their constant block settings, their scheme may cause recursion failure because they can not reduced the size of position map in the following layers [2].

In our scheme, we resolve this by combining several blocks into one in the position map and hence reducing its size instead of relying on large block size, and show that $O(\log_\alpha N)$ rounds of recursion is sufficient, where α is the compress factor in each recursion layer.

Idea of Our Scheme. While we follow the basic concepts in [16], our construction has some special properties, resulting in higher efficiency of our construction. Roughly speaking, we conceptually combine Q (to be decided later) *consecutive* blocks into a big block, called *trunk* in this paper, and always assign consecutive Q blocks in a trunk to consecutive S leaf nodes. Therefore we only store N/Q position in range $(1, N)$ each. This idea comes with a more aggressive (will be explained in details in the following sections) and efficient flush operation.[1] Thus, we improve the overhead to $O(\log^2 N \log \log N)$ instead of $log^3 N$. Also, our scheme achieves better performance than [16] when consecutive blocks are accessed which will be introduced in details in Sect. 3.6.

1.1 Our Contribution

Our scheme makes the following contributions.

Lower Computation Overheads. In Path Oram [16], they provide the scheme with $O(\log^2 N)$ overhead with $O(\log N)$ block size, and $O(\log N)$ overhead of $O(\log^2 N)$ block size. Therefore, it is indeed summed up to $O(\log^3 N)$ overhead. However, Our scheme can decrease the time overhead from $O(\log^3 N)$ to $O(\log^2 N \log \log N)$ mainly from by replacing the linear storage with searchable tree structure for the stash and to avoid $O(\log N)$ block size.

Better Performance in Continuous Access. Our scheme achieves better performance when continuous data blocks are read. In the construction of [16], if we read $\log N$ blocks *once*, the time overhead will be $O(\log^3 N) \cdot \log N$. In contrast, in our construction, we can reduce the overhead to as small as $O(\log^2 N \log \log N)$ when they are in the same trunk and we only have to read one path interval. In this case, we can reach amortizing $O(\log N \log \log N)$ overhead in average, which is nearly the asymptotic lower bound according to [4].

2 Preliminaries

Notations. We use N to denote the total number of blocks that can be stored in our ORAM. The block size is denoted by $C = O(\log N)$, and the capacity of

---

[1] Moreover, in our experiments, we found a problem in our experiments about an assertion (Lemma 3) made by [16]. When Lemma 3 claims that a N times, no duplicated block access can maximize the probability of stash size exceeding R (R can be any number). In other words, Lemma 3 claims that maximum number of stash will appear with one round after accessing all indexes. However, we find that the stash size is probably not maximal when each index is visited once, but will continue increasing until $O(\log N)$ number of rounds to converge.

buckets is denoted by Z, which is a constant. The height of the binary tree on the server's side, is denoted by h which is of size $O(\log N)$ (and the total number of leaves is $L = O(N)$). T, root, stash and PM denote the binary tree, the root of the tree, the stash and the position map respectively. The number of blocks and number of big blocks are denoted by $N(b)$ and $N(B)$ respectively. For any node n, the Z-sized bucket associated to it is denoted by n.bucket.

Trunk: For Q consecutive blocks whose position is stored in the same slot in position map, we call the big block formed by this consecutive blocks a Trunk.

Paths: For any leaf node l_i where $i \in \{0, 1, \ldots, 2^h - 1\}$, define the i-th path $P(i)$ to be the path from node l_i to the root. It is trivial that in a binary tree, this path is well-defined and unique, and contains $h + 1 = O(\log N)$ nodes. We call two paths to be *consecutive*, if and only if their corresponding leaf nodes are consecutive (i.e. their number differ by 1 modulo 2^h).

Path Intervals: Given the interval length $S = O(\log N)$ and interval start position $x \in \{0, 1, \ldots, 2^h - 1\}$, a path interval $PI(x, s)$ is defined to be the union of the S consecutive paths $P(x), P((x + 1) \mod 2^h), \ldots, P((x + s - 1) \mod 2^h)$. We further define the path interval on the i-th level, $PI(x, s, i)$, to be the intersection set of nodes of the i-th level and $PI(x, s)$.

We consider a client storing data at a remote untrusted server while preserving its privacy. While traditional encryption methods protect the content of the data, they fail to hide the data access pattern, which may reveal information to untrusted servers. We assume that the server is curious but honest (*i.e.*, do not modify the data), and small amount of memory is available at the client. Our ORAM scheme completely hides the data access pattern (the sequence of blocks read/write) from the server. From the server's perspective, the data access pattern from two sequence of read/write operations with the same length should be indistinguishable. Now we provide the followings:

Definition 1 (Access Pattern). *Let $A(y)$ denote the sequence of access to the remote server storage given the data request sequence y from client. Specifically, $y = (op_{L'}, a_{L'}, data_{L'}), \ldots, (op_1, a_1, data_1)$ ($L' = |y|$), and op_i denotes a operation of either $read(a_i)$ or $write(a_i, data_i)$. In addition, a_i is logical identifiers of the block.*

Definition 2 (Security Definition). *An ORAM construction is said to be secure if (1) For any two data request y and z of the same length, their access pattern $A(y)$ and $A(z)$ are computationally indistinguishable by anyone but the client, (2) the ORAM construction is correct in the sense that it returns correct results for any input y with probability $\leq 1 - negl(|y|)$.*

3   Our Scheme

3.1   Overview

Our Scheme follows the tree-based ORAM framework in [16], by building a binary tree with N leaves nodes. Each node is a bucket with capacity $Z = O(1)$

blocks. Furthermore, the client stores limited amount of local data in a stash. The blocks to be outsourced are denoted by $b_1, b_2, ..., b_N$. We combine every contiguous $Q = O(\log N)$ blocks into a trunk, denoted by $B_1, B_2, ..., B_M$, where $M = \frac{N}{\log N}$. i.e., $b_{kQ+1}, b_{kQ+2}, ..., b_{(k+1)Q}$ are contained in B_k.

We maintain the invariant that at any time, each trunk is mapped to a uniformly random interval of contiguous leaf buckets in the range of $(1, N)$, and every block b_{iQ+j} in the binary tree is always placed in some node of the Path Interval $PI(pos(i), S)$.

Whenever a block is read from the server, the nodes in the Path Interval is read into the stash and the trunk which contains the requested block is remapped to a new path interval. When the nodes are written back to the server, additional blocks in the stash may be evicted into the path as close to leaf level as possible there exists available spaces in the buckets.

3.2   Server Storage

Our server storage consist of three parts:

Tree: The server stores a binary tree data structure of height h and 2^h leaves, and we need $h = \lceil \log_2(N) \rceil$. the levels of the tree are numbered 0 to h where level 0 denotes the root of the tree and level h denotes the leaves. Each node in the tree contains one bucket that contains up to Z blocks. If a bucket has less than Z real blocks, it is padded with dummy blocks to always be of size Z.

Server Storage Size: There are $O(N)$ buckets in the tree and the total server storage used is about $Z \cdot O(N) = O(N)$ blocks.

3.3   Client Storage

Stash: When we write the blocks back to the tree after a read/write operation, a small number of blocks might overflow from the tree buckets and they would stay in the stash. We will show in the following sections that $O(\log^2 N)$ size of a shared stash for all recursive ORAM is enough to bound the overflow blocks with high probability. Specifically, we store the tuple of $(index, pos, data)$ for each block in the stash arranged. If we store stash as a binary searchable tree with pos as the key, which still has $O(\log^2 N)$ storage size. Therefore each access operation in the stash will cost $O(\log \log^2 N) = O(\log \log N)$ overhead.

Position Map: In our scheme, we have to keep a record of which *Path Interval* each *Trunk* is mapped to. We use p_i to denote the index of the start leaves and assume that a trunk B_i will be mapped to the leaves in $[p_i, p_i + S]$. $O(\log N)$ bits are needed to mark the leaves, so the size of position map is $\frac{N}{Q} \cdot O(\log N) = O(N)$ bits, which is $\frac{N}{O(\log N)} \cdot O(\log N) = O(N)$ bits when $Q = O(\log N)$. We can use recursion method to save position map in the server just like previous schemes to achieve constant position map storage on client side when we can achieve compress factor α in each recursion layer as much as $Q = O(\log N)$

Input: Tree T, position map PM, client stash stash

1 Construct binary tree T with height h and fill all buckets with Z dummies each;
2 $\emptyset \leftarrow$ stash;
3 **for** $i = 1$ **to** $N(B) - 1$ **do**
4      $PM[i] \leftarrow UniformRandom(0, 1, \ldots, L - 1)$;
5 **end**

Algorithm 1. Init(T, PM, stash)

Client Storage Size: The size of stash is $O(\log^2 N)$, which will be discussed later, and position map will be reduced to constant by the idea of recursive ORAM on server side. Therefore, the client storage size if $O(\log^2 N)$.

3.4 Detailed Scheme Description

Initialization. We require that the client stash S is initially empty, and each server buckets are initialized to contain Z random encryptions of the dummy block while the client's position map is filled with independent random numbers between 0 and $L - 1$. The algorithm is described in details in pseudocode in Algorithm 1.

Access Operation (a). In our construction, reading and writing a block to ORAM is done via a single protocol called Access. Specifically, to read block a, the client performs data $\leftarrow$ Access(read, a, None) and to write data* to a block a, the client performs Access(write, a, data*). The Access protocol can be summarized in following simple steps:

1. **Remap block** : We determine that which trunk B_i contains a by $i = a/Q$, and get the *PositionInterval* $p_i = PM(i)$ from position map. Then randomly remap the position of B_i to a new random position in range $(0, L - 1)$, and update the position map.
2. **Read path interval** : Read the path interval $PI(p_i, S)$ containing block a, and store all the blocks in this path interval in stash on the client side.
3. **Search Stash($p_i, .., p_i + S$)**: As described in Sect. 3.3, stash is the searchable binary tree with size of $O(\log^2 N)$ sorted by key *pos*. In our access operation, we have retrieved the positions of *Path Interval* of the target block in step 1. Supposed it contains the paths of $p_i, ..., p_i + S$ in the *Path Interval*, then we can search each path in the stash, which cost $O(\log \log^2 N) = O(\log \log N)$ for each access. Since S is set as constant in our scheme, the overhead for this step is $O(\log \log N)$.
4. **Update block** : If the operation is *write*, update the data stored for block a.

We provide the detailed algorithm in pseudocode in Algorithm 2.

Input: The index **index** of the entry required by the client; new value **data*** if
it is a *write* operation
Output: The content at **index**

```
1  found ← false;
2  index_trunk ← index/Q //the index of the trunk index belongs to;
3  curPos ← PM[index_trunk];
4  PM[index_trunk] ← UniformRandom(0, 1, ..., L − 1);
5  I ← PI(curPos, S);//the path interval we are going to search
6  for each node n in I do
7      if index is in the bucket of n then
8          b ← the required block; data ← contents of b;
9          found ← true;
10         if the operation is write then
11             b.content = data*;
12         end
13         delete b from bucket of n and add b to stash;
14     end
15     stash ← stash + bucket(n); set bucket(n) to empty;
16 end
17 if found != true then
18     search for index in stash;
19     if found then
20         data← the value found; found←true;
21     end
22     else
23         data← ⊥ and add it to stash;
24     end
25 end
26 return data;
```

Algorithm 2. Access(index)

Flush Operation. After an Access operation, we have to flush the elements
in the stash to the tree in order to avoid overflow. Hence any Access operation
is invariably succeeded by a flush operation. In a flush operation, we flush
the elements in the stash to the tree within a random path interval PI. When
the Access operation and the flush operation is considered as a whole, the
path interval we use in the flush operation is precisely the same interval we
search in the tree for the index we have just had accessed to. Before describing
the details of the algorithm, we first introduce a property of a node n in the
tree called *compatible*. Specifically, $n.compatible(i)$ is true if index i belongs to
the *Path Interval PI*, and there exists one path in PI whose ancestor is n.
Pseudo-code of flush operation is presented in Algorithm 3.

Intuitively, supposed we will evict the *Path Interval* $PI(p_i, S)$. Then we will
traverse nodes of this *Path Interval* from leaf level to root. For each node, we
will write back the blocks in stash that are compatible with the node. Specifically,
to write back a node n in $PI(p_i, s)$. It is easy to decide the path range (p_i, p_j)

that node n covers. Then choose a position $p_r \in (p_i, p_j)$ randomly, and search the stash for key p_r to retrieve a block subset S'. Obviously, the subset S' constructed in this way contain the blocks whose indexes are compatible with node n. Then write back Z blocks from S' to the node n if size of S' is larger than Z.

For example, the green nodes in Fig. 1 is the path interval $PI(4, 2)$. To flush this *Path Interval*, we start with node 13, we search the stash with key 13, and write back the blocks to the node. It is similar for node 14. Next, we move to node 6. Supposed that $S = 2$, then the position range for node 6 is 12–15. Then all blocks whose index mapped to $PI(3, 2), PI(4, 2), PI(5, 2)$ are compatible with the node 6. In this case, we will randomly pick one position in range of 12–15. For example, we will call search (13) in the binary searchable tree in stash if we pick $p_r = 13$. Then write back the retrieved blocks in S' to node 6. Likewise, we can get the position range (denoted as leaf id) for node 3 and node 1 is 12–16 and 8–16 respectively. Then pick random position and write back the corresponding nodes.

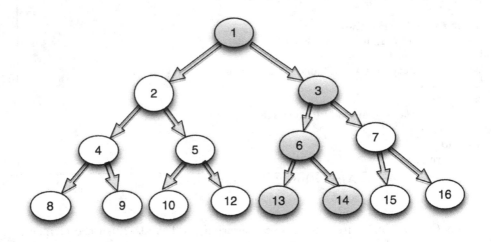

Fig. 1. Path interval

Combining the `Access` operation and `Flush` operation, we can now readily give our whole set of *read/write* operations. The pseudo-code for the complete protocol is written in Algorithm 4.

3.5 Security Analysis

To prove the security of our scheme, let y be a data request sequence of size M. The server sees $A(y)$ which is a sequence

$$p = (position_M[a_M], position_{M-1}[a_{M-1}], ..., position_1[a_1])$$

Input: PI, which is the path interval to be flushed

1 **for** $i=h$ **to** 0 **do**
2     $IL \leftarrow PI(i);$//the set of i-levelled nodes in the path interval
3   **for** *each node n in IL* **do**
4        $S' \leftarrow$ all blocks in stash that are compatible with n;
5   TEMP $\leftarrow$ any $\max\{Z, |S'|\}$ blocks from S';
6   add all blocks in TEMP into n.bucket, and fill with dummies if not full;
7   stash $\leftarrow$ stash $-$ TEMP;
8   **end**
9 **end**

Algorithm 3. Flush(PI)

Input: index, the index required by the client; v' which is the new value
           written if it is a *write* operation
Output: v, the value associating with the index

1 PI $\leftarrow$ the path interval corresponding to the big block index belongs to;
2 v $\leftarrow$ Access(index);
3 *Flush(PI)*;
4 return v;

Algorithm 4. RWWithFlush(index)

---

where $position_j[a_j]$ is the position of address a_j indicated by the position map for the j-th Access operation. Note that once $position_i[a_i]$ is revealed to the server, it is re-mapped to a completely new random label, hence, $position_i[a_i]$ is statistically independent of $position_j[a_j]$, when the i-th address and the j-th address correspond to the same trunk.

As for $a_j \neq a_i$, the i-th and j-th address are mapped to distinct trunks, with high probability. Their positions $position_i[a_i]$ and $position_j[a_j]$ are independent (*i.e.*, never affect each other) according to our flush mechanism. Therefore, the position sequence $\{position_j[a_j]\}_{j=0}^{M-1}$ consists of independent random integers from 0 to $L - 1$. So the server, after seeing the position sequence of y, guesses correctly with probability at most

$$\Pr[p] \leq \prod_{j=0}^{M-1} \Pr[position_j[a_j]] = (\frac{1}{2^h})^M = 2^{-hM} \tag{1}$$

which is negligible in h, where $\Pr[X]$ denotes the probability of a correct guess on the corresponding access step made by the server after seeing the corresponding position X. This indicates that $A(y)$ is computationally indistinguishable from random coins.

Now the security follows from the statement above and the fact that the $O(\log^2 N)$-sized stash will not overflow with high probability, which we will discuss in the following section.

3.6 Parametres and Complexities

Now we analyze our parametre settings and corresponding complexities.

Parametre Settings. We choose block size C as a constant, e.g. $C = \log N$ and $Z = 5$ as in [16]. Furthermore, the size of the trunk is set to $\frac{1}{2} \log N \leq S \leq \log N$(e.g. when $N = 2^{19}$ to 2^{24}, we have $S = 16$). Now we analyze the complexity of our scheme.

Recursion. We can follow the similar recursion in [16] to reduce the client space usage to $O(1)(i.e.,$ constant$)$. In each recursion, suppose initially we have N indexes in total, which make up $N * \log N$ bits originally. With the help of trunk, we should actually store $\frac{N * \log N}{Q}$ bits, which is $\frac{N * \log N}{Q * C} = O(\frac{N}{\alpha})$ blocks. α is denoted the compress factor in the recursive layer, and obviously $\alpha \geq 1$, which is decided by the size of trunk Q. The number of recursion layer is $\log \alpha N$. Particularly, the number of recursion is $\log N / \log \log N$ when $Q = O(\log N)$. Compared with the previous work [16] that rely on large block to achieve the compress factor $\alpha \geq 1$, our method can achieve lower overhead, and avoid the burden of bandwidth overhead caused by big block size, simultaneously, reduce the storage of position map to constant.

Time Complexity. First we consider time complexity. To analyze the time complexity of *read/write* operation, we have to figure out the number of blocks fetched from the path interval in each read/write operation. First we introduce the following theorem:

Theorem 1. *The total number of nodes in a path interval PI of length S (S is constant) is still $O(\log N)$.*

Proof. For a path interval PI of length $O(\log N)$, we consider $PI(j)$ for each level $j \in \{0, 1, \ldots, h\}$. Without loss of generality, we suppose the length of PI is $C \log N$ where C is a constant. By the definition of path interval, the size($i.e.,$ number of nodes) in $PI(h)$ is $C \log N$. Note that for any $PI(j)$, the nodes in $PI(j)$ are the parents of nodes in $PI(j+1)$. Since nodes in $PI(j+1)$ are consecutive, except for at most the leftmost and rightmost ones, every two adjacent nodes in $PI(j+1)$ share the same parent in $PI(j)$. So, the number of nodes in $PI(j)$ is at most

$$\frac{PI(j+1) - 2}{2} + 2 = \frac{PI(j+1)}{2} + 1 \tag{2}$$

Solving this recursion yields

$$PI(j) \leq 2^{-(h-j)}(PI(h) - 2) + 2 \tag{3}$$

Hence, adding them together, the total number of nodes is

$$\sum_{j=0}^{h} PI(j) \leq \sum_{j=0}^{h} 2^{-(h-j)}(PI(h) - 2) + 2h \leq 2PI(h) + 2h - 4 = O(\log N) \tag{4}$$

which comes from the fact that $PI(h) = O(\log N)$ and $h = O(\log N)$.   □

Time Overhead Analysis. An access in each recursive level consist of three sub-steps: 1. Read path in the binary tree totally visit $O(\log N)$ nodes (buckets) in a random path interval according to Theorem 1. Since the number of blocks held by a bucket is constant Z, the total time usage is $O(\log N)$. 2. Scan local stash: Supposed stash is maintained as a binary searchable tree with size $O(\log^2 N)$, the access of stash in total make up $O(\log \log N)$. 3. Flush cost: In a *flush* operation, according to Theorem 1, we visit $O(\log N)$ number of nodes.Adding up the three steps, we get the overhead for each layer to $O(\log N \log \log N)$.

$\log \alpha N$ is the number of recursive layer since we can achieve compress factor $\alpha = O(\log N)$. Take recursion into consideration , we can get overhead of $O(\log^2 N \log \log N)$.

Continuous Access. Our scheme is extremely suitable for continuous access. While accessing one block needs $O(\log^2 N \log \log N)$ overhead, the overhead will be at most $O(\log^2 N \log \log N)$ if we access continuous Q blocks, thus the amortized complexity will be $O(\log N \log \log N)$, nearly the asymptotic lower bound. The $O(\log \log N)$ comes from the flush operation: for each 'flushing' node, we need to find an appropriate block, taking an extra $O(\log \log N)$.

Bandwidth. Similar to the analysis in [16], in each read-write operation, by Theorem 1, the client reads a total number of $O(\log N)$ blocks from the tree and writes them back, inducing a bandwidth of $O(\log N)$.

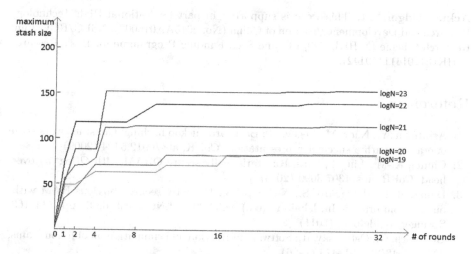

Fig. 2. Experiment results for stash size. As *log N* increase, so does the stash size. When the *log N* increases by one, the stash size increases nearly *log N*. Another observation is the maximum stash size usually does not appear at first round. Since the Path Oram [16] has a similar distribution depend on round, we think maybe one round is not enough for proof.

4   Discussion

In this section we show that our bound for stash size is $O(\log^2 N)$. Intuitively this complexity can be formed by results in [13], but we require some more actual evidences. In our experiment, we tested a number of cases with parameters $Z = 5$ and $\log N$ ranging from 19 to 23. The results show that the stash size is approx. $O(\log^2 N)$ and the maximum stash size will not increase after $O(\log N)$ rounds. We present the actual results in Fig. 2.

Note that the distance between any two adjacent lines is at most $O(\log N)$, indicating that the stash usage is bounded by $O(\log^2 N)$. We can also notice that after visiting all indexes once, the maximum stash usage is approximately half the total maximum stash usage, and only when approximately 16 rounds have been performed, then maximum stash usage reaches a balance.

5   Conclusion

We propose a new scheme of ORAM achieving $O(\log^2 N \log \log N)$ time overheads per access, and most importantly, attaining almost asymptotically lower bound time complexity if *continuous* data are requested. However, it is still an open question whether the lower bound can be achieved even when *random* addresses are visited, or, on the other hand, if the lower bound can be improved for general cases.

Acknowledgement. This work is supported in part by National High Technology Research and Development Program of China (No. 2015AA016008), NSFC/RGC Joint Research Scheme (N_HKU 729/13), and Seed Funding Programme for Basic Research of HKU (201411159142).

References

1. Arbitman, Y., Naor, M., Segev, G.: Backyard cuckoo hashing: Constant worst-case operations with a succinct representation. CoRR, abs/0912.5424 (2009)
2. Chung, K.-M., Liu, Z., Pass, R.: Statistically-secure ORAM with $\tilde{O}(\log^2 n)$ overhead. CoRR, abs/1307.3699 (2013)
3. Damgård, I., Meldgaard, S., Nielsen, J.B.: Perfectly secure oblivious RAM without random oracles. In: Ishai, Y. (ed.) TCC 2011. LNCS, vol. 6597, pp. 144–163. Springer, Heidelberg (2011)
4. Goldreich, O., Ostrovsky, R.: Software protection and simulation on oblivious rams. J. ACM **43**(3), 431–473 (1996)
5. Goodrich, M.T.: Randomized shellsort: a simple data-oblivious sorting algorithm. J. ACM **58**(6), 27: 1–27: 26 (2011)
6. Goodrich, M.T., Mitzenmacher, M.: Privacy-preserving access of outsourced data via oblivious RAM simulation. In: Aceto, L., Henzinger, M., Sgall, J. (eds.) ICALP 2011, Part II. LNCS, vol. 6756, pp. 576–587. Springer, Heidelberg (2011)

7. Goodrich, M.T., Mitzenmacher, M., Ohrimenko, O., Tamassia, R.: Oblivious ram simulation with efficient worst-case access overhead. In: Proceedings of the 3rd ACM Workshop on Cloud Computing Security Workshop, CCSW 2011, New York, pp. 95–100. ACM (2011)
8. Goodrich, M.T., Mitzenmacher, M., Ohrimenko, O., Tamassia, R.: Privacy-preserving group data access via stateless oblivious ram simulation. In: Proceedings of the Twenty-third Annual ACM-SIAM Symposium on Discrete Algorithms, SODA 2012, pp. 157–167. SIAM (2012)
9. Liu, Z., Chung, K.M., Lam, H., Mitzenmacher, M.: Chernoff-hoeffding bounds for markov chains: generalized and simplified. In: ACM (1998)
10. Chung, K.-M., Pass, R.: A simple oram (2013)
11. Goldreich, M.T.: Towards a theory of software protection and simulation by oblivious rams. STOC (1987)
12. Pinkas, B., Reinman, T.: Oblivious RAM revisited. In: Rabin, T. (ed.) CRYPTO 2010. LNCS, vol. 6223, pp. 502–519. Springer, Heidelberg (2010)
13. Raab, M., Steger, A.: "Balls into bins" - a simple and tight analysis. In: Proceedings of the Second International Workshop on Randomization and Approximation Techniques in Computer Science, RANDOM 1998, London, pp. 159–170. Springer-Verlag (1998)
14. Ostrovsky, R.: Efficient computation on oblivious rams. STOC (1990)
15. Shi, Elaine, Chan, T-HHubert, Stefanov, Emil, Li, Mingfei: Oblivious RAM with $o((\log n)^3)$ worst-case cost. In: Lee, Dong Hoon, Wang, Xiaoyun (eds.) ASIACRYPT 2011. LNCS, vol. 7073, pp. 197–214. Springer, Heidelberg (2011)
16. Stefanov, E., van Dijk, M., Shi, E., Fletcher, C., Ren, L., Xiangyao, Y., Devadas, S., Path oram: An extremely simple oblivious ram protocol. In: Proceedings of the ACM SIGSAC Conference on Computer & Communications Security, CCS 2013, New York, pp. 299–310. ACM (2013)
17. Wang, X., Chan, H., Shi, E.: Circuit oram: On tightness of the goldreich-ostrovsky lower bound. Cryptology ePrint Archive, Report /672 (2014). http://eprint.iacr.org/
18. Williams, P., Sion, R., Carbunar, B.: Building castles out of mud: practical access pattern privacy and correctness on untrusted storage. In: Proceedings of the 15th ACM Conference on Computer and Communications Security, CCS 2008, New York, pp. 139–148. ACM (2008)

A Self-Matching Sliding Block
Algorithm Applied to Deduplication
in Distributed Storage System

Chuiyi Xie[1,2(✉)], Ying Huo[2], Sihan Qing[3,4,5],
Shoushan Luo[1], and Lingli Hu[2]

[1] National Engineering Laboratory for Disaster Backup and Recovery,
Beijing University of Posts and Telecommunications, Beijing, China
gdxcy@163.com
[2] Department of Information and Computing Science,
Shaoguan University, Shaoguan, China
[3] Institute of Software,
Chinese Academy of Sciences, Beijing, China
[4] Institute of Information Engineering,
Chinese Academy of Sciences, Beijing, China
[5] School of Software and Microelectronics, Peking University, Beijing, China

Abstract. The deduplication technology can significantly reduce the amount of storage in data centers, thus to save network bandwidth and decrease the cost of construction and maintenance. Having inspired by the sliding block method of the Sliding Block (SB) algorithm and independent block-dividing thought of the Content Defined Chunking (CDC) algorithm, a Self-Matching Sliding Block (SMSB) algorithm for deduplication is proposed. Via communication with metadata node, the storage system client builds a matching table in local memory that contains fingerprint and checksum, based on the matching table to realize sliding block self-matching so as to detect the duplicate blocks. The experimental results show that the deduplication rate and the disk space utilization rate of SMSB algorithm is respectively 2.03 times and 1.28 times of the CDC algorithm and that the data processing speed is 0.83 times of the CDC algorithm. The SMSB algorithm is suitable for distributed storage system.

Keywords: Distributed storage · Deduplication · Sliding block algorithm · Rabin fingerprint · Adler-32 checksum

1 Introduction

Distributed storage system can store huge amounts of data. Due to its characteristics of high performance-cost ratio and good scalability, it is widely used in cloud storage, disaster recovery, backup and other purposes. But distributed storage system has a lot of duplicate data, which brings a waste of storage space and adds a lot of unnecessary network traffic. So it is quite necessary to employ deduplication technology for distributed storage.

© Springer International Publishing Switzerland 2016
S. Qing et al. (Eds.): ICICS 2015, LNCS 9543, pp. 406–413, 2016.
DOI: 10.1007/978-3-319-29814-6_34

By the difference of detection granularity, deduplication can process in file-level and block-level or byte/bit-level. The smaller detection granularity, the more detected redundant data will be, but the complexity and consume will correspondingly increase. The Content-Defined Chunking (CDC), a classic algorithm for deduplication, employs Sliding Window technology to determine the split point of chunking, has been applied in LBFS, [1] Pastiche backup system [2] and Deep Store archive storage system [3] and the like. The CDC is suitable for frequently updated data set and has more advantages of reducing the occupying of storage space over the Fixed-Sized Block method. [1] However, in the extreme case, if the entire data stream does not find the matching boundary point, the CDC will degenerate to the FSB. To process the blocks beyond a certain length, Eshghi and Tang [4] proposed a Two Thresholds Two Divisors (TTTD) algorithm supporting the size of chunk which bears two expectations and two thresholds. Lu et al. [5] proposed the solution of counting the frequency of occurrences of block to improve the effect of the block and raise the rate of deduplication. Zhang et al. [6] proposed an asymmetric extremum content defined chunking algorithm for fast and bandwidth-efficient data deduplication. Yu et al. [7] present a leap-based CDC algorithm which provides significant improvement in deduplication performance without compromising the deduplication ratio.

The chunks produced by CDC are varied with length; thereby more complexity of management appears. The Sliding Block (SB) algorithm [8] combines the advantages of fixed-size and variable-size, mainly produces fix-size chunks. The SB algorithm is efficient to solve the insert and delete problem. Wang et al. [9] employ backtracking sub-blocks strategy in SB algorithm, via backtracking the left/right 1/4 and 1/2 sub-blocks in matching-failed segments, improves the duplicate detection precision compared with the traditional SB algorithm and CDC algorithm. Zhu et al. [10] designed and implemented a backup system with intelligent data deduplication, which named Backup Ded up including four deduplication strategies, that is SIS, FSB, CDC and SB.

In this paper, a Self-Matching Sliding Block (SMSB) Algorithm applied to deduplication in distributed storage system is proposed. The SMSB creates a matching table in deduplication processing node and processes the self-matching on the fingerprint and checksum of sliding block. It ignores a large number of data blocks which do not meet the matching conditions, so as to improve the efficiency of deduplication. It is suitable for distributed environment.

2 Deduplication Problem in Distributed Storage

Distributed storage system, which is generally consisted of a single management node that can practice unified allocation and management of resources to all storage nodes and a plurality of data storage nodes, may be visited by multiple clients simultaneously. The management node saves data block information, the storage nodes store all data blocks. If need to perform deduplication in the distributed storage system, the task can be assigned to minor storage nodes or data sender. The transfer for duplicate data wastes so much bandwidth; therefore, the processing of eliminating redundant done before the transfer of data is a very appropriate option.

The deduplication rate of the SB algorithm ranks top in all types of the same data detecting method, but this algorithm needs to query checksum for matching the block when the sliding window move one byte forward. Since the metadata of distributed storage system is stored in one or more nodes, and the nodes performing task of matching cannot save the massive checksum and data, they can only complete the matching task by visiting metadata nodes via network. The processing speed is too slow! The CDC algorithm can take advantage of the internal characteristics of the data for deduplication without having to query the metadata node in the sub-block process, but compared with the SB algorithm, this algorithm has lower deduplication rate and disk space utilization.

3 SMSB Algorithm

In order to solve the deduplication problem in distributed storage, we proposed a novel Self-Matching Sliding Block (SMSB) algorithm. The SMSB uses a matching table as repetitive testing cache, and each node performing deduplication updates timely matching table data by querying metadata node in the process.

3.1 Description

The process of SMSB algorithm is shown in Fig. 1. Firstly, calculating the fingerprint and checksum of the data block in sliding window, if successfully matched, it shows that the block is likely to be repeated; and then calculate the hash value for further examination. If the match is not successful, it is probably not repeated block, and then the sliding window continues to move forward. When the sliding window has been moved to a block size distance, the block in it matching no blocks is likely a new one. The hash value of the block is calculated and stored, and later used as a comparison target block.

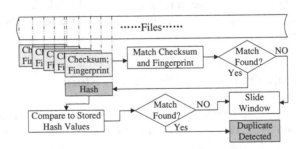

Fig. 1. Self-Matching Sliding Block method

3.2 Matching Table

The matching table consists of fingerprint and checksum. For a continuous string $[X_1, X_2,..., X_W, X_{W+1}, X_{W+2},...]$ (each character has 8 bits), any X_i represents polynomial $X_i(t)$ Select a irreducible polynomial $P(t)$ on Galois field $GF(2^n)$, the Rabin fingerprint [11] $R_1(t)$ and Adler-32 checksum [12] S_1 of string $[X_1, X_2, ..., X_W]$ are calculated as follows:

$$R_1(t) = \sum_{j=1}^{W} X_j(t) t^{8(W-j)} \bmod P(t) \tag{1}$$

$$\begin{cases} A_1 = 1 + \sum_{j=1}^{W} X_j \bmod 65521 \\ B_1 = \sum_{j=1}^{W} \left[(W - j + 1) \times X_j \right] + W \bmod 65521 \\ S_1 = B_i \ll 16 + A_i \end{cases} \tag{2}$$

For a string $[X_{1+1}, X_{1+2},..., X_W, X_{W+1}](i \geq 1)$, its fingerprint $R_{i+1}(t)$ and checksum S_{i+1} are calculated as follows:

$$R_{i+1}(t) = R_i(t) t^8 - X_1(t) t^{8w} + X_{1+w}(t) \quad mod P(t) \tag{3}$$

$$\begin{cases} A_{i+1} = A_i - X_i + X_{i+w} \bmod 65521 \\ B_{i+1} = B_i + A_{i+1} - W X_{i-1} \bmod 65521 \\ S_{i+1} = B_{i+1} \ll 16 + A_{i+1} \end{cases} \tag{4}$$

Equations (3) and (4) have the computation time complexity of $O(1)$.

3.3 Create and Maintain Matching Table

A matching table is created in memory, in order to achieve fast matching. Matching table is actually a simple index table stored in memory as an array, using the fingerprint of the data block as the array subscript (index), checksum as the value of the array element (index results). Matching table is updated by the latest block-priority strategy. When storing a new data block, according to the Rabin fingerprint(*rabin*) and Adler-32 checksum(*adler*) of the block, update Match[*rabin*] as *adler*.

3.4 Self-matching

Assume that storage space has processed a certain number of data blocks, in the matching table established based on this, checksum and fingerprint has a corresponding relationship as follows: (R1, S1), (R2, S2), (R3, S3), (R4, S4). When the sliding window moves forward, the fingerprint and checksum of each block corresponding to it will be calculated, and as a matching pair. The course of their work is shown in Fig. 2.

found..

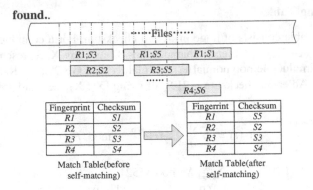

Fig. 2. Self-matching process

4   Experimental Results

The experiments use the actual data of the ordinary computer to extract three types of files (Word documents, source code, and BMP images) in the hard disk, less duplicate or identical files. The collected data sets are listed in Table 1.

In the experiments, the data sets on Table 1 were partitioned by using 64, 256, 512, 1024, 4096 bytes as a unit block. In CDC algorithm, the minimum block size is set to be a half of the maximum value.

Table 1.   Testing data set

File type	Quantity of documents	Size (Bytes)
Office document	57	21,978 K
Source code	368	4,769 K
BMP image	12	60,258 K

4.1   Deduplication Rate Test

The deduplication rates and comparison results are shown in Fig. 3.

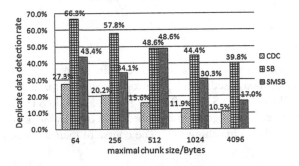

Fig. 3.   Compare with different chunk size

4.2   Disk Space Utilization Test

The rates of disk space utilization and comparison results are shown in Fig. 4.

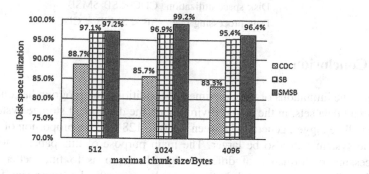

Fig. 4. Compare with different chunk size

4.3   The Data Processing Rate Test

The data processing rates and comparison results are shown in Fig. 5.

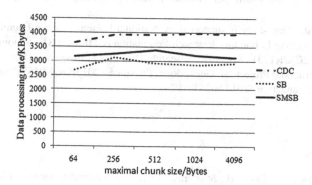

Fig. 5. Compare with different chunk size

4.4   Summary of Results

The comparison results of three algorithms by each evaluation criteria are summarized in Table 2. SMSB algorithm is better than the CDC algorithm in deduplication rate, disk space utilization, but it is lower in the data processing rate. The deduplication rate and the disk space utilization rate of SMSB algorithm is respectively 2.03 times and 1.28 times of the CDC algorithm and that the data processing speed is 0.83 times of the CDC algorithm. We are confident that the SMSB algorithm is more suitable than the CDC algorithm when used in a distributed storage system.

Table 2. Self-Matching Sliding Block

Evaluation criteria	Results
Deduplication rate	CDC < SMSB SB
Disk space utilization	CDC < SB SMSB
Data processing rate	SB < SMSB < CDC

5   Conclusion

Due to the limitations of the experimental conditions, the program has only been tested on small data sets, in the actual environment, the distributed storage system data block size will be bigger, generally between 4 KB to 128 KB, the proportion of duplicate data in the system will also be larger. The main purpose of this paper is to compare the processing performance of different algorithms, so as to find better deduplication method. Therefore, the work in this paper has a practical guiding significance.

For the distributed storage system with the feature of the Locality Preserved Caching (LPC), such as disaster recovery system and the backup system, we can modify the maintenance rules of the matching table according to this feature thus to identify the successor of duplicate blocks in the storage system, thus the coming block will be able to be predicted. We are ready to further improve and enhance the performance of SMSB algorithm for disaster recovery, backup storage system.

Acknowledgment. This study is supported by National Natural Science Foundation of China (61170282), Guangdong Laboratory Research Foundation (GDJ2014081), Shaoguan Innovation Foundation (2012CX/K123), Scientific Research Project of Shaoguan University (201216), Discipline Construction Project of Guangdong Province (2013KJCX0168), and Guangdong Natural Science Foundation (2014A030307029).

References

1. Muthitacharoen, A., Chen, B., Mazieres, D.: A low-bandwidth network file system. Proc. ACM Symp. Oper. Syst. Principles **35**(5), 174–187 (2001)
2. Cox, L.P., Murray, C.D., Noble, B.D.: Pastiche: making backup cheap and easy. ACM SIGOPS Oper. Syst. Rev. **36**, 285–298 (2002)
3. You, L.L., Pollack, K.T., Long, D.D.E.: Deep store: an archival storage system architecture. In: 2014 IEEE 30th International Conference on Data Engineering, pp. 804–815. IEEE Press, New York (2005)
4. Eshghi, K., Tang, H.K.: A framework for analyzing and improving content-based chunking algorithms. Technical report, Hewlett-Packard Labs (2005)
5. Lu, G.L., Jin, Y., Du, H.C.: Frequency based chunking for data de-duplication. In: Modeling Analysis & Simulation of Computer & Telecommunication Systems, pp.287–296. IEEE Press, New York (2010)
6. Zhang, Y.C., Jiang, H., Feng, D., Xia, W., Fu, M., Huang, F.T., Zhou, Y.K.: AE: an asymmetric extremum content defined chunking algorithm for fast and bandwidth-efficient data deduplication. In: 2015 IEEE Conference on Computer Communications (INFOCOM), pp.1337–1345. IEEE Press, Kowloon (2015)

7. Yu, C., Zhang, C., Mao Y., Li, F.L.: Leap-based content defined chunking — theory and implementation. In: 2015 31st Symposium on Mass Storage Systems and Technologies (MSST), pp.1–12. IEEE Press, Santa Clara (2015)
8. Bobbarjung, D.R., Jagannathan, S., Dubnicki, C.: Improving duplicate elimination in storage systems. ACM Trans. Storage **2**(4), 424–448 (2006)
9. Wang, G.P., Chen, S.Y., Lin, M.W., Liu, X.W.: SBBS: a sliding blocking algorithm with backtracking sub-blocks for duplicate data detection. Expert Syst. Appl. **41**, 2415–2423 (2014)
10. Zhu, G.F., Zhang X.J., Wang, L., Zhu, Y.G., Dong, X.S.: An intelligent data deduplication based backup system. In: 2012 15th International Conference on Network-Based Information Systems (NBiS), pp. 771–776. IEEE Press, New York (2012)
11. Rabin, M.: Fingerprint by random polynomials. Technical Report, Center for Research in Computing Technology, Harvard University (1981)
12. Deutsch, L.P., Gailly, J.L.: RFC 1950: ZLIB compressed data format specification version 3. In: RFC 1950, Aladdin Enterprises, Info-ZIP (1996)

Suffix Type String Matching Algorithms Based on Multi-windows and Integer Comparison

Hongbo Fan[1,2], Shupeng Shi[1,2], Jing Zhang[1,2(✉)], and Li Dong[1,2]

[1] Department of Computer Science,
Kunming University of Science and Technology, Kunming 650500, China
[2] Computer Technology Application Key Laboratory of Yunnan,
Kunming 650500, Yunnan, China
{hongbofan,shupengshi,jingzhang,lidong,
270677673}@qq.com

Abstract. In this paper, 3 classic suffix type algorithms: QS, Tuned BM and BMHq were improved by reducing the average cost of basic operations. Firstly, the multi-windows method was used to let the calculations of the jump distance run in parallel and pipelining. Secondly, the comparison unit was increased to integer to reduce the total number and the average cost of comparisons. Especially for BMHq, the jump distance was increased by good prefix rule and the operations to get the jump distance were simplified by unaligned integer read. Thus, 3 algorithms named QSMI, TBMMI and BMHqMI were presented. These algorithms are faster than other known algorithms in many cases.

Keywords: String matching · Single pattern · Multi-windows · Integer comparison algorithm

1 Introduction

String matching is the performance bottleneck and key issue in many important fields. The design of exact single pattern matching algorithm owns very important significance. Especially in our focus real-time information processing and security field, high performance matching is strongly demanded.

In the string $S = s_0 s_1 \ldots s_{m-1}$, for $0 < k \leq m$, we denote the prefix, suffix and factor of S of length k as $pref(S, k)/suff(S, k)/fac(S, k)$. SCW is used to denote the text in the slide window. All algorithms in this paper are belonging to exact single pattern matching algorithm, which means that for given alphabet Σ ($|\Sigma|=\sigma|$, Σ^* is closure of Σ), and for given text $T = t_0 t_1 \ldots t_{n-1}$ of length n/patten $P = p_0 p_1 \ldots p_{m-1}$ of length m, P, $T \in \Sigma^*$, seeking the window that $P[i] = SCW[i]$ for $\forall i \in [0 \ldots m-1]$ in all possible sliding window. Algorithms are described in C/C++.

This paper improved three classical suffix matching algorithms: Quick Search [1], Tuned BM [2] and BMHq [3]. We added Multi-window [4] and presented an integer comparison method in them. Thus the three series of algorithm named QSMI, TBMMI and BMHqMI were presented, and they are very fast for short patterns.

© Springer International Publishing Switzerland 2016
S. Qing et al. (Eds.): ICICS 2015, LNCS 9543, pp. 414–420, 2016.
DOI: 10.1007/978-3-319-29814-6_35

2   Accelerating Method: Multi-window and Integer Comparison

Multi-window [4] (shown in Fig. 1) let the text be equally divided as $k/2$ areas in k window mechanism (k is even). Each area has two windows and respectively matches from both ends toward the middle region until they are overlapped and each window matching procedure by tunes. It is a general accelerate method for string matching.

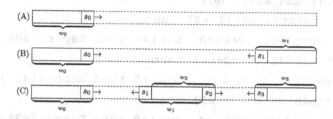

Fig. 1. Mechanism of two windows and multiple windows

There are many compares in suffix marching. Let the delay of branch prediction failure be signed *punishment*. The average character compare branch cost is about $1 - \sigma^{-1} + \sigma^{-1} * punishment$, e.g., 10.5 ticks on DNA sequence on Prescott. If unaligned read $pref(SCW, w)$ into an integer, compare with the integer of $pref(P, w)$. Only when they are equal, other compares are needed. One integer comparison is equivalent to w times of character comparison and the average cost of branch is reduced to $1 - \sigma^{-w} + \sigma^{-w} * punishment$. To compare uint16_t/uint32_t on Prescott and DNA sequence, the average branch cost will obviously reduce to 3.27/1.15 ticks.

3   Improved Algorithms Based on QS, Tuned BM and BMHq

By introducing above method into QS [1], a new algorithm called QSMI_*wkXc* was presented, which k is the number of windows and X is the integer type for comparison: S:short/uint16_t, I:int/uint32_t, L:long long/uint64_t. The code of QSMI_w4Ic is listed as Algorithm 1.

Algorithm 1. Algorithm of QSMI_w4Ic .

```
QSMI_w4Ic (P, T, m, n) {if m<4 then return ("Too short.");
for c∈∑ do qsBC[c]←qsBCr[c]←m+1;
for i∈[0......m-1] do qsBC[P[i]]←qsBCr[P[m-1-i]]←m-i;
s0←0;s1←n/2-1;s2←n/2;s3←n-m;
uint32_t IC; IC←*(uint32_t*)P;
while s0<s1 and s2<s3 do{
 if IC = *(uint32_t*)(T+s0) then
     if memcmp(P+4, T+4+s0, m-4)=0 then Report(s0);
 if IC = *(uint32_t*)(T+s1) then
     if memcmp(P+4, T+4+s1, m-4)=0 then Report(s1);
 if IC = *(uint32_t*)(T+s2) then
     if memcmp(P+4, T+4+s2, m-4)=0 then Report(s2);
 if IC = *(uint32_t*)(T+s3) then
     if memcmp(P+4, T+4+s3, m-4)=0 then Report(s3);
 s0←s0+qsBC[T[s0+m]];s1←s1-qsBCr[T[s1-1]];
 s2←s2+qsBC[T[s2+m]];s3←s3-qsBCr[T[s3-1]];}
matching T[s0...s1+m-1] and T[s2...s3+m-1] by QSMI_w2Ic;}
```

By introducing continuous jump method of Tuned BM into QSMI, TBMMI was proposed. Firstly, determine whether the window match occurs by integer comparison in the each window. And then, bad character jumping of Quick Search continuous jump once and bad character jumping of Horspool jump several times. We use once QS jump and twice Horspool jump twice in the TBMMI. TBMMI_w4Ic that is obtained only by the bad character jump table of QS are shown as Algorithm 2.

We improved BMHq [3], by using good-prefix rule to increase the jump distance, unaligned read to reduce read operation and add the method in Sect. 3, an algorithm named BMHqMI was proposed. BMH2MI_w4Ic is shown in Algorithm 3.

Algorithm2. Algorithm of TBMMI_w4Ic

```
TBMMI_w4Ic (P, T, m, n) {
 if m<4 return ("Too short."); IC←*(uint32_t*)P;
 for c∈Σ do qsBC[c]←qsBCr[c]←m+1;
 for i∈[0.......m-1]do qsBC[P[i]]←qsBCr[P[m-1-i]]←m-i;
 s0←0;s1←n/2-1; s2←n/2;s3←n-m;uint32_t IC;
 while s0<s1 and s2<s3 do{
 if IC = *(uint32_t*)(T+s0) then
   if memcmp(P+4, T+4+s0, m-4)=0 then Report(s0);
 if IC = *(uint32_t*)(T+s1) then
   if memcmp(P+4, T+4+s1, m-4)=0 then Report(s1);
 if IC = *(uint32_t*)(T+s2) then
   if memcmp(P+4, T+4+s2, m-4)=0 then Report(s2);
 if IC = *(uint32_t*)(T+s3) then
   if memcmp(P+4, T+4+s3, m-4)=0 then Report(s3);
 s0←s0+qsBC[T[s0+m]];s1←s1-qsBCr[T[s1-1]];
 s2←s2+qsBC[T[s2+m]];s3←s3-qsBCr[T[s3-1]];
 s0←s0+qsBC[T[s0+m-1]]-1;s1←s1-qsBCr[T[s1]]+1;
 s2←s2+qsBC[T[s2+m-1]]-1;s3←s3-qsBCr[T[s3]]+1;
 s0←s0+qsBC[T[s0+m-1]]-1;s1←s1-qsBCr[T[s1]]+1;
 s2←s2+qsBC[T[s2+m-1]]-1;s3←s3-qsBCr[T[s3]]+1;}
matching T[s0...s1+m-1] and T[s2...s3+m-1] by TBMMI_w2Ic;}
```

When $suff(SCW, q-1) \notin fac(P)$, BMHq make the window slide from the win0 to the win1 show as Fig. 2. If $suff(SCW, q-1) \neq pref(P, q-1)$ and win1 can not matching. So the window should keep sliding until find the first k satisfy $suff(SCW, k) = pref(P, k)$ (the window get extra jump to the win2).

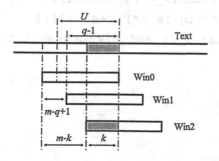

Fig. 2. Increase jump distance by good-prefix method.

To store the jump distance for q-grams needs q-Dimension table, which a table lookup need q times read. Unaligned read can simulate original q-Dimensional table lookup by once read and table lookup. Since on little-endian processor, *(uint16_t*) $(T + i + m - 2) = T[i+m-2] + b = T[i+m-1] * 256$. If the 2-Dimensional jump distance table is *shift*, build a 1-Dimensional table *shift*1D and for $\forall a, b \in \Sigma$, $shift1D[a + b * 256] = shift[a][b]$. So, $shift1D[*(uint\_16*)(T + i + m - 2)] = shift$ $[a][b]$. If the read string is $T[i + m - 2 \ldots i + m]$ for $q = 3$, * (uint32_t*)$(T + i+m-2)$ &0x00ffffffu $= T[i + m - 2] + (int)T[i + m - 1] * 256 + (int)T[i + m] * 65536$ can be used.

Algorithm3. Algorithm of BMH2MI_w4Ic

```
BMH2MI_w4Ic (P, T, m, n) {if m<4 return ("too short.");
uint32_t a, b, IC←*(uint32_t*)P, m1←m-1;
for a∈∑, b∈∑ do qs2BC[a+b*256]← qs2BCr[a+b*256]←m+1;
for a∈∑ do{qs2BC[P[m-1]+a*256]←qs2BCr[P[0]+a*256]←m;}
for i∈[0,……m-2] do { qs2BC[P[i]+(int)P[i+1]*256]←m-i-1;
qs2BCr[P[m-1-i]+(int)P[m-2-i]*256]←m-i-1;}
s0←n/2-1;s2←n/2;s3←n-m;
while s0<s1 and s2<s3 do{
 if IC = *(uint32_t*)(T+s0) then
     if memcmp(P+4, T+4+s0, m-4)=0 then Report(s0);
 if IC = *(uint32_t*)(T+s1) then
     if memcmp(P+4, T+4+s1, m-4)=0 then Report(s1);
 if IC = *(uint32_t*)(T+s2) then
     if memcmp(P+4, T+4+s2, m-4)=0 then Report(s2);
 if IC = *(uint32_t*)(T+s3) then
     if memcmp(P+4, T+4+s3, m-4)=0 then Report(s3);
 s0←s0+qs2BC[*(uint16_t*)(T+s0+m1)];
 s1←s1-qs2BCr[*(uint16_t*)(T+s1-1)];
 s2←s2+qs2BC[*(uint16_t*)(T+s2+m1)];
 s3←s3-qs2BCr[*(uint16_t*)(T+s3-1)];}
matching T[s0…s1+m-1] and T[s2…s3+m-1] by BMH2MI_w2Ic;}
```

4 Experiment and Results

We did the following experiment based on SMART 13.02 [6], it gave the implements of most known algorithms (in EI or SCI paper) as of Feb. 2013. The platform of this experiment is Intel Core2 E3400 @ 3.0 GHz/Ubuntu 12.10 64 bit desktop/g++4.6/-O3 optimization. The tested texts include three samples of text [8] listed as follow: DNA sequence (E.coil), pure English text (Bible.txt) and the sample of English nature language (world192.txt). This experiment compared all algorithms in SMART 13.02 and added some newer algorithms not be included in SMART, such as SBNDMqb [9], GSB2b [9], FSO [10], HGQSkip [11], kSWxC [12], SufOM [13], Greedy-QF [14], etc. If an algorithm with different parameters are called different algorithms, there were more than 1000 algorithms are compared, which covered most of known algorithms. The experiment data (dozens of thousands of records) can not be listed all. In this paper only list the highest performance of three algorithms under each match condition. The data of experiment show as Table 1 and the unit is MB/s.

Table 1. Matching speed of the fastest 3 algorithms and their optimal parameters

	m=4		m=8		m=16	
World192	TBMMI_w4Ic	3766.3	TBMMI_w4Ic	5254.2	QSMI_w4Lc	5736.2
	QSMI_w4Ic	3503.1	QSMI_w4Lc	5034.3	TBMMI_w4Lc	5602.4
	SBNDM2_2_sbi32	3007.7	SBNDM2_2_sbi32[16]	4610.4	SBNDM4_sbi32[9]	5556.2
Bible.txt	TBMMI_w4Ic	3531.8	TBMMI_w4Ic	5005.9	TBMMI_w4Lc	5604.5
	QSMI_w4Ic	3394.2	QSMI_w4Lc	4747.5	SBNDM4_4_sbi32	5600.4
	kSWxC_k6xI[12]	2945.6	SBNDM2_2_sbi32	4162.7	QSMI_w4Lc	5516.6
E.coli	BMH2MI_w4Ic	2799.6	BMH2MI_w4Lc	4570.8	BMH2MI_w4Lc	5310.5
	kSWxC_k4xI	2398.6	kSWxC_k4xL	3520.2	SBNDM4_3_sbi32	5252.3
	UFNDM4b_a64[9]	1187.9	SBNDM4_2_sbi32	3138.4	FSBNDMqb_q6f2i32[9]	4926.3

5 Conclusion

In this paper, three classical suffix match algorithms QS/TBM/BMHq are improved by introduce the method of Multi-window and unaligned read integer comparison, and three suffix match algorithms named QSMI/TBMMI/BMHqMI were proposed. It is shown in experiment results that these algorithms are faster than other known algorithm under multiple match conditions for matching short patterns.

6 Acknowledgements

This paper is supported by National Natural Science Foundation of Yunnan, China under Grant 2012FB131 and 2012FB137, Key Project of National Natural Science Foundation of Yunnan, China under Grant 2014FA029, and National Natural Science Foundation of China under Grant 61562051.

References

1. Daniel, M.S.: A very fast substring search algorithm. Commun. ACM **33**(8), 132–142 (1990)
2. Andrew, H.: Fast string searching. Softw. Pract. Exp. **21**(11), 1221–1248 (1991)
3. Kalsi, P., Hannu, P., Jorma, T.: Comparison of exact string matching algorithms for biological sequences. BIRD 2008, pp. 417–426. Springer, Berlin (2008)
4. Faro, S., Lecroq, T.: A multiple sliding windows approach to speed up string matching algorithms. In: Klasing, R. (ed.) SEA 2012. LNCS, vol. 7276, pp. 172–183. Springer, Heidelberg (2012)
5. Horspool, R.N.: Practical fast searching in strings. Softw. Pract. Exp. **10**(6), 501–506 (1980)
6. SMART: string matching research tools. http://www.dmi.unict.it/~faro/smart/
7. Simone, F., Simone, F., Thierry, L.: The exact online string matching problem: a review of the most recent results. ACM Comput. Surv. **45**(2), 13:1–13:42 (2013)
8. The large canterbury corpus. http://corpus.canterbury.ac.nz/descriptions/
9. Hannu, P., Jorma, T.: Variations of forward-SBNDM. In: PSC2011, pp. 3–14. Czech Technical University, Prague (2011)
10. Fredriksson, K., Grabowski, S.: Practical and optimal string matching. In: Consens, M.P., Navarro, G. (eds.) SPIRE 2005. LNCS, vol. 3772, pp. 376–387. Springer, Heidelberg (2005)
11. Wu, W., Fan, H., Liu, L., Huang, Q.: Fast string matching algorithm based on the skip algorithm. ICM 2012. LNEE, vol. 236, pp. 247–257. Springer, New York (2013)
12. Lv, Z., Fan, H., Liu, L., Huang, Q., et al.: Fast single pattern string matching algorithms based on multi-windows and integer comparison. In: IET International Conference on ICISCE 2012, pp. 1–5 (2012). doi:10.1049/cp.2012.2326)
13. Fan, H., Yao, N.: Tuning the EBOM algorithm with suffix jump. ICITSE 2012. LNEE, vol. 211, pp. 965–973 (2013)
14. Chen, Z., Liu, L., Fan, H., Huang, Q., et al.: A fast exact string matching algorithms based on greedy jump and QF. ICISCE 2012. In: IET International Conference (2012). doi:10.1049/cp.2012.2320
15. Fan, H., Yao, N.: Q-gram variation for EBOM. In: Proceedings of the 2012 International Conference on Information Technology and Software Engineering. LNEE, vol. 211, pp. 453–460 (2013)
16. Branislav, D., Jan, H., Hannu, P., Jorna T.: Tuning BNDM with q-grams. In: ALENEX 2009, pp. 29–37. SIAM, New York (2009)

Security-Enhanced Reprogramming with XORs Coding in Wireless Sensor Networks

Depeng Chen[1], Daojing He[1(✉)], and Sammy Chan[2]

[1] School of Computer Science and Software Engineering,
East China Normal University, Shanghai 200065, China
dpchen@ecnu.cn, djhe@sei.ecnu.edu.cn
[2] Department of Electronic Engineering, City University of Hong Kong,
Hong Kong SAR, China
eeschan@cityu.edu.hk

Abstract. Reprogramming is an important function required by wireless sensor networks (WSNs). Due to the openness of WSNs, more and more researchers pay attention to the security aspect of reprogramming, but confidentiality is often ignored in this process. However, in some special applications such as battlefield, sending messages demand high levels of confidentiality. Several protocols address this issue, but they use relatively complex cryptography methods, which consume more computational resources and energy. Moreover, those approaches require packets arrive at the receiver in order. However, out-of-order tolerance is often a required feature in some harsh environment. In this paper, we propose an efficient scheme to ensure confidentiality of reprogramming and out-of-order packet delivery can be tolerated. To enhance the confidentiality of code image, we design an encode-then-encrypt scheme. To mitigate the DoS attacks against digital signature packets, we provide an energy-efficient mechanism.

Keywords: Reprogramming · Security · Confidentiality · Dos attacks · Wireless sensor networks

1 Introduction

1.1 Motivation

With the development of sensor devices and wireless networking, wireless sensor networks (WSNs) have been widely used in a variety of areas. For example, WSNs can be deployed for structural health monitoring, habitat monitoring, pipeline monitoring, greenhouse monitoring, temperature and humidity monitoring [1], so and so forth. Once sensor nodes are deployed in a particular environment, it is often desirable and necessary to update or install software because of software bugs or new requirements. However, it is often difficult to reprogram sensor nodes one by one by hand, so some efficient reprogramming protocols need to be used. Many reprogramming protocols have been proposed to solve this problem,

© Springer International Publishing Switzerland 2016
S. Qing et al. (Eds.): ICICS 2015, LNCS 9543, pp. 421–435, 2016.
DOI: 10.1007/978-3-319-29814-6_36

such as [2–5], but none of them took security issues into consideration. Since WSNs are often deployed in unguarded harsh circumstances, it is vulnerable to attacks. Wireless network is an open system, so it is easier to be accessed than traditional network. Thus, the security of reprogramming in WSNs should not be ignored.

To ensure the security of reprogramming in WSNs, the proposed schemes should consider how to authenticate the sender, how to verify the integrity of updated program images and how to receive the code images efficiently. Moreover, some special application environment also requires high confidentiality in sending message. For example, in human health monitoring applications, the code image may be tapped by adversaries through wiretapping and analyzing of the program images [6]. To ensure the privacy of code images, many schemes exploit symmetric and asymmetric encryption algorithms. Due to the resource constraint of sensor nodes, it is inefficient to use asymmetric encryption algorithms to encrypt code images. To acheive relatively high confidentiality of updating program images, using noisy ciphertexts can be an appropriate choice, which makes the cryptanalysis by eavesdropper more difficult [7]. Since digital signature is an expensive operation [8], it is easy to be attacked by adversaries through repeatedly sending bogus data with fake signatures. And this authentication may exhaust sensors power rapidly. To mitigate such DoS (Denial-of-Service) attacks, a weak authentication as the first safety defense is proposed in some works [8–11]. However, if the malicious or faked packets only make up a very small proportion of the total packets in WSNs, the scheme using weak authentication mechanism may consume much more energy than those directly authenticating digital signature. In addition, packets received out of order in WSNs are pretty common, an effective scheme should take this into consideration. The goal of our work is to propose a novel approach to ensure high confidentiality, out-of-order tolerance, DoS-resistance as well as energy saving in code image dissemination.

1.2 Our Approach and Contributions

In this paper, we propose a novel enhanced security scheme which is tolerant to wiretapping attacks of reprogramming in WSNs. To enhance the confidentiality of updated program images, we exploit the encode-then-encrypt paradigm, using simple and effective XOR operation to encode original data. At the same time, we introduce multiple one-way hash chains to enhance the confidentiality of data dissemination in WSNs. A one-time pad is one of the most secure encryption methods; each time a sensor node can decode packets with a key. Even if attackers can acquire the former key, it is impossible to decode the packet next time. Thus, our approach can enhance the confidentiality of code image. Moreover, we propose a simple and efficient way to decode using XOR operation, which will cost less memory than other approaches such as AdapCode [5].

Motivated by [7,12–14], we propose a novel encode-then-encrypt scheme to enhance the security and provide efficient performance at the same time. The advantage of encode-then-encrypt scheme is that even if a wiretapper is in a known plaintext attacking scenario, he or she can learn only a noisy version of the data and keystream, so it becomes more complex to perform the cryptanalysis of the employed keystream generator [12].

To resist DoS-attacks against signature packets, many existing protocols mitigate these attacks using weak authentication as the first defense. And they all assume that the sensor networks have already been attacked by adversaries. However, in most of the time, there are no adversaries in sensor networks. Even if an adversary sends fake packets to the networks, it needs time to collect some useful messages or to compromise some nodes. In addition, such weak authentication will consume a lot of time and energy on the sender side [10]. Thus, in this paper, we put forward a mechanism that randomly adjusts the time to reboot the weak authentication defense to prolong the lifetime of the network. The details of this mechanism will be illustrated in Sect. 4.

The rest of this paper is organized as below. In Sect. 2, we give a brief review of related work in this area. Section 3 illustrates the background of our scheme. Our approach will be introduced in Sect. 4. Section 5 analyzes the security features of our proposed scheme. Finally, we give a conclusion of our work in Sect. 6.

2 Related Work

In this part, we briefly review the previous work in reprogramming WSNs. Researches in this field can be roughly classified into two types. One is basic reprogramming protocols and the other is security-enhanced protocols.

2.1 Basic Reprogramming Protocols

Reprogramming protocols play an important role in WSNs. After sensor nodes deployed in a given field, it is often difficult to change the software by hands. Thus, using reprogramming techniques is one of the best choices, as we can modify or install the software whenever we need. To provide such functionality, many protocols and schemes have been proposed. Among them Deluge [4] acts as the de facto standard. Deluge exploits Trickles [15] epidemic method to propagate data and maintain sensor nodes states. In Deluge, code image is divided into fixed pages and each page is further divided into fixed sized packets. Thus, Deluge sends code image packet by packet, and only if a page has been completely received, the sensor node can forward this page. This way can reduce the communication collision.

Other well known reprogramming protocols are MNP [3], MOAP [2] and AdapCode [5]. MNP is similar to Deluge. They both use negotiation mechanism to maintain effective code image dissemination. Compared with Deluge, MNP adds a sleep state which saves energy when there is no code image to be transmitted. MAOP exploits publish-subscribe mechanism to propagate code image around the neighborhood sensor nodes. In order to simplify the control about each code image, MOAP does not use pipeline mechanism. Thus, the snesor nodes using MOAP protocol cannot transmit any subsequent code image before having received the full program updates.

2.2 Secure Reprogramming Protocols

To ensure the security of reprogramming in WSNs, many schemes concentrated on the authentication and integrity of code updates. Sluice [16] adopted hash-chain and a single digital signature to ensure the authentication and integrity of code image. In Sluice, a sensor node first receives a signature and then it can leverage this signature to authenticate the first page and then use the hash value of the next page to authenticate the next page. Later, based on this work, Kim et al. proposed a symmetric cryptography mechanism called Castor [17] to reduce the computation load. Different from Sluice using digital signature to authenticate a code image, they adopted MACs to verify the source of code image. However, both of the schemes authenticate code image page by page. If one page is invalid, the whole page is discarded. This is inefficient in pipelining mechanism of code updates, because a page will be broken into fixed size packets and it is very common to lose some packets in harsh environment. Also, they take no consideration of code image privacy, which is pretty important in some harsh field such as military field, the code image should also be kept secret.

Shaheen et al. [18] suggested a one-way key chain to encrypt the code image. The main idea of the scheme is to use sequential keys to encrypt the propagation data. The propagation data is composed of the original segmented data and the next key of the encrypted key. Thus, the receiving sensor node can use the previous key to reveal the data as well as successor key. And then this new key can be used to decrypt the subsequent packet and get the next key. After iterating this procedure, the entire image can be received. However, this scheme is based on one-hop network reprogramming and only when the previous packet is correctly received can the next packet be decrypted.

Dutta et al. exploited a hash chain to bind each packet of the whole image code [19]. They first authenticate the advertisement packet which contains the hash value of the first packet and then use this hash value to authenticate the second packet, and so on. However, if packets arrive out of order, they have to wait and request the lost packet which will consume a lot of time and energy.

Seluge [11] exploited a weak authentication called specific message puzzle to resist Dos attacks based on digital signature authentication. However, it assumed that the networks have been attacked by adversaries. Thus, no matter there are adversaries or not, all received packets have to be authenticated first using such weak authentication, which will consume more energy of sensor nodes and decrease the lifetime of networks as each sensor node has limited power.

Tan et al. proposed a hash chain to encrypt the code image packets and combined CP (i.e. Cipher Puzzle) to provide a weak authentication to mitigate DoS attacks [8]. However, this approach has the same problem of [18] that need to receive packets in order.

Since sensor nodes have limited resources such as energy and memory, it is often inefficient to use asymmetric cryptography algorithms (such as RSA [20]). And symmetric cryptography algorithms have a fatal weakness that they use the same key for both encryption and decryption. However, using encoding mechanisms can mitigate such a drawback [12]. There are two main methods in

WSNs to encode data image packets. One is fountain code and the other is network coding. Both of them adopt XOR operation to encode packets. Moreover, their encoding and decoding mechanisms sometimes are too complex for sensor networks. For example, in [21] and [5] both have to wait for sufficient packets received and use Gaussian elimination to decode. However, the communication complexity of Gaussian elimination is $O(n^2)$, where n represents the number of packets. Thus, it will consume significant power resources to decode. In contrast, this paper only introduces the encoding idea of the two approaches to construct an effective encoding scheme. Even if an adversary can get a key to decrypt the code image, he or she still does not know the original program as not knowing the encoding scheme. However, sensor nodes can easily decode to get the original data image as the mechanism is easy to compute.

$$K_0 \xleftarrow{h(x)} K_1 \xleftarrow{h(x)} \cdots \xleftarrow{h(x)} K_{b-1} \xleftarrow{h(x)} K_b$$

Fig. 1. One-way hash chain

3 Background

3.1 One-Way Hash Chain

One-way hash chain is based on a hash function $h(.)$ with the feature that it is very easy to compute the hash value, whereas one can hardly calculate its inverse function $h^{-1}(.)$. That is to say that for an arbitrary x, it is easy to calculate $y = h(x)$. However when we know the value y, it is difficult to get $x = h^{-1}(y)$. And one-way hash chain (as shown in Fig. 1) is a sequential number of hash values which is generated by using $h(.)$ several times.

3.2 Merkle Hash Tree

The main idea of Merkle hash tree is to build a tree structure based on a hash function $h(.)$, the leaf nodes are the data items which can be verified through its authentication path information. Merkle hash tree is often combined with digital signature to verify code image packets sources. For example, consider a receiver sensor node wants to authenticate packets P_1, P_2, P_3 and P_4. The base station first uses hash function $H(.)$ to build a Merkle hash tree as shown in Fig. 2. Later, the base station will use its private key to sign the root packet $r = e_{1-4}$ to get signature packet $s = SIG_{K_{pr}}(e_{1-4})$. The base station first disseminates the root packet, and the receiver nodes verify it with the base stations public key K_{pb} to test the function $Ver_{K_{pb}}(r, s)$. If the answer is positive, the root packet is received and used to test other authentication path in the tree. Otherwise, the packet is discarded. When a sensor node receives an authentication path $(P_1 \| e_2 \| e_{3-4})$ ("$\|$" denotes concatenation operation), this node can promptly verify P_1 by checking whether $h(h(h(P_1) \| e_2) \| e_{3-4})$ equals to e_{1-4}.

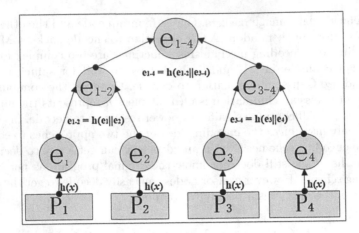

Fig. 2. An example of Merkle hash tree: Where e_1, e_2, e_3 and e_4 are the hash value of packet P_1, P_2, P_3 and P_4 respectively. $h(e_{1-2}) = h(e_1\|e_2)$, $h(e_{3-4}) = h(e_3\|e_4)$ and $h(e_{1-4}) = h(e_{1-2}\|e_{3-4})$.

4   Our Approach

Our scheme contains three phases: System initialization, Packets processing and Packets verification.

4.1   System Initialization Phase

This algorithm introduces a one-way key chain (as shown in Fig. 1) to ensure the confidentiality of code image. It is easy to calculate pseudo-function $F(.)$, but the inverse computation is pretty difficult. The base station first chooses a one-way hash function $F(.)$ such as SHA1 and generates a public key K_{pb} and the corresponding private key K_{pr} using a digital signature algorithm such as ECDSA. Then, the base station generates multiple one-way key chains (as shown in Fig. 3) according to the size of code image. For example, a code image contains n pages and each page has m packets. So, the base station will generate an n-way hash chain and the length of each chain is m. To create an n-way hash chain, the base station generates n nonce, and each nonce re-applies m times pseudo-function $F(.)$ to create the multiple one-way key chains.

Before WSNs are deployed in the environment, each sensor node will be preloaded hash function $F(.)$ to authenticate the elements of each hash key chain. In addition, the generated public parameters should be installed in each sensor node.
$K_i = F(K_{i+1})$, where $0 < i < m$ and $m \leq b$.

4.2   Packets Processing

Before code image dissemination, the base station will process code image data packet by packet. In this paper, we consider Deluge as the base protocol and

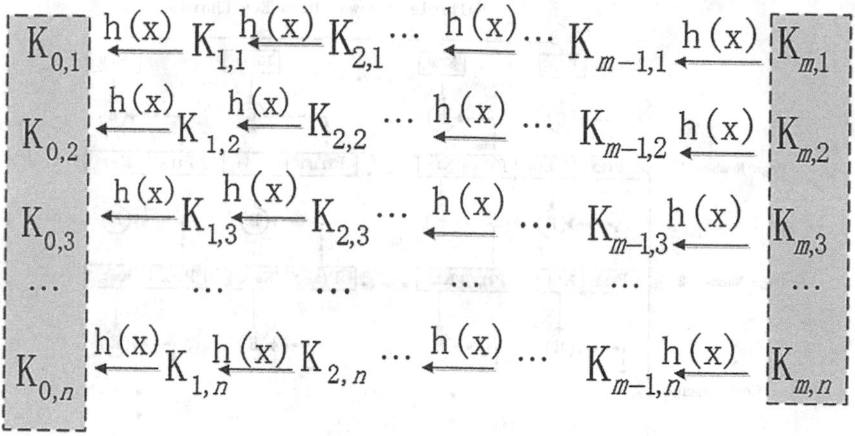

Fig. 3. Multiple one-way key chains: Each key chain is constructed by a random number and a one-way hash function. The value of m and n are determined by the number of pages of each code image and the number of packets of each page

exploit Deluge's pipeline mechanism. The whole code image will be divided into n fixed pages and each page contains m fixed packets (i.e. $S_{img} = n \cdot S_{page} = n \cdot m \cdot S_{pkt}$). To store and process each packet and page more conveniently, n and m need to be integer power of 2 (i.e. $n = 2^i, m = 2^j$, where i and j are integer). To get a relatively high cryptographic strength, we propose an encode-then-encrypt scheme with a light-weighted XOR operation to packets before encryption. Since each page contains m packets, we first use XOR operation to generate m encoded packets.

The rule is as follows:

In page j, it contains m packets (i.e. $Pt_{j,1}, Pt_{j,2}, Pt_{j,3}, ..., Pt_{j,m-1}, Pt_{j,m}$). The first encoded packet is produced by these m packets doing XOR operation one by one. That is $P_{c1} = Pt_{j,1} \oplus Pt_{j,2} \oplus Pt_{j,3} \oplus ... \oplus Pt_{j,m-1} \oplus Pt_{j,m}$. And other encoded packets are generated by $m - 1$ arbitrary packets doing XOR operation. Since choosing $m-1$ elements from m elements has $C(m, m-1) = m$ different situations, to reduce the calculation complexity, we use a parameter "salt" (value from 1 to m) to determine how to choose these $m - 1$ packets. For example, if salt equals to 1, that means the other $m - 1$ encoded packets in page j all contain $Pt_{j,1}$.

When getting m encoded packets, the base station will exploit n way key chains to encrypt these packets. Here, the encryption algorithm is AES. The first one-way key chain encrypts the first packet of each page and the second one-way key chain encrypts the second packet of each page. So, the ith one-way key chain encrypts the ith packet of each page. For example, $K_{1,0}$ encrypts $Pt_{1,1}$ and $K_{1,1}$ encrypts $Pt_{2,1}$ and so on (as shown in Fig. 4).

Then, the base station will use the encode-then-encrypt packets of the first page to construct a Merkle hash tree (as shown in Fig. 5). This hash tree will help

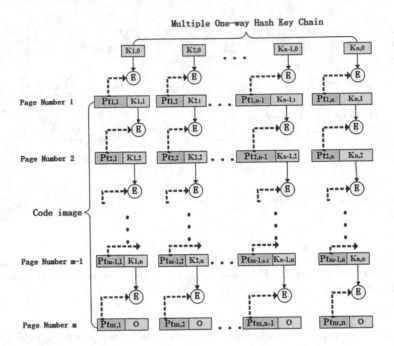

Fig. 4. Code image packets processing in the base station

sensor nodes to authenticate packets based on digital signature which can ensure the identity of the sender. We have illustrated how to construct and authenticate this tree in Sect. 3.

4.3 Packets Verification

Each sensor node in Deluge contains three phases (Maintenance-Request-Transmit), so three types of packets should be authenticated: Advertisement packets, Request packets and Code image Packets.

When receiving a data packet:

(1) Test timestamp
Check whether the timestamp has expired, if so just discards this packet.

(2) Test signature packet
If this packet is a signature packet, comparing the version number with current version. If the version number is larger than the current one, receive this packet; otherwise discard it.

Here, we set a parameter called F_Count to count the failures of authentication of digital signature packets. And we set the failure threshold times of signature authentication as F_MAX. When receiving a digital signature packet,

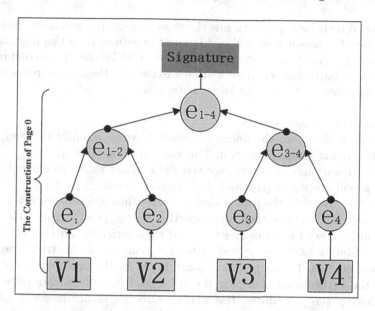

Fig. 5. The construction of page 0: When each page contains 48 packets and the leaves of the tree is 4, the hash packets of page 1 can be used to created 4 leaves of the Merkle hash tree. Thus, $V1 = h(E(Pt_{1,1}||K_{1,1}))||h(E(Pt_{1,2}||K_{2,1}))|| \cdots ||h(E(Pt_{1,12}||K_{12,1}))$. $V2, V3$ and $V4$ also contain the concatenation of other 12 hash packets of the page 1. And $e_i = h(V_i), 1 \leqslant i \leqslant 4$.

we first just verify it directly. If it fails, F_Count increase by 1. If the value of F_Count is larger than F_MAX, the sensor node regards it as an attack action and reboots the weak authentication to resist such DoS attacks. Moreover, our scheme will adjust the value of F_Count according to the successful authentication of digital signature. If the verification is successful and F_Count is larger than 1, the F_Count will decrease by 1. And when the value of F_Count equals to $ZERO$, the mechanism restores to its original state. Thus, our scheme can automatically adjust the defense methods, which will reduce the consumption of the energy and prolong the lifetime of the networks.

But how can we choose this threshold? We assume that malicious packets arrive as Poisson process, so we can adjust this threshold according to the probability and the collected data. In order to select an appropriate threshold for F_MAX, one should investigate the failure times of digital authentication in a specific time (such as one month). Thus, we can calculate the expectation of the failure times in normal situation. And this expectation can be set as F_MAX.

(3) Test Request packets

In our scheme, we use cluster keys for local request packets authentication which is similar to Seluge's local broadcast authentication. However, we add an additional array for this authentication which is a public parameter in each sensor node. The array in each sensor node records the number of requests of requesters. When one requester sends the same request packets more than a particular times, the sensor node will just ignore the request from this requester in a specific time period. As a result, even some sensor nodes have been compromised to pretend to be neighbors, they will be discovered. Hence, the request-based *DoS* attacks cannot destroy the entire networks.

(4) Test code image packets

If the node listens to the image summary is what recently received, it will adjust the Trickle listening interval. This can save node power.

If the version number of the received data is less than the current version number, it will propagate packets it has already stored.

Otherwise: We note the root packet as t and the signature packet as s. The first step is to receive t and then verify whether $Ver_{K_{pb}}(r, s)$ is true. If the answer is yes, that is to say t is a valid packet. And then verify the authentication path packets of Merkle hash tree according to the structure of this tree. The details can be seen in Sect. 3.2. As page 0 is constructed by the hash packets of page 1 packets, the authentication of page 0 can be used to authenticate page 1. And then following the procedures, the whole source pages are received using the Algorithms 1 and 2. Since our scheme exploits encode-then-encrypt method to process source packets, we use decrypt-then-decode method to recover source packets.

```
Algorithm 1: The process of decryption
   Require: Each sensor node has a session key set to decrypt code
             image packets.
   Ensure:  Confidentiality and integrity of each packet.
   Parameters:''BS'' is the base station, ''A'' is a sensor node
               and ''count'' is the number of decrypted packets.
   1. BS: BS->*: E(Ci||Ki,j)
   2. A: Receiving E(Ci||Ki,j)
   3. A: M <= DKi-1,j(E(Ci||Ki,j))
   4. if A: H(Ki,j)== Ki-1,j then
   5.     A: Ki,j <= Ki-1
   6.     A: count ++;
   7.     if count == n
   8.         try to decode packets
   9.     end if
   10. end if
   11. else drop this packet
   12. end
```

Algorithm 2: Decoding algorithm

When the packets of i-th page are arriving:
The parameter $pCount$ is used to calculate the number of different encoded data packets which have been correctly received.
$a_{t,1} \sim a_{t,n}$ are n coefficients, $b_t = a_{t,1} * p_1 + a_{t,2} * p_2 + ... + a_{t,n} * p_n$, Where pk is the k-th packet of page i and b_t is the coded packet.
Here, liner encoding is adopted in our scheme. Thus, $a_{t,1}$ $a_{t,n}$ belongs to $\{0,1\}$.
A nonce is chosen to determine the encoding way. For example, setting nonce to 1 means the coefficient of the first packet is 0, and other coefficients are all 1.
The first encode packet $C_1 = P_1 \oplus P_2 \oplus ... \oplus P_n$, other encoded packets are determined by nonce.
If $pCount$ equals to m
From 1 to $n - 1$: choosing an encoded packet to do XOR operation with C1
Store each packet in Pi (i is from 1 to $n - 1$)
Set P equals to the length of $m - 1$ sequence
$For(i = 1, i \leqslant n - 1, i + +)$
$P = P \oplus P_i \oplus C_1$
End

5   Performance and Analysis

5.1   Performance of Encode-then-encrypt

To test whether our scheme is efficient, we use a testbed composed Telosb, a TinyOS [22] supported hardware. Each sensor node contains a 8-MHz, 16-bit MSP430 microcontroller, 10-KB RAM, 48-KB ROM and 1-MB flash Memory. Here, each sensor node uses an AES algorithm as the underlying encryption algorithm and we test the impact of packet size on propagation delay. From Fig. 6, it can be seen that our scheme has a slight influence on the execution time. Thus, the proposed scheme is light-weighted. Moreover, from the experiment result, we can see that different size of data block has different influence on propagation delay. For example, when the size of data block is smaller than 36 bytes, it can be found that this effect to be small. So we can choose an appropriate pipeline scheme which is secure and light-weighted.

5.2   Enhanced Confidentiality with Light-Weighted Mechanism

We use an encode-then-encrypt mechanism to enhance the security of code image dissemination. Our security scheme can enhance the resistance against traffic analysis and brute force cryptographic. If the eavesdropper does not get the decryption key, he or she can only analyze the data traffic or use brute force to decrypt the encrypted message. Thus, the strength of this encode-then-encrypt process is measured by the amount of computations that a wiretapper needs to retrieve the plaintext from the ciphertext. If a wiretapper needs at least 2^{64} computing operations to decrypt the source code image, we note that the strength is 64-bit. Because of the encoding process, our scheme can enhance the

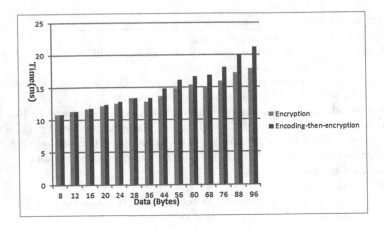

Fig. 6. Code image packets encryption propagation delay

security strength of this process. For example, if one code image page consists of 2 packets and each packet contains 32-*bit* data, the parameter salt is 32. When a wiretapper gets the first bit of the ciphertext, he or she not only needs to decrypt the ciphertext but also needs to decode the coding text. Since we use XOR operation to encode the packets, when the first bit is 0 it cannot tell whether this bit is 0 or 1 originally as $0 \oplus 0 = 0$ and $1 \oplus 1 = 0$. In this encoding situation, the security strength is 32-*bit*. However, in a pipeline reprogramming scheme a page may contain $n(n \geqslant 2)$ packets. Thus, our scheme can largely enhance the confidentiality with this light-weighted mechanism.

5.3   Efficiency and Resistance to DoS Attacks

In WSNs, packets arriving to sensors are a probabilistic event. Here, we assume that it follows Poisson distribution. So, not all of the packets arriving to sensors are coming from malicious nodes. However, almost all the security scheme with weak authentication to resist signature based DoS attacks assume that all the packets received are fake packets. Although some earlier works pointed out that such weak authentication (such as message specific puzzle in [11] and Cipher puzzle in [8]) is efficient to the receiver, it will consume a lot of energy and resources in senders. Thus, such weak authentication will lead to reduced lifetime of the networks.

Our approach modifies the scheme to reboot weak authentication according to the attack action in networks. Attackers in sensor networks are very different, some attackers only wiretap the code image message. Thus, we propose a method to save energy when there is no DoS attack against sensor networks. However, if an attacker launches DoS attacks against signature packets, we can react to this action promptly and reboot weak authentication to prevent this attacks. So, our scheme is more efficient than any other schemes which ignore this situation.

5.4 Out of Order Tolerance

Due to the collision of multiple senders in WSNs, out of order of packets dissemination often occurs. It will take a lot of resources and energy to deal with these packets especially in lossy channels. Thus, it is very helpful to tolerate packets received out of order. Our scheme exploits multiple one-way key chains to encrypt code image packets. Moreover, the first one-way key chain encrypts the first packet of each page and the *i-th* one-way key chain encrypts the *i-th* packet of each page. Thus, to decrypt the packets of the same page does not rely on each other, but only rely on packets of the previous page. Moreover, in Deluge a receiver node receives the next page only after all the packets of the previous page are received. So, our scheme is very appropriate to Deluge-based scheme.

5.5 Integrity and Data Freshness

The code image packets integrity can be ensured by digital signature and multiple one-way key chains. Before authenticating page 0, the base station first sends digital signature to each sensor node, which can be verified by the public key installed in sensor nodes. Since the digital signature packet can hardly be faked, the receiver can correctly authenticate page 0. The Merkle hash tree contains the hash message of page 1, so page 1 can be verified after authenticating the hash value. The later page can be authenticated with the multiple key chains. Thus, our scheme can ensure the integrity of code image program. In our scheme, when correctly receiving a packet, the key in the last page can be dynamically updated. Thus, adversaries cannot transmit the old version packets and launch replay attacks. Therefore, our scheme can ensure the freshness of each code image packet.

6 Conclusion

In this paper, we have proposed a novel and light-weighted scheme to ensure code image privacy and, at same time, resist *DoS* attacks against sensor nodes. To ensure the confidentiality of code image packets, we construct an *encode-then-encrypt* scheme. Our work is different from others in two main aspects. On one hand we exploit *encode-then-encrypt* mechanism to ensure confidentiality of code image dissemination. Unlike other encoding methods which need high computation to decode packets, such as Fountain codes [23] and network coding [24], we use a relatively simple rule to decode packets which is determined by the number of pages of code image and the random parameter salt. On the other hand, we manipulate multiple one-way key chains to encrypt code image packet by packet. This ensures that out-of-order packet delivery is tolerable, which is desirable in lossy channels.

Acknowledgement. This work was supported by the Natural Science Foundation of China (Grants: 51477056 and 61321064), the Shanghai Knowledge Service Platform for Trustworthy Internet of Things (No. ZF1213), the Pearl River Nova Program of Guangzhou (Grant: 2014J2200051), CCF-Tencent Open Research Fund, the Shanghai Rising-Star Program (No. 15QA1401700), and the East China Normal University graduate student to go abroad (boundary) short-term training special fund. Daojing He is the corresponding author of this article.

References

1. Khan, P., Ghosh, A., Konar, G., Chakraborty, N.: Temperature and humidity monitoring through wireless sensor network using shortest path algorithm. In: International Conference on Control, Instrumentation, Energy and Communication, CIEC 2014, pp. 199–203. IEEE, Calcutta (2014)
2. Stathopoulos, T., Heidemann, J., Estrin, D.: A remote code update mechanism for wireless sensor networks. Technical report, UCLA, Los Angeles, CA, USA (2003)
3. Kulkarni, S., Wang, L.: MNP: multihop network reprogramming service for sensor networks. In: Proceedings of 25th IEEE International Conference on Distributed Computing Systems, ICDCS 2005, pp. 7–16. IEEE, Columbus (2005)
4. Hui, J.W., Culler, D.: The dynamic behavior of a data dissemination protocol for network programming at scale. In: Proceedings of the 2nd International Conference on Embedded Networked Sensor Systems. SenSys 2004, pp. 81–94. ACM, Baltimore (2004)
5. Hou, I.H., Tsai, Y.E., Abdelzaher, T.F., Gupta, I.: Adapcode: adaptive network coding for code updates in wireless sensor networks. In: The 27th Conference on Computer Communications, INFOCOM 2008, pp. 2189–2197. IEEE, Phoenix (2008)
6. He, D., Chan, S., Zhang, Y., Yang, H.: Lightweight and confidential data discovery and dissemination for wireless body area networks. IEEE J. Biomed. Health Inform. 18(2), 440–448 (2014)
7. Wei, S., Wang, J., Yin, R., Yuan, J.: Trade-off between security and performance in block ciphered systems with erroneous ciphertexts. IEEE Trans. Inf. Forensics Secur. 8(4), 636–645 (2013)
8. Tan, H., Ostry, D., Zic, J., Jha, S.: A confidential and DoS-resistant multi-hop code dissemination protocol for wireless sensor networks. Comput. Secur. 32(1), 36–55 (2009)
9. Aura, T., Nikander, P., Leiwo, J.: DOS-resistant authentication with client puzzles. In: Christianson, B., Crispo, B., Malcolm, J.A., Roe, M. (eds.) Security Protocols 2000. LNCS, vol. 2133, pp. 170–177. Springer, Heidelberg (2001)
10. Ning, P., Liu, A., Du, W.: Mitigating DoS attacks against broadcast authentication in wireless sensor networks. ACM Trans. Sens. Netw. TOSN 4(1), 1–35 (2008)
11. Hyun, S., Ning, P., Liu, A., Du, W.: Seluge: secure and dos-resistant code dissemination in wireless sensor networks. In: Proceedings of the 7th International Conference on Information Processing in Sensor Networks, IPSN 2008, pp. 445–456. IEEE, St. Louis (2008)
12. Mihaljević, M., Oggier, F.: A wire-tap approach to enhance security in communication systems using the encoding-encryption paradigm. In: IEEE 17th International Conference on Telecommunications, ICT 2010, pp. 83–88. IEEE, Doha (2010)
13. Khiabani, Y.S., Wei, S.: Creation of degraded wiretap channel through deliberate noise in block ciphered systems. In: IEEE Workshops on GLOBECOM, GC Wkshps 2011, pp. 893–897. IEEE, Houston (2011)

14. Khiabani, Y.S., Wei, S., Yuan, J., Wang, J.: Enhancement of secrecy of block ciphered systems by deliberate noise. IEEE Trans. Inf. Forensics Secur. **7**(5), 1604–1613 (2012)
15. Levis, P., Patel, N., Culler, D.E., Shenker, S.: Trickle: a self-regulating algorithm for code propagation and maintenance in wireless sensor networks. In: Proceedings of the First USENIX/ACM Symposium on Networked Systems Design and Implementation, NSDI 2004, pp. 15–28. San Francisco (2004)
16. Lanigan, P.E., Gandhi, R., Narasimhan, P.: Sluice: secure dissemination of code updates in sensor networks. In: 26th IEEE International Conference on Distributed Computing Systems, ICDCS 2006, pp. 53–53. IEEE (2006)
17. Kim, D.H., Gandhi, R., Narasimhan, P.: Exploring symmetric cryptography for secure network reprogramming. In: 27th International Conference on Distributed Computing Systems Workshops, ICDCSW 2007, pp. 17–17. IEEE, Toronto (2007)
18. Shaheen, J., Ostry, D., Sivaraman, V., Jha, S.: Confidential and secure broadcast in wireless sensor networks. In: IEEE 18th International Symposium on Personal, Indoor and Mobile Radio Communications, PIMRC 2007, pp. 1–5. IEEE, Athens (2007)
19. Dutta, P.K., Hui, J.W., Chu, D.C., Culler, D.E.: Securing the deluge network programming system. In: Proceedings of the 5th International Conference on Information Processing in Sensor Networks, IPSN2006, pp. 326–333. IEEE, Nashville (2006)
20. Nilsson, D.K., Roosta, T., Lindqvist, U., Valdes, A.: Key management and secure software updates in wireless process control environments. In: Proceedings of the First ACM Conference on Wireless Network Security, Wisec 2008, pp. 100–108. ACM, New York (2008)
21. Rossi, M., Bui, N., Zanca, G., Stabellini, L., Crepaldi, R., Zorzi, M.: SYNAPSE++: code dissemination in wireless sensor networks using fountain codes. IEEE Trans. Mob. Comput. **9**(12), 1749–1765 (2010)
22. TinyOS.: An open-source OS for the networked sensor regime. http://www.tinyos.net/
23. Rossi, M., Zanca, G., Stabellini, L., Crepaldi, R., Harris, A.F., Zorzi, M.: Synapse: a network reprogramming protocol for wireless sensor networks using fountain codes. In: 5th Annual IEEE Communications Society Conference on Sensor, Mesh and Ad Hoc Communications and Networks, SECON 2008, pp. 188–196. IEEE, San Francisco (2008)
24. Katti, S., Rahul, H., Hu, W., Katabi, D., Mdard, M., Crowcroft, J.: XORs in the air: practical wireless network coding. IEEE/ACM Trans. Network. **16**(3), 497–510 (2008)

Preserving Context Privacy in Distributed Hash Table Wireless Sensor Networks

Paolo Palmieri[✉]

Department of Computing and Informatics, Bournemouth University,
Fern Barrow, Poole BH12 5BB, UK
ppalmieri@bournemouth.ac.uk

Abstract. Wireless Sensor Networks (WSN) are often deployed in hostile or difficult scenarios, such as military battlefields and disaster recovery, where it is crucial for the network to be highly fault tolerant, scalable and decentralized. For this reason, peer-to-peer primitives such as Distributed Hash Table (DHT), which can greatly enhance the scalability and resilience of a network, are increasingly being introduced in the design of WSN's. Securing the communication within the WSN is also imperative in hostile settings. In particular, context information, such as the network topology and the location and identity of base stations (which collect data gathered by the sensors and are a central point of failure) can be protected using traffic encryption and anonymous routing. In this paper, we propose a protocol achieving a modified version of onion routing over wireless sensor networks based on the DHT paradigm. The protocol prevents adversaries from learning the network topology using traffic analysis, and therefore p reserves the context privacy of the network. Furthermore, the proposed scheme is designed to minimize the computational burden and power usage of the nodes, through a novel partitioning scheme and route selection algorithm.

Keywords: Wireless sensor networks · Context privacy · Anonymity · Onion routing · Distributed hash table

1 Introduction

A Wireless Sensor Network (WSN) generally consist of a number of small, low-power computing sensors, deployed in an environment where they observe physical phenomena. The sensors, typically battery-powered and highly constrained in their computational capabilities, are nonetheless able to perform sensing, wireless communication and computation tasks. They collect and disseminate data about the supervised phenomena cooperatively, and collaborate in order to perform a common task. WSN's applications include health monitoring, smart agriculture, weather sensing, intrusion detection and industrial control [6,9]. However, in spite of the extensive research, WSN's still face many challenges, including security, privacy and network robustness and scalability. Wireless sensor networks share some of the above challenges with peer-to-peer networks: in particular,

© Springer International Publishing Switzerland 2016
S. Qing et al. (Eds.): ICICS 2015, LNCS 9543, pp. 436–444, 2016.
DOI: 10.1007/978-3-319-29814-6_37

both network designs aim at achieving a high level of scalability in a decentralized manner, and must be able to cope with nodes failing, entering or abandoning the network at any time. For this reason, some of the network constructions used in the peer-to-peer setting have been adopted in the design of WSN [10]. In particular, the Distributed Hash Table (DHT) network topology has found application in a number of WSN designs [5].

Privacy is also an increasing concern for WSN's [8]. The wireless nature of the communication link makes the network inherently vulnerable to eavesdropping. Moreover, nodes of the wireless sensor network are often deployed outdoor, in unsurveilled areas where they can be subject to tampering. An attacker might be able to gain control of one or more nodes. For this reason, privacy must be preserved even against internal adversaries. In particular, both the privacy of the data gathered and the privacy of the context should be protected. In order to preserve data privacy, nodes should not be able to build a more detailed picture of the data than it is required for their functioning (aggregation). With regard to context privacy, instead, the primary aim is to hide the location of sensors and base stations, the network topology and in certain cases the time data was collected. WSN's are in general highly vulnerable to attacks targeted at base stations, which coordinate network operation and gather data: the failure of a base station can in fact disrupt the whole network. The geographic location of base stations and the network topology should therefore be concealed [2]. Common strategies for hiding location and prevent traffic analysis are flooding, transmissions from fake sources [14], and random walks [7]. Random walks for the transmission of the information, in particular, have been adopted in a number of designs. Zhang proposed self-adjusting directed random walks in [15], while GROW (Greedy Random Walk) [13] introduced a two-way random walk, from both source and destination, to reduce the chance of an eavesdropper being able to collect location information. Finally, layers of encryption can be used to protect the information at each hop in the walk [3].

In this paper we propose a modified onion routing protocol for wireless sensor networks that are based on the distributed hash table topology. Onion routing, the anonymity protocol at the base of Tor and other privacy preserving technologies, can prevent tampering and preserve the secrecy of both the communication content and the location of the sender and receiver. Applied to wireless sensor networks, onion routing is an effective strategy to protect context privacy. However, the limited capabilities of sensing nodes, and the particular network infrastructure of a WSN make implementing onion routing a challenging task. For this reason, we aim at minimizing any computational overhead of onion routing. In particular, the processes of route selection and key distribution are fairly complex tasks in a WSN. Route selection is made difficult by the absence of a complete view of the network by each node. A node, in fact, might be able to communicate directly with only a fraction of all the nodes in the WSN, due, for instance, to distance or wireless signal visibility. We solve this issue by proposing a route selection algorithm based on Bloom filters, which takes into account the limited network view without compromising the secrecy of the route. Without a directory of all nodes, implementing the standard key distribution mechanism of onion routing is also impossible over a WSN. Therefore, we adopt a key distribution strategy designed for the DHT paradigm, making the network resilient to nodes failing, entering and abandoning it without disrupting the onion routing mechanism. The proposed protocol enables, for the first time, the implementation of a full-fledged onion routing mechanism over a wireless sensor network, overcoming the traditional limitations of the typical WSN infrastructure. This, in turn, will allow for better protection of context privacy and the location of nodes in the network, making WSN's more resilient to attacks targeting base stations or specific nodes.

2   Distributed Hash Table

Peer-to-peer networks are large distributed systems designed around three main principles: *decentralization, fault tolerance* and *scalability*. As wireless sensor networks are often required to satisfy the same properties, they sometimes integrate solutions first proposed in the peer-to-peer domain [10]. This is the case, in particular, for the family of WSN's designed around one of the most successful peer-to-peer designs, Distributed Hash Table (DHT) [5], used daily by millions of users through the BitTorrent protocol.

A DHT is defined over a *keyspace*, defined as the output range of a hash function. The keyspace is divided among the nodes in the network by using a partitioning scheme. For each DHT, a function defines the *distance* between any two values in the keyspace. The partitioning is achieved by assigning to each node in the network a value in the keyspace called *identifier*: the peer is responsible for the subset of values in the keyspace that have less than a predefined distance from his identifier value. Each node in the network maintains a connection to a number of other nodes, called *neighbors*. Neighbors are generally selected according to a certain structure, known as the network topology, which, together with the hash and distance functions, defines the specific DHT. For the purpose of this paper, we assume any WSN built over a DHT to specify: the keyspace K; the size of the keyspace s; the hash functions h used to map information generated by the sensors to values in the keyspace; the function f_{dist} determining the distance between two values in the keyspace; and the maximum distance d for which a node with identifier A is responsible for keys in the keyspace. We also assume the keyspace to be two-dimensional: given a distance d, a function f_{dist}, and a value v in the keyspace, there are exactly two values v^+ and v^- for which $f_{dist}(v^+) = f_{dist}(v^-) = d$.

3   Onion Routing

Onion routing is a mechanism allowing anonymous and privacy-preserving communication in a network. First proposed in 1997 [12], onion routing has recently seen widespread use thanks to the Tor implementation [4], which counts millions of active users. Onion routing can prevent surveillance and traffic analysis.

The identity, location and network activity of each node is protected by concealing to external observers both content and routing information of the node's traffic. This is achieved by relaying the traffic, including information about its destination, through a virtual *circuit* composed of three intermediary nodes (called *relays*). Each relay in the circuit only learns the preceding and following node, so that the sender remains anonymous to all relays except the first, and the destination remains secret to all relays except the last. In order to protect the actual content of the communication, messages are repeatedly encrypted with a public key encryption scheme in a layered manner, using in inverse order the public keys of all the relays in the circuit. Traffic going back to the source from the destination is similarly encrypted and routed from the last relay to the first one. Implementing onion routing is an effective strategy to protect communication in wireless sensor networks, especially when deployed in hostile environments, subject to both external and internal attacks. In particular, onion routing can prevent traffic analysis and packet eavesdropping, and at the same time prevent malicious nodes in the network from learning sensitive information about the network topology, such as the identity of base stations and data aggregation nodes. This information is generally being referred to as *context data*.

Each node participating in an onion routing protocol has a public and private key pair called *identity key*. This key serves the main purpose of authenticating the node and prove its identity to other nodes. The identity key pair is generated during the node startup, and is maintained for the entire life of the node. However, in order to minimize the impact of a compromised identity key, each node also generates at regular time intervals a second key pair: the *onion key*. The public key of the current onion key pair is signed using the identity key and then distributed to other nodes. The onion key is used during circuit creation: when establishing a circuit, each node being used as relay is challenged to prove knowledge of its (private) onion key. The actual communication over the circuit is encrypted using a symmetric *session key*, agreed on by each couple of consecutive nodes in the circuit. The key is discarded once the communication over the circuit stops, thus achieving forward secrecy. Onion circuits, in fact, are designed to be used only for a limited period of time. Similarly, onion keys are discarded and replaced after they reach the end of their intended lifetime.

4   Onion Routing over DHT Wireless Sensor Networks

Sensor nodes in a WSN are typically constrained devices: at the hardware level, due to the limited computational capabilities and often battery-powered nature, and at the network level, due to the restricted visibility of the network each node possesses. In order to satisfy these constraints, we design the proposed onion routing protocol so that each node in the wireless sensor network is able to operate both as a source of information and as a relay. However, not all nodes will cover both roles at the same time: for energy efficiency, we select a subset of nodes to act as relays for a given time, and rotate to the next subset of nodes after a predetermined amount of time. Therefore, a node will be in one of the following states at any time: *relay state*, during which the sensor node performs both sensing tasks and relays traffic of other nodes; *sensor state*, during which the node continues to sense information but does not accept traffic from other nodes for relay purposes. In order to be able to act as a relay, each node has an *identity key* pair, generated using a public key encryption scheme. The identity keys can be either loaded onto the device before deployment (to ease the computational burden) or created during bootstrap of the node. Additionally, when the node enters relay state, it also generates a temporary *onion key* pair, which is valid only for the current relay state. Nodes distribute the public keys of both identity and onion pairs following the strategy described in the following. We say that a node *owns* a key if it generated the key, while we say that a node is *responsible* for a key if it stores the key and distributes it to other peers requesting it. Keys are transmitted over the network by using the DHT underlying the WSN.

Identity Key Distribution. The subset of nodes in the network that are responsible for the identity key of a specific node are determined by hashing the identifier of the node using the hash function h defined by the DHT. A node X is responsible for the identity key $i_N \in K$ of the node N if:

$$f_{dist}\left(X - h\left(N\right)\right) < d. \tag{1}$$

This defines a subset I_N of size $2d$ of the keyspace K. The node owning the key distributes it to the nodes responsible for storing it. Should the value d increase during network operation, the nodes already responsible for the key distribute it to the new nodes in I_N. Should d instead decrease, the nodes that are no longer in I_N discard the key. It is important to note here that nodes in the WSN reply to request for keys both when in relay and sensor state.

Relay State Partitioning. Since we want only a subset of the nodes in the WSN to act as onion relays at any given time, we partition the WSN by using the identifier value of the nodes: we consider the first n bits of the identifier value in order to have 2^n different subsets. For instance, all peers with the first n bits of the identifier having value 0 are in the first subset.

Onion Key Distribution. The temporary onion keys are generated by the nodes when entering relay state, and are subsequently distributed to the nodes responsible for storing them similarly to the identity keys. However, we design the protocol so that the nodes that are responsible for storing an identity key will not also be responsible for the onion key of the same node. Moreover, a node responsible for the onion key of a node for the current relay state duration, will not be responsible for a key of the same node for a number of following relay states. We achieve this through the distribution mechanism described in the following, which follows that proposed in [11]. For each node N and its identifier $i_N \in K$, we divide the network into $u = \frac{s}{2d}$ partitions of size $2d$, such that one such partition is I_N, as defined by Eq. (1). Nodes in each partition except I_N cyclically store the onion key for N that is valid for the current relay state. The partitions are defined by an arbitrary function

$$f_{on}: \; K \to \{\text{all possible partitions of } K \text{ of size } 2d\}, \tag{2}$$

that takes as input an identifier $i \in K$ and outputs $\{O_1, \ldots, O_{u-1}\}$ (the set of partitions), such that $O_1, \ldots, O_{u-1}$ are disjoint subsets of K of equal size and

$$O_1 \cup \ldots \cup O_{u-1} = K \smallsetminus \{I_N\}. \tag{3}$$

For any $u - 1$ subsequent relay states, each partition is selected once for storing the onion key of the node, starting from O_1 and moving to the following partition until O_{u-1} is reached (the cycle starts anew after that).

Private Route Selection. Each node in a WSN has a limited visibility of the network, and may be able to communicate with only a subset of all the nodes. This has an impact on two basic functionalities of the proposed network: onion circuit creation, and reporting to the base station. In the former case, two successive relays may not be able to communicate with one another. We solve this by introducing the *relay filter*, an additional set of information generated by relays in relay state, and distributed similarly to the onion public key. The relay filter for a relay node r is the subset of the other currently available relays that are visible from r, encoded using a Bloom filter data structure [1]. Bloom filters allow us to keep the information secret to external observers as well as the nodes themselves. The filter is signed by the relay using its onion private key.

In order to preserve context privacy in the WSN, and therefore the identity and network location of the base stations, these particular nodes act similarly to other nodes for the purpose of onion routing. However, base stations own an additional set of keys, the *station key* pair. These keys are generated before the WSN deployment, and are embedded in each node reporting to the relative base station. Station keys are used to sign a filter similar to the relay filter, the *station filter*. The station filter encodes a randomly selected subset of all the relays that are visible from the relays the base station can connect to. Due to the property of Bloom filters, it is possible for the base station to generate the station filter based on the relay filters. The distribution of station filters and its impact on privacy are discussed in Sect. 4.1.

The mechanism for building an onion circuit between a sensor node and a base station is presented in Protocol 1. The proposed circuit building approach is alternative to that presented in [13], and to Tor hidden services [4].

4.1 Privacy Analysis

According to the distributed trust principle, no single relay in the circuit should learn the identity of both nodes at the two ends of the circuit. We achieve this by letting the nodes select independently the first relay, and by disclosing to each relay only the previous and following step in the circuit. This is possible thanks to the use of the intersection filters explained in step 2 and 3 of the circuit building protocol. Distributed trust provides protection for the context information of the wireless sensor network. We identify two private context information

---

Protocol 1. Building an Onion Circuit.

---

1 The sensor node S identifies the current relays through the partition function, and acquires relay information (current keys and filters) through the DHT, by querying the appropriate set of responsible nodes O_i. Then S selects among its neighbors a potential first relay for the sensor's end of the circuit.

2 S calculates the intersection filter $b_i = b_r \cap b_s$ between the filter of the selected first relay b_r and the station filter b_s. Then, S sends b_i to the relay and instructs it to build a circuit with one of its own neighbors whose identifier satisfies b_i.

3 Similarly to the sensor, and concurrently, the base station node B selects among its neighbors a potential first relay for the station's end of the circuit. Then, it instructs the relay to build a circuit with a neighboring second relay that satisfies a randomly selected subset of the first relay's filter.

4 Once second relays have been selected at both ends of the circuit, the sensor and the base station instruct the relative second relays to look for potential matches. The two relays start querying all neighboring relays for potential circuits, and open a new circuit each time they find open ends.

5 Among all the resulting circuits, S selects the right circuit by querying the node at the other end, and asking it to prove knowledge of the station private key. In case no suitable circuit is found, the node starts again from step 1.

---

that we aim to preserve: the network location (that is, the position within the DHT) and the identity of the nodes acting as base stations. Use of the proposed onion routing effectively conceals the context information to the sensor nodes communicating with the base station, as no information other than the station filter is required for communication. At the same time, relays used in the circuit cannot distinguish a sensor from a base station, as the same steps are taken by both S and B. This is true for as long as the base station does not select as first relay a sensor node that has access to B's station filter: considering that B has access to the list of sensors reporting to itself, we can safely assume this to be the case. For the same reason, station filters are distributed encrypted using the station public key. New station filters are generated at every change of state for the nodes. In order to preserve secrecy of the identity and position of the base station, the station filter distribution can follow two strategies: random walks (where the filter is passed on from node to node randomly, thus making it harder to identify the originating node) or distribution through an onion circuit (where the relay at the end of the circuit will propagate the filter through flooding). Finally, the identity key of a node is verified through a challenge by the node responsible for its distribution, while the onion key is verified by the node building the circuit. Since the node obtains the identity and onion keys from two different set of nodes (Sect. 4), an adversary would need to corrupt a majority of nodes in both sets in order to perform an attack. This would also have to be repeated at each change of state.

5 Conclusion

In this paper we proposed an onion routing protocol for wireless sensor networks based on the distributed hash table paradigm. The protocol minimizes the introduced overhead by partitioning the network and rotating relay responsibilities over time, which is particularly effective in battery-powered devices. The proposed construction allows for limited network visibility by the nodes, and is entirely decentralized. Context privacy is preserved by the distributed trust of the onion mechanism, and both sensor nodes and base stations remain anonymous within the network. The network topology is kept secret as a result, opening the way to implementation in WSN deployed in hostile settings.

References

1. Bloom, B.H.: Space/time trade-offs in hash coding with allowable errors. Commun. ACM **13**(7), 422–426 (1970)
2. Deng, J., Han, R., Mishra, S.: Intrusion tolerance and anti-traffic analysis strategies for wireless sensor networks. In: DSN 2004, pp. 637–646. IEEE (2004)
3. Deng, J., Han, R., Mishra, S.: Decorrelating wireless sensor network traffic to inhibit traffic analysis attacks. Pervasive Mob. Comput. **2**(2), 159–186 (2006)
4. Dingledine, R., Mathewson, N., Syverson, P.F.: Tor: The second-generation onion router. In: USENIX 2004, pp. 303–320 (2004)
5. Fersi, G., Louati, W., Jemaa, M.B.: Distributed hash table-based routing and data management in wireless sensor networks: a survey. Wireless Netw. **19**(2), 219–236 (2013)
6. Gaitan, S., Calderoni, L., Palmieri, P., Veldhuis, M.C.T., Maio, D., Riemsdijk, M.B.V.: From sensing to action: quick and reliable access to information in cities vulnerable to heavy rain. IEEE Sens. J. **14**(12), 4175–4184 (2014)
7. Kamat, P., Zhang, Y., Trappe, W., Ozturk, C.: Enhancing source-location privacy in sensor network routing. In: ICDCS 2005, pp. 599–608. IEEE (2005)
8. Li, N., Zhang, N., Das, S.K., Thuraisingham, B.M.: Privacy preservation in wireless sensor networks: a state-of-the-art survey. Ad Hoc Netw. **7**(8), 1501–1514 (2009)
9. Li, Y., Thai, M.T., Wu, W. (eds.): Wireless Sensor Networks and Applications. Signals and Communication Technology. Springer, New York (2008)
10. McGoldrick, C., Clear, M., Carbajo, R.S., Fritsche, K., Huggard, M.: TinyTorrents: integrating peer-to-peer and wireless sensor networks. In: WONS 2009, pp. 109–116. IEEE (2009)
11. Palmieri, P., Pouwelse, J.: Key management for onion routing in a true peer to peer setting. In: Yoshida, M., Mouri, K. (eds.) IWSEC 2014. LNCS, vol. 8639, pp. 62–71. Springer, Heidelberg (2014)
12. Syverson, P.F., Goldschlag, D.M., Reed, M.G.: Anonymous connections and onion routing. In: IEEE Symposium on Security and Privacy 1997, pp. 44–54. IEEE (1997)
13. Xi, Y., Schwiebert, L., Shi, W.: Preserving source location privacy in monitoring-based wireless sensor networks. In: IPDPS 2006, IEEE (2006)

14. Yang, Y., Shao, M., Zhu, S., Urgaonkar, B., Cao, G.: Towards event source unobservability with minimum network traffic in sensor networks. In: WISEC 2008. pp. 77–88. ACM (2008)
15. Zhang, L.: A self-adjusting directed random walk approach for enhancing source-location privacy in sensor network routing. In: IWCMC 2006, pp. 33–38. ACM (2006)

Prior Classification of Stego Containers as a New Approach for Enhancing Steganalyzers Accuracy

Viktor Monarev[1,2] and Andrey Pestunov[3](✉)

[1] Novosibirsk State University, Novosibirsk, Russia
viktor.monarev@gmail.com
[2] Institute of Computational Technologies SB RAS, Novosibirsk, Russia
[3] Novosibirsk State University of Economics and Management, Novosibirsk, Russia
pestunov@gmail.com

Abstract. We introduce a novel "prior classification" approach which can be employed in order to enhance the accuracy of stego detectors as well as to estimate it more subtly. The prior classification is intended for selection a subset of a testing set with such a property that a detection error, calculated over this subset, may be substantially lower than that calculated over the whole set. Our experiments demonstrated that it is possible to select about 30 % of the BOSSbase images for which HUGO 0.4 bpp is detected with the error less than 0.003, while the error over the whole set is 0.141. We also demonstrated that it is possible to find about 5 % of the BOSSbase images which provide the detection error for HUGO 0.1 bpp less than 0.05, while the error, calculated over the whole set, is about 0.37 which is not quite a reliable accuracy.

Keywords: Information hiding · Steganalysis · HUGO · Prior classification · Feature-based steganalysis · SRM features · Ensemble classifier

1 Introduction

A commonly used way for measuring the accuracy of binary stego detectors is to calculate a detection error

$$P_E = \frac{1}{2}(P_{FA} + P_{MD}),$$

where P_{FA} is the probability of false alarms, and P_{MD} is the probability of missed detections (see e.g. [4,5,11–14]). The strategic goal of steganalysis is to make this error as low as possible, therefore those detector is better, whose error is lower.

In practice, the statistical model of covers is unknown, that is why the detection error can not be calculated analytically and the solution of this problem lies in calculating an average error over a given set. For this purpose, steganalysts often utilize several "standardized" sets, like BOSSbase [1], BOWS2 [18] or NRCS [20]. However, the accuracy of the detectors may be different when

© Springer International Publishing Switzerland 2016
S. Qing et al. (Eds.): ICICS 2015, LNCS 9543, pp. 445–457, 2016.
DOI: 10.1007/978-3-319-29814-6_38

calculating over different image sets [14] because of various specific properties of the images (like noisiness, compression rate etc.). Moreover, a certain image set can be heterogenous and might be divided into subsets with different properties and different detection error values.

In this paper we introduce a novel approach to steganalysis, which we call a "prior classification". The idea of this approach is to add a stage before final classification in order to choose those images which will be reliably detected. The size of the subset of these images can be considered as an additional characteristic of the detector. The similar situation can be noticed in cryptography, where some attacks are applicable only for a certain subset of weak keys, and the size of this subset (or the ratio of this subset) is considered as an additional characteristic of the attack [2,10].

We introduce three possible methods of how to implement the prior classification approach: the naive splitting, the single classification, and a combination of these two methods. Our experiments demonstrated that it is possible to select about 30 % of the BOSSbase v1.01 images for which HUGO 0.4 bpp is detected with the error less than 0.003, while the error over the whole set is 0.141. We also demonstrated that it is possible to select about 5 % of the BOSSbase images which provide the detection error for HUGO 0.1 bpp less than 0.05, while the error, calculated over the whole set, is about 0.37 which is not quite a reliable accuracy. In our opinion, the prior classification has several potential practical applications which we discuss at the end of the paper.

2   Binary Classification

2.1   The Problem

In this paper we consider the binary classification problem, which is intended for building the detector which will distinguish between the two classes: empty (H_0) and stego (H_1) containers (see e.g. [11]). There are three assumptions behind binary steganalyzers:

1. The steganalyst has a set of covers which have statistical properties, similar to that of used by the steganographer.
2. The steganalyst knows the embedding algorithm and the payload size.
3. The steganalyst knows which object she must examine.

We do not touch quantitative steganalysis [15] when there is no knowledge about the payload.

The contemporary approaches to solving the binary classification problem are essentially based on image features and machine learning tools. There are two high-level components in binary classifiers: a feature extraction method and a classification algorithm. At first, we need to obtain some amount of empty containers as well as containers with a certain payload and extract features from all of them. Then, the classifier is trained in order to be able to distinguish between the empty containers features and features extracted from the stego containers.

The general scheme of the binary classification is as follows.

1. Extract the features from images in the training set which contains empty and stego images.
2. Train the classifier on this set to distinguish between features of empty and stego images.
3. Extract the features from the testing containers and classify them via the trained classifier.

2.2 Ensemble Classifier and Base Learners

The methods, which we introduce in this paper, are based on the idea of applying ensemble classifiers to steganalysis [12]. J. Fridrich et al. call them "a great alternative to support vector machines" because of their good performance and competitive accuracy [6]. The ensemble classifiers has been already applied for breaking HUGO during the public BOSS competition [6] by the winners. The ensemble classifier, as it was introduced in [12], works as follows.

1. Take d features (like SPAM [14], SRM [4], PSRM [9] etc.).
2. Obtain L random subsets of all the features, each of which of $d_{sub} < d$ features.
3. Train L base-leaners on the training set.

Let $N_{votes}(z)$ be the number of the base learners which voted in favor of the fact that z contains information:

$$N_{votes}(z) = \sum_{l=1}^{L} B_l(z).$$

Each base learned works as follows:

$$B_l(z) = \begin{cases} 0 & \text{the base learner } l \text{ votes that } z \text{ is empty;} \\ 1 & \text{the base learner } l \text{ votes that } z \text{ contains information;} \end{cases}$$

The final decision is made by the majority of voters according to the Algorithm 1.

ENSEMBLE-RULE(L, N_{votes})
  L — the number of the base learners,
  N_{votes} — the number of voices in favor of H_1.
  Estimate

$$B = \begin{cases} 0 & \text{if } N_{votes} < L/2; \\ 1 & \text{if } N_{votes} > L/2; \\ random(0,1) & \text{otherwise.} \end{cases}$$

  Result: B — the class number.

Algorithm 1. Ensemble classifier decision rule

3   Common Background and Designations

3.1   Images

We utilized the well-known standardized image database BOSSbase v1.01 [1, 19] which contains 10000 images captured by seven different cameras in RAW format (CR2 or DNG). These images had been converted into 8-bit grayscale format, resized and cropped to the size 512 x 512 pixels.

In order to prepare the training set $\mathcal{X}^p$ and the testing set $\mathcal{Y}^p$, where p identifies the embedding rate in bpp, the whole BOSSbase set was divided into two subsets $\mathcal{X}_0$ and $\mathcal{Y}_0$, where $|\mathcal{X}_0| = 8000$ and $|\mathcal{Y}_0| = 2000$. Then by random embedding p bpp into all the images from $\mathcal{X}_0$ and $\mathcal{Y}_0$ we obtained $\mathcal{X}_1^p$ and $\mathcal{Y}_1^p$ correspondingly. The training set was $\mathcal{X}^p = \mathcal{X}_0 \cup \mathcal{X}_1^p$ and the testing set $\mathcal{Y}^p = \mathcal{Y}_0 \cup \mathcal{Y}_1^p$. Thus, $|\mathcal{X}^p| = 16000$ and $|\mathcal{Y}^p| = 4000$. Both sets contain a half of empty images and a half of stego images.

Further in the paper we omit the payload index p (it will not confuse the reader) and designate the training set as $\mathcal{X}$ and the testing set as $\mathcal{Y}$.

3.2   Features

We utilize Spatial Rich Model (SRM) features [4] as one of the state-of-the-art instruments for steganalysis. The newer Projection Spatial Rich Model features (PSRM) [9] provide only slight improvement but require substantially greater complexity. SRM features have a total dimension of 34,671 and we took the extractor provided by [17].

3.3   Base Learners

There are several variants for choosing the base learners, but in our experiments we follow the recommendations of Kodovsky et al. [12] and exploit the Fisher Linear Discriminant [3] due to its low training complexity. There will be two types of the base learners in our paper, which we designate as B_l, $l = 1, \ldots, L$ and B'_m, $m = 1, \ldots, M$ correspondingly. Thus, the number of base learners is L or M. Each base learner is always assigned with 800 randomly chosen SRM features.

3.4   Embedding Algorithm

We used Highly Undetectable Steganography (HUGO) as an embedding algorithm [16]. This method is one of the hardest steganography to detect (see e.g. results in [9] where HUGO is compared to WOW [7] and UNIWARD [8] — the other content adaptive embedding algorithms). HUGO is based on the LSB matching but chooses the places for embedding probabilistically according to the SPAM-features [16] rather than randomly as LSB matching. This modification allows to lengthen the hidden message by 7 times comparing to LSB matching preserving the security level (the error).

3.5   State-of-the-Art

In our experiments we needed our own implementation of the ensemble classifier. There are many possible parameters of this classifier that is why we implemented it ourselves with some certain parameters and in the Table 1 we compare the original implementations of state-of-the-art classifiers from [9] with our implementation. We see that the detection errors of our implementation is rather close to original ones. These errors values will be used for comparison with our prior classification results.

Let $\mathcal{Y}^{good}$ be the set of "good" images, which were selected after the prior classification stage, and $P_E(\mathcal{Y}^{good})$ be the detection error calculated over this set. In our experiments we compare $P_E(\mathcal{Y}^{good})$ and $P_E(\mathcal{Y})$ and try to make $|\mathcal{Y}^{good}|/|\mathcal{Y}|$ as large as possible.

Table 1. State-of-the-art results on HUGO detection (ensemble classifier).

	Detection error $P_E(\mathcal{Y})$ over the whole BOSSbase 1.01	
Payload	Results from [9], various features and parameters	Our implementation, SRM features, $L = 500$
0.05 bpp	-	0.44
0.10 bpp	0.3564–0.3757	0.37
0.20 bpp	0.2397–0.2701	-
0.40 bpp	0.1172–0.1383	0.141

4   Prior Classification

4.1   Basic Idea

The basic idea behind all our methods consists in quite a natural assumption that if for an image z we have $N_{votes}(z)$ rather close to 0 or to L than we can be more sure in the decision. This idea is directly implemented in our first naive splitting method, which selects "good" images as images, for which

$$N_{votes}(z) \leq T^{left} \text{ or } N_{votes}(z) \geq T^{right}$$

for some fixed thresholds T^{left} and T^{right}.

The next, single classification method, consists in training an additional classifier to recognize the "good" images and use this classifier as the prior classification stage. At last, we give an algorithm of how to combine these two methods.

4.2 Method 1: Naive Splitting

Our first idea was to define some thresholds T^{left} and T^{right}, such that T^{left} is close to 0 and T_{right} is close to L (the number of the base learners), and split the testing set $\mathcal{Y}$ into "good" and "bad" subsets, according to the thresholds as follows

$$\mathcal{Y} = \mathcal{Y}^{good} \cup \mathcal{Y}^{bad}, \text{where}$$

$$\mathcal{Y}^{good} = \{ y \in \mathcal{Y} \mid N_{votes}(y) \leq T^{left} \text{ or } N_{votes}(y) \geq T^{right} \},$$

$$\mathcal{Y}^{bad} = \mathcal{Y} \setminus \mathcal{Y}^{good}.$$

This idea is implemented in the Algorithm 2.

NAIVE-SPLITTING$(\mathcal{Z}, t^{left}, t^{right})$
  $\mathcal{Z}$ — the set to be splitted,
  t^{left} — the left threshold,
  t^{right} — the right threshold.

1. Train the base learners $B_l, \ldots, B_L$ on the sets $\mathcal{X}_0$ and $\mathcal{X}_1$ to distinguish between the empty/stego containers.
2. For each $z \in \mathcal{Z}$ calculate the number of base learners votes
   $$N_{votes}(z) = \sum_{l=1}^{L} B_l(z).$$
3. Obtain the set $\mathcal{Z}^{good} = \{ z \in \mathcal{Z} \mid N_{votes}(z) \leq t^{left} \text{ or } N_{votes}(z) \geq t^{right} \}$.

Result: $\mathcal{Z}^{good} \subseteq \mathcal{Z}$ — the subset of the "good" containers.

Algorithm 2. Naive Splitting

Our hypothesis was that the detection error, calculated over $\mathcal{Y}^{good}$, would be smaller than that calculated over the whole $\mathcal{Y}$. The results were as we expected, but for 0.40 bpp they were really impressing. Prior classification allowed to select about one third of images with very low error — less than 0.003 (see Table 2). This error is approximately by 50 times lower than over the whole set (see Table 1). For the other two payloads the error lowered, but not so dramatically. Moreover, the sizes of the filtered subsets were rather small.

4.3 Method 2: Single Classification

In order to make $\mathcal{Y}^{good}$ bigger we built one more classifier (this method we call the simple classification) for distinguishing between the "good" and the "bad" images (see Algorithm 3). This classification gave a drastic increase in the size of $\mathcal{Y}^{good}$, but the detection error $P_E(\mathcal{Y}^{good})$ was rather high comparing to the simple splitting (see Table 3). However, it was lower than that calculated over the whole set (see Table 1).

Table 2. Naive splitting ($\% = 100 \cdot |\mathcal{Y}^{good}|/|\mathcal{Y}|$ — the percent of the "good" images, $T^{left} = 1$, $T^{right} = L - 1$).

	HUGO 0.05 bpp			HUGO 0.10 bpp			HUGO 0.40 bpp		
L	$\|\mathcal{Y}^{good}\|$	%	$P_E(\mathcal{Y}^{good})$	$\|\mathcal{Y}^{good}\|$	%	$P_E(\mathcal{Y}^{good})$	$\|\mathcal{Y}^{good}\|$	%	$P_E(\mathcal{Y}^{good})$
100	50	1.25	0.260	271	6.76	0.140	1651	41.28	0.0042
200	31	0.76	0.258	176	4.40	0.125	1462	36.55	0.0041
300	23	0.56	0.304	137	3.43	0.124	1384	34.60	0.0022
400	16	0.40	0.313	117	2.93	0.120	1323	33.08	0.0023
500	14	0.35	0.286	106	2.65	0.123	1285	32.13	0.0016

Table 3. Single classification ($\% = 100 \cdot |\mathcal{Y}^{good}|/|\mathcal{Y}|$ — the percent of the "good" images).

		HUGO 0.05 bpp			HUGO 0.1 bpp			HUGO 0.4 bpp		
T^{left}	T^{right}	$\|\mathcal{Y}^{good}\|$	%	$P_E(\mathcal{Y}^{good})$	$\|\mathcal{Y}^{good}\|$	%	$P_E(\mathcal{Y}^{good})$	$\|\mathcal{Y}^{good}\|$	%	$P_E(\mathcal{Y}^{good})$
1	499	292	7	0.353	1198	30	0.244	1903	48	0.0189
2	499	280	7	0.346	1139	28	0.227	2022	51	0.0218
3	499	455	11	0.365	1158	29	0.225	2061	52	0.0213
1	498	232	6	0.332	1510	38	0.273	1911	48	0.0167
2	498	337	8	0.359	1189	30	0.230	2132	53	0.0225
3	498	528	13	0.371	1302	33	0.247	2009	50	0.0184
1	497	284	7	0.357	1171	29	0.243	2045	51	0.0220
2	497	340	9	0.362	1204	30	0.236	2091	52	0.0210
3	497	347	9	0.378	1182	30	0.228	2048	51	0.0215

SINGLE-CLASSIFICATION($\mathcal{Z}, t^{left}, t^{right}$)

1. Obtain the set of "good" containers
   $\mathcal{X}^{good} :=$ NAIVE-SPLITTING($\mathcal{X}, t^{left}, t^{right}$).
2. Obtain the set of "bad" containers
   $\mathcal{X}^{bad} := \mathcal{X} \setminus \mathcal{X}^{good}$.
3. Train the base learners $B'_1, \ldots, B'_M$ on the sets $\mathcal{X}^{good}$ and $\mathcal{X}^{bad}$
   to distinguish between the "good"/"bad" containers.
4. Apply the ensemble classifier for each $z \in \mathcal{Z}$ in order to classify it
   as a "good" or a "bad" container.

   (a) Calculate the number of voices $N'_{votes}(z) = \sum_{m=1}^{M} B'_k(m)$.

   (b) Obtain the set
   $\mathcal{Z}^{good} = \{z \in \mathcal{Z} \mid$ ENSEMBLE-RULE($M, N'_{votes}(z)) = 1\}$.

Result: $\mathcal{Z}^{good} \subseteq \mathcal{Z}$ — the subset of the "good" containers.

Algorithm 3. Single classification

COMBINED-CLASSIFICATION$(\mathcal{Y}, t_1^{left}, t_1^{right}, t_2^{left}, t_2^{right})$
  $\mathcal{Z}_1^{good}$ = NAIVE-SPLITTING$(\mathcal{Y}, t_1^{left}, t_1^{right})$;
  $\mathcal{Z}_2^{good}$ = SINGLE-CLASSIFICATION$(\mathcal{Y}, t_2^{left}, t_2^{right})$;
  $\mathcal{Y}^{good} = \mathcal{Z}_1^{good} \cap \mathcal{Z}_2^{good}$;
Result: $\mathcal{Y}^{good} \subseteq \mathcal{Y}$ — the subset of the "good" containers.

Algorithm 4. Combined classification

4.4 Method 3: Combined Classification

In our aspiration to build a better prior classifier, we decided to combine the two introduced methods: the naive splitting and the single classification. According to our hypothesis, using appropriate thresholds T_1^{left} and T_1^{right} — for the naive splitting, and T_2^{left} and T_2^{right} — for the single classification, would allow to distinguish a reasonably large set $\mathcal{Y}^{good}$ such that the detection error $P_E(\mathcal{Y}^{good})$ would be noticeable smaller. The formal description of the combined classification is shown in the Algorithm 4.

Due to the big amount of parameters, there are several possible schemes can be used for testing this method. We tried the following. The goal was to search for the combination of the thresholds for getting the largest subset with a fixed detection error P_E^*.

In our experiments, we fixed the detection error P_E^* and searched for those thresholds $(T_2^{left}, T_2^{right})$ which provide the largest set

$$\mathcal{Y}^{good}(T_1^{left}, T_1^{right}, T_2^{left}, T_2^{right})$$

such that the detection error calculated over this set does not exceed P_E^*. More formally,

$$(T_2^{left}(P_E^*), T_2^{right}(P_E^*)) = \underset{t^{left}, t^{right}}{argmax} \, |\mathcal{Y}^{good}(T_l^{left}, T_l^{right}, t^{left}, t^{right})|,$$

under the limitation that

$$P_E(\mathcal{Y}^{good}(T_l^{left}, T_l^{right}, t^{left}, t^{right})) \leq P_E^*.$$

Table 4. Combined prior classification (HUGO 0.1 bpp, L=500, M=1).

| | $T_1^{left} = 1$, $T_1^{right} = 499$ | | | | $T_1^{left} = 2$, $T_1^{right} = 498$ | | | |
P_E^*	$|\mathcal{Y}^{good}|$	%	T_2^{left}	T_2^{right}	$|\mathcal{Y}^{good}|$	%	T_2^{left}	T_2^{right}
0.04	187	5	1	489	202	12	2	490
0.05	230	6	2	485	251	12	2	481
0.06	252	6	4	485	303	12	17	490
0.07	346	8	19	483	391	12	27	481
0.08	401	10	33	489	463	12	30	464

Table 5. Combined prior classification (HUGO 0.05 bpp, L=500, M=11, T_1^{left} = 10, T_1^{right} = 490).

P_E^*	$|\mathcal{Y}^{good}|$	%	T_2^{left}	T_2^{right}
0.15	21	0.5	0	487
0.18	28	0.7	3	487
0.21	58	1.5	20	486
0.24	92	2.3	42	470

Table 6. Combined prior classification (HUGO 0.4 bpp, L=500, M=11, T_1^{left} = 20, T_1^{right} = 480).

P_E^*	$|\mathcal{Y}^{good}|$	%	T_2^{left}	T_2^{right}
0.00000	1481	37	1	492
0.00125	1655	41	9	492
0.00225	1680	42	9	490
0.00325	1853	46	99	492

In Tables 4, 5, 6 and 7 there are the results. In the Table 7 it is demonstrated that it is possible to find about 5 % of the BOSSbase images which provide the detection error for HUGO 0.1 bpp less than 0.05, while the error, calculated over the whole set, is about 0.37 (see Table 1) which is not quite a reliable accuracy. Thus, here we see that not a very reliable detector turns into a more reliable one.

Table 7. Combined prior classification (HUGO 0.1 bpp, L=500, M=11)

P_E^*	$T_1^{left}=1, T_1^{right}=499$				$T_1^{left}=2, T_1^{right}=498$				$T_1^{left}=10, T_1^{right}=490$			
	$|\mathcal{Y}^{good}|$	%	T_2^{left}	T_2^{right}	$|\mathcal{Y}^{good}|$	%	T_2^{left}	T_2^{right}	$|\mathcal{Y}^{good}|$	%	T_2^{left}	T_2^{right}
0.01	0	0	-	-	0	0	-	-	0	0	-	-
0.02	157	3.9	1	471	0	0	-	-	0	0	-	-
0.03	181	4.5	2	464	175	4.4	1	485	0	0	-	-
0.04	191	4.8	2	455	227	5.7	1	464	203	5.1	2	490
0.05	209	5.2	3	438	255	6.4	2	455	284	7.1	2	470
0.06	267	6.7	27	455	336	8.4	28	464	334	8.4	27	490
0.07	293	7.3	45	464	388	9.7	45	455	460	11.5	27	455
0.08	354	8.9	90	438	456	11.4	93	442	518	13.0	33	434
0.09	378	9.5	90	403	482	12.1	96	418	567	14.2	33	403
0.10	386	9.7	98	403	499	12.5	98	401	626	15.7	93	453
0.11	388	9.7	98	401	499	12.5	98	401	710	17.6	95	403

4.5 Prior Classification On-The-Fly

Above, the prior classification algorithms were described in the terms of the sets, nevertheless, all of them can be easily applied to single images. Instead of creating the set $\mathcal{Z}^{good}$ we can test the next image via the classifiers, and, in such a way, the prior classifiers will work on-the-fly.

5 Possible Applications and Future Work

5.1 Increasing the Practical Significance of Weak Detectors

The prior classification can be used for making weak detectors more practically significant. If some detector is not reliable, i.e. when its detection error over the whole set is close to 0.5, maybe the prior classification will select some set of images such that the error over this subset will be lower. For instance, in our results with HUGO 0.05 bpp, the error over the whole BOSSbase was 0.37 (see Table 1) while the prior classification turned it into a lower one albeit over a small subset (see Table 5).

5.2 Spreading Images Between Different Detectors

The prior classification might be used in order to select the most accurate detector for a given image or an image subset. For instance, if there are several different detectors available to the steganographer, she can use the prior classification for the given image, then select those detectors which will classify this image as "good", and test the image only via them. The accuracy of such a testing scheme might be higher comparing to single detectors.

5.3 Splitting Image Sets into Subsets with Different Properties

There are at least two factors which may impact the detector's accuracy: image properties and the detector itself. Therefore, if one detector has a lower detection error than another on a certain set of images, it is not necessary that it will be always the case. There are no guarantee, that the second detector will not be more accurate on some other image set with specific properties. Thus, when comparing several detectors, it might be reasonable to estimate the detection error on such sets which are obtained by collecting images with common (in some sense) properties.

The introduced method for splitting an image set into subsets of "good" and "bad" images is suitable for obtaining such sets with common properties, and, moreover, it can be used for splitting the set into more that two parts, thereby creating layers of, for example, "very good", "good", "bad" and "very bad" images. Moreover, the prior classification can be used in order to provide a ceratin size of the "good" subset via adjusting detector's parameters. It will allow to pick out a certain (prescribed) percent of images where it will be possible to detect (the absence) of steganography reliably.

5.4 Potential Enhancement of Steganalytic Detectors

If portion of "good" images is significant (certainly, it depends on the image set), then adding the prior classification phase may be used for increasing the effectiveness (accuracy or throughput) of traditional classifiers. For instance, if there is some slow but highly accurate detector (like SVM), then it can be preceded by a quicker classifier (like ensemble) which will filter out "bad" images leaving only "good" ones for the slow detector.

5.5 Extended Definition of the Accuracy

Estimating the detectors accuracy over only a certain subset of the testing set is similar to that is used in cryptography when cryptanalysts develop attacks under the assumption of the weak keys [2,10]. Such attacks are characterized not only by their complexity or success probability, but by the cardinality of the weak keys class. Similarly, stego detectors can be characterized by the detection error and the size of the subset over which this error is estimated.

6 Conclusion

In this paper we introduced a new approach to steganalysis which we call the "prior classification". This approach assumes that there is an additional prior classification stage before the final classification, which allows to select those images which would be detected with the smaller detection error comparing to the error calculated over the whole containers set. There can be various ways of how to implement the prior classification in a given particular case. In such a way we presented the three possible methods of the prior classification: the naive splitting, the simple classification, and the combination of these two methods which we call the combined classification.

According to our experiments, the prior classifiers are sensitive to the choice of the parameters (the thresholds), therefore we presented our results via the tables, where the parameters varied. But, in our opinion, the most impressing results are as follows. We demonstrated that it is possible to select about 30 % of the BOSSbase images for which HUGO 0.4 bpp steganography is detected with the error less than 0.003, while the error over the whole set is 0.141. So the error decreased by almost 50 times for the rather large subset.

We also demonstrated that it is possible to select about 5 % of the BOSSbase images which provide the detection error for HUGO 0.1 bpp less than 0.05, while the error, calculated over the whole set, is about 0.37 which is not quite a reliable accuracy. Here we see an other application of the prior classification — it allowed to turn the unreliable detector into the reliable one, albeit for the small subset.

At the end of the paper several additional potential applications of the prior classification has been discussed, among them, the extended definition of the accuracy, ability to choose the size of the "good" subset by adjusting the parameters, splitting containers sets into several subsets with different properties.

Acknowledgment. This research has been supported by the Russian Foundation of Basic Research, grant no. 14-01-31484.

References

1. Bas, P., Filler, T., Pevný, T.: Break our steganographic system: the ins and outs of organizing BOSS. In: Filler, T., Pevný, T., Craver, S., Ker, A. (eds.) IH 2011. LNCS, vol. 6958, pp. 59–70. Springer, Heidelberg (2011)
2. Biryukov, A., Nakahara Jr., J., Preneel, B., Vandewalle, J.: New weak-key classes of IDEA. In: Deng, R.H., Qing, S., Bao, F., Zhou, J. (eds.) ICICS 2002. LNCS, vol. 2513, pp. 315–326. Springer, Heidelberg (2002)
3. Duda, R., Hart, P., Stork, D.: Pattern classification, 2nd edn. Wiley, New York (2001)
4. Fridrich, J.: Rich models for steganalysis of dugital images. IEEE Trans. Inf. Forensics Secur. **7**(3), 868–882 (2012)
5. Fridrich, J., Kodovský, J., Holub, V., Goljan, M.: Steganalysis of content-adaptive steganography in spatial domain. In: Filler, T., Pevný, T., Craver, S., Ker, A. (eds.) IH 2011. LNCS, vol. 6958, pp. 102–117. Springer, Heidelberg (2011)
6. Fridrich, J., Kodovský, J., Holub, V., Goljan, M.: Steganalysis of content-adaptive steganography in spatial domain. In: Filler, T., Pevný, T., Craver, S., Ker, A. (eds.) IH 2011. LNCS, vol. 6958, pp. 102–117. Springer, Heidelberg (2011)
7. Holub, V., Fridrich, J.: Designing steganographic distortion using directional filters. In: Proceedings 4th IEEE International Workshop on Information Forensics and Security, pp. 234–239. IEEE (2012)
8. Holub, V., Fridrich, J.: Digital image steganography using universal distortion. In: Proceedings 1th ACM Workshop Information Hiding and Multimedia Security, pp. 59–68 (2013)
9. Holub, V., Fridrich, J.: Random projections of residuals for digital image steganalysis. IEEE Trans. Inf. Forensics Secur. **8**(12), 1996–2006 (2013)
10. Kara, O., Manap, C.: A new class of weak keys for blowfish. In: Biryukov, A. (ed.) FSE 2007. LNCS, vol. 4593, pp. 167–180. Springer, Heidelberg (2007)
11. Ker, A., et al.: Moving steganography and steganalysis from the laboratory into the real world. In: Proceedings 1st ACM Workshop on Information Hiding and Multimedia Security, pp. 45–58. ACM (2013)
12. Kodovsky, J., Fridrich, J., Holub, V.: Ensemble classifiers for steganalysis of digital media. IEEE Trans. Inf. Forensics Secur. **7**(2), 434–444 (2011)
13. Monarev, V., Pestunov, A.: A known-key scenario for steganalysis and a highly accurate detector within it. In: Proceedings IEEE 10th International Conference on Intelligent Information Hiding and Multimedia Signal Processing, pp. 175–178. IEEE (2014)
14. Pevny, T., Bas, P., Fridrich, J.: Steganalysis by subtractive pixel adjacency matrix. IEEE Trans. Inf. Forensics Secur. **5**(2), 215–224 (2010)
15. Pevny, T.: Detecting messages of unknown length. In: Proceedings 8th Media Watermarking, Security and Forensics, pp. 1–12 (2011)
16. Pevný, T., Filler, T., Bas, P.: Using high-dimensional image models to perform highly undetectable steganography. In: Böhme, R., Fong, P.W.L., Safavi-Naini, R. (eds.) IH 2010. LNCS, vol. 6387, pp. 161–177. Springer, Heidelberg (2010)
17. Feature Extractors for Steganalysis. http://dde.binghamton.edu/download/feature_extractors/

18. Break our watermarking system 2nd ed. http://bows2.ec-lille.fr/
19. Break our steganographic system. http://www.agents.cz/boss/
20. NRCS photo gallery. http://photogallery.nrcs.usda.gov/

Eavesdropper: A Framework for Detecting the Location of the Processed Result in Hadoop

Chuntao Dong[1,2], Qingni Shen[1,2(✉)], Wenting Li[1,2], Yahui Yang[1,2], Zhonghai Wu[1,2], and Xiang Wan[1]

[1] School of Software and Microelectronics, Peking University, Beijing, China
{chuntaodong,wenlingli}@pku.edu.cn,
cowforkl990@hotmail.com,
{qingnishen,yhyang,wuzh}@ss.pku.edu.cn
[2] MoE Key Lab of Network and Software Assurance,
Peking University, Beijing, China

Abstract. Hadoop has become increasingly popular as it rapidly processes big data in parallel, while security mechanisms have been introduced or studied for Hadoop. In addition, other security issues that should not be neglected still exist. Data leakage is one of the major security challenges. This paper studies the vulnerability of authorization mechanism of services in Hadoop and the threat of information leakage. Some authorization mechanism allow all users to access services by default, an adversary can utilize these services to collect information of other users. We design and implement Eavesdropper, a framework which utilizes k-means clustering to address the nodes that store the processed results. We conduct a comprehensive of experiments, which clearly demonstrate that our detection framework is capable of detecting the nodes that store the results.

Keywords: Hadoop · MapReduce · YARN · Security · Data leakage · k-means

1 Introduction

Hadoop has become a major platform for big data. However, the research on Hadoop has mainly focused on the performance, and the security issues have not received sufficient attention. For Hadoop's initial purpose, it was always assumed that clusters in a trusted environment [9]. Therefore, since there were few security controls within Hadoop, many accidents and security incidents happened in such environments [8]. To enhance Hadoop system security, authentication and authorization are definitely necessary [2]. To our knowledge, insider attack can use the vulnerability of the security mechanisms configured by default to steal key value. We propose a framework for detecting the nodes that store the key value to prove the threat. Because the distributed characteristics of Hadoop, it is hard for insider attacker to locate the key value. To address these concerns, we propose Eavesdropper which is a novel, modular detection framework that can locate the key value.

© Springer International Publishing Switzerland 2016
S. Qing et al. (Eds.): ICICS 2015, LNCS 9543, pp. 458–466, 2016.
DOI: 10.1007/978-3-319-29814-6_39

Our Contribution. In summary, our work makes three key contributions:

- *The vulnerability analysis of the authorization mechanism in Hadoop:* If some authorization of services are configured by default is unsafe. We have highlighted the importance of ensuring the authorization of Hadoop is not configured by default.
- *A framework for detecting the nodes that store results:* If existing security mechanisms is not configured correctly, the adversary can get sensitive information of other users, but adversary cannot verify these nodes artificially. We propose a framework for detecting the DataNodes that store results.
- *Combination of vulnerability and detection framework:* Based on our detecting framework, we utilize the vulnerability of security mechanism that allows users to check information of applications in cluster and containers in a node to implement a detection scheme.

Paper Organization. We introduce the background in Sect. 2, and analyze threat and propose the detection framework in Sect. 3. The proposed detection scheme is elaborated in Sect. 4. Section 5 presents the implements and experimental results. We conclude the paper in Sect. 6.

2 Background

This section provides the background information on YARN and security mechanism of Hadoop [3–5].

YARN. In Hadoop 2.0 the classic MapReduce [7] module is upgraded into a new computing platform, called YARN [12]. YARN provides the ability to execute user code across machines in a cluster. This user code is executed in the container. Each container has an identity (Container ID). An application instance also has an identity (Application ID). There is a relation between them. Container ID is achieved by using the application ID along with a monotonically increasing counter for the container. This paper aims to address the vulnerability of unconstrained web port in Hadoop and the attacks of stealing high-value information to a Hadoop cluster with multi-tenancy. YARN provides system management interface for user to browse information of applications running in the cluster and containers running in the nodes. The default HTTP port is 8088, it is deployed on RM showing the Applications' information, such as the current queue backlog, resource utilization, application execution and so on, as illustrated in Fig. 1. This web UI opens up result in a number of potential issues [1].

The Security Mechanism of Hadoop. System security mechanism usually consists of two parts: authentication and authorization. Hadoop security relies on Kerberos and Tokens for authentication and relies on access control list (ACL) for authorization [10]. In Hadoop, Kerberos is used for client authentication at the "entry points" only. These entry points are master services like the NameNode, RM and HistoryServer. By default, the Kerberos authentication is disabled for Hadoop, which default is "simple".

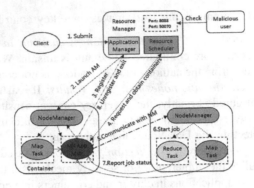

Fig. 1. The architecture of YARN

Hadoop relies on access control list (ACL) for authorization. According to the authorized entity, it can be divided into Map Reduce job Queue ACLs, Map Reduce Job ACLs, Service Endpoint ACLs [8]. Service Endpoint ACLs: All RPC endpoints can have ACLs applied at the protocol layer. These ACLs can control the users and groups that can access a given service protocol.

3 Vulnerability and Threat

In this section, we analyze the vulnerability of security mechanism in Hadoop and present a framework for detecting the DataNodes that store key value.

Vulnerability Analysis. As discussed in Sect. 2, Hadoop employ authentication and authorization to enhance system security. Hadoop relies on access control list (ACL) for authorization. These ACLs can control the users and groups that can access a given service protocol. By default, some protocols open to all users and groups. We believe that any shared web port left unconstrained will be a vulnerability. This vulnerability may be utilized by malicious to threaten system security and steal data of other users in the cluster. In the next part of this section, we propose a detection framework for detecting the DataNodes that store results to prove the threat of leaking key value pairs.

Threat Model. We assume adversary is regarded as trusted but have malicious intentions. He tries to steal sensitive results from other user that he is not allowed to access. The model of the detecting the nodes that store the results is depicted in Fig. 2. There are three types of entities:

User: These entities have data to be stored in the cluster and interact with the Hadoop Cluster to manage their data and submit applications on the cluster.
Adversary: The adversary intends to steal the processed results of other users in the cluster. He collects information by utilizing the service of cluster and analyzes the nodes that store results.
Hadoop Cluster: The Hadoop cluster provides resources and services for users.

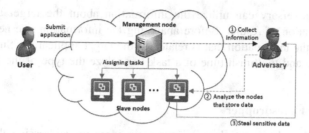

Fig. 2. The model of detecting the node storing the results

In the following section, we proposed a detection framework based on the threat model.

4   Detection Framework

We start with a sample scenario where the cluster is only shared between two parties, i.e., the adversary and the victim. Based on the threat model, we proposed Eavesdropper to locate the nodes that store results. Figure 3 demonstrates a sample architecture of Eavesdropper. The location detection mainly consists of two stages: Probing and Analysis. In our analysis for above identified threat, we have the following assumption.

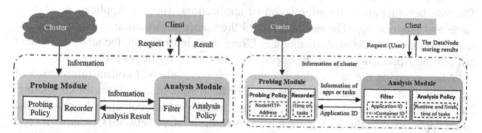

Fig. 3. A sample architecture of Eavesdropper. **Fig. 4.** A detailed architecture of Eavesdropper.

Assumption: The security mechanism is configured by default, users can easily access the services and get information of tasks in the cluster.

Probing. If an adversary and a victim are running synchronously, the adversary can trace the running process of victim's application and collect information about the application. For example, the adversary can utilize open service port to get information of the application. We should implement the probing policy according to practical scene. After capturing the information, we use the recorder to record the information.

Analysis. An adversary can utilize the information about the target application to analyze the location of results. Before analyzing the information, we need to use the filter to screen the information that is related to the target application. Such as, we can use the runtime and the finish time of a task to analyze the type of the task.

4.1 Detailed Eavesdropper

In the previous analysis, we describe our main ideas for addressing the two stages respectively. Note that we focus on the probing and analysis, and discuss the detailed design of the detection scheme in the next two part of the Section. We extend Eavesdropper by utilizing the open service port and related mechanism of YARN. Figure 4 demonstrates a detailed architecture of Eavesdropper. We realize Eavesdropper by utilizing the open service port and the relation between Application ID and Container ID. In the following of this section, we will describe our scheme in detail. We examine Eavesdropper in Sect. 5.

4.2 The Design of Probing Module

In this part, we will introduce the implement of probing module. The main function of probing module is that collect information of applications and tasks. The adversary intends to steal processed result of target user. He needs to collect and analyze information to confirm which application is submitted by the target user firstly. The adversary can achieve this by scanning the management interface of all applications. The interface including the information of applications, such as Application ID, user name and progress etc. The recorder record the related information of target user and send information to the analysis module. Using these information, the analysis module can get the Application ID of the application submitted by target user.

After receiving the application ID, the probing module will collect information of the application. An application needs to apply for a mass of containers for computing. Each node has a mass of containers, we must identify which container belongs to the target application. In the Sect. 2, we have known the relation between Container ID and Application ID. We will use this relation to collect information of target application. The process of collecting and recording information of the target application is cyclic until the application finish running. The steps are detailed below:

(1) Scan nodes management interface of the cluster to get the NodeHTTPAddress of all the nodes in the cluster. The address is the address to access each node of the cluster.
(2) Access the NodeHTTPAddress of each node to collect and record the information of containers that belong to the target application on the node.
(3) Using the relation between Container ID and Application ID to screen out the containers that belong to the target application.
(4) Using the recorder to record the container IDs, running node, start time and finish time of each container. We will use the record of containers to analyze the type of the task running in the container in the subsequent section.

4.3   The Design of Analysis Module

The analysis module is the critical module in proposed detection scheme and its main function is to analyze the node that store result of the target application. In the last part, we have recorded the information of containers. We need to analyze which container was used for a reduce task. Because we know that the result of a mapreduce job is generated by reduce task. Compared to map task, the reduce task finish later because the reduce task need to wait the relevant map task finish running. When the reduce task finish running, the node that the reduce task running on will upload the result to the HDFS at once [11]. HDFS's placement policy is to put one replication on the local node firstly, we can confirm that one replication of the result is on the local node.

The Analysis Policy. Our goal is to find out all the reduce task(s) of the target job. We provide a solution that utilizes k-means clustering [6]. In our solution, we utilize the runtime and the finish time of tasks to analyze the type of tasks. The runtime of reduce tasks is longer than that of map tasks and the reduce tasks finish later than map tasks. Our solution aims to partition the n observations into 2 sets $S = \{S_{map}, S_{reduce}\}$, where each observation is a 2-dimensional real vector that consists of the runtime R_n and finish time T_n of each tasks. The computing task that firstly start to run must be a map task, and the computing task that finish running last must be a reduce task. We initial $(T1, R1)$ to μ_1 and (T_n, R_n) to μ_2. The algorithm proceeds by alternating between two steps:

Assignment step: Assign each observation to the cluster whose mean yields the least within-cluster sum of squares. Our goal is make the value of J that in the formula (1) as small as possible, if data point n is categorized into cluster k, r_{nk} equals 1, otherwise r_{nk} equals 0.

$$J = \sum_{n=1}^{N} \sum_{k=1}^{K} r_{nk} \|x_n - \mu_k\|^2 \tag{1}$$

$$\mu_k = \frac{1}{N_k} \sum_{j \in clusterk} x_j \tag{2}$$

Update step: Calculate the new means to be the centroids of the observations in the new clusters. The value of μ_k is the average value of all the data points of cluster k. We use the formula (2) to calculate the new center point of each cluster.

After we have detected these DataNodes that store result, we need to find the result in the DataNode. We assume that we have invaded in these DataNodes. It is difficult to pick out the datablock of the target application in a DataNode. We utilize a relation between the finish time of reduce task and the modified time of data block to search the result. The modified time approximatively equals the finish time of reduce task plus the time that upload data. We can seek out the data block based on the relation.

The problem of the solution is that the failed tasks may be clustered by mistake. For example, when a map task may be delayed, the map task will run longer and finish later that may make it looks like a reduce job. The data that we aim to steal may be encrypted after computed, but encrypt do not mean safe completely. Our main focus is the process of computing data, data is unencrypted in the computing process, we can steal data before data encrypted and uploaded to HDFS.

5   Implementation and Experimental Results

5.1   Implementation

We have implemented a detection software in JAVA language. We conducted several experiments using the local 64-bit Centos operation system with an Intel Core i7 processor running at 3.4 GHz, 4096 MB of RAM, and run Hadoop 2.6.0. The configuration of our Hadoop cluster is of one NameNode, one RM, ten NodeManagers, ten NataNodes.

5.2   Experiment Results

In this section, we select a standard benchmark for evaluating our detection solution. The 7 benchmark applications cover a wide range of data-intensive tasks: compute intensive, shuffle intensive, database queries, and iterative. The size of the input data is between 1 GB and 1.5 GB in these case studies. We run 20 experiments of each benchmark applications to verify if our scheme can detect the reduce tasks accurately and efficiently.

In the first experiment, we run a wordcount job that consists 6 map tasks and 2 reduce tasks to verify the availability of our solution. We record the finish time and runtime of all the tasks and analyze the record. According to the analysis policy, we choose two initial means Container_03(C_03), Container_08 as μ_1, μ_2. Then, we use the k-means clustering to partition the n computing tasks into 2 sets S = {S_{map}, S_{reduce}}. The partition result is S_{map} = {C_02, C_03, C_04, C_05, C_06, C_07} and S_{reduce} = {C_08, C_09}. We run several jobs including target job and several other jobs in the other runs simultaneously. Our solution also detected the reduce tasks successfully and efficiently (Table 1).

Table 1. A wordcount job that consists of 6 map tasks and 2 reduce tasks.

Container ID	Start time	Finish time	Runtime(s)	Task type	Analysis result
Container_01	17:10:20	17:11:01	41	AplicationMaster	
Container_02	17:10:28	17:10:44	16	Map task	
Container_03	17:10:26	17:10:43	17	Map task	
Container_04	17:10:28	17:10:45	17	Map task	
Container_05	17:10:27	17:10:43	16	Map task	
Container_06	17:10:28	17:10:46	18	Map task	
Container_07	17:10:30	17:10:45	15	Map task	
Container_08	17:10:47	17:10:56	9	Reduce task	Rack1Node5
Container_09	17:10:48	17:10:55	7	Reduce task	Rack1Node3

We use other 6 benchmark applications to evaluate the accuracy of our solution. We summarize and analyze the accuracy of 7 benchmark applications, as shown in Table 2. We find that the analysis accuracy of some benchmark application is not 100 %. By analyzing the feature of each type of benchmark applications, we find out the applications which the runtime of map and reduce tasks is similar are easily interferential. We will improve our solution in the future work and make our detection software more reliable.

Table 2. Summary of the runtime of tasks and the analysis accuracy of 7 benchmark applications.

Job type	Num. of experiments	Num. of map tasks	Num. of reduce tasks	Runtime of map tasks	Runtime of reduce tasks	Num. of analysis successfully	Analysis accuracy
Wordcount	20	6	2	17.2	7.8	20	100 %
Index	20	8	5	50.5	15.7	19	100 %
Grep	20	8	5	18.9	15.4	16	80 %
Aggregate	20	16	8	4.7	10.1	18	90 %
Join	20	16	8	7.8	22.8	19	95 %
Pagerank	20	24	10	10.8	24.6	19	95 %
Kmeans	20	24	10	18.2	37.5	18	90 %

6   Conclusion

In this paper, we proposed a framework for detecting the node that stores key value and analyzed the vulnerability of the authorization mechanism of services in Hadoop. Combining these two aspects, we implemented a new detection scheme to detect the nodes that store the processed result in MapReduce successfully. Our experiment results demonstrated the effectiveness of our detecting framework of three cases in real-world systems, we had confirmed that the proposed detection program based on detection framework can detect the nodes that store the processed result.

Although our framework and detection scheme is implemented in experimental environment, we can improve and use it in the cloud with multiple users. In the future work, we aim at extending the approach to a larger set of application level vulnerabilities and propose a learning algorithm to classify type of tasks, as well as defining a sophisticated method able to detect Information Eavesdropping attacks in the cloud computing environment.

Acknowledgment. This work is supported by the National High Technology Research and Development Program ("863" Program) of China under Grant No. 2015AA016009, the National Natural Science Foundation of China under Grant No. 61232005, and the Science and Technology Program of Shen Zhen, China under Grant No. JSGG2014051 6162852628.

References

1. Apache hadoop. http://hadoop.apache.org
2. Sharma, A., Kalbarczyk, Z., Barlow, J.: Analysis of security data from a large computing organization. In: IEEE 41st International Conference on Dependable Systems Networks, pp. 506–517. IEEE (2011)
3. Hadoop in Secure Mode. http://hadoop.apache.org/docs/current/hadoop-project-dist/hadoop-common/SecureMode.html
4. Ulusoy, H., Colombo, P., Ferrari, E.: GuardMR: fine-grained security policy enforcement for mapreduce system. In: ASIACCS 2015, pp. 285–296. ACM (2015)
5. Lahmer, I., Zhang, N.: MapReduce: MR model abstraction for future security study. In: International Conference on Security of Information and Networks, pp. 392–398. ACM (2014)
6. Hartigan, J.A., Wong, M.A.: Algorithm AS 136: a k-means clustering algorithm. J. Roy. Stat. Soc. Ser. C **28**(1), 100–108 (1979). Wiley for the Royal Statistical Society
7. Dean, J., Ghenmawat, S.: Mapreduce: simplified data processing on large clusters. In: OSDI 2004, pp.137–150. ACM (2004)
8. Huang, J., Nicol, D.M., Campbell, R.H.: Denial-of-Service threat to hadoop/YARN clusters with multi-tenancy. In: IEEE International Congress on Big Data (2014)
9. Smith, K.T.: Big Data Security: The Evolution of Hadoop's Security Model (2013)
10. O'Malley, O., Zhang, K., Radia, S.: Hadoop security design. In: Yahoo! Tech Rep (2009)
11. White, T.: Hadoop: The Definitve Guide, 3rd Edition, pp. 43–79. O'Reilly, Sebastopol (2012)
12. Vavilapalli, V.K., Murthy, A.C., Douglas, C.: Apache hadoop YARN: yet another resource negotiator. In: Proceedings of the 4th Annual Symposium on Cloud Computing, vol. 5. ACM (2013)

Secret Picture: An Efficient Tool for Mitigating Deletion Delay on OSN

Shangqi Lai[1]([✉]), Joseph K. Liu[2],
Kim-Kwang Raymond Choo[3,4], and Kaitai Liang[5]

[1] Department of Computer Science,
The University of Hong Kong, Hong Kong, Hong Kong
aquas@connect.hku.hk
[2] Faculty of Information Technology, Monash University, Clayton, Australia
joseph.liu@monash.edu
[3] School of Information Technology and Mathematical Sciences,
University of South Australia, Adelaide, Australia
raymond.choo@unisa.edu.au
[4] INTERPOL Global Complex for Innovation, Singapore, Singapore
raymond.choo@fulbrightmail.org
[5] Department of Computer Science, Aalto University, Espoo, Finland
kaitai.liang@aalto.fi

Abstract. With the increasing popularity of online social networks (OSNs) and the ability to access and exchange sensitive user information, user privacy concerns become an important issue which have attracted the attention of researchers and policymakers. For example, deleted pictures or pictures in deleted posts may not be deleted from the OSN server immediately, and hence accessible to another unauthorized user. In this paper, we highlight the deletion delay issue in seven popular OSNs, namely: Facebook, Instagram, MySpace, Tumblr, Flickr, Google+ and Weibo, which can be exploited by another unauthorized user to gain access to these pictures. To ensure OSN users are able to achieve a higher level of privacy, we propose a conceptual privacy-preserving tool for photo sharing, without compromising on transparency and real-time sharing features. We demonstrate the utility of the tool by prototyping a browser extension, which does not require modification of existing OSN systems.

Keywords: Online social networks · Deletion delay · Privacy attacks · Privacy-preserving for social networks · Photo sharing

1 Introduction

Online social network (OSN) providers, such as Facebook, Twitter, and Google+, provide an effective platform for its users to conduct real-time communication. For example, users can update their status, check-in, post a comment and upload other user-generated content (e.g. text, picture, and video) in the social networks.

© Springer International Publishing Switzerland 2016
S. Qing et al. (Eds.): ICICS 2015, LNCS 9543, pp. 467–477, 2016.
DOI: 10.1007/978-3-319-29814-6_40

It is no surprising that the popularity of OSN has extended to users of different ages, countries and cultures.

However, when users disclose personal or sensitive information about themselves on the OSN, they are often unaware of the privacy implications. For example, who is able to access these information, and how these information can be mined or abused by, say, a cyberstalker or a criminal (e.g. publicly accessible home address information, holiday pictures, and wall posts such as "I am on holidays at Puerto Rico" will be targeted by opportunistic burglars). Consequently, OSN users may suffer financial loss, physical harm, etc. Although major OSN providers have put in place privacy and other related policies to ensure the security and privacy of user data, most users may not be familiar but the privacy settings. For example, OSN providers, such as Google+, can have in place extensive policies and measures to prevent accidental leakage of user information (e.g. public, and list of friends), for example, by providing users with the visibility of their data; users may not always choose the appropriate settings to preserve the privacy of their data. In addition, malicious actors, such as spammers and phishers, are on the constant lookout for ways to learn user data from OSNs.

In this paper, we discuss about the privacy issues associated with user-uploaded pictures as pictures may contain rich information, such as metadata, that can be extracted by a third-party (including a cybercriminal). For example, in a group picture taken at a kid's birthday party and uploaded to an OSN may provide a stalker with information such as the exact date of birth for the kid, who the parents and friends are, what school the kid go to, where the kid stay, what are the kid's interests, etc. More specifically, we want to highlight a less understood risk – **Deletion Delay**. In deletion delay, deleted pictures or pictures in deleted posts are preserved by the OSN providers and these pictures may be accessible to anyone with knowledge of the picture's URL.

In this paper, we study the deletion delay issue in popular OSNs. We then propose a privacy-preserving tool to address the deletion delay. In our solution, we design and implement the tool in a browser extension, which allows one to encrypt pictures at the user-end prior to uploading to the OSN. A third-party server is then used to store the secret key and sharing list of the user. By encrypting the online pictures, even if one of your friends decides to share the pictures with others, a new sharing list will be required to access these pictures.

2   Background

2.1   Problem Statement

Before introducing the problem, we briefly review the basic features available in OSNs [10]:

- Post/share picture: Almost all popular OSNs allow registered users to upload and share their pictures (and/or videos). For instance, Google+ users can click on the "photo" button and select a picture on the local device or a Google album to be posted. Users can generally control the extent of sharing. If they only choose to share the picture with a specified list of friends, then only friends in the list can access the picture. Hence, users can make the picture private by including only themselves in the sharing list. According to [10], OSNs such Facebook and Instagram use a similar mechanism to manage user access permission.

– Obtain URL of picture: Authorized users can access the pictures uploaded to OSNs via the URLs, which can be obtained by right-clicking on the particular picture and copying the URL (i.e. "Copy URL"). This method is available in popular OSNs, such as Facebook, Twitter, Tumblr and MySpace [10]. Although some OSNs providers do not provide such a feature, browsers such as Google Chrome has the "Inspect element" feature that allows the user to access the html code of the website, and locate the URL in the source code. Needless to say that the access control mechanism employ by these OSNs providers will not stop unauthorized user access to the pictures via URLs.

– Delete picture/post: The user can simply click "Delete" to remove the picture/post from the OSNs.

Deletion delay refers to the problem that when an user attempts to delete their posts. While the post will disappear from the user's profile (e.g. in Facebook, the user's wall) immediately, the picture is still stored on the OSN servers, perhaps with the exception of Twitter as noted in [10]. Therefore, anyone can access the deleted picture by accessing the original URL.

Table 1 details our study of eight popular OSNs. We found that with the exception of Twitter, most of the OSNs have a deletion delay of over three days. In the case of Weibo (the most widely used OSN in mainland China), many developers use this as a third-party Image Storage Service [15] because it has a long deletion delay. We found that pictures in the deleted post three years ago could still be accessible online.

Table 1. Deletion delay of different online social networks, adapted from [10]

Platforms	Day(s)
Facebook	7
Twitter	Immediately
Instagram	3
MySpace	> 30
Tumblr	> 30
Flickr	14
Google+	< 1
Weibo	> 1124

If the deleted pictures have been shared with other OSN users prior to deletion, the thumbnail images or a copy of the deleted picture may still be recoverable and accessible, as shown in recent studies (e.g. from Windows devices [11] and from Android [9] devices).

Observations from our study are as follow:

1. Some OSN providers may copy the link of the original picture directly. Hence, if the source platform has a deletion delay, then the target platform will have the same delay issue;
2. Some OSN providers use shared links associated with the original copy of the shared picture. These shared links will expire when the original copy is deleted; and
3. Although shared links can be removed, some OSN providers provide a thumbnail of the shared picture in the destination platform timeline. The thumbnail will be kept in the timeline when the original copy is deleted;

2.2   Countermeasures

While deletion delay can potentially compromise the privacy of a user's privacy, there are several potential solutions.

Eliminating the deletion delay is an obvious solution, and in theory, this is an action that can be easily undertaken by OSN providers. However, in practice, it had been noted by various independent sources (see [5,14]) that Facebook maintain copies of the user pictures on their servers after the users have decided to delete the pictures and posts. It was noted that from the calendar years 2010 to 2012, the deletion delay decreased from three years to 30 days, and in 2015 [10], the picture became unavailable seven days after the deletion. But from the perspective of the OSN providers, the practicality of this approach relies on the data structure. Searching and removing a single picture in more than a million resources is a very challenging task. Deletion requests may result in significant overhead and delay, as these requests needed to be forwarded to different data centers all over the world, and each data center deals with thousands of requests at any one time.

Users can also choose to encrypt the picture prior to uploading, such as using the traditional public key encryption [7,12], identity-based encryption [4,13], and attribute-based encryption [3,8]. It is more reliable as these measures ensure that any pictures uploaded and shared online are encrypted. In practice, ONS providers never offer such service, therefore, with the increasing number of friends and shared photos, the key management will become increasingly complex and unwieldy, if user should do it on his own. The user would need to deliver the decryption key to all friends in the sharing list after the user has uploaded an encrypted picture. Once the user decides to revoke this sharing, the user would need to use a new encryption key to encrypt the pictures and request the server to delete the old encrypted pictures. This is an inefficient and impractical solution.

In this paper, we address the following research challenge: "Can we design a new mechanism to mitigate the overhead in key generation and distribution, while managing shared list in a simple and efficient way?".

3   Our Conceptual Privacy Preserving Tool

3.1   Our Approach

To address the research challenge identified in the preceding section, we consider the principles. Firstly, there is no doubt that local encryption (i.e. encryption at the user-end) is preferred, as it provides the user more control over the picture (including shared links and thumbnails). Secondly, the solution should not burden users with key management, and this can be achieved using a sharing list and the encryption/decryption key approach as we will describe in this section (see our browser extension).

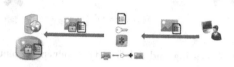

Fig. 1. Posting of picture

Posting of picture (see Fig. 1). Once a user posts / uploads a picture to an OSN platform using a browser, the browser extension generates a symmetric key randomly, and encrypts the picture using a pre-determined symmetric encryption algorithm. In our prototype described in Sect. 3.2, we use Advanced Encryption Standard (AES)-256 bit encryption [1]. The picture is then posted to the OSN platform. Upon receiving the request and encrypted picture from the browser, the OSN platform will store the encrypted picture and generate a URL for accessing the encrypted picture. The browser extension will call the corresponding API to upload the picture and obtain the URL, as well as storing the key-value pair of the symmetric key and the picture identity (i.e. the URL of original copy) on the local device by calling localStorage API in HTML5 [2]. Therefore, other OSN users will only be able to see an encrypted picture. Even if the users have the URL of the encrypted picture, they will not be able to view the picture without having access to the decryption key.

Accessing encrypted picture (see Fig. 2(a)). When the picture owner and users who have been granted the access right wish to access the encrypted picture, the OSN server will send the encrypted picture to the respective user's browser extension. This (plug-in) extension verifies the access rights specified by the sharing list. If the user is in the sharing list or the user is the owner, the extension will use the corresponding symmetric key to decrypt the encrypted picture, and present the (decrypted) picture to the user.

Deleting encrypted picture (see Fig. 2(b)). When the picture owner decides to delete the picture, then a "delete" request will be sent to the browser extension and the OSN platform. The extension then deletes the symmetric key associated with the picture. When an user who have been previously granted access to the

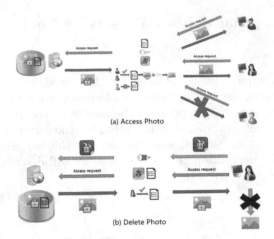

(a) Access Photo

(b) Delete Photo

Fig. 2. Accessing and deleting the encrypted picture

deleted picture wishes to view the picture, the extension will check and determine that the picture has been deleted (i.e. corresponding symmetric key cannot be located), and therefore, not able to decrypt the encrypted picture.

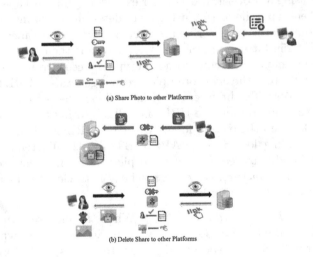

(a) Share Photo to other Platforms

(b) Delete Share to other Platforms

Fig. 3. Share and delete photo on other platforms

Sharing encrypted picture to other OSN platform (see Fig. 3(a)). When the (encrypted) picture is shared on other OSN platforms, the original OSN server generates a link for the third-party platform to access the encrypted picture. The browser extension obtains a new key-value pair of the symmetric key and picture identity. If a user on the third-party OSN platform requests for the encrypted picture, the extension will check against the sharing list and decrypt the picture if the requesting user is included in the sharing list. Otherwise, the decryption will not take place.

Deleting encrypted picture from other OSN platform (see Fig. 3(b)). When the user decides to delete the picture, the user will send a "delete" request to the browser extension and the OSN platform. Upon receipt, the OSN platform will delete the shared link. At the same time, the browser extension will also delete associated symmetric key. Subsequent request to access the deleted picture will be unsuccessful, as the decryption key associated with the encrypted picture has been deleted by the browser extension.

3.2   Our Prototype

We design a plug-in extension for Google Chrome – see Fig. 4.

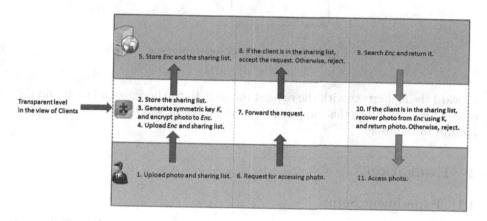

Fig. 4. An overview of our approach

The extension (see Fig. 5) uses the API from the respective OSNs, and consists of three components, namely: a popup interface, background and content script.

The popup interface allows an user to authorize the extension to access the respective API. Users also manage the sharing list using the popup interface. The users post / upload pictures using the page, and the pictures will be encrypted by Forge [6] prior to calling the corresponding OSN API. Immediately following this, the extension stores the sharing list and key-value pair on the local device.

Background is an invisible page, but both popup and the content script are able to access this page resource. Background plays the role of the daemon process to store sensitive information, such as the sharing list and key-value pair records. It also runs the decryption asynchronously.

Content script monitors specific webpage by registering listener. When the content script detects a picture identity, it will check against the sharing list, and

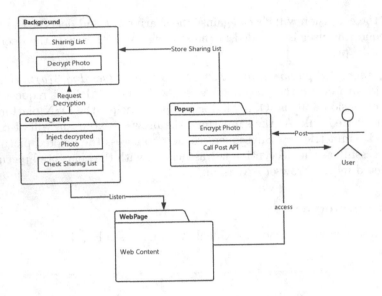

Fig. 5. An overview of our prototype

forward the ciphertext with the request message to the background to obtain the original picture. Once this happens, the content script will display the decrypted picture to the user.

4 Evaluation

4.1 Experiment Setup

To conduct the evaluation, we establish a developer account in Sina Weibo and for Google Chrome. We create a new App in Sina Weibo to facilitate the extension obtaining authorization and calling of the API. Meanwhile, we create an extension in Google Chrome store to obtain the application ID and provide callback URL for authorization.

In the evaluation, we upload pictures saved in JPG format to avoid compression by the OSN, and we change the settings to remove Weibo's watermark.

We measure the following performance metrics: time taken to encrypt pictures of different file sizes (as this affects performance), and the loading time of the encrypted picture.

4.2 Evaluation Result

Figure 6 shows the evaluation results of a picture saved in different resolutions and hence, file sizes. At a resolution of $3647 * 2736$, we need $20.424\,s$ to encrypt the picture. However, we remark that users seldom upload such high resolution pictures to Weibo. If the picture is compressed to $2048 * 1536$, it only takes a third of the time to encrypt the picture. The encryption time required descreases exponentially with the picture resolution. For example, a picture with $1024 * 768$ pixels only requires 1.736s, which may not be noticed by the average user.

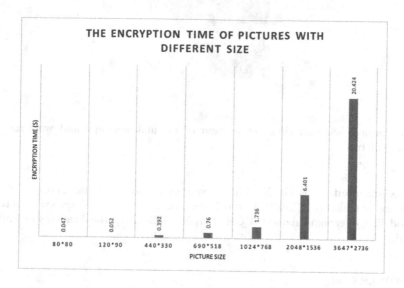

Fig. 6. The average encryption time of pictures with different size

When a webpage loads on the browser, it will firstly load the document object model (DOM, which assists front-end code to build the HTML) by parsing the respective element. It will then apply the CSS and execute the JavaScript code with the page load event, prior to rendering the webpage. Users can view the page contents, although the page may be incomplete during the page load stage. Figure 7 shows the average load time observed in our evaluations. As our extension will check the sharing list during the DOM loading stage, this process may slow down the DOM loading for up to 5 s, which will not adversely affect the average user's experience since users can continue to browse the webpage during this loading stage.

5   Conclusion

In this paper, we highlighted an understudied risk due to deletion delay of pictures from popular OSNs. We then presented the design of a novel privacy-preserving too to address the deletion delay issue. Based on the evaluation of our prototype (i.e. a Google Chrome plug-in extension), we demonstrated that our approach is practical and suitable for real-world deployment.

Future work will include improving the Google Chrome plug-in extension, building plug-ins for other popular browsers, and extending the support to more OSNs. We will also study the viability of other general approaches not restricted by API (i.e. only can be called several times per hour) to address deletion delay.

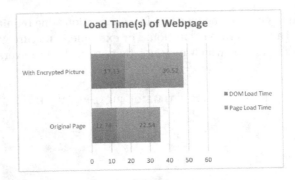

Fig. 7. The average load time comparison of original webpage and webpage with encrypted picture

Acknowledgments. Joseph K. Liu is supported by National Natural Science Foundation of China (61472083). Kaitai Liang is supported by privacy-aware retrieval and modelling of genomic data (PRIGENDA, No. 13283250), the Academy of Finland, Finland.

References

1. Announcing the ADVANCED ENCRYPTION STANDARD (AES). No. 197 in Federal Information Processing Standards Publication, United States National Institute of Standards and Technology (NIST) (2001)
2. HTML5 Specification. World Wide Web Consortium (W3C) (2015)
3. Bethencourt, J., Sahai, A., Waters, B.: Ciphertext-Policy Attribute-Based Encryption. In: 2007 IEEE Symposium on Security and Privacy (S&P 2007), pp. 321–334, Oakland, California, USA (2007)
4. Boneh, D., Franklin, M.: Identity-based encryption from the weil pairing. In: Kilian, J. (ed.) CRYPTO 2001. LNCS, vol. 2139, pp. 213–229. Springer, Heidelberg (2001)
5. Cheng, J.: Ars Technica: Three Years Later, Deleting Your Photos on Facebook Now Actually Works. http://arstechnica.com/business/2012/08/facebook-finally-changes-photo-deletion-policy-after-3-years-of-reporting
6. Digital Bazaar, I.: Forge: Javascript security and cryptography. http://digitalbazaar.com/forge/
7. Gamal, T.E.: A public key cryptosystem and a signature scheme based on discrete logarithms. IEEE Trans. Inf. Theor. **31**(4), 469–472 (1985)
8. Goyal, V., Pandey, O., Sahai, A., Waters, B.: Attribute-based encryption for fine-grained access control of encrypted data. In: Proceedings of the 13th ACM Conference on Computer and Communications Security, CCS 2006, pp. 89–98. ACM, Alexandria, VA, USA, October 30 - November 3, 2006
9. Leom, M.D., D'Orazio, C.J., Deegan, G., Choo, K.K.R.: Forensic collection and analysis of thumbnails in android. In: 14th IEEE International Conference on Trust, Security and Privacy in Computing and Communications, pp. 1059–1066. IEEE Computer Society Press (2015)
10. Liang, K., Liu, J.K., Lu, R., Wong, D.S.: Privacy concerns for photo sharing in online social networks. IEEE Internet Comput. **19**(2), 58–63 (2015)

11. Quick, D., Tassone, C., Choo, K.R.: Forensic Analysis of Windows Thumbcache files. In: 20th Americas Conference on Information Systems, AMCIS 2014, Savannah, Georgia, USA, 7–9 August, 2014

12. Rivest, R.L., Shamir, A., Adleman, L.M.: A method for obtaining digital signatures and public-key cryptosystems (reprint). Commun. ACM **26**(1), 96–99 (1983)

13. Shamir, A.: Identity-based cryptosystems and signature schemes. In: Blakely, G.R., Chaum, D. (eds.) CRYPTO 1984. LNCS, vol. 196, pp. 47–53. Springer, Heidelberg (1985)

14. Whittaker, Z.: ZDNet: Facebook Does Not Erase User-Deleted Content. http://www.zdnet.com/blog/igeneration/facebook-does-not-erase-user-deleted-content/4808

15. Zhu, Y.: Sina app: Weibo tuchuang (in Chinese). https://hk.v2ex.com/t/44453#reply149

A De-anonymization Attack on Geo-Located Data Considering Spatio-temporal Influences

Rong Wang[1,2]([✉]), Min Zhang[1,3], Dengguo Feng[1], Yanyan Fu[1],
and Zhenyu Chen[1,2]

[1] Trusted Computing and Information Assurance Laboratory, Institute of Software,
Chinese Academy of Sciences, Beijing, China
{wangrong,mzhang,feng,fuyy,chenzhenyu}@tca.iscas.ac.cn
[2] University of Chinese Academy of Sciences, Beijing, China
[3] State Key Laboratory of Computer Science, Institute of Software,
Chinese Academy of Sciences, Beijing, China

Abstract. With the wide use of smart phones, a large amount of GPS data are collected, while risks of privacy disclosure are also increasing. The de-anonymization attack is a typical attack which can infer the owner of an anonymous set of mobility traces. However, most existing works only consider spatial influences without considering temporal influences sufficiently. In this paper, we define a User Hidden Markov Model (UHMM) considering spatio-temporal influences, and exploit this model to launch the de-anonymization attack. Moreover, we conduct a set of experiments on a real-world dataset. The results show our approach is more accurate than other methods.

Keywords: De-anonymization attack · Spatio-temporal influences · Privacy disclosure · Hidden markov model

1 Introduction

Nowadays, smartphones equipped with GPS are becoming ubiquitous. Users' traces are collected and recorded by cellphones or service providers. However, they also increase the risks of individual privacy disclosure [1,2].

Although users' names are often anonymized to protect users' privacies, the anonymous traces are still threatened by many attacks. The de-anonymization attack [3,4] is a typical inference attack, which can re-identify the owner of an anonymous set of traces. To perform this de-anonymization attack, it is necessary to take spatio-temporal influences into full consideration.

In this paper, we propose a new model to profile users' spatio-temporal mobility behaviors and use the model to launch the de-anonymization attack further. The contributions of this paper are threefold:

- We define a User Hidden Markov Model (UHMM) to profile a user's mobility behavior.

© Springer International Publishing Switzerland 2016
S. Qing et al. (Eds.): ICICS 2015, LNCS 9543, pp. 478–484, 2016.
DOI: 10.1007/978-3-319-29814-6_41

– Based on the UHMMs, we propose a new de-anonymization attack using the Viterbi algorithm [6].
– We evaluate the proposed de-anonymization method through comprehensive experiments on a real-world dataset collected by Microsoft Research Asia. The experimental results show that: (1) Time has significant influences on users' mobility behaviors; (2) UHMMs are more suitable to describe users' mobility behaviors than other methods; (3) Our method is more accurate than other methods.

2   Related Work

The de-anonymization attack has been studied for a long time. Most of the studies only consider spatial influences. In [7], Zang and Bolot make a study of the top n most frequently visited places of an individual in a GSM network. They regard the set of the top n most frequently visited places as a quasi-identifier to re-identify a user. De Mulder et al. propose a Markov model [10] to profile a user's mobility behavior in a GSM network. Static GSM cells [15] are treated as the states of a Markov model. So the transitions are only possible between two neighboring GMS cells. Gambs and Killijian propose a Mobility Markov Chain (MMC) [3] to profile a user's mobility behavior, in which each state corresponds to a POI (Point Of Interest). They build an MMC for the testing set which belongs to a specific user, compute the distance between this MMC and all users' MMCs, and take the user corresponding to the minimum distance as a result. Their method does not consider temporal influences either.

In addition, some works consider temporal influences. Freudiger, Shokri and Hubaux [8] re-identify users from geo-located datasets. They label the place where a user stays mostly from 9 a.m. to 5 p.m. as "work", and the place where the user stays mostly from 9 p.m. to 9 a.m. as "home". The "home/work" pair is used as a quasi-identifier to de-anonymize users. De Montjoye et al. show that if a user has a unique pattern in an anonymous dataset, it is already enough to re-identify the user [9]. Their work indicates that 2 or 4 random spatio-temporal places are enough to re-identify a user, and they can re-identify 50 %-95 % of the anonymous users. But their method relies too much on the selection of random places. If tourist areas visited by a lot of users are selected, it cannot work well.

Some auxiliary information is also applied into de-anonymization attacks. Narayanan and Shmatikov use Internet Movie Database (IMDB) to re-identify the anonymous users of Netflix [11]. Srivatsa and Hicks de-anonymize users exploiting social relationships [12]. Semantic information is considered in [13], which relies on the notion of Semantic Location Histories (SLH) to compute the similarity between two users.

From the above analyses, we can figure out that most studies only focus on the regularity of location transitions, ignoring temporal influences which are non-negligible to profile users' mobility behaviors. Our method differentiates itself from all these existing ones, because it analyzes temporal influences on users' mobility behaviors and takes both temporal and spatial influences into consideration to profile users' mobility behaviors. Moreover, our de-anonymizer can work effectively even if the testing set does not intersect with the training set.

3   User Hidden Markov Model

In this paper, we take both spatial influences and temporal influences into consideration, and propose a UHMM to profile a user's daily mobility behavior. The UHMM $M = (S, \Pi, A, O, E)$ is defined as follows:

- First of all, we divide one day into 24 time spans, which constitute a set $S = \{s_0, s_1, \cdots, s_{23}\}$. Each element s_i is a time span. $S = \mathcal{S} \cup \{s_{24}\}$ is the state space set. Each element is taken as a hidden state and s_{24} is the final state. If the state transfers to s_{24}, then the user will stop visiting any location that day.
- Π is the initial probability distribution of the states. The initial probability of a state s_i is defined as

$$\pi_i = p(s_i) = \frac{\mathcal{D}_i}{\sum_{j=0}^{23} \mathcal{D}_j} \tag{1}$$

  where $\mathcal{D}_i$ represents how many days the user first visits a place in s_i.
- A is the set of probabilities of transitions between the states. Each element $a_{i,j}$ represents the probability of transferring from s_i to s_j:

$$a_{i,j} = \frac{\mathcal{D}_{i,j}}{\mathcal{D}_i} \tag{2}$$

  where $\mathcal{D}_i$ indicates how many days a user visits some place in s_i, while $\mathcal{D}_{i,j}$ indicates how many the user visits some place in s_i and visits the next place in s_j.
- $O = \{o_1, \cdots, o_{N_i}\}$ is the observation set, in which each element is a location visited by a user.
- E is the set of emission probabilities. Each element $e_k(o_i)$ is the emission probability that the observation is o_i when the current state is s_k, which is defined as

$$e_k(o_i) = p(o_i|s_k) = \frac{\Phi(o_i|s_k)}{\sum_{j=1}^{N_i} \Phi(o_j|s_k)} \tag{3}$$

  where $\Phi(o_i|s_k)$ indicates how many times the user visits o_i in s_k.

4   The New De-anonymization Attack

In this section, we introduce our de-anonymization attack, which is composed of two phases: the training phase and the testing phase.

In the training phase, for each user, a UHMM is built from his training set, which can be regarded as the profile of his daily mobility behavior. Then the set of all uses' UHMMs $\Gamma = \{M_1, \cdots, M_m\}$ can be constructed.

The testing phase consists of two steps: the ranking step and the voting step. In the ranking step, take the UHMMs and the records (elements) of an anonymous dataset $R = \{r_1, \cdots, r_n\}$ as the inputs. Each element $r_i = \{y_1, \cdots, y_T\}$ is a one-day record of an anonymous user's traces, in which y_i is an observation of O. Then we exploit the widely used Viterbi algorithm [6] to find out the top N users whose Viterbi output ranks in the top N.

In the voting step, from the top N users of all the records, find out the result user who is most probable to be the owner of the anonymous dataset. It takes the top user sets as the inputs, counts the occurrence number of the user in the top user sets, and outputs the re-identified user whose occurrence number is the largest. In the best case, there will be a user who exists in each top user set.

5   Experiments

In this section, we evaluate the accuracy of our method on a real-world geo-located dataset. We first briefly introduce the dataset used in our experiments, then list the methods to be evaluated, and finally demonstrate the experimental results.

5.1   Dataset

Our experiments exploit the *GeoLife* dataset collected by Microsoft Research Asia, which contains GPS traces of 178 users of Beijing captured at a very high rate of 1 to 5 s from April 2007 to October 2011. For each user who has more than 50 daily records, we divide his mobility into two disjoint trail of traces (Train 1, Test 1). The first half forms the training set Train 1, and the second half forms the testing set Test 1. We also construct two more sets Train 2 and Test 2. The former is composed of all the user's daily records, while the latter consists of half of his records which are randomly extracted. These two sets partially overlap, which is the main difference from the previous two datasets.

5.2   The De-anonymization Methods to be Evaluated

In our experiments, 5 methods are evaluated, which are listed in Table 1. In the table, the Rand2 and Rand4 methods are proposed in [9] which take 2 or 4 random locations respectively to characterize users' mobility patterns.

5.3   The Experimental Results

In this section, we conduct experiments to evaluate the above 5 methods. First of all, we compare the Rand2 and Rand4 methods. Figure 1 shows the accuracy

Table 1. Methods for comparison

Method	Descrption
Rand2 [9]	2 spatio-temporal locations are selected randomly as a quasi-identifier
Rand4 [9]	4 spatio-temporal locations are selected randomly as a quasi-identifier
Home/Work Pair [8]	The most frequently visited location between 9 p.m.-9 a.m. and the most frequently visited location between 9 a.m.-5 p.m. are treated as a quasi-identifier
UHMM (our method)	UHMMs are constructed for all users and will be used to perform the attack
MMC [3]	MMCs are constructed to profile users' mobility behaviors

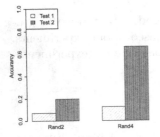

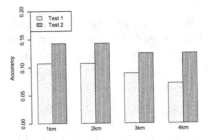

Fig. 1. Accuracy comparison between Rand2 and Rand4

Fig. 2. Accuracy analyses of the MMC method [3]

comparison between them for Test 1 and Test 2. We can see that the more spatio-temporal locations you have, the more users can be re-identified. In addition, the accuracy for Test 2 is much better than that for Test 1, because a record exists in Test 1 means it does not exist in Train 1, which may make the accuracy reduced.

Secondly, we evaluate the performance of the MMC method [3], which requires to set a distance threshold. When the state distance is less than the threshold, the method uses the state distance directly to compute the distance between two MMCs. Otherwise, the method uses the proximity distance. Here we set the threshold to range from 1 km to 4 km. As shown in Fig. 2, it can be observed that the accuracy for Test 2 is better than that for Test 1. Moreover, the shorter the distance threshold is, the better the attack performs. The reason is that the shorter the distance is, the better the MMC can profile the real user.

Our method is also evaluated for Test 1 and Test 2. In the ranking step, we compute the top 1, 2, 3 and 5 users, and use them to perform the attack

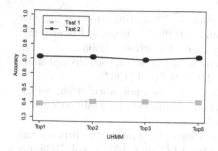

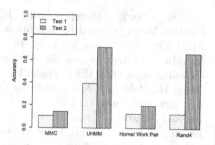

Fig. 3. Accuracy analyses of our method   **Fig. 4.** Comparison of four methods

respectively. The accuracy comparison is shown in Fig. 3, we can observe that the accuracy for Test 2 is higher than that for Test 1 and the parameter N does not influence the accuracy significantly.

The comparison between our attack and other methods is shown in Fig. 4, which shows that our attack outperforms other methods for both Test 1 and Test 2.

6   Conclusion

The de-anonymization attack is a typical attack that can predict the owner of an anonymous set of traces. However, most works do not consider temporal influences sufficiently. We define the UHMMs to profile users' mobility behaviors, and exploit the Viterbi algorithm to get the ranked users. Finally, we re-identify the anonymous user with our voting algorithm. In addition, we conduct sufficient experiments on a real-world dataset, which shows that our method is more accurate than other methods.

Acknowledgment. This work was supported by National Natural Science Foundation of China under Grant No. 61232005 and No. 91118006.

References

1. Gonzalez, M.C., Hidalgo, C.A., Barabasi, A.L.: Understanding individual human mobility patterns. Nature. **453**, 779–782 (2008)
2. Song, C., Qu, Z., Blumm, N.: Limits of predictability in human mobility. Science. **327**, 1018–1021 (2010)
3. Gambs, S., Killijian, M.O., del Prado Cortez, M.N.: De-anonymization attack on geolocated data. J. Comput. Syst. Sci. **80**, 1597–1614 (2014)
4. Gambs, S., Killijian, M.O., del Prado Cortez, M.N.: Show me how you move and i will tell you who you are. In: 3rd ACM SIGSPATIAL International Workshop on Security and Privacy in GIS and LBS, pp. 34–41. ACM, California (2010)

 5. Bettini, Claudio, Wang, XSean, Jajodia, Sushil: Protecting privacy against location-based personal identification. In: Jonker, Willem, Petković, Milan (eds.) SDM 2005. LNCS, vol. 3674, pp. 185–199. Springer, Heidelberg (2005)
 6. Viterbi, A.J.: Error bounds for convolutional codes and an asymptotically optimum decoding algorithm. IEEE Trans. Inf. Theor. **13**, 260–C269 (1967)
 7. Zang, H., Bolot, J.: Anonymization of location data does not work: a large-scale measurement study. In: 17th Annual International Conference on Mobile Computing and Networking, pp. 145–156. ACM, Las Vegas (2011)
 8. Freudiger, Julien, Shokri, Reza, Hubaux, Jean-Pierre: Evaluating the privacy risk of location-based services. In: Danezis, George (ed.) FC 2011. LNCS, vol. 7035, pp. 31–46. Springer, Heidelberg (2012)
 9. De Montjoye, Y.A., Hidalgo, C.A., Verleysen, M.: Unique in the Crowd: the privacy bounds of human mobility. Scientific reports, 3 (2013)
10. De Mulder, Y., Danezis, G., Batina, L.: Identification via location-profiling in GSM networks. In: 7th ACM Workshop on Privacy in the Electronic Society, pp. 23–32. ACM, Alexandria (2008)
11. Narayanan, A., Shmatikov, V.: Robust de-anonymization of large sparse datasets. In: the IEEE Symposium on Security and Privacy, pp. 111–125. IEEE, Washington, DC (2008)
12. Srivatsa, M., Hicks, M.: Deanonymizing mobility traces: using social network as a side-channel. In: the 2012 ACM conference on Computer and communications security, pp. 628–637. ACM, New York (2012)
13. Xiao, X., Zheng, Y., Luo, Q.: Finding similar users using category-based location history. In: 18th SIGSPATIAL International Conference on Advances in Geographic Information Systems, pp. 442–445. ACM, California (2010)
14. Zheng, Y., Li, Q., Chen, Y.: Understanding mobility based on GPS data. In: 10th International Conference on Ubiquitous Computing, pp. 312–321. ACM, Korea (2008)
15. Eagle, N., Pentland, A.: Reality mining: sensing complex social systems. Pers. Ubiquitous Comput. **10**, 255–268 (2006)

Author Index

Anand Sahu, Rajeev   252

Bai, Guoqiang   199, 212
Bao, Zhenzhen   18

Cao, Nairen   393
Cao, Weiqiong   62
Chan, Sammy   421
Chan, T.-H. Hubert   82
Chang, Jinyong   363
Chen, Depeng   421
Chen, Hua   62
Chen, Zhenyu   478
Chen, Zhifeng   10
Chen, Zhong   269
Choo, Kim-Kwang Raymond   467

Ding, Liping   295
Ding, Xuejie   141
Dong, Chuntao   458
Dong, Li   414
Du, Zhihui   311

Fan, Hongbo   414
Fan, Wenjun   311
Feng, Dengguo   152, 478
Feng, Jingyi   62
Fernández, David   311
Fu, Yanyan   478

Gao, Neng   184
Ge, Aijun   260
Geneiatakis, Dimitris   1
Ghorbani, Ali A.   282
Guo, Songhui   10
Guo, Wei   363

Han, Xucang   62
He, Daojing   421
Hirose, Shoichi   125
Hu, Bo   303
Hu, Lingli   406
Huang, Geshi   97
Huang, Weiqing   141, 303

Hui, Xinning   311
Huo, Ying   406

Ji, Yafei   346
Ji, Yuanyuan   220
Jia, Ping   97
Jia, Shijie   346
Jiang, Lihuan   50
Jiang, Ying   295

Kadobayashi, Youki   320

Lai, Shangqi   467
Lai, Xuejia   97
Li, Peili   220
Li, Qingbao   10
Li, Wenting   458
Li, Xiaochen   335
Liang, Kaitai   467
Lin, Dongdai   18
Lin, Jingqiang   346
Liu, Joseph K.   467
Liu, Muhua   363
Liu, Wanquan   169
Liu, Zeyi   184
Liu, Zhen   109
Liu, Zongbin   184
Luo, Peng   18
Luo, Shoushan   406
Lv, Kewei   37, 71

Ma, Chuangui   260
Ma, Yuan   184
Mamun, Mohammad Saiful Islam   282
Meng, Hongwei   269
Meng, Ziqian   269
Monarev, Viktor   445

Okuda, Takeshi   320

Palmieri, Paolo   436
Paundu, Ady Wahyudi   320
Pestunov, Andrey   445

Qin, Yu   152
Qing, Sihan   406
Qiu, Shuang   379

Sakurai, Kouichi   236
Saraswat, Vishal   252
Shen, Qingni   335, 458
Shi, Jun   141
Shi, Shupeng   414
Song, Chuck   269
Stakhanova, Natalia   282
Sun, Degang   303
Sun, Zizhou   335

Tang, Jiehui   379
Thiele, Lars   50
Tu, Chenyang   184

Wan, Xiang   458
Wang, Rong   478
Wang, Weijin   152
Wang, Wenwen   37
Wang, Xifeng   169
Wang, Xuanxuan   50
Wang, Yan   303
Wang, Yao   71
Wang, Ye   10
Wang, Yongming   50
Wong, Duncan S.   109
Wu, Wenling   62
Wu, Ying   363
Wu, Zhonghai   335, 458

Xia, Luning   346
Xiao, Siyu   260

Xie, Chuiyi   406
Xu, Haixia   220
Xu, Hong   97
Xue, Rui   363

Yamaguchi, Suguru   320
Yang, Bo   152
Yang, Kun   303
Yang, Yahui   335, 458
Yang, Yufang   393
Yasuda, Takanori   236
Yiu, SiuMing   393
Yu, Haibo   199
Yu, Xiaoqi   393

Zhang, Dan   212
Zhang, Guozhu   346
Zhang, Hailong   379
Zhang, Jie   260
Zhang, Jing   414
Zhang, Linru   393
Zhang, Meng   141
Zhang, Min   478
Zhang, Qian   295
Zhang, Rui   356
Zhang, Xue   356
Zhang, Yingjun   152
Zhao, Zhichao   82
Zheng, Xiaoguang   62
Zhou, Jian   184, 346
Zhou, Jianqin   169
Zhou, Yongbin   379
Zhu, Shaofeng   62

Printed in the United States
by Baker & Taylor Publisher Services